The Jossey-Bass Reader
on Nonprofit and Public Leadership

An Instructor's Manual is available online at: www.wiley.com/college/perry.

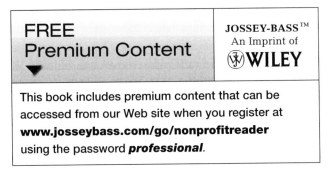

FREE
Premium Content
▼

JOSSEY-BASS™
An Imprint of
Ⓦ WILEY

This book includes premium content that can be
accessed from our Web site when you register at
www.josseybass.com/go/nonprofitreader
using the password *professional*.

Edited by

James L. Perry

—ᴧᴧ— The Jossey-Bass Reader on Nonprofit and Public Leadership

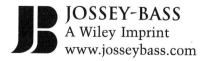

JOSSEY-BASS
A Wiley Imprint
www.josseybass.com

Published by Jossey-Bass

A Wiley Imprint

989 Market Street, San Francisco, CA 94103–1741—www.josseybass.com

Readers should be aware that Internet Web sites offered as citations and/or sources for further information may have changed or disappeared between the time this was written and when it is read.

Jossey-Bass books and products are available through most bookstores. To contact Jossey-Bass directly call our Customer Care Department within the U.S. at 800–956–7739, outside the U.S. at 317–572–3986, or fax 317–572–4002.

Jossey-Bass also publishes its books in a variety of electronic formats. Some content that appears in print may not be available in electronic books.

Library of Congress Cataloging-in-Publication Data

The Jossey-Bass reader on nonprofit and public leadership / edited by James L. Perry Jossey-Bass.
    p. cm.
  Includes index.
  ISBN 978-0-470-47949-0 (pbk.)
  1. Leadership. 2. Nonprofit organizations. 3. Public administration. I. Perry, James L. II. Title: Nonprofit and public leadership.
  HD57.7.J67 2009
  658.4'092—dc22
                    2009032201

Printed in the United States of America

FIRST EDITION

HB Printing   10 9 8 7 6 5 4 3 2

Contents

Technical Skills

Part Four: The Next Generation of Leaders and Leadership

~~~ On the Web

We are pleased to provide additional articles free on our website. Please visit www.josseybass.com/go/nonprofitreader to download pdf versions of the articles.

- *Zeroing In on Impact*, by Susan J. Colby, Nancy Stone, and Paul Cartar
  Originally appeared in the Fall 2004 issue of the Stanford Social Innovation Review *(www.SSIReview.org).*

- *Leading with Integrity*, by Mike Hudson
  Originally published in Managing at the Leading Edge: New Challenges in Managing Nonprofit Organizations *(2005).*

- *Leading Across Generations*, by Frances Kunreuther, Helen Kim, and Robby Rodriguez
  Originally published in Working Across Generations: Defining the Future of Nonprofit Leadership *(2009).*

- *Leading in a Leaderless World*, by Iain Somerville and D. Quinn Mills
  Originally published in Leading Beyond the Walls, *edited by Frances Hesselbein, Marshall Goldsmith, and Iain Somerville (1999).*

- *Artful Leadership*, by May Tschirhart
  Originally published in Artful Leadership: Managing Stakeholder Problems in Nonprofit Arts Organizations *(1996).*

INSTRUCTOR'S MANUAL

Instructors can access an Instructor's Manual at the following web address: www.wiley.com/college/perry.

~~~ Sources

In the interest of relevance and readability, the editor has slightly adapted the selections for this volume. For the complete texts, please refer to the original sources.

Chapter 1

Max DePree, "What Is Leadership?," *Leadership Is an Art.* (New York: Doubleday, 1989).

Chapter 2

John W. Gardner, "The Tasks of Leadership," *On Leadership.* (New York: The Free Press, 1990).

Chapter 3

James M. Kouzes and Barry Z. Pos*ner,* "The Five Practices of Exemplary Leadership," *The Leadership Challenge* (4th ed.). (San Francisco: Jossey-Bass, 2007).

Chapter 4

Ray Blunt, "Leaders Growing Leaders," *Growing Leaders for Public Service.* (Washington, DC: IBM Center for the Business of Government, 2003).

Chapter 5

John Carver, "Maintaining Board Leadership: Staying on Track and Institutionalizing Excellence," *Boards That Make a Difference* (3rd ed.). (San Francisco: Jossey-Bass, 2006).

Chapter 6

Montgomery Van Wart, "Public-Sector Leadership Theory: An Assessment," *Public Administration Review, 63.* (March/April 2003).

Chapter 7

Jim Keddy, "Human Dignity and Grassroots Leadership Development," *Social Policy.* (Summer 2001).

Chapter 8

Larry C. Spears, "Practicing Servant-Leadership," *Leader to Leader, 34.* (Fall 2004).

Chapter 9

Leslie Crutchfield and Heather McLeod Grant, "Share Leadership," *Forces for Good: The Six Practices of High-Impact Nonprofits.* (San Francisco: Jossey-Bass, 2008).

Chapter 10

Ann Marie Thomson and James L. Perry, "Collaboration Processes: Inside the Black Box," *Public Administration Review, 66.* (December/Special Issue, 2006).

Chapter 11

John M. Bryson, "The Strategy Change Cycle." In Robert Herman (Ed.), *The Jossey-Bass Handbook of Nonprofit Leadership and Management* (2nd ed.). (San Francisco: Jossey-Bass, 2004).

Chapter 12

Jeffrey L. Bradach, Thomas J. Tierney, and Nancy Stone, "Delivering on the Promise of Nonprofits," *Harvard Business Review, 86.* (December 2008).

Chapter 13

Robert D. Behn, "Performance Leadership: Eleven Better Practices That Can Ratchet Up Performance." (Washington, DC: IBM Center for the Business of Government, 2004).

Chapter 14

Edgar H. Schein, "The Learning Leader as Culture Manager," *Organizational Culture and Leadership.* (San Francisco: Jossey-Bass, 1996).

Chapter 15

Warren Bennis and Joan Goldsmith, "Maintaining Trust Through Integrity," *Learning to Lead.* (New York: Basic Books, 2003).

Chapter 16

Terry L. Cooper, "Administrative Responsibility: The Key to Administrative Ethics." In Terry Cooper (Ed.), *The Responsible Administrator: An Approach to Ethics for the Administrative Role* (5th ed.). (San Francisco: Jossey-Bass, 2006).

Chapter 17

Bill George, "Empowering People to Lead," *True North.* (San Francisco: Jossey-Bass, 2007).

Chapter 18

James M. Kouzes and Barry Z. Posner, "Enlist Others: Attracting People to Common Purposes," *The Leadership Challenge* (2nd ed.). (San Francisco: Jossey-Bass, 2007).

Chapter 19

R. Roosevelt Thomas, Jr., "Diversity Management: An Essential Craft for Leaders," *Leader to Leader, 41.* (Summer 2006).

Chapter 20

Lisa Blomgren Bingham, "Negotiating for the Public Good." In James L. Perry (Ed.), *Handbook of Public Administration* (2nd ed.). (San Francisco: Jossey-Bass, 1996).

Chapter 21

Talula Cartwright and David Baldwin, "Seeing Your Way: Why Leaders Must Communicate Their Visions," *Leadership in Action* (pp. 15–24). (July/August 2007).

Chapter 22

William F. Kumuyi, "Seven Communication Tips an Effective Leader Must Have," *New African* (July/August/September 2007).

Chapter 31

Jeffrey Yip, Serena Wong, and Christopher Ernst, "The Nexus Effect: When Leaders Span Group Boundaries," *Leadership in Action, 28.* (September/October 2008).

Chapter 32

Leslie Lenkowsky, "The Politics of Doing Good: Philanthropic Leadership for the Twenty-First Century." In William Damon and Susan Verducci (Eds.), *Taking Philanthropy Seriously: Beyond Noble Intentions to Responsible Giving.* (Bloomington, IN: Indiana University Press, 2006).

Chapter 33

Joseph S. Nye, Jr., "New Models of Public Leadership." In Frances Hesselbein, Marshall Goldsmith, and Iain Somerville (Eds.), *Leading Beyond the Walls.* (San Francisco: Jossey-Bass, 1999).

Chapter 34

Barbara Kellerman, "The Ties That Bind," *Reinventing Leadership.* (Albany, NY: State University of New York Press, 1999).

~~~ Foreword

By Jim Kouzes

Name an historical leader whom you greatly admire—a well-known leader from the distant or recent past whom you could imagine following willingly. Who is that leader?

We've asked thousands of people to do this over the last twenty-five years. Although no single leader receives a majority of the nominations, in the United States, the two most frequently mentioned are Abraham Lincoln and Martin Luther King, Jr. Other historical leaders who've made the list include Aung San Suu Kyi, Susan B. Anthony, Benazir Bhutto, César Chávez, Winston Churchill, Mahatma Gandhi, Mikhail Gorbachev, Miguel Hidalgo, Nelson Mandela, Golda Meir, His Holiness the Dalai Lama, His Holiness Pope John Paul II, Eleanor Roosevelt, Franklin D. Roosevelt, Mother Teresa, Margaret Thatcher, and Archbishop Desmond Tutu.

What do these leaders have in common? One quality stands out above all else. The most striking similarity we've found—and surely it's evident to you—is that the list is populated by people with strong beliefs about matters of principle. They all have, or had, unwavering commitment to a clear set of values. They all are, or were, passionate about their causes.

The lesson from this simple exercise is unmistakable. People admire most those who believe strongly in something, and who are willing to stand up for their beliefs. If anyone is ever to become a leader whom others would willingly follow, one certain prerequisite is that they must be someone of principle.

And there's something else striking about this list. The vast majority of people who are nominated as admired historical leaders are largely from the domains of nonprofit and public leadership. They are individuals who lead movements for social justice, who guided us through our darkest hours, and who seized the initiative to improve the quality of our lives. They are, in other words, leaders from the types of organizations that are the focus of this book. Far too often the discussion of leadership makes heroes of those who are driven to make money, failing to recognize the lasting contributions made by those who are driven to make meaning.

Famous figures from history, most assuredly, aren't the only leaders with strong beliefs on matters of principle. For over twenty-five years, Barry Posner and I have been researching personal-best leadership experiences, and the people we've studied are everyday leaders from all types of organizations. They could be leaders in the local community, the neighborhood school, ones down the hall from you, ones next door—and also you. The personal-best leadership cases we've collected are, at their core, the stories of individuals who remained true to deeply held values.

Representative of this group is Arlene Blum, biophysical chemist, mountaineer, and tireless campaigner for better policies for fire retardants and related chemicals. She's also the first woman to lead a team of all women to the summit of Annapurna, the tenth highest mountain in the world. She certainly knows firsthand the challenges of leadership under life-and-death conditions.

In talking about what separates those who make a successful ascent from those who don't, Arlene says, "The real dividing line is passion. As long as you believe what you're doing is meaningful, you can cut through fear and exhaustion and take the next step." Arlene could easily be talking about the leaders in nonprofits and public organizations. It's about the meaning of the work. What gets leaders—and all of us, really—through the tough times, the scary times, the times when you don't think you can even get up in the morning or take another step, is a sense of meaning and purpose. The motivation to deal with the challenges and uncertainties of life and work comes from the inside, and not from something that others hold out in front of you as some kind of carrot.

People commit to causes, not to plans. How else do you explain why people volunteer to rebuild communities ravaged by a tsunami, ride a bike from San Francisco to Los Angeles to raise money to fight AIDS, or rescue people from the rubble of a collapsed building after an earthquake? How else do you explain why people toil 24/7 to create the next big thing when the probability of failure is 60–70 percent? People are not committing to the plan in any of these cases. There may not even be a plan to commit to. They are committing to something much bigger, something much more compelling than goals and milestones on a piece of paper. That's not to say that plans aren't important to executing on grand dreams. They absolutely are. It's just to say that the plan isn't the thing that people are committing to.

Here's something else to consider. For a long time now we've been asking people about the leader role models in their own lives. Not the well-known historical leaders, but the leaders with whom they've had personal experience. We've asked them to identify the person they'd select as their most important role model for leadership, and then we've given them a list of eight possible categories from which these leaders might come. They can choose from business leader, community or religious leader, entertainer or Hollywood star, family member, political leader, professional athlete, teacher or coach, or other/none/not sure. From which category do you think the largest percentage of leader role models comes? Answer: Family member.

Regardless of whether one is young or old, when thinking back over our lives and selecting the most important leader role model, it's more likely to be a family member than anyone else. Nearly 50 percent of people find their leader role model among a member of their family. For respondents under 30, the second most frequently selected category is teacher-coach, and the third is community leader. For the over 30 crowd, business leader is number two. (And when we probe further, what people really mean when they say business leader is someone who was an immediate supervisor at work.) In third position is teacher-coach.

What does this selection of leader role models tell us? It says that leadership is not about position or title. Leadership is not about organizational power or authority. It's not about celebrity or wealth. It's not about being a CEO, president, general, or prime minister. And it's definitely not about being a superstar. Leadership is about relationships. The leader role models we most admire come from those people we know well and who know us well. They are the ones with whom we have had intimate contact. They are the people we are the closest to.

If you're a manager in an organization, to your direct reports you are the most important leader in your organization. You are more likely than any other leader to influence their desire to stay or leave, the trajectory of their careers, their ethical behavior, their ability to perform at their best, their drive to wow customers, their satisfaction with their jobs, and their motivation to share the organization's vision and values.

If you're a parent, teacher, coach, or community leader, you are the person who's setting the leadership example for young people. It's not hip-hop artists, movie stars, or professional athletes they seek guidance from. You are the one they are most likely going to look to for the example of how a leader responds to competitive situations, handles crises, deals with loss, or resolves ethical dilemmas. It's not someone else. It's you.

The leaders who have the most influence on us are those who are the closest to us. We have to challenge the myth that leadership is about position and power. And, once challenged, people can come to see leadership in a whole new light.

For example, when we asked Verónica Guerrero, one of the leaders we had the good fortune to interview, to name her most admired leader, she selected her father, José Luis Guerrero. And, in telling us his story, she underscored for us just how extraordinary those around us can be.

She told us about her father's leadership in the Unión Nacional Sinarquista (UNS) back in the early 1940s. She related in detail what her father did and then summed up his influence with this observation from José Luis: "I think the work that I did back then helped me extend myself and others to levels that I didn't know I could reach. . . . If you feel strongly about anything, and it's something that will ultimately benefit your community and your country, don't hold back. Fear of failing or fear of what might happen doesn't help anyone. . . . Don't let anyone or anything push you back."

Verónica closed her description of her father (who was then dying of pancreatic cancer) with this observation: "As I heard his story and I saw a sick, tired, and weak man, I couldn't help thinking that our strength as humans and as leaders has nothing to do with what we look like. Rather, it has everything to do with what we feel, what we think of ourselves . . . . Leadership is applicable to all facets of life." That's precisely the point. If you are to become a better leader, you must first believe that leadership applies to you and that you can be a positive force in the world.

The question for each of us is not Do I matter? but How do I matter? If others look to you for leadership, how are you doing in leading them right now? Not how is my boss doing, or how is the CEO doing, or how is that famous leader doing, but how am I doing?

None of us needs a ton of statistical studies to tell us how we respond when people are providing terrific leadership and when they're doing a lousy job of it. We just know. Developing better leaders really begins right here at home when we take a look at how we are doing.

Leadership is everyone's business. No matter what your position is, you have to take responsibility for the quality of leadership your constituents get. You—and that means all of us—are accountable for the leadership you demonstrate. And, because you are the most important leader to those closest to you, the only choice you really have is whether or not to be the best leader you can be.

That is what we hope to offer you in this book—the opportunity to make a few strides along the path to being the best leader you can be.

⚊⟿⚊ Preface

To paraphrase the title of a recent book, "leadership—if not now, when?" it seems that our public affairs are in a constant state of crisis. Crises have become so commonoplace—9/11, the subprime crisis, the credit crisis—that the word "crisis" may be in danger of losing its shock value. Our sense of constant crisis has elevated the salience of leadership for all of us. Recent crises have magnified flaws in some of our leaders, made heroes of others, and produced a longing among many that someone step forward to fix the mess in which the modern world finds itself.

The rise of a new American leader, Barack Obama, has also triggered renewed interest in leadership. For older generations, President Obama is a reminder of another youthful president, John F. Kennedy. To the world's youth, Obama represents possibility. Becoming the first African-American president opens the door to others in our diverse society who believed that ascending to the presidency was not possible. Both Obama's election and his leadership style symbolize a changing order.

This book seeks to provide some answers about leadership for people to whom leadership may have renewed salience because of crises and awareness of possibility. The book's domain of interest is the arena of public affairs—the nonprofit and public sectors. Leading in most public and nonprofit situations is a big challenge, and no one needs to exaggerate difficulties or equate them with recent public crises. Public and nonprofit leaders are confronted by the lights that shine on their public work, resource, authority, and power distributions that sometimes set off a free-for-all for influence among stakeholders and hard choices about who wins and who loses.

One question that may occur to some readers is, "Why bring readings about leadership in the nonprofit and public sectors together in the same book?" Several factors contribute to featuring readings about the nonprofit and public sectors in the same volume. I will touch on three of these factors here. One reason is the belief among many professionals and scholars that the nature of leadership in different sectors is converging. This perception is reflected as a theme in several of the readings contained in this reader, most prominently Barbara Kellerman's closing chapter. Some of the other readings treat leadership as a generic function in organizations, which presupposes some degree of convergence across sectors. I do not take a position about convergence in my editorial commentaries later in this reader, but the widespread perception that leadership tasks and skills are converging contributes to the rationale for including readings about the nonprofit and public sectors in the same volume.

Another factor contributing to presenting nonprofit and public sector readings in the same volume is that both nonprofit and government organizations are public-benefit organizations. Organizations from each sector are fundamentally about the public good. Government and nonprofit organizations also differ in many ways—for example, the distinctive voluntary character of nonprofit enterprises versus the coercive nature of much government activity. But their shared attention to the public or common good also unites them in important ways. The affinity of leaders in both the nonprofit and public sectors for the idea of servant-leadership is one indication that similarity around public purpose unites the ways in which leaders in each sector see themselves.

A final factor is that many parts of the two sectors are closely intertwined. As some of the authors note, public work that had once been done by government is now done by nonprofit organizations. What's more, large parts of the nonprofit sector, particularly at the local level, work hand-in-hand with government to deliver social services. The close working relationships across the sectors feeds some parallelism across the sectors and also demands that leaders from one sector appreciate the situation of their counterparts in the other sector. Just as important is the fact that the education of leaders in the nonprofit and government sectors often occurs in the same academic settings under the auspices of programs affiliated with American Humanics and the National Association of Schools of Public Affairs and Administration.

INTENDED AUDIENCE

The intended audience for this reader includes: (1) graduate and advanced undergraduate students who are preparing for leadership careers in the nonprofit and public sectors; (2) managers and professionals already working in nonprofit and public organizations who are seeking to broaden their perspectives about their enterprises; and (3) faculty members in professional schools that prepare students for the public, nonprofit, and social sectors. The readings are intended primarily for those who are embarking on leadership careers, but may also prove valuable to more experienced professionals who want to refresh or add to their stock of knowledge.

ORGANIZATION OF THE READER

The reader is organized in four parts. Part I, Aspirations for Leaders in the Nonprofit and Public Sectors, consists of five readings. They focus on the ends to which nonprofit and public leaders aspire as leaders. The readings begin with perspectives offered by two of the most acclaimed and articulate leaders of the late twentieth century, Max DePree and John Gardner. The third contribution in Part I, by James Kouzes and Barry Posner, indicates that the opening perspectives DePree and Gardner provide are not idiosyncratic, but are replicated in grounded research on a large sample of leaders. The final two readings in Part I look at intermediate steps toward leadership excellence in identifying the developmental processes by which leaders and boards grow in their capacities as leaders.

Part II, Leadership Theories for the Nonprofit and Public Sectors, also consists of five readings. It begins with a chapter that extensively reviews leadership theories developed during the last century. The opening chapter is followed by four chapters that explore theories that are particularly well suited to the contexts in which nonprofit and public leaders find themselves. In succession, the readings discuss grassroots, servant, shared, and collaborative leadership. As a whole, the readings in Part II provide a strong introduction to the range of what scholars and practitioners have come to know as leadership theory.

The largest number of readings in this volume appear in Part III, Critical Leadership Skills. As I explain in its introduction, Part III is a bridge between the high-minded principles introduced in Parts I and II and the "doing" of leadership. Given the volume of readings in Part III, thirteen in all, I organized the part around three skill-sets: *conceptual, human,* and *technical.* Within the conceptual set, the readings cover an important range of skills, including managing strategically, achieving results, shaping culture, leading ethically, and establishing trust. The human skills addressed involve motivating others, managing diversity, and negotiating for the public good. Part III concludes with two readings about technical skills, specifically communicating with stakeholders and evaluating achievements.

The reader concludes with Part IV, The Next Generation of Leaders and Leadership. This grouping of eleven readings looks to the future of leadership and leaders in the nonprofit and public sectors. The part begins with an article that looks at how leaders can institutionalize their impact beyond their tenure as leaders. The next readings about change and innovation explore the converse of institutionalization. The readings then shift to addressing who will be the next generation of leaders, how leadership transitions can be managed, and what can be done to ensure the quality of future leaders in the nonprofit and public sectors. The concluding readings in Part IV look holistically at leadership in the philanthropic, public, and business sectors.

~~~ About the Editor

James L. Perry is Distinguished Professor and Chancellor's Professor of Public and Environmental Affairs, Indiana University, Bloomington. He is also an adjunct professor of philanthropic studies and political science. He has held faculty appointments at the University of California, Irvine; Chinese University of Hong Kong; University of Wisconsin, Madison; Katholieke Universiteit Leuven; Yonsei University; and University of Hong Kong. He received an undergraduate degree from the University of Chicago and M.P.A. and Ph.D. degrees from the Maxwell School of Citizenship and Public Affairs at Syracuse University.

Dr. Perry's recent research focuses on public service motivation, community and national service, collaboration, and government reform. His research appears in such journals as *Academy of Management Journal, Administrative Science Quarterly, Journal of Public Administration Research and Theory, Nonprofit Management and Leadership, Nonprofit and Voluntary Sector Quarterly*, and *Public Administration Review*. He is author and editor of several books, including the *Handbook of Public Administration* (2nd ed.) (Jossey-Bass, 1996), *Civic Service: What Difference Does It Make?* (with Ann Marie Thomson; M. E. Sharpe, 2004), *Quick Hits for Educating Citizens* (with Steve Jones; Indiana University Press, 2006), and *Motivation in Public Management: The Call of Public Service* (with Annie Hondeghem; Oxford University Press, 2008).

Dr. Perry is recipient of several national awards. He received the Yoder-Heneman Award for innovative personnel research from the Society for Human Resource Management. He is recipient of two awards, the Charles H. Levine Memorial Award for Excellence in Public Administration and the Distinguished Research Award, given jointly by the American Society for Public Administration (ASPA) and the National Association of Schools of Public Affairs and Administration. He is recipient of the Best Book Award from the Public and Nonprofit Division of the Academy of Management. ASPA has recognized him with two awards, the Paul P. Van Riper Award for Excellence and Service and the Dwight Waldo Award for career contributions to the literature of public administration. He is a fellow of the National Academy of Public Administration.

PART ONE

Aspirations for Leaders in the Nonprofit and Public Sectors

Editor's Introduction

W
hen a U.S. President goes before a joint session of Congress to fulfill the constitutional injunction to "give to the Congress information of the state of the union," the President is usually prone to proclaim that the state of the union is strong. Can the same claim be made about the state of leadership in the nonprofit and public sectors? Well, the answer depends on whom you ask. One claim about which we are more certain is that we know a good deal about what leaders *should* do. Whether our leaders measure up, however, is sometimes another matter. And the divergence between what *ought* to be and what *is* helps to explain why leadership fascinates us.

Max DePree and the late John Gardner, whose writings open this volume, built outstanding careers by offering insights about the essence of leadership *and* practicing what they preached. DePree distinguished himself in the world of business as chairman of Herman Miller Incorporated, one of the world's largest and most successful office furniture designers and manufacturers. DePree is a member of the *Fortune* magazine National Business Hall of Fame. His four books about leadership, lectures, and philanthropy have disseminated widely his perspectives about leadership.

John Gardner's career was one of extraordinary breadth that included education, philanthropy, and politics. He served as president of the Carnegie Corporation of New York and the Carnegie Foundation for the Advancement of Teaching and Secretary of Health, Education, and Welfare under President Lyndon Johnson. Among his enduring legacies are founding Independent Sector, the leadership forum for charities, foundations, and corporate giving programs committed to advancing the common good, and Common Cause, a nonpartisan, nonprofit advocacy organization whose mission is to help citizens hold their elected leaders accountable to the public interest.

DePree and Gardner's understanding of the essence of nonprofit and public leadership, each drawing from more than forty years of accumulated wisdom in different arenas of American society, is surprisingly similar. They identify leadership in functional terms, that is, the tasks that leaders perform. As I hope you will agree after reading DePree and Gardner, the overlap in the tasks, although expressed in different ways, is striking. What is also striking are some of the underlying themes that unify DePree and Gardner's perspectives about leadership.

One of the themes of John Gardner's chapter, "The Tasks of Leadership," is the importance of leadership to the health and maintenance of *institutions*, which Gardner defines as "the structures and processes through which substantial endeavors get accomplished over time." Institutions, according to Gardner, are not only the means by which accomplishments are achieved, but the vehicles that leaders use to help others carry on after the leader's exit. In his contribution, "What Is Leadership?," Max DePree also gives institutions a central role: "Leadership is a concept of owing certain things to the institution."

Another theme shared in the two introductory readings is the centrality of *followership*. DePree writes: "The measure of leadership is not the quality of the head, but the tone of the body. The signs of outstanding leadership appear primarily among the followers." Gardner sounds a similar note, observing "that the purpose of leaders is not to dominate nor diminish followers but to strengthen and help them to develop. In the nonprofit and public sectors, followership merits a special status because the citizens of governments and constituencies of nonprofits are the *raison d'être* for these organizations."

The venerable management thinker Peter Drucker once described leadership in a *Wall Street Journal* article as "more doing than dash." To some extent, Gardner's task list evokes Drucker's contention, but both DePree and Gardner give extraordinary attention to values, obligation, and responsibility. DePree and Gardner leave no doubt that leadership is a moral enterprise.

The DePree and Gardner readings give us checklists for assessing what and how well public and nonprofit officials perform leadership functions. In "The Five Practices of Exemplary Leadership," James Kouzes and Barry Posner condense the essence of leadership to a handful of exemplary practices. Max DePree and John Gardner learned from many years of experience. Kouzes and Posner's insights come from grounded research spanning more than two decades looking at personal-best leadership experiences. The sample of leaders Kouzes and Posner studied cuts across a wide range of organized activities, including many government and nonprofit organizations. The breadth of their sample of leaders gives them confidence in the generalizability of their findings.

Kouzes and Posner emphasize, echoing a point from DePree, that "leadership is not about personality; it's about behavior." Their five exemplary practices therefore dwell on behaviors that can make a difference to leaders in nonprofit and public organizations. The first practice they offer, *model the way*, is one that you will encounter frequently in the leadership literature if you read enough of it. Being a good example to others is critical for developing bonds between leader and follower, establishing trust, and modeling practices you want others to follow.

The second practice involves *inspiring a shared vision*. Recognize this: inspiring a shared vision is not the same as having a vision. Inspiring a shared vision depends as much on expressing the vision in ways others comprehend it and communicating the vision to enlist support as it does on the content of the vision itself.

Kouzes and Posner's third practice is *challenge the process*. One thing we know about human behavior is that change is difficult. Leaders are the ones who must marshal people to act contrary to a natural tendency. They can do so by modeling the way for others and inspiring a shared understanding that the status quo must be abandoned.

The fourth practice arising from Kouzes and Posner's research is *enable others to act*. One facet of being an enabler is to build a climate within which trust flourishes and collaboration and cooperation are commonplace. Organizations that are endowed with rich climates of trust and collaboration empower their members.

Even if leaders do all the right things, they must help followers find ways to sustain commitment and effort. Kouzes and Posner call this practice *encourage the heart*, and the metaphor of a vital organ is well placed. Leaders who can help followers sustain effort and commitment are a vital part of organizational achievement.

After reviewing functional, philosophical, and behavioral imperatives for leadership, it might be appropriate to ask: What makes leaders in these images? Ray Blunt and John Carver offer sound advice for growing leaders in both nonprofit and public service. In "Leaders Growing Leaders," Blunt suggests several processes applicable for leader development in both the nonprofit and public sectors. These processes intersect directly with one of the practices suggested by Kouzes and Posner, which is growing leaders by personal example. Blunt goes beyond the power of example to suggest three other processes: mentoring, coaching, and teaching.

Although we associate leadership with managerial roles in organizations, the chapters throughout this book reinforce there are many other places in which we need to find and develop leadership. John Carver's "Maintaining Board Leadership: Staying on Track and Institutionalizing Excellence" illustrates the importance of leadership in governance forums and how leaders can be developed in these contexts. The principles Carver suggests for securing leadership from nonprofit boards apply to public forums as well. A city manager must be as concerned about the readiness of a city council to lead as is a nonprofit executive director about the readiness of her board.

The five chapters in Part I provide visible signposts for the aspirations of leaders in the nonprofit and public sectors. The signposts derive from the accumulated wisdom of DePree and Gardner, the grounded research of Kouzes and Posner, and the developmental insights of Blunt and Carver. They collectively offer a strong foundation for our exploration of leadership in this reader.

Reference

Drucker, Peter. "Leadership: More doing than dash." *Wall Street Journal*, January 6, 1988, p. 1.

CHAPTER ONE

What Is Leadership?

Max DePree

T he first responsibility of a leader is to define reality. The last is to say thank you. In between the two, the leader must become a servant and a debtor. That sums up the progress of an artful leader.

Concepts of leadership, ideas about leadership, and leadership practices are the subject of much thought, discussion, writing, teaching, and learning. True leaders are sought after and cultivated. Leadership is not an easy subject to explain. A friend of mine characterizes leaders simply like this: "Leaders don't inflict pain; they bear pain."

The goal of thinking hard about leadership is not to produce great, or charismatic, or well-known leaders. The measure of leadership is not the quality of the head, but the tone of the body. The signs of outstanding leadership appear primarily among the followers. Are the followers reaching their potential? Are they learning? Serving? Do

---

This chapter was originally published as "What Is Leadership?" in Max DePree's *Leadership Is an Art.* (New York: Doubleday, 1989).

they achieve the required results? Do they change with grace? Manage conflict?

I would like to ask you to think about the concept of leadership in a certain way. Try to think about a leader, in the words of the gospel writer Luke, as "one who serves." Leadership is a concept of owing certain things to the institution. It is a way of thinking about institutional heirs, a way of thinking about stewardship as contrasted with ownership.

The art of leadership requires us to think about the leader-as-steward in terms of relationships: of assets and legacy, of momentum and effectiveness, of civility and values.

Leaders should leave behind them assets and a legacy. First, consider assets; certainly leaders owe assets. Leaders owe their institutions vital financial health, and the relationships and reputation that enable continuity of that financial health. Leaders must deliver to their organizations the appropriate services, products, tools, and equipment that people in the organization need in order to be accountable. In many institutions leaders are responsible for providing land and facilities.

But what else do leaders owe? What are artful leaders responsible for? Surely we need to include people. People are the heart and spirit of all that counts. Without people, there is no need for leaders. Leaders can decide to be primarily concerned with leaving assets to their institutional heirs or they can go beyond that and capitalize on the opportunity to leave a legacy, a legacy that takes into account the more difficult, qualitative side of life, one which provides greater meaning, more challenge, and more joy in the lives of those whom leaders enable.

Besides owing assets to their institutions, leaders owe the people in those institutions certain things. Leaders need to be concerned with the institutional value system which, after all, leads to the principles and standards that guide the practices of the people in the institution. Leaders owe a clear statement of the values of the organization. These values should be broadly understood and agreed to and should shape our corporate and individual behavior. What is this value system based on? How is it expressed? How is it audited? These are not easy questions to deal with.

Leaders are also responsible for future leadership. They need to identify, develop, and nurture future leaders.

Leaders are responsible for such things as a sense of quality in the institution, for whether or not the institution is open to influence and open to change. Effective leaders encourage contrary opinions, an important source of vitality. I am talking about how leaders can nurture the roots of an institution, about a sense of continuity, about institutional culture.

Leaders owe a covenant to the corporation or institution, which is, after all, a group of people. Leaders owe the organization a new reference point for what caring, purposeful, committed people can be in the institutional setting. Notice I did not say what people can do—what we can do is merely a consequence of what we can be. Corporations, like the people who compose them, are always in a state of becoming. Covenants bind people together and enable them to meet their corporate needs by meeting the needs of one another. We must do this in a way that is consonant with the world around us.

Leaders owe a certain maturity. Maturity as expressed in a sense of self-worth, a sense of belonging, a sense of expectancy, a sense of responsibility, a sense of accountability, and a sense of equality.

Leaders owe the corporation rationality. Rationality gives reason and mutual understanding to programs and to relationships. It gives visible order. Excellence and commitment and competence are available to us only under the rubric of rationality. A rational environment values trust and human dignity and provides the opportunity for personal development and self-fulfillment in the attainment of the organization's goals.

Business literacy, understanding the economic basic of a corporation, is essential. Only a group of people who share a body of knowledge and continually learn together can stay vital and viable.

Leaders owe people space, space in the sense of freedom. Freedom in the sense of enabling our gifts to be exercised. We need to give each other the space to grow, to be ourselves, to exercise our diversity. We need to give each other space so that we may both give and receive such beautiful things as ideas, openness, dignity, joy, healing, and inclusion. And in giving each other the gift of space, we need also to offer the gifts of grace and beauty to which each of us is entitled.

Another way to think about what leaders owe is to ask this question: What is it without which this institution would not be what it is?

Leaders are obligated to provide and maintain momentum. Leadership comes with a lot of debts to the future. There are more immediate obligations as well. Momentum is one. Momentum in a vital company is palpable. It is not abstract or mysterious. It is the feeling among a group of people that their lives and work are intertwined and moving toward a recognizable and legitimate goal. It begins with competent leadership and a management team strongly dedicated to aggressive managerial development and opportunities. This team's job is to provide an environment that allows momentum to gather.

Momentum comes from a clear vision of what the corporation ought to be, from a well-thought-out strategy to achieve that vision, and from carefully conceived and communicated directions and plans that enable everyone to participate and be publicly accountable in achieving those plans.

Momentum depends on a pertinent but flexible research and development program led by people with outstanding gifts and unique talents. Momentum results when a corporation has an aggressive, professional, inspired group of people in its marketing and sales units. Momentum results when the operations group serves its customers in such a way that the customer sees them as their best supplier of tools, equipment, and services. Underlying these complex activities is the essential role of the financial team. They provide the financial guidelines and the necessary ratios. They are responsible for equity among the various groups who compose the corporate family.

Leaders are responsible for effectiveness. Much has been written about effectiveness—some of the best of it by Peter Drucker. He has such a great ability to simplify concepts. One of the things he tells us is that efficiency is doing the thing right, but effectiveness is doing the right thing.

Leaders can delegate efficiency, but they must deal personally with effectiveness. Of course, the natural question is "how?" We could fill many pages dealing with how to be effective, but I would like to touch on just two ways.

The first is the understanding that effectiveness comes about through enabling others to reach their potential—both their personal potential and their corporate or institutional potential.

In some South Pacific cultures, a speaker holds a conch shell as a symbol of a temporary position of authority. Leaders must understand who holds the conch—that is, who should be listened to and when. This makes it possible for people to use their gifts to the fullest for the benefit of everyone.

Sometimes, to be sure, a leader must choose who is to speak. That is part of the risk of leadership. A leader must assess capability. A leader must be a judge of people. For leaders choose a person, not a position.

Another way to improve effectiveness is to encourage roving leadership. Roving leadership arises and expresses itself at varying times and in varying situations, according to the dictates of those situations. Roving leaders have the special gifts, or the special strengths, or the special temperament to lead in these special situations. They are acknowledged by others who are ready to follow them.

Leaders must take a role in developing, expressing, and defending civility and values. In a civilized institution or corporation, we see good manners, respect for persons, an understanding of "good goods," and an appreciation of the way in which we serve each other.

Civility has to do with identifying values as opposed to following fashions. Civility might be defined as an ability to distinguish between what is actually healthy and what merely appears to be living. A leader can tell the difference between living edges and dying ones.

> To lose sight of the beauty of ideas and of hope and opportunity, and to frustrate the right to be needed, is to be at the dying edge.
>
> To be a part of a throwaway mentality that discards goods and ideas, that discards principles and law, that discards persons and families, is to be at the dying edge.
>
> To be at the leading edge of consumption, affluence, and instant gratification is to be at the dying edge.
>
> To ignore the dignity of work and the elegance of simplicity, and the essential responsibility of serving each other, is to be at the dying edge.

Justice Oliver Wendell Holmes is reported to have said this about simplicity: "I would not give a fig for the simplicity this side of complexity, but I would give my life for the simplicity on the other side of complexity." To be at the living edge is to search out the "simplicity on the other side of complexity."

In a day when so much energy seems to be spent on maintenance and manuals, on bureaucracy and meaningless quantification, to be a leader is to enjoy the special privileges of complexity, of ambiguity, of diversity. But to be a leader means, especially, having the opportunity to make a meaningful difference in the lives of those who permit leaders to lead.

—∿∿—

At the time of original printing Max DePree was chairman emeritus of Herman Miller, Inc., and a member of Fortune *magazine's Business Hall of Fame.*

CHAPTER TWO

The Tasks of Leadership

John W. Gardner

E xamination of the tasks performed by leaders takes us to the heart of some of the most interesting questions concerning leadership. It also helps to distinguish among the many kinds of leaders. Leaders differ strikingly in how well they perform various functions.

The following nine tasks seem to me to be the most significant functions of leadership, but I encourage readers to add to the list or to describe the tasks in other ways. Leadership activities implicit in all of the tasks (for example, communicating, relating effectively with people) are not dealt with separately.

ENVISIONING GOALS

The two tasks at the heart of the popular notion of leadership are goal setting and motivating. As a high school senior put it, "Leaders point us in the right direction and tell us to get moving." Although we take

Originally published as "The Tasks of Leadership," in John Gardner's *On Leadership*. (New York: The Free Press, 1990).

a more complicated view of the tasks of leadership, it is appropriate that we begin with the envisioning of goals. Albert Einstein said, "Perfection of means and confusion of ends seems to characterize our age."

Leaders perform the function of goal setting in diverse ways. Some assert a vision of what the group (organization, community, nation) can be at its best. Others point us toward solutions to our problems. Still others, presiding over internally divided groups, are able to define overarching goals that unify constituencies and focus energies. In today's complex world, the setting of goals may have to be preceded by extensive research and problem solving.

Obviously, a constituency is not a blank slate for the leader to write on. Any collection of people sufficiently related to be called a community has many shared goals, some explicit, some unexpressed (perhaps even unconscious), as tangible as better prices for their crops, as intangible as a better future for their children. In a democracy, the leader takes such shared goals into account.

The relative roles of leaders and followers in determining goals vary from group to group. The teacher of first-grade children and the sergeant training recruits do not do extensive consulting as to goals; congressional candidates do a great deal. In the case of many leaders, goals are handed to them by higher authority. The factory manager and the combat commander may be superb leaders, but many of their goals are set at higher levels.

In short, goals emerge from many sources. The culture itself specifies certain goals; constituents have their concerns; higher authority makes its wishes known. Out of the welter, leaders take some goals as given, and making their own contribution, select and formulate a set of objectives. It may sound as though leaders have only marginal freedom, but in fact there is usually considerable opportunity, even for lower-level leaders, to put their personal emphasis and interpretation on the setting of goals.

There is inevitable tension between long- and short-term goals. On the one hand, constituents are not entirely comfortable with the jerkiness of short-term goal seeking, and they value the sense of stability that comes with a vision of far horizons. On the other hand, long-term goals may require them to defer immediate gratification on at least some fronts. Leaders often fear that when citizens enter the voting booth, they will remember the deferral of gratification more vividly than they remember the reason for it.

Before the Civil War, Elizabeth Cady Stanton saw virtually the whole agenda for women's rights as it was to emerge over the succeeding century. Many of her contemporaries in the movement were not at all prepared for such an inclusive vision and urged her to play it down.

Another visionary far ahead of his time was the South American liberator, Simone Bolivar. He launched his fight in that part of Gran Colombia, which is now Venezuela, but in his mind was a vision not only of independence for all of Spain's possessions in the New World, but also a peaceful alliance of the new states in some form of league or confederation. Although he was tragically ahead of his time, the dream never died and has influenced generations of Latin American leaders striving toward unity.

AFFIRMING VALUES

A great civilization is a drama lived in the minds of a people. It is a shared vision; it is shared norms, expectations, and purposes. When one thinks of the world's great civilizations, the most vivid images that crowd in on us are apt to be of the physical monuments left behind—the Pyramids, the Parthenon, the Mayan temples. But in truth, all the physical splendor was the merest by-product. The civilizations themselves, from beginning to end, existing in the minds of men and women.

If we look at ordinary human communities, we see the same reality: A community lives in the minds of its members—in shared assumptions, beliefs, customs, ideas that give meaning, ideas that motivate. And among the ideas are norms or values. In any healthy, reasonably coherent community, people come to have shared views concerning right and wrong, better and worse—in personal conduct, in governing, in art, whatever. They define for their time and place what things are legal or illegal, virtuous or vicious, good taste or bad. They have little or no impulse to be neutral about such matters. Every society is, as Philip Rieff (1966) puts it, "a system of moralizing demands."

Values are embodied in the society's religious beliefs and its secular philosophy. Over the past century, many intellectuals have looked down on the celebration of our values as an unsophisticated and often hypocritical activity. But every healthy society celebrates its values. They are expressed in art, in song, in ritual. They are stated explicitly in historical documents, in ceremonial speeches, in textbooks. They are reflected in stories told around the campfire, in the legends kept alive by old folks, in the fables told to children.

In a pluralistic community there are, within the broad consensus that enables the community to function, many and vigorous conflicts over specific values.

THE REGENERATION OF VALUES. One of the milder pleasures of maturity is bemoaning the decay of once strongly held values. Values always decay over time. Societies that keep their values alive do so not by escaping the processes of decay but by powerful processes of regeneration. There must be perpetual rebuilding. Each generation must rediscover the living elements in its own tradition and adapt them to present realities. To assist in that rediscovery is one of the tasks of leadership.

The leaders whom we admire the most help to revitalize our shared beliefs and values. They have always spent a portion of their time teaching the value framework.

Sometimes the leader's affirmation of values challenges entrenched hypocrisy or conflicts with the values held by a segment of the constituency. Elizabeth Cady Stanton, speaking for now-accepted values, was regarded as a thoroughgoing radical in her day (Griffith, 1984). Jesus not only comforted the afflicted but afflicted the comfortable.

MOTIVATING

Chapter 16 [of *On Leadership*] is devoted to the task of motivation, so I deal with it briefly here. Leaders do not create motivation out of thin air. They unlock or channel existing motives. Any group has a great tangle of motives. Effective leaders tap those that serve the purposes of collective action in pursuit of shared goals. They accomplish the alignment of individual and group goals. They deal with the circumstances that often lead group members to withhold their best efforts. They call for the kind of effort and restraint, drive and discipline that make for great performance. They create a climate in which there is pride in making significant contributions to shared goals.

Note that in the tasks of leadership, the transactions between leaders and constituents go beyond the rational level to the non-rational and unconscious levels of human functioning. Young potential leaders who have been schooled to believe that all elements of a problem are rational and technical, reducible to words and numbers, are ill-equipped to move into an area in which intuition and empathy are powerful aids to problem solving.

MANAGING

Most managers exhibit some leadership skills, and most leaders on occasion find themselves managing. Leadership and management are not the same thing, but they overlap. It makes sense to include managing in the list of tasks leaders perform.

In the paragraphs that follow I focus on those aspects of leadership that one might describe as managing without slipping into a conventional description of managing as such. And I try to find terminology and phrasing broad enough to cover the diverse contexts in which leadership occurs in corporations, unions, municipalities, political movements, and so on.

1. *Planning and Priority Setting*. Assuming that broad goals have been set, someone has to plan, fix priorities, choose means, and formulate policy. These are functions often performed by leaders. When Lyndon B. Johnson said, early in his presidency, that education was the nation's number one priority, he galvanized the nation's educational leaders and released constructive energies far beyond any governmental action that had yet been taken. It was a major factor in leading me to accept a post in his Cabinet.

2. *Organizing and Institution Building*. We have all seen leaders enjoy their brilliant moment and then disappear without a trace because they had no gift for building their purposes into institutions. In the ranks of leaders, Alfred Sloan was at the other extreme. Although he sold a lot of automobiles, he was not primarily a salesman; he was an institution builder. His understanding of organization was intuitive and profound.

   Someone has to design the structures and processes through which substantial endeavors are accomplished over time. Ideally, leaders should not regard themselves as indispensable but should enable the group to carry on. Institutions are a means to that end. Jean Monnet (1978) said, "Nothing is possible without individuals; nothing is lasting without institutions."

3. *Keeping the System Functioning.* Presiding over the arrangements through which individual energies are coordinated to achieve shared goals sounds like a quintessential management task. But it is clear that most leaders find themselves occasionally performing one or another of the essential chores: mobilizing and allocating resources; staffing and ensuring the continuing vitality of the team; creating and maintaining appropriate procedures; directing, delegating, and coordinating; providing a system of incentives; reporting, evaluating, and holding accountable.

4. *Agenda Setting and Decision Making.* The goals may be clear and the organization well set up and smoothly operating, but there remain agenda-setting and decision-making functions that must be dealt with. The announcement of goals without a proposed program for meeting them is a familiar enough political phenomenon—but not one that builds credibility. There are leaders who can motivate and inspire but who cannot visualize a path to the goal in practical, feasible steps. Leaders who lack that skill must bring onto their team people who have it.

> One of the purest examples of the leader as agenda setter was Florence Nightingale (Huxley, 1975). Her public image was and is that of the lady of mercy, but under her gentle manner, she was a rugged spirit, a fighter, a tough-minded system changer. She never made public appearances or speeches and, except for her two years in the Crimea, held no public position. Her strength was that she was a formidable authority on the evils to be remedied, she knew what to do about them, and she used public opinion to goad top officials to adopt her agenda.

5. *Exercising Political Judgment.* In our pluralistic society, persons directing substantial enterprises find that they are presiding over many constituencies within their organizations and contending with many outside. Each has its needs and claims. One of the tasks of the leader/manager is to make the political judgments necessary to prevent secondary conflicts of purpose from blocking progress toward primary goals. Sometimes the literature on administration and management treats politics as an alien and disruptive force. But Aaron Wildavsky (1984), in his brilliant book, *The Nursing Father: Moses as a Political Leader*, makes the point that leaders are inevitably political.

ACHIEVING WORKABLE UNITY

A pluralistic society is, by definition, one that accepts many different elements, each with its own purposes. Collisions are inevitable and often healthy—as in commercial competition, in civil suits, and in efforts to redress grievances through the political process. Conflict is necessary in the case of oppressed groups that must fight for the justice that is due them. All our elective officials know the intense conflict of the political campaign. Indeed, one could argue that willingness to engage in battle when necessary is a sine qua non of leadership.

But most leaders most of the time are striving to diminish conflict rather than increase it. Some measure of cohesion and mutual tolerance is an absolute requirement of social functioning.

Sometimes the problem is not outright conflict but an unwillingness to cooperate. One of the gravest problems George Washington faced as a general was that the former colonies, although they had no doubt they were all on the same side, were not always sure they wanted to cooperate. As late as 1818, John Randolph declared, "When I speak of my country, I mean the Commonwealth of Virginia" (Bruce, 1922).

The unifying function of leaders is well illustrated in the actions of George Bush after winning the presidential election of 1988. He promptly met with his defeated opponent, Michael Dukakis; with his chief rival for the nomination, Senator Robert Dole; and with Jesse Jackson and Coretta Scott King, both of whom had opposed his election. He asked Jack Kemp, another of his rivals for the nomination, to be Secretary of Housing and Urban Development, and Senator Dole's wife, Elizabeth Hanford Dole, to be Secretary of Labor.

Leaders in this country today must cope with the fragmentation of the society into groups that have great difficulty in understanding one another or agreeing on common goals. It is a fragmentation rooted in the pluralism of our society, in the obsessive specialization of modern life, and in the skill with which groups organize to advance their concerns.

Under the circumstances, all our leaders must spend part of their time dealing with polarization and building community. There is a false notion that this is a more bland, less rigorous task than leadership of one of the combative segments. In fact, the leader willing to combat polarization is the braver person, and is generally under fire from both sides. I would suggest that Jean Monnet, the father of the European Common Market, is a useful model for future leaders.

When there were conflicting purposes, Monnet saw the possibility of shared goals, and he knew how to move his contemporaries toward those shared goals.

TRUST. Much depends on the general level of trust in the organization or society. The infinitely varied and complex doings of the society—any society—would come to a halt if people did not trust other people most of the time—trust them to observe custom, follow the rules, and behave with some predictability. Countless circumstances operate to diminish that trust, but one may be sure that, if the society is functioning at all, *some* degree of trust survives.

Leaders can do much to preserve the necessary level of trust. And the first requirement is that they have the capacity to inspire trust in themselves. In sixteenth-century Italy, where relations among the warring kingdoms were an unending alley fight, Machiavelli's chilling advice to the Prince—"It is necessary . . . to be a feigner and a dissembler," or, as another translator renders the same passage, "You must be a great liar and hypocrite"—may have been warranted (Machiavelli, 1952). And, under conditions of iron rule, Hitler and Stalin were able to live by betrayals. But in our society, leaders must work to raise the level of trust.

EXPLAINING

Explaining sounds too pedestrian to be on a list of leadership tasks, but every leader recognizes it. People want to know what the problem is, why they are being asked to do certain things, why they face so many frustrations. Thurman Arnold (1937) said, "Unhappy is a people that has run out of words to describe what is happening to them." Leaders find the words.

To be heard above the hubbub in the public forum today, explaining generally requires more than clarity and eloquence. It requires effective access to the media of communication or to those segments of the population that keep ideas in circulation—editors, writers, intellectuals, association leaders, advocacy groups, chief executive officers, and the like.

The task of explaining is so important that some who do it exceptionally well play a leadership role even though they are not leaders in the conventional sense. When the American colonies were struggling for independence, Thomas Paine was a memorable explainer. In the powerful environmentalist surge of the 1960s and 1970s, no activist leader had as pervasive an influence on the movement as did Rachel Carson (1963), whose book *Silent Spring* burst on the scene in 1963. Betty Friedan's (1963) *The Feminine Mystique* played a similar role for the women's movement.

Leaders teach. Lincoln, in his second inaugural address, provided an extraordinary example of the leader as teacher. Teaching and leading are distinguishable occupations, but every great leader is clearly teaching—and every great teacher is leading.

SERVING AS A SYMBOL

Leaders are inevitably symbols. Workers singled out to be supervisors discover that they are set apart from their old comrades in subtle ways. They try to keep the old camaraderie but things have changed. They are now symbols of management. Sergeants symbolize the chain of command. Parish religious leaders symbolize their churches.

In a group threatened with internal strife, the leader may be a crucial symbol of unity. In a minority group's struggle to find its place, combative leaders—troublesome to others—may be to their own people the perfect symbol of their anger and their struggle.

The top leader of a community or nation symbolizes the group's collective identity and continuity. For this reason, the death of a president produces a special reaction of grief and loss. Americans who were beyond childhood when John F. Kennedy was assassinated remember, despite the passage of decades, precisely where they were and what they were doing when the news reached them. Even for many who did not admire him, the news had the impact of a blow to the solar plexus. And those old enough to remember Franklin D. Roosevelt's death recognize the reaction.

For late eighteenth-century Americans, George Washington was the symbol of all that they had been through together. Thomas Jefferson became such a powerful symbol of our democratic aspirations that for generations politicians fought over his memory. Those who favored Hamiltonian views sought bitterly and unsuccessfully to shatter the Jefferson image. As Merrill Peterson (1960) has cogently argued, the man himself lost reality and the symbol took over. In the dark days of the Great Depression, the American impulse to face events in a positive spirit found its symbol in the ebullient Franklin D. Roosevelt.

Outside the political area, Albert Schweitzer, the gifted theologian and musician who in 1913 gave up a comfortable and respected life in his native Germany to spend the remainder of his years presiding over a medical mission in Equatorial Africa, stands as the pristine example of leader as symbol.

Some individuals newly risen to leadership have a hard time adjusting to the reality that they are symbols. I recall a visit with a young college president who had just come into the job fresh from a professorship, with no prior administrative experience. He confided that he was deeply irked by an incident the preceding day. In his first speech before faculty, students, trustees, and alumni he had simply been himself—a man of independent mind full of lively personal opinions—and many of his listeners were nonplussed and irritated. They were not interested in a display of idiosyncratic views. They had expected him to speak as their new leader, their symbol of institutional continuity, their ceremonial collective voice. I told him gently that they had expected him to be their spokesman and symbol, and this simply angered him further. "I'll resign," he said, "if I can't be myself!" Over time, he learned that leaders can rarely afford the luxury of speaking for themselves alone.

Most leaders become quite aware of the symbolic aspects of their roles and make effective use of them. One of the twentieth-century leaders who did so most skillfully was Gandhi (Erikson, 1969). In the issues he chose to do battle on, in the way he conducted his campaigns, in the jail terms and the fasting, in his manner of dress, he symbolized his people, their desperate need, and their struggle against oppression.

Needless to say, leaders do not always function as benign symbols. In the Iran-Contra affair of 1986–1987 it became apparent that men bound by their oath of office were lying to the public, lying to the Congress of the United States, and lying to one another. To some Americans they became symbols of all the falsehoods and betrayals committed by a distant and distrusted government.

REPRESENTING THE GROUP

In quieter times (we love to imagine that there were quieter times), leaders could perhaps concentrate on their own followers. Today, representing the group in its dealings with others is a substantial leadership task.

It is a truism that all of the human systems (organizations, groups, communities) that make up the society and the world are increasingly interdependent. Virtually all leaders at every level must carry on dealings with systems external to the one in which they themselves are involved—tasks of representing and negotiating, of defending institutional integrity, of public relations. As one moves higher in the ranks of leadership, such chores increase.

It goes without saying that people who have spent their careers in the world of the specialist or within the boundaries of a narrow community (their firm, their profession) are often ill-equipped for such leadership tasks. The young potential leader must learn early to cross boundaries and to know many worlds. The attributes that enable leaders to teach and lead their own constituencies may be wholly ineffective in external dealings. Military leaders who are revered by their troops may be clumsy with civilians. The business leader who is effective within the business culture may be lost in dealing with politicians. A distinctive characteristic of the ablest leaders is that they do not shrink from external representation. They see the long-term needs and goals of their constituency in the broadest context, and they act accordingly. The most capable mayors think not just of the city but of the metropolitan area and the region. Able business leaders are alert to the political climate and to world economic trends.

The most remarkable modern example of a leader carrying out the representative function is Charles De Gaulle. De Gaulle has his detractors, but none can fail to marvel at his performance in successfully representing the once and future France-as-a-great-power at a time when the nation itself was a defeated, demoralized, enemy-occupied land. By his own commanding presence, he kept France's place at the table through the dark days. Years later Jean Monnet wrote:

> "It took great strength of character for him, a traditional soldier, to cross the great dividing line of disobedience to orders from above. He was the only man of his rank with the courage to do so; and in the painful isolation felt by those Frenchmen who had decided to continue the Allied struggle, De Gaulle's rare example was a source of great moral strength."

RENEWING

Chapter 12 [in *On Leadership*] concerns the task of renewing, so I deal with it very briefly here.

Leaders need not be renewers. They can lead people down old paths, using old slogans, toward old objectives. Sometimes that is appropriate. But the world changes with disconcerting swiftness. Too often the old paths are blocked and the old solutions no longer solve anything. De Gaulle (1964), writing of France's appalling unpreparedness for World War II, said:

> "The Army became stuck in a set of ideas which had had their heyday before the end of the First World War. It was all the more inclined that way because its leaders were growing old at their posts, wedded to errors that had once constituted their glory."

Leaders must foster the process of renewal.

So much for the tasks of leadership. The individual with a gift for building a leadership team may successfully delegate one or another of those tasks to other members of the team. One function that cannot be delegated is that of serving as symbol. That the leader is a symbol is a fact, not a matter of choice. The task is to take appropriate account of that reality and to use it well in the service of the group's goals.

Another function that cannot be delegated entirely is the envisioning of goals. Unless the leader has a sense of where the whole enterprise is going and must go, it is not possible to delegate (or carry out personally) the other functions. To have "a sense of where the whole enterprise is going and must go" is, I am inclined to say, the very core and essence of the best leadership.

In a discussion of the tasks of leadership, a colleague of mine said, "I do not see 'enabling' or 'empowering' on the list. Aren't those the central tasks of leadership?" For those unfamiliar with contemporary discussions of leadership, I should explain that reference to *enabling* or *empowering* has become the preferred method of condensing into a single word the widely held conviction that the purpose of leaders is not to dominate nor diminish followers but to strengthen and help them to develop.

But enabling and empowering are not separable tasks. They require a variety of actions on the parts of leaders. For example:

- Sharing information and making it possible for followers to obtain appropriate kinds of education
- Sharing power by devolving initiative and responsibility

- Building the confidence of followers so that they can achieve their own goals through their own efforts
- Removing barriers to the release of individual energy and talent
- Seeking, finding, and husbanding the various kinds of resources that followers need
- Resolving the conflicts that paralyze group action
- Providing organizational arrangements appropriate to group effort

Any attempt to describe a social process as complex as leadership inevitably makes it seem more orderly than it is. Leadership is not tidy. Decisions are made and then revised or reversed. Misunderstandings are frequent, inconsistency inevitable. Achieving a goal may simply make the next goal more urgent; inside every solution are the seeds of new problems. And as Donald Michael (1983) has pointed out, most of the time most things are out of hand. No leader enjoys that reality, but every leader knows it.

It would be easy to imagine that the tasks described are items to be handled separately, like nine items on a shopping list, each from a separate store. But the effective leader is always doing several tasks simultaneously. The best antidote to the shopping list conception is to look at the setting in which all the tasks are mingled—the complex interplay between leaders and those "led."

References

Arnold, Thurman. *The Folklore of Capitalism*. New Haven: Yale University Press, 1937.

Bruce, William Cabell. *John Randolph of Roanoke*. New York: Putnam, 1922.

Carson, Rachel. *Silent Spring*. New York: Houghton Mifflin, 1963.

De Gaulle, Charles. *The War Memoirs, 1940–1946*. New York: Simon & Schuster, 1964.

Erikson, Erik. *Gandhi's Truth*. New York: W.W. Norton, 1969.

Friedan, Betty. *The Feminine Mystique*. New York: Dell, 1963.

Griffith, Elisabeth. *In Her Own Right: The Life of Elizabeth Cady Stanton*. New York: Oxford University Press, 1984.

Huxley, Elspeth. *Florence Nightingale*. New York: G.P. Putnam's Sons, 1975.

Machiavelli, Niccolo. *The Prince*. New York: New American Library, 1952.

Michael, Donald M. "Competence and Compassion in an Age of Uncertainty," *World Future Society Bulletin*, January–February 1983.

Monnet, Jean. *Memoirs*. (Richard Mayne, trans.). New York: Doubleday, 1978.

Peterson, Merrill D. *The Jefferson Image in the American Mind*. New York: Oxford University Press, 1960.

Rieff, Philip. *The Triumph of the Therapeutic*. New York: Harper and Row, 1966.

Wildavsky, Aaron. *The Nursing Father: Moses as a Political Leader*. Tuscaloosa: University of Alabama Press, 1984.

At time of original publication John W. Gardner had served six presidents of the United States in various leadership capacities. In addition he has served as director of several major U.S. corporations.

CHAPTER THREE

The Five Practices
of Exemplary Leadership

James M. Kouzes
Barry Z. Posner

Since 1983 we've been conducting research on personal-best leadership experiences, and we've discovered that there are countless examples of how leaders, like Dick and Claire, mobilize others to get extraordinary things done in virtually every arena of organized activity. We've found them in profit-based firms and nonprofits, manufacturing and services, government and business, health care, education and entertainment, and work and community service. Leaders reside in every city and every country, in every position and every place. They're employees and volunteers, young and old, women and men. Leadership knows no racial or religious bounds, no ethnic or cultural borders. We find exemplary leadership everywhere we look.[1]

This chapter was originally published as "The Five Practices of Exemplary Leadership" in James Kouzes and Barry Posner's *The Leadership Challenge* (4th ed.). (San Francisco: Jossey-Bass, 2007).

From our analysis of thousands of personal-best leadership experiences, we've discovered that ordinary people who guide others along pioneering journeys follow rather similar paths. Although each experience we examined was unique in expression, every case followed remarkably similar patterns of action. We've forged these common practices into a model of leadership, and we offer it here as guidance for leaders as they attempt to keep their own bearings and steer others toward peak achievements.

As we looked deeper into the dynamic process of leadership, through case analyses and survey questionnaires, we uncovered five practices common to personal-best leadership experiences. When getting extraordinary things done in organizations, leaders engage in these Five Practices of Exemplary Leadership:

- Model the Way
- Inspire a Shared Vision
- Challenge the Process
- Enable Others to Act
- Encourage the Heart

The Five Practices—which we discuss briefly in this chapter—aren't the private property of the people we studied or of a few select shining stars. Leadership is not about personality; it's about behavior. The Five Practices are available to anyone who accepts the leadership challenge. And they're also not the accident of a unique moment in history. The Five Practices have stood the test of time, and our most recent research confirms that they're just as relevant today as they were when we first began our investigation more than twenty-five years ago.

MODEL THE WAY

Titles are granted, but it's your behavior that wins you respect. As Tom Brack, with Europe's SmartTeam AG, told us, "Leading means you have to be a good example, and live what you say." This sentiment was shared across all the cases that we collected. Exemplary leaders know that if they want to gain commitment and achieve the highest standards, they must be models of the behavior they expect of others. *Leaders model the way.*

To effectively model the behavior they expect of others, leaders must first be clear about guiding principles. They must *clarify values.* As Lindsay Levin, chairman for Whites Group in England, explained, "You have to open up your heart and let people know what you really think and believe. This means talking about your values." Leaders must find their own voices, and then they must clearly and distinctively give voice to their values. As the personal-best stories illustrate, leaders are supposed to stand up for their beliefs, so they'd better have some beliefs to stand up for. But it's not just the leader's values that are important. Leaders aren't just representing themselves. They speak and act on behalf of a larger organization. Leaders must forge agreement around common principles and common ideals.

Eloquent speeches about common values, however, aren't nearly enough. Leaders' deeds are far more important than their words when one wants to determine how serious leaders really are about what they say. Words and deeds must be consistent. Exemplary leaders go first. They go first by *setting the example* through daily actions that demonstrate they are deeply committed to their beliefs. As Prabha Seshan, principal engineer for SSA Global, told us, "One of the best ways to prove something is important is by doing it yourself and setting an example." She discovered that her actions spoke volumes about how the team needed to "take ownership of things they believed in and valued." There wasn't anything Prabha asked others to do that she wasn't willing to do herself, and as a result, "While I always trusted my team, my team in turn trusted me." For instance, she wasn't required to design or code features, but by doing some of this work she demonstrated to others not only what she stood for but also how much she valued the work they were doing and what their end-user expected from the product.

The personal-best projects we heard about in our research were all distinguished by relentless effort, steadfastness, competence, and attention to detail. We were also struck by how the actions leaders took to set an example were often simple things. Sure, leaders had operational and strategic plans. But the examples they gave were not about elaborate designs. They were about the power of spending time with someone, of working side by side with colleagues, of telling stories that made values come alive, of being highly visible during times of uncertainty, and of asking questions to get people to think about values and priorities.

Modeling the way is about earning the right and the respect to lead through direct involvement and action. People follow first the person, then the plan.

INSPIRE A SHARED VISION

When people described to us their personal-best leadership experiences, they told of times when they imagined an exciting, highly attractive future for their organization. They had visions and dreams of what *could* be. They had absolute and total personal belief in those dreams, and they were confident in their abilities to make extraordinary things happen. Every organization, every social movement, begins with a dream. The dream or vision is the force that invents the future. *Leaders inspire a shared vision.* As Mark D'Arcangelo, system memory product marketing manager at Hitachi Semiconductor, told us about his personal-best leadership experience, "What made the difference was the vision of how things could be and clearly painting this picture for all to see and comprehend."

Leaders gaze across the horizon of time, imagining the attractive opportunities that are in store when they and their constituents arrive at a distant destination. They *envision exciting and ennobling possibilities.* Leaders have a desire to make something happen, to change the way things are, to create something that no one else has ever created before. In some ways, leaders live their lives backward. They see pictures in their mind's eye of what the results will look like even before they've started their project, much as an architect draws a blueprint or an engineer builds a model. Their clear image of the future pulls them forward. Yet visions seen only by leaders are insufficient to create an organized movement or a significant change in a company. A person with no constituents is not a leader, and people will not follow until they accept a vision as their own. Leaders cannot command commitment, only inspire it.

Leaders have to *enlist others in a common vision.* To enlist people in a vision, leaders must know their constituents and speak their language. People must believe that leaders understand their needs and have their interests at heart. Leadership is a dialogue, not a monologue. To enlist support, leaders must have intimate knowledge of people's dreams, hopes, aspirations, visions, and values. Evelia Davis, merchandise manager for Mervyns, told us that, while she was good at telling people where they were going together, she also needed to do a good job of explaining why they should follow her, how they could help reach the destination, and what this meant for them. As Evelia put it, "If you don't believe enough to share it, talk about it, and get others excited about it then it's not much of a vision!"

Leaders breathe life into the hopes and dreams of others and enable them to see the exciting possibilities that the future holds. Leaders forge a unity of purpose by showing constituents how the dream is for the common good. Leaders stir the fire of passion in others by expressing enthusiasm for the compelling vision of their group. Leaders communicate their passion through vivid language and an expressive style.

Whatever the venue, and without exception, the people in our study reported that they were incredibly enthusiastic about their personal-best projects. Their own enthusiasm was catching; it spread from leader to constituents. Their belief in and enthusiasm for the vision were the sparks that ignited the flame of inspiration.

CHALLENGE THE PROCESS

Every single personal-best leadership case we collected involved some kind of challenge. The challenge might have been an innovative new product, a cutting-edge service, a groundbreaking piece of legislation, an invigorating campaign to get adolescents to join an environmental program, a revolutionary turnaround of a bureaucratic military program, or the start-up of a new plant or business. Whatever the challenge, all the cases involved a change from the status quo. Not one person claimed to have achieved a personal best by keeping things the same. All leaders *challenge the process.*

Leaders venture out. None of the individuals in our study sat idly by waiting for fate to smile upon them. "Luck" or "being in the right place at the right time" may play a role in the specific opportunities leaders embrace, but those who lead others to greatness seek and accept challenge. Jennifer Cun, in her role as a budget analyst with Intel, noted how critical it is for leaders "to always be looking for ways to improve their team, taking interests outside of their job or organization, finding ways to stay current of what the competition is doing, networking, and taking initiative to try new things."

Leaders are pioneers. They are willing to step out into the unknown. They *search for opportunities to innovate, grow, and improve.*

But leaders aren't the only creators or originators of new products, services, or processes. In fact, it's more likely that they're not: innovation comes more from listening than from telling. Product and service innovations tend to come from customers, clients, vendors, people in the labs, and people on the front lines; process innovations, from the people doing the work. Sometimes a dramatic external event thrusts an organization into a radically new condition. Leaders have to continually be looking outside of themselves and their organizations for new and innovative products, processes, and services. "Mediocrity and status quo will never lead a company to success in the marketplace" is what Mike Pepe, product marketing manager at O3 Entertainment, told us. "Taking risks and believing that taking them is worthwhile," he went on to say, "are the only way companies can 'jump' rather than simply climb the improvement ladder."

When it comes to innovation, the leader's major contributions are in the creation of a climate for experimentation, the recognition of good ideas, the support of those ideas, and the willingness to challenge the system to get new products, processes, services, and systems adopted. It might be more accurate, then, to say that leaders aren't the inventors as much as they are the early patrons and adopters of innovation.

Leaders know well that innovation and change involve *experimenting and taking risks.* Despite the inevitability of mistakes and failures, leaders proceed anyway. One way of dealing with the potential risks and failures of experimentation is to approach change through incremental steps and small wins.

Little victories, when piled on top of each other, build confidence that even the biggest challenges can be met. In so doing, they strengthen commitment to the long-term future. Not everyone is equally comfortable with risk and uncertainty. Leaders must pay attention to the capacity of their constituents to take control of challenging situations and to become fully committed to change. You can't exhort people to take risks if they don't also feel safe.

It would be ridiculous to assert that those who fail over and over again eventually succeed as leaders. Success in any endeavor isn't a process of simply buying enough lottery tickets. The key that unlocks the door to opportunity is learning. Claude Meyer, with the Red Cross in Kenya, put it to us this way: "Leadership is learning by doing, adapting to actual conditions. Leaders are constantly learning from their errors and failures." Life is the leader's laboratory, and exemplary leaders use it to conduct as many experiments as possible.

Try, fail, learn. Try, fail, learn. Try, fail, learn. That's the leader's mantra. Leaders are learners. They learn from their failures as well as from their successes, and they make it possible for others to do the same.

ENABLE OTHERS TO ACT

Grand dreams don't become significant realities through the actions of a single person. It requires a team effort. It requires solid trust and strong relationships.

It requires deep competence and cool confidence. It requires group collaboration and individual accountability. To get extraordinary things done in organizations, leaders have to *enable others to act.*

After reviewing thousands of personal-best cases, we developed a simple test to detect whether someone is on the road to becoming a leader. That test is the frequency of the use of the word *we.* In our interviews, we found that people used *we* nearly three times more often than *I* in explaining their personal-best leadership experiences. Hewlett-Packard's Angie Yim was the technical IT team leader on a project involving core team members from the United States, Singapore, Australia, and Hong Kong. In the past, Angie told us, she "had a bad habit of using the pronoun *I* instead of *we,*" but she learned that people responded more eagerly and her team became more cohesive when people felt part of the *we.* "This is a magic word," Angie realized. "I would recommend that others use it more often."

Leaders *foster collaboration and build trust.* This sense of teamwork goes far beyond a few direct reports or close confidants. They engage all those who must make the project work—and in some way, all who must live with the results. In today's virtual organizations, cooperation can't be restricted to a small group of loyalists; it must include peers, managers, customers and clients, suppliers, citizens—all those who have a stake in the vision.

Leaders make it possible for others to do good work. They know that those who are expected to produce the results must feel a sense of personal power and ownership. Leaders understand that the command-and-control techniques of traditional management no longer apply. Instead, leaders work to make people feel strong, capable, and committed. Leaders enable others to act not by hoarding the power they have but by giving it away. Exemplary leaders *strengthen everyone's capacity* to deliver on the promises they make. As Kathryn Winters learned working with the communications department at NVIDIA Corporation, "You have to make sure that no one is outside the loop or uninvolved in all the changes that occur." She continually ensures that each person has a sense of ownership for his or her projects. She seeks out the opinions of others and uses the ensuing discussion not only to build up their capabilities but also to educate and update her own information and perspective. "Inclusion (not exclusion)," she finds, "ensures that everyone feels and thinks that they are owners and leaders—this makes work much easier." Kathryn realized that, when people are trusted and have more discretion, more authority, and more information, they're much more likely to use their energies to produce extraordinary results.

In the cases we analyzed, leaders proudly discussed teamwork, trust, and empowerment as essential elements of their efforts. A leader's ability to enable others to act is essential. Constituents neither perform at their best nor stick around for very long if their leader makes them feel weak, dependent, or alienated. But when a leader makes people feel strong and capable—as if they can do more than they ever thought possible—they'll give it their all and exceed their own expectations. Authentic leadership is founded on trust, and the more people trust their leader, and each other, the more they take risks, make changes, and keep organizations and movements alive. Through that relationship, leaders turn their constituents into leaders themselves.

ENCOURAGE THE HEART

The climb to the top is arduous and long. People become exhausted, frustrated, and disenchanted. They're often tempted to give up. Leaders *encourage the heart* of their constituents to carry on. Genuine acts of caring uplift the spirits and draw people forward. In his personal-best leadership experience, Ankush Joshi, the service line manager with Informix USA, learned that "writing a personal thank-you note, rather than sending an e-mail, can do wonders." Janel Ahrens, marcom manager with National Semiconductor, echoed Ankush's observation. Janel would make notes about important events in other people's lives and then follow up with them directly after or simply wish them luck prior to an important event. Every person was "genuinely touched that I cared enough to ask them about how things are going."

She told us that in her organization "work relationships have been stronger since this undertaking." Janel's and Ankush's experiences are testimony to the power of a "thank you."

Recognizing contributions can be one-to-one or with many people. It can come from dramatic gestures or simple actions. One of the first actions that Abraham Kuruvilla took upon becoming CEO of the Dredging Corporation of India (a government-owned, private-sector company providing services to all ten major Indian ports) was to send out to every employee a monthly newsletter (*DCI News*) that was full of success stories. In addition, he introduced, for the first time, a public-recognition program through which awards and simple appreciation notices were given out to individuals and teams for doing great work. Abraham made sure that people were recognized for their contributions, because he wanted to provide a climate in which "people felt cared about and genuinely appreciated by their leaders."

It's part of the leader's job to show appreciation for people's contributions and to create a culture of *celebrating values and victories*. In the cases we collected, we saw thousands of examples of individual recognition and group celebration. We've heard and seen everything from handwritten thank-yous to marching bands and "This Is Your Life"–type ceremonies. Recognition and celebration aren't about fun and games, although there is a lot of fun and there are a lot of games when people encourage the hearts of their constituents. Neither are they about pretentious ceremonies designed to create some phony sense of camaraderie. When people see a charlatan making noisy affectations, they turn away in disgust. Encouragement is, curiously, serious business. It's how leaders visibly and behaviorally link rewards with performance. When striving to raise quality, recover from disaster, start up a new service, or make dramatic change of any kind, leaders make sure people see the benefit of behavior that's aligned with cherished values. Leaders also know that celebrations and rituals, when done with authenticity and from the heart, build a strong sense of collective identity and community spirit that can carry a group through extraordinarily tough times.

LEADERSHIP IS A RELATIONSHIP

Our findings from the analysis of personal-best leadership experiences challenge the myth that leadership is something that you find only at the highest levels of organizations and society. We found it everywhere. These findings also challenge the belief that leadership is reserved for a few charismatic men and women. Leadership is not a gene and it's not an inheritance. Leadership is an identifiable set of skills and abilities that are available to all of us. The "great person"—woman or man—theory of leadership is just plain wrong.

Or, we should say, the theory that there are only a few great men and women who can lead others to greatness is just plain wrong. Likewise, it is plain wrong that leaders only come from large, or great, or small, or new organizations, or from established economies, or from start-up companies. We consider the women and men in our research to be great, and so do those with whom they worked. They are the everyday heroes of our world. It's because there are so many—not so few—leaders that extraordinary things get done on a regular basis, especially in extraordinary times.

To us this is inspiring and should give everyone hope. Hope, because it means that no one needs to wait around to be saved by someone riding into town on a white horse. Hope, because there's a generation of leaders searching for the opportunities to make a difference. Hope, because right down the block or right down the hall there are people who will seize the opportunity to lead you to greatness. They're your neighbors, friends, and colleagues. And you are one of them, too.

There's still another crucial truth about leadership. It's something that we've known for a long time, but we've come to prize even more today. In talking to leaders and reading their cases, there was a very clear message that wove itself throughout every situation and every action. The message was: *leadership is a relationship*. Leadership is a relationship between those who aspire to lead and those who choose to follow. It's the quality of this relationship that matters most when we're engaged in getting extraordinary things done. A leader-constituent relationship that's characterized by fear and distrust will never, ever produce anything of lasting value. A relationship characterized by mutual respect and confidence will overcome the greatest adversities and leave a legacy of significance.

Evidence abounds for this point of view. For instance, in examining the critical variables for executive success in the top three jobs in large organizations, Jodi Taylor and Valerie Sessa (1998) at the Center for Creative Leadership found the number one success factor to be "relationships with subordinates."[2] We were intrigued to find that, even in this nanosecond world of e-everything, opinion is consistent with the facts. In an online survey, respondents were asked to indicate, among other things, which would be more essential to business success in five years—social skills or skills in using the Internet. Seventy two percent selected social skills; 28 percent, Internet skills (FR Roper Starch Survey, 1999). Internet literati completing a poll online realize that it's not the web of technology that matters the most; it's the web of people. *Leadership is a relationship.*

Similar results were found in a study by Public Allies, an AmeriCorps organization dedicated to creating young leaders who can strengthen their communities. Public Allies sought the opinions of eighteen- to thirty-year-olds on the subject of leadership. Among the items was a question about the qualities that were important in a good leader. Topping the respondents' list is "Being able to see a situation from someone else's point of view." In second place is "Getting along well with other people" (Public Allies, 1998).

Success in leadership, success in business, and success in life have been, are now, and will continue to be a function of how well people work and play together. Success in leading will be wholly dependent upon the capacity to build and sustain those human relationships that enable people to get extraordinary things done on a regular basis.

THE TEN COMMITMENTS OF LEADERSHIP

Embedded in The Five Practices of Exemplary Leadership are behaviors that can serve as the basis for learning to lead. We call these The Ten Commitments of Leadership (Table 3.1). These ten commitments serve as the guide for our discussion of how leaders get extraordinary things done in organizations and as the structure for what's to follow. Before delving into the practices and commitments further, however, let's consider leadership from the vantage point of the constituent. If leadership is a relationship, as we have discovered, then what do people expect from that relationship? What do people look for and admire in a leader? What do people want from someone whose direction they'd be willing to follow?

Practice	Commitment
Model the Way	1. Clarify values by finding your voice and affirming shared ideals.
	2. Set the example by aligning actions with shared values.
Inspire a Shared Vision	3. Envision the future by imagining exciting and ennobling possibilities.
	4. Enlist others in a common vision by appearing to share aspirations.
Challenge the Process	5. Search for opportunities by seizing the initiatives and by looking outward for innovative ways to improve.
	6. Experiment and take risks by constantly generating small wins and learning from experience.
Enable Others to Act	7. Foster collaboration by building trust and facilitating relationships.
	8. Strengthen others by increasing self-determinations and developing competence.
Encourage the Heart	9. Recognize contributions by showing appreciation for individual excellence.
	10. Celebrate the values and victories by creating a sprit of community.

Table 3.1.   The Five Practices and Ten Commitments of Leadership

Source: The Leadership Challenge by James M. Kouzes and Barry Z. Posner. Copyright © 2007.

Notes

1. Unless otherwise noted, all quotations are taken from personal interviews or from personal-best leadership case studies written by the respondent leaders. The titles and affiliations of the leaders may be different today from what they were at the time of their case study or publication of this volume. We expect that many have moved on to other leadership adventures while we were writing, or will do so by the time you read this.

2. Telephone interview with Jodi Taylor, Center for Creative Leadership, Colorado Springs, Colorado, April 1998.

References

"FC Roper Starch Survey: The Web," *Fast Company*. October 1999.

Public Allies. *New Leadership for a New Century*. Washington, DC: Public Allies, 1998.

The Five Practices of Exemplary Leadership

—◁∿∿▷—

James M. Kouzes and Barry Z. Posner are preemine
award-winning writers, and highly sought-after teacher
leadership. Their groundbreaking studies, pioneered in
to create a model of leadership that has been embraced by more than
one million people around the world.

CHAPTER FOUR

How Leaders Are Grown
The Lessons of Example and Experience

Ray Blunt

Ⅰf growing public service leaders is imperative for tomorrow's changing world, if there is a surfeit of managers and a dearth of public service leaders, if systematic approaches to developing future leaders are rare, and if the task of a leader is to help shape the culture within which leaders develop, what is the best course to take?

By now, it is better understood that, for the most part, leaders are not born—they are made; they are grown. The capabilities that are needed by leaders—the behaviors, skills, mindsets, and attitudes—can be learned; the character qualities of leaders can be shaped within an organization's culture. This puts to rest the most common myth that leaders are born. Both the excellent capabilities and the proven character needed in public service leaders can be "grown" within the organization itself.

Originally published as "Leaders Growing Leaders" in Ray Blunt's *Growing Leaders for Public Service.* (Washington, DC: IBM Center for the Business of Government, 2003).

These conclusions emerge from probably the best longitudinal body of research on growing leadership available today: the years of study and gathering of data on leaders by the Center for Creative Leadership (CCL) in Greensboro, North Carolina. In studies of leaders in the private sector, the nonprofit world, and the public sector, the findings are highly consistent. Successful leaders grow through particular sets of experiences. CCL's findings place leader learning into four broad categories:

- Challenging job assignments—42 percent
- Learning from others' examples—22 percent
- Hardships and setbacks—20 percent
- Other events—16 percent (including training and education)

Challenging job assignments are those that stretch the individual. CCL has identified the types of job experiences that produce leadership learning:

- A change in the scope of a job;
- A job that requires a "fix it" opportunity;
- A job that needs to be started from scratch;
- Line to staff or staff to line switches (including headquarters to field); and
- Projects and task forces that require new skills or learning but where the individual remains on the job.

All of these job-based experiences challenge, stretch, and grow the individual—and produce leader learning. For the leader who wishes to grow leaders, such an understanding is critical. This is, however, a notion that runs counter to the way that government managers typically develop—within their functional, organizational, and geographic "stovepipes," and through training programs attended by individuals—"largely serendipitously."

LEADERS BEGET LEADERS AND LEAVE A LEGACY

We see clearly that the task of growing leaders may be as important a task as can be found today in public service and as important a "result." That there are more leaders needed, particularly leaders with new capabilities and solid character, is perhaps intuitively obvious. That leaders develop within a leader-centered culture—one best shaped by leaders themselves—and that leaders develop over time primarily through challenging and diverse experiences is also clear. But, more importantly, what also emerges is that the central role in this drama is not played by leadership training programs alone, though they are important; nor by replicating "best practices," although they are certainly instructive.

The Critical Players in Growing Future Public Service Leaders Are the Senior Leaders

Noel Tichy (1997), University of Michigan professor, former head of executive development for General Electric (GE), and long-time consultant to GE and numerous other top organizations, benchmarked many of the best organizations in the world in growing excellent leaders. These included Hewlett-Packard, the U.S. Special Operations Command, Tenneco, AlliedSignal, ServiceMaster, Shell Oil, and the exemplary nonprofit Focus: HOPE, among others. What he found in the very best organizations was highly consistent:

> "Winning companies win because they have good leaders that nurture the development of other leaders at all levels of the organization. *The key ability of winning organizations and winning leaders is creating leaders.*" (emphasis added)

He saw certain fundamentals demonstrated over and over again, despite wide disparity in the types of organizations (including public sector), the leaders, and the cultures. The leaders with a proven track record of successfully growing leaders:

- Assume personal responsibility for developing other leaders.
- Have a "teachable point of view" that they can articulate and show others how to make the organization work effectively, how to grow others, what behaviors are needed, and what values are essential.
- Embody their teachable point of view in "stories" about the past and stories about a visionary future.
- Generate positive energy and encourage other leaders while making tough decisions.

- Devote considerable time to developing other leaders and have approaches that normally involve vulnerability, openness, and a willingness to admit mistakes, thus serving as effective role models.

We now turn to an examination of how these principles can be employed by senior leaders to help grow the next generation of public service leaders—leaders with capability and character who will serve the American people. Then we will take a look at how these principles have been embodied in the lives of three outstanding public service leaders in their roles as exemplar, mentor, coach, and teacher.

LESSONS IN HOW TO GROW PUBLIC SERVICE LEADERS

The ultimate test for a leader is not whether he or she makes smart decisions and takes decisive action, but whether he or she teaches others to be leaders and builds an organization that can sustain its success even when he or she is not around.

Noel Tichy, 1997.

We are accustomed now to the notion of a leader being a life-long learner and someone who helps build a learning organization. "Teaching," as a generic term, is simply the transmission of personal learning and wisdom from a leader to others. Exemplary leaders see it as their responsibility and their legacy to grow the next generation. At the end of the day, that is the only way that successful change is sustained.

In that respect, leaders not only learn to be leaders, they learn to be effective "growers"—developers of other leaders able to translate the lessons of their experience into helping others to become leaders. Leaders beget leaders. So where do you begin if this is your objective as a senior leader?

This section focuses on four roles—four areas of action where you can focus your efforts in growing the next generation of public service leaders:

- Growing leaders through personal example—as an *exemplar*
- Growing leaders through significant relationships—as a *mentor*

- Growing leaders through varied experiences—as a *coach*
- Growing leaders through development programs—as a *teacher*

Three outstanding leaders are profiled in *Growing Leaders for Public Service*. These are public service leaders who have produced significant results and have made a priority of successfully growing other leaders.

Growing Leaders Through Personal Example: As an *Exemplar*

Leadership by example is not a new concept. As Peter Drucker cogently pointed out, leaders are defined by having followers. Leaders are followed more for who they are as observed by their behavior than for what title they have or how expert they are. In essence, followers choose their leaders. What may be new, however, is the perspective that people learn leadership from you *whether you intend for them to or not*; whether you are an excellent leader or not. Simply think about the leaders who have had the greatest influence on you—the ones you want to emulate and the ones you never wanted to be like. Both have helped to shape you. Now think about the people who have worked for you and with you over the years. If they were interviewed about your leadership story, what would they have learned?

The Center for Creative Leadership found that some of the most telling leadership lessons came from simply observing leaders in action. Ironically, the lessons learned came from both good and bad leaders. That knowledge alone should spur leaders to be more aware of the congruency between their talk and action—walk the talk—and to be more conscious of involving younger leaders in their sphere of action. But that can often produce a need to project perfection. Actually the contrary is true.

As Tichy (1997) discovered, the best role models were also the ones who were personally vulnerable, open, and honest about their mistakes. As we will see in the lives of the three exemplary leaders identified for this report, it is primarily the personal and character qualities that stand out in people's minds when they discuss leaders they have known. It is those aspects of personal character they exemplify that win them the "right," if you will, to serve others through mentoring, coaching, and teaching. Character and capability in a leader cannot be separated.

While this may be the most important aspect of leaders growing leaders—by their example of character and capability—it is certainly the most elusive to "learn." How can you know if you are setting an example that others want to follow, and how can you become a more effective example?

Many, if not most, who benchmark leadership programs use a method that is designed to get at this issue—360-degree feedback. It is a common best practice to help leaders identify their strengths and weaknesses; examine the consistency between what they believe about themselves and what others see; and analyze the relationship between "walk" and "talk." Why? Simply because most senior leaders receive less and less feedback the further up the ladder they go. Often their view of their own strengths goes back several years, and those so-called strengths now may be weaknesses.

For example, the self-starting, highly reliable independent thinker may find herself in a situation that calls for significant collaborative relationships and team building. What worked and was valued has now become a hindrance and a factor that separates her from her colleagues and subordinates. For reasons such as this, many top-flight organizations have identified not only their corporate culture values, but the behaviors that they want to embed in the culture by the example of their leaders. Such feedback from peers and subordinates as well as from superiors—360-degree feedback—combines to provide self-awareness and the opportunity to make changes. Not only is the solicitation of such feedback an opportunity to learn and to change, but it also exhibits an openness and a vulnerability that are important components of exemplary leadership.

Another important place to begin setting an example is in serving rather than seeking to be served.

> If our ... organizations are going to live up to their potential, we must find, develop, and encourage more people to lead in the service of others. Without leadership, [organizations] cannot adapt to a fast moving world. But if leaders do not have the hearts of servants, there is only the potential for tyranny.
>
> *Kotter and Heskett, 1992.*

It was Robert Greenleaf, former head of Management Research for AT&T, who brought the notion of servant-leadership into board rooms and executive suites. In his book *Servant-Leadership*, he lays out the long-known principles and precepts that those who seek to lead must first seek to serve others—to live out a selfless attitude. A motivation of serving others first is one that is particularly appropriate for leaders in the public service, but it goes beyond customer or public service. It includes the sense that a leader is willing to devote his time, attention, and energies to the development of the careers of others—not simply his own. The political culture often subtly affects the already inherent bent that we all have toward self-promotion. Counter-intuitively, it is in seeking to serve the development needs of others and their careers that leaders can best set an example that others will emulate and follow.

When the agenda is all about "my needs, my demands, my schedule, my priorities, and my 'face time' with superiors," then it is unlikely that any initiatives to coach, mentor, or teach others will have any more credibility than a formal speech. To get at this, 360-degree feedback may be extremely helpful, but this is also an area that can use some self-reflection. Most of us rarely stop to seriously consider what we are doing with our lives and our time in relationships at work (or outside work, for that matter). The thirty-day calendar exercise may be one way to get at this and to begin a systematic plan of serving the next generation of leaders.

Being congruent in action and speech and seeking to serve others before self are two character qualities that distinguish a leader who grows other leaders through example. These qualities also are essential for growing others through mentoring relationships.

Growing Leaders Through Relationships: As a *Mentor*

When Odysseus went off to war, he placed his young son, Telemachus, in the care of an older, wiser man who would advise the young boy and help him to mature should his father not return. By the time Odysseus returned after the war and his long journey home, Telemachus was a man. He had matured not only physically, but in character and wisdom and in war-fighting skill: he was all that his father had dreamed of. Odysseus owed much to the man who helped raise his son. That man's name? Mentor.

To clarify some things about this role, a mentor is not a supervisor, although supervisors can be mentors. A mentor is not a "coach," although coaches can be mentors as well; coaches typically focus on certain skills, not the whole person's potential. (We will discuss the role of leader as coach in the next section.) And a mentor is not a teacher in the strictest sense. While there are clearly aspects of formal teaching in being a mentor, teachers usually work with groups, not individuals. Even within the context of this chapter, a leader is not necessarily a mentor, but *all leaders should become mentors who help a few others learn to lead*. That is one lesson that Noel Tichy learned from looking at great organizations. And that is a lesson today's public service leaders must heed if the next generation of leaders is to be grown effectively.

> Ideally, mentoring is a lifelong relationship in which a mentor helps a protégé reach her or his God-given potential.
> *Bobb Biehl, 1996.*

Being a mentor is not complex, does not require extensive training, and is not a full-time job. In the best organizations where mentoring occurs, mentoring is not even a formal program, although it can be. All that said, a senior leader can easily become a mentor by keeping a couple of things in mind and then doing just a few key things.

We have already discussed the importance of blocking time on your calendar and reflecting on some of your "stories," which form the basis for others to learn from your experience.

Remember, it's not about you. It is about the people you are mentoring. This is not a power trip or recognition that you know best what is right for another or that you want this person to champion your cause in the organization. At its best, this leader/mentor role is simply servant-leadership. Your role is to serve the learning needs of another by building and sustaining a long-term relationship whose objective is to help the other person grow, learn, and reach his or her potential. To do this you give up some of yourself, including your time, for building toward the future.

You must also keep in mind that the coin of the realm in mentoring is trust, earned trust. Above all, this is a trusting relationship, normally between an older and a younger person. Before you begin mentoring, understand that to effectively build trust there needs to be both mutual honesty and mutual vulnerability laced with deep respect for confidences. A mentor is not to feel as if she needs to be a heroine with no visible flaws. Openness to mistakes of the past and learning from them is one of the best "stories" that can be shared. Honesty about fear, doubt, nervousness, and uncertainty are lessons of life that help protégés understand that a leader doesn't always feel inside what is seen from the outside.

So what do you do? First, find a protégé. Look around you at the people who have potential. This is harder than you think. Most of us want to mentor someone just like us—people we are the most comfortable with. But if your interest is in the future of the person and of the organization, you may want to step back and ask yourself whether the person you might want as your protégé is really the person with the most potential. You might also want to consider individuals with whom you already have some connection other than a strictly boss-to-employee situation. Are there people who already ask your advice from time to time? This is a good place to start. Now what do you do?

In a way, it's like being a good parent—you simply spend some time together in a variety of settings: breakfast, lunch, taking a walk, sitting in your office, at your home, playing racquetball, taking a bike ride—you get the point.

What is the content? Bobb Biehl (1996) recommends that you start by asking a couple of questions and using this simple framework as a point of departure. The questions are: What are your priorities? How can I help you? The easiest topics will likely surround work issues—a problem employee, to stay or not to stay in public service, when to look for a new position elsewhere, how to deal with a pushy congressional staffer, what to do about a boss who won't make a decision.

The key skill you will need is listening—really listening to the words and the tone of voice—and observing the body language. Most leaders find it far easier to simply solve the problem for a person or to tell him what to do. Mentors need to be about helping people make their own way while sharing their experiences and perhaps some options to think about. Similar situations help serve as illustrations, particularly if it is something you struggled with and didn't have a slam-dunk success.

Mentoring, in the sense discussed here, has as its objective not simply helping people to learn, but to learn to become better leaders. That can often mean encouragement to take risks, to break cultural "rules," to get outside the comfort zone, or to get out of a career stovepipe. Sometimes it can be helping a person get his or her life into balance when it has become overloaded with work, with no time for "saw sharpening" or decompression, or being with the family, or just having fun. Sometimes it's helping with parenting advice when the burden has become too heavy. So while listening is key, if the objective is leadership, some judicious and caring encouragement (gentle pushing) is often called for as well.

Finally, a good mentor understands the organization culture and the external stakeholders' worlds as well. Introducing your protégés to people and helping them to become exposed to a level of the organization that they will be part of in the future are also an important part of helping them to grow. It's not playing politics; exposure and an opportunity to observe are critical. Let them see you in action if that is not a part of their normal routine and let them give you input. Part of what is learned is "caught" from simply "hanging out" in a work setting with a more experienced person and observing what occurs.

One additional note: If senior leaders take responsibility to mentor two or three others, much like the example of Paul Barnes, at the Social Security Administration (his profile begins on page 20 [of *Growing Leaders for Public Service*]), this relationship does not depend entirely on being in a formal position. Certainly experience is the critical commodity, but it is not one that diminishes significantly over time. A mentoring relationship is one that can extend into formal retirement from public service and is a role that more senior leaders should consider establishing—even after they retire. Public service has lost many good senior leaders over the past several years, many to early retirement. They are a scarce resource who still have something to contribute.

Growing Leaders Through Experiences:
As a *Coach*

Any senior leader potentially can be a mentor of another whether they are in the same organization or even whether the mentor is actively employed or retired, because the essence of mentoring lies in the relationship. However, being a coach typically requires some form of a leadership role in the organization because here the focus is experiential.

Returning to how leaders are grown, the most significant factors that grow leaders are challenging job-based experiences. A good leadership coach will make it a matter of utmost priority not only to have strong relationships with future leaders at all levels, but also to invest in their growth through intentionally ensuring they get the necessary experiences to become future leaders.

> At its best, "coaching is the process of equipping people with the tools, knowledge, and opportunities they need to develop themselves and become more effective" [leaders].
>
> *Peterson and Hicks, 1996.*

Senior leaders do not "manufacture" other leaders. What you can do, however, is to create the conditions and shape the culture under which people with potential learn and acquire the leadership attributes needed by the organization and public service. You help them to grow in the capabilities and the character which enlarge their capacity to produce change and significant results through others. How would this work? What are some of the things you might do?

Take a look at some of the examples of the three leaders profiled [in *Growing Leaders for Public Service*, beginning on page 19]. Leo Wurschmidt of the Veterans Benefits Administration would take many casual, informal opportunities to talk to people, encouraging them to take new assignments, to take a risk and move to a different type of job or to a different location. Paul Barnes did the same both informally and by reassigning people to work for him in ways that would stretch them. Dr. Janet Woodcock at the Center for Drug Evaluation and Research would spend time with small groups of future leaders, listening to their experiences and offering options. They each made it a point to get younger managers into programs that would allow for developmental assignments and likely job changes.

Each of these individuals created and encouraged developmental opportunities, spent time with both groups and individuals, and had a hand in shaping the infrastructure that supported such leader growth. These examples suggest three actions that senior leaders in their role as coach can take to help grow other leaders.

FORMING INDIVIDUAL COACHING RELATIONSHIPS. Coaching, by its nature, has many elements of individual relationship. In that sense, it is like mentoring. However, the intent of coaching is to create job-based conditions where people learn leadership. This involves:

- Challenging others to take initiatives to get out of their comfort zone;

- Creating specific opportunities for such stretch work through job changes, job rotation, reassignments, team projects;
- Advocating for them to others for such changes; and
- Being a "noodge"—helping others to reflect on what they are learning, being a sounding board for problems, and encouraging and even prodding at times to make sure that stagnancy and discouragement don't set in.

Such learning isn't always comfortable. There are organizational cultures in which coaching is expected, and cultures in which it never occurs. The military, sports, and performing arts are examples of where active coaching for the development of individuals and groups is the norm. Those may be environments that are worthwhile benchmarking for lessons to be applied to certain public service cultures in which development is often more passive and individualistic.

"TEACHING" HOW TO LEARN LEADERSHIP. Here is one place where reflecting on your own leadership and life stories can pay dividends. Many people you will coach do not take the time to reflect on what they are learning or even have a framework for doing so. Typically, early in one's career the habit of simply "churning" at the work for the day is about all that can be managed. By telling others your stories of how you learned from situations similar to the ones they are experiencing, you give them a framework into which their experiences can be fit. You don't have to give them answers; in fact, that doesn't promote learning. Rather, let them use your metaphors and experiences as a means for encouraging their own reflection and learning.

You can also ask questions—a central coaching technique—which helps others learn by reflecting on what is occurring or may occur at work. No lesser light than Socrates pioneered this technique and it remains a good method. Simply asking your protégés questions that cause them to think about what they are seeing or what actions they might take or what they may have missed can be very helpful in leader learning without micromanaging—a deadly leadership sin that takes energy right out of a person.

You can also do periodic organizational "post mortems" after key stages of projects. Putting the entire team in the room and engaging in an honest self-critique—senior leaders included—does much to make the point that we are all able to learn from our experiences.

The Army uses such an approach in "after action" debriefings of exercises, where all of the members of a team are quizzed on what happened in a particular scenario, what was going through their minds, why certain decisions were made or certain actions taken, why hesitancy occurred—from colonel on down to second lieutenant. Candid feedback among everyone, without regard to rank, is strongly encouraged as a means to build more openness and enhance the synergy of a team. It is a more active and vulnerable approach to coaching, but one that demonstrates that everyone can learn and profit from each other. You might want to try it out as a coaching technique and as a means of setting an example of openness to constructive criticism.

ACTIVE INVOLVEMENT. There are many opportunities for more active involvement—some of which are suggested in the approaches of the three exemplary leaders [profiled in *Growing Leaders for Public Service*]. These can range from reassigning a promising person to your staff, rotating a high-potential person into a temporary executive assistant or special assistant role, selecting a person to head a special projects team, or intervening with one of your colleagues to transfer a key member of your organization to their area for developmental purposes.

Growing Leaders Through Development Programs: As a *Teacher*

While the culture of public service and the lack of role models are often seen as barriers to growing excellent leaders, so too is the lack of sufficient resources to grow leaders. Translated this means that with the wholesale and often random downsizing that has been occurring in the last decade, there simply are not the financial resources available for leadership programs.

The options for many organizations are seen as cutting even more people or cutting the margins. The margins are quite often identified as training, travel, and equipment or supplies. Hence, there is a tacit assumption that little can be done to develop leaders if resources are short. While this assumption can easily be challenged on its merits (if people are our top priority, why do we cut people programs first?), among the very best practices for growing leaders are those that are in-house, leader-led, and experiential.

Typically, the role of trainer or facilitator in a leadership development program is considered to be the domain of expert consultants, in-house trainers, or the HR development staff. But, as Tichy found, the very best companies and the very best leaders are themselves the leadership program trainers. This does not mean the token appearance of the "boss" to give the opening remarks in a program or to drop by to see how things are going. Leaders have learned practical lessons, most likely grounded in good theory as well, that only they can pass on in a way that others will want to learn. A "classroom" setting is a good place for such wisdom to be transferred.

Adult learning is centered on what is practical, not simply what is factually true. That is why even the best, most entertaining speakers, trainers, and consultants rarely have a long-term impact. The stories that a leader can tell—often about hard-won experiences, sometimes about failure—are stories that stick and can be applied. (Another good reason to develop your stories.)

GE's Jack Welch, one of the most respected leaders in business today, prides himself on having taught every two weeks at their leadership course in Crotonville, New York, for over fifteen years. He actively teaches, passes on his stories of change, helps embed the corporate values and "no boundaries" mindset, and serves as a coach to participants in these programs. Over the years, he has influenced thousands of today's leaders at GE—many who now run the company. But perhaps what GE may be best known for is their use of action learning as a means of developing future leaders. We turn now to what is perhaps one of the best approaches that a leader-teacher can use to grow other leaders.

The effectiveness of action learning and its use in the best organizations build on the basic understanding of how leaders are grown that was outlined earlier, aspects of which can be seen in the approaches of the three exemplary leaders.

> Perhaps the best way of describing action learning is as a parallel universe.... Accomplishments that might take months or even years to happen ... occur in a matter of weeks. Learning and action are compressed.
>
> *Dotlich and Noel, 1998.*

How would it work in your organization? There are seven key elements—each of which can occur as part of a leadership development program without significant expenditure of resources. Such initiatives depend strongly on the direct involvement of senior leaders in the process to produce two things every organization covets: real results and the growth (and testing) of future leaders.

A SPONSOR. It is important that a senior person sponsor the commissioning of an important project that is essential to the organization—a strategic imperative—and which will take a team to do it successfully. Typically it should be a project that will require out-of-the-box thought, benchmarking of private-sector and public-sector organizations, and the learning of some new skills. The sponsor both gives the charge to the team and is the person who holds the team accountable for final, well-documented recommendations. The sponsor should also be in a position to make a decision or to get a decision promptly.

A PROCESS. This is a leadership learning process. As such, some idea of the approach to be taken needs development. While not complex, it will need to be explained to the team that is formed. Typically it consists of a selected strategic issue; a timeframe for work and bringing recommendations back for decision; the use of experienced coaches who are currently leaders in the organization; and the provision of some form of "just in time" training on team skills, benchmarking, or any technical expertise that will be needed. The key point is to have an approach firmly fixed, and the senior "faculty" and staff identified and briefed.

A TEAM(S). The team is often composed of individuals from various parts of the organization, selected because of leadership potential for participation in this project. There could also be more than one team to look at various aspects of a problem or vision challenge or to tackle the same project with competing approaches. It is similar to what Dr. Janet Woodcock has done at CDER in using the Council for Excellence in Government Fellows to spearhead special projects and to build their vision and mission. Keep in mind the purpose is twofold: learning leadership through challenging experience and producing a significant change initiative or problem solution.

A PROJECT. The sponsor or the senior team identifies the nature of the project. The project team then proceeds to gather data, conduct analyses, and frame findings, conclusions and recommendations for presentation for decision. The primary basis of the learning is in the doing.

A LEARNING OF NEW APPROACHES AND APPLICATIONS. Here is where periodic forums such as short skill workshops can be interjected. Other useful resources might include a speaker from an organization that has done something similar, a benchmarking visit to such an organization, bringing in someone from the staff or elsewhere in government with expertise in an area needed, an excellent video presentation, or outside workshop. There might also be time set aside for coaches to tell their leadership stories or for interim check-ins to explore problems or issues.

A PRESENTATION. At the point allotted in the project, a formal presentation, often accompanied by a written report, is delivered to the sponsor or the senior team. It is a decision-making forum during which tough questions are asked and professional quality work is expected. A thorough airing of what was done and how and why the recommendations are being made is expected. A decision within a short period of time by the sponsor or the senior team is also part of the agreement. Team members can also be selected for implementing the decision.

A DEBRIEF AND REFLECTION. The key to embedding the learning is to learn from the experiences of the project. Here is where senior coaching is critical—to help individuals ask themselves the tough questions, to share candid observations about each individual's contributions and areas for learning, to provide opportunity for team feedback to each other. Areas for further individual development and for organizational process improvement are typically identified as a result of this reflection.

References

Biehl, Bobb. *Mentoring: Confidence in Finding a Mentor and Becoming One.* Nashville, TN: Broadman and Holman, 1996.

Dotlich, David, and Noel, James L. *Action Learning: How the World's Top Companies Are Re-Creating Their Leaders and Themselves.* San Francisco: Jossey-Bass, 1998.

Kotter, John P., and Heskett, James L. *Corporate Culture and Performance.* New York: The Free Press, 1992.

Peterson, David B., and Hicks, Mary Dee. *The Leader as Coach: Strategies for Coaching and Developing Others.* Minneapolis: Personnel Decisions International, 1996.

Tichy, Noel. *The Leadership Engine: How Winning Companies Build Leaders at Every Level.* New York: HarperCollins, 1997.

Ray Blunt serves as associate director and teaching Fellow, The Washington Institute, and as senior consultant, Leadership Institute at the National Center for Leadership.

CHAPTER FIVE

Maintaining Board Leadership
Staying on Track and Institutionalizing Excellence

John Carver

P erformers—whether humans or machines—can perform only up to their capability. That capability can be diminished or improved, so it is a commodity that deserves care. The concept of investment is crucial, for the board can choose to see training as a troublesome cost or as an opportunity to reap a return. If sophisticated and experienced board members find training an offensive concept, then find another word for it. But by no means should any board think it has skills that never fade, for even perfect board members have much to learn and relearn about teamwork and the exercise of group authority.

RECRUIT THOSE WHO CAN AND WILL GOVERN

Raw material makes a difference. If the board is able to select its own new members, it should start with a well-deliberated set of qualifications. If the members are selected by others, whenever

Originally published as "Maintaining Board Leadership: Staying on Track and Institutionalizing Excellence" in John Carver's *Boards That Make a Difference* (3rd ed.). (San Francisco: Jossey-Bass, 2006).

possible, the board should enlist the appointing authorities to use the board's desired qualifications. Aggressive recruiting involves not only selling prospective members on board membership but excluding those who do not fulfill the requirements.

Entrusting recruitment to a nominating committee can be useful, but integrity is maintained only if the board as a body has decided what types of people it desires. Too often, nominating committees are left completely to their own judgment. They cannot help but develop implicit criteria, but they rarely develop explicit criteria prior to becoming entangled in the personality-loaded interactions of recruiting. Even if they were to use a two-step process (a good idea if the board defaults), the board will not have been party to a matter that is critical to future board performance.

If the nominating committee has board-stated qualifications in hand (recorded as a Governance Process policy), it can render better service. The board should phrase its committee charge (also in the Governance Process category) so that finding the right people is given greater priority than filling vacancies. Boards "don't do a very good job of assessing prospective board members," says Edward Able, executive director of the American Association of Museums. Many boards have the wrong people on them. Indeed, boards would do well to tolerate a few empty seats instead of rushing to fill them. Recruiting would be more diligent if it were made known that membership on this board is an honor. After all, the board is selecting those who will bear the privilege and burden of trusteeship. With a more rationally defined board job, the California Park & Recreation Society, Sacramento, saw "an increase in the number of members who wish to serve on the board, as the board is now seen as doing 'important work,'" according to executive director Jane H. Adams.

What qualifications are important? These vary, of course, but with governance construed as I have described in this text, a few universal characteristics logically follow. Naturally, we all want Renaissance people, but to be more realistic and specific, we must start with the job to be done, so we begin by consulting the governance process policies on the board job description and style of governing. Members need to have the understanding, skills, and willingness to contribute to the governance task that the board has so carefully set forth. To promote the degree of strategic leadership championed in these pages, five qualifications, among others, are necessary.

1. *Commitment to the ownership and to the organization's specific area of endeavor.* As agents of the organization's ownership, board members must be committed to that trust. Commitment to the ends as currently stated is important, though less so, for ends are a continuing creation of the board itself. Therefore, fidelity to those in whose name ends are created is more essential than fidelity to the current wording.

2. *Propensity for thinking in terms of systems and context.* Some people focus quickly on parts. Whatever the relationship of whole to part might be, these persons more readily focus on the part itself for inspection, discussion, and decision. Such persons, with all good intentions, place distractions, if not massive roadblocks, in the way of strategic leadership. Prospective members who are more comfortable with parts have a valuable gift, but one that can more usefully be shared as a volunteer adviser to staff than as a board member. The board needs members who are cybernetically aware, drawn naturally to the harmony of the whole.

3. *Ability and eagerness to deal with values, vision, and the long term.* The board members who make the best contributions are those who have a natural propensity for looking not only beyond the stream of single events but beyond systems to the values on which they are based. It is only a small step from divining today's values as they currently are to planning tomorrow's values as they should be. What stronger argument can be made that a board member's greatest gift to enterprise is educing, weighing, challenging, and frequently fighting over values?

4. *Ability to participate assertively in deliberation.* Productive board deliberation depends on bringing the foregoing characteristics to the governance struggle. Boards are overly tolerant of members who fail to share their capacities in a way that enhances the deliberative process. It is not enough to have the potential to be a good board member; the potential must be manifested through participation.

5. *Willingness to delegate, to allow others to make decisions.* Board members, with respect to one another, must be able to share

power in the group process and, with respect to staff, must be able to delegate. Board members who are loath to delegate will impair the board's leadership by constantly bringing small issues up for consideration. They will impair staff by denying them the opportunity to grow.

Some prospective members are required to attend board meetings prior to assuming membership. Others are chosen from a pool of persons who are already familiar with board operations. These are useful tactics. At a minimum, a board should determine that a prospective member understands the board's governance model, bylaws, policies, current condition, and suspending issues. Frankly, a prospective member who fails to ask about such things is probably not a good candidate. Selection of the most qualified members deserves careful thought and design. *Qualified,* as is clear from the foregoing list, need not refer to academic credentials or high position.

It need not relate to gender, color, or income. It is more likely to relate to grasp, mentality, connectedness, and commitment. As an assessment of past selection, consider this test: if fewer than half the board's members would make good chief governance officers, the selection needs improvement.

PREPARE NEW MEMBERS AND OLD

Orienting new members can help institutionalize the board's governance process and prepare new members for immediate participation. Excellence can be lost simply through the influx of new members who have not agonized through the process of improvement. As they bring in their expectations about governance from other settings, they may cause a regression to the norm. Institutionalizing the hard-won process calls for helping new members understand the system of governance that has already been implemented by their colleagues. It is crucial that new members learn the principles of policy governance as quickly as possible. When this has been done, says Nash Williams, executive director of Southeast Georgia Regional Development Center in Waycross, "New board members can start making meaningful contributions almost immediately." Orientation is important enough to be a mandatory step rather than an optional exercise. The bylaws can require that a new member complete orientation prior to voting on any issue. That members who are ignorant of the organization are regularly given a voice in board decisions is an absurdity that only tradition can explain.

Continued education is needed by all board members, so orientation is merely one part of a larger commitment to having the necessary skills and insights for governance. Boards too infrequently invest in their own competence as much as good governance warrants. The board of Migrant/Immigration Shelter and Support in Owensboro, Kentucky, formulated a Governance Process policy committing the board to proper "knowledge, understanding, and skills" for all board members, new and old, in the service of what Tom Gregory (2003) calls "erosion prevention."

Part of the problem may lie in the word *orientation*, which may smack of learning where the lavatory, coffee pot, and desk supplies are located. Adequate preparation to shoulder the burden of strategic leadership requires something a bit more substantial. What is called for is *job training*, although that term may be offensive to new members who are accomplished in their occupation or in other board service. Whatever it is called, proper preparation of new board members requires that they become thoroughly familiar with the process and the current values of the board they are joining.

Present board members are the best persons to impart this training, although staff can certainly acquaint new board members with operational matters. *Acquaint* is the operative word inasmuch as new members' primary need is not for operational information. Such information may help members form impressions of the whole and even to ask good, board-relevant questions, but operational information is the domain of management, not of governance. No matter how well this information is presented and learned, it still will not equip the new member with the tools he or she needs to participate constructively in the board process. New member training must be built primarily around preparation for strategic leadership.

CAREFULLY MANAGE INFORMATION AND KNOWLEDGE

All jobs require those who perform them to continually update their skills and refurbish their understanding of the position. Turnover would perpetuate this need, even if it were capable of being met for all time for a given group of persons. Greater skills and understanding can often be obtained without the expenditure of dollars. If dollars are necessary, the outlay is best approached from the standpoint of investment rather than cost; instead of depicting training as an irritating cost, see it as an investment made for its expected return.

Consequently, return-on-investment criteria are applied. Although the return in terms of more effective governance will always be subjective because quantification is difficult, the idea is the same. Boards learn that education per se is not the issue; it is education about the right things. Similarly, it is not just information that is the issue, but the right information. Moreover, decisions about board skill building and the supply of appropriate information would give appropriate consideration not only to the cost of training but to the cost of ignorance as well.

Because of its carefully structured separation of issues, policy governance is ready-made for the use of modern technology for process, record keeping, and displaying the status of issues at a given moment. Emergence of this capability—in effect, an Internet-based governance "secretariat"—is under way as this edition goes to press. Ray Tooley (2004) argued for a system that is instantaneously updated, "easily navigated from the broadest policy statement to the most detailed," with "current monitoring reports for each policy" (p. 7). Such a computerized system can enable task scheduling; historical access to board documents; management of board work between meetings; sharing of policies among boards of similar type; integration of multitiered organizations such as those with national, regional, and local boards; online voting; and audio and video conferencing via the Internet. One beauty of such a system is that it not only makes using policy governance easier and, therefore, more likely to succeed, but can actually be a source of continuing education about the model due to its structure. Further, as Tooley says, "Time to get up to full policy governance speed is dramatically reduced" and "sustainability becomes much less of an issue."

COMMIT TO STRUCTURED PRACTICE

It has been observed that "boards rarely practice as a team. [Boards] meet to govern, not to rehearse" (Chait, Holland, and Taylor, 1996). It is true that armies, rock bands, and football teams practice more frequently than they perform, while boards act as if practice is unnecessary. But for a board that is committed to the rigor of the policy governance model, practice is not only useful but crucial for maintaining skills. As situations arise that would otherwise be problems, the board must be able to use the model (or, more directly, the policies it has created by using the model) to reach a solution. Practicing skills will allow the board to maintain disciplined teamwork and prevent a few excited board members from taking the board off into top-of-the-head reactions.

Miriam Carver developed a structured practice methodology, which she and co-author Bill Charney later published in a workbook, that lays out a step-by-step series of rehearsals. Frequent use of this method will help a board not only maintain but elevate its governance skills. Frequent rehearsals during easy times makes it more likely that a board will stay the course during problematic times. Ian R. Horen, CEO of Painting and Decorating Contractors of America, St. Louis, accurately warns, "Preserving the concept of policy governance in an organization requires significant diligence. There is enormous temptation among the elected leadership to revert back to the abandoned structure and behaviors at the first sign" of difficulties.

Hence, Carver and Charney (2004) urge, "Since the point of rehearsal is to build board skill, practicing on a regular and frequent basis makes a good deal of sense, especially as board composition changes due to turnover. Accordingly, we suggest that boards set aside a brief period of time during each board meeting to solve a scenario presented either in this book or by a board member, staff member, or any interested party." However, they caution, "governance rehearsal can be a meaningful concept only if the expectations and requirements of a governing board are clearly articulated. In other words, boards must rehearse in order to be effective, but unless there are established rules and expectations, *there is nothing to be rehearsed*" (p. 5; italics in original). I realize that boards, already pressed for time, will find it difficult to sustain such rehearsals. But devoting a relatively small amount of time to effective skill maintenance will pay for itself many times over.

SURMOUNT THE CONVENTIONAL WISDOM

Until the prevailing understanding of governance changes, leaders must be aware of the deleterious influence of conventional wisdom. Current norms drag down boards that aspire to a higher standard. A board must continually overcome regressive pressures based in the general expectations people have of boards, the requirements foisted by funders and authorities, and even the well-intended advice of experts.

Influence of Those Who Expect

When observers see a board behaving atypically, they are surprised, maybe bewildered. Their discomfort with deviation has little to do with whether the departure from the norm is productive. When members of a national association watch their board or members of the public scrutinize an elected board, they may be confused, suspicious, and even angered if it does not behave in the way they expect. In the public sector, the ownership's commitment to a better system is largely rhetorical. We do not petition our public boards to create more effective systems; we assail them for some small instance of implementation that offends us. So the board that would create a better system will find few committed supporters among the onlookers. A survey of what lobbyists lobby for would indicate which aspects of a system truly command our attention. We pursue fixes in regard to the element that concerns us, not more integrity in the process itself.

Rituals and symbols of responsible board behavior have grown over the years. Observers (not to mention board members themselves) have come to expect a responsible board to look a certain way: it approves budgets, monthly financial statements, and personnel "policies." It might adopt long-range plans, but these are expected to originate from staff recommendations for board reaction and revision. Observers have come to believe that boards that skip these steps are mere rubber stamps for staff wishes. They have seen occasional excesses and even disasters. So there is every reason to believe that boards who follow the prescribed route are responsible and those who do not are not. A board that forges new symbols does so at its own peril. The unmasking of empty symbols rarely receives as much attention as their absence.

Boldness and inclusion are keys to success in overcoming these impediments. Boldness is needed to do anything new against the pressure to conform. Inclusion of all relevant parties in the adventure helps to defuse opposition. In other words, the board can seek to include observers throughout its discussion of governance principles and during its adoption of a new model. Those included might be journalists, advocacy groups, unions, lawmakers, and any other relevant stakeholders.

Influence of Those Who Demand

Those who have power over the board constitute a special class of observers. Funding bodies, regulatory agencies, and lawmakers incorporate the conventional wisdom into their demands. After all, in the development of federal or state regulations, statutory language, association certification, and standards of accreditation, there has been little but traditional concepts of governance to guide the authors. Consequently, even vastly improved governance can run afoul of accreditation or law because of the improvements themselves. Mediocrity can pass tests that excellence fails.

The board has an obligation to lawfulness, of course, but finding a way to preserve good governance while being lawful often requires creativity. Frequently, it requires legal counsel that is schooled in Policy Governance as well as in the law. It is not uncommon for standard-setting bodies to be very prescriptive about what constitutes good governance. National associations might dictate that a local board have a certain set of committees, particular officers, or monthly meetings. Federal legislation and regulations might dictate that grantees meet similar requirements. Hospital accreditation may require the board to go through certain approval procedures. State laws require school boards to take action on a host of personnel and expenditure matters.

Often, little can be done aside from implementing the consent (automatic approval) agenda.... If possible, a board would be well advised to interact with funders, regulators, and accreditors in a manner that takes those parties' perceptions of threat to their authority into account as compassionately as possible. Sometimes it is possible to maintain a good governance model while giving the controllers what they are looking for—that is, evidence that they are in control and will not be viewed as lax by those who evaluate them. Enrolling them in the board's adventure in governance innovation may be one approach. Another may be to proceed through the ritual behaviors expected but not take them seriously.

Influence of Those Who Help

Vast experience and expertise are accessible in the literature and from educators and consultants. Competent help can be obtained on strategic planning, financial oversight, fundraising, endowment building, administrative controls, audits, bylaws, corporate restructuring, and on and on. As part of their ongoing education as well as for specific issues that arise, boards should avail themselves of this body of knowledge, but very cautiously.

Because much expertise and many helpful formats have been developed within the conventional governance framework, the board must be a wise consumer. Texts, academic courses, and advice from consultants are likely to be topic-specific. The board needs assistance with its peculiar conceptual segment of budget, personnel, or planning activities, not with all budget, personnel, or planning activities.

The board's role can be more easily confused than helped when the board becomes smarter about administrative or programmatic topics in their entirety, because the board can expend a great deal of energy on learning how to do the wrong things better. The challenge facing boards is how to take advantage of accumulated knowledge yet reframe that wisdom so that it contributes to better governance within a conceptually useful model, not simply to more information within an impaired model. Some helpers can adapt to this challenge quite well, but boards should not expect adaptation to be either automatic or voluntary. A conceptual struggle might be involved, not to mention a little ego. Staff members, for example, may find that their training advice is not as useful to a board that is fulfilling an appropriate role. Although staff members may have expertise in many areas, governance is not typically one of these areas. To adapt their expertise to what the board needs to learn, staff must have an understanding of advanced governance.

That understanding is not so widespread that boards can expect to find it easily, even in skilled educators and consultants. Help helpers to be helpful by querying them about competing value issues in the area under discussion. Rather than seeking their recommendation as to what a selected value might be, draw them out on the range of value alternatives available and what they see as the implications of options within that range. Implications are not only the predictable consequences but also the industry averages with regard to others' experience in making certain choices.

Particularly with regard to developing Executive Limitations policies, helpers can bring a great deal to a board's struggle to set the ranges within which staff members are allowed to act. They can assist the board in discovering, debating, and deciding what the conditions of jeopardy might be in, say, financial condition or personnel management. On these two topics, accountants and labor lawyers can be extremely enlightening if their counsel is taken in a way that relates to the board's proper role in such matters. Do not expect accountants or attorneys to know the proper board role, for they, too, will be operating from the conventional view. Following the raw advice of an accountant or attorney can, indeed, result in poor governance. The use of consultants has always been an important skill; good consultees are made, not born.

MAKE SELF-EVALUATION A REGULAR EVENT

There is no possibility of a board's governing with excellence in the absence of regular and rigorous self-evaluation. Like evaluation of organizational performance, board self-evaluation should be against pre-established criteria. In Policy Governance, those criteria are embedded in Governance Process and Board-Management Linkage policies, for they set out how the board will function, the discipline it will follow, and the products it will produce. So while organizational performance evaluation tests organizational behavior and achievement, self-evaluation tests board behavior and achievement.

Exhibit 5.1 shows the "Monitoring Governance Process Policies" policy adopted by the publicly elected board of Adams 12 Five Star Schools in Thornton, Colorado. The Adams 12 board policy illustrates clearly the connection between Governance Process policies and regular board self-evaluation. Notice that the board recognizes that its CGO (in this case, the president) is empowered to determine any reasonable interpretation he or she chooses for all Governance Process policies (including, incidentally, this one). The policy makes obvious that a board's self-evaluation has much in common with the board's evaluation of executive performance: they are both mandatory; they are both ongoing rather than sporadic or infrequent activities; and they both use pre-established criteria. For self-evaluation to have practical effect, it must be frequent.

Governance Process Policy

"Monitoring Governance Process Policies"

Systematic monitoring of the Board's adherence to Governance Process Policies will be against the policies themselves. Accordingly:

1. Monitoring is simply to determine the degree to which the Board is adhering to Governance Process policies.

2. Monitoring data will be acquired by three methods: (a) by direct Board inspection, in which a designated member or members of the Board assess compliance with the appropriate policy criteria, (b) by DSIT, in which a designated member or members of the committee assess compliance with the appropriate policy criteria, and (c) by external report, in which an external, disinterested third party selected by the Board assesses compliance with Board Governance Process policies.

3. In every case, the standard for compliance shall be *any reasonable President interpretation* of the Board policy being monitored. The Board is final arbiter of reasonableness, but will always judge with a "reasonable person" test rather than with interpretations favored by Board members or by the Board as a whole.

4. All policies will be monitored at a frequency and by a method chosen by the Board. The Board can monitor any policy at any time by any method, but will ordinarily depend on the attached monitoring report schedule.

Exhibit 5.1.   Adams 12 Five Star Schools, Thornton, Colorado

Note: The monitoring schedule to which the policy refers has been omitted.

In fact, frequent crude evaluations have a far greater effect than infrequent precise ones. For that reason, boards should devote at least a brief amount of time in each meeting to evaluating whether they are on course. An annual, more meticulous evaluation may be used as well, but it will not have as great an effect on ongoing board performance. In no event should board self-evaluation be a matter of downloading some generic form from the Internet.

REMEMBER THAT EXCELLENCE BEGINS IN THE BOARDROOM

Boards can be successful strategic leaders if they nurture their group responsibility. That responsibility must be accepted by every board member, not just officers. All members must participate in the discipline and productivity of the group. All members must be willing to challenge and urge one another on to big dreams, lucid values, and fidelity to their trusteeship. All members must cherish diversity as well as an unambiguous, single board position derived from diversity. All members must strive for accountability in the board's job, confident that if quality dwells in the boardroom, the rest of the organization will take care of itself. For in the long run, as surely as excellence ends with clients, patients, students, or other customers, it begins with governance.

Governing well is difficult, but the greatest difficulty may lie in shifting from old to new paradigms. "Just as managerial ability is distinct from technical expertise," says Elaine Sternberg (1994) in an apt comparison, "so the qualities needed for being a director are not the same as managerial skill." Successful strategic leadership demands powerful engagement with trusteeship, obsessive concern with results, enthusiastic empowerment of people, bigness in embracing the farsighted view, and the commitment to take a stand for dreams of tomorrow's human condition. Re-creating governance can generate a zestful new genre of strategic leadership in the boardroom, to be sure, but the effects go far beyond. Douglas K. Smith (1996) points out the compelling opportunity to provide leadership through modeling: "When leaders are learning and growing, everything about them communicates the same opportunity to other people.

They're excited; they do things differently. One of the most profound—and unusual—experiences people can have on the job is to see their leaders grow."

References

Chait, Richard, Holland, Thomas P., and Taylor, Barbara E. *Improving the Performance of Governing Boards*. Phoenix, AZ: Oryx Press, 1996.

Gregory, T. "Board Erosion Prevention." *Governing Excellence* (International Policy Governance Association), Winter 2003.

Smith, Douglas K. *Taking Charge of Change: 10 Principles for Managing People and Performance*. Reading, MA: Addison-Wesley, 1996.

Sternberg, Elaine. *Just Business: Business Ethics in Action*. London: Warner, 1994.

Tooley, R. "Using Information Technology to Sustain Policy Governance." *Board Leadership*, 2004, p. 76.

—w—

At time of original publishing John Carver was a theorist, consultant, and the world's most published author on the design of governance.

PART TWO

Leadership Theories for the Nonprofit and Public Sectors
Editor's Introduction

Any effort to put leadership theories into perspective quickly confronts a stark reality. In the opening chapter of Part II, Montgomery Van Wart refers to a comment about the state of leadership theory by political historian James MacGregor Burns. In his 1978 classic, *Leadership*, Burns observed, "Leadership is one of the most observed and least understood phenomena on earth" (p. 1). Van Wart is more affirmative about the state of leadership theory in the period following Burns' observation, but any effort to grasp the leadership field must confront the crowding of the theory landscape.

I deal here with the theory clutter in two ways. First, this part of the book begins with an excellent literature review, Montgomery Van Wart's "Public-Sector Leadership Theory: An Assessment," that puts the leadership theory into historical perspective. His review establishes the contours of the leadership theory landscape that has developed over more than a century of writing and research about leadership. The second way I address the crowding of leadership theory is by drawing upon leadership theories selectively rather than comprehensively. I identify readings related to four theories that are particularly salient for the nonprofit and public sectors: grassroots leadership, servant-leadership, collective leadership, and collaborative leadership.

Although Van Wart's review does not explicitly discuss leadership theories applied to the nonprofit sector, the scope of his review covers the whole range of leadership theory scholars and practitioners have applied in the nonprofit, public, and private sectors. It is also noteworthy that leadership theories have frequently migrated from the sectors in which they originated to other settings, suggesting both the breadth and appeal of some theories. Transformational leadership, for instance, was originally formulated by James MacGregor Burns based on his studies of the American presidency. Servant-leadership, which has become closely identified with the nonprofit sector, was first formulated by Robert Greenleaf, a forty-year executive at AT&T. Thus, many leadership theories transcend their original contexts, implying the need for caution not to pigeonhole them.

Despite the long-standing popularity of the community organizing process that Saul Alinsky (1971) popularized, Barack Obama's election has brought grassroots leadership new visibility and popularity. In "Human Dignity and Grassroots Leadership Development," Jim Keddy presents a view of grassroots leadership quite different from the mobilization or campaign-style organizing introduced by Alinsky in the mid-twentieth century. Keddy describes a model of grassroots leadership in which the human development of leaders and followers is central. Grassroots leadership prepares local leaders, regular people in their communities, to become powerful actors who are part of the long-term human infrastructure in the places where they live. Keddy summarizes the key to the grassroots leadership process: "the interplay between human dignity and the leadership development process is what enables this kind of organizing to have a deep and long-lasting impact" (p. 49).

The concepts of servant leader and stewardship, surfaced by both Max DePree and John Gardner in the opening chapters of this reader, are taken up in greater depth by Larry Spears in "Practicing Servant-Leadership." When the article was first published, Spears was president and CEO of the Robert K. Greenleaf Center for Servant-Leadership. Thus, he writes with close familiarity about Greenleaf's legacy, the ideas embodied in servant-leadership, and its diffusion as a leadership philosophy and set of practices. In reflecting about Greenleaf's development of his servant-leadership philosophy,

Spears writes: "True leadership emerges from those whose primary motivation is a deep desire to help others" (p. 8). In light of the centrality of this perspective, it is not surprising that leaders in the nonprofit and public sectors would be attracted to servant-leadership.

In "Share Leadership," Leslie Crutchfield and Heather McLeod Grant acknowledge a radical turn in thinking about leadership. They distinguish between *leaders* and *leadership* and argue that too much attention is given the former and too little the latter concept. Leadership may be the sum of the parts for what is referred to variously as "integrated," "shared," "collective," or "distributed" activities (Fernandez, Cho, and Perry, 2008) across a broad category of contributors. Referring to The Heritage Foundation as an exemplar, they write:

> "This triumvirate of leadership—the shared executive leadership, a broad tier of senior managers, and a strong and supportive board—has created an unstoppable organization. This model of shared leadership is not what we expected to find. After all, in business—and in much leadership literature—the individual heroic leader is often exalted." (p. 155)

Changing the unit of leadership analysis from individuals to social collectives (groups, organizations, communities) would radically change leadership theory and research. At the same time, like servant-leadership, collective leadership seems eminently well matched to the institutional nexus within which nonprofit and public organizations operate.

The final reading in Part II looks at settings in which collective leadership may be the rule rather than the exception. These settings are referred to as *collaborations*, which typically bring together individuals and organizations, usually in the absence of a hierarchical order, to solve complex problems. In "Collaboration Processes: Inside the Black Box," Ann Marie Thomson and James Perry discuss leadership imperatives for building effective collaboration. Much like John Gardner's "tasks of leadership" from Part I, Thomson and Perry identify five processes that collaboration participants must manage to help lead collaborations toward collectively valued outcomes. They define the processes as governance, administration, organizational autonomy, mutuality, and norms of trust and reciprocity.

As I note above, the five readings in Part II are not intended to present a comprehensive picture of leadership theory. They are, instead, rich in variety and insights about leadership in the contexts in which nonprofit and public leaders work. As a group, these readings also provide a strong orientation to the range of what scholars and practitioners have come to know as leadership theory.

References

Alinsky, S. D. *Rules for Radicals*. New York: Vintage Books, 1971.

Fernandez, S., Cho, Y. J., and Perry, J. L. (Forthcoming). "Exploring the Link Between Integrated Leadership and Public Sector Performance." *Leadership Quarterly*.

CHAPTER SIX

Public-Sector Leadership Theory

An Assessment

Montgomery Van Wart

———

In 1995, Larry Terry noted the neglect of administrative or "bureaucratic leadership" in the public-sector literature. This article assesses the state of the administrative leadership literature. It examines the following questions:

- Is the study of administrative (that is, bureaucratic) leadership important?

- What are the reasons for the neglect of administrative leadership, including the difficulties associated with this type of research?

- Has the administrative leadership literature made significant strides since Terry's observation in 1995? If not, why?

- What are the specific strengths and weaknesses of the literature, whatever its overall robustness? In particular, how does

Originally published as "Public-Sector Leadership Theory: An Assessment" in *Public Administration Review*, 63. (March/April 2003).

it compare with the mainstream (that is, largely private-sector-focused) literature?

• What areas are ripe for research?

To address these questions, a relatively exhaustive review of public-sector leadership was conducted, as well as a thorough review of the major schools in the mainstream literature. Because of the many weaknesses in the literature (in scope, in numerous gaps, and in theory building), it is hoped this article can make a major contribution in defining the terrain of this complex and difficult area so that more rapid and coherent progress can be made.

THE IMPORTANCE AND CHALLENGES OF LEADERSHIP RESEARCH

The Importance of Leadership

To most people, the importance of leadership is self-evident no matter what the setting. In organizations, *effective* leadership provides higher-quality and more efficient goods and services; it provides a sense of cohesiveness, personal development, and higher levels of satisfaction among those conducting the work; and it provides an overarching sense of direction and vision, an alignment with the environment, a healthy mechanism for innovation and creativity, and a resource for invigorating the organizational culture. This is no small order, especially in contemporary times.

Leadership is difficult in all eras, to be sure, but it seems that today's leaders face additional challenges. While the shared-power environment created in the second half of the twentieth century enhanced many aspects of democracy, "it also makes leadership more difficult" (Henton, Melville, and Walesh, 1997). The public has greater access to view leaders today—especially public-sector leaders—through the media focus, the Internet, and greater levels of public awareness. Yet the public shows less tolerance for leaders' mistakes, foibles, and structural challenges as its skepticism has grown (Yankelovich, 1991). Further, there is evidence that as competition in the organizational universe has intensified in the new global economy, even among public-sector organizations, the range of skills necessary for leaders has grown (Bass, 1985).

Reasons for Neglect and Difficulties
in Administrative Leadership Research

If we accept—as most people do—that leadership is important and that leaders have a tough job in the best of times, it stands to reason that leadership research would be both prolific and valuable. Although the first part of this statement is documentably true in the mainstream literature—more than 7,500 empirical and quasi-empirical references were cited in the major handbook for the literature in 1990 (Bass, 1990)—the latter is disputed among leadership experts. The most prominent researcher of his day, Ralph Stogdill urged his colleagues to largely abandon forty years' of work as utterly inconclusive in 1948 (which, as a whole, they did). In his landmark 1978 study on leadership thirty years later, James MacGregor Burns acidly stated:

> "Leadership is one of the most observed and least understood phenomena on earth" (p. 1). Another particularly eminent scholar—Warren Bennis—came to the same conclusion in the mid-1980s: "Never have so many labored so long to say so little," and "leadership is the most studied and least understood topic of any in the social sciences." (Bennis and Nanus, 1985)

Although I will argue the situation improved dramatically in the mainstream in the 1990s, it is easier to understand the incredibly slow progress of leadership research, for all the attention, when one examines the challenges leadership research faces in generalizing beyond relatively small subsets.

One set of difficulties has to do with what Brunner calls "contextual complexity" (1997). While there are significant similarities among leaders that are generally agreed upon (for instance, they have followers and affect the direction of the group), from a research perspective, the differences among leaders are far greater and more challenging.

For example, the leader of paid employees and the leader of volunteers have very different jobs. Issues of contextual complexity apply to mission, organizational, and environmental culture, structure, types of problems, types of opportunities, levels of discretion (Baliga and Hunt, 1988), and a host of other critically important areas. These types of issues led one of the earliest commentators on public-sector administrative leadership to conclude that "the differences in individuals who find themselves in executive positions and the variations in the life cycles of organizations produce practically limitless permutations and combinations" (Stone, 1945). As if these contextual, complex challenges were not enough, however, a researcher has other problems that inhibit generalizations in social science research when highly complex human phenomena are studied. An additional confounding factor in our list is the issue of proper definition, which is ultimately a normative problem. Because science cannot solve normative issues (Dahl, 1947), this problem is central to the ability to build a body of work that is coherent as research and applied use. The final technical problem is the effect of observation and the observer. Even the "hardest" of the sciences has rediscovered this problem (Kiel, 1994), yet it is a particularly pesky dilemma in amorphous areas such as leadership. One version of the predicament, simply stated, is that observed phenomena change through the act of observation. A second version of the problem is that because the observer determines the conceptual framework of the issue, the methods to be used, and the context to be studied, the results are affected far more by the investigators' biases than might be supposed.

For all of these challenges and all of the seemingly nonadditive (but certainly not nonproductive) leadership research done until the 1980s, efforts at more sophisticated, multifaceted approaches for comprehensive models have made a substantial improvement (Chemers, 1997; Hunt, 1996). However, administrative leadership research (literature that is most interested in leadership in public-sector bureaucratic settings) has experienced neither the volume nor the integration of the mainstream. Why? Building on the ideas of Doig and Hargrove (1987), Terry (1995) speculates on some reasons beyond the technical issues raised above, which certainly have not slowed down mainstream interest in leadership research. He offers three types of reasons.

First, there may be some belief that administrative leadership does not (or should not) exist to an appreciable degree because of a belief in a highly instrumental approach to leadership in the public sector. This is a legacy of both scientific management, with its technocratic focus, and beliefs in a strong model of overhead democracy (Redford, 1969). The stronger these beliefs, the less likely administrative leadership would receive attention. Second, bureaucracies may be guided by powerful forces that are largely beyond the control of administrative leaders, making their contributions relatively insignificant. Both arguments tend to delimit the role and contribution of public administration.

Finally, there may be a problem with attention being diverted from leadership research by related topics. Given the relatively small size of the pool of researchers compared to the number of possible topics in the field, this is a significant possibility. Researchers who are more empirically inclined may find bureaucratic routines (frontline and mid-level management) more accessible. Many of those interested in executive leadership may find political leadership more attractive, with its dramatic and accessible policy debates and discussions, rather than administrative leadership, with its more subtle and nuanced decision-making routines. Finally, those interested in the philosophical nature of leadership may be pulled into the normative debates about the amount of and manner in which discretion should be exercised by administrative leaders, rather than the changing and unchanging characteristics of administrative leadership. Although it is not conclusive, my assessment of the causal weights will be offered in the conclusion.

Operationally, "administrative leadership" in this article refers to leadership from the frontline supervisor (or even lead worker) to the nonpolitical head of the organization. The focus is not on elected legislative leaders and only on elected executives and their political designees, such as agency secretaries and directors, commissioners, or legislatively approved directors, to the degree that they include non-policy functions as a significant component of their responsibilities. There are many instances in which the line is hard to draw. The article first will review the mainstream leadership research as well as the administrative (public-sector) research. Next, the perennial debates (and research questions) of mainstream leadership theory will be compared to administrative leadership theory. This will culminate in a discussion of the state-of-the-art in administrative leadership research and a conclusion suggesting areas that may be productively mined in the future by scholars and pursued by practitioners.

BACKGROUND ON LEADERSHIP RESEARCH
Dominant Themes in the Mainstream Leadership Literature

It is certainly impossible to pigeonhole all of the mainstream leadership literature[1] into tight eras with sharp demarcations; however, it is possible to capture the dominant themes and interests for a heuristic

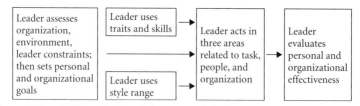

Figure 6.1.   A Generic Practitioner Model of Organizational Leadership

overview. For those interested in a detailed history and more complex analysis, an excellent, exhaustive review can be found in *Bass and Stogdill's Handbook of Leadership* (Bass, 1990). However, Figure 6.1 provides a simple, contemporary, practitioner-oriented model as a mental framework for the development of the leadership literature. Such practitioner models emphasize leader assessment, leader characteristics, and leader styles, all of which affect actual leader behaviors. As leaders evaluate their own and their organizations' effectiveness, they begin the cycle again. Scientific models tend to de-emphasize the leader-assessment phase (as difficult to observe) and emphasize intervening organizational variables that affect leader success.

The nineteenth century was dominated by the notion of the "great man" thesis. Particular great men (women invariably were overlooked despite great personages in history such as Joan of Arc, Elizabeth I, or Clara Barton) somehow move history forward because of their exceptional characteristics as leaders. The stronger version of this theory holds that history is a handmaiden to men; great men actually change the shape and direction of history.

Philosophers such as Friedrich Nietzsche and William James firmly asserted that history would be different if a great man suddenly were incapacitated. Thomas Carlyle's 1841 essay on heroes and hero worship is an early popular version of this, as is Galton's 1869 study of hereditary genius (cited in Bass, 1990). Such theories generally have an explicit class bias. A milder version of the theory is that as history proceeds on its irrevocable course, a few men will move history forward substantially and dramatically because of their greatness, especially in moments of crisis or great social need. Although these lines of thinking have more sophisticated echoes in the later trait and situational leadership periods, "hero worship" is certainly alive and well in popular culture and in biographies and autobiographies.

Its core belief is that there are only a few, very rare, individuals in any society at any time with the unique characteristics to shape or express history. Although this thesis may serve sufficiently for case studies (essentially biographies), it is effectively irrefutable and therefore unusable as a scientific theory.

The scientific mood of the early twentieth century fostered the development of a more focused search for the basis of leaders. What traits and characteristics do leaders seem to share? Researchers developed personality tests and compared the results against those perceived to be leaders. By the 1940s, researchers had amassed very long lists of traits from numerous psychologically oriented studies (Bird, 1940; Jenkins, 1947). This tactic had two problems: First, the lists became longer and longer as research continued. Second—and more importantly—the traits and characteristics identified were not powerful predictors across situations. For example, leaders must be decisive, but they also must be flexible and inclusive. Without situational specificity, the endless list of traits offers little prescriptive assistance and descriptively becomes little more than a laundry list. In 1948, Ralph Stogdill published a devastating critique of pure trait theory, and it fell into disfavor as being too one-dimensional to account for the complexity of leadership (Stogdill, 1948).

The next major thrust was to look at the situational contexts that affect leaders in order to find meaningful patterns for theory building and useful advice. One early example was the work that came out of the Ohio State Leadership Studies (Hemhill, 1950; Hemhill and Coons, 1957), which started by testing 1,800 statements related to leadership behavior. By continually distilling the behaviors, researchers arrived at two underlying factors: consideration and initiation of structure. *Consideration* describes a variety of behaviors related to the development, inclusion, and the good feelings of subordinates. *Initiating structure* describes a variety of behaviors related to defining roles, control mechanisms, task focus, and work coordination, both inside and outside the unit. Coupled with the humanist or human relations revolution that was occurring in the 1950s and 1960s, these (and similar studies) spawned a series of useful—if often simplistic and largely bimodal—theories (Argyris, 1957; Blake and Mouton, 1964, 1965; Fiedler, 1967; Fiedler, Chemers, and Mahar, 1976; Hersey and Blanchard, 1969, 1972; Likert, 1959; Maslow, 1965; McGregor, 1960).

These early implicit and explicit situational theories were certainly useful, for several reasons. First, they were useful as an antidote to the excessively hierarchical, authoritarian styles that had developed in the first half of the twentieth century with the rise and dominance of large organizations in both the private and public sectors. Second, they were useful as teaching tools for incipient and practicing managers, who appreciated the elegant constructs even though they were descriptively simplistic. As a class, however, these theories generally failed to meet scientific standards because they tried to explain too much with too few variables. Among the major theories, only Vroom's normative decision model broke out of this pattern because it self-consciously focused on a single dimension of leadership style—the role of participation—and identified seven problem attributes and two classes of cases (group and individual) (Vroom and Jago, 1988; Vroom and Yetton, 1973).

Although the situational perspective still forms the basis of most leadership theories today, it has done so either in a strictly managerial context (that is, a narrow level of analysis) on a factor-by-factor basis, or it has been subsumed by more comprehensive approaches to leadership at the macro level.

While ethical dimensions were mentioned occasionally in the mainstream literature, the coverage was invariably peripheral because it avoided normative issues. The first major text devoted to ethical issues was Robert Greenleaf's book, *Servant Leadership* (1977), but it did not receive mainstream attention. In contrast, James MacGregor Burns' book on leadership burst on the scene in 1978 and had unusually heavy ethical overtones.[2] However, it was not the ethical dimension that catapulted it to prominence, but its transformational theme. Both Greenleaf (a former business executive) and Burns (a political scientist) were outside the normal academic circles in leadership, which primarily came from business and psychology. A number of contemporary mainstream leadership theorists, both popular and academic, continue in this tradition to one degree or another, such as DePree (1989), Rost (1990), Block (1993), Gardner (1989), Bennis, Parikh, and Lessem (1994, in contrast with Bennis's other work), and Zand (1997), among others. This theme was covered earlier and more frequently (at least in terms of ethical uses of discretion) in the public-sector literature, but that was not part of the mainstream literature and will be discussed separately.

Until 1978, the focus of the mainstream literature was leadership at lower levels, which was amenable to small group and experimental methods and simplified variable models, while executive leadership (and its external demands) and the more amorphous abilities to induce dramatic change were largely ignored.[3] Burns' book on leadership dramatically changed that interest by introducing the notion that transactional leadership was what was largely being studied, and that the other highly important arena—transformational leadership—was largely being ignored.[4] This hit an especially responsive cord in the non-experimental camp, which had already been explicitly stating that, nationally, there was a surfeit of managers (who use a "transactional" mode) and a terrible deficit of leaders (who use a "transformational" mode) (Zaleznik, 1977). Overall, this school agreed that leaders have a special responsibility for understanding a changing environment, that they facilitate more dramatic changes, and that they can energize followers far beyond what traditional exchange theory would suggest.

Overstating for clarity, three subschools emerged that emphasized different aspects of these "larger-than-life" leaders.[5] The transformational school emphasized vision and overarching organizational change (Burns, 1978; Bass, 1985; Bennis and Nanus, 1985; Tichy and Devanna, 1986). The charismatic school focused on the influence processes of individuals and the specific behaviors used to arouse inspiration and higher levels of action in followers (Conger and Kanungo, 1998; House, 1977; Meindl, 1990). Less articulated in terms of leadership theory was an entrepreneurial school that urged leaders to make practical process and cultural changes that would dramatically improve quality or productivity; it shared a change emphasis with the transformational school and an internal focus with the charismatic school (Champy, 1995; Hammer and Champy, 1993; Peters and Austin, 1985).

The infusion of the transformational leadership school(s) led to both a reinvigoration of academic and nonacademic studies of leadership and a good deal of confusion initially. Was the transactional leadership that the situationalists had studied so assiduously really just mundane management? Or was the new transformational leadership just an extension of basic skills that its adherents were poorly equipped to explain with more conventional scientific methodologies? Even before the 1980s, some work had been done to create holistic models that tried to explain more aspects of leadership (Winter, 1979; Yukl, 1971). Yet it was not until the 1980s that work began in earnest and that conventional models routinely incorporated transactional and transformational elements.

Bass's work is a good example in this regard. Even his original work on transformational leadership (1985) has strong transactional elements (transformational leaders being those who not only master transactional skills, but capitalize on transformational skills as well),[6] which were strengthened in later work (Bass, 1996; Bass and Avolio, 1990). In the authoritative *Bass and Stogdill's Handbook of Leadership*, Bass asserted that the field "has broken out of its normal confinement to the study of [small group and supervisory] behaviors" to more studies on executives, more inclusion of perspectives from political science, and more cross-fertilization among schools of thought (Bass, 1990, p. xi). Not surprisingly, fresh efforts to find integrative models were common in the 1990s (Chemers, 1997; Hunt, 1996; Yukl, 1998) (see Table 6.1 for a summary of the eras of mainstream leadership theory and research). To be sure, this cursory review does not do justice to the wealth of perspectives on specific leadership topics, but space and purpose preclude a more in-depth treatment.[7]

The Public-Sector Literature on Leadership Theory and Research

Although the literature on leadership with a public-sector focus is a fraction of that in the private sector, it has been substantial albeit relatively unfocused. One way to begin a brief review is to look at the track record of *PAR*. In doing an informal content analysis of the journal since its inception—using a rather loose definition of leadership that includes the broader management topics, most executive topics, much of the explicit discretion literature, and that part of the organizational change literature that has a strong leadership component—the author found 110 articles relating to the topic in sixty-one years. However, using a stricter criterion—that leadership was an explicit focus of the article—only about twenty-five articles qualified, or about four per decade on average.

In the 1940s, articles by Finer (1940) and Leys (1943) defined the administrative discretion debate—how much discretion should public administrators have, and under what conditions—that was taken up so vigorously again in the 1990s. Donald Stone wrote "Notes on the Government Executive: His Role and His Method" in 1945, which is as good an equivalent to Follett's "The Essentials

Era	Major Time Frame	Major Characteristics/Examples of Proponents
Great Man	Pre-1900; continues to be popular in biographies.	• Emphasis on emergence of a great figure such as a Napoleon, George Washington, or Martin Luther, who has substantial effect on society. • Era influenced by notions of rational social change by uniquely talented and insightful individuals.
Trait	1900–1948; current resurgence of recognition of importance of natural talents.	• Emphasis on the individual traits (physical, personal, motivational, aptitudes) and skills (communication and ability to influence) that leaders bring to all leadership tasks. • Era influenced by scientific methodologies in general (especially industrial measurement) and scientific management in particular (for instance, the definition of roles and assignment of competencies to those roles).
Contingency	1948–1980s; continues as the basis of most rigorous models but with vastly expanded situational repertoire.	• Emphasis on the situational variables leaders must deal with, especially performance and follower variables. Shift from traits and skills to behaviors (for example, energy levels and communication skills to role clarification and staff motivation). Dominated by bimodal models in its heyday. • Era influenced by the rise of human relations theory, behavioral science (in areas such as motivation theory), and the use of small group experimental designs in psychology.
Transformational	1978–present.	• Emphasis on leaders who create change in deep structures, major processes, or overall culture. Leader mechanisms may be compelling vision, brilliant technical insight, and/or charismatic quality.

Table 6.1.   Eras of Mainstream Leadership Theory and Research

Era	Major Time Frame	Major Characteristics/Examples of Proponents
		• Era influenced by the loss of American dominance in business, finance, and science and the need to re-energize various industries that had slipped into complacency.
Servant	1977–present.	• Emphasis on the ethical responsibilities to followers, stakeholders, and society. Business theorists tend to emphasize service to followers; political theorists emphasize citizens; public administration analysts tend to emphasize legal compliance and/or citizens. • Era influenced by social sensitivities raised in the 1960s and 1970s.
Multifaceted	1990s–present.	• Emphasis on integrating the major schools, especially the transactional schools (trait and behavior issues largely representing management interests) and transformational schools (visionary, entrepreneurial, and charismatic). • Era affected by a highly competitive global economy and the need to provide a more sophisticated and holistic approach to leadership.

Table 6.1. *(continued)*

of Leadership" ([1933] 1996) or Barnard's *Functions of the Executive* ([1938] 1987) as ever appeared in the journal.

The trickle of high-quality pieces continued in which Lawton (1954) followed in Stone's footsteps, and Dimock (1958) provided a well-grounded assessment of leadership development. The first piece based exclusively on empirical evidence was by Golembiewski (1959), in which he brought together the literature on small groups in public-sector settings.

Guyot (1962) presented the only empirical study in the 1960s to study variation in the motivation of public and private leaders. Fisher (1962) complained that federal managers do not have management training, and James Fesler (1960) provided a superb editorial comment on the importance of studying leadership and its many contexts. Other topics addressed were influence and social power (Altshular, 1965; Lundstedt, 1965).

No important articles appeared in the 1970s, which mirrors the low profile of leadership publication in the popular literature. Yet the lacuna is made up by the resurgence of interest in leadership topics in the 1980s. DiIulio (1989) reasserted the importance of both leadership and the management component. Probably the three best articles on the training and development of leaders were written during this time (Faerman, Quinn, and Thompson, 1987; Flanders and Utterback, 1985; Likert, 1981). Stone (1981) and Dimock (1986) wrote essays on the importance and nurturing of innovation and creativity in organizations by leaders. Empirical pieces also appeared on followership (Gilbert and Hyde, 1988) and leader action planning (Young and Norris, 1988).

Because leadership is so highly related to reform, and because of the volume and debate over the proper type of reforms to make that occurred throughout the decade, leadership is at least indirectly discussed in nearly every issue after 1992. This is particularly true for the debate about administrative discretion, which largely pitted an "entrepreneurial" camp against a "stewardship" camp. Although they cannot do justice to the full range of topics in these two idealized perspectives, good examples are provided in Bellone and Goerl's "Reconciling Public Entrepreneurship and Democracy" (1992) and Terry's "Administrative Leadership, Neo-Managerialism, and the Public Management Movement" (1998). Some of the best and most focused empirically based studies in *PAR* appeared in the 1990s (Borins, 2000; Considine and Lewis, 1999; Hennessey, 1998; Moon, 1999).

Generalizing about the leadership literature in *PAR* as one barometer of the field, the following observations can be made: First, until the last decade, leadership was largely considered an executive phenomenon, and thus when small group and lower-level leadership was the focus of the mainstream leadership literature in the 1960s and 1970s, leadership topics were lightly covered. Second, there were only a handful of empirical pieces on leadership in the first fifty years of the journal. Finally, in terms of the "thoughtful essay" tradition, many of the best examples occur in book reviews, with Donald Stone, John Corson, and Paul Appleby being frequent contributors. Although important, *PAR* is but one source—what other contributions were being made to a distinctively public-sector leadership literature?

In the first half of the century during the trait period, public-sector sites were frequently examined, although no distinctive perspective emerged (Jenkins, 1947). The first in an important genre of executive studies was done by Macmahon and Millett (1939), in this case regarding federal administrators. The tradition of biographies and autobiographies of important administrative leaders was also established (Pinchot, 1947). In the 1950s, a series of good leadership studies in the administrative realm was produced, most notably by Bernstein (1958). However, Selznick's classic, *Leadership in Administration* (1957), is probably the single best overall treatment of the subject in terms of timelessness. In the 1960s, Corson (with Shale) wrote his second book on senior administrative leaders (1966), and Graubard and Holton edited a series of essays on political and administrative leadership (1962). Downs' (1967) well-known book on bureaucracy is notable for its popular, if negative, typology of leaders. Again, the 1970s produced little of special note, with the exception of the administrative role in iron-triangle politics (Heclo, 1977) and several good studies of military and quasi-military leadership (Jermier and Berkes, 1979; Winter, 1979).

With the introduction of the transformational and charismatic literatures in the 1980s, the resurgence of more general interest in leadership was mirrored in the administrative leadership literature. The administrative leader as entrepreneur was introduced by Eugene Lewis (1980) and expanded upon by Doig and Hargrove (1987). Kaufman provided a definitive executive study (1981); Cleveland (1985) and Gardner (1989) provided masterfully well rounded essays in the Selznick tradition. The more specialized studies on public-sector leadership continued to be primarily for the military (Taylor and Rosenback, 1984; Van Fleet and Yukl, 1986).

The volume of materials produced in the 1990s requires more selectivity for the present purpose. Many public-sector leadership books have elements that are applicable for administrative leaders but really focus on local and national policy makers (such as councils, mayors, state legislators, etc.) and civic leaders (Chrislip and Larson, 1994; Heifetz, 1994; Luke, 1998; Henton, Melville, and Walesh, 1997;

Svara, 1994). Some emphasize specific elements of leadership such as planning (Bryson and Crosby, 1992), complexity (Kiel, 1994), problem focus (R. Terry, 1993), public-service values (Fairholm, 1991; Riccucci, 1995; Rost, 1990), and frontline leaders (Vinzant and Crothers, 1998). Larry Terry (1995) provided a full-length argument supporting leadership as stewardship (which he calls conservatorship). Much of the more narrowly focused leadership literature continued to be for the military (Hunt, Dodge, and Wong, 1999). The *International Journal of Public Administration* sponsored a symposium about transformational leadership, edited by the distinguished leadership expert Bernard Bass in 1996. In 2001, Rusaw provided the first book designed as an overarching textbook with a review of the literature. Previously, broad treatments had been available only in chapter formats in most of the standard generic textbooks in the field.

No review of the literature would be complete without some mention of leadership education and training—that is, the application of scholarly work and the genesis of applied research from training settings. Although some of the larger public administration programs with greater resources have substantial offerings in organizational leadership, few of the moderate and smaller programs nationally have the faculty resources to do so. Nonetheless, leadership books and articles are sprinkled throughout management classes in educational curricula, even if in an auxiliary capacity. There are numerous leadership training programs for leaders at all levels of government and at various levels in organizations. Many use leadership-feedback instruments (often called 360-degree instruments) that provide anonymous feedback from subordinates, superiors, and sometimes colleagues. For example, the Center for Creative Leadership uses the proprietary assessment tool "Benchmarks" as the basis of one of its programs. Some rely heavily on case studies, such as the State and Local Executive Program at Harvard's Kennedy School. Many are eclectic or holistic, such as the Federal Executive Institute. Nearly all major federal agencies have their own leadership programs, and the military and public safety areas are particularly keen on leadership training. Many fine state and local programs are located at universities, such as the University of Virginia (Center for Public Service), University of Texas–Austin (Governor's Center), and Arizona State University (Advanced Public Executive Program). A number of the scholars who publish in this area are affiliated with such programs. Finally, it should be noted that the Office of Personnel Management has done a good deal of applied research (OPM, 1997, 1999), which it shares with its partners in state governments.

Why do the literatures vary today? The mainstream was pushed into more integrative leadership models in the 1980s by the "new economy," which was triggered by the economic shocks of the 1970s. Substantially higher levels of productivity and customer focus required a much more encompassing model or set of models than the largely transactional approaches had achieved. Reformation efforts in the public sector lagged by nearly a decade (despite the fanfare of 1992–1994). Integrative models tailored to public-sector settings simply may be following traditional delayed development, but they also may have been stymied by the enormous normative debates that typified the field in the 1990s.

PERENNIAL DEBATES IN MAINSTREAM LEADERSHIP THEORY

Another way to review the leadership literature is to examine the major debates that have shaped both leadership paradigms and research agendas. For simplicity, only four of the broadest are discussed here:

- The "proper" focus?
- Does it make a difference?
- Are leaders born or made?
- The best style?

What Should Leaders Focus On: Technical Performance, Development of People, or Organizational Alignment?

We expect leaders to "get things done," to maintain good systems, to provide the resources and training for production, to maintain efficiency and effectiveness through various controls, to make sure that technical problems are handled correctly, and to coordinate functional operations. These and other more technical aspects of production are one level of leadership focus. This focus is implicit in much of the management literature from scientific management, classical management (for example, POSDCORB), the productivity literature, and the contemporary measurement and benchmark literature. It is particularly relevant for leadership in the lower levels of the organization closest to production.

Another perspective is that leaders do not do the work: They depend on followers to actually do the work. Therefore, followers' training, motivation, maturation and continued development, and overall satisfaction are critical to production and organizational effectiveness. Indeed, some of the foremost researchers on the stumbling blocks for leaders state, "many studies of managerial performance have found that the most critical skill for beginning managers, and one most often lacking, is interpersonal competence, or the ability to deal with 'people problems' " (McCall, Lombardo, and Morrison, 1988, p. 19). This strain of thought blossomed during the humanist era, beginning with Maslow in the 1940s and peaking during the 1960s with writers like Argyris, McGregor, and Likert and the situationalists in the 1970s. In the situational leadership research, it was the other half of the task–people dualism. It is still very popular today, especially in the team leadership literature (Katzenbach and Smith, 1993), the excellence literature such as Tom Peters (1994), and the charismatic elements of the transformational leadership literature. The emergence of the transformational leadership paradigm in the 1980s brought the idea that "the essential function of leadership is to produce adaptive or useful change" (Kotter, 1990). This notion was, in reality, resurrected from the great man theories in political science and Weberian charismatic theory in sociology. Similarly, Edgar Schein asserted that *the only thing of real importance that leaders do is to create and manage culture* (1985, p. 2, emphasis in original).

Certainly not a major theme in the mainstream, if not altogether absent, was the notion that leadership is a service to the people, end consumers, society, and the public interest (rather than followers). It is common for biographies of religious and social leaders to advance this most strongly, but exemplars in public service do so nearly as strongly (Cooper and Wright, 1992; Riccucci, 1995). This notion does not displace technical performance, follower development, or organizational alignment, but it often largely ignores these dimensions as "givens." Although relatively uncommon in the mainstream, it has been a prominent element of the scholarly discussion in the public administration literature.

Last—and logically—leadership can be seen as a composite of several or all of these notions. Such a composite perspective has both logical and emotional appeal. Leaders typically are called upon to do and be all of these things—perform, develop followers, align their organizations, and foster the common good. Yet it also sidesteps the problem to some degree. Most leaders must make difficult choices about what to focus on and what they should glean from the act of leadership. What is the appropriate balance, and who determines it? Such normative questions loom large when reckoning the merits of the checkered histories of administrative leaders such as Robert Moses (Caro, 1974), J. Edgar Hoover (Powers, 1987), and more recently, Robert Citrone. For an array of possible definitions related to administrative leadership, see Exhibit 6.1 below.

Leadership can focus strictly on the ends (getting things done), the means by which things get done (the followers), or aligning the organization with external needs and opportunities (which can result in substantive change). A definition of leadership can also emphasize the spirit with which leadership is conducted: In the public sector, this is invariably a public service commitment. Of course, definitions are a blend of several of these elements but with different emphases. One's definition tends to vary based on normative preferences and one's concrete situation and experience.

1. *Administrative leadership is the process of providing the results required by authorized processes in an efficient, effective, and legal manner.* (This narrower definition might apply well to a frontline supervisor and would tend to be preferred by those endorsing strict political accountability.)

2. *Administrative leadership is the process of developing/supporting followers who provide the results.* (Since all leaders have followers, and since it is the followers who actually perform the work and provide its quality, it is better to focus on them than the direct service/product. This is a common view in service industries with mottoes such as Our Employees Are Our Number 1 Priority.)

3. *Administrative leadership is the process of aligning the organization with its environment, especially the necessary macro-level changes necessary, and realigning the culture as appropriate.* (This definition tends to fit executive leadership better and emphasizes the "big picture." Many public-sector analysts are concerned about the application of this definition because of a breakdown in democratic accountability.)

4. *The key element to administrative leadership is its service focus.* (Although leadership functions and foci may vary, administrative leaders need to be responsive, open, aware of competing interests, dedicated to the common good, etc., so that they create a sense of public trust for their stewardship roles.)

5. *Leadership is a composite of providing technical performance, internal direction to followers, external organizational direction—all with a public service orientation.* (This definition implicitly recognizes the complex and demanding challenge for leaders; however, it eschews the tough decision about defining the proper emphasis or focus that leaders may need to—and operationally do—make.)

Exhibit 6.1.   Possible Definitions of Leadership in an Administrative Context

To What Degree Does Leadership Make a Difference?

Burns (1978, p. 265) tells the cynical story of a Frenchman sitting in a cafe who hears a disturbance, runs to the window, and cries: "There goes the mob. I am their leader. I must follow them!" Such a story suggests that, at a minimum, we place too great an emphasis on the effect that leaders have. At its loftiest level—Do leaders make a difference?—the question is essentially philosophical because of its inability to provide meaningful control groups and define what leadership means, other than in operational terms. No matter whether it is the great man or transformational theorists comparing Hitlers to Chamberlains, or situational theorists working with small groups comparing the results of finite solution problems, the answer is generally yes. Nonetheless, it is important to remember that leaders do not act in a vacuum—they are a part of the flow of history and set in a culture filled with crises, opportunities, and even dumb luck. In practical terms, however, the question of whether leaders make any difference gets translated into the questions of how much difference and when?

In its various permutations, the question of how much difference leaders make takes up the largest part of the literature, especially when the question relates to the effect of specific behaviors, traits, and skills or their clusters. At a global level, the transformational and great man devotees generally assert that great leaders can make a great difference. Some of the best practical writers, however, caution that leaders' effects are only modest because of the great constraints and the inertia they face (Barnard, [1938] 1987; Gardner, 1989). The stories about Truman pitying the incoming Eisenhower, because his orders would not be followed as in the Army, and Kennedy ordering the missiles out of Turkey, only to find out during the Cuban missile crisis that they were still there, reflect this perspective.

It is likely that this wisdom is directed at the excessive reliance on formal authority and insulated rationalistic thinking that some inexperienced or weaker leaders exhibit.

Another particularly important dimension of the effect of leadership relates to the levels at which leadership occurs. At the extreme, some theorists emphasize leadership that is almost exclusively equivalent to grand change (Zaleznik, 1977) and minimize and even denigrate the notion that leadership occurs throughout the organization. To the contrary, the small group research of the 1950s through the 1970s seemed to suggest that leadership is fundamentally similar at any level. A few, especially the customer service and excellence literatures, emphasize the importance of frontline supervisors (Buckingham and Coffman, 1999; Peters, 1994). More comprehensive models of the current leadership literature tend to emphasize the idea that different types of leadership are required at different levels, especially because of the increasing levels of discretion allowed as one climbs higher in the organization (Hunt, 1996). Different styles simply require different types of skills (Katz, 1955).

Are Leaders Born or Made?[8]

An implicit assumption of the great man theory is that leaders (invariably the heads of state and major businesses such as banks and mercantile houses) are essentially born, probably allowing for some significant early training as well. That is, you either have the "stuff" of leadership or you don't, and most do not. Of course, in an age when leadership generally required either membership in the privileged classes (that is, the "right stuff" included education, wealth, connections, and senior appointments) or, in rare instances, extraordinary brilliance in a time of crisis (such as a Napoleon),[9] this has more than a little truth to it. In a more democratic era, such factors have less force, especially because leadership is conceived so much more broadly in terms of position.

Today, the question is generally framed as one of degree rather than as a strict dichotomy. To what degree can leaders be "made," and how? The developmental portion actually has two major components according to most researchers and thoughtful practitioners. While part of leadership is the result of formal training, it actually may be the smaller component. Experience is likely the more important teacher. In the extreme, this position states that leadership cannot be taught, but it can be learned. More formal training is not without its virtues, too, providing technical skills and credibility, management knowledge, external awareness, coaching, and encouragement for reflection. Leaders must have (or in some instances acquire) the basic technical knowledge of the organization, often more for credibility than the executive function itself; formal training can assist greatly here. Management is a different profession altogether from doing line work; again, training can greatly facilitate the learning process, especially for new managers. Thus, while the black-and-white debate about leaders being made or born is largely considered sophomoric, the more sophisticated debate about the *relative* importance of innate abilities, experience (unplanned or rotational), and formal training is alive and well.

What Is the Best Style to Use?

Although leadership style is really just an aggregation of traits, skills, and behaviors, it has been an extremely popular topic of research and debate in its own right. One of the most significant issues has been definitional: What is leadership style? Although leadership style can be thought of as the cumulative effect of *all* traits, skills, and behaviors, it generally describes what is perceived as the key—or at least a prominent—aspect of the universal set of leadership characteristics. Examples include follower participation, such as Zand (1997, p. 143), who discusses command, consign, consult, and concur styles; change styles, such as risk averse or risk accepting; and personality styles, such as those based on the Myers-Briggs Type Indicator. Other leadership style definitions involve communication, individual versus group approaches to leadership, value orientations—especially involving integrity, and power-and-influence typologies.

A slightly different approach to style looks at it related to function. Much of the situational literature addresses style in this light. Leaders have to get work done ("initiate structure") and work through people ("consideration"). How they are perceived to balance these factors can be defined operationally as their style. A somewhat different, but very useful, insight into functional style preference has to do with the type of situation the leader prefers or excels in: a maintenance situation, a project or task force situation, a line versus function situation, a startup, or turning a business around (McCall, Lombardo, and Morrison, 1988).

Another important set of issues regarding style has to do with whether and to what degree style can be changed in adults.[10] Not many have taken the hard line that changing style is nearly impossible. Fiedler (1967; Fiedler, Chemers, and Mahar, 1976) is probably most prominent in this regard, largely advising that it is better to figure out the situation first and find the appropriate leader second. Yet, even assuming that change in style is possible, most serious researchers warn against excessive expectations of dramatic change, although radical style change anecdotes pepper the popular literature. If style can be changed, then the important issue that emerges is *how* (which largely becomes an applied training issue)? Hersey and Blanchard (1969, 1972) have been the most popular in this regard, teaching people to compare their style preference (defined by worker participation in decision making) with the style needs of various situations. In addition to style need (situational demands), style preference, and style range (a leader's repertoire of different styles) is the issue of style quality. Just because one practices a style extensively does not mean that one is proficient in its use.

Although these debates have strong echoes in the public-sector literature, the differences in the debate structures are as important as the similarities.

DEBATES AND DISCUSSIONS
IN ADMINISTRATIVE LEADERSHIP THEORY

Of the four major questions, only the first (focus) is discussed as robustly in the public-sector literature as it is in the mainstream; indeed, from a normative philosophical basis, the administrative leadership literature probably argues this issue even more thoroughly. However, the question of proper focus is translated into the discretion debate, which has taken numerous forms affecting the proper role of administrative leaders. For the sake of simplicity, the first era (1883–1940s) can be conceptualized as a time when the dichotomy between the political world of policy decisions and the world of technical and neutral implementation was the overarching ideal. It was argued that good administrative leaders made many technical decisions but referred policy decisions to their political superiors. The role of discretion was largely ignored or downplayed.

The second era (1940–1980s) was a less idealistic model that recognized that the interplay of the political and administrative worlds is far more intertwined than a simple dichotomy would explain. The dominant model during this period was administrative responsibility, that is, the appropriate and modest use of significant discretion. The recent era (since the 1990s), driven by a worldwide government reform agenda, has interjected entrepreneurial uses of discretion for public administrators. The debate about what to reform in government (the size, the cost, the processes, the structures, the accountability mechanisms, etc.) and how to reform it has stirred huge controversies in the scholarly community. To the degree that it is embraced, the newest model encourages creative and robust uses of discretion and diffuses authority among more stakeholders and control mechanisms.

The discretion debate has shaped the proper focus debate primarily in terms of a management orientation (transactional) versus a change orientation (transformational). If leaders should not exercise significant discretion or be too activist, then they should *not* play a substantial change role but should focus more on management issues. In a contrary position, many in the New Public Management school echo the mainstream school of the 1980s in asserting that public administrators are uniquely qualified to play a large role, which otherwise would leave a critical leadership vacuum. Another element in the proper focus discussion that is robust in the public-sector literature adds—or sometimes substitutes altogether—the inclusion of customers/clients/citizens and the public good generally. Although the different schools disagree rather caustically about the way to frame these notions and the proper terms to use, there tends to be rather impressive agreement that external constituencies and the common good are a fundamental focus of public-sector administrators that is not to be taken for granted.

The debate about the importance of leadership is much more muted and underdeveloped. Although some argue from the perspective of democratic theory that administrative leaders should *not* be important from a strictly political perspective, most public administration scholars and almost all practitioners simply assume or assert the importance of public administrators. Unfortunately, there is a tendency to treat all situations in which leadership is important as a single monolith, rather than exploring the ramifications of different types of leadership in different contexts with varying missions, organizational structures, accountability mechanisms, environmental constraints, and so on. This means that the technology of leadership is much less articulated on the public-sector side than the private-sector side. Attempts at scholarly syntheses that reflect sophisticated multifunctional, multilevel, and multi-situational models that were in evidence in the mainstream by the 1990s are largely lacking in either monographs or the journal literature in the public sector.

Part of the weakness of the literature resides in its nonintegrated character, with the ironic exception of many surprisingly good chapter overviews on leadership in general public administration and public management textbooks. The serious debate about the best style to use is cut into many parts and is rarely as explicitly or holistically discussed as in the mainstream leadership literature. Fragments of this literature are found in management topics such as total quality management, motivation, and routine problem solving in places such as *Public Productivity and Management Review*, and part of the literature is found in executive topics such as strategic planning and organizational change and development in journals such as *Public Administration Quarterly*. The ethics–values literature, for all of its normative robustness, generally offers few concrete recommendations on this score beyond general admonitions to be responsive, trustworthy, honest, courageous, and prudent.

The final debate, about whether leaders are born or made, is also not particularly well developed from a theoretical perspective. In the 1960s, the situational models presented relatively elementary task–people matrices. Both task and people skills could be taught, and a more humanistic approach that was less reliant on directive styles was generally encouraged. This was generally adopted in the public-sector literature. In the 1980s, when the mainstream field was searching for a more comprehensive and complex model, some good examples of sophisticated training models did emerge on the public-sector side (Faerman, Quinn, and Thompson, 1987; Flanders and Utterback, 1985) but this part of the literature was largely dormant in the 1990s. The "born" side of the argument recognizes the importance of recruitment and selection of exceptional individuals. Such discussions have been relatively common in a human resources context, especially in reports recommending ways to strengthen the public sector (for instance, the Volcker Commission in 1990 and the Winter Commission in 1993), but have not been integrated into an explicit leadership discussion.

CONCLUSION

The mainstream leadership literature, which is a multidisciplinary field dominated by business administration and psychology, has been huge. Although the field has been active for a century, partial and simplistic approaches to this complex phenomenon did not really contribute much to the overall understanding of leadership until the 1980s, when transformational approaches were (re)introduced. That is, many of the elements of leadership—select traits, skills, or behaviors—were better understood, but a more sophisticated model that could accommodate entirely different missions and environments was lacking. A major effort in the 1990s was to provide syntheses that are sophisticated enough for researchers and elegant enough for practitioners. Although some have contributed or used public-sector examples in the mainstream literature, that has not been integrated into a distinctive public-sector leadership literature focusing on the significant constraints and unique environment of administrative leaders. The administrative leadership literature is substantial if very broadly defined, especially in the last decade. However, the broader, tangential literature about administrative leadership is dispersed in topics such as reform, ethics, and management, and an explicit focus on the detailed dynamics of leadership is largely lacking.

Although it is hard to determine the exact reasons for neglect in this area, it is possible to assess the broad reasons. The technical difficulties of leadership research, especially the empirical elements, have not deterred those in the mainstream. Yet given the subtle nature of decision making by administrators in a system of democratically elected leaders with multiple branches of government, this seems to have been a significant detraction for public-sector researchers. This has been compounded by a noticeable lack of administrative leadership theory development that has not been in the service of organizational, ethical, policy, or political studies. Beliefs that activist administrative leadership styles are not appropriate, or insignificant given the other powerful players, seem to have produced self-selection before the decision to research the area. That is, those with these beliefs have already largely gone into political science and policy areas rather than public administration and public management. If this has been a significant problem in the past, it seems the call for organizational excellence, reform, entrepreneurialism, and robust stewardship over the last twenty years has compensated for this tendency. The final problem—the diversion of attention—seems to be a major problem when examining much of the leadership-related materials. Most of the best empiricism, coupled with disciplined theory building and testing, is at the management level. The most problematic diversion (in terms of extending understanding of administrative leadership), albeit a healthy discussion in its own right, has been the normative debate about administrative discretion in which schools use extreme cases to make arguments rather than more balanced assessments and recommendations of realistic trends.

The strength of the administrative leadership literature, such as it is, has been its hearty normative discussions about the proper role of administrators in a democratic system. Entrepreneurial behavior cannot be blithely endorsed when public administrators are entrusted with the authority of the state. Yet the increased size, cost, and regulatory intervention of the state mean that new modes must also be considered—no matter whether they are explicitly entrepreneurial or more robust stewardship roles—as enormous pressures for reform escalate.

As a literature, the weaknesses are more pronounced than the strengths. The normative debate about the right amount and use of more activist leadership approaches for administrative leaders has long since stopped producing useful insights in terms of leadership studies. All schools of thought have tended to treat transformational elements of leadership either too simplistically or too universally. After all, the leadership of a frontline supervisor and a chief executive officer, or the leadership of an auditor as opposed to a state lottery executive, is likely to be remarkably different. Good leadership theory, if it is at the macro level, must accommodate these substantial differences. The field has had remarkably few empirical studies that are not largely descriptive and has overly emphasized leadership as an executive function. Finally, contemporary syntheses of public-sector leadership models that define the actual relationships of the numerous leadership competencies in various environmental contexts are simply absent. Indeed, no matter where you look in or for this subfield, the needs are great and the research opportunities are manifold.

These needs can be crystallized into a dual leadership agenda. First, there is a striking need for a comprehensive leadership model that integrates transactional and transformational elements. While simplistic models such as Figure 6.1 are good for heuristic purposes, such a comprehensive model must be far more articulated to have the requisite explanatory power for the variety of situations and factors inherent in the vast world of public-sector leadership.[11]

Second, such comprehensive models must be subjected to empirical research to test the strength of relationships under various conditions and over time. This is particularly important in an age when change skills, vision articulation, and innovation are in greater demand. With well-articulated models, this is not as difficult as it might seem. Such models should undergird leadership survey feedback programs (360-degree instruments used in leadership training), which in turn provide excellent (and large) databases.

Another way to examine such models is through the types of surveys commissioned by the International City/County Management Association. Yet another way is to do a series of in-depth interviews with key organizational leaders. The key is to discipline ourselves to create models that are powerful enough to handle the complex leadership phenomenon and then to harness them in our research. Not only will it produce better science, it will be extremely useful in sharing our insights with the practitioner community.

Notes

1. By "mainstream," I refer to literature that self-consciously labels itself as a part of the leadership literature and addresses itself to broad audiences. I exclude literatures that are meant for the consumption of a single discipline with specialized interests and terms. Thus, although many of the studies of public-sector administration are found in the mainstream, many of the issues and materials are not. Needless to say, as with all distinctions regarding large bodies of work, such differentiations are meant more for general insight and convenience than as rigorous taxonomies.

2. For example, Burns states that "moral leadership emerges from and always returns to, the fundamental wants and needs of followers," and later he adds that "transforming leadership ultimately becomes moral in that it raises the level of human conduct and ethical aspiration of both the leader and the led, and thus it has a transforming effect on both."

3. Of course, Weber ([1922] 1963) introduced the notion of charismatic leadership quite clearly, and it had been used by those influenced by sociology and political science such as Willner (1968), Dow (1969), and Downton (1973). Even Freud made it clear that leadership involved more than simple exchange processes implicit in most situational theories.

4. Although part of this avoidance may have been the result of a pro-experimental or positivist perspective, part of it may have been an eschewal

of the great man school (which clearly has transformational trappings), which was disdained as antiscientific.

5. Because the overlap is so extensive for the subschools, these distinctions are more for analytical insight than articulation of groups that would necessarily self-identify with these monikers.

6. For example, he notes, "We find that leaders will exhibit a variety of patterns of transformational and transactional leadership. Most leaders do both but in different amounts" (1985, p. 22).

7. Examples of these topics include the types of leaders, leadership styles, the types and effects of followers, the relevance of societal and organizational cultures on leadership, and the operation of power, or mid- and micro-level theory such as leader role theory, group development theory, path-goal theory, leader–member exchange theory, and attribution theory, among many others.

8. This is a variation of the nature–nurture debate found in some form in most of the social sciences.

9. The time-of-crisis motif is prominent in the change literature (Kanter, Stein, and Jick, 1992) as well as the leadership literature. Transformationalists reminded us there are exceptional leadership opportunities, which may or may not be filled, when there is a dramatic crisis, a leadership turnover, or at select stages of the organizational life cycle (especially the birth-to-growth and the maturity-to-decline phases).

10. This debate is related to the made–born argument, but with a critical difference. While the made–born argument is about whether a leader can master any style, the style debate focuses on whether a leader can learn styles other than their native or preferred style.

11. For example, I am completing a book that uses an overarching framework somewhat more articulated than Figure 6.1 and that incorporates sixty-two sub-elements.

References

Altshular, Alan. "Rationality and Influence in Public Service." *Public Administration Review*, 1965, *25*(3), 226–233.

Argyris, Chris. *Personality and Organization*. New York: Harper, 1957.

Baliga, B. Rajaram, and Hunt, James G. "An Organizational Life Cycle Approach to Leadership." In James G. Hunt, B. Rajaram Baliga, H. Peter Dachler, and Chester A. Schriesheim (Eds.), *Emerging Leadership Vistas*. Lexington, MA: Lexington Books, 1988.

Barnard, Chester I. *The Functions of the Executive*. In Jay M. Shafritz and Albert C. Hyde (Eds.), *Classics of Public Administration*. Chicago: Dorsey Press, 1987. (Originally published 1938.)

Bass, Bernard M. *Leadership and Performance Beyond Expectations*. New York: The Free Press, 1985.

Bass, Bernard M. *Bass and Stogdill's Handbook of Leadership*. New York: The Free Press, 1990.

Bass, Bernard M. *A New Paradigm of Leadership: An Inquiry into Transformational Leadership*. Alexandria, VA: U.S. Army Research Institute for the Behavioral and Social Sciences, 1996.

Bass, Bernard M., and Avolio, Bruce J. "The Implications of Transactional and Transformational Leadership for Individual, Team, and Organizational Development." In William Pasmore and Richard W. Woodman (Eds.), *Research in Organizational Change and Development*. Vol. 4. Greenwich, CT: JAI Press, 1990.

Bellone, Carl J., and Goerl, George F. "Reconciling Public Entrepreneurship and Democracy." *Public Administration Review*, 1992, *52*(12), 130–134.

Bennis, Warren, and Nanus, Burt. *Leaders: Strategies for Taking Charge*. New York: Harper and Row, 1985.

Bennis, Warren, Parikh, Jagdish, and Lessem, Ronnie. *Beyond Leadership: Balancing Economics, Ethics and Ecology*. Oxford, UK: Basil Publishing, 1994.

Bernstein, Marver H. *The Job of the Federal Executive*. Washington, DC: Brookings Institution, 1958.

Bird, Charles. *Social Psychology*. New York: Appleton-Century, 1940.

Blake, Robert R., and Mouton, Jane S. *The Managerial Grid*. Houston, TX: Gulf, 1964.

Blake, Robert R., and Mouton, Jane S. "A 9, 9 Approach for Increasing Organizational Productivity." In Edgar H. Schein and Warren G. Bennis (Eds.), *Personal and Organizational Change Through Group Methods*. New York: John Wiley & Sons, 1965.

Block, Peter. *Stewardship: Choosing Service Over Self-Interest*. San Francisco: Berrett-Koehler, 1993.

Borins, Sandford. "Loose Cannons and Rule Breakers? Some Evidence About Innovative Public Managers." *Public Administration Review*, 2000, *60*(6), 498–507.

Brunner, Ronald D. "Teaching the Policy Sciences: Reflections on a Graduate Seminar." *Policy Sciences*, 1997, *39*(2), 217–231.

Bryson, John M., and Crosby, Barbara C. *Leadership for the Common Good: Tackling Problems in a Shared-Power World*. San Francisco: Jossey-Bass, 1992.

Buckingham, Marcus, and Coffman, Curt. *First, Break All the Rules: What the World's Greatest Managers Do Differently*. New York: Simon and Schuster, 1999.

Burns, James MacGregor. *Leadership*. New York: Harper and Row, 1978.

Caro, Robert A. *The Power Broker: Robert Moses and the Fall of New York*. New York: Vintage Books, 1974.

Champy, James. *Reengineering Management: The Mandate for New Leadership*. New York: HarperBusiness, 1995.

Chemers, Martin M. *An Integrative Theory of Leadership*. Mahwah, NJ: Lawrence Erlbaum Associates, 1997.

Chrislip, David D., and Larson, Carl E. *Collaborative Leadership: How Citizens and Civic Leaders Can Make a Difference*. San Francisco: Jossey-Bass, 1994.

Cleveland, Harlan. *The Knowledge Executive: Leadership in an Information Society*. New York: E.P. Dutton, 1985.

Conger, Jay A., and Kanungo, Rabindra N. *Charismatic Leadership in Organizations*. Thousand Oaks, CA: Sage, 1998.

Considine, Mark, and Lewis, Jenny N. "Governance at Ground Level: The Frontline Bureaucrat in the Age of Markets and Networks." *Public Administration Review*, 1999, *59*(6), 467–480.

Cooper, Terry L., and Wright, N. Dale. (Eds.). *Exemplary Public Administrators: Character and Leadership in Government*. San Francisco: Jossey-Bass, 1992.

Corson, John J., and Shale, Paul R. *Men Near the Top: Filling Key Posts in the Federal Service*. Baltimore, MD: Johns Hopkins University Press, 1966.

Dahl, Robert A. "The Science of Public Administration: Three Problems." *Public Administration Review*, 1947, *7*(1), 1–11.

DePree, Max. *Leadership Is an Art*. New York: Doubleday, 1989.

DiIulio, John J., Jr. "Recovering the Public Management Variable: Lessons from Schools, Prisons, and Armies." *Public Administration Review*, 1989, *49*(2), 127–133.

Dimock, Marshall E. "Executive Development After Ten Years." *Public Administration Review*, 1958, *18*(2), 91–97.

Dimock, Marshall E. "Creativity." *Public Administration Review*, 1986, *46*(1), 3–7.

Doig, Jameson W., and Hargrove, Erwin C. *Leadership and Innovation: A Biographical Perspective on Entrepreneurs in Government*. Baltimore, MD: Johns Hopkins University Press, 1987.

Dow, Thomas. "The Theory of Charisma." *Sociological Quarterly*, 1969, *10*(3), 306–318.

Downs, Anthony. *Inside Bureaucracy*. Boston, MA: Little, Brown, 1967.

Downton, James V. *Rebel Leadership: Commitment and Charisma in the Revolutionary Process.* New York: The Free Press, 1973.

Faerman, Sue R., Quinn, Robert E., and Thompson, Michael P. "Bridging Management Practice and Theory: New York State's Public Service Training Program." *Public Administration Review*, 1987, *47*(4), 310–319.

Fairholm, Gilbert. *Values Leadership: Toward a New Philosophy of Leadership.* New York: Praeger, 1991.

Fesler, James W. "Leadership and Its Context." *Public Administration Review*, 1960, *20*(2), 122.

Fiedler, Fred E. *A Theory of Leadership Effectiveness.* New York: McGraw-Hill, 1967.

Fiedler, Fred E., Chemers, Martin M., and Mahar, L. *Improving Leadership Effectiveness: The Leader Match Concept.* New York: John Wiley & Sons, 1976.

Finer, Herman. "Administrative Responsibility in Democratic Government." *Public Administration Review*, 1940, *1*(4), 335–350.

Fisher, John. "Do Federal Managers Manage?" *Public Administration Review*, 1962, *22*(2), 59–64.

Flanders, Lorretta R., and Utterback, Dennis. "The Management Excellence Inventory: A Tool for Management Development." *Public Administration Review*, 1985, *45*(3), 403–410.

Follett, Mary Parker. *Mary Parker Follett: Prophet of Management.* Boston, MA: Harvard Business School Press, 1996. (Originally published 1933.)

Gardner, John. W. *On Leadership.* New York: The Free Press, 1989.

Gilbert, G. Ronald, and Hyde, Albert. "Followership and the Federal Worker." *Public Administration Review*, 1988, *48*(6), 962–968.

Golembiewski, Robert T. "The Small Group and Public Administration." *Public Administration Review*, 1959, *19*(3), 149–156.

Graubard, Stephen R., and Holton, Gerald. (Eds.). *Excellence and Leadership in a Democracy.* New York: Columbia University Press, 1962.

Greenleaf, Robert K. *Servant Leadership: A Journey into the Nature of Legitimate Power and Greatness.* New York: Paulist Press, 1977.

Guyot, James F. "Government Bureaucrats *Are* Different." *Public Administration Review*, 1962, *22*(4), 195–202.

Hammer, Michael, and Champy, James. *Reengineering the Corporation: A Manifesto for Business Revolution.* New York: HarperCollins, 1993.

Heclo, Hugh. *A Government of Strangers: Executive Politics in Washington.* Washington, DC: Brookings Institution, 1977.

Heifetz, Ronald A. *Leadership Without Easy Answers.* Cambridge, MA: Belknap Press, 1994.

Hemhill, John K. *Leader Behavior Description.* Columbus, OH: Ohio State University, Personnel Research Board, 1950.

Hemhill, John K., and Coons, Alvin E. "Development of the Leader Behavior Questionnaire." In Ralph M. Stogdill and Alvin E. Coons (Eds.), *Leader Behavior: Its Description and Measurement.* Columbus, OH: Ohio State University, Bureau of Business Research, 1957.

Hennessey, J. Thomas. "Reinventing Government: Does Leadership Make the Difference?" *Public Administration Review,* 1998, *58*(6), 522–532.

Henton, Douglas, Melville, John, and Walesh, Kimberly. *Grassroots Leaders for a New Economy: How Civic Entrepreneurs Are Building Prosperous Communities.* San Francisco: Jossey-Bass, 1997.

Hersey, Paul, and Blanchard, Kenneth H. "Life Cycle Theory of Leadership." *Training and Development Journal,* 1969, *23*(1), 26–34.

Hersey, Paul, and Blanchard, Kenneth H. "The Management of Change." *Training and Development Journal,* 1972, *26*(2), 20–24.

House, Robert J. "A 1976 Theory of Charismatic Leadership." In James G. Hunt and Lars L. Larson (Eds.). *Leadership: The Cutting Edge.* Carbondale, IL: Southern Illinois University Press, 1977.

Hunt, James G. *Leadership: A New Synthesis.* Newbury Park, CA: Sage, 1996.

Hunt, James G., Dodge, George E., and Wong, Leonard (Eds.). *Out-of-the-Box Leadership: Transforming the Twenty-First-Century Army and Other Top-Performing Organizations.* Stamford, CT: JAI Press, 1999.

Jenkins, William O. "A Review of Leadership Studies with Particular Reference to Military Problems." *Psychological Bulletin,* 1947, *44*(1), 54–79.

Jermier, John M., and Berkes, L. J. "Leader Behavior in a Police Command Bureaucracy: A Closer Look at the Quasi-Military Model." *Administrative Science Quarterly,* 1979, *24*(1), 1–23.

Kanter, Rosabeth Moss, Stein, Barry A., and Jick, Todd D. *The Challenges of Organizational Change: How Companies Experience It and Leaders Guide It.* New York: The Free Press, 1992.

Katz, Robert L. "Skills of an Effective Administrator." *Harvard Business Review,* 1955, *33*(1), 33–42.

Katzenbach, Jon R., and Smith, Douglas K. *The Wisdom of Teams: Creating the High Performance Organization.* Boston, MA: Harvard Business School Press, 1993.

Kaufman, Herbert. *The Administrative Behavior of Federal Bureau Chiefs.* Washington, DC: Brookings Institution, 1981.

Kiel, L. Douglas. *Managing Chaos and Complexity in Government.* San Francisco: Jossey-Bass, 1994.

Kotter, John P. *A Force for Change: How Leadership Differs from Management*. New York: The Free Press, 1990.

Lawton, Frederick J. "The Role of the Administrator in the Federal Government." *Public Administration Review*, 1954, *14*(2), 112–118.

Lewis, Eugene. *Public Entrepreneurship: Toward a Theory of Bureaucratic Political Power*. Bloomington, IN: Indiana University Press, 1980.

Leys, Wayne A. R. "Ethics and Administrative Discretion." *Public Administration Review*, 1943, *3*(1), 10–23.

Likert, Rensis. "Motivational Approach to Management Development." *Harvard Business Review*, 1959, *37*(4), 75–82.

Likert, Rensis. "System 4: A Resource for Improving Public Administration." *Public Administration Review*, 1981, *41*(6), 674–678.

Luke, Jeffrey S. *Catalytic Leadership: Strategies for an Interconnected World*. San Francisco: Jossey-Bass, 1998.

Lundstedt, Sven. "Administrative Leadership and Use of Social Power." *Public Administration Review*, 1965, *25*(2), 156–160.

Macmahon, Arthur W., and Millett, John D. *Federal Administrators: A Biographical Approach to the Problem of Departmental Management*. New York: Columbia University Press, 1939.

Maslow, Abraham. *Eupsychian Management*. Homewood, IL: Dorsey, 1965.

McCall, Morgan W., Lombardo, Michael M., and Morrison, Ann M. *The Lessons of Experience: How Successful Executives Develop on the Job*. Lexington, MA: Lexington Books, 1988.

McGregor, Douglas. *The Human Side of Enterprise*. New York: McGraw-Hill, 1960.

Meindl, John R. "On Leadership: An Alternative to the Conventional Wisdom." In B. M. Staw and L. L. Cummings (Eds.). *Research in Organizational Behavior*, Vol. 12. Greenwich, CT: JAI Press, 1990.

Moon, Myung Jae. "The Pursuit of Managerial Entrepreneurship: Does Organization Matter?" *Public Administration Review*, 1999, *59*(1), 31–43.

National Commission on the Public Service (Volcker Commission). *Leadership for America*. Lexington, MA: Lexington Books, 1990.

National Commission on the State and Local Public Service (Winter Commission). *Hard Truths/Tough Choices: An Agenda for State and Local Reform*. Albany, NY: Nelson A. Rockefeller Institute of Government, 1992.

Office of Personnel Management (OPM). *MOSAIC: Occupational Study of Federal Executives, Managers, and Supervisors*. Washington, DC: Office of Personnel Management, 1997.

Office of Personnel Management (OPM). *High-Performing Leaders: A Competency Model.* Washington, DC: Office of Personnel Management, 1999.

Peters, Thomas, and Austin, Nancy. *A Passion for Excellence: The Leadership Difference.* New York: Random House, 1985.

Peters, Tom. *The Pursuit of WOW! Every Person's Guide to Topsy-Turvy Times.* New York: Vintage Books, 1994.

Pinchot, Gifford. *Breaking New Ground.* New York: Harcourt, Brace, 1947.

Powers, Richard G. *Secrecy and Power: The Life of J. Edgar Hoover.* New York: The Free Press, 1987.

Redford, Emmette. *Democracy in the Administrative State.* New York: Oxford University Press, 1969.

Riccucci, Norma M. *Unsung Heroes: Federal Execucrats Making a Difference.* Washington, DC: Georgetown University Press, 1995.

Rost, Joseph C. *Leadership for the Twenty-First Century.* Westport, CT: Praeger, 1990.

Rusaw, A. Carol. *Leading Public Organizations: An Integrative Approach.* Orlando, FL: Harcourt, 2001.

Schein, Edgar H. *Organizational Culture and Leadership: A Dynamic View.* San Francisco: Jossey-Bass, 1985.

Selznick, Philip. *Leadership in Administration.* New York: Row, Peterson, and Company, 1957.

Stogdill, Ralph M. "Personal Factors Associated with Leadership: A Survey of the Literature." *Journal of Psychology,* 1948, *25*(1), 35–71.

Stone, Donald C. "Notes on the Government Executive: His Role and His Methods." *Public Administration Review,* 1945, *5*(3), 210–225.

Stone, Donald C. "Innovative Organizations Require Innovative Managers." *Public Administration Review,* 1981, *41*(5), 507–513.

Svara, James H. (Ed.). *Facilitative Leadership in Local Government: Lessons from Successful Mayors and Chairpersons.* San Francisco: Jossey-Bass, 1994.

Taylor, Robert L., and Rosenback, William E. (Eds). *Military Leadership: In Pursuit of Excellence.* Boulder, CO: Westview Press, 1984.

Terry, Larry D. *Leadership of Public Bureaucracies: The Administrator as Conservator.* Thousand Oaks, CA: Sage, 1995.

Terry, Larry D. "Administrative Leadership, Neo-Managerialism, and the Public Management Movement." *Public Administration Review,* 1998, *58*(3), 194–200.

Terry, Robert. *Authentic Leadership: Courage in Action.* San Francisco: Jossey-Bass, 1993.

Tichy, Noel M., and Devanna, Mary Anne. *The Transformational Leader.* New York: John Wiley & Sons, 1986.

Van Fleet, David D., and Yukl, Gary. *Military Leadership: An Organizational Perspective*. Greenwich, CT: JAI Press, 1986.

Vinzant, Janet C., and Crothers, Lane. *Street-Level Leadership: Discretion and Legitimacy in Front-Line Public Service*. Washington, DC: Georgetown University Press, 1998.

Vroom, Victor H., and Jago, Arthur G. *The New Leadership: Managing Participation in Organizations*. Englewood Cliffs, NJ: Prentice Hall, 1988.

Vroom, Victor H., and Yetton, Phillip W. *Leadership and Decision-Making*. Pittsburgh, PA: University of Pittsburgh Press, 1973.

Weber, Max. *The Sociology of Religion*. Beacon, NY: Beacon Press, 1963. (Originally published 1922.)

Willner, Ann Ruth. *Charismatic Political Leadership: A Theory*. Princeton, NJ. Princeton University, Center for International Studies, 1968.

Winter, David G. *Navy Leadership and Management Competencies: Convergence Among Tests, Interviews and Performance Ratings*. Boston, MA: McBer, 1979.

Yankelovich, Daniel. *Coming to Public Judgment: Making Democracy Work in a Complex World*. Syracuse, NY: Syracuse University Press, 1991.

Young, Frank, and Norris, John. "Leadership Challenge and Action Planning: A Case Study." *Public Administration Review*, 1988, *48*(1), 564–570.

Yukl, Gary. *Leadership in Organizations*. Englewood Cliffs, NJ: Prentice Hall, 1971.

Yukl, Gary. *Leadership in Organizations* (4th ed.). Englewood Cliffs, NJ: Prentice Hall, 1998.

Zaleznik, Arthur. "Managers and Leaders: Are They Different?" *Harvard Business Review*, 1977, *55*(5), 67–78.

Zand, Dale E. *The Leadership Triad: Knowledge, Trust, and Power*. New York: Oxford University Press, 1997.

—⌇⌇—

At time of original publishing Montgomery Van Wart was the director of the Center for Public Service and an associate professor at Texas Tech University. His research interests include administrative ethics, public management, human resources management, and leadership.

CHAPTER SEVEN

Human Dignity and Grassroots Leadership Development

Jim Keddy

Over the last fifteen years, organizers with the Pacific Institute for Community Organization (PICO) have developed a model of organizing that differs significantly from the most prevalent approach to organizing in practice today, that of mobilization or campaign-style organizing. In the mobilization model, a small group of organizers engage community members in a short-term campaign focused on a particular issue or election. These kinds of campaigns can generate a great deal of activity in a limited period of time, but frequently do not leave much behind when the campaign ends. The majority of community members who participate in such campaigns do so at the level of task. The campaign organizers plug people into a set of pre-ordained activities and usually end their relationship with the volunteers at the close of the campaign.

In contrast to the mobilization style of organizing, PICO's model places primary emphasis on the development of local community

Originally published as "Human Dignity and Grassroots Leadership Development" in *Social Policy*. (Summer 2001).

leaders who build their own organizations, identify their own issues, and learn how to create issue campaigns. This kind of organizing, with its focus on leadership development, is dedicated to helping regular people become powerful actors in their own neighborhoods, cities, and states and to building the human infrastructure of communities over the long term. Another distinguishing characteristic of PICO's work is that it is faith-based. PICO draws upon faith traditions as a source of motivation for the fight for justice and to provide the organization with a value base to undergird the organizing process. A local PICO organization typically will have two hundred or more community leaders regularly engaged in building the organization and in acting on issues. Many of our leaders have been active with our organizations for ten or fifteen years and have invested a large part of their lives in the organizing effort. In addition to these core leaders, a local organization will have a few thousand community members involved in a less regular way, who will join with the organization a few times a year at key moments.

I would like to suggest that much of PICO's effectiveness in developing the capacity of local communities to organize arises from how PICO views people. At the center of the PICO model is an understanding of the human person rooted in the notion of human dignity. The remainder of this article will examine the dynamic relationship between human dignity and the leadership development process used in PICO's work. At the end of the article, I will argue that the interplay between human dignity and the leadership development process is what enables this kind of organizing to have a deep and long-lasting impact. This kind of organizing is ultimately about much more than politics or the issues of the day. It is a culture-shaping enterprise which can serve as a critical source of resistance to the dehumanizing aspects of capitalism and consumerism.

Before discussing the relationship between dignity and grassroots leadership development, I will briefly explain what we, as a network of organizers, mean by these words. PICO believes that people have an inalienable dignity which stems from their creation in God's image. The inherent value of every person, regardless of his or her ethnicity, income, or religion, is a key assumption which underlies all of our efforts. Regarding leadership development, we believe that every person has the potential to become a leader in his/her community. People become leaders one step at a time through a process of action and reflection. Leaders learn to build relationships and engage in the public arena incrementally, and reflect along the way on what they are learning about themselves and the world in which they live.

As people become involved in the organizing process, they grow in their awareness of their own worth. This growing sense of dignity propels people to challenge the status quo and to confront those conditions in the community which threaten their values and that of their neighbors. In our work, leadership development is not simply a set of skills or learned behaviors. Rather it is a dynamic process of *becoming*. This process of *becoming* goes beyond the mere learning of organizing skills and extends into other areas of a person's life. As people become leaders, they are transformed; they become *bigger* people. Their lives become a more true reflection of their God-given dignity.

To further explore the interplay between dignity and leadership development, I will discuss four aspects of PICO's understanding of how leaders are developed. For the sake of this article, I am naming these aspects: awakening, participation, community, and learning.

AWAKENING

Organizers seek to awaken people to a sense of their own worth. Many of us are, at best, half awake to our own dignity. This process of awakening begins with one-to-one conversations, in which organizers agitate people's anger at those conditions in the community which demean them, their family, and their neighbors. Organizers ask questions which surface suppressed feelings. They ask people to imagine a different reality and then challenge them to do something about it. We all become experts at rationalizing what is going on. Organizers put our rationalizations for inaction in front of us and make us confront our own complicity. When leaders tap into their anger, they are also rediscovering their dignity. There is an intimate relationship between dignity and righteous anger. People who have a deep awareness of their own dignity are those with the greatest anger at injustice.

PICO's basic trust that all people can become leaders is a persistent source of agitation in and of itself. When leaders and organizers challenge new members of an organizing effort to take a leadership role, they send a message to that person about his/her inherent worth. The challenge to act like a leader is a challenge to own one's dignity as a person.

PARTICIPATION

The vast majority of people, in any community, are spectators in public life. We seek to live out our values in our private lives, but do not imagine that we have the ability to act in the public arena as well. We may be concerned about decisions made by public officials, and may be directly affected by those decisions, but we feel powerless to do anything about them. We sit on the sidelines while local corporations take their profits out of our communities, or lay off hundreds of workers while paying their CEOs in the millions.

It's no accident that we live as spectators. Our public institutions frequently carry out public business in a way that makes meaningful participation difficult, if not impossible. They pay lip service to public accountability at the same time they have practices in place that intimidate and obscure. Corporations, by their nature, are unaccountable to the broader community and make decisions with little consideration for their impact on the community's well-being. The result is that a small elite in any community regularly make decisions of great impact on our families and communities with little public input.

Access to the major systems which structure the life of a community is largely confined to the wealthy and to those already in the system. As people become awakened to their own dignity, they are compelled to move beyond being spectators to become leaders in the public arena. Their understanding of who they are, of their "self," grows exponentially. They are not only school aides or roofers.

They are school aides or roofers who just met with the mayor. Their renewed sense of their value and that of their neighbors emboldens them to step beyond their private lives into a new world. Their rediscovery of their dignity gives them the courage to challenge the same institutions and their leaders which, in the past, had overlooked them and their community. As they step into the public arena, they bring a new voice and perspective to the public debate and begin to reshape how those institutions interact with their communities. They face discouragement and at times defeat, but remain grounded in who they are. This grounding enables them to persist and carry out the long-term organizing campaigns critical to creating any real change. Through participation in public life, they expand their own identity, and develop a public self, which in turn transforms their private self.

COMMUNITY

Another critical aspect of PICO's understanding of dignity and leadership development is that people emerge as leaders through relationships with others. The first step taken by a leader in the PICO model is to do "one-to-one's," that is, to carry out intentional conversations with others and to build long-lasting relationships based on common interests and values. PICO defines a leader to be a person with a following. A leader is not the most charismatic person in a group, or the most formally educated, or the one with the greatest social status. A leader is one who leaves the television behind to sit in a church hall with others, and who visits her or his neighbors.

In placing relationship building at the center of leadership, PICO organizations actively challenge our culture of individualism. Our society tends to elevate the rights of the individual above all else. This stress on the individual is a two-edged sword. On one hand, it empowers the individual and restricts a community's claims on the individual.

On the other hand, it can lead to the isolation of the person and can impede a community's ability to act together. A person who leads an isolated life is further distanced from recognition of his or her own dignity and that of others.

To be a leader in PICO also means to be in relationships with people of diverse backgrounds. PICO organizations bring people together from different ethnic groups, from different neighborhoods, and from different social classes. Leaders build relationships with those who live in their same neighborhoods but who may be from a different country or who speak a different language. But they also get to know those who live "across the tracks" from them. Frequently, in any given community, the PICO organization is the one place where people from diverse backgrounds have the opportunity to discuss their most deeply felt concerns and to dream together. As leaders of diverse backgrounds work together, they recognize their common humanity. Any true grasp of one's own dignity must be accompanied by the recognition of the dignity of those who are not like us.

LEARNING

Our dignity as human persons compels us toward our own spiritual growth and intellectual development. As leaders become engaged in an organizing process, they become active learners. They become conversant in public policy issues, are able to analyze complex issues, and learn new skills in public speaking and group facilitation. They discover how to use tension creatively and to hold institutions accountable that otherwise would overlook or exploit them. They learn about how government works and about how government and the private sector interact, and collude with one another. They examine the history of their community with a critical eye to understand why things are the way they are. They are involved in ongoing research on how to improve their community's most dire problems.

PICO organizations are structured to maximize the learning of each member of an organizing effort. No one leader chairs every meeting. Tasks typically rotate among the members of an organizing committee so that each person has the opportunity to learn a new skill. Many leaders find that the skills they learn in organizing enable them to find better jobs and to be more effective in their home lives. The community organization serves as a place for continuing education in social analysis and moral reasoning.

COMPETING NOTIONS OF THE HUMAN PERSON

The above paragraphs sketch out how we understand the person and build organizations based on human dignity. We must recognize, however, that our understanding of the person with its emphasis on human dignity is not the dominant notion in our present society. Our understanding exists in competition with other societal forces that put forward a very different understanding.

One competing understanding of the person may be found in elitist systems that essentially value the participation of some people over others, usually due to factors of wealth, ethnicity, family background, and/or formal education. These systems grant access easily to those with the right credentials and will tend to exclude those without.

Examples of such elitism abound in our present political system. A wealthy campaign contributor often is able to meet with a political leader on a moment's notice, whereas community leaders frequently have to kick down the door of the politician's office to obtain a meeting.

Another competing notion arises from, and is fueled by, the marketplace, where the person is treated primarily as a consumer. Advertising tells us that we are what we own. In order to feel good about ourselves, we need the latest products. This understanding of the person has gained an even greater foothold in our wider culture as corporations have learned to target their messages to children. Children are bombarded daily with consumer messages. Longitudinal surveys of college students show that this advertising strategy is working. Today's college students are much more likely to see success in terms of their future income and possessions than in regard to their contributions to their community.

Finally, a long-standing notion of the person present in American culture revolves around perceptions of poverty and wealth. In this thinking, people are poor because they are somehow morally inferior. People who are middle class or affluent are morally superior to people who are poor. This notion surfaces frequently in our work with training teachers in low-income schools to visit parents in the home. When teachers return from making such visits, they report their amazement at discovering that, even though their parents are poor, they still care about their kids. Another common perception is that people are poor because they are lazy. They are responsible for their poverty, and hence worthy of blame. This mindset overlooks the present reality of our market economy, whose structure guarantees that we will have large numbers of people earning low wages. Our economy generates many more low-wage jobs than high-wage jobs and enables a few to have lavish wealth at the expense of the many. It's easier to blame poor people than to struggle with the implications of our economic system.

THE PERSON AND CULTURE

There is an intimate connection between the understanding of the person and human culture. The understanding of the nature of the person underlies the values and norms which make up culture. In its best moments, PICO's organizing efforts stimulate and energize people's awareness of their own dignity. In doing so, this kind of organizing becomes about something beyond an issue campaign or the mechanics of social and political change. It acts as a countervailing force to our dominant culture. I believe that many community leaders stay with PICO organizations over the long haul and invest countless hours of their own lives in the organization because they find that this kind of organizing offers them an alternative cultural space. In this space they are able to return to the roots of who they are and to resist the influence on their self-identity of the dominant messages of our consumer culture. Yet this alternative cultural space is not only the domain of those who participate in the organization. By acting consistently in the public arena and by persistently seeking out new leaders, PICO organizations bring this notion of human dignity into the public debate and into the community at large. In this way, the organizing process functions as a culture-shaping enterprise with whose influence reverberates in the world of individuals, in our collective understanding, and in our public life.

—/\/\/—

Jim Keddy is director of the California Project, a statewide organizing effort affiliated with the Pacific Institute for Community Organization.

CHAPTER EIGHT

Practicing Servant-Leadership

Larry C. Spears

———✺———

As many small trickles of water feed the mightiest of rivers, the growing number of individuals and organizations practicing servant-leadership has increased into a torrent, one that carries with it a deep current of meaning and passion.

Robert K. Greenleaf's idea of servant-leadership, now in its fourth decade as a concept bearing that name, continues to create a quiet revolution in workplaces around the world. Since the time of the Industrial Revolution, managers have tended to view people as tools, while organizations have considered workers as cogs in a machine. In the past few decades we have witnessed a shift in that long-held view. In countless for-profit and nonprofit organizations today we are seeing traditional, autocratic, and hierarchical modes of leadership yielding to a different way of working—one based on teamwork and community, one that seeks to involve others in decision making, one strongly based in ethical and caring behavior, and one that is attempting to enhance the personal growth of people

Originally published as "Practicing Servant-Leadership" in *Leader to Leader*, *34.* (Fall 2004).

while improving the caring and quality of our many institutions. This emerging approach to leadership and service began with Greenleaf.

The term *servant-leadership* was first coined by Greenleaf (1904–1990) in a 1970 essay titled "The Servant As Leader." Since that time, more than half a million copies of his books and essays have been sold worldwide. Greenleaf spent most of his organizational life in the field of management research, development, and education at AT&T. Following a forty-year career at AT&T, Greenleaf enjoyed a second career that lasted twenty-five years, during which time he served as an influential consultant to a number of major institutions, including Ohio University, MIT, the Ford Foundation, the R.K. Mellon Foundation, the Mead Corporation, the American Foundation for Management Research, and the Lilly Endowment. In 1964 Greenleaf also founded the Center for Applied Ethics, which was renamed the Robert K. Greenleaf Center in 1985 and is now headquartered in Indianapolis.

Slowly but surely, Greenleaf's servant-leadership writings have made a deep, lasting impression on leaders, educators, and many others who are concerned with issues of leadership, management, service, and personal growth. Standard practices are rapidly shifting toward the ideas put forward by Greenleaf, as witnessed by the work of Stephen Covey, Peter Senge, Max DePree, Margaret Wheatley, Ken Blanchard, and many others who suggest that there is a better way to lead and manage our organizations. Greenleaf's writings on the subject of servant-leadership helped to get this movement started, and his views have had a profound and growing effect on many people.

WHAT IS SERVANT-LEADERSHIP?

The idea of the servant as leader came partly out of Greenleaf's half-century of experience in working to shape large institutions. However, the event that crystallized Greenleaf's thinking came in the 1960s, when he read Hermann Hesse's short novel *Journey to the East*—an account of a mythical journey by a group of people on a spiritual quest.

After reading this story, Greenleaf concluded that its central meaning was that the great leader is first experienced as a servant to others, and that this simple fact is central to the leader's greatness. True leadership emerges from those whose primary motivation is a deep desire to help others.

The great leader is first experienced as a servant to others.

In his works, Greenleaf discusses the need for a better approach to leadership, one that puts serving others—including employees, customers, and community—as the number one priority. Servant-leadership emphasizes increased service to others, a holistic approach to work, promoting a sense of community, and the sharing of power in decision making. The words *servant* and *leader* are usually thought of as being opposites. When two opposites are brought together in a creative and meaningful way, a paradox emerges. So the words *servant* and *leader* have been brought together to create the paradoxical idea of servant-leadership.

Who *is* a servant-leader? Greenleaf said that the servant-leader is one who is a servant first. In "The Servant As Leader" he wrote, "It begins with the natural feeling that one wants to serve, to serve first. Then conscious choice brings one to aspire to lead. The difference manifests itself in the care taken by the servant—first to make sure that other people's highest-priority needs are being served. The best test is: Do those served grow as persons? Do they, while being served, become healthier, wiser, freer, more autonomous, more likely themselves to become servants? And what is the effect on the least privileged in society? Will they benefit or at least not be further deprived?"

At its core, servant-leadership is a long-term, transformational approach to life and work—in essence, a way of being—that has the potential for creating positive change throughout our society.

Characteristics of the Servant-Leader

After some years of carefully considering Greenleaf's original writings, I have extracted the following set of characteristics central to the development of servant-leaders:

1. *Listening.* Leaders have traditionally been valued for their communication and decision-making skills. While these are also important skills for the servant-leader, they need to be reinforced by a deep commitment to listening intently to others. The servant-leader seeks to identify the will of a group and helps clarify that will. He or she seeks to listen receptively to what is being said. Listening, coupled with regular periods of reflection, is essential to the growth of the servant-leader.

2. *Empathy.* The servant-leader strives to understand and empathize with others. People need to be accepted and recognized

for their special and unique spirits. One assumes the good intentions of co-workers and does not reject them as people, even if one finds it necessary to refuse to accept their behavior or performance.

3. *Healing*. One of the great strengths of servant-leadership is the potential for healing one's self and others. Many people have broken spirits and have suffered from a variety of emotional hurts. Although this is part of being human, servant-leaders recognize that they also have an opportunity to "help make whole" those with whom they come in contact. In "The Servant As Leader" Greenleaf writes: "There is something subtle communicated to one who is being served and led if implicit in the compact between servant-leader and led is the understanding that the search for wholeness is something they share." Able leaders are usually sharply awake and reasonably disturbed.

4. *Awareness*. General awareness, and especially self-awareness, strengthens the servant-leader. Awareness also aids one in understanding issues involving ethics and values. It lends itself to being able to view most situations from a more integrated, holistic position. As Greenleaf observed: "Awareness is not a giver of solace—it is just the opposite. It is a disturber and an awakener. Able leaders are usually sharply awake and reasonably disturbed. They are not seekers after solace. They have their own inner serenity."

5. *Persuasion*. Another characteristic of servant-leaders is a primary reliance on persuasion rather than positional authority in making decisions within an organization. The servant-leader seeks to convince others rather than coerce compliance. This particular element offers one of the clearest distinctions between the traditional authoritarian model and that of servant-leadership. The servant-leader is effective at building consensus within groups.

6. *Conceptualization*. Servant-leaders seek to nurture their abilities to "dream great dreams." The ability to look at a problem (or an organization) from a conceptualizing perspective means that one must think beyond day-to-day realities. For many managers this is a characteristic that requires discipline and practice. Servant-leaders are called to seek a delicate balance

between conceptual thinking and a day-to-day focused approach.

7. *Foresight*. Foresight is a characteristic that enables the servant-leader to understand the lessons from the past, the realities of the present, and the likely consequence of a decision for the future. It is also deeply rooted within the intuitive mind. Foresight remains a largely unexplored area in leadership studies, but one most deserving of careful attention.

8. *Stewardship*. Peter Block has defined stewardship as "holding something in trust for another." Robert Greenleaf's view of all institutions was one in which CEOs, staffs, and trustees all played significant roles in holding their institutions in trust for the greater good of society. Servant-leadership, like stewardship, assumes first and foremost a commitment to serving the needs of others. It also emphasizes the use of openness and persuasion rather than control.

9. *Commitment to the growth of people*. Servant-leaders believe that people have an intrinsic value beyond their tangible contributions as workers. As a result, the servant-leader is deeply committed to the growth of each and every individual within the institution. The servant-leader recognizes the tremendous responsibility to do everything possible to nurture the growth of employees.

10. *Building community*. The servant-leader senses that much has been lost in recent human history as a result of the shift from local communities to large institutions as the primary shaper of human lives. This awareness causes the servant-leader to seek to identify some means for building community among those who work within a given institution. Servant-leadership suggests that true community can be created among those who work in businesses and other institutions. Greenleaf said: "All that is needed to rebuild community as a viable life form for large numbers of people is for enough servant-leaders to show the way, not by mass movements, but by each servant-leader demonstrating his own unlimited liability for a quite specific community-related group."

These ten characteristics of servant-leadership are by no means exhaustive, but they serve to communicate the power and promise that this concept offers to those who are open to its invitation and challenge.

The Growing Impact of Servant-Leadership

Many individuals and organizations have adopted servant-leadership as a guiding philosophy. For individuals it offers a means to personal growth—spiritually, professionally, emotionally, and intellectually. It has ties to the ideas of M. Scott Peck (*The Road Less Traveled*), Parker Palmer (*The Active Life*), Ann McGee-Cooper (*You Don't Have to Go Home from Work Exhausted!*), and others who have written on expanding human potential. A particular strength of servant-leadership is that it encourages everyone to actively seek opportunities to both serve and lead others, thereby setting up the potential for raising the quality of life throughout society.

An increasing number of companies have adopted servant-leadership as part of their corporate philosophy or as a foundation for their mission statement. Among these are the Toro Company (Minneapolis, Minnesota), Synovus Financial Corporation (Columbus, Georgia), ServiceMaster Company (Downers Grove, Illinois), the Men's Wearhouse (Fremont, California), Southwest Airlines (Dallas, Texas), and TDIndustries (Dallas, Texas).

TDIndustries, one of the earliest practitioners of servant-leadership in the corporate setting, is a heating and plumbing contracting firm that has consistently ranked in the top ten of *Fortune* magazine's 100 Best Companies to Work for in America. The founder, Jack Lowe Sr., came upon "The Servant As Leader" in the early 1970s and began to distribute copies of it to his employees. They were invited to read through the essay and then to gather in small groups to discuss its meaning. The belief that managers should serve their employees became an important value for TDIndustries.

Thirty years later, Jack Lowe Jr. continues to use servant-leadership as the company's guiding philosophy. Even today, any TDPartner who supervises even one person must go through training in servant-leadership. In addition, all new employees continue to receive a copy of "The Servant As Leader," and TDIndustries has developed elaborate training modules designed to encourage the understanding and practice of servant-leadership.

Servant-leadership has influenced many noted writers, thinkers, and leaders. Max DePree, former chairman of the Herman Miller

Company and author of *Leadership Is an Art* and *Leadership Jazz*, has said, "The servanthood of leadership needs to be felt, understood, believed, and practiced." And Peter Senge, author of *The Fifth Discipline*, has said that he tells people "not to bother reading any other book about leadership until you first read Robert Greenleaf's book, *Servant-Leadership*. I believe it is the most singular and useful statement on leadership I've come across."

Servant-leadership is also increasingly in use in both formal and informal education and training programs. This is taking place through leadership and management courses in colleges and universities, as well as through corporate training programs. A number of undergraduate and graduate courses on management and leadership incorporate servant-leadership within their syllabi. Several colleges and universities now offer specific courses on servant-leadership.

In the world of corporate education and training programs, many management and leadership consultants now employ servant-leadership materials as part of their ongoing work with corporations. Through internal training and education, organizations are discovering that servant-leadership can truly improve how business is developed and conducted, while still successfully turning a profit.

> Servant-leadership has influenced many noted writers, thinkers, and leaders.

A Growing Movement

Interest in the philosophy and practice of servant-leadership is now at an all-time high. Hundreds of articles on servant-leadership have appeared in various magazines, journals, and newspapers over the past decade. Many books on the general subject of leadership have been published that recommend servant-leadership as a more holistic way of being. And there is a growing body of literature available on the understanding and practice of servant-leadership.

The Greenleaf Center for Servant-Leadership (www.greenleaf.org) is an international nonprofit educational organization that seeks to encourage the understanding and practice of servant-leadership. The Center's mission is to fundamentally improve the caring and quality of all institutions through a servant-leader approach to leadership, structure, and decision making.

Life is full of curious and meaningful paradoxes. Servant-leadership is one such paradox that has slowly but surely gained hundreds of thousands of adherents over the past thirty-five years. The seeds that have been planted have begun to sprout in many institutions, as well as in the hearts of many who long to improve the human condition. Servant-leadership is providing a framework from which many thousands of known and unknown individuals are helping to improve how we treat those who do the work within our many institutions.

Servant-leadership truly offers hope and guidance for a new era in human development, and for the creation of better, more caring institutions.

—*∿∿*—

At time of original publishing Larry C. Spears had served as president and CEO of the Robert K. Greenleaf Center for Servant-Leadership since 1990. He had edited or co-edited nine books on servant-leadership, including Practicing Servant-Leadership: Succeeding Through Trust, Bravery, and Forgiveness, *on which this article is based.*

CHAPTER NINE

Share Leadership

Leslie Crutchfield
Heather McLeod Grant

Edwin Feulner is not a shy and retiring person. The president of The Heritage Foundation reminds you of a burly football coach as he vigorously shakes your hand. The oversize desk in his office is cluttered with political tchotchkes and awards for speaking, policy leadership, and work with several presidential administrations.[1]

Feulner loves to regale visitors with stories of political brinkmanship, and recounts going head-to-head with an arch nemesis: "I was in a debate with Ralph Nader, who accused us of being a 'Coors foundation,'" he recalls. (Joseph Coors provided a seed grant in 1973.) "And I said, 'We actually receive only 1 percent of our funds from them, and we have over *two hundred thousand supporters*, while you won't tell us how many you have.' Point, set, match." Feulner likes a good fight—and even more, he loves to win.

Originally published as "Share Leadership" in Leslie Crutchfield and Heather McLeod Grant, *Forces for Good: The Six Practices of High-Impact Nonprofits.* (San Francisco: Jossey-Bass, 2008).

Over the years, Feulner has helped turn The Heritage Foundation into "the most influential public-policy think tank in Washington, D.C." (Edwards, 1997). It wasn't always smooth sailing, however. During its first few years, the nonprofit went through several early directors before members of the board approached Feulner to become president in 1977. He was staff director of the House Republican Study Committee, so he knew the ins and outs of politics. But unlike many policy wonks, who are often more comfortable behind the scenes, Feulner had the makings of a great, and charismatic, leader.

By now, you might think that the point of this story is that nonprofits need a larger-than-life figure at the helm. But you'd be missing the most important aspect of Feulner's strength as a leader: *his ability to share power with others.*

When you ask people outside the Beltway to name the president of The Heritage Foundation, many scratch their heads. Policy experts we spoke to rarely mentioned Feulner's name in the same breath as Heritage. Unlike Focus on the Family, which is closely identified with its founder, Dr. James Dobson, or Ralph Reed, the former director of the Christian Coalition who is a brand unto himself, The Heritage Foundation is not overly associated with any individual. And that's just the way Feulner wants it. "The objective has always been to build an institution that will outlive me," he says. "It has been deliberate. I don't claim to be unduly modest or humble, but it is more important that the institution has made its mark."

Feulner's secret? He has a unique combination of charismatic yet egoless leadership. He gives power away, rather than hoards it.

Perhaps the most telling example of his leadership style occurred when Feulner was first offered the job. He immediately called up his friend Phil Truluck, who was working on the Hill, and said: "I'll take the job, but you have to come with me." Truluck accepted, becoming Feulner's second-in-command. For more than thirty years now, the two men have built a powerful organization. Today, Heritage has a budget of $40 million, two hundred employees, a network of two thousand informal grassroots affiliates and policy leaders, and 275,000 members who work on behalf of the ideas it champions. Heritage's remarkable success owes a lot to the shared leadership of Feulner and Truluck. They possess highly complementary skills: Feulner is an extrovert who exudes energy and vision, whereas Truluck is more internally oriented. From the outset, Feulner positioned Heritage as part of a larger movement, and focused on marketing conservative ideas to Congress and the public. Truluck focused more on managing and growing the organization, building up Heritage's signature policy research program. "They have a great partnership: Ed's a visionary, Phil is very practical, and they are both very savvy," says Kim Holmes, vice president of the organization's Davis Institute for International Studies.

Beyond their shared leadership, Feulner and Truluck have built an institution of leaders, starting with a powerful executive team of eight vice presidents, many of whom have been with the nonprofit twenty years or more. Truluck recalls when they first adopted this organizational structure: "It was around 1981, and we had grown. . . . All of a sudden I had sixty-five people reporting to me, and Ed [Feulner] had five. No one had designated me 'Number Two,' but I was. So we did a simple organizational chart: Ed was at the top, I was underneath, and we created a tier of VPs under me. That has enabled us to continue to grow."

We spent a great deal of time studying Heritage's success, and came to see that this structure, with its broadly distributed leadership, provided the critical capacity Heritage needed to sustain its growth and impact. Not only does Heritage have two long-tenured leaders at the helm, but it has built bench strength throughout the organization in the form of a large and empowered executive team. In addition, Heritage is governed by a highly engaged board, with many members who have served for decades.

By having so many leaders, Heritage has been able to cultivate critical relationships, influence federal policy, develop a large individual donor base, and run high-powered marketing campaigns to promote its message. This triumvirate of leadership—the shared executive leadership, a broad tier of senior managers, and a strong and supportive board—has created an unstoppable organization.

THE POWER OF COLLECTIVE LEADERSHIP

This model of shared leadership is not what we expected to find. After all, in business—and in much leadership literature—the individual heroic leader is often exalted. Many books on leadership focus on the traits and behaviors of leaders, or the relationship between leaders and followers. In just the past decade, theories of "collective leadership" have begun to gain traction, but for the most part, leadership is still thought of as an individual act. Great leaders are praised for their individual competencies, attributes, or distinguished personalities. In other words, attention has focused more on leaders than on leadership.

Within the social sector, older models of individual, heroic leadership endure. The social entrepreneurship movement is fascinated with the role of the lone entrepreneur; less attention is paid to collective leadership or entrepreneurship as a collaborative act (Light, 2006). Fellowship programs like Ashoka and Echoing Green emphasize and reward the individual over the organization. Many nonprofit leadership programs and awards still focus on the executive director, rather than on an entire team. And too many nonprofits are known for their charismatic, visionary founders who have a hard time sharing leadership and who use their organizations to promote their grandiose visions rather than build institutions that will outlast them.

We're not discounting the role of the individual as a leader— indeed, the twelve organizations featured in this book [*Forces for Good: The Six Practices of High-Impact Nonprofits*] would not have achieved such high levels of impact without the exceptionally gifted entrepreneurs who led them in their growth. These nonprofits have all had highly strategic, extremely intelligent leaders who have stayed with their organizations for long periods of time, whether the leader was the founder or joined the organization later in its history. (See Table 9.1, which highlights the tenure of these leaders.)

But strong leadership doesn't only exist at the very top of high-impact nonprofits; rather, it extends throughout the organization. CEOs of high-impact nonprofits share a commitment that goes beyond their own egos, and they use their leadership to empower others. Every one of the twelve groups we studied now has an empowered executive team and a strong second-in-command. And like Heritage, they almost all have large, enduring, and engaged boards. They have distributed leadership throughout their organization, and often throughout their larger network of allies and affiliates as well.

Although we can't prove a simple cause-and-effect link between collective leadership and organizational performance, we have come to believe that sharing leadership has in fact enabled these nonprofits to have more impact. Because they focus so much on influencing players outside their organizational boundaries, they need to manage hundreds of relationships and access many networks. Further, working across sector boundaries to advocate for policy change, partner with business, build a network, or engage thousands

	Number of CEOs (as of 2006)	Tenure (in Years), Name of Founder or Growth Leader ⚲
The Heritage Foundation	⚲ ⚲	33 (Feulner)
National Council of La Raza	⚲ ⚲ ⚲ ⚲	31 (Yzaguirre)
Habitat for Humanity	⚲ ⚲	29 (Fuller)
Self-Help	⚲	26 (Eakes)
Center on Budget and Policy	⚲	25 (Greenstein)
Share Our Strength	⚲	23 (Shore)
Environmental Defense	⚲ ⚲ ⚲ ⚲	21 (Krupp)
City Year	⚲	19 (Khazei and Brown)
Teach For America	⚲	17 (Kopp)
YouthBuild USA	⚲	17 (Stoneman)
Exploratorium	⚲ ⚲ ⚲ ⚲	16 (Oppenheimer, Delacôte)
America's Second Harvest	⚲ ⚲ ⚲ ⚲ ⚲ ⚲ ⚲	4.5 (average for all seven)

Table 9.1.   Long-Tenured Leaders

of individuals takes many different skills—not all of which can be found in one person. And the problems these groups are trying to solve are complex, requiring large-scale systemic solutions involving many stakeholders.

Recent research suggests that a collaborative model is more effective in such a complex environment. "A more collective orientation to leadership is often considered especially appropriate for complex, messy situations that lack clear answers or even clearly defined problems," writes Betsy Hubbard in a recent report on the field of nonprofit leadership development (Hubbard, 2005). "In such situations, a top-down model of leadership—a traditional approach in which a single leader operates primarily from his or her own perspective, experience, and judgment—is unlikely to prove successful."

Our research strongly supports the notion that leading a nonprofit is quite different from leading a business—and therefore requires a more collaborative type of leadership. The CEO of a business has formal authority, and can use a more executive style of leadership to compel people to act. By contrast, leaders in the social sector lead through influence, not authority, and must convince others to act by force of their convictions alone.

This doesn't mean that the role of the executive director isn't important—on the contrary, the top leader sets the tone for the whole organization. "The point of the collaborative leadership paradigm is not that leaders are unnecessary," writes leadership scholar Greg Markus (Markus, 2001, cited in Hubbard, 2005). "Rather ... organizations are more likely to thrive within complex, continuously changing environments when leadership comes from many places within the organization, drawing upon the complementary assets of group members and not confusing leadership with formal authority."

Although the executive director of a high-impact nonprofit might have vision, he or she can't single-handedly build an organization while catalyzing a larger movement and changing entire systems. No single director could possibly have as much impact by hoarding power, relationships, or information, or by making himself or herself the decision-making bottleneck. In fact, only by giving power away and empowering others do these groups develop networks and movements large enough to catalyze widespread social change.

ONE STYLE DOESN'T FIT ALL

Thousands of articles and books have been written about leadership, many of which focus on the individual attributes of a leader. Business management author Jim Collins, in his book *Good to Great,* described the "Level 5" leader as an individual who paradoxically embraces both personal humility and professional will. These leaders possess strong professional resolve and focus more on building their organizations than on feeding their egos. "Level 5 leaders channel their ego needs away from themselves and into the larger goal of building a great company," writes Collins. "[T]heir ambition is first and foremost for the institution, not themselves" (Collins, 2001).

In this respect, our findings are similar to those of Collins's—great nonprofit leaders, like the best business leaders, are successful because they put their organization's interests ahead of their own egos. In fact, we believe that the CEOs of the twelve great nonprofits we studied take the "Level 5 leadership" concept one step further. They not only put the interests of their *organizations* ahead of their personal egos, they often put their *overall cause* ahead of their organization's interests.

Where our findings about successful nonprofit leaders differ from Collins's description of great corporate CEOs is in the realm of personality styles. Collins observed that Level 5 leaders are most often described as "quiet, humble, modest, reserved, shy" (Collins, 2001). However, the *Forces for Good* leaders couldn't all be described as humble, shy, or particularly mild-mannered. No one would say that Millard Fuller of Habitat for Humanity International, Ed Feulner of The Heritage Foundation, Dorothy Stoneman of YouthBuild USA, or Alan Khazei of City Year are quiet, or that they operate behind the scenes. Although these leaders can check their egos at the door, that does not mean they lack personality. On the contrary, many of the leaders we studied are highly dynamic, extroverted, outwardly inspirational individuals.

We actually found that the leaders of high-impact nonprofits are quite different from one another in their individual leadership styles. The myth of a single type of leader who can succeed is just that—a myth. Many kinds of leaders can be successful at running high-impact social sector organizations.

For example, Wendy Kopp was initially so introverted that she would avoid interactions with Teach For America corps members, because she didn't know what to say to them (Koop, 2001). She was much more interested in staying up all night developing fund-raising plans than in chit-chatting over coffee.

Yet despite her shyness, Kopp was still able to persuade countless others to support her cause—from donors who wrote big checks to college graduates who turned down lucrative job offers to teach in inner-city schools. Because Kopp was so passionate about fixing American education, she turned her personal conviction into inspiration—and used this to overcome her initial weaknesses as a leader.

Today Kopp is described as an incredibly focused and disciplined leader who inspires her staff to achieve greater results. She leads by example, setting a tone for the whole organization. "Wendy is the magic bullet at Teach For America," says vice president Kevin Huffman. "People outside the organization tend to label her as a visionary, but that damns with faint praise. She is astonishingly efficient and effective at both the people and project level. She gets things done at a very high level, and sets a higher bar for the office. It's different from any place I've ever worked."

And those who have heard Billy Shore of Share Our Strength speak so eloquently in public would be surprised to learn that he has had to work at addressing large crowds. Like Kopp, Shore is an introvert.

By his own account, he spends a third of his time thinking deeply, riding his bike, and reading books on diverse topics like science and religion. Shore uses this solitary time to dream up new ideas, remain inspired, and write. In addition to building an organization that has raised more than $200 million for hunger relief, Shore has authored three books that explore people's motivations to give back through nonprofit work. He has also transcended his own introversion to become a highly effective and inspirational speaker.

Unlike Kopp, Shore is less interested in managerial details and more externally focused. He is described as an inspirational leader who spends much of his time building relationships and persuading others to act—whether by writing a check, hosting a dinner, or entering into a multimillion-dollar cause-marketing partnership. "Billy is just an amazing asset because he can speak about the cause, and write so well," says sister and cofounder Debbie. Adds Chuck Scofield, development director: "He is a connector of ideas and people. He's an innovative and creative thinker. He is inspirational—he's the reason I'm still here."

On the other end of the extroversion spectrum are leaders like Alan Khazei of City Year, Dorothy Stoneman of YouthBuild USA, Fred Krupp of Environmental Defense, and Ed Feulner of Heritage. Khazei is like a nonstop politician—but rather than campaigning for elected office, he is stumping for national service. Krupp is widely credited with helping to professionalize Environmental Defense, but he's equally effective lobbying politicians, corporate CEOs, or billionaires to support solutions to global warming.

Dorothy Stoneman, by contrast, has been described as "an organizer straight out of the 1960s." She is also brilliant at politics and lobbying, but comes across as more of a grassroots activist than as a polished insider. But anyone who has met her—Republican or Democrat—quickly realizes that she is a force to be reckoned with. Her staff describe her as "relentless, dogged, and determined," a reputation confirmed by YouthBuild USA's success at obtaining large federal appropriations for YouthBuild programs, regardless of which party is in power.

Self-Help founder Martin Eakes is also cut from the 1960s activist mold. His staff describe him as passionate and humble, and "a Level 5 leader, a servant leader," quoting Jim Collins. He doesn't look the part of a powerful financial mover and shaker, but he's a man who controls $1 billion in assets and wields significant influence with such industry titans as Sandy Weill, former Citigroup CEO and chairman. Eakes has also been accused of micromanagement, as he gets involved at all levels of the organization—from lobbying the state legislature to reprogramming computers.

Twelve high-impact nonprofits—and more than twelve inspirational leaders, with radically different personalities. Yet the more we looked, the more we realized that they all had one critical quality in common: *they shared power and leadership in their quest to be a greater force for good.*

Despite their individual differences, these leaders have all demonstrated a willingness to distribute leadership among others both inside and outside their organizations. Although they may not have started out this way, they all now recognize that they cannot increase their impact by hoarding power. The only way to get to the top in the social sector is to give power away.

TWO AT THE TOP: THE SECOND-IN-COMMAND

Although several of these nonprofits might appear to have been started by a lone social entrepreneur, a number of them had shared executive leadership from the outset. City Year was cofounded by friends Alan Khazei and Michael Brown, just as Share Our Strength was cofounded by brother and sister Billy and Debbie Shore. Heritage had Feulner and Truluck from very early on. And YouthBuild USA, although strongly identified with founder and president Stoneman, was actually cofounded along with her husband, John Bell, who currently spearheads leadership development within the network. The National Council of La Raza (NCLR) was founded by a collective group of Hispanic leaders, but early on appointed Raul Yzaguirre as director. He in turn built a larger leadership team.

A few of the organizations we studied, such as Teach For America, America's Second Harvest, and the Center on Budget and Policy Priorities, were started by a single individual, but fairly quickly grew into a shared leadership model. Others, such as Self-Help, Habitat for Humanity, and the Exploratorium, were started by one charismatic social entrepreneur and took much longer to evolve into collective leadership. Their founders had a harder time letting go.

But regardless of the timing, the primary leader eventually realized the need to appoint a strong second-in-command to help run the organization. All these organizations now have the equivalent of a chief operating officer (COO) working closely with the executive director. It really is two at the top—whether this second-in-command is called a COO, an executive vice president, or senior vice president, the role is similar. This second leader is more often an internal manager, focused on operational issues, while the executive director is more often the external leader, concerned with vision, strategy, issue leadership, relationship building, or fund raising. The split echoes the distinction between leadership and management drawn by authors Warren Bennis and Burt Nanus (1997): "Managers are people who do things right, and leaders are people who do the right thing."

The timing for appointing a second-in-command—and the precipitating factors—varied from organization to organization. For some nonprofits, such as YouthBuild USA, the board prompted the founder to let go and appoint a COO. As one board member recalls, "When I first joined the board, I had concern that the organization was purely directed by Dorothy [Stoneman]. She was doing everything without an executive management team. With board encouragement, she set out to find a COO." Tim Cross was promoted to COO; now Stoneman is the public face, and Cross manages internal operations and international expansion.

In several of the cases we studied, it took a crisis moment for the primary leader to let go. These moments occurred when the founder-director either contemplated leaving or in fact left the nonprofit for a brief time, allowing a second leader to assume more power and responsibility. Often this break with routine also allowed the founder to release some control and begin to share power and leadership more broadly.

After ten years as cofounder and CEO of City Year, Alan Khazei left on a one-year sabbatical to get married and travel around the world. During this time, other City Year leaders, including cofounder Michael Brown, took on more responsibility. Khazei eventually left the organization in 2006, but only after he and Brown ensured that there was a strong leadership team at the top. They named Brown as CEO, internally promoting COO Jim Balfanz, and recruiting Colonel Robert Gordon, a military leader from West Point who shares Khazei's relationship skills, as the senior vice president for civic leadership.

In some cases, it was the original second-in-command, or cofounder, who needed to be moved aside as the organization grew.

Share Our Strength was cofounded by executive director Billy Shore and his sister, associate director Debbie Shore. Their longtime friend Kathy Townsend managed internal operations. After twelve years of this arrangement, it became apparent that the organization had grown beyond the skills of the founding team. It needed real operational expertise. Billy Shore recruited Pat Nicklin—a former McKinsey consultant who had run several businesses—as managing director, a role that she still holds today.

"We were really late in doing it," says Billy Shore. "The managers of the organization were the people who had been there the longest, not those with management skills. It was hard, but Pat was really graceful, and my sister was really graceful at moving over." Debbie Shore concedes that it wasn't easy for her to let go. "I was on the border of not being able to evolve," she says. "You have to learn that it's not about you, or your way—it's about the organization. You really have to keep evolving as a leader, but most founders don't do this well." Debbie Shore still plays a senior leadership role in the nonprofit.

Self-Help went through a similar transition more recently—one also precipitated by the growth of the organization. As founder Martin Eakes recalls, "We reached a point where we had twenty senior people reporting to me. Nobody can adequately do feedback or intervention with twenty people! We had an organizational consultant come in who made a joke that 'Half the people report to Martin, and the other half think they do.' Up to a certain size that worked, but then I became the bottleneck."

Eakes put in place a new structure that elevated four senior staff members to the senior management level. At the same time, he appointed Eric Stein as COO. "Eric has the authority," says Randy Chambers, CFO. "If Martin [the CEO] is out of the office, all the staff knows that we can count on Eric to cover for Martin."

LETTING EXECUTIVES LEAD

In addition to having a strong second-in-command, these nonprofits have something else that sets them apart: a remarkably strong senior executive team. It's not just "two in a box," but a whole team at the top. Often this shared leadership extends beyond the headquarters of the organization to include the executive directors of local sites, in the cases where the group has formal affiliates.

"At a typical nonprofit, the person at the head is almost the whole organization, but that's not really true here," says Charles Clark, YouthBuild USA's vice president of asset development. "YouthBuild is not successful just because of Dorothy [Stoneman]. She enables the two hundred executive directors of local sites out there who are really doing the work. She has been more of a founder and enabler."

It is of interest that most of the nonprofits we studied have a handful of senior leaders who have been with the organization an extraordinarily long time. These executives are not only loyal but also empowered to speak and act on behalf of the group. They have both authority and accountability for their divisions, and make decisions like hiring and firing without executive director approval. On the basis of our knowledge of the sector and our experience with many other nonprofits, we believe that these strong, empowered, and enduring executive teams differentiate high-impact nonprofits from their less successful counterparts.

Many leaders are never able to evolve and truly share power at the top. Although they may have executives in title, they are unable to let go, or to retain their senior staff. "I know an organization with a strong reputation, but it's built on the charisma of a single individual," says Emily Gantz McKay, former executive vice president of NCLR. "I do know they've had a real problem keeping senior staff. When you see an organization whose success is all based on the individual, and it is not able to maintain strong [managers], you worry about it."

By contrast, NCLR is an excellent example of a high-impact nonprofit with an empowered and enduring executive team.[2] Initially launched by a collective of Hispanic leaders in Phoenix as the Southwest Council of La Raza, the organization went national in 1972 and moved its headquarters to Washington, D.C. NCLR grew significantly after Raul Yzaguirre was named executive director in 1974 and worked to strengthen the nonprofit's mission, key programs, and organization. (Former Clinton staffer Janet Murguia took over as its first woman president and CEO in 2005, when Raul Yzaguirre retired after more than thirty years at the helm.) Yzaguirre is thoughtful and soft-spoken. His former staff describe him as "old-world" and patrician without being paternalistic—he has a quiet power. Born in the 1930s, he grew up with activist parents in the American Southwest, and began doing community organizing at age fifteen.

An early formative experience came later when he worked for the War on Poverty under Sergeant Shriver. When originally appointed as director of NCLR at the age of thirty, Yzaguirre had the insight to hire strong leaders who would complement his own strengths and weaknesses. "One of my most important talents is being creative," says Yzaguirre. "I have ten ideas and eight of them are worthless; but the two that are good are what makes the organization. And I surround myself with people who are not shy about telling me which are which."

By 1978, Yzaguirre had too many direct reports, and the organization moved to a structure with several vice presidents. He came to rely on Emily Gantz McKay as his second-in-command, and she was named executive vice president in 1983. Although Gantz McKay left NCLR in 1994, she spent more than twenty years with the nonprofit in various roles.

As the organization grew, it recruited a number of younger leaders who have subsequently evolved into senior roles. For example, Charles Kamasaki, a local activist from NCLR's Texas office, joined the national office in 1982 and has been with the organization ever since, currently serving as senior vice president. Among the other NCLR senior staff with exceptionally long tenure are Cecilia Muñoz, vice president of the Office of Research, Advocacy, and Legislation (ORAL) (eighteen years); Sonia Pérez, vice president of affiliate member services (sixteen years); and Lisa Navarrete, vice president of public information (eighteen years). Several others who had equally long tenure have only recently left or retired.[3]

"One of the ways Raul [Yzaguirre] and NCLR were effective was [in creating] the vice president tier—it was very critical," says Marco Davis, NCLR leadership director. "There was a core of vice presidents who really knew what they were doing, and had a great relationship with each other. So Raul could let them go—they were able to excel and make day-to-day decisions." This structure also freed up Yzaguirre to focus on developing new program ideas, building external relationships, fund raising, and executing high-level strategy.

The most critical point to emphasize is that these are not vice presidents in title only—they play a substantial leadership role both inside and outside the organization. "We empowered and trained our staff to become spokespersons for our organization," says Yzaguirre. One good signal that Yzaguirre truly shared power came when

Muñoz was awarded a MacArthur Fellowship "genius grant" in 2000, an honor usually reserved for executive directors. She has had a major impact as a leader on immigration policy in her own right.

The Exploratorium presents a slightly different case in shared leadership—and illustrates the dangers of not developing a strong executive team as an organization grows.[4] In fact, it took the founder's death, and a new executive director, before the Exploratorium evolved to a more collective leadership model.

Founded by the visionary and charismatic Frank Oppenheimer in the late 1960s, the museum operated informally under his leadership. Oppenheimer was less interested in building an organization than in catalyzing a movement to change science education, so he didn't spend much time on things like management, budgets, or systems. The nonprofit was thrown into chaos when he died in 1985. There was no formal management structure, second-in-command, or empowered leadership team—and no succession plan.

"After his death, [the Exploratorium] almost didn't survive," says Christina Orth, chief of staff. "But people were committed to his vision and legacy. People didn't want to let this die." The organization operated under several interim directors while a search was conducted. The first executive director brought in from the outside was rejected by the staff after only two years as not being a good cultural fit. Ultimately, five years passed before the board hired Goéry Delacôte, a director at the National Center for Science Research in France.

"I took over when it was almost ready to die and took it to the grown-up phase," says Delacôte, who introduced professional management practices to the organization. (In 2006, Delacôte decided to move back to Europe after nearly fifteen years running the nonprofit; he was replaced by a former Exploratorium executive, Dennis Bartels, who had most recently been running another science education nonprofit.)

Part of Delacôte's strategy, in addition to building management systems, was to develop a strong executive team. "Goéry [Delacôte] wasn't a publicity hound; the spotlight wasn't on him," says board member Ann Bowers. "In contrast to other nonprofits, Goéry was building a team. Their ideas were listened to, they were respected, and they were definitely part of the decision-making process. In other organizations, the sun shines on the director—but I don't think you build an organization that way."

GREAT LEADERS LAST

In studying these successful executive directors and their top teams, we were struck by the fact that many of them have extraordinarily long tenure. Although about half of the groups we studied have been through at least one executive transition (some have withstood several), half are still founder led. Almost all of them, however, have had one executive director at the helm for decades. In the cases in which the founder left early, it was an early successor we call the "growth leader" who took on a founder-like role and who stayed with the nonprofit a long time.

This finding was surprising because the data show that most nonprofit executives last an average of only four years on the job. A recent CompassPoint study titled *Daring to Lead* looked at executive turnover in the social sector and found that just 25 percent of nonprofit executives expect to stay in their jobs for more than five years (Bell, Moyers, and Wolfred, 2006). In the business sector, most CEOs last around five to seven years. Leaders like Jack Welch at GE—who was in the CEO role for twenty years—are much more rare.

But among the groups we studied, the leaders stay, on average, twenty years (see Figure 9.1). Further, many of them have a few senior executives who have also been with the organization for a long period of time, as in the case of NCLR.

Why have these high-impact leaders stayed so long? After all, it's not for the money. By nonprofit standards, these executives are well-compensated, but they could all earn more in the private sector.

Average for nonprofit sector = 4 yrs

Figure 9.1.   CEO Tenure Much Longer Than Average

Note: Figure illustrates CEO or growth leader tenure as of 2006.

And it's not like these jobs are easy—on the contrary, leading in complex, changing environments without a lot of formal power is challenging, to say the least. From our interviews with nonprofit CEOs we came to see that they stayed because they are so passionate about their cause—their role is not just a job, but a *calling.* "The novelty doesn't wear off," says Fred Krupp, president of Environmental Defense. "If what you really want to do with your life is have an impact on things that matter, then what I am doing is so satisfying." These leaders all share a relentless focus on results and a desire to have real impact—which often takes decades, not years.

Further, we believe that the very success of these executive directors has enabled them to stay longer—success breeds success. As these organizations achieve real impact, their leaders accumulate more reasons for staying, both financial and emotional. *Daring to Lead* noted that larger organizations have leaders with longer tenure, speculating that "presumably the nature of working at a larger organization—higher pay, more staff support, and perhaps prestige and community influence—make sticking it out longer seem more desirable" (Bell, Moyers, and Wolfred, 2006) Nonprofit boards are less likely to force a transition if both the leader, and the organization, are successful.

Although some might argue that such long tenure is unhealthy (and with a megalomaniac director, it would be), we believe that continuity among these executives and senior managers contributes to success. For one thing, executive directors and senior managers spend much of their time cultivating relationships—if a leader leaves, some of these are lost. Similarly, most nonprofit work relies on tacit knowledge embodied in the staff; when top leaders leave, the organization loses accumulated wisdom and skills. And because the issues that nonprofits are trying to solve are so complex, constant leadership turnover causes the organization to focus more internally, rather than on external results. Leadership continuity keeps them headed down their path to success.

FOUNDER'S SYNDROME AND SUCCESSION PLANNING

Not surprisingly, many less successful nonprofits do not share the longevity, depth, or breadth of leadership of these high-impact organizations. Within the sector as a whole, turnover is rampant, burnout rates are high, and many organizations struggle just to stay afloat. We know many cases of nonprofits led by charismatic but egocentric individuals who are unable to let go and truly share leadership—a phenomenon known as founder's syndrome. These groups run the risk of imploding, as the Exploratorium almost did, when their founder either leaves or dies. Succession planning is an important, but often-neglected, issue within the field.

As Phil Truluck of The Heritage Foundation observes of his peers, "Quite frankly, a lot of these conservative groups were started by strong individuals who were never willing to release control of the organization," he says. "It will be a real problem over the next ten years as they retire. A lot of them have never delegated things down."

Habitat for Humanity is the only nonprofit we studied that is only now moving toward a model of greater shared leadership—after a difficult founder transition.[5] Habitat was started by the classic visionary entrepreneur, Millard Fuller, who was uninterested in organizational management and did not develop a broad and empowered executive team—although he did have a small group of critical people on whom he relied.

Habitat was cofounded in the late 1970s by Fuller and his wife, Linda, as a Christian housing mission. Fuller was tireless in his efforts to promote Habitat, and the organization's success can be attributed in large part to his entrepreneurial and inspirational leadership. "You can't discount the necessity of the charismatic, visionary founder," says Denny Bender, former senior vice president of communications. "Habitat flourished because of Millard's insatiable drive to rid the world of substandard housing. It's an engine that's essential to rapid growth; it attracts the support and resources necessary to grow. A good idea is not enough—it takes someone to lead the parade."

Despite his ability to inspire others, however, Fuller was much more interested in building a movement than an organization—and he expected others to be as tireless and self-sacrificing as he was. "The key ingredient of a movement is abandon—you sell out to the movement," says Fuller. "Martin Luther King sold out to the cause and gave his life for it. You don't hold back: You get up at 5 a.m. and go until midnight. That's what it takes: passion, commitment, dedication. You don't build a movement being concerned about pension plans and salaries."

Not surprisingly, Fuller didn't pay much attention to things like staff capacity, salaries, or other management systems—all of which started to cause problems as the organization grew. Ultimately, senior staff and the Habitat board worried that the movement would collapse without a strong organization to sustain it. "The board said, 'We don't want to be called a movement—you can't plan a movement, and we want Habitat to be something you can plan and move forward,'" recalls Clive Rainey, director of community relations. "Movements don't last; organizations do."

Eventually, the Habitat movement was in danger of eclipsing the organization's ability to effectively manage its network and sustain its impact. Despite sensational external impact and a fabulous reputation, Habitat was chaotic internally. Staff morale was low, and the organization was stretched too thin and was dependent on many volunteers who didn't necessarily have the skills to manage a multimillion-dollar global nonprofit. Although the board wanted to build internal capacity, Fuller was less interested. He and the board disagreed on his authority and succession planning. The struggles became public knowledge when a former employee accused Fuller of sexual harassment. Eventually, Fuller was fired by the board.

The transition that followed was difficult for some staff members, but Habitat came through it successfully. Fuller went on to launch another housing organization, and the board conducted a national search for a replacement, while an interim leader filled in.

The nonprofit ended up hiring a CEO with impeccable credentials: Jonathan Reckford, a self-described born-again Christian, a former executive with Best Buy and Disney, an executive pastor of a large Presbyterian church, and an MBA from Stanford. Reckford combines passion for the housing cause, a personal commitment to the faith-based community, and the managerial experience needed to run a billion-dollar global organization.

As the Habitat case illustrates, founder's syndrome is a significant issue in the nonprofit sector—and one that can imperil an organization if not handled well. Of the twelve organizations we studied, seven are still led by founders (or the primary growth leaders), and are only now beginning to discuss succession planning. The other organizations we studied have all undergone at least one leadership transition, if not several. One organization—America's Second Harvest—has had a new executive director nearly every five years, in part because it is a "bottom-up" nonprofit whose headquarters report to its many local food-bank members.

In fact, during the course of our research, five of the twelve organizations we studied underwent a leadership transition at the top.

In addition to Habitat, NCLR, the Exploratorium, and City Year, in 2006 America's Second Harvest brought on former Delta Airlines senior executive Vicki Escarra as their seventh CEO. Interestingly, none of these nonprofits appointed a CEO successor from within, despite having strong executive teams. By contrast, most successful for-profit businesses promote new CEOs from within their own company (Collins, 2001). The fact that these high-impact organizations have all recruited a new executive director from outside is somewhat surprising, given their bench strength. We attribute this to the fact that high-impact nonprofits often need a charismatic, externally oriented leader to speak on behalf of the organization and appeal to outside constituents, whereas the COO and executive teams often perform a more managerial function.

Many of the other organizations we studied have just begun to address the issue of founder transition. YouthBuild USA has only recently developed a senior management team and expanded organizational leadership beyond founder and president Dorothy Stoneman. Although it doesn't yet have a formal succession plan in place, its leadership is much stronger than even five years ago. "If I were hit by a truck, YouthBuild would survive," says Stoneman. "We now have a COO, four senior vice presidents, and five vice presidents—and another level of senior program managers with five to ten years' experience."

Share Our Strength is another organization strongly identified with its founder, Billy Shore. It has not yet addressed the issue of succession planning, although there is a strong executive team in place. "Billy Shore is inseparable from Share Our Strength—he is a huge asset," says Mike McCurry, board member and former Clinton presidential adviser. "But I think there is some recognition that we will have to be able to project stability and continuity beyond the founder. An organization has to transcend the founder if it is to be successful."

THE INVISIBLE, INVINCIBLE BOARD

No discussion of nonprofit leadership would be complete without addressing the fundamental role of the board in leading an organization. Many experts we interviewed, however, almost uniformly failed to mention this role. It didn't come up as a critical success factor among senior managers, outside stakeholders, or even board members themselves. This was somewhat surprising, given the amount of attention paid to building strong boards within the social sector.

However, most of the *executive directors* we interviewed maintained that their relationship with the board was critical. It is "true but not new": if the board isn't effective, it can sink an organization, but if things are going well, the board rarely gets credit. Perhaps that's the hallmark of a truly great nonprofit board—it plays a significant role leading the organization, but it does so from behind the scenes.

Some fascinating trends emerged once we started teasing out the various threads of our research. The high-impact boards we studied are fairly large in size, and they have a handful of long-tenured members. The executive directors share power with their boards—neither one is really on top or has ultimate control of the organization. The boards are highly engaged; they work well with the executive leadership and have evolved as the organization has grown, although their governance models and roles vary depending on the context in which they operate.

The size of these boards, particularly in comparison with corporate boards, was eye opening, ranging from twenty to forty people (see Table 9.2). Perhaps this is because high-impact nonprofits must engage so many stakeholders, both internal and external, to have impact. They need broad boards that represent a range of skills, backgrounds, and social networks. "It has to be a mix: You have to have people with money and people representing the community," says the Exploratorium's Delacôte. "A board has to be a mirror of the society in which it is functioning."

Nonprofit	Number of Board Members
Environmental Defense	42
Exploratorium	28
National Council of La Raza	26
Teach For America	26
Habitat for Humanity	25
America's Second Harvest	21
City Year	21
The Heritage Foundation	20
Share Our Strength	20
Center on Budget and Policy Priorities	16
YouthBuild USA	15

Table 9.2.   Larger Than Average Boards

Like the continuity of leadership among the executive directors and senior staff we studied, there is also a great deal of continuity of leadership on the boards of high-impact organizations. Many of these groups have board members who have been around for years—although they balance this continuity with some turnover to allow for new energy and ideas. "We have six board members who have been here for more than twenty-five years," says Virginia Carollo Rubin, development director of the Exploratorium who also served as interim director during several executive transitions. "They are really dedicated. There's something about this place that feeds them—the activity, the mission, the vitality of the place. People aren't here for a personal agenda or for the distinction."

The executive directors and top teams have all found a way to actively share leadership with the board to further their mission. In most cases, the organization is equally led by the executive director and the board—each has a critical but different role to play. This was an interesting finding given that many boards tend to micromanage or play an incredibly hands-on role, often doing much of the work, particularly in startup or early growth phases. But in these high-impact nonprofits, the board balances its power with that of the executive director and senior staff, or works in partnership with them, rather than dominating. We believe that this balance reflects both a shared leadership model internally and that these groups are in a more mature stage in the life cycle of organizational growth.

In some cases, an organization started out being led and dominated by a founding board, but then transitioned to stronger executive director leadership and shared power. For example, NCLR had a controlling but unaccountable board when Raul Yzaguirre first took over in 1974. (The nonprofit was founded by a collective group who then appointed Yzaguirre director.) He didn't have either the authority or accountability he needed as executive director, so he confronted the board with a request for change—and threatened to walk away if they wouldn't give him more power to make critical operating decisions without board approval. In other words, he lobbied for shared leadership, rather than a hierarchical model with the board on top.

"We had a strong board chair with a political agenda, and we were defined by his relationships and affiliations," recounts Yzaguirre. "It was just a runaway board. It was unaccountable and it made the staff unaccountable." To its credit, the board gave up some of its power in order to prevent Yzaguirre from quitting. From that time on, he and the board were able to operate effectively together in a true balance of power.

These boards have a high level of engagement; more critical, they have a positive relationship with the executive director. Research shows that many nonprofit executives do not have constructive relationships with their boards, a factor often cited as a reason for high turnover. "Executives who are unhappy with their boards are more than twice as likely to be planning near-term departures as those who have positive perceptions of their boards," according to *Daring to Lead* (Bell, Moyers, and Wolfred, 2006). The study found that only one in three nonprofit executives strongly agreed that their "boards challenge them in ways that make them more effective" or viewed their boards as "an engaged leadership body."

Our research seems to echo this general perception. Although we don't have deep data on the board-executive relationship, our observation is that these executives have a strong and supportive relationship with their boards. "Most of my colleagues were always saying, 'I hate my board,'" says Delacôte of other science museum directors. "But I was always saying the opposite. The work relationship was superb."

The role that the board plays varies from organization to organization. Most play a fund-raising role (with the exception of YouthBuild USA and Self-Help), and board members help the nonprofit access resources either directly or indirectly, through social networks. "Fred pays a lot of attention to building a very engaged board," says Marcia Aronoff, vice president for programs at Environmental Defense. "A lot of cultivation [of donors] comes from the board making introductions to their networks. It's a huge part of our resource strategy." Board members are often the group's most powerful evangelists, helping make introductions or broker critical relationships in government and business.

Further, most of these executives say their board is quite involved in helping set high-level strategy and in advising the top executives on critical issues. For this reason, they are often deliberately diverse, rounding out the skills or backgrounds of the senior team, with a mix that often includes people with legal, marketing, or finance expertise, or experience and networks in government or business. (This may be another reason for their large size.)

Many boards have also gone through transitions as the organizations themselves have evolved. For example, the Share Our Strength board "started out as friends and family—a founder's board, really," says Billy Shore. "We didn't pick people for their name or ability to give resources. We picked them for their ability to think strategically. Then we outgrew that board and looked for communications experience, corporate experience, and so on. It's a very different board today but still pretty engaged."

One thing is certain, however: strong leadership requires that an organization maintain a delicate balance of power among the executive director, the executive team, and the board. As F. Van Kasper, chairman emeritus and board member of the Exploratorium says, "You have people [on the board] who have bought into a mission statement that is strong, and they are very committed. So it can create a very dedicated staff and board environment. I think that consistency of the two working together has really provided for the success of the organization."

LEADERSHIP MATTERS

At a time when the social sector is growing in size and importance, the need for skilled leadership has never been greater. And as our findings illustrate, leadership is needed not just at the executive director level but also among senior managers, board members, and site staff. Despite the importance of shared leadership, however, it's not always easy to find the top talent that nonprofits need.

All the organizations in our research cited lack of talent as the second most significant barrier to growing their organization and expanding their impact, just after lack of funding. And studies show that the social sector is facing an impending leadership crisis. Just as demand is growing, supply is falling, due to the number of baby boomers retiring, a high rate of burnout among nonprofit executives, and the failure of most organizations to develop human resources within their organizations. Although these nonprofits have done a good job cultivating leadership within their organizations—including paying top talent, as we'll see in the next chapter [of *Forces for Good*]—that doesn't mean it has been easy for them. They go out of their way and invest time, money, and significant energy in sharing leadership throughout their organizations.

As Tom Tierney, founder of the nonprofit consulting firm Bridgespan, wrote in an important report on the topic, more nonprofits should follow this example: "It takes long, hard work to build an excellent leadership team. Many successful business CEOs spend well over half their time on people-related issues. In contrast, executive directors of nonprofits tend to devote the lion's share of their time to fund-raising" (Tierney, 2006).

Leadership matters a great deal to nonprofits, in part because they are primarily service organizations whose assets are intangible; their programs and services are only as good as the people they hire and retain. All the more reason that the social sector needs to wake up to new models of leadership. A report from the Center for Creative Leadership says, "To expand leadership capacity, organizations must not only develop individuals, but also develop the leadership capacity of collectives (for example, work groups, teams, and communities). They must develop the connections between individuals, between collectives within the organization, and between the organization and key constituents and stakeholders in its environment" (Van Velsor and McCauley, 2004). Of course, all of this is easier said than done, but our nonprofits provide some examples of how to get started.

By cultivating internal leadership and building bench strength, high-impact nonprofits have shored up their capacity to support growth. By building strong and engaged boards and developing a supportive partnership between the board and the executive director, they ensure longer tenure. Ultimately, these nonprofits have learned that true power, both professionally and organizationally, comes not from concentrating authority and responsibility at the top, but rather from spreading it as widely as possible. It comes from a culture of leadership that permeates the organization, one that freely gives power away.

Chapter Highlights

- *Great nonprofit leaders share power.* Wise CEOs recognize that they must share power if they are to unleash and magnify the potential of their organizations. They learn to let go to have greater impact.

- *Let many leadership styles bloom.* There is no one type of leader who is most successful at creating a high-impact organization. Instead, many different styles can succeed (charismatic, humble, strategic, detail-oriented) if leaders are willing to put their cause, and their organization, above their own egos.

- *To relinquish control, hire a COO.* Many CEOs either start with or eventually hire a second-in-command. Regardless of his or her title, this person usually focuses more on internal management, so that the director can focus more on external leadership.

- *Empower your executive team.* The best nonprofit leaders build their bench strength by creating strong executive teams and giving these top managers real authority and accountability for the organization's success. This approach helps retain top talent over time.

- *Great leaders last.* Many of the executives at these nonprofits have been with their organizations much longer than the sector average, or even the typical CEO. Longevity and leadership continuity help these nonprofits succeed.

- *Develop a succession plan.* Great leaders also know when it's time to go. Create a transition plan with the board that prepares for that day. Get ready for the change by cultivating leadership within the organization and preparing to hire a new director from the outside.

- *Build a big and strategic board.* Although the trend these days is toward smaller boards, the nonprofits discussed in this book all have relatively large and diverse boards. But quality matters, too. Board members should be highly committed and should bring a diverse range of skills, perspectives, and social networks to help the organization and its cause.

- *Balance power.* Many leaders try to minimize their interactions with their board, or they perpetually fight with them, whereas great nonprofits have a positive relationship with the board. They share leadership to advance the larger cause.

Notes

1. All facts and quotations presented in this case were taken from interviews with Heritage Foundation staff or from internal or publicly available organizational information.
2. All facts and quotations presented in this case were taken from interviews with National Council of La Raza staff or from internal or publicly available organizational information.
3. NCLR tenure data were taken from interviews and original research in 2005.

4. All facts and quotations presented in this case were taken from interviews with Exploratorium staff or from internal or publicly available organizational information.

5. Interviews with Millard Fuller and other Habitat staff.

References

Bell, J., Moyers, R., and Wolfred, T. *Daring to Lead 2006: A National Study of Nonprofit Executive Leadership*. A joint project of Compass-Point Nonprofit Services and the Meyer Foundation. San Francisco: CompassPoint, 2006.

Bennis, W., and Nanus, B. *Leaders: Strategies for Taking Charge*. New York: HarperBusiness, 1997.

Collins, J. *Good to Great: Why Some Companies Make the Leap ... and Others Don't*. New York: HarperBusiness, 2001.

Edwards, L. *The Power of Ideas*. Ottawa, IL: Jameson Books, 1997.

Hubbard, B. *Investing in Leadership: Vol. 1. A Grantmaker's Framework for Understanding Nonprofit Leadership Development*. Washington, DC: Grantmakers for Effective Organizations, 2005.

Kopp, W. *One Day, All Children ..: The Unlikely Triumph of Teach For America, and What I Learned Along the Way*. New York: Perseus Books, 2001.

Light, P. C. "Reshaping Social Entrepreneurship." *Stanford Social Innovation Review*, 2006, 4(3), 46–51.

Markus, G. *Building Leadership: Findings from a Longitudinal Evaluation of the Kellogg National Fellowship Program*. Battle Creek, MI: W. K. Kellogg Foundation, 2001.

Tierney, T. J. *The Nonprofit Sector's Leadership Deficit*. San Francisco: Bridgespan Group, February 2006.

Van Velsor, E., and McCauley, C. "Our View of Leadership Development." In *The Center for Creative Leadership Handbook of Leadership Development* (2nd ed.). San Francisco: Jossey-Bass, 2004. Cited in Hubbard, 2005.

—◦◦◦—

At time of original publishing Leslie R. Crutchfield was a managing director of Ashoka and a research grantee of the Aspen Institute's Nonprofit Sector and Philanthropy Program. Heather McLeod Grant was an adviser to the Stanford Center for Social Innovation and research fellow with Duke University's Center for the Advancement of Social Entrepreneurship (CASE).

CHAPTER TEN

Collaboration Processes
Inside the Black Box

Ann Marie Thomson
James L. Perry

Social science research contains a wealth of knowledge for people seeking to understand collaboration processes. The authors argue that public managers should look inside the "black box" of collaboration processes. Inside, they will find a complex construct of five variable dimensions: governance, administration, organizational autonomy, mutuality, and norms. Public managers must know these five dimensions and manage them intentionally in order to collaborate effectively.

Collaboration is the act or process of "shared creation" or discovery. [It] involves the creation of new value by doing something new or different.

[It] is transforming in the sense that you don't leave the same way you came in. There's some sort of change. You give up part of yourself. Something new has to be created. Something happens differently because of the process.

Collaboration is when everybody brings something to the table (expertise, money, ability to grant permission). They put it on the table, take their hands off and then the team creates from there.

— *Comments from public agency directors*

Originally published as "Collaboration Processes: Inside the Black Box" in *Public Administration Review*, 66. (December/Special Issue, 2006).

Although skeptics believe that relatively little collaboration happens in the real world, practicing managers, such as the public agency directors just quoted, know collaboration when they see it. One reason for the skepticism about collaboration is its transient qualities and the demands it places on participating actors. An AmeriCorps program director in Michigan, for example, summarized managers' uneasiness about collaboration: "Collaboration is like cottage cheese. It occasionally smells bad and separates easily" (Thomson and Perry, 1998). Yet collaboration is becoming an imperative for public managers. Devolution, rapid technological change, scarce resources, and rising organizational interdependencies are driving increasing levels of collaboration.

The roots of collaboration are buried deep in American life and public administration. When placed within the context of an American public ethos, collaboration can be understood as a process that is rooted in two competing political traditions: classic liberalism and civic republicanism (Perry and Thomson, 2004). Classic liberalism, with its emphasis on private interest, views collaboration as a process that aggregates private preferences into collective choices through self-interested bargaining. Organizations enter into collaborative agreements to achieve their own goals, negotiating among competing interests and brokering coalitions among competing value systems, expectations, and self-interested motivations. Civic republicanism, on the other hand, with its emphasis on a commitment to something larger than the individual (whether that be a neighborhood or the state), views collaboration as an integrative process that treats differences as the basis for deliberation in order to arrive at "mutual understanding, a collective will, trust and sympathy [and the] implementation of shared preferences" (March and Olsen, 1989, p. 126).

Public managers often find themselves pulled between these two competing views of collaboration, and the literature on collaboration tends to mirror this tension. Huxham (1996), for example, argues that a necessary requirement for successful collaboration is the self-interest motive—each organization must be able to justify its involvement in a collaboration first by how it furthers the organization's goals. Bardach agrees: "Collaboration," he writes, "should be valued only if it produces better organizational performance or lower costs than can be had without it" (1998, p. 17).[1] These and other collaboration scholars (Gray, 1989, 2000; Huxham, 1996; Huxham and Vangen, 2005)—as well as precursor literatures on inter-organizational relations (Ring and Van de Ven, 1994) and organizational behavior (Hellriegel, Slocum, and Woodman, 1986)—strongly support an integrative view of collaboration as a process "through which parties who see different aspects of a problem can constructively explore their differences and search for solutions that go beyond their own limited vision of what is possible" (Gray, 1989, p. 5).

These literatures—outside traditional public administration research—provide insight into the complex nature of collaborative processes. We believe an important piece of the collaboration

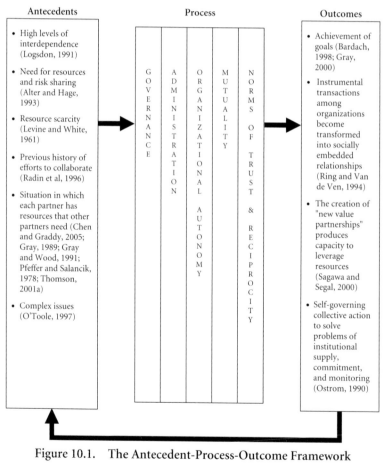

Figure 10.1.   The Antecedent-Process-Outcome Framework

Source: Adapted from Wood and Gray, 1991.

puzzle is lost by failing to explore the multidisciplinary literature on collaboration, as this broader scan yields valuable insights about what public managers need to know in order to "do" collaboration. In their review of collaboration research, Wood and Gray (1991) frame the discussion in terms of an antecedent-process-outcome model (Figure 10.1).[2] The "doing" of collaboration—the process component—is, in Wood and Gray's terminology, a "black box." They argue that the interactive process of collaboration is least understood. We agree.

Our thesis in this article is twofold: First, we believe that the research about collaboration, much of it emanating from outside public administration,[3] is quite useful for illuminating valuable knowledge for public managers. Second, before we can manage collaboration, we need to know what it is. We argue that collaboration is not an either/or: When public managers look inside the black box of collaboration processes, they find a complex construct consisting of five variable dimensions. Public managers must know these five dimensions and manage them intentionally in order to collaborate effectively.

INSIDE THE BLACK BOX: WHAT IS COLLABORATION?

A process framework for collaboration suggests that collaboration occurs over time as organizations interact formally and informally through repetitive sequences of negotiation, development of commitments, and execution of those commitments. Scholars have described the collaboration process in terms of a continuum of stages. For example, Gray's (1989) three-phase framework involves problem setting, direction setting, and implementation, and Himmelman's (1996) view of the collaboration process sees it as a continuum of strategies that range from bettering the community to transforming it through "empowerment collaboration."

Ring and Van de Ven (1994) provide a particularly useful framework for thinking about the process of collaboration (Figure 10.2). They conceive of the process as iterative and cyclical rather than linear. Using this logic, if organizations that are engaged in collaboration can negotiate minimal, congruent expectations regarding their collective action, then they will commit to an initial course of action. If the collective action is executed in a reciprocal fashion, then participating organizations will continue or expand their mutual commitments. If

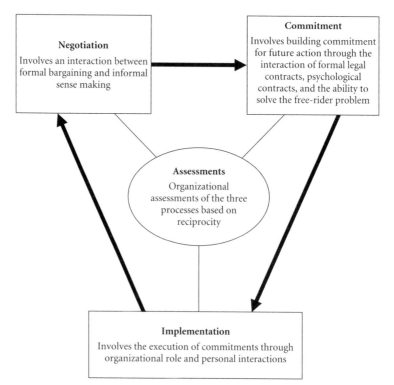

Figure 10.2.   A Process Framework of Collaboration

Source: Adapted from Ring and Van de Ven, 1994.

these commitments are not implemented in a reciprocal fashion, then participants will initiate corrective measures either through renegotiation or by reducing their commitments. The extent to which organizations exercise their voice or exit often depends on the extent to which they have an aggregative or an integrative perspective on collaboration. As Figure 10.2 suggests, collaboration implies a cyclical process of renegotiation.

A process-oriented definition of collaboration, then, must take into account the nonlinear and emergent nature of collaboration, suggesting that collaboration evolves as parties interact over time. Findings from game theory support a process-oriented perspective on collaboration (Axelrod, 1984, 1997; Ostrom, 1990, 1998). Experimental and field research confirms that "individuals temporarily caught in a social-dilemma structure are likely to invest resources to innovate and change the structure itself in order to improve joint outcomes . . . [Learning occurs through a] continuous trial-and-error process until a rule system is evolved that participants consider yields substantial net benefits" (Ostrom, 1998, p. 8).

Ring and Van de Ven's (1994) process framework implies that in order for collaboration to evolve, the integrative elements manifest in personal relationships, psychological contracts, and informal understandings and commitments need to supplant the aggregative elements manifest in formal organizational roles and legal contracts. Finding the right balance between integration and aggregation—not relying on formal institutional structures such as memoranda of agreement and standard operating procedures—may be the key to sustaining collaboration over time.

Defining Collaboration

Using Ring and Van de Ven's (1994) process to frame our understanding of collaboration, we employ a definition of collaboration developed by Thomson (2001a) as a starting point for our analysis:

> "Collaboration is a process in which autonomous actors interact through formal and informal negotiation, jointly creating rules and structures governing their relationships and ways to act or decide on the issues that brought them together; it is a process involving shared norms and mutually beneficial interactions."[4]

This definition suggests a higher-order level of collective action than cooperation or coordination. Although the extensive literature on collaboration is without agreement on terms—drawing as it does from a wide variety of perspectives, including inter-organizational relations (Alexander, 1995; Ring and Van de Ven, 1994; Warren, Burgunder, Newton, and Rose, 1975), networks (Alter and Hage, 1993; O'Toole, 1997; O'Toole, Meier, and Nicholson-Crotty, 2005; Powell, 1990), and the logic of collective action (Olson, 1971; Ostrom, 1990)—most scholars would agree that cooperation and collaboration differ in terms of their depth of interaction, integration, commitment, and complexity, with cooperation falling at the low end of the continuum and collaboration at the high end (Alter and Hage, 1993; Himmelman, 1996; Mattessich and Monsey, 1992).

In her groundbreaking book on collaboration, *Collaborating: Finding Common Ground for Multiparty Problems*, Gray points out that although both cooperation and coordination may occur as part of the early process of collaboration, collaboration represents a longer-term integrated process "through which parties who see different aspects of a problem ... constructively explore their differences ... search for solutions that go beyond their own limited vision of what is possible" (1989, p. 5) and implement those solutions jointly. In her interviews with public agency directors between 1995 and 2000, Thomson (2001a) found that, in contrast to the ease with which they described cooperation, agency directors frequently used metaphors to describe collaboration, such as "stepping into other people's shoes," "the combination of hydrogen and oxygen atoms to form water," and "combining yellow and green circles to form a larger blue circle."

One public manager's comments help to summarize the distinction. "It's indicative," he pointed out,

> "... that we ... think of [collaboration] as a residual of cooperation and coordination. It's not coordination, it's not cooperation. Cooperation involves reciprocities, exchange of resources (not necessarily symmetrical). Cooperation for a *mutual goal* moves this to collaboration. The whole is greater than the sum of its parts. It may be achieving individual ends, but there's an *additional outcome* that is shared (though not mutually exclusive) separate from the individual ends." (Thomson, 2001b).

A thesis of this article is that in order to arrive at that "additional outcome that is shared [and] separate from individual ends," public managers need to understand the multidimensional nature of collaboration.

A Multidimensional Model of Collaboration

The achievement of shared outcomes implies synergistic processes rather than stepwise movement from one phase to another (Brinkerhoff, 2002; Huxham and Vangen, 2005; Thomson, 2001a). In their review of numerous cases studies over many years, for example, Huxham and Vangen (2005) describe five fundamental characteristics of collaborative situations, each of which implies a messy, contradictory, dynamic process that is defined by multiple viewpoints and unintended outcomes. Other scholars identify different elements of collaboration. For example, Roberts and Bradley (1991) argue that the principal elements of collaboration are a trans-mutational purpose, explicit and voluntary membership, organization, an interactive process, and a temporal property. For Gray (1989), collaboration involves interdependence, dealing constructively with differences to arrive at solutions, joint ownership of decisions, and collective responsibility that recognizes collaboration is an emergent process.

Thomson (2001a) builds on this earlier research by systematically reviewing and analyzing a wide variety of definitions of collaboration found in the multidisciplinary research. She concludes that the essence of collaboration processes can be distilled into five key dimensions.[5] These dimensions, though distinct variables, are interdependent in the sense that movement from one dimension to another does not necessarily occur sequentially. Instead, the dimensions are part of a larger covariance model in which variation across each dimension is influenced by variation in the others. Movement along the five dimensions depends on a wide variety of factors, including but not limited to internal relationships (Bardach, 1998; Huxham and Vangen, 2005; Ospina and Sag-Carranza, 2005; Sink, 1996; Williams, 2002) and external factors such as antecedent conditions (Gray and Wood, 1991), uncertainty, ambiguity, shifting membership, and multiple accountabilities (Huxham and Vangen, 2000; Ospina and Sag-Carranza, 2005). The dimensions vary from low to high, but the complexity and uncertainty of the process suggest that linking inputs to outputs is difficult, and we are unable, at this juncture, to specify an optimal level for all five dimensions. Rather than insisting on reaching the highest levels on all five dimensions, the challenge for public managers and partners in collaboration is to seek a balance among the dimensions through mutual accommodation and incentives for renegotiation.

This perspective is consistent with the empirical research. Among the 422 collaborations that Thomson and Miller (2002) studied, for example, they found wide variations on the five dimensions. Although the average collaboration in the sample exhibited relatively high levels of joint decision making, administration, mutuality, and trust and fairly low levels of tension between individual and collective interests, achieving exceptionally high levels of collaboration proved difficult; moving substantially *above* the average seldom occurred. Ostrom's research on self-governance of common pool resources suggests that instead of presuming that optimal institutional solutions can be designed easily and imposed at a low cost by external authorities, "getting the institutions right is a difficult, time-consuming, conflict-ridden process" (1990, p. 14).

A collective action perspective, such as Ostrom uses, is a particularly useful way to think about the process of collaboration. Movement along the five dimensions occurs as partners try to solve the collective action problem of changing a situation "from one in which appropriators act independently to one in which they adopt coordinated strategies to obtain higher joint benefits or reduce their joint harm" (Ostrom, 1990, p. 39). These five key dimensions are critical pieces of the puzzle, and public managers and their partners in collaboration need to balance them in order to solve this collective action problem.

Five Key Dimensions of Collaboration

Of the five dimensions summarized in Figure 10.1, two are structural dimensions (governing and administering), two are dimensions of social capital (mutuality and norms), and one is an agency dimension (organizational autonomy). We believe that public managers would benefit from a systematic and careful analysis of the process by which partners interact by focusing on these five key dimensions that together signify collaborative action.

When collaborative partners are unwilling to monitor their own adherence to the agreed-upon rules, the ability to build credible commitment is lost, and joint decision making is unlikely.

THE PROCESS OF COLLABORATIVE GOVERNING: THE GOVERNANCE DIMENSION. Partners who seek to collaborate must understand how to jointly make decisions about the rules that will govern their behavior and relationships; they also need to create structures for reaching agreement on collaborative activities and goals through shared power arrangements. These ideas are at the heart of collaboration and encompass both the negotiation and commitment processes depicted in Figure 10.2. The literature on collaboration describes governance variously as participative decision making (McCaffrey, Faerman, and Hart, 1995; Wood and Gray, 1991); shared power arrangements (Clift, Veal, Holland, Johnson, and McCarthy, 1995; Crosby and Bryson, 2005); and problem solving (Hellriegel, Slocum, and Woodman, 1986).

Each of these terms implies (1) a lack of authoritative structure or hierarchical division of labor (Huxham, 1996); (2) an awareness that participants are not only directly responsible for reaching an agreement but must also impose decisions on themselves (Gray, 1989); (3) a willingness to accept that all participants have legitimate interests, such that outcomes "reflect group consensus, not coalitional or power politics" (McCaffrey, Faerman, and Hart, 1995, p. 612); and (4) an understanding that this kind of governance emphasizes openness in information sharing, respect for others' opinions, and potentially lengthy negotiations to reach agreement (Thomson, 2001a). Reaching agreements that are compatible with all interests does not mean groupthink. As one public manager put it, collaboration does not mean everyone has to agree on the best possible solution; it only means that they have to be willing to support the decision once it is made (Thomson, 2001a).

When parties come together to collaborate, they make choices that govern a variety of collective action problems implicit in joint decision making—how to collectively develop sets of working rules to determine who will be eligible to make decisions, which actions will be allowed or constrained, what information needs to be provided, and how costs and benefits will be distributed (Ostrom, 1990). The key to the success of these choices rests in participants' willingness to monitor themselves and each other and to impose credible sanctions on noncompliant partners. When collaborative partners are unwilling to monitor their own adherence to the agreed-upon rules, the ability to build credible commitment is lost, and joint decision making is unlikely. For Ostrom (1998), a reputation for trustworthiness is one of three core factors (the other two are trust and reciprocity) that increases the likelihood of collective action. Closely related to the process of building credible commitment is the value of face-to-face communication (Mattessich and Monsey, 1992; Ostrom, 1998) and the creation of an "ethic of collaboration" (Radin et al., 1996), which allows partners to give each other the benefit of the doubt while they build the reputations needed for joint decision making.

As a process, then, governance in collaboration is not static, nor is there one universal way to go about creating what Bardach (1998) calls "jointness." Warren (1967) conceives of general consensus as a process of arriving at an equilibrium in which contest and conflict among partners still occur, but only at the margins and within a larger framework of agreement on the appropriateness of jointly determined rules that ensure a collaborative environment. To arrive at this kind of equilibrium, public managers need to understand the shared responsibility that accompanies this form of governance when they engage in collaboration (Himmelman, 1996; Pasquero, 1991).

In his study of a Canadian initiative to develop national environmental policy, for example, Pasquero (1991) found that when people and organizations were able to demonstrate a deeper appreciation for the interconnected nature of the problems of environmental pollution, they were more likely to collaborate. Instead of blaming particular partners (especially polluters), Pasquero found that the stakeholders he studied began to adopt collective responsibility for the problems they faced. This allowed them to focus directly on addressing the problem rather than on assigning individual responsibility. A shared vision and commitment to a supraorganizational goal allowed them to move toward problem solving rather than problem blaming.

THE PROCESS OF COLLABORATIVE ADMINISTRATION: THE ADMINISTRATION DIMENSION. Collaborations are not self-administering enterprises. Organizations collaborate because they intend to achieve a particular purpose. To achieve the purpose that brought the organizations to the table in the first place, some kind of administrative structure must exist that moves from governance to action. This reality is hardly new to public managers! In her interviews with public managers, Thomson (2001a) found administration to be a critical dimension of collaboration. When asked about their best and worst experiences with collaboration, the agency directors interviewed repeatedly identified the presence (or absence) of clear roles and responsibilities, the capacity to set boundaries, the presence of concrete achievable goals, and good communication as the key characteristics of their experiences.

The implementation of collaboration is complex, not only because participation is voluntary and actors are autonomous (Gray, 2000; Huxham, 1996) but also because traditional coordination mechanisms such as hierarchy, standardization, and routinization are less feasible across units than within them, and communication among partners is based more on interdependent relationships than on contractual agreements (Huxham and Vangen, 2005; O'Toole, 1996; Powell, 1990). The potential to withdraw from the relationship may be particularly high if collaborations are unable to achieve short-term success (Thomson, 1999) as a result of collaborative inertia (Huxham, 1996).

The key administrative functions identified in the top-down management literature—functions such as coordination, clarity of roles and responsibilities, and monitoring mechanisms—are also stressed in the collaboration research (Bardach, 1998; Mattessich and Monsey, 1992; Ring and Van de Ven, 1994), but they take on new meaning in light of the more symmetrical (at least in theory) and horizontal relationships found in collaborations. Pressman and Wildavsky's (1984) classic recommendation to simplify the implementation chain of action does not work for getting things done in collaboration given the interdependence (and thus increased complexity) that characterizes partner relationships.

Yet as public managers know all too well, decentralized administrative structures still require a central position for coordinating communication, organizing and disseminating information, and keeping partners alert to the jointly determined rules that govern their relationships—what Freitag and Winkler describe as "social coordination" (2001, p. 68). In her case study of the Barani Area Development Project in Pakistan, for example, Brinkerhoff (2002) found that this multilevel partnership (which included government departments, nongovernmental organizations, and local communities) proved relatively successful because the trust building among participants and the political will to work together in new ways were augmented by administrative will in the use of bureaucratic mechanisms that helped to maximize some degree of predictability.

Most scholars of collaboration agree, however, that the key to getting things done in a collaborative setting rests in finding the right combination of administrative capacity (through coordination and elements of hierarchy) and social capacity to build relationships. In their study of business and nonprofit collaboration, for example, Sagawa and Segal (2000) suggest that coordinating roles need to be augmented by "relationship managers" whose specific task is to manage and build inter-organizational relationships, not just make sure collaboration requirements are being met. Williams (2002) also makes a strong case for the importance of boundary spanners—individuals who have the skill to build and manage interpersonal relationships. In his examination of boundary spanners operating in several different policy domains in the United Kingdom, Williams found that particular boundary-spanning skills enhanced the likelihood of collaboration. These skills include the ability to build and sustain effective interpersonal relationships among partners, the ability to play an "honest broker role" (p. 117) among contested power structures, and the ability to manage interdependency—a skill that is developed especially through "accumulated 'on-the-job' inter-organizational experience" (p. 119).

This perspective suggests that partners in collaboration play different administrative roles. The leader-manager distinction of traditional public management, for example, whereby leaders set and managers implement particular agendas (Rainey, 2003), appears less relevant as the same participants in collaboration simultaneously set and implement agendas. Different partners, then, lead and manage by playing different roles (e.g., convener, advocate, technical assistance provider, facilitator, funder), each of which is necessary for the collaboration as a whole to achieve its goals (Himmelman, 1996). Drawing on findings from a study of the National Rural Development Council, however, Radin suggests that boundary-spanning responsibilities may not rest in a single individual playing a single role but instead are "integral to [any] manager's competencies" (1996, p. 159). Whether partners in collaboration play distinctive roles or whether they begin to develop competency in multiple roles, one of the principal administrative dilemmas for leaders and managers in collaboration is managing the inherent tension between self-interests and collective interests.

THE PROCESS OF RECONCILING INDIVIDUAL AND COLLECTIVE INTERESTS: THE AUTONOMY DIMENSION. A defining dimension of collaboration that captures both the potential dynamism and the frustration that is implicit in collaborative endeavors is the reality that partners share a dual identity: They maintain their own distinct identities and organizational authority separate from (though simultaneously with) the collaborative identity. This reality creates an intrinsic tension between self-interest—achieving individual organizational missions and maintaining an identity that is distinct from the collaborative—and a collective interest—achieving collaboration goals and maintaining accountability to collaborative partners and their stakeholders (Bardach, 1998; Tschirhart, Christensen, and Perry, 2005; Van de Ven, Emmett, and Koenig, 1975; Wood and Gray, 1991). Huxham refers to this tension as the autonomy-accountability dilemma and concludes that because "collaboration is voluntary, partners generally need to justify their involvement in it in terms of its contribution to their own aims" (1996, p. 15) or refrain from collaborating altogether.

This dimension is especially problematic because collaborations typically form around intractable problems that partners cannot solve on their own (Finn, 1996; Gray, 1989; Huxham, 1996; Pasquero, 1991). Partners need each other if such problems are to be adequately addressed, yet their own missions (which may or may not be directly related to the particular problem collaboration forms to address) can create a difficult choice. One partner in a collaboration addressing homelessness described it well when he said,

> "Tension exists because of [our blinders]. You have to prove you are meeting [your organization's] mission. In the case of the Center [we collaborate on], ministry is the mission of our church. [The other organization's] mission wasn't about ministry at all but about meeting the needs of the homeless. [The question is] how do we keep our identity as a church? Because of your constituency, your resource base, you have to watch out for your [own] identity." (Thomson 2001a, p. 88)

When collaboration's goals conflict with the autonomous goals of individual partner organizations, identities are at stake. Unless the particular problem is of sufficient urgency to all partners, it is likely that individual missions will trump collaboration missions.

The autonomy dimension contrasts shared control with individual control (Wood and Gray, 1991). The aggregative elements in collaboration suggest that partners protect their own identities in collaboration by maintaining individual control. Shared control, on the other hand, involves partners' willingness to share information, not only about their own organizations' operations but also about what they can and cannot offer the collaboration. This willingness to share information *for the good of partners* (even at the risk of compromising a particular organization's autonomy) is the distinguishing characteristic of collaboration for Himmelman (1996). For Gray (1989) and Wood and Gray (1991), sharing information in collaboration needs to be seen in terms of increasing partners' understanding of the problem they are jointly seeking to address.

The creative tension between individual and collective interests is a recurring theme in much of the case research on collaboration. In her study of how California's Silicon Valley business community and public officials jointly responded to traffic congestion, for example, Logsdon (1991) found that reconciling private interests with collective interests became possible only when partners began to understand the problem in terms of the high stakes of *not* engaging in a shared solution. Selsky (1991), on the other hand, in his study of twelve collaborative projects involving 148 small nonprofit organizations in the Philadelphia area, found that by mobilizing the managers of these organizations around the exchange of resources, a "more developed organizational community" was created. He implies that collaboration among these agencies resulted in a transformation of the community in which these organizations reside.

In general, though, reconciling individual interests with collective interests is often too difficult for many collaborative endeavors, as evidenced by the common conclusion of collaboration scholars that although "greater collaboration is not a very new idea in public administration, it has never fulfilled its promising potential" (Vigoda-Gadot, 2003, p. 147). In the words of Huxham and Vangen, "In the fifteen years that we have been researching collaboration we have seen no evidence to shift our 'don't do it unless you have to'—or unless the stakes are really worth pursuing—position" (2005, p. 42). Forging commonalities out of differences, however, can yield highly satisfying results, and this is also a recurring theme in the literature on collaboration.

THE PROCESS OF FORGING MUTUALLY BENEFICIAL RELATIONSHIPS: THE MUTU-ALITY DIMENSION. Although information sharing is necessary for collaboration, it is not sufficient for it to thrive. Without mutual benefits, information sharing will not lead to collaboration. Mutuality has its roots in interdependence. Organizations that collaborate must experience mutually beneficial interdependencies based either on differing interests—what Powell (1990) calls "complementarities"—or on shared interests, which are usually based on homogeneity or an appreciation and passion for issues that go beyond an individual organization's mission—such as the moral imperative of environmental degradation or a humanitarian crisis. Complementarity describes a situation in which "parties to a network agree to forego the right to pursue their own interests at the expense of others" and accommodation serves as the modus operandi of interaction (Powell 1990, p. 303). It occurs when one party has unique resources (skills, expertise, or money) that another party needs or could benefit from (and vice versa). Such exchange relationships are well documented in inter-organizational relations (Levine and White, 1961; Warren, Burgunder, Newton, and Rose, 1975; Van de Ven, Emmett, and Koenig, 1975) and supported by resource dependence theory (Pfeffer, 1997; Pfeffer and Salancik, 1978).

Mutuality provides a foundation for forging common views out of differences (Cropper, 1996; Gray, 1989; Wood and Gray, 1991). "Collaboration," write Wood and Gray, "can occur as long as stakeholders can satisfy one another's differing interests without loss to themselves" (1991, p. 161). In their study of Los Angeles County's Family Preservation Program, for example, Chen and Graddy found that the most important variable in explaining collaboration outcomes was the organizations' need to "acquire resources from other organizations that they need and do not have but are critical for their continuing functioning" (2005, p. 17). For organizational behavior scholars, mutuality in collaboration is seen as a win-win problem-solving technique that addresses the conflicts inherent in differing interests (Hellriegel, Slocum, and Woodman, 1986). The more consensus partners can forge out of differences based on each other's needs, the greater the likelihood they will be able to collaborate.

In contrast to negotiation, which begins with differences, other scholars begin with shared interests, jointly identifying commonalities among organizations such as similarity of mission, commitment to similar target populations, or professional orientation and culture (Lax and Sebenius, 1986). In her study of collaborations in national service, Thomson (1999) found that commitment to similar target populations proved to be one of the most important factors in holding collaborations together. In one case, the power of this commitment was so great that when the promised funding did not come through, partner organizations "forked out [their own] money" (p. 37), at a cost of $20,000, to keep the collaboration going. This kind of commitment is unlikely without the presence of the final defining dimension of collaboration: norms of reciprocity and trust.

Although information sharing is necessary for collaboration, it is not sufficient for it to thrive. Without mutual benefits, information sharing will not lead to collaboration.

THE PROCESS OF BUILDING SOCIAL CAPITAL NORMS: THE TRUST AND RECIPROCITY DIMENSION. Reciprocity can be conceptualized in two different ways: one that is short term and contingent, and one that is long term and rooted in a sociological understanding of obligation (Axelrod, 1984; Ostrom, 1990; Powell, 1990). In collaboration, individual partners often demonstrate a willingness to interact collaboratively only if other partners demonstrate the same willingness. This "I will if you will" mentality (tit-for-tat reciprocity) is based on the perceived degree of obligation, such that partners are willing to bear initial disproportional costs because they expect their partners will equalize the distribution of costs and benefits over time out of a sense of duty—what Ring and Van de Ven (1994) call "fair dealing." Axelrod (1984, 1997), Ostrom (1990, 1998), and Powell (1990) all identify reciprocity as a key factor in successful collective action. Axelrod (1984), for example, found that tit-for-tat reciprocity in prisoner's dilemmas games, when accompanied by repeated interaction, can lead to collective action, and Ostrom (1998) concludes that evidence from laboratory experiments shows that a large proportion of the population in these experiments believes that others will reciprocate, making collective action possible. These findings, however, do not conform to Olson's (1971) prediction that whenever participation in collective action is voluntary, the members whose marginal costs exceed the marginal benefits of participating will stop contributing before a group optimum is reached.

The emphasis on repeated interactions in the game theory literature underscores the longer-term view of obligation based on the social and cultural tenets that form the basis of social interaction in society and give reciprocal exchanges meaning (Powell, 1990). Furthermore, over time, as collaboration partners learn what works and what does not work, "highly rationalized myths" may develop that gain both intrinsic and instrumental legitimacy and then form the basis of reciprocal exchange (Meyer and Rowan, 1977), such as individual partner roles that are perceived as critical to the collaboration itself. Here, a reputation for trustworthiness proves critical to any collaborative enterprise, as Ostrom (1998) demonstrates in her comprehensive review of the literature on collective action.

Closely related to reciprocity, then, is the second facet of norms—trust—which can be defined as a common belief among a group of individuals that another group (1) will make "good-faith efforts to behave in accordance with any commitments both explicit and implicit," (2) will "be honest in whatever negotiations preceded such commitments," and (3) will "not take excessive advantage of another even when the opportunity is available" (Cummings and

Bromiley, 1996, p. 303). Trust is a central component of collaboration because it reduces complexity and transaction costs more quickly than other forms of organization (Chiles and McMackin, 1996; Ostrom, 1998; Smith, 1995).

Bardach (1998) identifies trust as a key element in one of two dimensions of interagency collaborative capacity, and the findings of Huxham and Vangen's (2005) extensive action research on collaboration lead them to conclude that trust is a critical component of collaboration, but trust building takes an inordinate amount of time and nurturing. In her study of 422 collaborations, Thomson (2001a) found evidence to support Huxham and Vangen's conclusion. As one AmeriCorps director put it:

> "Collaboration can't be rushed. [It is] very energy intensive. You have to be willing to invest inordinate amounts of time at low productivity to establish relationships and trust building. Organizations don't initially start with a cost-benefit analysis. They start with a kind of idealism. Then, as they start to accomplish things, they realize that they're going to have to pay a cost. When organizations are willing to make the costs that is when you have moved to collaboration." (Thomson, 2001a, p. 93)

For Ostrom (1998), collective action depends on three key core relationships—reciprocity, trust, and reputation. As collaborative partners interact and build reputations for trustworthy behavior over time, they may find themselves moving away from the more contingent "I will if you will" reciprocity to longer-term commitments based on institutionalized "psychological contracts" (Ring and Van de Ven, 1994). When personal relationships supplement formal organizational role relationships, psychological contracts substitute for legal contracts, and formal organizational agreements mirror informal understandings and commitments, inter-organizational relationships may be sustained over time (Ring and Van de Ven, 1994).

CONCLUSION

"There is a fine line," write Huxham and MacDonald, "between gaining the benefits of collaborating and making the situation worse" (1992, p. 50). Given the complexity of collaboration, public managers may find themselves overwhelmed by the dynamism that collaborations can create or the inertia that often transpires as partners seek to achieve collective goals. Public managers who understand the variable and complex nature of the five dimensions that compose the black box of collaboration processes are better prepared to engage in collaborative activities than those who focus merely on achieving individual goals through collaboration.

The five collaboration process dimensions we have presented provide one systematic approach to collaboration that public managers can use in their daily experiences with collaboration partners. One lesson can be taken away from this review: *Don't collaborate unless you are willing to thoughtfully consider and educate yourself about the nature of the process involved.* Collaborating for collaboration's sake or to achieve only individual goals is likely to result in failure given the complexity of the collaboration process. This is largely because collaboration is costly.

The most costly resources of collaboration are not money but time and energy, neither of which can be induced. Huxham (1996) distinguishes between two sorts of time that anyone who has collaborated will recognize: *actual* time (e.g., achieving mutual understanding, building credible commitments and goodwill, and negotiating bases for action and coordination) and *lapsed* time (coping with accountability issues and other organizational priorities outside the collaboration). The amount of actual and lapsed time that is demanded of collaboration partners can be demotivating, particularly when partners do not recognize or budget time as one of the principal resources of collaboration (Huxham, 1996). Public managers must take this time element seriously if the benefits of collaboration are to be realized. How they do so depends on their capacity to work with partners to negotiate an equilibrium among the five dimensions that will allow them to achieve small gains in the short term, which will, over time, allow them to develop the trust and negotiated agreements necessary to realize longer-term benefits.

Stone's (2000) case study of Washington County's Welfare-to-Work Partnership illustrates how the five dimensions of collaboration can interconnect over time. The partnership, which originated in response to the Personal Responsibility and Work Opportunity Reconciliation Act of 1996, was generously supported with planning and implementation grants from the McKnight Foundation. Stone reports that members of the collaboration were initially highly competitive because they perceived the partnership as a threat to their autonomy. In the absence of prior interactions, partners had no foundation for trusting other partners. The partnership began to coalesce as small collective successes built interpersonal trust among partners. Increases in trust decreased the constraining effects of organizational autonomy. Increasing trust, in turn, triggered an expansion of common interests—mutuality—that stimulated increased commitments to new governance initiatives and administrative support.

The time required to find this equilibrium among the five dimensions, however, underscores the reality that collaborations are inherently fragile systems. They are fragile because, as Wood and Gray argue, although they "may make environments more predictable in some respects, they also cause new dependencies to be created, thus *increasing* environmental complexity and turbulence" while decreasing partners' control over their environment (1991, p. 158). Zucker (1988), Stone (2000), and Ring Van de Ven (1994) agree. The resolution of social dilemmas can be fragile, writes Zucker, because self-interest, a tendency toward disorganization, and partial institutionalization all conspire against it. Ring and Van de Ven conclude that the "seeds for disintegration of relationships are contained within the very governance structures, safeguards, and processes that lead to their formation and growth" (1994, p. 108). Public managers would do well to appreciate the fragility of many collaborative relationships—especially new and immature ones—as a result of the autonomy and competing accountabilities that participants bring to collaborative endeavors.

By simulating different scenarios in which players have a choice between working together or defecting from the game, Axelrod (1997) demonstrates how the advantages of acting in one's own self-interest in the short run conflict with the achievement of success in the long run by working together. Public managers who understand that this tension will always exist in collaborative endeavors (the essence of the organizational autonomy dimension) will be more likely to appreciate and take seriously what Axelrod describes as "the deep consequences of the fundamental processes involved in dealing with this tension" (1997, p. 6).

Greater awareness of the organizational autonomy dimension will give managers a more realistic perspective of what it takes to manage the paradoxical environments that are modeled on game theory simulations but are indicative of the realities of collaboration (Ospina and Sag-Carranza, 2005; Tschirhart, Christensen, and Perry,

2005). In examining the paradox between branding (characterized as a competitive process) and collaboration (characterized by cooperative activities), Tschirhart, Christensen, and Perry suggest managers may use several strategies to address the inherent tensions produced by this paradox. These include acceptance (living with the contradictions of the paradox), confrontation (confronting the paradox by mitigating negative effects or developing ways to manage tensions), and transcendence (reframing meanings to achieve shared and independent goals). Repeated interaction helps managers weigh the costs and benefits of pursuing one or another of these strategies. We believe that public managers, if they enter collaborations with their eyes open, will be more likely to appreciate, reflect on, and support the relationships that are so critical to collaboration efforts.

Like the ideal of civic republicanism, collaboration represents an ideal to which we aspire but sometimes fall short of achieving. Despite the reality that collaboration is hard to do, we are encouraged that when collaboration partners experience something new being created, they engage in repeated interactions with one another, allowing trial-and-error learning to occur. Ostrom (1998) argues that our evolutionary heritage has "hard-wired us" to learn norms of reciprocity and trust, so that over time, institutional change is possible. Public managers need to budget the time necessary to negotiate with collaboration partners across the five dimensions—governing, administering, paying attention to the tension between self-interests and collective interests, forging mutually beneficial relationships, and building reciprocal and trusting relationships—to allow for trial-and-error learning and the building of credible commitments.

The process of collaboration involves movement along the five dimensions as partners renegotiate a new equilibrium that reinforces the learning achieved at a previous equilibrium. "Because individuals are boundedly rational," writes Ostrom, "they do not calculate a complete set of strategies for every situation they face" (1998, p. 9). Each situation demands a different equilibrium among the five key dimensions to achieve an optimal mix for the partners in that context. Time, respect for the fragility of the process, and close attention to the five dimensions cannot ensure positive collaboration outcomes, but these actions will increase the likelihood that this will occur.

It may be that the focus on antecedents and enhancing collaborative performance in much of the public management literature—at the expense of wrestling with the process itself—means tha[are missing an important piece of the puzzle. Developing a more systematic approach to the process of collaboration by focusing on the five defining dimensions presented here increases the likelihood that public managers will be able to manage the intrinsic challenges of collaboration. For scholars, a more systematic attention to understanding the process of collaboration will further the public value of this emerging field of study.

Notes

1. Bardach argues that "substantial public value is being lost to insufficient collaboration" because political pluralism tends to create institutional and political pressures that "push for differentiation rather than integration [where] the basis for differentiation is typically political rather than technical" (1998, p. 11).
2. Wood and Gray (1991) use the antecedent-process-outcome framework to review the literature on collaboration. The literature abounds with antecedents. Because we are focused here on the process of collaboration, we have provided only a small sampling in Figure 10.1.
3. Space limitations prevent us from citing what has become a large public administration literature. One of the most comprehensive contributions is Agranoff and McGuire (2003).
4. This definition of collaboration is strongly influenced by Wood and Gray's (1991) definition. Thomson expands on Wood and Gray's definition by (1) incorporating key phrases and words from a much broader review of the literature, (2) using commonalities among multiple theoretical perspectives, (3) expanding the governance and administration aspects of collaboration, and (4) identifying distinctive key dimensions of collaboration tested empirically using a higher-order confirmatory factor analysis model (Thomson, 2001a).
5. For a description of the analysis of the collaboration literature from which these five dimensions are derived, see Thomson (2001a), especially Tables 5.1 through 5.3.

References

Agranoff, Robert, and McGuire, Michael. *Collaborative Public Management: New Strategies for Local Governments.* Washington, DC: Georgetown University Press, 2003.

Alexander, Ernest R. *How Organizations Act Together: Interorganizational Coordination in Theory and Practice.* Australia: Gordon and Breach, 1995.

Alter, Catherine, and Hage, Jerald. *Organizations Working Together.* Newbury Park, CA: Sage, 1993.

Axelrod, Robert. *The Evolution of Cooperation.* Princeton, NJ: Princeton University Press, 1984.

Axelrod, Robert. *The Complexity of Cooperation: Agent-Based Models of Competition and Collaboration.* Princeton, NJ: Princeton University Press, 1997.

Bardach, Eugene. *Getting Agencies to Work Together: The Practice and Theory of Managerial Craftsmanship.* Washington, DC: Brookings Institution Press, 1998.

Brinkerhoff, Jennifer M. *Partnership for International Development: Rhetoric or Results?* Boulder, CO: Lynne Rienner, 2002.

Chen, Bin, and Graddy, Elizabeth A. "Inter-Organizational Collaborations for Public Service Delivery: A Framework of Preconditions, Processes, and Perceived Outcomes." Paper presented at the 2005 ARNOVA Conference, Washington, DC, November 2005.

Chiles, Todd H., and McMackin, John F. "Integrating Variable Risk Preferences, Trust, and Transaction Cost Economics." *Academy of Management Review,* 1996, *21*(1), 73–96.

Clift, Renee T., Veal, Mary Lou, Holland, Patricia, Johnson, Marlene, and McCarthy, Jane. *Collaborative Leadership and Shared Decision Making: Teachers, Principals, and University Professors.* New York: Teachers College Press, 1995.

Cropper, Steve. Collaborative Working and the Issue of Sustainability. In Chris Huxham (Ed.), *Creating Collaborative Advantage.* Thousand Oaks, CA: Sage, 1996.

Crosby, Barbara C., and Bryson, John M. *Leadership for the Common Good: Tackling Public Problems in a Shared Power World.* San Francisco: Jossey-Bass, 2005.

Cummings, L. L., and Bromiley, Philip. "The Organizational Trust Inventory." In Roderick M. Kramer and Tom R. Tyler (Eds.), *Trust in Organizations* (pp. 302–330). Thousand Oaks, CA: Sage, 1996.

Finn, Charles B. "Utilizing Stakeholder Strategies for Positive Collaborative Outcomes." In Chris Huxham (Ed.), *Creating Collaborative Advantage.* Thousand Oaks, CA: Sage, 1996.

Freitag, Matthias, and Winkler, Ingo. "Development of Cooperation in Regional Networks: Mechanisms of Coordination and Support

Measures." In Thars Taillieu (Ed.), *Collaborative Strategies and Multi-Organizational Partnerships*. Leuven, Belgium: Grant, 2001.

Gray, Barbara. *Collaborating: Finding Common Ground for Multiparty Problems*. San Francisco: Jossey-Bass, 1989.

Gray, Barbara. "Assessing Inter-Organizational Collaboration: Multiple Conceptions and Multiple Methods." In David Faulkner and Mark de Rond (Eds.), *Cooperative Strategy: Economic, Business, and Organizational Issues*. New York: Oxford University Press, 2000.

Gray, Barbara, and Wood, Donna. "Collaborative Alliances: Moving from Practice to Theory." *Journal of Applied Behavioral Science*, 1991, *27*(2), 3–22.

Hellriegel, Don, Slocum, John W., and Woodman, Richard W. *Organizational Behavior* (4th ed.). New York: West, 1986.

Himmelman, Arthur T. "On the Theory and Practice of Transformational Collaboration: From Social Service to Social Justice." In Chris Huxham (Ed.), *Creating Collaborative Advantage*. Thousand Oaks, CA: Sage, 1996.

Huxham, Chris. "Collaboration and Collaborative Advantage." In Chris Huxham (Ed.), *Creating Collaborative Advantage*. Thousand Oaks, CA: Sage, 1996.

Huxham, Chris, and MacDonald, David. "Introducing Collaborative Advantage: Achieving Interorganizational Effectiveness Through Meta-Strategy." *Management Decision*, 1992, *30*(3), 50–56.

Huxham, Chris, and Vangen, Siv. "Ambiguity, Complexity, and Dynamics in the Membership of Collaboration." *Human Relations*, 2000, *53*(6), 771–801.

Huxham, Chris, and Vangen, Siv. *Managing to Collaborate: The Theory and Practice of Collaborative Advantage*. New York: Routledge, 2005.

Lax, David A., and Sebenius, James K. *The Manager as Negotiator: Bargaining for Cooperation and Competitive Gain*. New York: The Free Press, 1986.

Levine, Sol, and White, Paul E. "Exchange as a Conceptual Framework for the Study of Inter-Organizational Relationships." *Administrative Science Quarterly*, 1961, *5*(4), 581–601.

Logsdon, Jeanne M. "Interests and Interdependence in the Formation of Problem-Solving Collaborations." *Journal of Applied Behavioral Science*, 1991, *27*(1), 23–37.

March, James G., and Olsen, Johan P. *Rediscovering Institutions: The Organizational Basis of Politics*. New York: The Free Press, 1989.

Mattessich, Paul W., and Monsey, Barbara R. *Collaboration—What Makes It Work*. St. Paul, MN: Amherst H. Wilder Foundation, 1992.

McCaffrey, David P., Faerman, Sue R., and Hart, David W. "The Appeal and Difficulties of Participative Systems." *Organization Science*, 1995, *6*(6), 603–627.

Meyer, John W., and Rowan, Brian. "Institutional Organizations: Formal Structure in Myth and Ceremony." *American Journal of Sociology*, 1977, *83*(2), 341–363.

Olson, Mancur. *The Logic of Collective Action: Public Goods and the Theory of Groups*. Cambridge, MA: Harvard University Press, 1971.

Ospina, Sonia, and Sag-Carranza, Angel. "Paradox and Collaboration in Coalition Work." Paper presented at the Annual Meeting of the Academy of Management, Honolulu, HI, August 2005.

Ostrom, Elinor. *Governing the Commons: The Evolution of Institutions for Collective Action*. Cambridge, MA: Cambridge University Press, 1990.

Ostrom, Elinor. "A Behavioral Approach to the Rational Choice Theory of Collective Action." *American Political Science Review*, 1998, *92*(1), 1–22.

O'Toole, Laurence J., Jr. "Rational Choice and the Public Management of Inter-Organizational Networks." In Donald E. Kettl and H. Brinton Milward (Eds.), *The State of Public Management*. Baltimore: Johns Hopkins University Press, 1996.

O'Toole, Laurence J., Jr. "Treating Networks Seriously: Practical and Research-Based Agendas in Public Administration." *Public Administration Review*, 1997, *57*(1), 45–52.

O'Toole, Laurence J., Jr., Meier, Kenneth J., and Nicholson-Crotty, Sean. "Managing Upward, Downward, and Outward: Networks, Hierarchical Relationships, and Performance." *Public Management Review*, 2005, *7*(1), 45–68.

Pasquero, Jean. "Supra-Organizational Collaboration: The Canadian Environmental Experiment." *Journal of Applied Behavioral Science*, 1991, *27*(1), 38–64.

Perry, James L., and Thomson, Ann Marie. *Civic Service: What Difference Does It Make?* Armonk, NY: M.E. Sharpe, 2004.

Pfeffer, Jeffrey. *New Directions for Organization Theory: Problems and Prospects*. New York: Oxford University Press, 1997.

Pfeffer, Jeffrey, and Salancik, Gerald R. *The External Control of Organizations: A Resource Dependence Perspective*. New York: Harper & Row, 1978.

Powell, Walter W. "Neither Market nor Hierarchy: Network Forms of Organization." In Barry M. Staw and Larry L. Cummings (Eds.), *Research in Organizational Behavior*, Vol. 12. Greenwich, CT: JAI Press, 1990.

Pressman, Jeffrey L., and Wildavsky, Aaron. *Implementation: How Great Expectations in Washington Are Dashed in Oakland* (3rd ed.). Berkeley, CA: University of California Press, 1984.

Radin, Beryl A. "Managing Across Boundaries." In Donald F. Kettl and H. Brinton Milward (Eds.), *The State of Public Management.* Baltimore: Johns Hopkins University Press, 1996.

Radin, Beryl A., Agranoff, Robert, Bowman, Ann O. M., Buntz, C. Gregory, Ott, J. Steven, Romzek, Barbara S., and Wilson, Robert H. *New Governance for Rural America: Creating Intergovernmental Partnerships.* Lawrence, KS: University Press of Kansas, 1996.

Rainey, Hal G. *Understanding and Managing Public Organizations* (3rd ed.). San Francisco: Jossey-Bass, 2003.

Ring, Peter Smith, and Van de Ven, Andrew H. "Development Processes of Cooperative Interorganizational Relationships." *Academy of Management Review*, 1994, *19*(1), 90–118.

Roberts, Nancy C., and Bradley, Raymond Trevor. "Stakeholder Collaboration and Innovation: A Study of Public Policy Initiation at the State Level." *Journal of Applied Behavioral Science*, 1991, *27*(2), 209–227.

Sagawa, Shirley, and Segal, Eli. *Common Interest, Common Good: Creating Value Through Business and Social Sector Partnerships.* Boston: Harvard Business School Press, 2000.

Selsky, J. W. "Lessons in Community Development: An Activist Approach to Stimulating Inter-Organizational Collaboration." *Journal of Applied Behavioral Science*, 1991, *27*(1), 91–115.

Sink, David. "Obstacles to Community-Based Collaboration." In Chris Huxham (Ed.), *Creating Collaborative Advantage.* Thousand Oaks, CA: Sage, 1996.

Smith, Steven Rathgeb. *Social Capital, Community Coalitions, and the Role of Institutions.* Durham, NC: Duke University, Sanford Institute of Public Policy, 1995.

Stone, Melissa M. "Exploring the Effects of Collaboration on Member Organizations: Washington County's Welfare-to-Work Partnership." *Nonprofit and Voluntary Sector Quarterly*, 2000, *29*(1), S98–S119.

Thomson, Ann Marie. *AmeriCorps Organizational Networks on the Ground: Six Case Studies of Indiana AmeriCorps Programs.* Washington, DC: Corporation for National Service, 1999.

Thomson, Ann Marie. Collaboration: Meaning and Measurement. Ph.D. dissertation, Indiana University–Bloomington, 2001a.

Thomson, Ann Marie. Unpublished field notes, 2001b.

Thomson, Ann Marie, and Miller, Ted. "Knowledge for Practice: The Meaning and Measurement of Collaboration." Paper presented at the 2002 ARNOVA Conference, Montreal, Canada, November 2002.

Thomson, Ann Marie, and Perry, James L. "Can AmeriCorps Build Communities?" *Nonprofit and Voluntary Sector Quarterly*, 1998, *27*(4), 399–420.

Tschirhart, Mary, Christensen, Robert K., and Perry, James L. "The Paradox of Branding and Collaboration." *Public Performance and Management Review*, 2005, *29*(1), 67–84.

Van de Ven, Andrew H., Emmett, Dennis C., and Koenig, Jr., Richard "Theoretical and Conceptual Issues in Inter-Organizational Theory." In Anant R. Negandhi (Ed.), *Inter-Organizational Theory*. Kent, OH: Kent State University Press, 1975.

Vigoda-Gadot, Eran. *Managing Collaboration in Public Administration: The Promise of Alliance Among Governance, Citizens, and Businesses.* Westport, CT: Praeger, 2003.

Warren, Roland L. "The Interorganizational Field as a Focus for Investigation." *Administrative Science Quarterly*, 1967, *12*, 396–419.

Warren, Roland L., Burgunder, A. F., Newton, J. W., and Rose, S. M. "The Interaction of Community Decision Organizations: Some Conceptual Considerations and Empirical Findings." In Anant R. Negandhi (Ed.), *Inter-Organizational Theory*. Kent, OH: Kent State University Press, 1975.

Williams, Paul. "The Competent Boundary Spanner." *Public Administration*, 2002, *80*(1), 103–124.

Wood, Donna, and Gray, Barbara. "Toward a Comprehensive Theory of Collaboration." *Journal of Applied Behavioral Science*, 1991, *27*(2), 139–162.

Zucker, Lynne G. "Where Do Institutional Patterns Come From?" In Lynne Zucker (Ed.), *Institutional Patterns and Organizations: Culture and Environment*. Cambridge, MA: Ballinger, 1988.

———

At time of original publishing Ann Marie Thomson was an adjunct assistant professor in the School of Public and Environmental Affairs at Indiana University-Bloomington.

At time of original publishing James L. Perry was Chancellor's Professor of Public and Environmental Affairs in the School of Public and Environmental Affairs at Indiana University-Bloomington.

PART THREE

Key Leadership Skills
Editor's Introduction

The readings in Parts I and II provided a conceptual and theoretical orientation to the meaning and processes of leadership in nonprofit and public organizations. In Part III, we pivot in another direction—toward translating theory to practice—by focusing on leadership skills. Skills are generally understood as abilities acquired by training or experience. If the first two parts of this handbook were about what Peter Drucker described as "dash," then this part most certainly focuses on "doing." How do nonprofit and public leaders translate high-minded principles and visions into reality in the arenas in which they perform?

A quandary we confront as we move from leadership theory to practice is that the skill set needed to translate broad ideas into reality grows exponentially by virtue of the greater specificity of skills in contrast to general principles. Scholars and observers have suggested, however, ways to think about skills that make them more manageable even as their numbers grow. Montgomery Van Wart's chapter on leadership theory in Part II offered one way to categorize skills. Figure 6.1 in his chapter identifies leader skills in three areas—task, people, and organization. Robert Katz (1994), in a classic *Harvard*

Business Review article, "Skills of an Effective Administrator," offered another framework for organizing skills. He proposed grouping skills into three categories: conceptual, human, and technical. I use Katz's scheme to organize the thirteen articles in Part III. Although I group skills into Katz's three categories, it is important to recognize that the leadership skills are not exclusive to any category but are likely to serve leaders in a variety of situations.

The first subset of six articles in Part III focus on Katz's *conceptual skills* category. Conceptual skills permit leaders to see the big picture—helping leaders to envision how resources, people, events, and decisions are linked in time and space. I place among the conceptual skills a leader's skills for managing strategically, achieving results, shaping culture, and leading ethically and establishing trust.

In the opening chapter of Part III, John Bryson provides a general model of what public and nonprofit leaders must consider to guide strategy development in their organizations. "The Strategy Change Cycle" presents a ten-step process for strategic planning and management as a means for identifying and responding to fundamental issues confronting nonprofit and public organizations. Although Bryson lays out the ten steps in a linear sequence, he contends the process is far more fluid and should be seen as iterative, wherein participants go back and forth between steps in the process. For leaders, the strategy process is often critical. It is the context in which vision and values can be articulated, ideas communicated, and participants develop understandings and partnerships with leaders.

If strategy skills are the foundation for leaders to create a big picture, skills for achieving results involve transporting organizations, causes, and communities toward the ends they envision. Two articles, one discussing results-oriented skills in the nonprofit sector and the other performance in the public sector, illustrate the skills for achieving results. In the first of the two articles, "Delivering on the Promise of Nonprofits," Jeffrey Bradach, Thomas Tierney, and Nan Stone make a case for how difficult it is to deliver results in the nonprofit sector because of a variety of centripetal forces working to scatter the efforts of nonprofit stakeholders. Bradach and company show how nonprofits can discipline themselves by answering four basic questions that are central to mission accomplishment.

In the second of the two articles about results-oriented skills, Harvard lecturer Robert Behn details eleven practices for leading performance in the public sector. "Performance Leadership: Eleven

Better Practices That Can Ratchet Up Performance" grows from Behn's observations of successful public managers at all levels of government. Behn begins his presentation with an important point about leaders' focus. He notes that most government organizations pursue better *systems*, but this approach is seldom effective. He contends that government needs better *practices*. Better practices, Behn argues, put public managers in the position to become performance leaders.

Although leaders have come to know the importance of culture for pursuing their visions, the skills to manage culture are seldom placed on a par with conceptual skills associated with developing strategies and achieving results. Edgar Schein, the foremost thinker about managing organizational cultures, enumerates the skills that leaders need to command to be "perpetual learners" who can examine and manage the cultures in which they are embedded. Schein's argument in "The Learning Leader as Culture Manager" is that leaders are central figures in culture formation, evolution, transformation, and destruction. The continuous nature of culture transformations in organizations requires, Schein contends, that leaders become "perpetual learners." Schein enumerates the skills and abilities that he perceives as necessary for leaders to become perpetual learners.

The final two readings in the conceptual skills segment of Part III focus broadly on the ethics of leaders and skills that they can develop to be perceived by followers as trustworthy and responsible. In "Maintaining Trust Through Integrity," Warren Bennis and Joan Goldsmith focus on mechanisms by which leaders are perceived by followers as principled and thereby worthy of their followers' trust. Bennis and Goldsmith argue that four conditions "engender trust: having a clear, articulate vision; practicing consistent empathy; behaving with reliable consistency; and acting with impeccable integrity." They employ several experiential exercises to illustrate their points about each of these conditions.

Integrity also plays an important role in Terry Cooper's "Administrative Responsibility: The Key to Administrative Ethics." Cooper is interested in specifying a systematic way for public leaders to think about responsibility. He acknowledges a frequent tension between two types of responsibility, what he calls objective and subjective responsibility. He identifies a process for leaders to discern these different senses of responsibility so that they can act with integrity, which he defines as imagining "an alternative that satisfies the need for consistency in our fundamental self-image."

Human skills, the second category of skills identified by Katz (1974), encompass a range of familiar skills that have long been associated with both management and leadership. The essence of human skills is that they are essential for fostering the cooperative activity that is at the heart of nonprofit and public enterprises. Human skills include motivating others, managing diversity, and negotiating for the public good. Four articles in Part III address these human skills.

In "Empowering People to Lead," the first of two articles about motivational skills, Bill George sets out simple norms that leaders can use to create trust and empower people. George contends that the foundation for developing trusting relationships is mutual respect. Although George does not propose a formula for establishing mutual respect, he points to several tested behaviors for which mutual trust grows—treating others as equals, being a good listener, learning from people, and sharing life stories. Once trusting relationships are created, then leaders are in positions to empower people. George again suggests some behavioral rules, among them engaging people and helping teammates, that will empower people. The combination of trusting relationships and empowered people, argues George, brings out the best in people.

In "Enlist Others: Attracting People to Common Purposes," James Kouzes and Barry Posner propose another approach to leading high performance. The key to their approach is inspiring followers by appealing to common ideals and animating the leader's vision. Appealing to common ideals has a good deal in common with parts (for example, aligning the leader's "dream" with the people's "dream") of Bill George's perspective. Kouzes and Posner's advice to animate the vision is vivid and distinctive. They urge leaders to learn to create images of the future, express emotions, and speak from the heart as skills for engendering passion and pride among followers.

Motivational skills have long been recognized as essential for the leadership function. R. Roosevelt Thomas, Jr., discusses a relatively new human skill that is increasingly important in twenty-first century nonprofit and public organizations. In "Diversity Management: An Essential Craft for Leaders," Thomas defines diversity as "the behavioral differences, similarities, and tensions that can exist among people when representation has been achieved." Thomas leaves no doubt that mastering leadership for diversity requires experience and practice. Among the skills he suggests are part of effective diversity management are the ability to analyze diversity mixtures and to decide about appropriate responses.

In the shared power world that most nonprofit and public leaders inhabit, negotiating differences—a skill that emanates from and complements diversity skills—is an incredibly important skill. In "Negotiating for the Public Good," Lisa Bingham succinctly reviews a large body of theory and research that is fundamental for leaders seeking to master negotiation skills. Bingham defines negotiating for the public good broadly to include techniques of principled negotiation, mediation, and facilitation. As she notes in her conclusion, mastery of negotiation skills to resolve differences is a far better way to pursue the public good than adversarial processes are.

Not all leaders need to possess *technical skills*, the third and final category of skills identified by Katz, but technical skills can be important for public and nonprofit leaders, particularly at lower levels of organizational hierarchies and within communities. The two skills that are taken up in the three readings that conclude Part III involve communicating with stakeholders and evaluating achievements.

Talula Cartwright and David Baldwin take up a vital communication skill, which was first introduced in Max DePree's chapter in Part I and reinforced in Kouzes and Posner's chapter earlier in Part III. "Seeing Your Way: Why Leaders Must Communicate Their Visions" revisits why and how leaders communicate their visions. The distinct contribution of Cartwright and Baldwin's chapter is that it translates ideas about transmitting leaders' visions into requisite communication skills. Leaders must pay attention to the messages they transmit, understand the audiences they seek to reach and communication channels by which they reach them, and reinforce their message frequently. Cartwright and Baldwin's chapter gives leaders an excellent template for evaluating how effectively their vision is communicated.

In "Seven Communication Tips an Effective Leader Must Have," William Kumuyi offers additional advice about communication skills for leaders. Kumuyi's chapter again emphasizes important skills distilled from research and experience about communicating in organizational settings. His logic for sharing the leadership communication skills he presents is compelling. He writes: "I'm out to share with you the factors of good communication that enhance organizational growth and stability. Factors that most leaders can testify play a crucial workplace role in calming storms, fuelling zeal and making the workforce go marching as to war."

In the concluding chapter of Part III, Salavatore Alaimo takes up another important skill for nonprofit and public leaders as public-benefit enterprises are increasingly judged by the results they achieve. "Nonprofits and Evaluation: Managing Expectations from the Leader's Perspective" takes up the issue of how nonprofit executive directors build capacity for program evaluation. He finds that human-service organization leaders who are attentive to their external and internal contexts and have the skill to effectively balance external and internal forces are better able to develop capacity for program evaluation. Given the proliferation of results-based systems [for example, the Government Performance and Results Act (GPRA) and Program Assessment Rating Tool (PART) in the federal government and United Way of America's Common Good Index] across the nonprofit and public sectors, Alaimo's conclusions are broadly relevant for leadership skills to enhance program evaluation.

The readings in Part III go a long way toward translating theory to practice by identifying abilities that can be acquired by training or experience. In the words of Peter Drucker, the skills are the "doing" that complements perfectly the "dash" to which leaders aspire. The three types of leadership skills discussed in Part III position nonprofit and public leaders to translate high-minded principles and visions into reality.

Reference

Katz, R. Skills of an effective administrator. *Harvard Business Review*, 1974, *52*, 90–102.

CHAPTER ELEVEN

The Strategy Change Cycle

An Effective Strategic Planning Approach for Nonprofit Organizations

John M. Bryson

This chapter presents an approach to strategic planning for nonprofit organizations and collaboratives. The process, called the Strategy Change Cycle, does what Poister and Streib (1999, pp. 309–310) assert strategic planning should do. Specifically, they believe strategic planning should

- Be concerned with identifying and responding to the most fundamental issues facing an organization

- Address the subjective question of purpose and the often competing values that influence mission and strategies

- Emphasize the importance of external trends and forces as they are likely to affect the organization and its mission

---

Originally published as "The Strategy Change Cycle." In Robert Herman (Ed.), *The Jossey-Bass Handbook of Nonprofit Leadership and Management* (2nd ed.). (San Francisco: Jossey-Bass, 2004).

- Attempt to be politically realistic by taking into account the concerns and preferences of internal, and especially external, stakeholders

- Rely heavily on the active involvement of senior-level managers and, in the case of nonprofits, board members, assisted by staff where needed

- Require the candid confrontation of critical issues by key participants in order to build commitment to plans

- Be action-oriented and stress the importance of developing plans for implementing strategies

- Focus on implementing decisions now in order to position the organization favorably for the future

The Strategy Change Cycle becomes a *strategic management* process—and not just a *strategic planning* process—to the extent that it is used to link planning and implementation and to manage an organization in a strategic way on an ongoing basis (Poister and Streib, 1999). The Strategy Change Cycle draws on a considerable body of research and practical experience, applying it specifically to nonprofit organizations (Bryson, 2004a).

Two quotes help make the point that strategic thinking, acting, and learning are more important than any particular approach to strategic planning. Consider first a humorous statement from Daniel Boone, the famous American frontiersman: "No, I can't say as I ever was lost, but once I was bewildered pretty bad for three days" (Faragher, 1992, p. 65). When you are lost in the wilderness—*bewildered*—no fixed plan will do. You must think, act, and learn your way to safety. Boone had a destination of at least a general sort in mind, but not a route. He had to wander around reconnoitering, gathering information, assessing directions, trying out options, and in general thinking, acting, and learning his way to where he wanted to be. In Karl Weick's words (1979), he had to "act thinkingly," which often meant acting first and then thinking about it. Or as Bob Behn (1988) put it, he had to "manage by groping along." Ultimately—but not initially, or even much before he got there—Boone was able to establish a clear destination and a route that worked to get him there. Boone thus had a strategy of purposeful wandering—because although he was not exactly lost, he had to work at finding himself where he wanted to be. Wandering with a purpose is therefore an important aspect of strategic planning, in which thinking, acting, and learning matter most.

Next, consider a quote from poet and essayist Diane Ackerman: "Make-believe is at the heart of play, and also at the heart of so much that passes for work. Let's make-believe we can shoot a rocket to the moon" (1999, p. 7). She makes the point that almost anything is possible with enough imagination, ambition, direction, intelligence, education and training, organization, resources, will, and staying power. We have been to the moon, Mars, the rings of Jupiter, and a host of other places. We as citizens of the world have won world wars and cold wars, ended depressions, virtually eliminated smallpox, unraveled the human genome, watched a reasonably united and integrated Europe emerge, and seen democracy spread where it was not thought possible. Now let's think about having a good job for everyone, adequate food and housing for everyone, universal health care coverage, drastically reduced crime, effective educational systems, secure pensions and retirements, a dramatic reduction in greenhouse gas emissions, the elimination of weapons of mass destruction, the elimination of HIV/AIDS, the realization in practice of the Universal Declaration on Human Rights, more peace and cooperation on a global scale, and so on. And then let us get to work. We can create institutions, policies, projects, products, and services of lasting public value by drawing on our diverse talents—and have done so again and again throughout history (Boyte and Kari, 1996), and clearly, nonprofit organizations have an important role to play (Letts, Ryan, and Grossman, 1999; Light, 2002). We can use strategic planning to help us think, act, and learn strategically—to figure out what we should want, why, and how to get it. Think of strategic planning as the organization of hope, as what makes hope reasonable (Forester, 1989; Baum, 1997).

A TEN-STEP STRATEGIC PLANNING PROCESS

Now, with the caution that strategic thinking, acting, and learning matter most, let us proceed to a more detailed exploration of the ten-step Strategy Change Cycle. The process, presented in Figure 11.1, is more orderly, deliberative, and participative than the process followed by an essayist such as Ackerman or a wanderer like Boone. The process is designed to "create public value" (Moore,

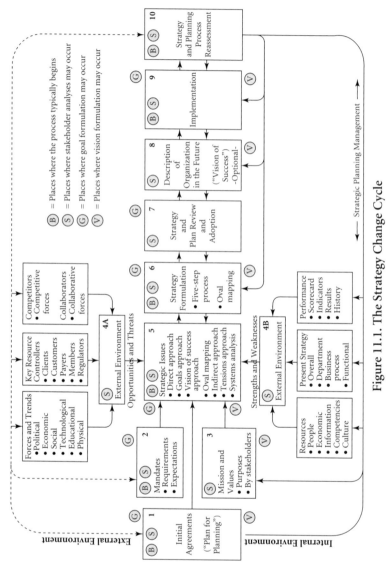

Figure 11.1. The Strategy Change Cycle

Source: Copyright © 1995, 2003 by John M. Bryson.

2000) through fashioning an effective mission, meeting applicable mandates, organizing participation, creating ideas for strategic interventions, building a winning coalition, and implementing strategies. The Strategy Change Cycle may be thought of as a *process strategy* (Mintzberg, Ahlstrand, and Lampel, 1998) or *processual model of decision making* (Barzelay, 2001), whereby a leadership group manages the process but leaves much of the content of what the strategies will be to others. The ten steps (or occasions for dialogue and decision) are as follows:

1. Initiate and agree on a strategic planning process.
2. Identify organizational mandates.
3. Clarify organizational mission and values.
4. Assess the external and internal environments to identify strengths, weaknesses, opportunities, and threats.
5. Identify the strategic issue facing the organization.
6. Formulate strategies to manage the issues.
7. Review and adopt the strategic plan or plans.
8. Establish an effective organizational vision.
9. Develop an effective implementation process.
10. Reassess strategies and the strategic planning process.

These ten steps should lead to actions, results, evaluation, and learning. It must be emphasized that actions, results, evaluative judgments, and learning should emerge at each step in the process. In other words, implementation and evaluation should not wait until the "end" of the process but should be an integral and ongoing part of it.

The process is applicable nonprofit organizations and collaboratives. The only general requirements are a "dominant coalition" (Thompson, 1967), or at least a "coalition of the willing" (Cleveland, 2002), able to sponsor and follow the process, and a process champion willing to push it. For small nonprofit organizations, many well-informed strategic planning teams that are familiar with and believe in the process should be able to complete most of the steps in a two- or three-day retreat, with an additional one-day meeting scheduled three to four weeks later to review the resulting strategic plan. Responsibility for preparing the plan can be delegated to a planner assigned to work with the team, or the organization's chief executive may choose to draft the plan personally. Additional reviews and signoffs by key decision-makers might take additional time. Extra time might also be necessary to secure information or advice for specific parts of the plan, especially its recommended strategies. For large organizations, however, more time and effort are likely to be needed for the process. And when applied to a collaborative, the effort is likely to be considerably more time-consuming in order to promote the involvement of substantial numbers of leaders, organizations, and perhaps members or citizens (Huxham, 2003).

Note that, in practice, the Strategy Change Cycle bears little resemblance to the caricature of strategic planning occasionally found in the literature as a rigid, formal, detached process (see Mintzberg, Ahlstrand, and Lampel, 1998). Instead, the Strategy Change Cycle is intended to enhance strategic thinking, acting, and learning; to engage key actors with what is, as well as with what can be; to engage with the important details while abstracting the strategic message in them; and to link strategy formulation with implementation in wise, technically workable, and politically intelligent ways.

Step 1: Initiating and Agreeing on a Strategic Planning Process

The purpose of the first step is to negotiate agreement among key internal (and perhaps external) decision-makers or opinion leaders about the overall strategic planning effort and the key planning steps. The support and commitment of key decision-makers are vital if strategic planning in an organization is to succeed. Further, the involvement of key decision-makers outside the organization is usually crucial to the success of nonprofit programs if implementation will involve multiple parties and organizations (Eden and Ackermann, 1998; Huxham, 2003; Light, 1998; Nutt and Backoff, 1992).

Obviously, some person or group must initiate the process. One of the initiators' first tasks is to identify exactly who the key decision-makers are. The next task is to identify which persons, groups, units, or organizations should be involved in the effort. These two tasks will require some preliminary stakeholder analysis, which we will discuss in more detail shortly. The initial agreement will be negotiated with at least some of these decision-makers, groups, units, or organizations. In practice, a *series* of agreements must typically be struck among various parties as support for the process builds and key stakeholders and decision-makers sign on. Strategic planning for a nonprofit organization or collaborative is especially likely to work well if an effective policymaking body is in place to oversee the effort.

The agreement itself should cover:

- The purpose of the effort
- Preferred steps in the process
- The form and timing of reports
- The role, functions, and membership of any group or committee empowered to oversee the effort, such as a strategic planning coordinating committee (SPCC)
- The role, functions, and membership of the strategic planning team
- The commitment of necessary resources to proceed with the effort
- Any important limitations or boundaries on the effort

As noted, at least some stakeholder analysis work will be needed in order to figure out whom to include in the series of initial agreements. A *stakeholder* is defined as any person, group, or organization that can place a claim on an organization's (or other entity's) attention, resources, or output or is affected by that output. Examples of a nonprofit organization's stakeholders include clients or customers, third-party payers or funders, employees, the board of directors, members, volunteers, other nonprofit organizations providing complementary services or involved as partners in joint ventures or projects, banks holding mortgages or notes, and suppliers.

Attention to stakeholder concerns is crucial: *the key to success in nonprofit organizations and collaboratives is the satisfaction of key stakeholders* (Light, 1998; Moore, 2000). A stakeholder analysis is a way for the organization's decision-makers and planning team to immerse themselves in the networks and politics surrounding the organization. An understanding of the relationships—actual or potential—that help define the organization's context can provide valuable clues to identifying strategic issues and developing effective strategy (Bryson, 2004b; Moore, 2000). In this regard, note that the stakeholder definition is deliberately quite broad for both practical and ethical reasons. Thinking broadly, at least initially, about who the stakeholders are is a way of opening people's eyes to the various webs of relationships within which the organization exists (Feldman and Khademian, 2002) and of ensuring that the organization is alerted to its ethical and democratic accountability responsibilities, since they always involve clarifying *who* and *what* counts (Behn, 2001; Mitchell, Agle, and Wood, 1997).

For many nonprofit organizations, the label "customer" will be given to their key stakeholder, particularly if an organization is trying to "reinvent" itself (Osborne and Plastrik, 1997, 2000), "reengineer" its operations (Cohen and Eimicke, 1998; Hammer and Champy, 1993), or employ continuous improvement processes (Cohen and Eimicke, 1998). The customer label can be useful, particularly for organizations that need to improve their "customer service." In other situations, the customer language can actually be problematic. One danger is that focusing on a single "customer" may lead these organizations inadvertently to ignore other important stakeholder groups. Another danger is that the customer label can undermine the values and virtues of active citizenship that many nonprofit organizations are trying to promote (de Leon and Denhardt, 2000; Denhardt and Denhardt, 2000). In addition, many community-based nonprofit organizations and those relying on government funding also face very complex stakeholder environments.

The organizers of the planning effort should count on using several different techniques, including what I call the "basic stakeholder analysis technique" (Bryson, 2004a, 2004b). This technique requires the strategic planning team to brainstorm a list of who the organization's stakeholders are, what their criteria are for judging the performance of the organization (that is, what their "stake" is in the organization or its output), and how well the organization performs against those criteria *from the stakeholders' points of view*. If there is time, additional steps (perhaps involving additional analysis techniques) should be considered, including understanding how the stakeholders influence the organization, identifying what the organization needs from its various stakeholders (money, staff, political support), and determining in general how important the various stakeholders are. Looking ahead, a stakeholder analysis will help clarify whether the organization needs to have different missions and perhaps different strategies for different stakeholders, whether it should seek to have its mandates changed, and in general what its strategic issues are. Indeed, planners should expect to perform stakeholder analyses of various kinds at various points in the process as a way of understanding what stakeholders want or need and how stakeholder support can be generated (see Figure 11.1) (Bryson, 2004b).

Step 2: Identifying Organizational Mandates

The formal and informal mandates placed on the organization consist of the various "musts" it confronts, the requirements, restrictions, and expectations it faces. It is surprising how few organizations know precisely what they are—and are not—formally mandated to do. Typically, few members of any organization have ever read, for example, the relevant legislation, policies, ordinances, charters, articles, and contracts that outline the organization's formal mandates. Many organizational members also do not understand the informal mandates—which are primarily political in the broadest sense—that the organization faces. It may not be surprising, then, that most organizations make one, two, or all of three fundamental mistakes. First, by not articulating or learning what they must do, they are unlikely to do it. Second, they may believe they are more tightly constrained in their actions than they actually are. And third, they may assume that if they are not explicitly told to do something, they are not allowed to do it.

Step 3: Clarifying Organizational Mission and Values

An organization's mission, or purpose, in tandem with its mandates, provides the organization's raison d'être, the social justification for its existence. An organization's mission and mandates also point the way toward the ultimate organizational end of creating public value. For a nonprofit organization, this means that there must be identifiable social or political demands or needs that the organization seeks to fill in a way that accords with its nonprofit status (Bryce, 2000). Viewed in this light, nonprofit organizations must always be seen as a means to an end, not as an end in and of themselves. For a collaborative, it means identifying the collaborative advantage to be gained by working together—that is, what can be accomplished together that creates public value that cannot be achieved alone (Huxham, 2003).

Identifying the mission, however, does more than merely justify the organization's existence. Clarifying purpose can eliminate a great deal of unnecessary conflict in an organization and can help channel discussion and activity productively (Nutt, 2002; Terry, 2001; Thompson, 2001). Agreement on purpose also defines the arenas in which the organization will collaborate or compete and, at least in broad outline, charts the future course of the organization. Agreement on purpose thus serves as a kind of "primary framework" (Bryant, 2003; Goffman 1986) that bounds the plausibility and acceptability of arguments. Agreement on purpose can go even further and provide a kind of premise control that constrains thinking, learning, and acting (Perrow, 1986; Weick, 1995) and even legitimacy (Suchman, 1995). Moreover, an important and socially justifiable mission is a source of inspiration and guidance to key stakeholders, particularly employees (Kouzes and Posner, 2002; Weiss and Piderit, 1999). Indeed, it is doubtful if any organization ever achieved greatness or excellence without a basic consensus among its key stakeholders on an inspiring mission (Collins and Porras, 1997; Light, 1998).

Some careful stakeholder analysis work should precede development or modification of a mission statement so that attention to purpose can be informed by thinking about purpose *for whom*. If the purposes of key stakeholders are not served, the organization may be engaging in what historian Barbara Tuchman (1984) aptly calls "folly." The mission statement itself might be very short, perhaps not more than a sentence or a slogan. But development of the mission statement should grow out of lengthy dialogue about the organization's identity, its abiding purpose, desired responses to key stakeholders, its philosophy and core values, and its ethical standards. These discussions may also provide a basic outline for a description of the organization in the future, or its "vision of success," described in step 8. Considerable intermediate work is necessary, however, before a complete vision of success can be articulated.

Step 4: Assessing the Organization's External and Internal Environments

The planning team should explore the environment outside the organization to identify the opportunities and threats (or more euphemistically, the challenges) the organization faces (step 4a). It should explore the environment inside the organization to identify strengths and weaknesses (step 4b). Basically, "outside" factors are those not under the organization's control, while "inside" factors are those that are (Pfeffer and Salancik, 1978). Opportunities and threats are usually (though not necessarily) more about the future than about the present, whereas strengths and weaknesses are about the present and not the future (Nutt and Backoff, 1992).

Monitoring a variety of forces and trends, including political, economic, social, educational, technological, and physical environmental ones, can help planners and decision-makers discern opportunities and threats. Unfortunately, organizations all too often focus only on the negative or threatening aspects of these changes and not on the opportunities they present, so care must be taken to ensure a balanced view (Borins, 1998; Dutton and Jackson, 1987; Nutt, 2001). In other words, attending to threats and weaknesses should be seen as an opportunity to build strengths and improve performance (Weick and Sutcliffe, 2001).

Besides monitoring trends and events, the strategic planning team also should monitor various important external stakeholder groups, including especially those that affect resource flows (directly or indirectly). These groups would include customers, clients, payers or funders, dues-paying members, regulators, and relevant policy bodies. The team also should attend to competitors, competitive forces, and possible sources of competitive advantage; as well as to collaborators, collaborative forces, and potential sources of collaborative advantage.

The organization might construct various scenarios to explore alternative futures in the external environment, a practice typical of much strategic planning in large private-sector organizations. Scenarios are particularly good at demonstrating how various forces and trends are likely to interact, which are amenable to organizational influence, and which are not. Scenarios also offer an effective way of challenging the organization's "official future" when necessary. The official future is the presumed or taken-for-granted future that makes current strategies sensible. Organizations unwilling to challenge this future are the ones most likely to be blindsided by changes (Schwartz, 1991; van der Heijden and others, 2002).

Members of an organization's governing body (particularly if they are elected) may be better at identifying and assessing external threats and opportunities (especially present ones) than the organization's employees. This is partly due to a governing board's responsibility for relating an organization to its external environment and vice versa

(Carver, 1997; Scott, 1987). Unfortunately, neither governing boards nor employees usually do a systematic or effective job of external scanning. As a result, most organizations are like ships trying to navigate troubled or treacherous waters without benefit of human lookouts, global positioning systems, radar, or sonar. All too often, the result is unwelcome surprises (Weick and Sutcliffe, 2001).

Because of this, both employees and governing board members should consider relying on a somewhat formal external assessment process to supplement their informal efforts. The technology of external assessment is fairly simple and allows organizations to cheaply, pragmatically, and effectively keep tabs on things that are happening in the larger world that are likely to have an effect on the organization and the pursuit of its mission. Clip services, discussion groups, and periodic retreats, for example, might be used to explore forces and trends and their potential impact. The key, however, is to avoid being captured by existing categories of classification and search, since they tend to formalize and routinize the past rather than open one to the surprises of the future (Mintzberg, Ahlstrand, and Lampel, 1998; Weick and Sutcliffe, 2001).

Attention to opportunities and threats, along with a stakeholder analysis, can be used to identify the organization's "critical success factors" (Johnson and Scholes, 2002). These may overlap with mandates, in the sense that they are the things the organization must do, or criteria it must meet, in order for it to be successful in the eyes of its key stakeholders, especially those in the external environment. Ideally, the organization will excel in these areas, and it must do so in order to outperform or stave off competitors.

To identify internal strengths and weaknesses, the organization might monitor resources (inputs), present strategy (process), and performance (outputs). Most nonprofit organizations, in my experience, have volumes of information on many of their inputs, such as salaries, supplies, physical plant, and full-time equivalent personnel. Unfortunately, too few organizations have a very clear idea of their philosophy, core values, distinctive competencies, and culture, a crucial set of inputs for both ensuring stability and managing change.

Organizations also tend to have an unclear idea of their present strategy, either overall, by subunit, or by function. And typically, they cannot say enough about their outputs, let alone the effects, or outcomes, those outputs create for clients, customers, or payers, although this, too, is changing. The difficulties of measuring performance are well known (Kaplan, 2001; Osborne and Plastrik, 2000), but regardless of the difficulties, organizations are continually challenged to demonstrate effective performance to their stakeholders.

In this regard, some nonprofit organizations have been able to pull their input, process, and outcome measures together in the form of a "balanced scorecard" (BSC) that shows, in effect, the organization's "theory of action" and allows it to monitor how it is doing in terms of the theory's components (Kaplan, 2001; Niven, 2003). BSCs are likely to become far more widely used in the future by nonprofit organizations. Table 11.1 presents a BSC for the United Way of Southeastern New England. The BSC identifies desired financial, customer, and internal process outcomes and strategic objectives designed to help produce the outcomes. Many BSCs also include a category of learning and growth outcomes (Niven, 2003).

A lack of performance information presents problems both for the organization and for its stakeholders. Stakeholders judge an organization according to the criteria *they* choose, which are not necessarily the same criteria the organization would choose. For external stakeholders in particular, these criteria typically relate to performance. If an organization cannot effectively meet its stakeholders' performance criteria, then regardless of its "inherent" worth, the stakeholders are likely to withdraw their support. An absence of performance information may also create—or harden—major organizational conflicts. Without performance criteria and information, there is no way to objectively evaluate the relative effectiveness of alternative strategies, resource allocations, organizational designs, and distributions of power. As a result, organizational conflicts are likely to occur more often than they should, serve narrow partisan interests, and be resolved in ways that don't further the organization's mission (Flyvbjerg, 1998; Terry, 1993).

A consideration of the organization's strengths and weaknesses can also lead to an identification of its "distinctive competencies" (Selznick, 1957), or what have been termed more recently "core competencies" (Johnson and Scholes, 2002; Prahalad and Hamel, 1990) or "capabilities" (Stalk, Evans, and Shulman, 1992). These are the organization's strongest abilities, or the most effective strategies and actions, or resources (broadly conceived), on which it can draw routinely to perform well. What makes these abilities "distinctive" is the inability of others to replicate them easily, if at all, because of the way they are interlinked with one another (Eden and Ackermann, 2000).

Outcomes	Strategic Objectives
Financial	
External growth	Increase net amount of funds raised
Internal stability	Balance internal income and expenses to maintain our 100 percent guarantee to others
Community building	Increase amount of funds that go to services
	Increase amount of funds that go to proprietary products
Customer	
Customer satisfaction	Recognition, ease of giving
Market growth	Products that customers care about and that will improve the community
Customer retention	Information on results; quality, timely service
Internal	
Key internal business processes	Improve key internal processes in the following areas:
	• Fundraising • Fund distribution • Community building • Information processing and communications • Pledge processing • Product development • Volunteer and staff development • Customer service • Interdepartmental communications
Innovative products	Develop a research and development process to come up with new, innovative products
Viable product line	Develop a consistent process for evaluating existing products and services

Table 11.1.   Balanced Scorecard for the United Way of Southeastern New England

Source: Kaplan, 2001. Used with permission of United Way of Rhode Island (formerly United Way of Southeastern New England).

Step 5: Identifying the Strategic Issues the Organization Must Face

Together the first four elements of the process lead to the fifth, the identification of strategic issues. *Strategic issues* are fundamental policy questions or critical challenges affecting the organization's mandates, mission and values, product or service level and mix, clients, users or payers, cost, financing, organization, or management. Finding the best way to frame these issues typically requires considerable wisdom, dialogue, and deep understanding of organizational purposes, operations, stakeholder interests, and external demands and possibilities. The first four steps of the process are designed deliberately to slow things down so that there is enough information and interaction for the needed wisdom to emerge. The process is designed, in other words, to "unfreeze" people's thinking (Dalton, 1970; Lewin, 1951) so that knowledge exploration, development, and learning might occur (Crossan, Lane, and White, 1999; March, 1991). This knowledge will be exploited in this and later phases.

Strategic planning focuses on achieving the best "fit" between an organization and its environment. Attention to mandates and the external environment can therefore be thought of as planning from the outside in. Attention to mission and organizational values and the internal environment can be considered planning from the inside out. Usually, it is vital that pressing strategic issues be dealt with expeditiously and effectively if the organization is to survive and prosper. An organization that does not respond to a strategic issue can expect undesirable results from a threat or a missed opportunity (or both).

The iterative nature of the strategic planning process often becomes apparent in this step when participants find that information generated or discussed in earlier steps presents itself again as part of a strategic issue. For example, many strategic planning teams begin strategic planning with the belief that they know what their organization's mission is. They often find out in this step, however, that one of the key issues their organization faces is determining exactly what its mission ought to be. In other words, if the organization's present mission is found to be inappropriate, given the team members' new understanding of the situation the organization faces, a new mission must be selected and embraced.

Strategic issues, virtually by definition, involve conflicts of one sort or another. The conflicts may involve ends (what), means (how or how much), philosophy (why), location (where), timing (when), and who might be advantaged or disadvantaged by different ways of resolving the issue (who). For the issues to be raised and resolved effectively, the organization must be prepared to deal with the almost inevitable conflicts that will occur. Conflict, shifts in understanding, and shifts in preferences will all evoke participants' emotions (Bryant, 2003; Weick, 1995). It is therefore in this stage that the importance of emotion will become dramatically apparent, along with the concomitant need for "emotional intelligence" on the part of participants if the emotions are to be dealt with effectively (Goleman, 1995; Goleman, Boyatzis, and McKee, 2002; Heifetz and Laurie, 1997).

A statement of a strategic issue should contain three elements. First, the issue should be described succinctly, preferably in a single paragraph. The issue should be framed as a question that the organization can do something about. If the organization cannot do anything about it, it is best not to think of it as an issue for the organization; it is simply a *condition* (Wildavsky, 1979). An organization's attention is limited enough without wasting it on issues it cannot address effectively. The question also should have more than one answer, as a way of broadening the search for viable strategies. Too often organizations focus too quickly on a specific solution, without first learning more about the context within which the issue arose and without exploring the full range of possible responses (Eden and Ackermann, 1998; Nutt, 2002).

Second, the factors that make the issue a fundamental challenge should be listed. In particular, what is it about the organization's mandates, mission, values, internal strengths and weaknesses, and external opportunities and threats that make this a strategic issue for the organization? Listing these factors will become useful in the next step, strategy development. Every effective strategy builds on strengths and takes advantage of opportunities while minimizing or overcoming weaknesses and threats. The framing of strategic issues is therefore very important because it will provide much of the basis for the issues' resolution (Eden and Ackermann, 1998; Bryant, 2003; Nutt, 2002).

Finally, the planning team should prepare a statement of the consequences of failure to address the issue. This will help organizational leaders decide just how strategic or important various issues are. If no consequences will ensue from failure to address a particular issue, it is not a strategic issue (at least not yet). At the other extreme, if the organization will be destroyed or will miss a valuable opportunity by failing to address a particular issue, the issue is clearly *very* strategic and is worth attending to immediately. Thus the step of identifying strategic issues is aimed at focusing organizational attention on what is truly important for the survival, prosperity, and effectiveness of the organization.

Once statements of the issues are prepared, the organization will know what kinds of issues it faces and just how strategic they are. There are several kinds of strategic issues. *Developmental issues* have the potential to alter the organization and its "core business" but have no real precedent (Nutt, 2001). They involve a fundamental change in products or services, customers or clients, service or distribution channels, sources of revenue, identity or image, or some other aspect of the organization for which there is no real organizational precedent.

Nondevelopmental issues involve far less ambiguity because most of the aspects of the organization's overall strategy will not change. Most existing decision premises can be presumed still to apply (Nutt, 2001).

Then there are issues that require an immediate response and therefore cannot be handled in a more routine way. There are issues that are coming up on the horizon and are likely to require some action in the future or perhaps some action now; for the most part, these issues can be handled as part of the organization's regular strategic planning cycle. And finally, there are issues that require no organizational action at present but must be continuously monitored.

There are seven basic approaches to the identification of strategic issues. The *direct approach* goes straight from a discussion of mandates, mission, and SWOTs (strengths, weaknesses, opportunities, and threats) to the identification of strategic issues. The *indirect approach* begins with brainstorming about several different sets of options before identifying issues. The sets of options include actions the organization could take to meet stakeholders' performance expectations; to build on strengths, take advantage of opportunities, and minimize or overcome weaknesses and threats; and to incorporate any other important aspect of background studies or reports or present circumstances. Each option is put on a separate card or self-adhesive label. These options are then merged into a single set of potential actions, and the actions are regrouped into clusters, with each cluster representing a potential issue category. A category label is developed for each cluster that identifies the subject or theme of the cluster.

The *goals approach* starts with goals (or performance indicators) and then identifies issues that must be addressed before the goals (or indicators) can be achieved. And the *"vision of success" approach* starts with at least a sketch of a vision of success in order to identify issues that must be dealt with before the vision can be realized. This approach is probably necessary in situations involving developmental decisions—where fundamental change is needed but the organization lacks a precedent (Nutt, 2001). For example, development of a vision is often recommended for organizations about to engage in a serious way in e-commerce (Abramson and Means, 2001).

The *oval mapping approach* grew out of the Strategic Options Development and Analysis (SODA) method developed by Colin Eden, Fran Ackermann, and their associates (Eden and Ackermann, 2001; Bryson, Ackermann, Eden, and Finn, 2004). Oval mapping involves creation of word-and-arrow diagrams in which ideas about actions the organization might take, how it might take them, and why, are linked by arrows indicating the cause-and-effect or influence relationships between them (see Eden and Ackermann, 1998, and especially Bryson, Ackermann, Eden, and Finn, 2004). In other words, the arrows indicate that action A may cause or influence B, which in turn may cause or influence C, and so on; if the organization does A, it can expect to produce outcome B, which may in turn be expected to produce outcome C. These "maps" can consist of hundreds of interconnected relationships, showing differing areas of interest and their relationships to one another. The approach's name comes from the fact that ideas are usually written on oval-shaped pieces of paper, one idea per oval, and then placed on a flip-chart-sheet-covered wall; arrows linking ideas are then drawn on the flip-chart sheets.

Important clusters of potential actions may indicate strategic issues. A strategy in response would be to determine actions to undertake in the issue area, how to undertake them, and why (see step 6). The approach is particularly useful when participants are having trouble making sense of complex issue areas, when time is short, when the emphasis must be on action, and when commitment on the part of those involved is particularly important.

The *tensions approach* was developed by Nutt and Backoff (1992) and elaborated in Nutt, Backoff, and Hogan (2000). These authors argue that there are always four basic tensions around any strategic issue, in various combinations. These tensions involve human resources, especially *equity* concerns; *innovation and change*; maintenance of *tradition*; and *productivity improvement*. The authors suggest critiquing the way issues are framed using these tensions separately and in combination in order to find the best way to frame the issue. The critiques may need to run through several cycles before the wisest way to frame the issue is found. Finally, a *systems analysis approach* can be used to help discern the best way to frame issues when the system contains complex feedback effects and must be formally modeled in order to understand it (Senge, 1990; Sterman, 2000).

By stating that there are seven different approaches to the identification of strategic issues, I may raise the hackles of some planning theorists and practitioners who believe that one should always start with issues or goals or vision or analysis. I argue that what will work best depends on the situation and that the wise planner should choose an approach accordingly.

Step 6: Formulating Strategies and Plans to Manage the Issues

A *strategy* is defined as a pattern of purposes, policies, programs, actions, decisions, or resource allocations that define what an organization is, what it does, and why it does it. Strategies can vary by level, function, and time frame. Strategies are developed to deal with the issues identified in step 5.

This definition is intentionally broad in order to focus attention on the creation of consistency across *rhetoric* (what people say), *choices* (what people decide and are willing to pay for), *actions* (what people do), and the *consequences* of those actions. Effective strategy formulation and implementation processes link rhetoric, choices, actions, and consequences into reasonably coherent and consistent patterns across levels, functions, and time (Eden and Ackermann, 1998). They will also be tailored to fit an organization's culture, even if the purpose of the strategy or strategies is to reconfigure that culture in some way (Johnson and Scholes, 2002). Draft strategies, and perhaps drafts of formal strategic plans, will be formulated in this step to articulate desired patterns. They may also be reviewed and adopted at the end of this step if the strategic planning process is relatively simple and small-scale and involves a single organization. (Such a process would merge this step with step 7.)

A FIVE-PART STRATEGY DEVELOPMENT PROCESS. There are numerous approaches to strategy development (Bryson, 2001, 2003; Bryson and Anderson, 2000; Holman and Devane, 1999). I generally favor either of two approaches. The first is a fairly speedy five-part process based on the work of the Institute of Cultural Affairs (Spencer, 1996). The second can be used if there is a need or desire to articulate more clearly the relationships among multiple options, to show how they fit together as part of a pattern.

The first part of the five-part process begins with identification of practical alternatives and dreams or visions for resolving the strategic issues. Each option should be phrased in action terms; that is, it should begin with an imperative, such as *do, get, buy,* or *achieve.* Phrasing options in action terms helps make the options seem more "real" to participants.

Next, the planning team should enumerate the barriers to achieving those alternatives, dreams, or visions. Focusing on barriers at this point is not typical of most strategic planning processes, but doing so is one way of ensuring that any strategies developed deal with implementation difficulties directly rather than haphazardly.

Once alternatives, dreams, and visions, along with barriers to their realization, have been listed, the team develops major proposals for achieving the alternatives, dreams, or visions, either directly or else indirectly by overcoming the barriers. (Alternatively, the team might solicit proposals from key organizational units, various stakeholder groups, task forces, or selected individuals.)

After major proposals have been submitted, two final tasks remain in order to develop effective strategies. Actions to implement the major proposals that must be taken over the next two to three years must be identified. And finally, a detailed work program for the next six to twelve months must be spelled out to implement the actions. These last two tasks shade over into the work of step 9, but that is good, because strategies should always be developed with implementation in mind. As Mintzberg (1994, p. 25) explains, "Every failure of implementation is, by definition, also a failure of formulation." In some circumstances, steps 6 and 9 may be merged—for example, when a single organization is planning for itself. In addition, in collaborative settings, implementation details must often be worked out first by the various parties before they are willing to commit to shared strategic plans (Bardach, 1998; Bryant, 2003; Innes, 1996). In such situations, implementation planning may have to precede strategy or plan adoption.

USING OVAL MAPPING TO STRUCTURE RELATIONSHIPS AMONG STRATEGIC OPTIONS TO DEVELOP STRATEGIES. Developing strategies using the oval mapping process builds on the oval mapping approach to strategic issue identification; if strategic issues were developed using the oval mapping method, the transition from issues to strategy development is quite easy (Bryson, Ackermann, Eden, and Finn, 2004).

The method involves making a list of multiple options to address each strategic issue, on which each option is again phrased in imperative, action, terms. The options are then linked by arrows indicating which options cause or influence the achievement of other options. An option can be a part of more than one chain. The result is a "map" of action-to-outcome (cause-and-effect, means-to-an-end) relationships; the options toward the end of a chain of arrows are possible goals or perhaps even mission statements. Presumably, these goals can be achieved by accomplishing at least some of the actions leading up to them, although additional analysis and work on the arrow chains may be necessary to determine and clearly articulate action-to-outcome relationships. The option maps can be reviewed and revised, and particular action-to-outcome chains can be selected as strategies. Additional detail and numerous examples will be found in Bryson, Ackermann, Eden, and Finn (2004).

An effective strategy must meet several criteria. It must be technically workable and politically acceptable to key stakeholders, and it must fit the organization's philosophy and core values. Further, it should be ethical, moral, and legal and should further the creation of public value. It must also deal with the strategic issue it was supposed to address. All too often, I have seen strategies that were technically, politically, morally, ethically, and legally impeccable but did not deal with the issues they were presumed to address. Effective strategies thus meet a rather severe set of tests. Careful, thoughtful dialogue—and often bargaining and negotiation—among key decision-makers who have adequate information and are politically astute is usually necessary before strategies can be developed that meet these tests. Some of this work must occur in this step, and some is likely to occur in the next step.

Step 7: Reviewing and Adopting the Strategies and Plan

Once strategies have been formulated, the planning team may need to obtain an official decision to adopt them and proceed with their implementation. The same is true if a formal strategic plan has been prepared. This decision will help affirm the desired changes and move the organization toward "refreezing" in the new pattern (Dalton, 1970; Lewin, 1951), where the knowledge exploration of previous steps can be exploited (March, 1991). When strategies and plans are developed for a single organization, particularly a small one, this step may actually merge with step 6. But a separate step will likely be necessary when strategic planning is undertaken for a large organization, network of organizations, or community. The SPCC will need to approve the resulting strategies or plan; relevant policymaking bodies and other implementing groups and organizations are also likely to have to approve the strategies or plan, or at least parts of it, in order for implementation to proceed effectively.

To secure passage of any strategy or plan, it will be necessary to continue to pay attention to the goals, concerns, and interests of all key internal and external stakeholders. Finding or creating inducements that can be traded for support can also be useful. But there are numerous ways to defeat any proposal in formal decision-making arenas. So it is important for the plan to be sponsored and championed by actors whose knowledge of how to negotiate the intricacies of the relevant arenas can help ensure passage (Bryson and Crosby, 1992).

Step 8: Establishing an Effective Organizational Vision

In this step, the organization develops a description of what it should look like once it has successfully implemented its strategies and achieved its full potential. This description is the organization's "vision of success." Few organizations have such a description or vision, yet the importance of such descriptions has long been recognized by well-managed companies, organizational psychologists, and management theorists (Collins and Porras, 1997; Kouzes and Posner, 2002). Such descriptions can include the organization's mission, its values and philosophy, basic strategies, its performance criteria, some important decision rules, and the ethical standards expected of all employees.

The description, to the extent that it is widely circulated and discussed within the organization, allows organizational members to know what is expected of them without constant managerial oversight. Members are free to act on their own initiative on the organization's behalf to an extent not otherwise possible. The result should be a mobilization of members' energy toward pursuing the organization's purposes and a reduced need for direct supervision (Nutt, 2001).

Some people might question why developing a vision of success comes at this point in the process rather than much earlier. There are two basic answers to this question. First, it does not have to come here for all organizations. Some organizations are able to develop a clearly articulated, agreed-on vision of success much earlier in the process. And some organizations start with "visioning" exercises in order to develop enough of a consensus on purposes and values to guide issue identification and strategy formulation efforts. Figure 11.1 therefore indicates the many different points at which participants may find it useful to develop some sort of guiding vision. Some processes may start with a visionary statement. Others may use visions to help them figure out what the strategic issues are or to help them develop strategies. And still others may use visions to convince key decision-makers to adopt strategies or plans or to guide implementation efforts. The farther along in the process a vision is found, the more likely it is to be more fully articulated.

Second, most organizations will typically not be able to develop a detailed vision of success until they have gone through several iterations of strategic planning—if they are able to develop a vision at all. A challenging yet achievable vision embodies the tension between what an organization wants and what it can have (Senge, 1990). Often several cycles of strategic planning are necessary before organizational members know what they want, what they can have, and the difference between the two. A vision that motivates people will be challenging enough to spur action yet not so impossible to achieve that it demotivates and demoralizes people. Most organizations, in other words, will find that their visions of success are likely to serve more as a guide for strategy implementation than for strategy formulation.

Further, for most organizations, development of a vision of success is not necessary in order to produce marked improvements in performance. In my experience, most organizations can demonstrate a substantial improvement in effectiveness if they simply identify and satisfactorily resolve a few strategic issues. Most organizations simply do not address often enough what is truly important; just gathering key decision-makers to deal with a few important matters in a timely way can enhance organizational performance substantially. For these reasons, the step is labeled "optional" in Figure 11.1.

Step 9: Developing an Effective Implementation Process

Just creating a strategic plan is not enough. The changes indicated by the adopted strategies must be incorporated throughout the system for them to be brought to life and for real value to be created for the organization and its stakeholders. Thinking strategically about implementation and developing an effective implementation plan are important tasks on the road to realizing the strategies developed in step 6. For example, in some circumstances, direct implementation at all sites will be the wisest strategic choice, while in other situations, some form of staged implementation may be best (Joyce, 1999).

Again, if strategies and an implementation plan have been developed for a single organization, particularly a small one, or if the planning is for a collaborative, this step may need to be combined with step 7, strategy formulation. On the other hand, in many multi-organizational situations, a separate step will be required to ensure that relevant groups and organizations do the action planning necessary for implementation success.

Action plans should detail the following:

- Implementation roles and responsibilities of oversight bodies, organizational teams or task forces, and individuals
- Expected results and specific objectives and milestones
- Specific action steps and relevant details
- Schedules
- Resource requirements and sources
- A communication process
- Review, monitoring, and midcourse correction procedures
- Accountability procedures

It is important to build into action plans enough sponsors, champions, and other personnel—along with sufficient time, money, attention, administrative and support services, and other resources—to ensure successful implementation. You must "budget the plan" wisely if implementation is to go well. In inter-organizational situations, it is almost impossible to underestimate the requirements for communication, the nurturance of relationships, and attention to operational detail (Huxham, 2003).

It is also important to work quickly to avoid unnecessary or undesirable competition with new priorities. Whenever opportunities to implement strategies and achieve objectives arise, they should be taken. In other words, it is smart to be opportunistic as well as deliberate. And it is important to remember that what actually happens in practice will always be some blend of what is intended with what emerges along the way (Mintzberg, Ahlstrand, and Lampel, 1998).

Successfully implemented and institutionalized strategies result in the establishment of a new "regime," a "set of implicit or explicit principles, norms, rules, and decision-making procedures around which actors' expectations converge in a given area" (Krasner, 1983, p. 2; see also Crossan, Lane, and White, 1999). Regime building is necessary to preserve gains in the face of competing demands. Unfortunately, regimes can outlive their usefulness and must be changed, which involves the next step in the process.

Step 10: Reassessing Strategies and the Strategic Planning Process

Once the implementation process has been under way for some time, it is important to review the strategies and the strategic planning process as a prelude to a new round of strategic planning. Much of the work of this phase may occur as part of the ongoing implementation process. However, if the organization has not engaged in strategic planning for a while, this will be a separate phase. Attention should be focused on successful strategies and whether they should be maintained, replaced by other strategies, or terminated for one reason or another. Unsuccessful strategies should be replaced or terminated. The strategic planning process also should be examined, its strengths and weaknesses noted, and modifications suggested to improve the next round of strategic planning. Effectiveness in this step really does depend on effective organizational learning, which means taking a hard look at what is really happening and being open to new information. As Weick and Sutcliffe (2001, p. 18) say, "The whole point of a learning organization is that it needs to get a better handle on the fact that it doesn't know what it doesn't know." Viewing strategic planning as a kind of action research can help embed learning in the entire process and make sure that the kind of information, feedback, and dialogue necessary for learning occur (Eden and Huxham, 1996).

TAILORING THE PROCESS TO SPECIFIC CIRCUMSTANCES

The Strategy Change Cycle is a general approach to strategic planning and management. Like any planning and management process, it must therefore be tailored carefully to the specific situation if it is to be useful (Alexander, 2000; Christensen, 1999). A number of adaptations—or variations on the general theme—are discussed in this section.

Sequencing the Steps

Although the steps (or occasions for dialogue and decision) are laid out in a linear sequence, it must be emphasized that the Strategy Change Cycle, as its name suggests, is iterative in practice. Participants typically rethink what they have done several times before they reach final decisions. Moreover, the process does not always begin at the beginning. Organizations typically find themselves confronted with a new mandate (step 2), a pressing strategic issue (step 5), a failing strategy (step 6 or 9), or the need to reassess what they have been doing (step 10), and that leads them to engage in strategic planning. Once engaged, the organization is likely to go back and begin at the beginning, particularly with a reexamination of its mission. Indeed, it usually does not matter where you start; you always end up back at mission.

In addition, implementation usually begins before all of the planning is complete. As soon as useful actions are identified, they are taken, as long as they do not jeopardize future actions that might prove valuable. In other words, in a linear, sequential process, the first eight steps of the process would be followed by implementing the planned actions and evaluating the results.

However, implementation typically does not, and should not, wait until the eight steps have been completed. For example, if the organization's mission needs to be redrafted, then it should be. If the SWOT analysis turns up weaknesses or threats that need to be addressed immediately, they should be. If aspects of a desirable strategy can be implemented without awaiting further developments, they should be. And so on. As noted earlier, strategic thinking *and* acting *and* learning are important, and all of the thinking does not have to occur before any actions are taken. Or as Mintzberg, Ahlstrand, and Lampel (1998, p. 71) note, "Effective strategy making connects acting to thinking, which in turn connects implementation to formulation. We think in order to act, to be sure, but we also act in order to think." And learn, they might have added. Strategic planning's iterative, flexible, action-oriented nature is precisely what often makes it so attractive to nonprofit leaders and managers.

Making Use of Vision, Goals, and Issues

In the discussion of step 8, it was noted that different organizations or collaboratives may wish to start their process with a vision statement. Such a statement may foster a consensus and provide important inspiration and guidance for the rest of the process, even though it is unlikely to be as detailed as a statement developed later in the process. As indicated in Figure 11.1, there are other points at which it might be possible to develop a vision statement (or statements). Vision thus may be used to prompt the identification of strategic issues, guide the search for and development of strategies, inspire the adoption of strategic plans, or guide implementation efforts. The Amherst H. Wilder Foundation of Saint Paul, Minnesota, for example, has a current vision in its 2000–2005 Strategic Plan of "a vibrant Saint Paul where individuals, families, and communities can prosper, with opportunities for all to be employed, to be engaged citizens, to live in decent housing, to attend good schools, and to receive support during times of need" (Amherst H. Wilder Foundation, 2000). It had a similar vision in each of its previous plans and used it to help identify issues to be addressed and to develop strategies to be used to realize the vision. The decision to develop a vision statement should hinge on whether one is needed to provide direction to subsequent efforts; whether people will be able to develop a vision that is meaningful enough, detailed enough, *and* broadly supported;

and whether there will be enough energy left after the visioning effort to push ahead.

Similarly, as indicated in Figure 11.1, it is possible to develop goals in many different places in the process (Behn, 1999; Borins, 1998). Some strategic planning processes will begin with the goals of new boards of directors, executive directors, or other top-level decision-makers. These goals embody a reform agenda for the organization or collaborative. Other strategic planning processes may start with goals that are part of mandates. For example, government agencies often require the nonprofit organizations on which they rely for policy implementation to develop plans that include results and outcome measures that will show how the intent of the legislation is to be achieved. A *starting* goal for these nonprofits, therefore, is to identify results and outcomes they want to be measured against that are also in accord with legislative intent. The goal thus helps these organizations identify an important strategic issue—namely, what the results and outcomes should be. Subsequent strategic planning efforts are then likely to start with the desired outcomes the organization thinks are important.

Still other strategic planning processes will articulate goals to guide strategy formulation in response to specific issues or to guide implementation of specific strategies. Goals developed at these later stages of the process are likely to be more detailed and more specific than those developed earlier in the process. Goals may be developed anytime they would be useful to guide subsequent efforts in the process *and* when they will have sufficient support among key parties to produce desired action.

In my experience, however, strategic planning processes generally start neither with vision nor with goals. In part, this is because in my experience, strategic planning rarely starts with step 1. Instead, people sense that something is not right about the current situation—they face strategic issues of one sort or another, or they are pursuing a strategy that is failing or about to fail—and they want to know what to do (Borins, 1998; Nutt, 2001). One of the crucial features of issue-driven planning (and political decision making in general) is that you do not have to agree on goals to agree on next steps (Bryant, 2003; Huxham, 2003; Innes, 1996). You simply need to agree on a strategy that will address the issue and further the interests of the organization or collaborative and its key stakeholders. Goals are likely to be developed once viable strategies have been developed to address the issues. The goals will typically be strategy-specific.

Articulating goals or describing a vision in this way may help provide a better feeling for where an agreed strategy or interconnected set of strategies should lead (Behn, 1999; Nutt, 2001). Goals and vision are thus more likely to come toward the end of the process than near the beginning. But there are clear exceptions—the Wilder Foundation, for example—and process designers should think carefully about why, when, and how—if at all—to bring goals and vision into the process.

Applying the Process Across Organizational Subunits, Levels, and Functions on an Ongoing Basis

Strategic thinking, acting, and learning depend on getting key people together, getting them to focus wisely and creatively on what is really important, and getting them to do something about it. At its most basic, the technology of strategic planning thus involves deliberations, decisions, and actions. The steps in the Strategy Change Cycle help make the process reasonably orderly to increase the likelihood that what is important will actually be recognized and addressed and to allow more people to participate in the process. When the process is applied to an organization as a whole on an ongoing basis (rather than as a one-shot deal), or at least to significant parts of it, it is usually necessary to construct a *strategic planning system*. The system allows the various parts of the process to be integrated in appropriate ways and engages the organization in strategic *management*, not just strategic planning (Poister and Streib, 1999). In the best circumstances, the system will include the actors and knowledge necessary to act wisely, foster systems thinking, and prompt quick and effective action, since inclusion, systems thinking, and speed are increasingly required of nonprofit organizations (Bryson, 2003; see also Schachtel, 2001).

The process might be applied across subunits, levels, and functions in an organization as outlined in Figure 11.2. The application is based on the "layered" or "stacked units of management" system used by many corporations. The system's first cycle consists of "bottom-up" development of strategic plans within a framework established at the

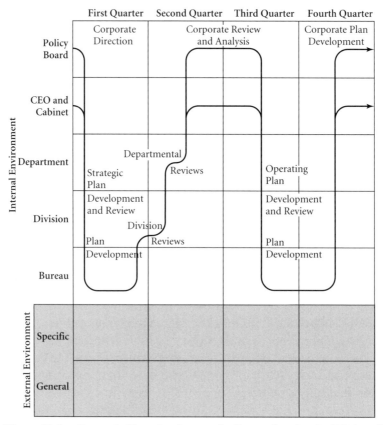

Figure 11.2.   Strategic Planning System for Layered or Stacked Units of Management

Source: Adapted from Bryson and Roering, 1987, p. 16.

top, followed by reviews and reconciliations at each succeeding level. In the second cycle, operating plans are developed to implement the strategic plans. Depending on the situation, decisions at the top of the organizational hierarchy may or may not require policy board approval (which is why the line depicting the process flow diverges at the top). The system may be supported by a set of performance indicators and strategies embodied in a balanced scorecard (Kaplan, 2001); see Table 11.1.

Strategic planning systems for nonprofit organizations are usually not as formalized and integrated as the one outlined in Figure 11.2. More typical is a "strategic issues management" system, which attempts to manage specific strategic issues without seeking integration of the resultant strategies across all subunits, levels, and functions. Tight integration is not necessary because most issues do not affect all parts of the organization, are subject to different politics, and are on their own time frame. Other common nonprofit strategic planning systems include the *contract model*, in which there is a contract or agreement between a "center" and related units, such as between a headquarters organization and local affiliates; the *goal model*, in which there are goals but little else to ensure implementation; the *portfolio model*, in which organizational subunits or programs are managed as part of an overall organizational portfolio; and *collaboration*, which itself can take a variety of forms (Gray, 1989; Huxham, 2003).

If the organization is fairly large, specific linkages will be necessary in order to join the process to different functions and levels in the organization so that it can proceed in a reasonably orderly and integrated manner. One effective way to achieve such a linkage is to appoint the heads of all major units to the strategic planning team. All unit heads can then be sure that their units' information and interests are represented in strategy formulation and can oversee strategy implementation in their unit.

Indeed, key decision-makers might wish to form themselves into a permanent strategic planning committee or cabinet. I would recommend this approach if it appears workable for the organization, as it emphasizes the role of line managers as strategic planners and the role of strategic planners as facilitators of decision making by the line managers. Pragmatic and effective strategies and plans are likely to result. Temporary task forces, strategic planning committees, or a cabinet can work, but whatever the arrangement, there is no substitute for the direct involvement of key decision-makers in the process.

Applying the Process to Collaboratives

When applied to a collaborative, the process will probably need to be sponsored by a committee or task force of key decision-makers, opinion leaders, "influentials," or "notables" representing important stakeholder groups. Additional working groups or task forces will probably need to be organized at various times to deal with specific strategic issues or to oversee the implementation of specific strategies. Because so many more people and groups will have to be involved, and because implementation will have to rely more on consent than on authority, the process is likely to be much more time-consuming and iterative than strategic planning applied to an organization (Bardach, 1998; Bryant, 2003; Huxham, 2003).

Roles for Planners, Decision-Makers, Implementers, and Citizens

Planners can play many different roles in a strategic planning process. In many cases, the planners are not people with the word *planner* in their job title but are in fact policymakers or line managers (Mintzberg, Ahlstrand, and Lampel, 1998). The people with the title of planner often act primarily as facilitators of decision making by policymakers or line managers or as technical experts in substantive areas. In other cases, planners operate in a variety of roles. Sometimes the planner is an "expert on experts" (Bolan, 1971) who eases different people with different expertise in and out of the process for different purposes at different times. At still other times, planners are "finders" of strategy, who do their job by interpreting existing actions and recognizing important patterns in the organization and its environment; "analysts" of existing or potential strategies; "catalysts" for promoting strategic thought and action; or "strategists" themselves (Mintzberg, 1994).

Since the most important thing about strategic planning is the development of strategic thought, action, and learning, it may not matter much which person does what. However, it does seem that strategic planning done by boards, executive directors, or line managers is most likely to be implemented. Exactly how people formally designated as planners contribute to that formulation is unclear. In any particular situation, they should be involved in a way that promotes strategic thought, action, and learning and enhances commitment to agreed-on strategies.

When a nonprofit organization is the principal focus of attention, few "outsiders" other than board members are ordinarily involved in the planning process. One reason may be that the organization may already possess the necessary knowledge and expertise in-house, so outsider involvement would be redundant and time-consuming. In addition, insiders are typically the chief implementers of strategies, so their ownership of the process and resultant decisions may be most crucial. Furthermore, participation by outsiders may not be necessary to legitimate the process because the board is directly involved and its members are seen as legitimate representatives of larger constituencies. The absence of participation by ordinary outsiders would parallel much private-sector corporate planning practice. On the other hand, it is easy to be wrong about how much one "knows," or needs to know, and how much perceived legitimacy the process needs (Nutt, 2002; Suchman, 1995). Interviews, focus groups and surveys of outsiders, and external sounding boards of various sorts, such as advisory boards or councils, are often worth their weight in gold when they open insiders' eyes to information they have missed, add legitimacy to the effort, and keep insiders from reaching the wrong conclusions or making wrong decisions (Feldman and Khademian, 2001; Thomas, 1995). So a word of caution is in order, and that is to remember, as the Greeks believed, that nemesis always walks in the footsteps of hubris!

Program-focused strategic planning appears to be much more likely to involve outsiders, particularly in their capacity as clients or customers. Outsider involvement in program planning is thus roughly analogous to consumer involvement in private-sector marketing research and development projects. Finally, planning on behalf of a collaborative almost always involves substantial participation, but who is inside and who is outside can be difficult to determine (Huxham, 2003).

SUMMARY

This chapter has outlined a process called the Strategy Change Cycle for promoting strategic thinking, acting, and learning in nonprofit organizations and collaboratives. Although the process is presented in a linear, sequential fashion for pedagogical reasons, it proceeds iteratively as groups continuously rethink connections among the various elements of the process, take action, and learn on their way to formulating effective strategies. In addition, the process often does not start with step 1 but instead starts somewhere else and then cycles back to step 1. The steps also are not steps precisely but are more like occasions for deliberation, decision, and action as part of a continuous flow of strategic thinking, acting, and learning; knowledge exploration and exploitation; and strategy formulation and implementation. Mintzberg, Ahlstrand, and Lampel (1998, p. 195) assert that "all real strategic behavior has to combine deliberate control with emergent learning." The Strategy Change Cycle is designed to promote just that kind of strategic behavior.

References

Abramson, D., and Means, G. *E-Government 2001*. Lanham, MD: Rowman & Littlefield, 2001.

Ackerman, D. *Deep Play*. New York: Vintage Books, 1999.

Alexander, E. R. "Rationality Revisited: Planning Paradigms in a Post-Postmodernist Perspective." *Journal of Planning Education and Research*, 2000, *19*, 242–256.

Amherst H. Wilder Foundation. Strategic Plan, 2000–2005. Saint Paul, MN: Amherst H. Wilder Foundation, 2000.

Bardach, E. *Getting Agencies to Work Together*. Washington, DC: Brookings Institution Press, 1998.

Barzelay, M. *The New Public Management: Improving Research and Policy Dialogue*. Berkeley: University of California Press; New York: Russell Sage Foundation, 2001.

Baum, H. *The Organization of Hope: Communities Planning for Themselves*. Albany: State University of New York Press, 1997.

Behn, R. D. "Managing by Groping Along." *Journal of Policy Analysis and Management*, 1988, *7*, 643–666.

Behn, R. D. "The New Public-Management Paradigm and the Search for Democratic Accountability." *International Public Management Journal*, 1999, *1*, 131–165.

Behn, R. D. *Rethinking Democratic Accountability*. Washington, DC: Brookings Institution Press, 2001.

Bolan, R. S. "Generalist with a Specialty: Still Valid? Educating the Planner: An Expert on Experts." In American Society of Planning Officials, *Planning 1971: Selected Papers from the ASPO Conference*. Chicago: American Society of Planning Officials, 1971.

Borins, S. *Innovating with Integrity*. Washington, DC: Georgetown University Press, 1998.

Boyte, H. C., and Kari, N. *Building America: The Democratic Promise of Public Work*. Philadelphia: Temple University Press, 1996.

Bryant, J. *The Six Dilemmas of Collaboration: Inter-Organisational Relationships as Drama*. Chichester, England: John Wiley & Sons, 2003.

Bryce, H. J. *Financial and Strategic Management for Nonprofit Organizations* (3rd ed.). San Francisco: Jossey-Bass, 2000.

Bryson, J. M. "Strategic Planning." In N. J. Smelser and P. B. Baltes (Eds.), *International Encyclopedia of the Social and Behavioral Sciences*. Oxford, England: Pergamon, 2001.

Bryson, J. M. "Strategic Planning and Management." In B. G. Peters and J. Pierre (Eds.), *Handbook of Public Administration*. Thousand Oaks, CA: Sage, 2003.

Bryson, J. M. *Strategic Planning for Public and Nonprofit Organizations* (3rd ed.), San Francisco: Jossey-Bass, 2004a.

Bryson, J. M. "What to Do When Stakeholders Matter: Stakeholder Identification and Analysis Techniques." *Public Management Review*, 2004b, *6*, 21–53.

Bryson, J. M., Ackermann, F., Eden, C., and Finn, C. *Causal Mapping for Individuals and Groups: What to Do When Thinking Matters.* Chichester, England: John Wiley & Sons, 2004.

Bryson, J. M., and Anderson, S. R. "Applying Large-Group Interaction Methods to the Planning and Implementation of Major Projects." *Public Administration Review*, 2000, *60*, 143–162.

Bryson, J. M., and Crosby, B. C. *Leadership for the Common Good: Tackling Public Problems in a Shared-Power World.* San Francisco: Jossey-Bass, 1992.

Bryson, J. M., and Roering, W. D. "Applying Private Sector Strategic Planning in the Public Sector." *Journal of the American Planning Association*, 1987, *53*, 9–22.

Carver, J. *Boards That Make a Difference: A New Design for Leadership in Nonprofit and Public Organizations* (2nd ed.). San Francisco: Jossey-Bass, 1997.

Christensen, K. S. *Cities and Complexity: Making Intergovernmental Decisions.* Thousand Oaks, CA: Sage, 1999.

Cleveland, H. *Nobody in Charge: Essays on the Future of Leadership.* Hoboken, NJ: John Wiley & Sons, 2002.

Cohen, S., and Eimicke, W. *Tools for Innovators.* San Francisco: Jossey-Bass, 1998.

Collins, J. C., and Porras, J. I. *Built to Last: Successful Habits of Visionary Companies.* New York: HarperBusiness, 1997.

Crossan, M. M., Lane, H. W., and White, R. E. "An Organizational Learning Framework: From Intuition to Institution." *Academy of Management Review*, 1999, *24*, 522–537.

Dalton, G. W. "Influence and Organization Change." In G. W. Dalton, P. Lawrence, and L. Greiner (Eds.), *Organization Change and Development*. Homewood, IL: Irwin, 1970.

de Leon, L., and Denhardt, R. B. "The Political Theory of Reinvention." *Public Administration Review*, 2000, *60*, 89–97.

Denhardt, R. B., and Denhardt, J. "The New Public Service: Serving Rather Than Steering." *Public Administration Review*, 2000, *60*, 549–559.

Dutton, J. E., and Jackson, S. E. "Categorizing Strategic Issues: Links to Organizational Action." *Academy of Management Review*, 1987, *12*, 76–90.

Eden, C., and Ackermann, F. *Making Strategy: The Journey of Strategic Management.* London: Sage, 1998.

Eden, C., and Ackermann, F. "Mapping Distinctive Competencies: A Systematic Approach." *Journal of the Operational Research Society*, 2000, *51*, 12–20.

Eden, C., and Ackermann, F. "SODA: The Principles." In J. Rosenhead and J. Mingers (Eds.), *Rational Analysis in a Problematic World Revisited.* London: John Wiley & Sons, 2001.

Eden, C., and Huxham, C. "Action Research for Management Research." *British Journal of Management*, 1996, *7*, 75–86.

Faragher, J. M. *Daniel Boone: The Life and Legend of an American Pioneer.* New York: Henry Holt, 1992.

Feldman, M. S., and Khademian, A. "Managing for Inclusion and Control: Balancing Control and Participation." *International Public Management Journal*, 2001, *3*, 149–167.

Feldman, M. S., and Khademian A. "To Manage Is to Govern." *Public Administration Review*, 2002, *62*, 541–554.

Flyvbjerg, B. *Rationality and Power: Democracy in Practice.* Chicago: University of Chicago Press, 1998.

Forester, J. *Planning in the Face of Power.* Berkeley: University of California Press, 1989.

Goffman, E. *Frame Analysis: An Essay on the Organizational Experience.* Boston: Northeastern University Press, 1986.

Goleman, D. *Emotional Intelligence.* New York: Bantam Books, 1995.

Goleman, D., Boyatzis, R., and McKee, A. *Primal Leadership: Realizing the Power of Emotional Intelligence.* Boston: Harvard Business School Press, 2002.

Gray, B. *Collaborating: Finding Common Ground for Multiparty Problems.* San Francisco: Jossey-Bass, 1989.

Hammer, M., and Champy, J. *Reengineering the Corporation: A Manifesto for Business Revolution.* New York: HarperBusiness, 1993.

Heifetz, R. A., and Laurie, D. L. "The Work of Leadership." *Harvard Business Review*, Jan.–Feb. 1997, pp. 124–134.

Holman, P., and Devane, T. E. *The Change Handbook: Group Methods for Shaping the Future.* San Francisco: Berrett-Koehler, 1999.

Huxham, C. "Theorizing Collaborative Practice." *Public Management Review*, 2003, *5*, 401–423.

Innes, J. E. "Planning Through Consensus Building: A New View of the Comprehensive Planning Ideal." *Journal of the American Planning Association*, 1996, *62*, 460–472.

Johnson, G., and Scholes, K. *Exploring Corporate Strategy* (6th ed.). Upper Saddle River, NJ: Prentice Hall, 2002.

Joyce, P. *Strategic Management for the Public Services.* Buckingham, England: Open University Press, 1999.

Kaplan, R. S. "Strategic Performance Measurement and Management in Nonprofit Organizations." *Nonprofit Management and Leadership,* 2001, *11*, 353–370.

Kouzes, J. M., and Posner, B. Z. *The Leadership Challenge: How to Get Extraordinary Things Done in Organizations* (3rd ed.). San Francisco: Jossey-Bass, 2002.

Krasner, S. D. "Structural Causes and Regime Consequences: Regimes as Intervening Variables." In S. D. Krasner (Ed.), *International Regimes.* Ithaca, NY: Cornell University Press, 1983.

Letts, C. W., Ryan, W. P., and Grossman, A. *High-Performance Nonprofit Organizations: Managing Upstream for Greater Impact.* Hoboken, NJ: John Wiley & Sons, 1999.

Lewin, K. *Field Theory in Social Sciences.* New York: HarperCollins, 1951.

Light, P. *Sustaining Innovation: Creating Nonprofit and Government Organizations That Innovate Naturally.* San Francisco: Jossey-Bass, 1998.

Light, P. *Pathways to Nonprofit Excellence.* Washington, DC: Brookings Institution Press, 2002.

March, J. G. "Exploration and Exploitation in Organizational Learning." *Organization Science,* 1991, *2,* 71–87.

Mintzberg, H. *The Rise and Fall of Strategic Planning.* New York: The Free Press, 1994.

Mintzberg, H., Ahlstrand, B., and Lampel, J. *Strategy Safari: A Guided Tour Through the Wilds of Strategic Management.* New York: The Free Press, 1998.

Mitchell, R. K., Agle, B. R., and Wood, D. J. "Toward a Theory of Stakeholder Identification and Salience: Defining the Principle of Who and What Really Counts." *Academy of Management Review,* 1997, *22,* 853–886.

Moore, M. H. "Managing for Value: Organizational Strategy in For-Profit, Nonprofit, and Governmental Organizations." *Nonprofit and Voluntary Sector Quarterly,* 2000, *29* (suppl.), 183–204.

Niven, P. R. *Balanced Scorecard Step-by-Step for Government and Nonprofit Agencies.* Hoboken, NJ: John Wiley & Sons, 2003.

Nutt, P. C. "Strategic Decision-Making." In M. A. Hitt, R. E. Freeman, and J. S. Harrison (Eds.), *Blackwell Handbook of Strategic Management.* Oxford, England: Blackwell Business, 2001.

Nutt, P. C. *Why Decisions Fail: Avoiding the Blunders and Traps That Lead to Debacles.* San Francisco: Berrett-Koehler, 2002.

Nutt, P. C., and Backoff, R. W. *Strategic Management of Public and Third Sector Organizations: A Handbook for Leaders.* San Francisco: Jossey-Bass, 1992.

Nutt, P. C., Backoff, R. W., and Hogan, M. F. "Managing the Paradoxes of Strategic Change." *Journal of Applied Management Studies,* 2000, *9,* 5–31.

Osborne, D., and Plastrik, P. *Banishing Bureaucracy: The Five Strategies for Reinventing Government.* Reading, MA: Addison-Wesley, 1997.

Osborne, D., and Plastrik, P. *The Reinventor's Fieldbook: Tools for Transforming Your Government.* San Francisco: Jossey-Bass, 2000.

Perrow, C. *Complex Organizations.* New York: Random House, 1986.

Pfeffer, J., and Salancik, G. *The External Control of Organizations: A Resource Dependence Perspective.* New York: HarperCollins, 1978.

Poister, T. H., and Streib, G. D. "Strategic Management in the Public Sector: Concepts, Models, and Processes." *Public Productivity and Management Review,* 1999, *22,* 308–325.

Prahalad, C. K., and Hamel, G. "The Core Competence of the Corporation." *Harvard Business Review,* 1990, May–Jun, 79–91.

Schachtel, M. R. B. "CitiStat and the Baltimore Neighborhood Indicators Alliance: Using Information to Improve Communication and Community." *National Civic Review,* 2001, *90,* 253–265.

Schwartz, P. *The Art of the Long View: Planning for the Future in an Uncertain World.* New York: Doubleday Currency, 1991.

Scott, W. R. *Organizations: Rational, Natural and Open Systems* (2nd ed.). Upper Saddle River, NJ: Prentice Hall, 1987.

Selznick, P. *Leadership in Administration: A Sociological Interpretation.* Berkeley: University of California Press, 1957.

Senge, P. M. "The Leader's New Work: Building Learning Organizations." *Sloan Management Review,* 1990, Fall, 7–23.

Spencer, L. *Winning Through Participation.* Dubuque, IA: Kendall-Hunt, 1996.

Stalk, G., Jr., Evans, P., and Shulman, L. "Competing on Capabilities: The New Rules of Corporate Strategy." *Harvard Business Review,* 1992, Mar–Apr., 57–69.

Sterman, J. D. *Business Dynamics: Systems Thinking and Modeling for a Complex World.* New York: McGraw-Hill, 2000.

Suchman, M. C. "Managing Legitimacy: Strategic and Institutional Approaches." *Academy of Management Review,* 1995, *20,* 571–610.

Terry, R. W. *Authentic Leadership: Courage in Action*. San Francisco: Jossey-Bass, 1993.

Terry, R. W. *Seven Zones for Leadership: Acting Authentically in Stability and Chaos*. Palo Alto, CA: Davies-Black, 2001.

Thomas, J. C. *Public Participation in Public Decisions: New Skills and Strategies for Public Managers*. San Francisco: Jossey-Bass, 1995.

Thompson, J. D. *Organizations in Action*. New York: McGraw-Hill, 1967.

Thompson, L. *The Mind and Heart of the Negotiator*. Upper Saddle River, NJ: Prentice Hall, 2001.

Tuchman, B. *The March of Folly: From Troy to Vietnam*. New York: Knopf, 1984.

van der Heijden and others. *The Sixth Sense: Accelerating Organizational Learning with Scenarios*. Chichester, England: John Wiley & Sons, 2002.

Weick, K. E. *The Social Psychology of Organizing*. Reading, MA: Addison-Wesley, 1979.

Weick, K. E. *Sensemaking in Organizations*. Thousand Oaks, CA: Sage, 1995.

Weick, K. E., and Sutcliffe, K. M. *Managing the Unexpected: Assuring High Performance in an Age of Complexity*. San Francisco: Jossey-Bass, 2001.

Weiss, J. A., and Piderit, S. K. "The Value of Mission Statements in Public Agencies." *Journal of Public Administration Research and Theory*, 1999, *9*, 193–223.

Wildavsky, A. *Speaking Truth to Power: The Art and Craft of Policy Analysis*. Boston: Little, Brown, 1979.

—∾∾—

John Bryson is a professor of planning and public affairs in the Hubert H. Humphrey Institute of Public Affairs at the University of Minnesota, Minneapolis. He consults widely on leadership and strategic planning with public, nonprofit, and for-profit organizations in the United States and abroad.

CHAPTER TWELVE

Delivering on the Promise of Nonprofits

Jeffrey L. Bradach
Thomas J. Tierney
Nancy Stone

—◦◦◦—

Ending violence in inner-city communities, education-disadvantaged children, stemming the loss of rain forests or marine wildlife—U.S. nonprofits are being asked to take on an increasing share of society's most important and difficult work. At the same time, the expectations being placed on these organizations to show results—by their staff members, their boards, and public and private donors—are rising. How are nonprofits responding? By being much more explicit about the results they intend to deliver and the strategies and organizations they'll create to achieve those outcomes.

Consider the following example. Ten years ago, Rheedlen Centers for Children and Families had a $7 million budget and a truly herculean mission: to improve the lives of poor children in America's most devastated communities. It provided New Yorkers

---

Originally published as Jeffrey L. Bradach, Thomas J. Tierney, and Nancy Stone, "Delivering on the Promise of Nonprofits," *Harvard Business Review*, 86. (December 2008).

with family-support networks, a homelessness-prevention program, a senior center, and a host of programs to meet the needs of troubled and impoverished children and teenagers. Among them was the Harlem Children's Zone, a fledgling neighborhood initiative based in a twenty-four-block area in south-central Harlem.

- U.S. nonprofits face mounting pressure to demonstrate the effectiveness of their programs—but the sector's orientation toward mission statements rather than market forces actually undermines their ability to focus on results.

- To push back and develop pragmatic plans for making a difference, nonprofit leaders should rigorously answer several interdependent questions, suggested by the authors as a framework for change: Which results will we hold ourselves accountable for? How will we achieve them? What will results really cost, and how can we fund them? How do we build the organization we need to deliver results?

- Successful organizations are willing to make hard trade-offs based on objective information to increase their impact.

Exhibit 12.1.   Idea in Brief

Despite Rheedlen's many good programs, however, the prospects for Harlem's children appeared to be getting worse, not better. For Geoffrey Canada, the nonprofit's longtime DEO, the imperative was clear: to help the greatest possible number of kids lead healthy lives, stay in school, and grow up to become independent, productive adults. Rheedlen would have to step up its performance. So in 2002, it changed its name and sharpened its focus. Now simply called the Harlem Children's Zone (HCZ), the agency linked its original mission to a very concrete statement of the impact it intended to have: namely, that three thousand children, ages 0 to 18, living in the zone should have demographic and achievement profiles consistent with those found in an average U.S. middle-class community.

With support from the board and major funders, particularly the Edna McConnell Clark Foundation, Canada and his team discontinued or transitioned out of activities that were no longer in line with HCZ's intended impact (such as homelessness-prevention programs outside the zone) and took on new ones (such as a Head Start program and a charter elementary school). They also diversified HCZ's funding, shook up and expanded its management ranks, and invested precious dollars in evaluating results. By 2004, HCZ had more than doubled in scope, encompassing sixty square blocks that housed some

6,500 children. In 2007, the organization added another thirty-seven square blocks—housing four thousand kids—to the zone. Over the same five-year period, its budget grew from $11.6 million to $50 million. Civic and nonprofit leaders in other cities have expressed interest in replicating HCZ's approach.

HCZ is not an isolated case. During the past eight years, we have worked with more than 150 nonprofits whose executive directors and boards are committed to increase their organizations' social impact. We have yet to find one "best way" to do that, and we wouldn't expect to. Every organization faces unique challenges and opportunities, and the decisions its leaders make necessarily reflect those realities. The one constant, however, is a willingness to rigorously confront a few essential, interdependent questions:

- Which results will we hold ourselves accountable for?
- How will we achieve them?
- What will results really cost, and how can we fund them?
- How do we build the organization we need to deliver results?

Together, these questions create a framework that executive directors can use in candid conversations with stakeholders and in developing pragmatic, specific plans for making a tangible difference, whether that is measured in more high school graduates or in healthier oceans. Although the questions look easy and generic, answering them—and acting on the recommendations—is remarkably hard for many reasons. Ironically, the dynamic driving the nonprofit sector actually undermined its organizations' ability to focus on results, despite the mounting pressure to do just that.

THE CHALLENGE OF DELIVERING RESULTS IN THE NONPROFIT SECTOR

A day in the life of an executive director is filled with fund raising, board tending, and "fire" extinguishing. Meanwhile, staff members work long hours in bare-bones facilities. These are stereotypes, sure, but like most stereotypes, they contain a kernel of truth. Leaders and employees of nonprofit organizations are constantly being pulled in different directions to serve multiple constituencies. This "scatterization" is as much a function of how the nonprofit sector is organized as it is of how the organizations themselves operate.

In the business world, market forces serve as feedback mechanisms. Companies that perform well are rewarded by customers and investors; underperformers are penalized. Performance is relatively easy to quantify through quarterly earning, ROI, customer loyalty, scores, and the like. Moreover, such metrics can be calibrated and compared, ensuring that the companies producing the best results will attract capital and talent. Managers are encouraged to invest in the people, systems, and infrastructure needed to continue delivering superior performance. And internal feedback mechanisms, from up-to-the-minute operating data to performance reviews, keep everyone focused on critical activities and goals.

In the nonprofit world, missions, not markets, are the primary magnets attracting essential resources—from donors inspired by organizations' audacious goals; from board members, who not only volunteer their time and expertise but also often serve as major funders; and from employees, who accept modest paychecks to do work they care passionately about. But missions are typically better at providing inspiration than direction. So it is not uncommon for key stakeholders to have deeply felt but divergent views about what the organizations' chief priorities ought to be—and for those differences to be masked by the broad aspirations of the mission statement.

Assessing and comparing performance is also a more subjective and values-driven exercise for nonprofits than for companies. Given the diversity of the goals nonprofits pursue, there is no single quantitative or qualitative metric against which performance can be evaluated and ranked. Even when several organizations are aiming for the same goal—reducing school dropout rates, say—the absence of standard outcomes measures makes it impossible to compare their performance.

Quirky, too, are the sector's funding flows, which often fail to reward high performance and are seldom reliable enough to justify significant investments in organizational capacity. A nonprofit's very success can provide an excuse for donors to stop giving, because the organization no longer "needs" their money. Both public and private funders overwhelmingly want to support programs (especially new ones) rather than overhead. So program proliferation trumps investment in existing programs, and the organization is strained on every front: Management ends up being under-compensated and overstretched. Operating systems and technology are often rudimentary.

Committing to deliver a defined set of results may sound unremarkable, but it is not easy for nonprofits given these dynamics. It involves forging new relationships with the external stakeholders who provide the funding and with the internal stakeholders who do the work—changes as profound and revolutionary as those that U.S. business leaders experienced when they embraced the quality movement decades ago.

WHICH RESULTS WILL WE HOLD OURSELVES ACCOUNTABLE FOR?

The most fundamental—and perhaps most difficult—decision a nonprofit can make is to define the results it must deliver in order to be successful. That process entails translating the organization's mission into goals that are simultaneously compelling enough to attract ongoing support from stakeholders and specific enough to inform resources allocations.

One approach is for nonprofit leaders to formulate and agree upon what we call its *intended impact*. A strong intended-impact statement identifies both the beneficiaries of a nonprofit's activities and the benefits the organization will provide—that is, the change in behavior, knowledge, or status quo its programs are designed to effect. Such specificity gives decision-makers a powerful lens to use when they have to make tradeoffs among worthy, competing priorities. To see the difference between a mission and an intended-impact statement, consider this example from Larkin Street Youth Services, a San Francisco-based nonprofit that is nationally recognized for its work with homeless and runaway youths. Larkin Street's mission is "to create a continuum of service that inspires youth to move beyond the street. We will nurture potential, promote dignity, and support bold steps by all." The intended-impact statement drills down further: Help homeless youths, ages 12 to 24, in the San Francisco Bay area develop the self-sufficiency and skills to live independently.

In response to the growing pressure for nonprofits to demonstrate that they are achieving results, their leaders should be able to answer the following key questions:

Which results will we hold ourselves accountable for?

Example: Despite the variety of programs Rheedlen Centers for Children and Families (now the Harlem Children's Zone) offered to help inner-city youths, outcomes for kids weren't improving. So the organization revamped itself around a very concrete set of goals: namely that three thousand children, ages 0 to 18, living in a twenty-four-block area in south-central Harlem should have demographic and achievement profiles consistent with those found in an average U.S. community.

How will we achieve results?

Example: Expeditionary Learning Schools (ELS) trains teachers to educate students through real-world projects. To achieve results in a low-performing school, ELS staff members must work on-site thirty days a year for at least three years. When the organization assessed its existing network, it found that few schools were as engaged as they needed to be to attain excellent results. ELS made the painful decision to exit sites to devote the time required to implement its curricular approach.

What will results really cost, and how can we fund them?

Example: Larkin Street Youth Services relies heavily on government funding. Because grants and contracts often set arbitrary limits on overhead, obscuring the real cost of essential activities, the organization has had to clearly articulate what it needs financial support for and identify appropriate sources to meet those needs.

How do we build the organization we need to deliver results?

Example: Geoffrey Canada, CEO of Harlem Children's Zone, actively engaged staff members and funders in a disciplined process of organizational change. In drawing up their plan, the CEO and his team were willing to question just about every aspect of the organization. They discontinued some activities, diversified funding, shook up and expanded management ranks, and invested money in new IT systems. After doing that, Canada was able to secure multiyear financial commitments from several major funders.

Exhibit 12.2.   Idea in Practice

Discussion about an organization's intended impact tends to be iterative, inclusive (drawing in board as well as staff members), and incredibly hard. One source of difficulty is that legitimate needs invariably outstrip any single organization's ability to meet them. So by clarifying its strategy and scope, the nonprofit is also determining what it will *not* do. Should the Natural Resources Defense Council's oceans program work to block offshore oil drilling or promote more responsible management of fisheries? Should STRIVE, a job-training organization, focus on the chronically unemployed, who are the most difficult to serve, or on those with the best chance of rapidly reentering the workforce? These are touch choices, without "right" answers. But only by making them can a nonprofit align its limited resources with the activities that will have the greatest impact.

There is no standard template for an intended-impact statement, but organizational values, data, and a willingness to make tough decisions are all part of the mix.

Organizational values. An especially helpful way to begin a discussion about intended impact is to identify an anchor that is embedded in the organization's values and history. Four types exist: target population (in Larkin Street's case, homeless youths, ages 12 to 24), target outcomes (self-sufficiency), geography (San Francisco), and approach (continuum of care). The organization ultimately must address all these dimensions—who, what, where, and how—in order to develop an intended-impact statement that can be acted on. But it helps to have one fixed starting point on which all the stakeholders can agree.

Data. Objective information plays an equally critical role in developing a realistic intended-impact statement: What is the magnitude and nature of the need for our activities? What are our relative strength and weaknesses? What resources are required to achieve the outcomes we hope for, and how likely are they to be available? Bringing hard data to bear on questions like these promotes better decision making and builds consensus. Although Larkin Street's decision to keep its direct services focused on the Bay Area may have been rooted in the organization's history, it was solidly reinforced by statistics showing that there were nearly four times as many homeless youths in San Francisco as there were providers to help them.

Making tough choices. Because hard choices, especially those with tangible human costs, need to be made, nonprofit leaders must be able to build agreement among stakeholders while avoiding the paralysis of endless discussions about what the organization should be doing. When the Harlem Children's Zone decided to hand the management of its senior center over to another agency, it was extremely difficult for many staff members—not so much because of the effect on them personally but because of the effect of the people who would no longer be assisting. What ultimately made it possible for everyone to rally around was analysis showing how much of HCZ's discretionary funding the center was absorbing—dollars that could be reallocated to help kids.

HOW WILL WE ACHIEVE RESULTS?

When time and money have to be allocated among various programs and activities, identifying the most effective initiatives isn't easy. Nor is the logic supporting those decisions likely to be transparent. That is why theory-of-change work—explaining how the organization, working alone or with others, will achieve its intended impact—is so critical. The process ensures that stakeholders understand why strategic decisions are being made as they are. It also unearths assumptions about programs and services that can then be tested and revisited as necessary. A strong theory of change is broad enough to show the scope of an organization's beliefs about how social change occurs (including, where appropriate, the activities of others) but specific enough to show the scope of an organization's beliefs about how social change occurs (including, where appropriate, the activities of others) but specific enough to allow decision-makers to map programs and resources against it. (See Exhibit 12.3.)

Like intended-impact work, theory-of-change discussions are iterative, and several options may be plausible for achieving a given set of results. For example, teacher training, curriculum reform, an extended school day, and personalized instruction might be levers for improving graduation rates among disadvantaged youths in urban high schools. The "right" approach will depend in part on what the leaders of an organization believe they ought to be doing. An even bigger factor will be what they learn as they analyze their origination's capabilities and economics, and gather information about what others are doing—for example, whether similar programs already exist and which ones are being funded by whom.

Several issues pop up routinely in theory-of-change work. One is the question of proof: Which elements have been shown to create positive results? Formal evaluations, which document the link between a particular program or activity and a set of positive outcomes, are time-consuming, costly, and difficult to get funded, so most organizations can't answer this question definitively. Even so, many fields do have a growing body of academic research about what really works—for instance, studies on climate change or early childhood development. Decision-makers need to be familiar with any such information, especially since what may look like a nuance—whether a tutor meets with a child once a week or twice, for example—can be central to a program's success.

Another challenge is determining where one organization's work begins and ends relative to the work of others. JumpStart, a national nonprofit that mentors young children in Head Start programs who are falling behind, offers a good illustration. JumpStart focuses on providing tutors who are well trained to support the intellectual and emotional development of their tutees. But should the organization also develop programs focused on the children's families? JumpStart's leadership had to wrestle with that question because the organization's intended impact is school readiness, and it is abundantly clear that families are crucial in helping children succeed in school. But given JumpStart's limited resources, and the fact that it couldn't drive change on both fronts, the organization decided to stay focused on increasing the number of kids it could serve.

Since its founding in 1984, San Francisco-based Larkin Street Youth Services has become a model of innovative and effective service provision for homeless and runaway youths. The organization's theory of change, refined in 2007 and presented here, articulates its beliefs about how Larkin Street can achieve its intended impact.

Mission

"To create a continuum of service that inspires youth to move beyond the street. We will encourage potential, promote dignity, and support bold steps by all."

Theory of Change

Larkin Street's continuum of care raises the hope, optimism, and self-esteem of youths by

- Making homeless youths aware of services through outreach
- Meeting youth where they are and addressing immediate needs
- Providing a stable living situation and supportive environment
- Increasing life skills and connecting youths with jobs and education

This continuum of care is continually refined through collaboration across programs and across evaluation data.

Direct Impact

- Larkin Street helps homeless youths ages 12 to 24 in San Francisco to live independently.
- Larkin Street disseminates best practices and informs thought leaders through presentations, publication of brief reports, and advocacy activities.

Indirect Impact

- Other organizations employ Larkin Street's best practices for serving homeless youths.
- Thought leaders and policy makers envision and enact better policies for homeless youths.

Exhibit 12.3.   One Blueprint for Delivering Results

Finally, theory-of-change work highlights gaps between what is supposed to happen and what is actually occurring. It is not unusual to find, for instance, that people using a nonprofit's services are not the intended beneficiaries. Or an organization may discover a discrepancy between what its leaders think is required for its program to be effective (the length of time that people participate, say) and how the programs are being delivered. This was the case for Expeditionary Learning Schools (ELS), which trains teachers to educate students through real-world projects called learning expeditions.

Multiple evaluations by independent research showed that the ELS model could improve student learning and performance when implemented with fidelity. For a low-performing school, that meant having ELS staff members work on-site with its leadership and faculty thirty days a year for at least three years. In 2004, ELS received significant funding from the Bill and Melinda Gates Foundation to extend its work to new small high schools in needy areas. Before expanding, however, ELS leadership wanted to assess the existing network. The results were bracing: Few of the schools were as highly engaged as they needed to be to achieve excellent results. After several soul-searching conversations, the ELS leadership team and board made the painful decisions to exit schools unwilling to devote the time required to implement the nonprofit's curricular approach. Although that decision initially reduced the size of the network by nearly 25 percent, within three years the addition of new schools, excited by the model's rigor and thoughtfulness, had more than compensated for the loss.

WHAT WILL RESULTS REALLY COST, AND HOW CAN WE FUND THEM?

A theory of change that can't be funded isn't real. And yet nonprofits almost never have enough money to cover everything they are already doing, let alone surplus funds to support new activities and investments. So hard choices inevitably appear as leaders determine which outcomes they can reasonably achieve given current and potential levels of support. If they are to make the necessary tradeoffs, reaching financial clarity has to be their first order of business: This entails understanding the full costs of current programs and how each is affecting the organization's overall financial health. Does the program cover its own costs? Does it require a subsidy? Generate a surplus? Although it might seem as though such information ought to be obvious, the environment in which nonprofits operate tends to make it opaque.

What do things cost? Nonprofits' financial systems typically are rudimentary. Much of Finance's time goes to preparing individual reports for multiple funders about their specific program grants or contracts. Moreover, grants and contracts usually set arbitrary limits—invariable too low—on how much of the money can be used for overhead. This pattern of constraining overhead, which we will talk more about later, both obscures the real costs of essential activities and inhibits investments in the very systems and staff that would enable the nonprofit to achieve its intended impact.

Financial clarity often leads to surprising insights. For example, a youth-development nonprofit launched a culinary enterprise, which involved building a commercial kitchen and hiring local kids to work in it. Believing that a bottle of salad dressing cost $3.15 to produce, the organization sold it for $3.50, yielding a putative 35-cent profit. However, that estimate captured only direct expenses. When indirect expenses such as the kitchen manager's salary, facility expenses, and organizational overhead were appropriately allocated, the cost shot up to $90. What looked like a money-maker was in fact a dramatic money-loser.

Financial clarity also allows decision-makers to assess the impact of their programs on both the organization's mission and its margins. (See Exhibit 12.4.) The objective is not to do away with those that aren't earning their keep: Many essential programs cannot fully cover their own costs. Rather, it is to determine whether discretionary dollars are being used to support activities with the greatest potential to help the organization achieve its intended impact. It's not uncommon for nonprofits to discover—as HCZ did—that they are subsidizing programs that lack such potential. Or, conversely, to find that programs not completely aligned with the strategy are nonetheless worth maintaining because they throw off cash that can be applied to other areas.

Once a nonprofit's leaders hone their organization's intended impact and get an accurate picture of its finances, they can use the matrix below to classify their programs and identify strategic options.

Delivering on the Promise of Nonprofits

Alignment with intended impact (strategy)	high	These programs **require funding.** Pursue opportunities for additional funding and/or cost improvements.	These programs are **self-sustaining.** Invest in and grow them.
	low	These programs are **potential distractions.** Find ways to improve them, or reconsider participation.	These programs **generate income.** Pursue them unless they become a management distraction.
		negative	positive
		Financial contribution (revenue minus cost)	

Exhibit 12.4.   Strategic and Financial Clarity

Where does the money come from? In the for-profit sector, customers drive an organization's performance. If no one is willing to pay for a product or service, we say, "The market has spoken" and shut down the product line or even the organization. In the nonprofit sector, weak market forces exist—donors do decide whom to support, for example. But funders' choices are often influenced by personal relationships or the emotional appeal of the mission rather than by organizational performance. People will give millions of dollars to their alma maters without requiring clear evidence of performance. Yet they may stop funding organizations delivering demonstrable results when their personal interests shift, a phenomenon called donor fatigue.

As a consequence, nonprofits can be quite fragile financially. For example, a Bridgespan study of seventeen well-known and successful youth-serving organizations found that two-thirds experienced at least one year of declining revenues between 1999 and 2003. Nearly one-third dipped twice—and setbacks unrelated to performance led half to lay off staff and 45 percent to cut entire programs.

How can nonprofit leaders develop a reliable funding base? There is no simple answer, but they identify appropriate sources to meet those needs. Larkin Street relies extensively on government funding, which has accounted for two-thirds of its revenues for many years. In contrast, HCZ relies heavily on individual contributions. The activities nonprofits pursue may lend themselves to one financial model or another (and the model may change as an organization gets larger), so it is important to invest over time in building the capabilities to attract and manage appropriate type of funding. Cultivating private donors requires capabilities very different from those needed to apply for government grants and respond to RFPs, for example.

Nonprofit leaders also must look hard at the true costs—both tangible and intangible—associated with potential revenue. Will accepting proffered funds mean executing on the donor's strategy instead of the organization's own? Will the value of the funding be reduced by the donors' excessive reporting requirements, overly long and unpredictable decision processes, or aversion to covering appropriate overhead?

Perhaps most important, both nonprofit leaders and funders need to stop pulling punches—with themselves and others—and confront the reality of what it will cost to deliver results. Knowing that a new program will require $500,000 to implement, raising one-fifth of that, and then attempting to initiate it with the hope that "more will come in later on" or that "something is better than nothing" is standard operating procedure among too many nonprofits. That is a recipe for disappointment and disillusion all around.

HOW DO WE BUILD THE ORGANIZATION WE NEED TO DELIVER RESULTS?

When it comes to delivering and sustaining results, having the right people in the right positions trumps having the right strategy or even a reliable source of capital. In this respect, many nonprofits are fortunate. Their leaders are passionate, entrepreneurial, and hard-working. Their ranks are filled with dedicated people motivated more by the opportunity to help others than by personal economic incentives.

But while nonprofits tend to be strongly led, they also tend to be undermanaged. As a result, they are often marked by persistent confusion about roles and responsibilities and by opaque decision making. These issues play out at every level of the organization—between the board and the executive director, between the executive director and the staff—and, in larger networks, between the center and the affiliates. As the executive director of Communities in Schools observed before bringing in a chief operating officer, "There were a whole series of issues around who had access to decisions, who would get money, who wouldn't.... We had absolutely no framework for defining what were reasonable expectations and what were not."

Such confusion leads to the repeated reinvention of virtually every process, especially in organizations filled with volunteers whose institutional memory can be very short. The costs show up both in a weakened ability to achieve results for beneficiaries and in burnout among volunteers and staff members. As Rob Waldron noted when he was the CEO of JumpStart, "We have to muscle everything we do, and eventually you just get tired!"

Creating better processes. Staff members may feel passionate, but in Bridgespan surveys they also report feeling under-supported and underdeveloped professionally. The absence of processes for setting employees' goals and obtaining feedback, for instance, disconnects individuals and their performance from the organization's strategy. In one nonprofit that pairs mentors with disadvantaged kids, staff members were repeatedly told that the organization's priorities extended beyond the number of matches made to include other dimensions, such as their quality and presence in hard-to-serve communities. But when the time came for performance reviews, staffers were assessed and rewarded only on the first, most easily quantifiable metric. Recognizing this problem, senior leadership redesigned the process to include data and qualitative feedback on the other dimensions and began to regard people who performed well against all the priorities. This story is an exception, however. Few nonprofit directors devote much energy to improving processes.

The basic imbalance between philanthropists and nonprofits—one group has the money the other group desperately needs—gives donors enormous power. Whether their money actually helps the recipients deliver greater results depends on how they give it, not just how much they give. To that end, here are four guideposts for individual donors and foundations.

Understand that the results aren't "ours." Donors can influence the behavior of the nonprofits they fund, but when they impose their own priorities, they risk compromising the nonprofits' ability to deliver results. Such consensus building takes time and effective collaboration. Personal opinions must yield to data and personal motivations must take a backseat to common goals.

Realize that everything takes longer and costs more. Like nonprofits, philanthropists have an alarming tendency to underestimate what it costs to produce results. Instead of placing appropriately sized bets on well-defined strategies, donors often spread too little money among too many recipients. Sophisticated donors recognize when nonprofits are ripe for deeper investment in the form of more money over longer periods of time.

Invest in good overhead. B-level leadership teams will not deliver A-level results. Yet donors are inclined to fund programs while minimizing overhead, including essential expenses such as basic infrastructure and leadership development. Donors must be willing to invest in capacity building for the organizations they support and hold them clearly accountable for generating results.

Remember that excellence is self-imposed. Philanthropy exists in a world without marketplace pressures. Donors don't actually have to do much good in order to feel good. Nor do foundations go out of business because they miss their numbers in consecutive quarters. Quite the contrary. Thanks to the unfailingly positive feedback donors receive, mediocrity is easily perpetuated. Those who are serious about making a real impact must first establish the results for which they hold themselves accountable and then align their grant-making appropriately.

Exhibit 12.5.   How Donors Can Help Nonprofits Achieve Results

Building leadership capacity. Although nonprofits are growing in scales and facing increased pressure to perform, they're not doing nearly as much as they must to attract, retain, and develop a cadre of leaders and managers. A recent study by the Eugene and Agnes E. Meyer Foundation and CompassPoint Nonprofit Services reported that three-quarters of the executive directors surveyed planned to leave their positions within five years. Among the reasons, anxiety about fund-raising and shaky financial sustainability—their organizations' and their own—loomed large. And even though many organizations need executives with specialized skills (such as chief operating and chief financial officers) to implement their strategies, the comparatively low compensation levels in the nonprofit sector can be a significant barrier to filling those positions—and to retain talented people more generally. That is why the willingness to provide fair play in exchange for top-flight executive performance will be a key differentiator between nonprofits that can deliver great results consistently and those that cannot.

Distinguishing between good and bad overhead. The phenomenon most to blame for inefficiencies in nonprofits is something we noted earlier: resistance by just about everyone, including the general public, to supporting overhead. The word itself is disparaging, suggesting wasteful or unnecessary expenses. But there is a difference between good overhead and bad. Investing in an IT system that can track program results is good; paying excessive rent for opulent office space is bad. Attempts to limit all overhead blur this distinction and severely undermine nonprofits' ability to invest in the people and HR processes necessary to deliver great results year after year.

Nonprofits' most common and pernicious response to this phenomenon is to both under-invest in infrastructure and to underreport what they've spent—thereby reinforcing external expectations about what is (and is not) appropriate. In the short run, staff members may be able to "do more with less," but ultimately the organization's beneficiaries suffer.

Nonprofit leaders who understand the link between developing capacity and achieving results are pushing back—by identifying the positions and infrastructure that will be required to implement their strategies, by making those needs transparent to funders, and by communicating the logic that supports those investments throughout their organizations and to their boards.

SUMMARY

No question, a nonprofit's journey from aspirations to impact is a challenging one. Moreover, this pursuit is largely self-imposed, as nonprofits do not typically confront the customer defections, market-share battles, and quarterly earnings reports that shape executive behavior in the for-profit world. There is still a lot of voluntarism in these organizations: Board members donate both time and money. Executives serve a cause rather than maximize their own compensation. Philanthropists donate their hard-earned wealth. Legions of community members contribute their time. So the executive director of a nonprofit cannot simply impose her or his perspective on this diverse group of personally motivated stakeholders.

Instead, the discipline of leadership must replace the discipline of markets. The executive director shoulders the heavy burden of engaging key stakeholders in a rigorous consensus-building process, in which all parties confront the fundamental questions in this article—and fully embrace the subsequent answers.

When such leadership is complemented by donors, board members, and staff members who are equally committed to excellence, the results—whether measured in clearer skies, fewer homeless families, or more college graduates—can be outstanding.

At the time of original printing Jeffrey L. Bradach was the managing partner and a cofounder of the Bridgespan Group, a nonprofit that provides strategy consulting and executive search services to nonprofits and philanthropy organizations. Thomas J. Tierney was the chairman and a cofounder of Bridgespan and a former worldwide managing director of Bain & Company. Nan Stone was a knowledge partner at Bridgespan and a former editor of the Harvard Business Review. *The authors were based in Boston. For a closer look at the case studies and research behind this article, visit www.bridgespan.org.*

CHAPTER THIRTEEN

Performance Leadership

Eleven Better Practices That Can Ratchet Up Performance

Robert D. Behn

H ow can the leaders of a public agency improve its performance? What can the leaders of a governmental organization possibly do that might have a positive effect on the results that their agency produces? This is an important question. This is a leadership question.

THE FUTILE SEARCH FOR A PERFORMANCE SYSTEM

This *leadership question* is not, however, the question about government performance that is usually asked. Traditionally, we have asked the *systems question*. Rather than develop public managers with the leadership capacity to improve the performance of their agencies, we have sought to create performance systems that will impose such

---

Originally published as *Performance Leadership: Eleven Better Practices That Can Ratchet Up Performance*. (Washington, DC: IBM Center for the Business of Government, 2004).

improvements. We have sought to create government-wide schemes that will somehow require performance from all departments, agencies, and bureaus. Thus, we have tended (if only implicitly) to ignore the leadership question and, instead, have focused on the systems question: How can we compel, command, or coerce public agencies into improving their performance?[1]

This systems approach is unlikely to prove very effective (Behn, 2003a). Yes, it is possible for a legislature, a budget office, or a central administrative agency to force public agencies to do things that—if done with genuine enthusiasm and subtle intelligence—could contribute to improved performance. Those upon whom such requirements are imposed, however, are not likely to view them as helpful. They will see these requirements as another complex confusion of administrative regulations with which they must dutifully comply—not as a coherent collection of supportive principles that, if deployed discernibly and employed adaptively, might actually help. Administrative requirements (for performance or anything else) are not designed to elicit discernment and adaptation. They are created to impose obedience and conformity.

Moreover, the senior managers upon whom such compliance is imposed have seen all this before. They have learned how to cope. Indeed, they became senior managers precisely because they learned how to cope. They learned that administrative requirements are hoops through which they must jump. And, as they moved up the organizational hierarchy, they learned to become very good hoop jumpers. They can now jump nimbly through big hoops and small hoops, red hoops and green hoops; they can even jump through flaming hoops without getting the least bit singed.

MAKE, LET, OR HELP THE MANAGERS MANAGE

Still, some of those who have become master hoop-jumpers may desire to do more. They may seek to progress from complying with the requirements of the latest performance-management system to doing something that might help improve the performance of their agency. What should they do? What could they do? How might they exercise leadership so as to ratchet up their organization's performance? If we can provide public-sector executives with a proven strategy—or even with just a few helpful suggestions—we would be doing a useful service.

Over the last two decades, "new public management" has come to represent a collection of managerial philosophies, ideas, and practices designed to improve the performance of government (Behn, 2001). Donald Kettl and others have organized these various ideas and practices into two basic strategies: (1) make the managers manage and (2) let the managers manage. Based on the assumption that public managers lacked clear incentives to improve performance, the make-the-managers-manage strategy was designed to induce public-sector executives to concentrate on improving performance in specific ways. In contrast, the let-the-managers-manage strategy reflected the assumption that these officials knew how to improve performance but were constrained from doing so by the multitude of rules and regulations. Thus, this strategy was designed to ensure that public-sector executives possessed the flexibility necessary to do what was required to improve performance (Kettl, 1997).

Both of these approaches, however, are based on one additional assumption: The people who manage public agencies do know how to improve performance. That is, they possess the capacity—the leadership and managerial skills—necessary to produce real results. Thus, all that is required is to give them either the correct incentives or the necessary flexibility, and they will do it—they will just know what managerial actions will most effectively improve performance.

Whether these public officials have inherited this managerial talent from their ancestral genes or have absorbed it from their organizational and political environment is never stated. The assumption is strictly implicit. Nevertheless, it lurks behind both new-public-management strategies. If we change the condition within which public managers must work—by creating either better incentives or more flexibility—the existing managers will significantly improve organizational performance.

Perhaps, however, the managers do not know what to do. Perhaps managerial talent is difficult to acquire, either from one's parents or one's environment. Perhaps changing the rules is not enough. After all, the private sector devotes significant resources to developing the managerial skills and leadership talents of individuals whom it expects to assume significant responsibilities in the future. And the private sector, it is assumed, has better incentives and more flexibility than government has. Businesses do not assume that managerial talent is acquired genetically or absorbed experientially. Businesses assume that managerial talent can—and should—be learned. In comparison, government significantly under-invests in developing its own managerial capacity (National Commission on the Public Service, 1999).

Maybe we should do more than make or let public managers manage. Maybe we also need a help-the-managers-manage strategy. Maybe we should help officials in the executive branches of our governments advance from administrators to managers to leaders. If we wish to improve the performance of public agencies, maybe we should find a way to help them learn how to exercise performance leadership.[2]

THE SEARCH FOR BETTER PRACTICE

The following approach to performance leadership makes no claim to be a *best practice*. It might be, however, in Eugene Bardach's phrase, a "smart practice" (Bardach, 1998). If employed with thoughtful discernment of the underlying principles and deployed with intelligent adaptation to the characteristics and needs of the particular organization and its environment, this approach might help some public managers improve their agency's performance, marginally or even significantly.

After all, to ratchet up performance a notch or two, most public managers do not require a best practice. All they need is a *better practice*—a set of operational principles, or just one good idea, that is an improvement over what they are currently doing.

This approach is just that—an approach. It is not a rule. It is not a requirement. It is not a prescription. It is certainly not a system.[3] I make no claim that it is the *only* way for public managers to improve the performance of their organization—or even that it is the *best* way. It is merely a way—one *possible* way. It reflects my observations of a variety of efforts by managers of public agencies large and small to improve performance. Some of these observations have been my own. Some of these I have examined in detail;[4] others I have viewed only fleetingly. Still others I have "observed" strictly through the eyes of others.[5]

This approach to performance leadership contains little that is wholly novel or overwhelmingly revolutionary. Indeed, most of its eleven components[6] have been advocated by numerous scholars and practitioners. Yet, too few public managers exploit the advantages of these practices. (Perhaps they have to devote too much time, resources, and energy jumping through multiple hoops.) Fewer still exploit the advantages that may accrue from employing several of these practices simultaneously.

I make no claim that employing all eleven practices is necessary to improve a public agency's performance. Still, each practice is, if the agency manager is not already using it, a *better* practice. Moreover, the eleven do reinforce each other. (Several of these practices are based on the same underlying principles, so that employing one practice without another is often difficult.) Consequently, public managers who employ several of them will have a better opportunity to exploit their reinforcing benefits.

The eleven practices that might be better than current practices are organized into three categories:

- The leaders of the agency can employ four practices to *create a performance framework.*

- The leaders can employ four other practices to *mobilize the organization's resources* to ratchet up performance in some tangible way.

- The leaders can employ three additional practices to *learn how to improve* performance.

These eleven practices offer *one approach* to performance leadership.

ONE APPROACH TO PERFORMANCE LEADERSHIP: ELEVEN BETTER PRACTICES THAT CAN RATCHET UP PERFORMANCE

Creating the Performance Framework: What would it mean to do a better job?

Practice 1: Articulate the organization's mission. Proclaim—clearly and frequently—what the organization is trying to accomplish.

Practice 2: Identify the organization's most consequential performance deficit. Determine what key failure is keeping the organization from achieving its mission.

Practice 3: Establish a specific performance target. Specify what new level of success the organization needs to achieve next.

Practice 4: Clarify your theoretical link between target and mission. Define (for yourself, at least) your mental model that explains how meeting the target will help accomplish the mission.

Driving Performance Improvement: How can we mobilize our people?

Practice 5: Monitor and report progress frequently, personally, and publicly. Publish the data so that every team knows that you know (and that everyone else knows) how well every team is doing.

Practice 6: Build operational capacity. Provide your teams with what they need to achieve their targets.

Practice 7: Take advantage of small wins to reward success. Find lots of reasons to dramatize that you recognize and appreciate what teams have accomplished.

Practice 8: Create "esteem opportunities." Ensure that people can earn a sense of accomplishment and thus gain both self-esteem and the esteem of their peers.

Learning to Enhance Performance: How must we change to do even better?

Practice 9: Check for distortions and mission accomplishment. Verify that people are achieving their targets in a way that furthers the mission (not in a way that fails to help or actually undermines this effort).

Practice 10: Analyze a large number and a wide variety of indicators. Examine many forms of data—both quantitative and qualitative—to learn how your organization can improve.

Practice 11: Adjust mission, target, theory, monitoring and reporting, operational capacity, rewards, esteem opportunities, and/or analysis. Act on this learning, making the modifications necessary to ratchet up performance again.

CREATING THE PERFORMANCE FRAMEWORK

The first question that an agency's leadership team must address is: "What would it mean to do a better job?" Regardless of the level at which the organization is performing, it can still improve. So what might this improvement look like?

The answer to this question is a judgment call. Different people will make this call differently. In some circumstances, the answer may appear obvious. In others, it may be open to much debate. But this debate should not go on forever. If the organization is actually to improve performance, it cannot go on forever. Moreover, regardless of how smart the leaders are, they are unlikely to get this (or any other aspect of their performance strategy) perfectly right the first time.

They ought to accept that they will not get it perfectly right the second time or even the hundredth time, and that they will have to grope along.[7] From the very beginning, they ought to accept that their efforts will make some performance improvements, which can be improved upon further, but only later. That is what the third category of practices is all about: learning how to improve even more.

Historically, however, public-policy practitioners have followed (and public-policy theorists have advocated) some variant of the get-all-of-the ducks-lined-up-before-you-do-anything strategy. But getting all of the ducks lined up can take a lot of time—as measured in years. To line up all of the ducks, the leaders have to create an elaborate strategic plan. They have to get all of the key stakeholders and all of the key legislators to agree to the basic approach outlined in the strategic plan, plus numerous key details. They have to get the funding approved by the budget office, the ways and means committee, and the entire legislature. They have to get the personnel office, and the procurement office, and a few other overhead agencies to sign off on the necessary waivers. And before they know it, the agency's leaders have outlived their appointing authority's tenure.

This is not, however, the only possible strategy. The leaders of public agencies can also employ the groping-along strategy. Indeed, behind my approach to performance leadership lies the assumption that, to create a performance strategy, an organization's leaders need to "get it up and running and then fix it" (Behn, 1991).

Practice 1: Articulate the Organization's Mission

This first practice is hardly profound. It is advocated by numerous management gurus and followed by many practicing managers. Everyone in the organization needs to understand the big picture. Thus, the leaders of the organization need to proclaim, clearly and frequently, what the organization is trying to accomplish.

When you walk into the main lobby of many business firms, government agencies, and nonprofit organizations, you will find the mission statement displayed on the wall. Yet, how many people know what these words say? How many appreciate the values that these words are designed to represent? How many act daily (or even occasionally) to further the basic purposes that are proclaimed in the mission statement and that thus constitute the rationale for the organization's existence? How many public employees go about their assigned tasks completely oblivious to how these tasks contribute (or not) to their agency's mission?

For any organization, particularly for a public agency, it is not enough to form a committee or engage a consultant to write or update the mission statement. After all, in the words of Scott Adams, a mission statement is nothing more than "a long awkward sentence that demonstrates management's inability to think clearly" (Adams, 1996). Even if a public agency's mission statement is neither long, nor awkward, nor convoluted, posting the statement on the wall is not enough. If the agency's leaders want everyone in the organization to take the mission seriously, they need to reiterate its fundamental points at every opportunity.

Practice 2: Identify the Organization's Most Consequential Performance Deficit

The mission of any organization—public, private, or nonprofit—is necessarily vague. It may be inspirational; nevertheless, it lacks specificity. It fails to provide any useful guidance about what to do next: What specific problem does the organization need to attack now to significantly improve its performance? The words in the mission statement do not answer this operational question. Thus, the organization needs to determine what key failure is keeping it from achieving its mission: "What is our most consequential performance deficit?"

Naturally, the organization will have a variety of failures and performance deficits. Just as naturally, it cannot attack all of them at once. It must choose. This is the first challenge to the organization's leadership—to figure out, from the variety of problems inhibiting its ability to produce results, that one performance deficit (or, at most, a very few) on which the organization should now focus its intelligence and energies. This performance deficit can be anywhere along the causal or value chain that runs from inputs to processes to outputs to outcomes:

INPUTS. The big performance deficit might be in the inputs. The organization, for example, might not possess people with the necessary knowledge or skills. If the leaders of a school district believe the caliber of its teachers to be the major cause of its under-performance—that is, why the schools are not doing a better job of educating the children—then the biggest performance deficit is at the input end of the causal chain.

PROCESSES. Alternatively, the big performance deficit might be in the processes. The organization might not be employing the strategies, tactics, plans, structures, procedures, routines, or habits that are most effective in converting its inputs into the desired outputs. For example, the leaders of a school district might conclude that they have recruited excellent teachers but are asking them to teach the wrong curriculum—that the teachers are using textbooks or curriculum guidelines that fail to match the content covered on the statewide tests employed to define the district's performance. Or it could be that these excellent teachers have the right curriculum, but that their allocation of time among the various items on the curriculum does not mesh with the knowledge and skills emphasized on the statewide test.

OUTPUTS. Or the most significant deficit might be the organization's failure to focus on the desired outputs. The leaders might have obtained the necessary inputs and created effective processes. Yet, the people within the organization might be merely employing those inputs and following those processes without any dedication to the outputs they were charged with producing.

Government agencies are particularly prone to this kind of performance failure. After all, public employees are required to follow so many processes that devotion to these processes often displaces their devotion to results. Consequently, the agency's performance deficit might be that it has forgotten what it is actually trying to accomplish—that it is following all of the required standard operating procedures without thinking about how they do (or do not) contribute to the mission. A school system might have hired a staff of talented teachers, and it might have selected a truly effective curriculum. At the same time it might be so arrested by the need to follow all procedures required by the city council, the state board of education, and (now) the federal government that it fails to devote much attention to teaching its students important skills and essential knowledge.

OUTCOMES. Unfortunately, government agencies (like all organizations) do not produce outcomes. Organizations produce outputs. The outcomes are what happens outside the organization. Automobile manufacturers do not produce transportation; they produce cars. County health departments do not produce health; they produce measles immunizations and hypertension testings. Society takes the outputs of many organizations and converts them into outcomes. Society needs public organizations that produce good, effective outputs. Citizens might like to believe that government produces societal outcomes (so that they need not worry about their own contribution), but public agencies can produce only outputs.

When the leaders of a public agency are seeking to identify their organization's most consequential performance deficit, they have to work from a list of inputs, processes, and outputs—but not outcomes. They have to concentrate on the aspects of performance that the organization, and its collaborators, can influence.[8] They want to select a performance deficit that is significantly impairing the agency's ability to influence the outcomes to which its mission tells it to contribute. Nevertheless, this performance deficit will lie in the domains of either inputs, processes, or outputs.

The leaders have to understand the workings of their causal chain. They have to possess an idea about what causes what. They have to understand how their inputs are combined by their organizational processes—how the operations and behaviors that go on inside their organizational black box produce their outputs. They have to understand how their outputs interact with societal processes to produce outcomes.

Identifying the organization's performance deficit is clearly a subjective judgment. Every organization—no matter whether public or private; no matter how well it is performing—has multiple performance deficits. It has a variety of things that, if it did them better, would enhance its outputs, and thus the outcomes to which it contributes. Someone has to choose. This is a leadership requirement. If the individuals at the top of the organizational hierarchy fail to select the performance deficits on which their organization should focus, they have no claim to the title of leader.

The leaders of the organization can make this selection brilliantly or haphazardly. They can put some serious thought into the question, "On which performance deficit should our organization focus?" They can deliberately choose a big deficit that, when eliminated, will have a major impact on the organization's performance. Or they can just as deliberately select a small deficit that, when eliminated, will demonstrate to those working in the organization (and perhaps to multiple stakeholders) that they can accomplish even more. Of course, even if they choose deliberately, the organization's leaders can choose badly.

Still, the biggest mistake is not to choose at all—to avoid the responsibility for determining what the organization should fix next.

Practice 3: Establish a Specific Performance Target

Having made the admittedly subjective judgment about the aspect of the organization's performance deficit on which it will focus, the leaders need to make a second judgment. They need to create an explicit performance target for closing that deficit. That is, the leaders of the organization need to specify what new level of success the organization should attempt to achieve next and by when.

Does the school system need to hire twenty more highly qualified teachers before next September 1? Or does it need to hire two hundred of them? Does the school system need to select a new curriculum package by June 1 (so that the teachers can study it over the summer and be ready to use it by September 1)? Or does it need to select the new curriculum by January 30 (so that the teachers can experiment with it during the spring)? Or, if the school system has suitable teachers and an appropriate curriculum, should it concentrate on ratcheting up its output—on, say, improving its average test scores in math from 75 to 85 in two years, or on reducing the percentage of students with math scores below 50 from 30 percent to 5 percent in three years?

Note that the school system need not have recruited the best teachers or have identified the ideal curriculum before deciding to declare that its most critical performance deficit is its test scores in math or writing or history. It simply needs to make the (again, admittedly subjective) judgment that the performance deficit on which it can make the biggest improvement is at the output end of the causal chain. If, in trying to improve test scores, it discovers that it needs a different mix of teachers with pedagogical skills more suited to its students or its curriculum, or a different curriculum with a pedagogical strategy that reflects the learning style of its students, it can then make the necessary adjustments.

Regardless of whether an agency's leaders choose an input, a process, or an output as their performance target, they need to ensure that it possesses two characteristics:

1. They need to specify their target in sufficient detail to ensure that a vast majority of people will agree when it has been achieved.

2. They need to attach to their target a specific deadline.

Unless they have constructed a target with these two characteristics, they have not created a real performance target.

AN INPUT PERFORMANCE TARGET. The leaders of a health department might pick as their target the introduction, by the end of the next calendar year, of a new computer system to track obesity in children. They might recognize that the county's children have recently become significantly overweight and that they need to attack this problem. At the same time, they might have observed from the experiences of other counties that, before creating some new organizational processes for attacking the problem or before beginning to focus on specific outputs, they need to improve their operational infrastructure. Of course, while some in the department are bringing the new computer online, others can work on improving the processes they will employ or on identifying the appropriate outputs to produce. Nevertheless, the leaders have concluded (given their professional experience, recent research, and knowledge of the department's culture) that the biggest cause of their inadequate performance is this input. Thus, their first performance target is to eliminate this particular deficit.

A PROCESS PERFORMANCE TARGET. Alternatively, this health department's leaders might choose as their target a complete redesign, within two months, of the strategic mechanism for conducting adult hypertension testing and education. The leaders recognize that the department is completely ineffective at convincing adults to get tested and at educating those whose results are dangerously high. Thus, it decides that it cannot begin to focus on the output of the number of individuals it tests and educates until it develops a completely new strategy and procedures for doing so.

AN OUTPUT PERFORMANCE TARGET. Finally, the leaders of a health department might select as their target the immunization of 99.5 percent of the county's three-year-olds against measles by June 30. The county has an adequate supply of the vaccine and has developed an effective strategy for reaching parents; it simply needs to energize county employees to focus on output production. Sure, there may be some dispute about how many three-year-olds live in the county (should we count the children of migrant farm workers who move into the county in late May?), and even some (although fewer) dispute about how many children actually received a proper immunization. Nevertheless, a rudimentary accounting system should be able to certify, to most people's satisfaction, whether or not the target has been achieved.

Practice 4: Clarify Your Theoretical Link Between Target and Mission

Unfortunately, no performance target is precisely the same as the organization's mission. By achieving the target, the organization should further its mission. Otherwise the leadership team would not have chosen to focus on the related performance deficit or have selected this as its next target. Still, the leaders need to make this connection very clear. They need to define (for themselves individually, at least, and perhaps collectively) a mental model that explains how meeting the target will help accomplish the mission.

In some circumstances, the causal connection will be obvious. If a health department delivers the proper measles immunization to a child, that child's probability of actually being immune to measles, and thus healthier, is greater than 99 percent.[9] The output of immunization is directly connected to the outcome of a healthier child. Moreover, the immunization process is relatively simple and, if followed by certified personnel, does not have a lot of defects; if a certified nurse follows the standard operating procedures for measles immunization, the immunization will take. The theoretical linkage between achieving the performance target and furthering the agency's mission is not theoretical at all. It has been well established, very empirically.

Unfortunately, most actions taken by most public agencies are not connected this closely to their mission. The causal link between the actions taken by the agency to close its performance deficit and the achievement of its mission may be indirect, vague, poorly understood, or nonexistent. Consequently, the leaders of public agencies cannot merely define a performance deficit, select a performance target, and mobilize their organization to achieve this target—all under the (implicit) assumption that this will further its mission. These leaders need first to clarify explicitly the nature of their theory that connects reaching the target and furthering the mission. Then, once they have reached the target, they need to check to see whether this effort has, indeed, produced some real improvement.

DRIVING PERFORMANCE IMPROVEMENT

Having created their performance framework, the agency's leaders must address a second question: "How can we mobilize our people?" Having created their performance target, the leaders have to convince the people in the agency to work intelligently and energetically to achieve this target.

This effort to mobilize the resources of the organization is hardly mechanical. It, too, requires leadership, but it does not require charisma. Certainly, it would help if the leaders could walk into an agency conference on a Friday afternoon and so dazzle their staff that everyone leaves determined to produce twice as much the next week. Most leaders cannot do that. Instead, they do a large number of mundane things that, collectively, can have the same kind of gripping impact on individual and organizational behavior.

Practice 5: Monitor and Report Progress Frequently, Personally, and Publicly

Again, this better practice is hardly mysterious. The leaders of the organization have to track and publish the performance data so that every team knows that the leadership knows (and that everyone else knows) how well every team is doing.[10]

This is the first step in motivating teams (and the individuals on these teams) to achieve their performance targets. The mechanism chosen to monitor and report progress depends on both the culture of the organization and the nature of the performance targets. Still, whatever mechanism the leaders choose, they need to ensure that it provides several kinds of information.

First, this practice of monitoring and reporting needs to dramatize that the organization's leaders are paying attention to its progress. The people in any organization have an easy instrument for determining what their leaders care about; they measure how much time the leaders spend on their various initiatives. If the leaders do not spend time monitoring progress toward their performance targets, the entire organization quickly realizes that the leaders do not really care.

After all, the leaders' most valuable resource is their own time. They can invent clever ways to get around budgetary limits and regulatory constraints. But they face one eternal, immutable constraint; like all other humans, they have only 168 hours in any week. They cannot squeeze 169 hours out of any week, save an hour from one week to the next, or borrow an hour from a colleague or friend. Thus, the metaphor about "spending time" is not a metaphor at all. It is reality. People "spend" time just as they spend money. Both are extremely valuable resources—and time is scarcer than money.

Performance measurement is not performance leadership. Performance measurement is a passive activity easily delegated to a few wonks in a back office. Performance leadership, however, requires the ceaseless, active engagement of the organization's leaders.

If these leaders do not spend time monitoring the organization's performance targets, everyone soon figures out that they are really not interested. If, however, these leaders do spend the time necessary to dramatize that they are carefully following progress, many in the organization will begin to take the performance targets—and their part in achieving them—seriously.

Second, this practice of monitoring and reporting needs to dramatize how well different teams or individuals are contributing to the overall target. In many circumstances, effective reporting can be done on a single piece of paper. If the responsibility for achieving the performance target is allocated among various teams within the agency, the single piece of paper need contain only two columns: Column A lists all the teams that made their target for the last month, last quarter, or last year; Column B lists all the teams that did not make their target. I call this "The List" (Behn, 2003b).

For example, if a state health department creates a production target for immunizations—during the fiscal year give 95 percent of the state's one-year-olds the first dose of the measles vaccine—it can allocate this target among the counties. Each county also has a production target: give 95 percent of its one-year-olds the first dose of the measles vaccine. At the end of the year, the reporting mechanism is quite simple: Column A lists every county that made its 95 percent target; Column B lists every county that did not make this target.[11] One consequence of such a reporting system is that it can motivate improved performance.

What will the members of each county team do when this report arrives? First, they will look to see whether their own county is in Column A or B. Next, they will look to see whether the counties of their closest colleagues are in Column A or B. Finally, they will realize that their colleagues are checking to see whether their own county is in Column A or B. To motivate performance, a reporting mechanism needs to provide everyone with three essential pieces of information:[12]

- It needs to tell every individual how well his or her team is doing in achieving its assigned target.
- It needs to tell every individual how well every other team is doing in achieving its assigned target.
- It needs to tell every individual that everyone else knows how well his or her team is doing in achieving its assigned target.

The performance target could be allocated among individuals rather than teams. Teams, however, have several obvious advantages. The performance of most organizations depends on cooperation among individuals (otherwise, we would not need the organization). And to foster such cooperation, leaders need to both select and assign targets to teams. In fact, they ought to create targets that can be assigned to teams.[13]

Whether the targets are allocated among teams or individuals, however, everyone in the organization must be part of a personal or collective unit with responsibility for achieving a specified target. And every individual must get the three pieces of information about progress toward all of these targets, be they for individuals or for teams.

The leader of each team, naturally, faces an extra burden and thus extra pressure, but the three pieces of information should be made available to everyone in the organization. After all, everyone wants to be a winner. Everyone wants to be in Column A. No one wants to be in Column B. Consequently, if they have an opportunity to move themselves from Column B to Column A, they may try to do so. And if they see some of their colleagues in Column A—teams composed of individuals who, they believe, are neither smarter nor more talented—making their targets, their own ego may drive them to do what is necessary to get themselves listed in Column A.

This is competition, but not of the conventional sort. When we think of the concept of competition, we typically (if only implicitly) think about athletics. At the end of the season, one team is the winner and all of the other teams are losers. Traditional competition is a zero-sum game. But the kind of competition created by The List does not necessarily have only one winner. In fact, every team can be a winner because every team can achieve its own target. These teams are not competing against each other. Each team competes against its own goal, and if it achieves its goal, it moves to Column A—it becomes a winner. Every team can be a winner (or a loser); its success is not limited by the successes of other teams.

I call this "friendly competition" (Behn, 2003c). It is still competition. Some teams can win; some teams can lose. But neither the number of winners nor the number of losers is predetermined before the competition begins. Because everyone has the opportunity to be a winner, the competition need not be cutthroat.[14] Teams that share their secrets with their colleagues are not penalized. This is the difference between *competition against each other* and *competition against a goal.* The latter is friendly competition.[15]

Competition motivates. This belief is a fundamental component of the American ideology. But what exactly does it motivate? It does not necessarily motivate people to win. It can motivate people to simply quit. Competition will motivate people to strive to win only if they believe they have a real chance to win. If the members of a team conclude that their chances of winning are, effectively, zero, the competition will hardly motivate them to ratchet up performance. Friendly competition can motivate everyone because it gives every team—and thus everyone—a chance to win.[16]

Practice 6: Build Operational Capacity

Of course, no team can win unless the organization's leaders provide their teams with whatever they need to achieve their targets.

W. Edwards Deming did not like goals or, as he often called them, "quotas." One of his reasons was that he believed most organizations set goals for individuals or teams but failed to provide them with the operational capacity to achieve the goals. "I have yet to see a quota that includes any trace of a system by which to help anyone to do a better job," wrote Deming. Personal "goals are necessary" and people should set them for themselves, he argued; "but numerical goals set for other people, without a road map to reach the goal, have effects opposite to the effects sought." Deming (1986) was, admittedly, talking about "numerical quotas for hourly workers," the classical "work standards" of scientific management. Nevertheless, Deming's general point still applies. If the leaders of an organization wish to improve performance, they cannot just assign targets to individuals or teams. They have to provide everyone in the organization with the "system," the "road map"—whatever it takes to create the operational capacity necessary to achieve the targets.

This operational capacity might include money and other resources, people and training, technology and production systems, the cooperation of essential partners, and a road map of tactics and strategies that help teams achieve their targets. Leaders cannot simply demand improved performance. They cannot simply set new, demanding performance targets. The organization's leadership has to give teams the capabilities necessary for achieving these targets.

Practice 7: Take Advantage of Small Wins to Reward Success

Having established a performance target, the agency's leaders need to dramatize that they recognize and appreciate what teams (and the individuals on those teams) have accomplished. And although moving a team from Column B to Column A on a widely distributed piece of paper (or the home page on the agency's intranet) is itself a reward, the leaders can do more. When a team achieves its annual target—or even makes significant quarterly progress toward it—effective leaders understand how to celebrate the success. Some accomplishments warrant the simple recognition of a sincere thank you. Other triumphs require the leaders to kill the fatted calf. The magnitude of the ceremony should match the significance of the victory.

In public agencies, celebrating successes is undervalued.[17] So is saying "thank you." There can be a danger in over-celebrating a minor achievement. In most organizations, however, the more common mistake is to under-acknowledge achievements of all sizes. Most public executives do not say thank you enough. As William James (1920) once wrote: "I now perceive one immense omission in my psychology—the deepest principle of Human Nature is the *craving to be appreciated,* and I left it out altogether from the book, because I never had it gratified till now."

To foster an environment in which successes will be celebrated more frequently, an agency's leaders can create more milestones. Do not just create a performance target for the year. Break that target down into quarterly and monthly targets. And when a team has an important breakthrough, the agency's leaders need to find a way to signal, both to this team and to everyone else throughout the agency, that this group of individuals has done something truly worthwhile.

This is Karl Weick's (1984) "strategy of small wins." Do not try to solve the problems of the world by establishing one cosmic performance target. Do not try to bring about international peace and harmony by the end of the fiscal year. Instead, create performance targets that move the organization closer to achieving its mission. "Pick a winner," advocates Robert Schaffer (1988). Create performance targets that give the people in the organization the opportunity to win—to achieve something that they (and those whose opinions they value) recognize as consequential. Then the agency's leaders have to create a vehicle for making sure that the team's members (and, again, those whose opinions they value) understand that the leaders recognize the significance of the achievement.[18]

This addiction strategy is really quite simple. Create performance targets that people can hit. Get them hooked on success. Give them an opportunity to earn the adrenaline rush that comes from accomplishing something worthwhile, and then give them the challenge of accomplishing even more.

This is why I describe this leadership approach as a way to *ratchet up* performance. Each small win creates not just a sense of accomplishment but also a new and higher plateau—a new baseline from which future performance must be compared.

Practice 8: Create "Esteem Opportunities"

Rewarding success is one way to ensure that the members of high-performing teams can earn a sense of accomplishment and thus gain both self-esteem and the esteem of their peers. And the opportunity to earn such esteem can be an important motivational strategy for any organization's leaders.

After all, once people have satisfied their three most basic needs on Abraham Maslow's hierarchy, they come to the "esteem needs"—the needs "for self-respect, or self-esteem, and for the esteem of others." These needs, Maslow (1943) argues, must be "soundly based upon real capacity, achievement, and respect from others." Thus, the need for esteem includes the desire "for achievement, for adequacy, for confidence in the face of the world." But it also includes "the desire for reputation or prestige (defining it as respect or esteem from other people), recognition, attention, importance or appreciation."

The leaders of a public agency can contribute to the esteem needs of their organization's employees and collaborators. The leaders can give people an opportunity to take pride in a real achievement. They can give people an opportunity to gain a reputation for real achievement. Moreover, in doing so, the agency's leaders can contribute to their organization's ability to do even more. For, writes Maslow (1943), "satisfaction of the self-esteem need leads to feelings of self-confidence, worth, strength, capability and adequacy of being useful and necessary in the world."

The strategy of small wins creates successes that can convince people that they possess the ability to achieve even bigger wins. Thus, one of the better practices that the leaders of public agencies can employ to ratchet up performance is to create opportunities for individuals to earn this esteem—both self-esteem and the esteem of others.

The List—the two columns of teams that did and did not achieve their targets—might be described as an effort to create peer pressure. But the phrase "peer pressure" has come to mean (both in the vernacular and in the psychological literature) the coercion that groups place on individual members to engage in some kind of antisocial or pathological behavior. Most commonly, the phrase "peer pressure" refers to the efforts of teenagers to convince their socially responsible peers to participate in the three evils of contemporary culture: sex, drugs, and rock and roll.

To distinguish this better practice from the corrupting influence normally associated with peer pressure, I am experimenting with the label "esteem opportunities." Leaders create esteem opportunities for the people in their organization by giving them a chance to shine. To do so, the leaders have to create two opportunities. First, they have to give people a chance to accomplish something worthwhile. Second, they have to give people a chance to be recognized for the accomplishment, particularly by colleagues, friends, and others whose esteem they value. By setting performance targets, the leaders give people the opportunity to do something useful and important. By saying thank you and hosting celebrations, these leaders recognize people's achievements.

Leaders have many ways to recognize accomplishment and thus to generate esteem. The List is one. Saying thank you and hosting ceremonies are others. But how can the leadership team signal that a team has done exceptionally well? If every team has the opportunity to "win," and if a team can earn only two rankings—the success of Column A or the failure of Column B—how can the leaders create extra esteem for those whose performance warrants special recognition?

One practice (that I have seen employed in a variety of public organizations) is to ask the head of a particularly successful team: "Would you please come back to next month's meeting and tell us how you did it?" In doing so, the organization's leaders thereby reward the team's head by giving him or her an esteem opportunity. At the same time, they have rewarded this individual by giving him or her more work. For now, this team leader must (1) keep up team performance during the coming month so as not to be embarrassed by having to explain why the team regressed and (2) devote additional time to preparing a coherent presentation to somehow explain the team's success. Still, the message will be clear. Everyone will get it. This team has been asked to report on its strategy, tactics, and processes precisely because it is a high-performing team.

This esteem opportunity need not be limited to the head of the team. The agency's leaders could also ask: "Would you please bring your team to next month's meeting and tell us how you all did it?" Like saying thank you, esteem opportunities are not a scare resource that can be awarded to just a few elites. They can be created for multiple individuals and teams throughout the organization.

Moreover, this kind of esteem opportunity provides for technology transfer, and thus helps to build operational capacity. It gives those on the less successful teams—and often those on the more successful teams, too—the chance to learn new strategies, tactics, and processes. Although the explanations offered by some team members may not be as articulate or clear as ones that the agency's leaders might produce, such imperfect explanations come with one added advantage. Those listening to a convoluted explanation of what everyone accepts to be a significant success can easily conclude: "They aren't so smart. If they can do it, we certainly can do it, too."

LEARNING TO ENHANCE PERFORMANCE

Achieving a performance target, however, is not enough. Once a public agency has made its first performance target, it cannot stop. The leaders of the organization have to address a third question: "How must we change to do even better?"

To answer this question, they have to answer several others: "How has our performance deficit changed?" "What is our performance deficit now?" "Have we reduced our deficit but not enough, so that we need to concentrate on reducing it even more?" "Or have we eliminated it—or at least reduced it to such a small level—so that we ought to concentrate on a bigger and more significant performance deficit?" And finally: "What should be our new performance target?" To answer these questions, the leaders of public organizations need data and analysis.

The organization's leaders can make such adjustments at any time; but they certainly ought to think carefully about their targets before the beginning of the next fiscal year. Then, once they have created their new performance target for the next year, next quarter, next month, or next week, they have to figure out how to mobilize the people in their organization and their collaborators to achieve this new, more demanding level of performance: "What operational capacity do we need to achieve this new target?" "How can we monitor and report progress so as to create friendly competition?" "How should we reward success, and how can we create esteem opportunities?"

To answer such questions, the agency's leaders need to examine carefully what they have accomplished and why: "Does our theory about causal links between targets and mission still hold? Or must we revise it?" "What can we learn from our past successes and failures, and how can we apply these lessons to ratchet up performance even further?" Like everyone else in the organization, the leaders are hooked. Having achieved a significant success, they know people are expecting even more. They have to ask: "How do we ratchet performance up again?"

Practice 9: Check for Distortions and Mission Accomplishment

Unfortunately, achieving the performance target does not guarantee that the organization achieves its mission. Achieving the target does not even guarantee that the organization has helped to accomplish its mission. Thus, the leaders of the organization need to verify that people are pursuing their targets in ways that do, indeed, further the mission (not in ways that either fail to help or even undermine the effort). They need to check for a variety of distortions in which achieving the target may not have contributed significantly to accomplishing the mission.

After all, the leader's theoretical link between target and mission may not be perfect. Indeed, this link may not even exist. It is always difficult, in any organization, to predict cause-and-effect relationships—to understand the complex interactions that are going on inside the organizational black box. The organization's leaders can take specific actions based on the perfectly reasonable prediction (derived from established theory or personal experience) that it will create behavior that will then produce the results they desire—or, at least, something close to these results—only to discover that actual consequences of these actions are quite different. They have no guarantee that the mental model they used to create their theoretical link between target and mission is correct, or even close to correct.

The leaders need to check carefully to be sure that the agency has, by achieving its performance target, indeed helped further its true purpose. Did their organizational black box respond as they predicted? If their theoretical link does not appear to work as they predicted, they have to figure out why.

The target could have encouraged perverse behavior. Mason Haire's oft-quoted observation, "What gets measured gets done," is very specific. If an organization measures progress toward a performance target, people will do things that help achieve that target. Haire, however, makes no guarantee that they will do things that help further the organization's mission. People will focus their efforts not on the difficult-to-accomplish mission but on the easy-to-measure targets. Consequently, if the leaders have chosen the wrong targets—if they have chosen the wrong thing to measure—they will distort the behavior of people within the organization in such a way as to hit the targets but contribute little or nothing to the mission.

This can be true even if everyone in the organization is purely dedicated to the mission. Their behavior will be influenced by the visibility of the target, by the periodic monitoring and reporting, and by the recognition and esteem that come from hitting interim and final targets. (This is one reason why the leadership needs to continue to emphasize not only the specific targets but also the overall mission.)

Moreover, if people in the agency feel too much pressure to achieve their targets, they will begin to cheat. As the twentieth-century American philosopher William Claude Dukenfield (a.k.a. W. C. Fields) once observed, "A thing worth having is a thing worth cheating for."[19] And, just as the nineteenth-century American philosopher George Washington Plunkitt distinguished between dishonest graft (which was illegal) and honest graft (which was perfectly legal, though everyone knew it was graft) (Riordon, 1963),[20] I want to distinguish between two types of cheating: honest cheating and dishonest cheating (Behn, 1998).

Dishonest cheating is illegal. You can go to jail for it (though you may only lose your job). In recent years, in response to the pressure to improve student test scores, some educators have engaged in dishonest cheating. After an exam, some teachers have driven up individual student scores, and thus school scores, by erasing wrong answers and replacing them with correct answers. Some district officials have driven up district scores by doctoring the data that they report. And, of course, during a test, a teacher can help improve an individual student's score by leaning over and saying, "Johnny, you might want to recheck your answer to question five."[21]

Honest cheating, however, is perfectly legal. Yet, we think of it as cheating. Honest cheating involves focusing strictly on achieving the target while ignoring the mission. Honest cheaters do not care about the mission, only about the target (and its associated rewards). Of course, by emphasizing the importance of the target—and by rewarding teams that reach their targets—the organization's leaders are simultaneously encouraging this honest cheating. They should not be surprised that people and teams, in their rush to achieve their performance targets, will tend to neglect (or even subvert) the mission.

In education, honest cheating is called "teaching to the test." It is perfectly legal to teach to the test. Indeed, in many ways, we want our teachers to do so; we want them to help their students learn the knowledge and capabilities necessary to pass the test. At the same time, we do not want teachers to devote so much effort to teaching their students precisely what will be tested in the annual, standardized exam that they fail to cover other kinds of knowledge and capabilities that are important but will not, and perhaps cannot, be on the standardized test. As one education expert often notes, "The challenge in educational testing is designing a test worth teaching to."

The same is true for other performance targets. The challenge of performance leadership is to create a target that we really want people to achieve—a target that it would be worth cheating *honestly* to achieve. The leaders of a public agency need to establish a performance target such that when people adjust their behavior to achieve it, they are simultaneously adjusting their behavior in ways that further the agency's mission.

Practice 10: Analyze a Large Number and a Wide Variety of Indicators

The leaders of the organization need to learn not only whether they have created any distortions, whether their agency has engaged in any cheating, and whether their agency is making progress toward achieving its mission. Regardless of how well the agency has done, they also need to learn how to improve. For all of these purposes, the leaders need to examine many forms of data—both quantitative and qualitative.

Some of this learning will be quantitatively sophisticated. After all, doing a conscientious evaluation of a public agency's impact is a complex undertaking. It requires a sophisticated analysis of a multitude of potential influences as well as some subtle judgments about how to measure progress toward the mission.[22] It also requires a lot of very clean, quantitative data.[23]

Some of this learning, however, will rely on data that are significantly less quantitative and significantly less verifiable. It will come in the form of anecdotes and casual observations that may, however, be no less helpful. Particularly when the challenge is to uncover distortions and to develop ways to improve for next year, the organization's leaders may find that examining such qualitative data analytically (though not mathematically) can be of significant help.

The leaders can employ quantitative analysis to determine whether their agency is accomplishing its mission. But what they really want to know is whether they are moving their organization in the proper direction. A public agency's leaders need not seek to determine whether they have *achieved* their mission, for they never will. Instead, they need to learn whether or not they have done a better job recently. They need to learn whether or not their performance strategy is truly *furthering* their mission.

Once they are convinced that they are making progress, the leaders have to determine why: What are the things that they have done that have contributed significantly to their progress? It would be nice to be able to use quantitative analysis to answer this question—to determine precisely what actions contributed *most* to their progress. Their organization's data set, unfortunately, will rarely be robust enough to answer this question. But, then, the leaders do not need to determine *the best practice.* They need to uncover only *a better practice*—or two. Then they can employ these better practices in a way that ratchets up performance some more.

Thus, the analytical task of determining what has worked, what has not worked, and what needs to be done to improve performance requires examining a diversity of indicators. Some indicators will be found in formal data sets collected by the agency or by other organizations. Additional indicators will be found in careful, if serendipitous, observations in the reports from the heads of successful teams about how (they think) they achieved their targets, and in the complaints about inadequate resources, perverse incentives, or distortions.

Practice 11: Adjust Mission, Target, Theory, Monitoring and Reporting, Operational Capacity, Rewards, Esteem Opportunities, and/or Analysis

The learning that results from checking for distortions, from evaluating mission accomplishment, and from analyzing numerous indicators, itself, accomplishes very little. The leaders of the agency need to act on this learning, making the modifications necessary to ratchet performance up another notch.

The leaders may change any of the key components of their performance strategy—creating a new performance target, modifying how they monitor and report performance, reallocating resources, creating new operational capacity, revising rewards, inventing new esteem opportunities, or adjusting how they conduct their analyses.

They might even decide to modify their mission. If they have significantly improved their operational capacity, they might extend their agency's operating mandate to include other authorized (but underemphasized) purposes.[24] Or, on discovering that they lack some key capability—be that essential funding or cooperative collaborators—they might contract their ambitions.

THE PERFORMANCE TREADMILL

Thus, the cycle begins all over again. But I do not think of this as a neatly drawn, annual circle, containing eleven boxes with eleven (unidirectional) arrows connecting Box N to Box N+1 (and, at the end, Box 11 to Box 1). Rather, my operational diagram is quite messy.[25] After all, if the leaders of a public agency learn something in month three, rather than waiting until the end of the year to make the implied change, they will make the change immediately. Indeed, if they are truly trying to ratchet up performance, they are constantly making changes.[26]

Thus, this approach to performance leadership is a treadmill—a treadmill for the organization's leaders, for its employees, and for its collaborators. And once they jump on the treadmill, they cannot get off. They have to keep running—with the success on one lap requiring even more success on the next.

Business executives are accustomed to this treadmill. Shareholders do not say, "Because you did such a good job this year, you can take next year off." Instead, this year's performance becomes the baseline for measuring next year's accomplishments. In business, the expectations of the investors create the performance treadmill. Every year, the investors demand that a firm ratchet up its performance.

Although these eleven better practices reflect observations of public-sector organizations and are designed specifically for them, they can help any organization—public, private, or nonprofit— ratchet up performance. The leaders of a public sector organization are not, however, required to jump on the performance treadmill. After all, they have a lot of other responsibilities. Citizens are not single-minded in demanding that this year's performance become the baseline for next year's improvements. They are at least as focused on demanding that the leaders of public agencies deploy their financial assets precisely as prescribed by legislation and that they treat citizens, employees and applicants, vendors and bidders very, very fairly. These demands are enough to keep any self-respecting public manager quite busy. Why not focus on meeting the accountability demands for finances and fairness, and leave the demands for improving performance to a successor?[27]

If, however, the leaders of a public agency do wish to ratchet up performance—if they choose to jump on the performance treadmill—these eleven better practices offer one approach that they can employ to exercise performance leadership.

Notes

1. I make a clear distinction between "performance systems" and "performance management." A performance system is a government-wide effort. One kind of performance system is performance measurement; another is performance budgeting. It is a system just like a procurement system or a personnel system. Like any system, it requires public agencies to follow rules and regulations, to publish annual reports, and to leave paper trails that permit others to audit compliance with these rules and regulations. The Government Performance and Results Act is one such system.

    Performance management is not a system. Performance management is more than performance measurement. To me, performance management is the active, conscious efforts of the leadership of a public agency to produce more, or better, or more consequential results that citizens value. In both the academic and political worlds, however, the phrase "performance management" is commonly used to mean a mere performance system. Thus, to emphasize my distinction, I will use the contrasting labels of (1) performance systems, and (2) performance leadership.

    Are CompStat and CitiStat performance systems? They are certainly government-wide (or, at least, agency-wide) efforts to require different units to do specific things. But, the public leaders who created these efforts hardly thought of them as systems that, once created, would continue to function on automatic pilot. Instead, Commissioner William Bratton of the New York Police Department and Mayor Martin O'Malley of Baltimore both recognized that to make their approach work to improve performance required the constant attention of top leadership. If the top leaders of the department or the city stop going to the meetings, the system will have no impact on the behavior of the managers at the next level.

2. The following does not reflect the personality trait school of leadership. Instead of examining the individual attributes and virtues that may convert an individual into a leader, I am focusing on the leadership activities and

actions that can help public managers improve the performance of their agencies.

3. A note to legislators, budget officers, and other overhead regulators: Please do not attempt to impose this "approach" on all of the departments, agencies, and bureaus within your jurisdiction by requiring them to jump through eleven more hoops. Please do not demand that they file an eleven-chapter annual report explaining in detail how they followed each of the eleven practices. If you really want to improve the performance of particular agencies, *help* the managers become leaders by providing them with opportunities to learn how to use these eleven (and other) leadership practices.

4. Those that I have investigated in some detail include the Massachusetts Department of Public Welfare, the Massachusetts Department of Revenue, the New York City Bureau of Motor Equipment, the Washington Department of Labor and Industries, and Homestead Air Force Base. These investigations include not only the traditional after-the-fact interviews with key individuals at multiple levels in the organization, but also, for many of these organizations, in-process observations of the leaders in action at internal meetings and other settings.

5. For example, much has been written about the CompStat strategy for improving the performance of the New York City Police Department (and the police departments of other cities):

- William Bratton with Peter Knobler, *Turnaround: How America's Top Cop Reversed the Crime Epidemic* (New York: Random House, 1998).
- James Lardner, "The C.E.O. Cop," *The New Yorker* (February 6, 1995), pp. 45–46, 51–57.
- Jack Maple with Chris Mitchell, *The Crime Fighter: How You Can Make Your Community Crime-Free* (New York: Doubleday, 1999).
- Paul E. O'Connell, *Using Performance Data for Accountability: The New York City Police Department's CompStat Model of Police Management* (Washington, D.C.: The IBM Center for The Business of Government, August 2001).
- Eli B. Silverman, NYPD *Battles Crime: Innovative Strategies in Policing* (Boston: Northeastern University Press, 2001).
- Chris Smith, "The NYPD Guru," *New York* (April 1, 1996), pp. 29–34.
- Dennis C. Smith and William J. Bratton, "Performance Management in New York City: CompStat and the Revolution in Police Management," in *Quicker, Better, Cheaper? Managing Performance in American Government*, Dall Forsythe (Ed.). (Albany, NY: Rockefeller Institute Press, 2001).

For another example of performance leadership, see Burton Rosenthal, "Lead Poisoning (A)," C14-75-123.0, and "Lead Poisoning (B)," C14-75-124.0 (John F. Kennedy School of Government, Harvard University, 1975).

6. I apologize for having eleven practices; the original version of this list had an even six practices (Behn, 1991, "Managing for Performance," pp. 49–82). Indeed, when producing a list of almost anything, it is incumbent upon the list producer to edit the elements so that they number ten or twelve, or perhaps five, six, or eight. Lists of seven or nine or thirteen have been traditionally inadmissible. David Letterman never reads a top-eleven list.

Nevertheless, as I have attempted to observe and define some better practices for performance management, I have been unable to justify cutting the list to ten or to warrant expanding it to twelve. I put each item on this list because I wanted to emphasize it. For example, I could have combined Practice 9 (Check for cheating, distortions, and mission accomplishment) with Practice 10 (Analyze a large number and a wide variety of indicators). After all, Practice 10 is how you do Practice 9. But I wanted to make both of these activities stand out. Similarly, Practice 3 (Establish a performance target) is hardly more than an obvious extension of Practice 2 (Identify the organization's most consequential performance deficit). Yet, again, I wanted to distinguish the two actions and emphasize the importance of both; thus I gave them separate numbers.

Nevertheless, it would be nice to add one item (but not two) to create a list containing an even dozen practices, thus eliminating the dissonance that readers will feel when confronted with an oddball list of eleven. Any suggestions?

7. For a discussion of "management by groping along," see Robert D. Behn, "Management by Groping Along," *The Journal of Policy Analysis and Management*, 1998, 7(4), pp. 643–663; and Behn, 1991, Chapter Seven, "Management by Groping Along."

8. This argument depends, of course, on my definition of *outputs* and *outcomes*. Many people use these two words as if their distinction were self-obvious, at least at the abstract level. When faced with a specific public agency with a particular set of responsibilities, however, people will not necessarily define the agency's output or outcome in the same way. My definition of an *output* is what the agency itself produces—what it puts out the door.

For a school system, the *output* is students with diplomas, knowledge, and skills. But, of course, the *outcome* arrives only many years later when the school system's students have become adults. The outcome to which we citizens want a school system to contribute is that its graduates grow up to be *productive employees and responsible citizens*. Obviously, numerous societal influences affect what a community's children become when they grow up; the school system is only one such influence.

For a health department, the *output* might be the children immunized against measles and the adults tested for hypertension. But, of course, the *outcome* that we care about is the *health of people* in the community. And a county health department cannot control the behavior of adults who have dangerously high blood pressure, even if it gives these adults the latest warnings and advice in the most persuasive of ways. Similarly, the department cannot even ensure that all of the community's parents will respond to its immunization announcements and warnings and get their children immunized (although requiring immunization for school attendance can help).

The leaders of a public agency can broaden the boundaries of their organization by recruiting collaborators to contribute to their *outputs*. A school superintendent can convince parents and civic leaders to take responsibility for contributing to the education of the district's students. A county health officer can recruit others to help convince adults with hypertension that they should eat differently and exercise more or to help convince parents to get their children immunized. Such entrepreneurship broadens the operational boundary of the "organization" and thus helps to create better outputs—and, we assume and hope, better outcomes. Still, even the most creative public managers cannot completely control (what I define as) the *outcomes*. Society simply comes with too many other influences.

9. "Studies indicate that more than 99 percent of persons who receive two doses of measles vaccine (with the first dose administered no earlier than the first birthday) develop serologic evidence of measles immunity" (Atkinson, Wolfe, Humiston, and Nelson, 2002).

10. Here I assume that responsibility for achieving the agency's performance target will be divided among several teams rather than individuals. If the target was to immunize 99.5 percent of the children in a county against measles, the county could be divided into districts; then a team could be assigned to each district and given its own target. If the target was to introduce a new computer system, that task could be broken down into subtasks; different teams could be assigned to complete each such subtask. Of course, these targets or tasks could be assigned to individuals rather than to teams.

11. The creation of Column B can be considered an effort to shame those who failed to make their targets. Thus, being listed in Column B can be considered a punishment. But if the original targets were fair, if other teams

made their (equally demanding) targets, and if the teams listed in Column B were not arbitrarily prevented from making their targets (and thus moving to Column A), the shame or punishment is self-inflicted.

Of course, The List needs to contain only Column A. Column B can be left off. But will the shame or punishment be any less? After all, everyone who sees Column A can immediately calculate who is in the missing Column B.

Note that for some people in some circumstances, shaming may be an effective motivational strategy. For example, King and Mathers (1997) report that "rewards, recognition, and the avoidance of negative publicity and sanctions are important to upwardly mobile [school] principals."

12. For an example of how the leader of one public agency used a single piece of paper to convey these three pieces of information, see Behn, *Leadership Counts*, pages 70–73. For an example of how the leader of a quite different public organization used billboards to convey the same three pieces of information, see Robert D. Behn, "Homestead Air Force Base" and "Homestead Air Force Base: Sequel."

13. I am grateful to Frederick Thompson for not letting me forget this point. Personal communication, October 23, 2003.

14. Several years ago, while visiting the campus of Johns Hopkins University at the beginning of the fall semester, I picked up a copy of the first issue of the student newspaper, which, as a courtesy to freshmen, included a glossary of key university slang. And perhaps the most valuable service contained in this list was an explanation of the practice of "throating." Many undergraduates have chosen to attend Johns Hopkins as a pathway to medical school. Of course, each medical school admits only a fixed number of Johns Hopkins graduates. Consequently, this is a fixed-sum game. For every Johns Hopkins undergraduate who is admitted to the medical school at Harvard, Duke, or the University of San Francisco, one other student is not. So the premed undergraduates see themselves in very unfriendly competition with each other. In fact, some see it to be in their direct interest to sabotage the laboratory experiments of their colleagues. This is "throating."

15. For an example of friendly competition, see Behn, "Homestead Air Force Base" and "Homestead Air Force Base: Sequel."

16. Note that different people can have different definitions of winning. For example, Peter Vaill (1991) observes that, even for a sports team, it is not easy to define winning: "A former college basketball coach once told me that one of the coach's key problems is to get all the players to define 'winning' in the same way. For some, winning can mean always being willing to play hurt; for others, it can mean never playing hurt. Where one player

may believe in starting fast and hanging on, another will take it easy early in the game and go all out at the end. For one, each game can be an individual freestanding challenge; for another, the challenge is a series of games, or even a whole season. Some players regard all opponents equally; for others, some opponents are much more important than other opponents, and winning against one of the others isn't really 'winning.'"

Yet if the definition of winning is "*open*" for a sports team, how unsettled is the definition of winning—the definition of success—for a public agency? This is why setting the performance target is a responsibility of the organization's leadership. Without an explicit performance target—for the entire organization and for individual teams—each individual and unit can define winning in his, her, or its own way. This definition of winning can reflect the particular role these people have in the organization—a role that they (of necessity must) believe is important. It can reflect their own interpretation of the organization's mission. Or it can reflect simply the idiosyncrasies of personality or history.

If the organization's leaders want the employees and collaborators of the organization to strive to achieve the same purpose, they need to set an explicit performance target that defines what winning is. They need to get everyone using the same definition of winning. Leadership, Vaill writes, is "getting everybody on the same wave length regarding what winning is going to mean for the team and keeping them there." This is because, he continues, what an organization "thinks winning is drives action on a minute-to-minute basis" (Vail, 1991).

17. Tom Peters is, perhaps, the biggest advocate for celebrating successes. Yet, he does confess that "no short-term cost/benefit analysis will provide justification" for such celebrations. And here, Peters (1985) is talking about the private sector. Instead, he argues that "you simply must believe in people and believe that people like to be around one another and share one another's successes."

18. Note that I have focused on rewards for success, not punishments for failure. Punishment might motivate people to do better; but that is not the only response punishment can motivate. Punishment might be an effective motivator for conscripts. After all, they have few alternatives. But if people are volunteers, punishment can simply motivate them to quit. And most of the employees of a public agency—and most of its collaborators—are volunteers. They don't have to work for the agency. They don't have to help it. They can exit. For a discussion of "Shame, Voice, Exit, and Enter," see Robert D. Behn, "Rethinking Accountability in Education," *International Public Management Journal*, 6(1) (2003), pp. 53–55.

19. This line comes from the mouth of Larson E. Whipsnade, as played by W. C. Fields, in the 1939 film, *You Can't Cheat an Honest Man.* Mark A. R. Kleiman calls this "Dukenfield's Law of Incentive Management" [http://mkpolitics.blogspot.com/2002_08_25_mkpolitics_archive.html #85399552.]

20. Since Plunkitt's day, we have taken many of the activities he classified as honest graft and converted them into dishonest graft by making them illegal. Nevertheless, we still have activities that could be classified as honest graft: They are called campaign contributions (Riordin, 1963).

21. For examples of dishonest (and honest) cheating in K–12 education, see:

   • Abby Goodnough, "Teachers Are Said to Aid Cheating: Answers Allegedly Supplied in Test in New York City," *The New York Times,* December 8, 1999, pp. A1, A24.
   • Randal C. Archibold, "Teachers Recall How Students Got Right Answers, and School Scores Were Raised," *The New York Times,* December 8, 1999, p. A24.
   • John Bohte and Kenneth J. Meier, "Goal Displacement: Assessing the Motivation for Organizational Cheating," *Public Administration Review, 60*(2) (March–April, 2000), pp. 173–182.
   • Behn, "Rethinking Accountability in Education," pp. 52–53, 66–67 (particularly endnote, 26).
   • Behn, "Cheating-Honest and Dishonest."

22. If the performance target is highly correlated with the mission, as in the case of measles immunizations, the evaluation task will be relatively simple. In most cases, however, the first challenge is to figure out how to value progress toward the mission. The second challenge is to figure out how to attribute various factors—from the agency's work to the collection of possible outside influences—to changes in this mission value.

23. For a discussion of the kind of performance measures needed to evaluate performance, see Robert D. Behn, "Why Measure Performance? Different Purposes Require Different Measures," *Public Administration Review, 63*(5) (September–October 2003), pp. 586–606. Note that the kinds of measures needed to evaluate past performance are usually quite different from the kinds needed to motivate better performance in the future.

24. This suggestion—that the leaders of public agencies think of their new or improved operational capacity as a license to pursue additional purposes—strikes some as unacceptable in a democracy. Of course, this depends on your perception of the responsibility of those who manage executive-branch agencies. Those who believe that public managers should

do no more than obey the specific directions provided by legislators and elected chief executives will find this suggestion illegitimate—even illegal. Those who believe, as Mark Moore (1995) writes, that public managers "are *explorers* commissioned by society to search for public value" will not merely find this suggestion reasonable; they will think it is an imperative.

25. In my mental map of this approach to performance leadership, every box is connected in some way (with bidirectional arrows) with every other box. These boxes could, of course, be mapped on a single surface, but the fifty-five bidirectional arrows would obliterate any meaning to the diagram. And, if you decide to locate the eleven boxes not on a two-dimensional surface but in three dimensions, you can more easily follow individual arrows; but how do you diagram the collection? It is difficult to move a three-dimensional model from room to room, carry it on an airplane, or send it as an e-mail attachment; and we humans have yet to invent three-dimensional paper.

26. For an example of an agency making such changes, see Behn, *Leadership Counts*, note 2, pp. 226–227.

27. I have called this "the accountability dilemma—the tradeoff between accountability for finances and fairness and accountability for performance." Behn, *Rethinking Democratic Accountability*, pp. 10–11.

References

Adams, Scott. *The Dilbert Principle: A Cubicle's-Eye View of Bosses, Meetings, Management Fads & Other Workplace Afflictions.* New York: HarperBusiness, 1996.

Atkinson, William L., Wolfe, Charles, Humiston, Sharon G., and Nelson, Rick (Eds.), *Epidemiology and Prevention of Vaccine-Preventable Diseases* (7th ed.). Atlanta, GA: The Centers for Disease Control and Prevention, 2002.

Bardach, Eugene. *Getting Agencies to Work Together: The Practice and Theory of Managerial Craftsmanship.* Washington, DC: The Brookings Institution, 1998.

Behn, Robert D. *Leadership Counts: Lessons for Public Managers from the Massachusetts Welfare, Training, and Employment Program.* Cambridge, MA: Harvard University Press, 1991.

Behn, Robert D. "Cheating—Honest and Dishonest." *The New Public Innovator*, May/June 1998.

Behn, Robert D. *Rethinking Democratic Accountability.* Washington, DC: The Brookings Institution, 2001.

Behn, Robert D. "Creating Leadership Capacity for the Twenty-First Century: Not Another Technical Fix." In John D. Donahue and Joseph S. Nye, Jr. (Eds.), *For the People: Can We Fix Public Service?* Washington, DC: The Brookings Institution, 2003a.

Behn, Robert D. "On the Motivational Impact of: The List." *Bob Behn's Public Management Report*, 2003b, *1*(2) [http://www.ksg.harvard.edu/ TheBehnReport/October2003.pdf.]

Behn, Robert D. "On the Characteristics of: Friendly Competition." *Bob Behn's Public Management Report*, 2003c, *1*(3) [http://www.ksg. harvard.edu/TheBehnReport/November2003.pdf.]

Deming, W. Edwards. *Out of the Crisis*. Cambridge, MA: Center for Advanced Engineering Study, Massachusetts Institute of Technology, 1986. (Original copyright 1982.)

James, William. *The Letters of William James*. Henry James (Ed.), Boston: The Atlantic Monthly Press, 1920.

Kettl, Donald F. "The Global Revolution in Public Management: Driving Themes, Missing Links." *Journal of Policy Analysis and Management*, 1997, *16*(3).

King, Richard A., and Mathers, Judith K. "Improving Schools Through Performance-Based Accountability and Financial Rewards." *Journal of Education Finance*, 1997, *23*.

Maslow, A. H. "A Theory of Human Motivation." *Psychological Review*, 1943, *50*(4).

Moore, Mark H. *Creating Public Value: Strategic Management in Government*. Cambridge, MA: Harvard University Press, 1995.

National Commission on Public Service. *The Report of the National Commission on the Public Service, Leadership for America, Rebuilding the Public Service*. Washington, DC: The National Commission on the Public Service, 1999.

Peters, Tom, and Austin, Nancy. *A Passion for Excellence: The Leadership Difference*. New York: Random House, 1985.

Riordon, William L. *Plunkitt of Tammany Hall*. New York: E. P. Dutton, 1963.

Schaffer, Robert H. *The Breakthrough Strategy: Using Short-Term Successes to Build the High Performance Organization*. New York: Harper Business, 1988.

Vaill, Peter B. *Managing as a Performing Art: New Ideas for a World of Chaotic Change*. San Francisco: Jossey-Bass, 1991.

Weick, Karl E. "Small Wins: Redefining the Scale of Social Problems." *American Psychologist*, 1984, *39*(1).

—ɯɯ—

At time of original printing Robert D. Behn was a lecturer at Harvard University's John F. Kennedy School of Government and the faculty chair of the school's executive education program on "Driving Government Performance: Leadership Strategies That Produce Results." He specialized in governance, leadership, and the management of large public agencies.

CHAPTER FOURTEEN

The Learning Leader as Culture Manager

Edgar H. Schein

—〜〜—

Leaders create, embed, develop, and sometimes deliberately attempt to change cultural assumptions.

Though typically exemplified by the founder, owner, or professional manager who has been promoted to be CEO, leadership can occur anywhere in the organization. Leadership is the attitude and motivation to examine and manage culture. Accomplishing this goal is more difficult lower down in the organization but by no means impossible in that subcultures can be managed just as can overall organizational cultures.

The issues that make the most difference to the kind of leadership required are twofold. First, different stages of organizational development require different kinds of culture management. Second, different strategic issues require a focus on different kinds of cultural dimensions. Each of these points is briefly examined here.

Originally published as "The Learning Leader as Culture Manager" in Edgar H. Schein, *Organizational Culture and Leadership.* (San Francisco: Jossey-Bass, 1996).

LEADERSHIP IN CULTURE CREATION

In a growing organization leaders externalize their own assumptions and embed them gradually and consistently in the mission, goals, structures, and working procedures of the group. Whether we call these basic assumptions the guiding beliefs, the theories-in-use, the mental models, the basic principles, or the guiding visions on which founders operate, there is little question that they become major elements of the organization's emerging culture (for example, Argyris, 1976; Bennis, 1989; Davis, 1984; Donaldson and Lorsch, 1983; Dyer, 1986; Kotter and Heskett, 1992; Pettigrew, 1979; Schein, 1983).

In a rapidly changing world, the learning leader/founder must not only have vision but must be able to impose it and to develop it further as external circumstances change. Inasmuch as the new members of an organization arrive with prior organizational and cultural experiences, a common set of assumptions can only be forged by clear and consistent messages as the group encounters and survives its own crises. The culture creation leader therefore needs persistence and patience, yet as a learner must be flexible and ready to change.

As groups and organizations develop, certain key emotional issues arise. These have to do with dependence on the leader, with peer relationships, and with how to work effectively. Leadership is needed to help the group identify the issues and deal with them. During this process leaders must often absorb and contain the anxiety that is unleashed when things do not work as they should (Hirschhorn, 1988; Schein, 1983). Leaders may not have the answer, but they must provide temporary stability and emotional reassurance while the answer is being worked out. This anxiety-containing function is especially relevant during periods of learning, when old habits must be given up before new ones are learned. Moreover, if the world is increasingly changing, such anxiety may be perpetual, requiring learning leaders to assume a perpetual supportive role. The traumas of growth appear to be so constant and so powerful that unless a strong leader takes the role of anxiety and risk absorber, the group cannot get through its early stages of growth and fails. Being in an ownership position helps because everyone then realizes that the founder is in fact taking a greater personal financial risk; however, ownership does not automatically create the ability to absorb anxiety. For many leaders this is one of the most important things they have to learn.

When leaders launch new enterprises, they must be mindful of the power they have to impose on those enterprises their own assumptions about what is right and proper, how the world works, and how things should be done. Leaders should not apologize for or be cautious about their assumptions. Rather, it is intrinsic to the leadership role to create order out of chaos, and leaders are expected to provide their own assumptions as an initial road map into the uncertain future. The more aware leaders are of this process, the more consistent and effective they can be in implementing it.

The process of culture creation, embedding, and reinforcement brings with it problems as well as solutions. Many organizations survive and grow but at the same time operate inconsistently or do things that seem contradictory. One explanation of this phenomenon that has been pointed out repeatedly is that leaders not only embed in their organizations what they intend consciously to get across, but they also convey their own inner conflicts and the inconsistencies in their own personal makeup (Kets de Vries and Miller, 1984; Miller, 1990; Schein, 1983). The most powerful signal to which subordinates respond is what catches leaders' attention consistently, particularly what arouses them emotionally. But many of the things to which leaders respond emotionally reflect not so much their conscious intentions as their unconscious conflicts. The organization then either develops assumptions around these inconsistencies and conflicts and they become part of the culture, or the leader gradually loses a position of influence if the behavior begins to be seen as too disruptive or actually destructive. In extreme cases the organization isolates or ejects the founder. In doing so, however, it is not rejecting all of the founder's assumptions but only those that are inconsistent with the core assumptions on which the organization was built.

The period of culture creation, therefore, puts an additional burden on founders—to obtain enough self-insight to avoid unwittingly undermining their own creations. Founding leaders often find it difficult to recognize that the very qualities that made them successful initially, their strong convictions, can become sources of difficulty later on and that they also must learn and grow as their organizations grow. Such insights become especially important when organizations face issues of leadership succession because succession discussions force into the open aspects of the culture that may not have been previously recognized.

What all of this means for leaders of developing organizations is that they must have tremendous self-insight and recognize their own role not only in creating the culture but also their responsibility in embedding and developing culture. Inasmuch as the culture is the primary source of identity for young organizations, the culture creation and development process must be handled sensitively with full understanding of the anxieties that are unleashed when identity is challenged.

LEADERSHIP AT ORGANIZATIONAL MIDLIFE

As the organization develops a substantial history of its own, its culture becomes more of a cause than an effect. As subgroups develop their own subcultures, the opportunities for constructive use of cultural diversity and the problems of integration both become greater. The leader must be able to pay attention to diversity and assess clearly how much of it is useful for further organizational development and how much of it is potentially dysfunctional. The culture is now much less tied to the leader's own personality, which makes it easier to assess objectively, though there are likely to be sacred cows, holdovers from the founding period, that have to be delicately handled.

The leader at this stage must be able to detect how the culture influences the strategy, structure, procedures, and ways in which the group members relate to one another. Culture is a powerful influence on members' perceptions, thinking, and feeling, and these predispositions, along with situational factors, influence members' behavior. Because culture serves an important anxiety-reducing function, members cling to it even if it becomes dysfunctional in relationship to environmental opportunities and constraints.

Leaders at this stage need diagnostic skill to figure out not only what the cultural influences are, but also what their impact is on the organization's ability to change and learn. Whereas founding leaders most need self-insight, midlife leaders most need the ability to decipher the surrounding culture and subcultures. To help the organization evolve into whatever will make it most effective in the future, leaders must also have culture management skills. In some instances this may mean increasing cultural diversity, allowing some of the uniformity that may have been built up in the growth stage to erode. In other instances it may mean pulling together a culturally diverse set of organizational units and attempting to impose new common assumptions on them. In either case the leader needs (1) to be able to analyze the culture in sufficient detail to know which cultural assumptions can aid and which ones will hinder the fulfillment of the organizational mission and (2) to possess the intervention skills to make desired changes happen.

Most of the prescriptive analyses of how to maintain the organization's effectiveness through this period emphasize that the leader must have certain insights, clear vision, and the skills to articulate, communicate, and implement the vision, but these analyses say nothing about how a given organization can find and install such a leader. In U.S. organizations in particular, the outside board members probably play a critical role in this process. If the organization has had a strong founding culture, however, its board may be composed exclusively of people who share the founder's vision. Consequently, real changes in direction may not become possible until the organization experiences serious survival difficulties and begins to search for a person with different assumptions to lead it.

One area to explore further here is the CEO's own role in succession. Can the leader of a midlife organization perceive the potential dysfunctions of some aspects of the culture to a sufficient extent to ensure that his or her successor will be able to move the culture in an appropriate new direction? CEOs have a great deal of power to influence the choice of their successor. Do they use that power wisely in terms of cultural issues? For example, it is alleged that one of the main reasons why Reginald Jones as CEO of General Electric "chose" Jack Welch to be his successor was because he recognized in Welch a person who would create the kinds of changes that were necessary for GE to remain viable. Similarly, Steve Jobs "chose" John Sculley to head Apple even though at some level he must have sensed that this choice might eventually lead to the kind of conflict that in the end forced Jobs to leave. The ultimate paradox here is that truly learning leaders may have to face the conclusion that they must replace themselves, that they do not have the vision needed to bring the midlife organization into alignment with a rapidly changing world.

LEADERSHIP IN MATURE AND POTENTIALLY DECLINING ORGANIZATIONS

In the mature stage if the organization has developed a strong unifying culture, that culture now defines even what is to be thought of as leadership, what is heroic or sinful behavior, and how authority and power are to be allocated and managed. Thus, what leadership has created now either blindly perpetuates itself or creates new definitions of leadership, which may not even include the kinds of entrepreneurial assumptions that launched the organization in the first place. The first problem of the mature and possibly declining organization, then, is to find a process to empower a potential leader who may have enough insight to overcome some of the constraining cultural assumptions.

What the leader must do at this point in the organization's history depends on the degree to which the culture of the organization has, in fact, enabled the group to adapt to its environmental realities. If the culture has not facilitated adaptation, the organization either will not survive or will find a way to change its culture. If it is to change its culture, it must be led by someone who can, in effect, break the tyranny of the old culture. This requires not only the insight and diagnostic skill to determine what the old culture is, but to realize what alternative assumptions are available and how to start a change process toward their acceptance.

Leaders of mature organizations must, as has been argued repeatedly, make themselves sufficiently marginal in their own organization to be able to perceive its assumptions objectively and non-defensively. They must, therefore, find many ways to be exposed to their external environment and, thereby facilitate their own learning. If they cannot learn new assumptions themselves, they will not be able to perceive what is possible in their organizations. Even worse, they may destroy innovative efforts that arise within their organizations if those innovative efforts involve countercultural assumptions.

Leaders capable of such managed culture change can come from inside the organization if they have acquired objectivity and insight into elements of the culture. Such cultural objectivity appears to be related to having had a non-conventional career or exposure to many subcultures within the organization (Kotter and Heskett, 1992). However, the formally designated senior managers of a given organization may not be willing or able to provide such culture change leadership. Leadership then may have to come from other boundary spanners in the organization or from outsiders. It may even come from a number of people in the organization, in which case it makes sense to talk of turnaround teams or multiple leadership.

If a leader is imposed from the outside, she or he must have the skill to diagnose accurately what the culture of the organization is, what elements are well adapted and what elements are problematic for future adaptation, and how to change that which needs changing. In other words the leader must be a skilled change manager who first learns what the present state of the culture is, unfreezes it, redefines and changes it, and then refreezes the new assumptions. Talented turnaround managers seem to be able to manage all phases of such changes, but sometimes different leaders will be involved in the different steps over a considerable period of time. They will use all the mechanisms previously discussed in the appropriate combinations to get the job done provided that they have the authority and power to use extreme measures, such as replacing the people who perpetuate the old cultural assumptions.

In summary, leaders play a critical role at each developmental stage of an organization, but that role differs as a function of the stage. Much of what leaders do is to perpetually diagnose the particular assumptions of the culture and figure out how to use those assumptions constructively or to change them if they are constraints.

LEADERSHIP AND CULTURE IN STRATEGY FORMULATION

Many companies have found that they or their consultants can think of new strategies that make sense from a financial, product, or marketing point of view, yet they cannot implement those strategies because such implementation requires assumptions, values, and ways of working that are too far out of line with the organization's existing assumptions. In some cases, the organization cannot even conceive of certain strategic options because they are too out of line with shared assumptions about the mission of the organization and its way of working, what Lorsch (1985) has aptly called "strategic myopia."

The Multi Company built its businesses by capitalizing on the intensive efforts of its research labs to develop "important" products that were "useful to society." Members viewed themselves as a company that produced life-saving drugs, pesticides that enabled countries to improve their food crops, sophisticated chemicals that made other industries possible, and so on. The company's success was based on brilliant research work and the protection from competition that patents allowed.

When the company began to compete in more diversified and mature markets, where patent protection had run out and product utility was not nearly as important as product marketability, some senior managers argued for a more pragmatic marketing strategy. Those managers wanted to decrease the research and development budget, increase marketing expenditures, and teach their colleagues how to think like marketers. But they were unable to convince senior management as a whole, leaving parts of the company in a financially vulnerable position. Clearly, the traditions, values, self-concepts, and assumptions about the nature of Multi made some aspects of the proposed new marketing strategy unthinkable or unacceptable to senior management.

Another example is provided by the Action Company, which became successful by developing a very complex product marketed to very sophisticated customers. The company later developed some smaller, simpler, less expensive versions of this product, which could have been further developed and marketed to less sophisticated customers. Even senior management argued that such low-end products had to be developed, but the product designers and marketers could not deal with the new customer type. The sales and marketing people could not imagine what the concerns of the new, less knowledgeable customer might be, and the product designers continued to be convinced that they could judge product attractiveness themselves. Neither group was motivated to understand the new customer because, unconsciously, they tended to look down on such a customer. The assumption that "dumb users" were not worth designing for was, in fact, held throughout the company, even by senior managers who were advocating low-end products.

To put this in the proper perspective, we must remember that cultural assumptions are the product of past successes. As a result they are increasingly taken for granted and operate as silent filters on what is perceived and thought about. If the organization's environment changes and new responses are required, the danger is that the changes will not be noticed or, even if noticed, that the organization will not be able to adapt because of embedded routines based on past success. Culture constrains strategy by limiting what the CEO and other senior managers are able to think about and what they perceive in the first place.

One of the critical roles of learning leadership, then, is first of all to notice changes in the environment and then to figure out what needs to be done to remain adaptive. I am defining leadership; in this context in terms of the role, not the position. The CEO or other senior managers may or may not be able to fulfill the leadership role, and leadership in the sense that I am defining it can occur anywhere in the organization. However, if real change and learning are to take place, it is probably necessary that the CEO or other very senior managers be able to be leaders in this sense.

Leaders must be somewhat marginal and must be somewhat embedded in the organization's eternal environment to fulfill this role adequately. At the same time, leaders must be well connected to those parts of the organization that are themselves well connected to the environment—sales, purchasing, marketing, public relations and legal, finance, and R&D. Leaders must be able to listen to disconfirming information coming from these sources and to assess the implications for the future or the organization. Only when they truly understand what is happening and what will be required in the way of organizational change can they begin to take action in initiating a learning process.

Much has been said about the need for vision in leaders, but too little has been said about their need to listen, to absorb, to search the environment for trends, and to build the organization's capacity to learn. Especially at the strategic level, the ability to see and acknowledge the full complexity of problems becomes critical. The ability to acknowledge complexity may also imply the willingness and emotional strength to admit uncertainty and to embrace experimentation and possible errors as the only way to learn. In our obsession with leadership vision, we may have made it possible for learning leaders to admit that their vision is not clear and that the whole organization will have to learn together. Moreover, as I have repeatedly argued, vision in a mature organization helps when the organization has already been disconfirmed and members feel anxious and in need of a solution. Much of what learning leaders must do occurs before vision even becomes relevant.

To summarize, the critical roles of leadership in strategy formulation and implementation are (1) to perceive accurately and in depth what is happening in the environment, (2) to create enough disconfirming information to motivate the organization to change without creating too much anxiety, (3) to provide psychological safety by either providing a vision of how to change and in what direction or by creating a process of visioning that allows the organization itself to find a path, (4) to acknowledge uncertainty, (5) to embrace errors in the learning process as inevitable and desirable, and (6) to manage all phases of the change process, including especially the management of anxiety as some cultural assumptions are given up and new learning begins . . . .

LEADERSHIP AND CULTURE IN JOINT VENTURES AND STRATEGIC ALLIANCES

Joint ventures and strategic alliances require cultural analysis even more than mergers and acquisitions because cross-national boundaries are more often involved in today's rapidly globalizing world. Deciphering differences between two companies in the same national culture is not as difficult as deciphering both national and company differences when one engages in a joint venture across national boundaries, as research by Salk (1992) shows. One special difficulty is to determine whether the differences that we perceive are attributable to national or organizational cultures. Yet it is important to make this determination because one would have to assume that the likelihood of changing national characteristics is very low.

The role of leadership in these situations is much the same as in the foregoing scenarios, except here leaders must even surmount their national identities. The European subsidiary of a U.S. company that could never find local managers to put on its board because they were all "too emotional" never came to terms with its own stereotype of managers as intrinsically non-emotional people and never realized or accepted that this was based on their U.S. assumptions. Many organizations make international assignments a requirement for a developing general manager. The explicit notion here is that such experience is essential if potential leaders with broader outlooks are to emerge. In other words, the learning leader must become marginal not only with respect to the organizational culture, but even with respect to national and ethnic culture.

IMPLICATIONS FOR THE SELECTION AND DEVELOPMENT OF LEADERS

A dynamic analysis of organizational culture makes it clear that leadership is intertwined with culture formation, evolution, transformation, and destruction. Culture is created in the first instance by the actions of leaders; culture is embedded and strengthened by leaders. When culture becomes dysfunctional, leadership is needed to help the group unlearn some of its cultural assumptions and learn new assumptions. Such transformations sometimes require what amounts to conscious and deliberate destruction of cultural elements. This in turn requires the ability to surmount one's own taken-for-granted assumptions, seeing what is needed to ensure the health and survival of the group, and orchestrating events and processes that enable the group to evolve toward new cultural assumptions. Without leadership in this sense, groups will not be able to adapt to changing environmental conditions. Let us summarize what is really needed to be a leader in this sense.

Perception and Insight

First, the leader must be able to perceive the problem, to have insight into himself or herself and into the culture and its dysfunctional elements. Such boundary-spanning perception can be difficult because it requires one to see one's own weaknesses, to perceive that one's own defenses not only help in managing anxiety but can also hinder one's efforts to be effective. Successful architects of change must have a high degree of objectivity about themselves and their own organizations, and such objectivity results from spending portions of their careers in diverse settings that permit them to compare and contrast different cultures. International experience is therefore one of the most powerful ways of learning.

Individuals often are aided in becoming objective about themselves through counseling and psychotherapy. One might conjecture that leaders can benefit from comparable processes such as training and development programs that emphasize experiential learning and self-assessment. From this perspective one of the most important functions of outside consultants or board members is to provide the kind of counseling that produces cultural insight. It is therefore far more important for the consultant to help the leader figure out for himself or herself what is going on and what to do than to provide recommendations on what the organization should do. The consultant also can serve as a "cultural therapist," helping the leader figure out what the culture is and what parts of it are more or less adaptive.

Motivation

Leadership requires not only insight into the dynamics of the culture but the motivation and skill to intervene in one's own cultural process. To change any elements of the culture, leaders must be willing to unfreeze their own organization. Unfreezing requires disconfirmation, a process that is inevitably painful for many. The leader must find a way to say to his or her own organization that things are not all right and, if necessary, must enlist the aid of outsiders in getting this message across. Such willingness requires a great ability to be concerned for the organization above and beyond the self, to communicate dedication or commitment to the group above and beyond self-interest.

If the boundaries of organization become looser, a further motivational issue arises in that it is less and less clear where a leader's ultimate loyalty should lie—with the organization, with industry, with country, or with some broader professional community whose ultimate responsibility is to the globe and to all of humanity.

Emotional Strength

Unfreezing an organization requires the creation of psychological safety, which means that the leader must have the emotional strength to absorb much of the anxiety that change brings with it and the ability to remain supportive to the organization through the transition phase even if group members become angry and obstructive. The leader is likely to be the target of anger and criticism because, by definition, he or she must challenge some of what the group has taken for granted. This may involve closing down the company division that was the original source of the company's growth and the basis of many employees' sense of pride and identity. It may involve laying off or retiring loyal, dedicated employees and old friends. Worst of all, it may involve the message that some of the founder's most cherished assumptions are wrong in the contemporary context. It is here that dedication and commitment are especially needed to demonstrate to the organization that the leader genuinely cares about the welfare of the total organization even as parts of it come under challenge. The leader must remember that giving up a cultural element requires one to take some risk, the risk that one will be very anxious and in the end worse off, and yet the leader must have the strength to forge the way into this unknown territory.

Ability to Change the Cultural Assumptions

If an assumption is to be given up, it must be replaced or redefined in another form, and it is the burden of leadership to make that happen.

In other words, the leader must have the ability to induce cognitive redefinition by articulating and selling new visions and concepts. The leader must be able to bring to the surface, review, and change some of the group's basic assumptions.

At Multi this process had just begun. Many managers were beginning to doubt that the organization's commitment to science-based technical products could sustain the company in the long run. However, to that point no strong leader had emerged to convince the organization that consumer goods marketing through strong customer-oriented organizations could be a source of pride for the company.

The situation in the Action Company is highly ambiguous and difficult at the present time because it is neither clear whether Murphy will be able to sustain some of the original assumptions that he still believes in as the company faces economic downturns and a mature market requiring much tighter cost controls, or whether Murphy's assumptions about what the company needs today are correct, given the rapidly changing environment. Many of the basic assumptions on which Action was built are less and less sustainable as the company finds itself leveling off in sales and shrinking in terms of people, which poses the serious question of whether or not the basic cultural paradigm must be deliberately changed. If Murphy's belief in internal entrepreneurship and empowerment of his organization is to be sustained, he has to find a leadership succession process that will ensure that his successor has assumptions similar to his own.

Ability to Create Involvement and Participation

A paradox of culture change leadership is that the leader must be able not only to lead but also to listen, to emotionally involve the group in achieving its own insights into its cultural dilemmas, and to be genuinely participative in his or her approach to learning and change. The leaders of social, religious, or political movements can rely on personal charisma and let the followers do what they will. In an organization, however, the leader has to work with the group that exists at the moment, because he or she is dependent on the group members to carry out the organization's mission. The leader must recognize that, in the end, cognitive redefinition must occur inside the heads of many members and that will happen only if they are actively involved in the process. The whole organization must achieve some degree of insight and develop motivation to change before any real change will occur, and the leader must create this involvement.

The ability to involve others and to listen to them also protects leaders from attempting to change things that should not be changed. When leaders are brought in from the outside this becomes especially important because some of the assumptions operating in the organization may not fit the leader's own assumptions yet be critical to the organization's success. To illustrate the kinds of mistakes that are possible, we need remember only the period in the Atari Company's history when Warner Communications, the parent company, decided to improve Atari's marketing by bringing in as president an experienced marketing executive from the food industry. This executive brought with him the assumption that the key to success is high motivation and high rewards based on individual performance. He created and imposed an incentive system designed to select the engineers who were doing the best job in inventing and designing new computer games and gave them large monetary rewards. Soon some of the best engineers were leaving, and the company was getting into technical difficulty. What was wrong?

The new executive had created and articulated clear symbols, and everyone had rallied around them. Apparently, what was wrong was the assumption that the incentives and rewards should be based on individual effort. What the president failed to understand, coming from the food industry with its individualistic product management orientation, was that the computer games were designed by groups and teams and that the engineers considered the assignment of individual responsibility to be neither possible nor necessary. They were happy being group members and would have responded to group incentives, but unfortunately, the symbol chosen was the wrong symbol from this point of view. The engineers also noted that the president, with his nontechnical background, was not adept at choosing the best engineers, because their key assumption was that "best" was the product of group effort, not individual brilliance. Given the incompatible assumptions, it is no surprise that the president did not last long. Unfortunately, damage in terms of the loss of employees and in esprit had been done.

Ability to Learn a New Culture

Culture change leaders often have to take over a company in which they did not previously have any experience. If they are to diagnose and possibly change the culture they have entered, it is, of course, mandatory that they first learn what the essence of that culture is. This point raises the question of how much an individual can learn that is totally new. My hypothesis, based on various streams of research on leadership and management, is that leaders can cross boundaries and enter new organizational cultures fairly easily if they stay within a given industry, as defined by a core technology. A manager growing up in one chemical company can probably become the successful CEO of another chemical company and can learn the culture of that company. What appears to be much more difficult is to cross industry or national boundaries, because cognitive frames that are built up early in the manager's career are fundamentally more embedded. The ability of a John Sculley to become a successful leader of Apple is unusual. More typical is the Atari Company story mentioned above. The Action Company has had a series of senior financial officers drawn from the auto industry, and, though they were effective in bringing some new financial methods to the company, one always heard many stories concerning their inability to understand the Action culture and, consequently, to be ultimately ineffective.

In any case, the leader coming into a new organization must be very sensitive to his or her own need to truly understand the culture before assessing it and possibly changing it. A period of learning lasting a year or more, if the situation allows that much time, is probably necessary. If the situation is more critical, the leader could speed up his or her own learning by systematically involving the layers of the organization below him or her in culture deciphering exercises.

SUMMARY AND CONCLUSIONS

It seems clear that the leaders of the future will have to be perpetual learners. This will require (1) new levels of perception and insight into the realities of the world and also into themselves; (2) extraordinary levels of motivation to go through the inevitable pain of learning and change, especially in a world with looser boundaries in which one's own loyalties become more and more difficult to define; (3) the emotional strength to manage their own and others' anxiety as learning and change become more and more a way of life; (4) new skills in analyzing and changing cultural assumptions; (5) the willingness and ability to involve others and elicit their participation; and (6) the ability to learn the assumptions of a whole new organizational culture.

Learning and change cannot be imposed on people. Their involvement and participation are needed in diagnosing what is going on, figuring out what to do, and actually doing it. The more turbulent, ambiguous, and out of control the world becomes, the more the learning process will have to be shared by all the members of the social unit doing the learning. If the leaders of today want to create organizational cultures that will themselves be more amenable to learning, they will have to set the example by becoming learners themselves and involving others in the learning process.

The essence of that learning process will be to give organizational culture its due. Can we as individual members of organizations and occupations, as managers, teachers, researchers, and, sometimes, leaders recognize how deeply our own perceptions, thoughts, and feelings are culturally determined? Ultimately, we cannot achieve the cultural humility required to live in a turbulent culturally diverse world unless we can see cultural assumptions within ourselves. In the end, cultural understanding and cultural learning start with self-insight.

References

Argyris, Chris. *Increasing Leadership Effectiveness*. New York: Wiley-Interscience, 1976.

Bennis, Warren. *On Becoming a Leader*. Reading, MA: Addison-Wesley, 1989.

Davis, Stanley M. *Managing Corporate Culture*. New York: Ballinger, 1984.

Donaldson, Gordon, and Lorsch, Jay W. *Decision Making at the Top*. New York: Basic Books, 1983.

Dyer, William G., Jr. *Culture Change in Family Firms*. San Francisco: Jossey-Bass, 1986.

Hirschhorn, Larry. *The Workplace Within: Psychodynamics of Organizational Life*. Cambridge, MA: MIT Press, 1988.

Kets de Vries, Manfred F. R., and Miller, Danny. *The Neurotic Organization: Diagnosing and Changing Counterproductive Styles of Management*. San Francisco: Jossey-Bass, 1984.

Kotter, John P., and Heskett, James L. *Corporate Culture and Performance*. New York: The Free Press, 1992.

Lorsch, Jay W. "Strategic Myopia: Culture as an Invisible Barrier to Change." In R. H. Kilmann, M. J. Saxton, R. Serpa, and others, *Gaining Control of the Corporate Culture*. San Francisco: Jossey-Bass, 1985.

Miller, Danny. *The Icarus Paradox.* New York: Harper & Row, 1990.

Pettigrew, Andrew M. "On Studying Organizational Cultures." *Administrative Science Quarterly*, 1979, *24*, 570–581.

Salk, J. E. "International Shared Management Joint Venture Teams: Their Development Patterns, Challenges, and Possibilities." Unpublished doctoral dissertation, Sloan School of Management, Massachusetts Institute of Technology, 1992.

Schein, Edgar H. "The Role of the Founder in Creating Organizational Culture." *Organizational Dynamics*, Summer 1983, pp. 13–28.

—◁∧∧▷—

At time of publishing Edgar H. Schein was professor emeritus at the Sloan School of Management, Massachusetts Institute of Technology, and a consultant.

CHAPTER FIFTEEN

Maintaining Trust
Through Integrity

Warren Bennis
Joan Goldsmith

Trust, is fragile. Like a piece of china, once cracked it is never quite the same. And people's trust in business, and those who lead it, is today cracking. To many, it seems that executives no longer run their companies for the benefit of consumers, or even of their shareholders and employees, but for their personal ambition and financial gain. A Gallup poll conducted early this year found that 90 percent of Americans felt that people running corporations could not be trusted to look after the interest of their employees, and only 18 percent thought that corporations look after their shareholders a great deal. Forty-three percent, in fact, believed that senior executives were only in it for themselves. In Britain, that figure, according to another poll, was 95 percent.

> *Charles Handy, "What's a Business For?"* Harvard Business
> Review, *December 2002.*

Originally published as "Maintaining Trust Through Integrity" in Warren Bennis and Joan Goldsmith's *Learning to Lead*. (New York: Basic Books, 2003).

Why did India's poor march to the sea with Gandhi against the salt tax? What was it about Margaret Sanger that emboldened women to break with husbands and families and adopt birth control? What did Dr. Martin Luther King Jr. do to inspire poor, uneducated sharecroppers who were tied to the soil of the American South to register to vote? We know that each of these leaders believed in the correctness of his or her cause at a moment in history when action was called for. Their impact was profound because the trust they enjoyed was based on invincible integrity and powerful commitment. Trust is the essential quality that creates a following for leaders and enables them to make a difference. It is the key ability that inspires those who join them to create movements for social change and build organizations to realize their dreams.

We want and need leaders we can trust. Trust is a whole lot harder to come by than competence, which is why we have so many more managers than leaders. Unlike competence, trust can't be acquired by would-be leaders but can only be voluntarily given by their followers.

Our perception of a leader's performance is more important than her actual performance. In general, the people we trust "walk their talk." And when they do, what they espouse is what they do, and what they espouse and do is in synch with what we want and need. Leaders we trust are there when we need them, and they are on our side. They can perform the functions of the office and have a kind of steadiness, or "trusted thumb." They are able to control themselves in difficult situations, and under pressure, they do not act recklessly.

Leaders don't care a whit about posterity or even wonder how they'll be remembered. They do what needs to be done as well as they can do it, without a thought as to what the media will say about them today, or what historians will say about them ten years from now. They neither grandstand nor suffer from delusions of grandeur.

Leaders are ambitious, or they wouldn't have made it to the top, but they are ambitious for all of us, and they trust us as much as we trust them. Such leaders are so good at what they do that they bring out the best in us.

TRUST AND ORGANIZATIONAL EFFECTIVENESS

Trust provides the motivation and energy that make it possible for organizations to be successful. It is hard to imagine an institution in which leaders do not inspire some semblance of trust. It is what motivates heroism, sells products, and keeps communication humming. Trust is the source of organizational integrity. Like leadership, trust is hard to describe, let alone define. We know when it is present, and we know when it is not. We are aware that it is essential and that it is based on predictability. We trust people who are predictable, whose positions are known and who keep at it; leaders who are trusted make themselves known and make their positions clear. Organizations without trust would resemble the nightmare of Kafka's *Castle*, where nothing can be certain and no one can be relied on or held accountable. The ability to predict the outcomes of leadership with a high probability of success generates and maintains trust.

In this chapter we explore trust by focusing on the four qualities of leadership that, when practiced, engender trust: Having a clear, articulate vision; practicing consistent empathy; behaving with reliable consistency; and acting with impeccable integrity. A leader who is trusted demonstrates these four characteristics:

- Trusted leaders have inspiring *visions* for the organization that are clear, attractive, and attainable. Their vision provides a context of shared beliefs and a common organizational purpose with which we can identify. As a result we feel that we belong. The leader involves us in their vision, empowers us to make it real, and enables us to integrate it into our lives.

- Trusted leaders have unconditional *empathy* for those who live in their organizations. We tend to trust leaders who can walk in our shoes and are able to let us know that. Although they may have different points of view, they can see the world as we see it and understand the sense we are making of it.

- The behaviors of trusted leaders are consistent with their values and the *commitments* they have. We tend to trust leaders when we know where they stand in relation to their organizations, as well as how they seek to orient their organizations in relation to the larger environment. We understand how these leaders' commitments have evolved and we know they are willing to reconsider them in the face of new evidence.

- The *integrity* of trusted leaders is unquestionable. We tend to trust leaders who stand for a higher moral order and who demonstrate their ethics and values through actions we can observe. Leaders uphold a standard of ethics, encourage others to act on their shared values, and call themselves and others to account for deviations from what they know is right.

As we continue our exploration of trust, we will investigate the concepts of vision, empathy, commitment, and integrity in greater depth.

SUPPORT THROUGH EMPATHY

A basic ingredient of leadership is a guiding vision. Leaders who are trusted have a clear idea of what they want to do both professionally and personally. They draw on their vision to give themselves and their followers the strength to persist in the face of setbacks, even failures. Unless they know where they are going and why, they cannot possibly get there, and if they are not inspired they will give up. Thus a vision for the future is crucial to producing any *strategic* result at all.

If leaders only have a vision, however, they may end up successfully prophesying the future yet they may feel frustrated, lonely, and ineffectual. Leaders cannot achieve their dreams without recruiting people to support their vision. How do they do that? Ultimately, the ability of leaders to galvanize co-workers resides both in a clear understanding of themselves as well as the needs and wants of co-workers, and a strong, abiding belief in their mission to lead. Sydney Pollack, the successful film director, described a leader's ability to bring people to his side this way:

> "Up to a point, I think you can lead out of fear, intimidation, as awful as that sounds. You can make people follow you by scaring them, and you can make people follow by having them feel obligated. You can lead by creating guilt. There is a lot of leadership that comes out of fear, dependence, and guilt. The Marine boot camp is famous for it. But the problem is that you're creating obedience with a residue of resentment. If you want to make a physics analogy, you'd be moving through the medium but you'd be creating a lot of drag, a lot of

backwash. There are two other qualities that I think are more positive reasons to follow someone. One is an honest belief in the person you're following. The other is selfish. The person following has to believe that following is the best thing to do at the time. I mean it has to be apparent to them that they are getting something better by following you than they ever would by not following you. You don't want people to follow you just because that's what they're paid for. Sometimes you can teach them something. 'You're going to learn more by doing this move than you would by doing another move' let's say. You try to make everyone feel they have a stake in it."

Visionary leaders invite people to feel they have a stake in realizing the vision. They empower them to experience the vision as their own. They offer opportunities to join them and create their own visions. They explore what the vision will mean to their jobs and lives. They envision a future that clarifies the purpose and values of the organization. They have the ability to connect with others and at the same time they see them as separate from themselves. In some deeper sense, they know that they are also alike. This ability is an expression of the leader's capacity for empathy.

Our friend and colleague Dr. Norman Paul, a leading psychiatrist, believes empathy is a key to successful relationships. In his essay "Parental Empathy" he describes the qualities that are necessary for empathetic leadership:

"Empathy is different from sympathy; the two processes are, in fact, mutually exclusive. In sympathy, the subject is principally absorbed in his own feelings as they are projected into the object and has little concern for the reality and validity of the object's special experience. Sympathy bypasses real understanding of the other person, and that other is denied his own sense of being. Empathy, on the other hand, presupposes the existence of the object as a separate individual, entitled to his own feelings, ideas and emotional history. The empathizer makes no judgments about what the other *should* feel, but solicits the expression of whatever he *does* feel and, for brief periods, experiences these feelings as his own. The empathizer oscillates between such subjective involvement and a detached recognition of the shared feelings. The periods of his objective detachment do not seem to the other to be spells of indifference, as they would in sympathy; they are, instead, evidence that the subject respects himself and the object as separate people. Secure in his sense of self and his own emotional boundaries, the empathizer attempts to nurture a similar security in the other."

Most of us know when a leader with whom we interact is able to empathize with us. We experience being understood on a deep level. It feels as though we are more than understood—we are *known*. But empathetic leaders do not merge with us or violate our personal boundaries. They do not take away our feelings or responses. They do not overpower us with the resonance they have with us. An empathetic leader is able to acknowledge who we are and walk in our shoes.

PRACTICING EMPATHY

Learning to empathize means making a conscious effort to listen to the other person and hear what she is saying in the context of *her own* orientation, needs, and perceptions. When you empathize, your attention is on the other person rather than on yourself. Letting other people know you empathize with their situation, their position, their feelings means:

- Feeding back to them what you hear them say or see them do;
- Asking them questions to learn more about what they really feel or believe;
- Repeating their comments back to show them you have heard them without inserting your own ideas; and
- Understanding their point of view from the inside out, as though it were your own.

An empathic leader does not judge the responses of others or stifle them with his own agenda. Rather, the leader listens to the other person in silence, gives her the space to have her own reactions, and lets her know that she has been heard.

When we live and work in a world we cannot fully trust.... We have a choice between three fundamental options. We can approach what happens that does not match our expectations with a *negative* attitude and treat it as a burden, or we can approach it with a *positive* attitude and affirm its beneficial features, or we can *transcend* both categories, reject them, and stop the ceaseless, complicated interplay between them.

In Joan's recent book with Ken Cloke, *The Art of Waking People Up: Cultivating Awareness and Authenticity at Work*, they explore the transcendent approach to leadership, which integrates the negative truth of harsh reality with the positive truth of generous possibility. Transcendence acknowledges the presence of necessity and opportunity, frustration and dedication, inadequacy and abundance, disaster and opportunity that are present in all change efforts. Leaders who transcend their circumstances do not accept the world as it is; rather, they work to transform it.

When we are negative or unhappy about life or its circumstances, it is easy to become apathetic or cynical and simply give up. When we are positive or happy, we easily become complacent and develop a stake in preserving the status quo. Either of these choices causes us to fix problems superficially or become dulled to the creative, transcendent possibilities that come from exploring the sources of negativity. Taking a negative approach to problems is useful in that it is the first step in recognizing the problem, but it is one that easily leads to cynicism and apathy, thereby disarming change efforts and perpetuating the problem. Taking a positive approach leads us to alternatives, but it can also promote denial of the importance of the problem and can result in superficial solutions.

When we recognize the higher, *combined* truth that lies hidden in both these alternatives, we start to recognize the deeper sources of our problems, shift them where they originate, and transcend the attitudes and ideas that got us into trouble in the first place. We can then move on to discover newer, higher orders of problems and generate more profound solutions. Taking a transcendent approach means seeing the problem in all its manifestations but not being discouraged by the seriousness or difficulty of the task ahead. At the same time, if we focus only on ourselves and ignore the external conditions that continually generate new problems, we will not succeed in overcoming them. We will merely escape the immediate need to face them and we will allow them to reappear in different guises. When we transform the systems that produced these problems and transcend our inner vulnerability to them, we more easily understand how we got into difficulty in the first place, how to collaborate in ending them, and how to avoid similar problems in the future. An enhanced commitment within ourselves to transcend the problem produces a determination to overcome it within the organization, or even in society as a whole. We become far more powerful and effective in solving problems when we have already solved them *within ourselves* and are able to approach them from a distant perspective; when we adopt an outlook that transcends negative and positive characterizations; when we create a context that is oriented toward the future and avoids getting stuck in the past.

TRUST THROUGH CONSISTENCY

The current disarray in corporations, church hierarchies, governments, and nonprofit agencies caused by revelations of fraud, corruption, theft, and betrayal has created an urgent need for leaders who are above suspicion and can be counted on to consistently adhere to moral, ethical, and value-based behavior.

The quagmire of inappropriate campaign contributions to candidates in exchange for favors in the political sector; the violation of honest audit practices by major accounting and auditing firms in the corporate world; the misuse of grants and donated contributions to nonprofit agencies; the cover-up of sexual abuse of minors by Catholic priests—all have stimulated an urgent demand for leaders we can trust.

Time magazine's cover story a few years back asked the right question: "What Ever Happened to Ethics? Assaulted by Sleaze, Scandals, and Hypocrisy, America Searches for Its Moral Bearings." The editors went on to say:

> "At a time of moral disarray, America seeks to rebuild a structure of values.... Large sections of the nation's ethical roofing have been sagging badly, from the White House to churches, schools, industries, medical centers, law firms, and stock brokerages—pressing down on the institutions and enterprises that make up the body and blood of America. At the same time, the collapse of standards brings ethical issues to the forefront. Many Americans feel a need to start rebuilding the edifice, to reevaluate the basis of public morality. In so doing, says Joseph Kockelmans, professor of philosophy at Pennsylvania State University, 'People may finally begin to take responsibility for their lives, instead of just being sheep.'"

We have become numb to scandal and corruption in high places. Although it may not be condoned, it is often accepted, causing us to abandon our trust in leaders, leaving cynicism in its place. This country desperately needs leaders who uphold values against self-interest and consistently stand for moral and ethical integrity. How do we reestablish trust? We have to develop leaders who have a clear and compelling vision, consistently demonstrate empathy, and can be counted on to practice ethical behavior. It is consistent integrity that we are seeking, as well as courageous ethical action. We seek reliability, or what we prefer to call "constancy," in those who lead us.

A recent national study indicates that people would much rather follow individuals on whom they can count, even when they disagree with their viewpoint. They prefer leaders with ideas that are contrary to their beliefs to people with whom they agree but flip-flop in their positions or change willy-nilly. We cannot emphasize strongly enough the significance of constancy, of staying the course. A leader's regular and consistent pattern of integrity provides security and builds trust. In the long haul, strong moral and ethical values allow trust to fully blossom between a leader and followers. Leaders generate and sustain trust by exemplifying the following characteristics:

CONSTANCY. The surprises leaders themselves face are not passed on to their followers. They maintain continuity and create security by being consistently ethical, even when their ideas and positions evolve to reflect changing circumstances.

CONGRUITY. There is no gap between the theories that leaders espouse and the ones they practice. Their morality is found in their behavior.

RELIABILITY. Leaders are there when it counts. They are ready to support their co-workers in the moments that matter.

INTEGRITY. Leaders honor their commitments and promises. They are ethical in their relationships.

Harold Williams, former president of the J. Paul Getty Trust, clarifies this idea when he describes his early experiences as chairman of the Securities and Exchange Commission (SEC):

> "If there is anything I feel good about [at the SEC], it's the way I came through in terms of my own personal values and my personal self. If you believe in your course, you gotta stay with it in terms of course and timing. I think it's tough at times—when the press are all over you and you start hearing from Capitol Hill and you know that

even some of your own staff are feeding the stories and the corporate community is up in arms, and there were several times when it was all going that way and it gets kind of heavy.... But if you believe you're right, and you've got your own integrity—and I think that's where it really ends up—I mean: 'Do you believe in what you're doing?'—And if you believe it you stay with it. I couldn't change course and still respect myself."

In our current organizational and political environment, the only constant is change, and a sense that the integrity, to which Williams points, is slowly disappearing. The dilemma for each of us is this: How can a leader maintain consistent commitments without seeming to be rigid and unresponsive to shifting realities? It is a fine line to walk in today's volatile climate to steer a clear and consistent course while empathizing with, responding to, and addressing constant change. Leaders are expected to acknowledge uncertainties and deal effectively with the present while simultaneously anticipating and responding to the future. This means endlessly expressing, explaining, extending, expanding, and, when necessary, revising the organization's mission as well as their own vision. Leaders can change their minds, but they need to be consistent in their values, which includes being open to change. They need to demonstrate this same value—constancy—in how they communicate these changes, how they behave in relation to change, and how they explain the thinking process that got them to a new position.

Thomas L. Friedman, writing in *The New York Times* about then-President Bill Clinton, who had then been in the White House for one month, describes his problem of constancy as follows:

"How will Mr. Clinton respond when the screaming starts? One friend of Mr. Clinton compares him to a character in the television show 'Star Trek: The Next Generation.' The character is an 'Empath,' one of a race of people born with an ability to empathize with and absorb the feelings of others. As he prepares his economic program, the Empath President is clearly uneasy. 'More than anything else he doesn't want to anger people,' said the friend. 'He wants to be loved. He doesn't want to do things that will hurt people, but that is fundamentally incompatible with the Presidency.'"

In retrospect, it is clear that Clinton, like the rest of us, wanted to be loved. Staying the course, maintaining a consistent focus, and being predictable in terms of what a leader believes will not always end in his being loved, but it will lead to effective leadership and increased trust. Yet as the later stages of the Clinton presidency reveal, people soon begin to distrust a leader who does not consistently uphold the values he preaches or tell the truth about his mistakes.

We are not advocating that leaders take a position and stick to it no matter what. In today's organizations, which require flexible, responsive, innovative leadership, digging in one's heels and sticking to one's guns are strategies that are doomed to failure. But we *are* urging constancy in ethics, values, and integrity. Leaders are responsible for the ethics and norms that govern the behavior of people in their organizations. Leaders can lead through ethics and values in several ways. One is to demonstrate their commitment to the ethics and values they want to institutionalize by matching their own behavior with their values. Leaders set the moral tone in organizations by carefully choosing the people with whom they surround themselves, by communicating a sense of purpose to the organization, by empowering employees to articulate and live by their shared values, by reinforcing value-based behaviors, and by articulating strong ethical positions to external and internal constituencies. John Gardner, writing in *No Easy Victories*, describes a leader's role with regard to ethics and values as follows:

> "Leaders have a significant role in creating the state of mind that is the society. They can serve as symbols of the moral unity of the society. They can express the values that hold the society together. Most important, they can conceive and articulate goals that lift people out of their petty preoccupations, carry them above the conflicts that tear a society apart, and unite them in pursuit of objectives worthy of their best efforts."

In the end, vision, empathy, constancy, and integrity are all different faces of leadership. If organizations are successful in creating ethical, value-based leadership, they can operate as a single organism that is in harmony with itself and comfortable in its environment.

—⁓—

Warren Bennis, a Distinguished Professor of Business Administration and Founding Chairman of the Leadership Institute at the University of Southern California, draws on over forty years of experience as a best-selling author, a prestigious educator, renowned consultant, and award-winning visionary. During most of the 1960s and 1970s, Bennis was an innovative university administrator, serving as president of the University of Cincinnati for seven years. He has been an adviser to four U.S. presidents and has served as professor at such institutions as the Massachusetts Institute of Technology, Harvard College, and Boston University. A recipient of eleven honorary degrees, Bennis has advised many Fortune 500 companies. He lives in Santa Monica, California.

Joan Goldsmith is an organizational consultant, coach, and educator, specializing in leadership development, organizational change, conflict resolution, and team building.

CHAPTER SIXTEEN

Administrative Responsibility

The Key to Administrative Ethics

Terry L. Cooper

R esponsibility is the key concept in developing an ethic for the administrative role. Frederick Mosher (1968, p. 7) once observed, "Responsibility may well be the most important word in all the vocabulary of administration, public and private." Two major aspects of that concept, as defined by Mosher, are used here: subjective and objective responsibility.

When you are confronted with a problem over what you should do in a given situation, you are experiencing the need to define your responsibility in the administrative role. For example, assume that you are an administrator in a federal agency that allocates funds to state agencies for highway construction. Your organization's mission is to review proposed highway routes for their anticipated environmental impact. Highway projects that significantly affect the environment require an environmental impact statement (EIS);

Originally published as "Administrative Responsibility: The Key to Administrative Ethics." In Terry Cooper (Ed.), *The Responsible Administrator: An Approach to Ethics for the Administrative Role* (5th ed.). (San Francisco: Jossey-Bass, 2006).

others do not. One section of a federal law mandates that highways constructed with federal money may not have an impact on or use public parkland, unless it has been determined that there is no feasible and desirable alternative—a question that is normally determined in the EIS.

A member of your staff comes to you with a problem. She has recently met with officials from a certain state to discuss a proposed highway improvement. The existing highway is narrow, with no shoulders, and is heavily used by elementary school students on bicycles and on foot. It is extremely unsafe, as the number of accidents clearly indicates. The school board, the parents' association, the local newspaper, the council of churches, and state highway officials are all calling for immediate action to widen the highway and alleviate these hazardous conditions. The problem, according to the state highway planners, is that widening the road sufficiently would require taking a strip of land five feet wide by one hundred feet long from a fifty-acre municipal park. This can be done within the law, but an EIS must be prepared to identify and justify the environmental impact. This process typically takes two years to complete.

You are responsible for complying with the law under which your organization operates, but you also believe your responsibility is to help reduce the hazardous road condition as quickly as possible. Two types of responsibility can be identified in this case. They are sometimes referred to as *objective* and *subjective* responsibility (Mosher, 1968; Winter, 1966). Objective responsibility has to do with expectations imposed from outside ourselves, whereas subjective responsibility concerns those things for which we feel a responsibility. As we shall see, this is not to be understood as a difference between real and unreal; subjective responsibility, as an expression of our beliefs, personal and professional values, and character traits, is just as real as the more tangible manifestations of objective responsibility. These concepts are the main focus of this chapter, as they seem to represent the most common ways in which administrators actually experience problems in defining their responsibility in concrete situations.

OBJECTIVE RESPONSIBILITY

The specific forms of objective responsibility discussed here include two dimensions: accountability and imposed obligation. All objective responsibility involves responsibility to someone, or some collective body, and responsibility *for* certain tasks, subordinate personnel, and goal achievement. The former is accountability and the latter is obligation. Accountability and obligation, responsibility *to* someone else *for* something—these are the dual dimensions of objective administrative responsibility.

Principal-agent theory, in its current use drawn largely from economics, attempts to describe and explain objective responsibility in terms of relationships between those with the primary right to exercise authority (principals) and those charged with carrying out their wishes (agents). Sappington (1991) identifies the central concern of this perspective as "how the principal can best motivate the agent to perform as the principal would prefer, taking into account the difficulties in monitoring the agent's activities" (p. 45).

The limitations of this perspective for use in administrative ethics are that it oversimplifies the principal-agent relationship; it focuses on the single value of efficiency and fails to deal with the ethical dimensions. The public administrator's role as an agent is complicated by responsibility to multiple principals, including organizational superiors, political officials, professional associations, and the citizenry. Although efficiency is highly important in administrative work, it is not necessarily the most important value; justice, rights (such as privacy), honesty, and a whole host of other values must also be considered. The need to deal with conflicts among principals and competing values, and between accountability and obligation, requires ethical reflection and analysis generally ignored by principal-agent theory (Dees, 1992; De George, 1992).

In terms of relative importance, obligation is the more fundamental; accountability is the means for ensuring the fulfillment of obligation in a hierarchical structure. Accountability implies superior-subordinate relationships and the exercise of authority from the top down to maintain the flow of work toward the achievement of mandated goals. If we explicate these two aspects of objective responsibility in the organizational and political contexts of the public administrative role, we can clarify the relationship of responsibility among the key actors in the policy process. These will be ordered from more to less proximate relationships of accountability, and from less to more fundamental relationships of obligation.

First, public administrators are most immediately responsible to their organizational superiors for carrying out their directives or mutually agreed-on goals and for the conduct of their subordinates.

They must be able to explain their conduct and allocation of time and other resources as consistent with the work plan and objectives of the organization, whether these result from orders originated in a strict hierarchical fashion or from some collaborative decision-making process. This is the most proximate relationship of accountability, involving a regular reporting process. However, the relationship of obligation here is the least fundamental. The organization's work plan, specific objectives, and task assignments are simply instrumental in nature. They are pursuant to policies established in the political arena.

Objective responsibility also for the actions of subordinates is essential to the Weberian bureaucratic ideal type. Superiors must direct the activities of those under their supervision, provide resources for accomplishing the work, delegate adequate authority for assigned duties, and monitor performance. They in turn are held accountable for how their subordinates use the resources provided and exercise delegated authority toward the fulfillment of an assignment. This assumes, of course, that superiors are also accountable for clearly defining the assigned duties in the first place and, wherever discretion is allowed, delineating its boundaries. Subordinates are instructed to refer to their superiors any decisions that exceed the stipulated bounds of discretion, and thus the superiors maintain ultimate responsibility.

Second, public administrators are responsible to elected officials for carrying out their wishes as embodied in public policies. Such policies are collectively determined for legislative acts, singly determined for executive orders. As we have seen previously, this obligation includes both preparing policy proposals and implementing legislation and executive orders. Administrators must be able to explain their actions and use of resources as consistent with legislative intent or the intent of executive orders. This relationship of legal accountability is less proximate than the first because it involves relatively infrequent reporting, but it is a more fundamental obligation. As public policy is the basis for the organizational mandate and mission, obligations to those who establish policy supersede obligations to organizational superiors.

Finally, public administrators are responsible to the citizenry for discerning, understanding, and weighing their preferences, demands, and other interests. They may respond by changing programs within existing law or recommending new legislation to elected officials. Administrators must be able to explain their conduct to the citizenry as consistent with either the wishes of the citizenry or the larger public interest. This is the least proximate relationship of accountability, with only very infrequent and often indirect reporting of conduct and achievements. It is, however, the most fundamental relationship of obligation, because the citizenry are sovereign and public administrators are their fiduciaries. Sharing representative and fiduciary functions with elected officials in modern democratic society means that this relationship of obligation is also shared. For both groups, this is the source of role ambiguity and conflict.

One final word about the nature of accountability in all three relationships is in order. Accountability may be understood in both practical and ethical terms. The responsible administrator must be prepared to answer for conduct from both perspectives, but ethical accountability must finally prevail. Generally we should assume that an administrator will be expected to explain actions from a practical perspective in terms such as cost-effectiveness, efficiency, economy, feasibility, and productivity, and from an ethical perspective according to values and principles such as equity, equality, freedom, truthfulness, beneficence, human dignity, privacy, and democracy. The practicality of conduct is never sufficient in and of itself. Unless a course of action can be adequately explained on ethical grounds, it is not a responsible act. The full meaning of responsibility requires ethical as well as practical accountability. To illustrate these concepts, think back to the federal highway case described above.

Responsibility to Elected Officials Through Support for the Law

Your responsibility to elected officials through compliance with the law is a matter of objective responsibility. You are expected to behave according to the wishes of those set in authority over you. Here the expectations are those of duly elected legislators expressed in a legally codified statement. That legislation prescribes how you shall conduct yourself when the construction of highways affects public parkland, apart from your own feelings about the matter.

Objective responsibility involves accountability to someone else and obligation for a particular standard or category of performance. It is objective in that the source of accountability and obligation lies outside yourself. Objective responsibility is not the result of a series of decisions you made about what ought to be done.

Rather it flows from the decisions of others about what someone occupying your administrative position ought to do. Your decision to accept the position is understood to be tantamount to accepting these expectations and constraints. Objective responsibility projects generalized obligations for all who fill this type of position without any attempt to acknowledge the individual needs, limitations, preferences, or predilections of a particular incumbent. It is through these external generalized obligations that the role is structured, given its distinctive content, and maintained through changing times, incumbents, and situations. It is through hierarchical arrangements that accountability is maintained. The stability and continuity of the role are rooted in these two aspects of objective responsibility.

Responsibility to the laws governing your organization and your conduct within it is one form of objective responsibility for your role as a public administrator. Ultimately, of course, legal responsibility includes an obligation to uphold the Constitution. Through the Constitution and specific pieces of legislation consistent with it, the intentions of the citizenry for those employed in the public service are presumed to be formally expressed. Inherent in the fiduciary nature of the public administrative role is the objective responsibility to the law. Legal mandates for public agencies are a manifestation of primary obligation to serve the public's interests, not those of the people employed by the agencies. Responsibility to the law is a constant reminder that public organizations and their administrators exist on behalf of the public.

Thus, in the highway-widening case, you are held accountable for acting consistently with your obligations under the law that governs the use of parkland. Your own personal opinion about the relative importance of highway safety versus park space is not the controlling factor, but rather the course of action that the law requires of you as an agent of the public. In accounting for your conduct and justifying your decision, it will not be sufficient to explain that you "have loved that park since you were a kid and just couldn't stand to see it whittled away for a highway." This would likely be viewed as irresponsible conduct.

Responsibility to Superiors and for Subordinates

In addition to law, there are numerous other objective sources of responsibility for public administrators: organizational rules and policies, official job descriptions, and professional standards.

However, alongside law, the most prominently experienced objective responsibility is to the hierarchical accountability structure of the organization for which you work: your responsibility to organizational superiors and your responsibility for the conduct of subordinates.

Paul Appleby (1952) has argued that hierarchy is "the formal structure and instrument of responsibility" (p. 340). The chain of command, with its successive delegations of responsibility, is the means by which the generalized intentions of the law are approximated in concrete programs and services. Successive approximations of general legal intent are achieved by specifying accountability for particular aspects of the total task. Particular organizations and individuals are held responsible for implementing specific portions of the legal mandate or providing support for others in fulfilling their responsibility.

Whatever individuals working within the hierarchies of governmental organizations may feel about them, they are the formally accountable means of maintaining conduct that is consistent with the wishes of the citizenry. Appleby insists that only through "loyalty upward disciplined by the sanctions of hierarchy" (p. 228) can the public be maintained at the highest level in democratic decision making. Public servants may very well feel constrained and limited in their range of discretion by the chain of command, but that is one of the intended functions of organizational structure. The personal preferences of individual public employees must be subjugated to the popular will, presumably as communicated through the organizational chain of command.

From Appleby's perspective, this is accomplished by making officials at the top of the hierarchy responsible for the conduct of those below. Then, as diverse public preferences and demands are introduced at various subordinate levels of the organizational structure, they are pushed upward for resolution. Those with greater objective responsibility for conformity to law and popular will are held accountable for reconciling these multiple, often conflicting, demands. According to Bailey (1965, p. 283), this view of the objective responsibility of hierarchies assumes that "the basic morality of the system is in its forcing of unitary claims into the mill of pluralistic considerations," as they move upward.

Once again, the case of the highway and the park exemplifies this process. The member of your staff who laid the problem before you recognized that there were conflicting public demands that she was not competent to resolve at her level of responsibility. The law, expressing the presumed intent of the citizenry of the nation, clearly required an EIS, but the local public, as represented by the newspaper, churches, school board, parent associations, and state highway officials, was primarily concerned about the expeditious widening of the road. Her only responsible option was to carry the problem up the chain of command to the next level.

Authority and *politics* are the key concepts for understanding this upward movement. The pressure of political conflict, combined with insufficient authority to resolve it at any given level in the hierarchy, creates the necessity for moving the problem up the ladder of responsibility. When it reaches an organizational level at which there is both responsibility for resolving the conflict and authority to do so, then a decision can and should be made. If, for example, you have been delegated the authority to make exceptions to the legal requirement for an EIS, then you are obligated to decide whether to do so in this case. However, if you have not been authorized by your superiors to grant exceptions, the problem will need to be pushed upward until it reaches someone with that authority and obligation.

Or, if you have the authority to resolve the issue and attempt to do so but some significant actors in the political arena are not satisfied with the outcome, they may appeal to those higher in the chain of command to review and override your decision. In matters of serious consequence, this movement up the hierarchy may reach the top of the organizational pyramid without being settled and eventually find its way into the judicial system for resolution.

One of the pathologies of bureaucratic organizations is a failure to exercise responsibility when you are in fact authorized and obligated to make a given decision (Barnard, 1952). Passing the buck up the chain of command because you do not want to bear your obligation for deciding is just as irresponsible as acting when you are not authorized to do so or allowing subordinates to engage in misconduct. This reluctance to accept the share of the responsibility delegated to you results in superiors being inundated with decisions they should not have to make, thus leaving subordinates without adequate direction. It distorts the organizational structure and impedes the flow of work.

However, the objective responsibility that an administrator experiences from the organizational hierarchy must not be viewed as the rigid one-way process exemplified by the strictest interpretation of the Weberian ideal type (Weber, 1946). Carl Friedrich (1952) has criticized Weber's model precisely at this point; it does not sufficiently acknowledge the possibility of consultation and cooperation between levels of the organization. The exercise of objective responsibility to the hierarchy should not involve a simple flow of directives from top to bottom; it should be far more complex and dynamic. The apparently fixed subordinate-superior relationships should be more fluid because of the need for consultation and sharing information up and down the hierarchy. Superiors in any bureaucratic organization are highly dependent on the specialized knowledge and experience of subordinates. Subordinates, in turn, need to consult regularly with those above them about legal requirements, clarification of agency regulations, and political considerations. Appleby's normative view of this process has been described by Egger (1965, p. 307) as "the structuring of a network of intelligence and communication which provides a matrix of abundantly diverse and catholic values and influences for the decisions of a pluralistic society."

Hugh Heclo (1975) has described the responsibility of individual public administrators in terms that are generally consistent with those of Appleby. It was Appleby's belief that, far from being the docile submissive implementer, "the function of an administrator was to complicate the lives of his political masters at least to the extent of assuring that they did not resolve complex issues on the basis of disingenuously simple criteria" (Egger, 1965, p. 307). Heclo referred to this active, even aggressive, role of the administrator as one of exercising "neutral competence." By that he meant not the conduct of a docile and simply compliant automaton but "a strange amalgam of loyalty that argues back, partisanship that shifts with the changing partisans, independence that depends on others" (p. 82). Both Appleby and Heclo were describing the responsibility of the top levels of administration to political officials; however, the mode of conduct they suggest seems generally appropriate for all levels of the administrative hierarchy.

The objective responsibility of any public administrator to the chain of command does not imply a passive acceptance of directives from above or the unilateral issuance of orders to those below. It includes the systematic filtering upward of information that will complicate the lives of superiors in the sense of providing a more accurate representation of issues and the regular clarification downward of acceptable norms for conduct. If democratic government is to be maintained in a modern pluralistic society, those with authority and responsibility for making decisions should do so with full knowledge of relevant technical information, public opinion trends, positions of interest groups, interpretations of the law, past practice, the views of interested elected officials, the perspectives of other governmental agencies, and the best informed judgment of subordinates, both practical and ethical. Those in subordinate positions should act with clear directives from above about the publicly mandated mission of the organization, and these directives should be based on full knowledge of all relevant factors.

When your staff member came to you with the problem of the highway and the park, she was acting responsibly from the perspectives of Appleby and Heclo if she complicated your life with relevant information about a decision she did not have authority to make. If, for example, she informed you that, in addition to support of the project from the churches, school board, parent association, newspaper, and state highway officials, there was also opposition from other quarters, she would be carrying out her objective responsibility. She might have told you that the state environmental agency, the municipal parks and recreation commission, the local chapter of the Sierra Club, a home owners' association in the area surrounding the park, and a city council member from that district were strongly opposing the highway project and threatening litigation. Also, she should have apprised you of the possibility of a more expensive alternative course of action that would involve a realignment of the highway but would permit the use of industrial property on the opposite side of the roadway instead of the parkland.

The objective responsibility of public administrators to the hierarchy of an organization includes not only taking decisions up the chain of command when their authority has been transcended by the magnitude of an issue, but also passing along as much information as needs to be considered in arriving at a decision. This is not only a matter of individual responsibility, but when summed throughout an entire organization or an entire government, it amounts to the responsible conduct of the public's business. Wilensky (1967) has demonstrated that the flow of intelligence through an organization is essential not only for the organization's survival but, more important, for achieving democratic values.

The dysfunctions of this hierarchical system are well documented (Merton, 1952). With particular concern for the flow of information, both Tullock (1965) and Perrow (1972) identify two different types of problems. Tullock describes the tendency for subordinates to withhold or distort information, whereas Perrow argues that superiors often receive appropriate information but are unwilling to use it. The common motivation in both cases is the desire to protect self-interests. Subordinates tend to filter out information that may upset the boss and create problems for themselves, and those higher in the chain of command tend to suppress information that is not favorable to their positions.

The difficulty here is centered in a lack of congruence between subjective and objective responsibility.... Suffice it to say that the assumption here is that it is not necessarily bureaucratic organization itself that gives rise to these problems. Based on years of experience in applied research on hierarchical organizations, Elliott Jaques (1976, p. 2) argues that bureaucracies are "dependent institutions, social instruments, taking their initial objectives and characteristics from the associations which employ them." Jaques insists that bureaucratic organizations can be effective and humane tools for a democratic society....

Responsibility to the Citizenry

A third form of objective responsibility is an obligation to serve the public interest. Whether by formal oath, governmental code of ethics, or legislative mandate, all public administrators are ultimately responsible to measure their conduct in terms of the public interest. However, it is impossible to identify any definition of "the public interest" that would receive widespread support among either scholars or practitioners. The public interest has been examined by political theorists like Richard Flathman (1966), but in 1990 Charles Goodsell commented that there had been no serious treatment of the concept in the public administration literature since 1957. That situation has improved only slightly since 1990 with a recent treatment of the concept by Douglas Morgan (2001). However, it remains true that public administrators have shown little sustained interest in public interest theory. The result is that public administrators are confronted with an array of alternatives for conceptualizing the public interest, left to fend for themselves, and expected to serve this confusing idea even though it is a far less specific and concrete form of objective responsibility than either the will of elected officials embodied in law or the organizational chain of command (Held, 1970).

The confounding paradox is that it is assumed that an indefinite concept of this kind should guide our judgment in responding to these two far more definite and proximate sources of obligation. It is not surprising then that as a practical matter, we either treat it as the object of lip-service, along with the flag, motherhood, and apple pie, or we reduce it to balancing power in a political struggle along the lines of the pluralist tradition, with its interest group theory.... In the former case, we may have been exposed to abstract philosophical treatises that have convinced us that the public interest is impossible to define and has little to do with the realities of life in a governmental agency (Friedrich, 1962). In the latter instance, we may have internalized the pluralist notion that balancing organized interests is the way democracy in a mass society approximates the general well-being of the citizenry (Harmon, 1969).

The public interest is clearly a problematic concept. None of the attempts at defining it has been very useful in providing guidance for the practicing administrator. And yet it remains in our political tradition, our legislation, our official codes of ethics, our political debates, our campaign rhetoric, and our deepest reflections during times of profound crisis such as Watergate and the Vietnam War. It remains a part of our thinking about the ends of public policy and the responsibility of public servants—and rightly so.

The function served by the concept of public interest is not so much one of defining specifically what we ought to do or even providing operational criteria for particular decision-making problems. Rather it stands as a kind of question mark before all official decisions and conduct. The primary obligation to serve the public interest as a member of the citizenry should cause the administrator to ask whether all relevant interests have been considered, whether "the interests and welfare of more inclusive populations than self, family, clan, or tribe" are accounted for in the decision (Waldo, 1974, p. 267).

Has the range of viewpoints represented in the development of your policy recommendations, program implementation plans, or service delivery guidelines been too restricted? Are you and your staff listening to opinions that run contrary to your own or to those that would not benefit the organization politically? Have you seriously considered the gains and losses of those not represented in the hearing room, or the advice of experts, or the lobbying process?

The obligation to serve the public interest should always cause administrators and elected officials to feel a little uneasy, not quite sure that everyone worth hearing has been heard. That is its most practical function. The fulfillment of this objective responsibility is to be found neither in adopting a Benthamite utilitarian formula nor in a universal blueprint for society, but in a mind-set. It is a matter of carrying out your duties as though you might be required to stand before the assembled populace and explain your conduct.

Walter Lippmann's oft-quoted words are appropriate here (1922). He observed that the public interest is "what men would choose if they saw clearly, thought rationally, acted disinterestedly and benevolently" (as quoted in Held, 1970, p. 205). Admittedly this is an extremely general statement with a significant *if* in the middle. However, it does suggest an attitude in dealing with the public's business that is more than rhetoric. It is not unlike the conditions stipulated by John Rawls (1971) as the necessary prerequisites for arriving at principles of justice that could be defined as "fair."

Rawls insists that anyone who attempts to reflect on this problem should do so from the "original position," that is, without consideration for one's own social, cultural, economic, or biological circumstances. We should attempt to reason about the requirements of justice as though we did not know our own social class, natural assets and abilities, intelligence, strength, or even the political and economic characteristics of our society. He terms this perspective "the veil of ignorance." One of the basic conclusions Rawls (1971) reaches by reasoning from this assumed vantage point is this: "All social primary goods—liberty and opportunity, income and wealth, and the bases of self-respect—are to be distributed equally *unless an unequal distribution of any or all of these goods is to the advantage of the least favored*" (p. 19, emphasis added). In other words, if none of us actually knew what our situation in society might be, according to Rawls, we would all think it just to distribute these goods equally unless we could increase the advantages of those who turn out to be among the least favored. We would do so because from behind "the veil of ignorance," it would be in our interest to do so; none of us would want to run the risk of winding up among the disadvantaged without these provisions.

This very limited treatment of the complex and carefully reasoned philosophy of John Rawls is included only to suggest the attitude required of administrators in serving the public interest, an attitude built on rationality and benevolence, both inclusive and projected over the long run. It is an attitude that attempts to eschew short-run personal gains and resists immediate pressures. It is a frame of mind that struggles to maintain a commitment to an evolving social system, a vision of the distant future, and a sense of equity that excludes none. It assumes that public servants can realize that they are primarily members of the public, whose fortunes will rise or fall with the concern and fairness exercised in the conduct of the public's business.

SUBJECTIVE RESPONSIBILITY

Externally imposed obligations are only one dimension of responsibility. Alongside these are our own feelings of, and beliefs about, responsibility. Objective responsibility arises from legal, organizational, and societal demands on our role as public administrator, but subjective responsibility is rooted in our own beliefs about loyalty, conscience, and identification. Subjective responsibility in carrying out our administrative role reflects the kind of professional ethic developed through personal experience.... We believe in being legal, and so we are compelled by our conscience to act in a particular way, not because we are required to do so by a supervisor or the law but because of an inner drive composed of beliefs, values, and character understood as predispositions to act in certain ways. These internal sources of responsibility may begin as external standards and expectations that become internalized over time through training and socialization.

Faced with the highway problem, for example, although you may have no specific objective responsibility for reducing hazardous conditions, nevertheless you may have an intense concern for the safety of children. All the law requires of you is to prepare an environmental impact statement when parkland is involved. That is also what the hierarchy of your agency expects of you. The one source of objective responsibility that may require more of you is the obligation to serve the public interest. However, that is such an abstract and elusive notion that it may not serve even the purpose of expanding the perspective of the decision maker, unless there is a strong sense of subjective responsibility. Sometimes subjective responsibility reinforces a person's objective responsibilities, and sometimes not. Sometimes it moves the public interest obligation to the forefront, and at other times it obscures it altogether.

Our feelings and beliefs about responsibility to someone or for something emerge from the socialization process. They are manifestations of values, attitudes, and beliefs we acquire from family, school, religious affiliation, friends, professional training, and organizational involvement. Through these experiences, we begin to perceive patterns in physical nature and in the behavior of others that become a part of our cognitive system.

According to Rokeach (1970, pp. 112–113), these beliefs may be descriptive ("I believe rain is a form of water"), evaluative ("I believe rain is good for the earth"), or prescriptive ("I believe experiments to increase rainfall should be encouraged"). These beliefs, Rokeach explains, are organized into attitudes as they become oriented around types of situations. They are relatively enduring and tend to create within us predispositions to respond in a consistent fashion to these situations—another way of saying that they contribute to the development of both character (predispositions) and integrity (consistency of conduct over time).

Values are types of beliefs more basic than other beliefs we may hold; they are central to our belief systems and thus to our attitudes. They are beliefs about how we ought to behave and about the desirability of certain end states. Figure 16.1 shows three concentric circles: values are located in the innermost circle, indicating their fundamental relationship to the more specific beliefs one holds; beliefs lie in the middle ring; and attitudes are placed in the outer circle to suggest that they are generalized composites of values and beliefs (see also Wright, 1971).

Values are powerful influences in human experience. Although we have referred to subjective responsibility as involving feelings, it is important to note that the values from which this kind of responsibility emerges are not simply emotional expressions. They have three components, which affect the way we live: cognitive, affective, and behavioral. Values not only emerge from our cognitive interaction with our environment, but they also shape our perceptions as we continue to experience the world. Values also evoke emotional responses to what we perceive; we have positive and negative feelings associated with what we believe about what we perceive (Drews and Lipson, 1971). This combination of cognitive and affective responses to the physical and social environment creates predispositions within

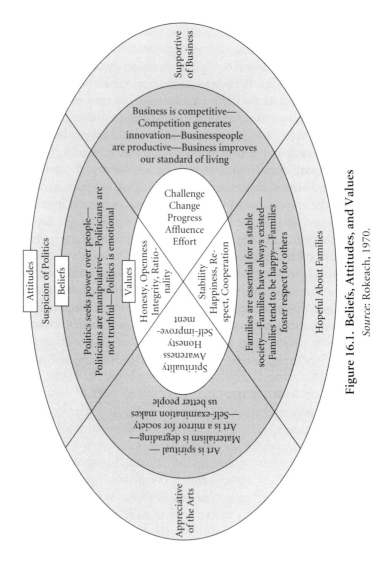

Figure 16.1. Beliefs, Attitudes, and Values
Source: Rokeach, 1970.

us toward certain kinds of behavior. In other words, what we believe and how we feel about that belief affect our character, which shapes our conduct. A value functions as a powerful imperative to action; it is "a standard or yardstick to guide actions" (Rokeach, 1970, p. 160).

As a federal administrator considering the hazardous highway, you may have formed an *attitude* of support for any effort that proposes to alter highways for the increased safety for children. This attitude may be composed of a number of *beliefs* about the accident rate on narrow highways, the best means for reducing that rate, the vulnerability of pedestrians and bicycle riders, the special vulnerability of children traveling by these means, and the desirability of walking and riding bicycles instead of driving motor vehicles. At a deeper and more determinative level in your cognitive system, there may be some fundamental values about preserving the dignity of human life and the particular importance of protecting children. These values motivate you to feel responsible for expediting the widening of the highway. They cause you to want to take action in that direction.

These sources of subjective responsibility may be rooted in one or more of our other roles, such as member of a professional or religious association, citizen, or parent. For example, our membership and involvement in the American Society for Public Administration (ASPA) may create, through the experiences it provides, a sense of subjective responsibility that influences our conduct in our work roles. This may arise from ASPA's de facto ethical standards expressed through the informal norms of its culture. We acquire these through participation in its activities. Note that these may be more or less consistent with ASPA's espoused ethics set forth explicitly in its code of ethics.

Subjective responsibility is rooted in these basic determinative beliefs that we refer to as values, which become more or less elaborated as principles. These principles connect values to broad criteria for conduct. As we confront problems and issues, our values, and the principles associated with them, give rise to feelings and inclinations to behave in a certain way or to seek the fulfillment of a particular goal.

Chester Barnard, in *The Functions of the Executive* (1964), has argued that these values and principles are organized into various constellations, which he terms private, unwritten "codes" governing the conduct of an individual (p. 262). His notion of codes suggests that values and principles are not merely ranked hierarchically but also are structured into subsystems. These normative subsystems are functionally related to the various types of activities in which we are involved. They serve as unwritten, internal codes of conduct for particular aspects of our lives. Although Barnard does not relate these internal codes specifically to the roles we occupy, it is generally consistent with his conceptual scheme to do so. Identifying internal codes with roles helps to clarify both how they are organized and how they are linked to behavior. Values that are appropriate for defining and structuring a given role function as a subsystem of our total value system, functionally oriented around conduct in a particular role but related also to other value subsystems for other roles.

Roles are ... bundles of obligations and interests. Now the description needs to be elaborated in a more complex fashion. There are two components in the enactment of a role: the objective and the subjective. The objective component consists of those external obligations that were discussed under objective responsibility. They give to the role a structure, stability, predictability, and continuity that approximate the will of the citizenry. The subjective component consists of a subsystem of values and principles that we construct in the process of responding to those objective obligations and expectations. As we assume the role and begin to act it out in making particular decisions, we organize a set of values and principles that guide our specific, personal, individual responses to the generalized objective definition of the role. In this process, elements of a role that began as external expectations may be internalized through socialization and become part of our system of subjective responsibility. The more we internalize the values and principles of a role, the more our behavior is guided by our subjective responsibility and the less we depend on external structures.

In other words, we develop a structure of subjective responsibility that is the counterpart of the objective responsibility imposed from outside ourselves. This is the way we mesh our own needs and idiosyncratic perspectives with the demands of the role. A role evokes within us a need to create a value subsystem, a code for living out its objective responsibilities in a way that is compatible with our own inner inclinations.

This inner code may or may not be significantly informed by some professional consensus about the responsibility of public administrators. Sometimes when an administrator has not been socialized by a professional community, idiosyncratic personal values derived from other roles provide the only source for subjective responsibility; no identifiable public service ethical norms shape the conduct of the administrator. In these cases, the public role is carried out on the basis of personal values that may or may not be consistent with public expectations. Inconsistency may be discovered only when some significant action by the administrator is found by superiors, political officials, or the public to be at odds with public service norms.

Barnard (1964) also makes a useful distinction between moral status and responsibility. Moral status has to do with the attributes of the inner code for a particular role: "simple or complex, high or low, comprehensive or narrow." Responsibility is "the power of a particular private code of morals to control the conduct of the individual in the presence of strong contrary desires or impulses" (p. 263). Thus we may have a clearly worked out code for any given role, but may not behave consistently in a manner that is congruent with the code. To the extent that our codes do not consistently control our behavior, we may be described as irresponsible. A responsible person's conduct is not at odds with his or her code for that role.

Sometimes we say that those whose actions are in conflict with what they believe are lacking in integrity. They cannot be trusted because their inner controls are so weak that their behavior is unpredictable and inconsistent. Maintaining a high degree of subjective responsibility is important not only for the sake of our sense of wholeness, self-esteem, and identity—essential as these are to mental health—but also for the fulfillment of our objective responsibility. As Srivastva and Cooperrider (1988) suggest, integrity involves wholeness, not only within ourselves but in our relationships. They maintain that integrity is not a single character trait and not limited to particular roles, but rather "a sophisticated state of processing experience in the world that encompasses moral judgment, creativity, and intuitive capability, as well as rational-analytic powers" (p. 5). They further assert that executives who have this kind of integrity "invite trust from others" because they are "consistent in word and deed" (p. 5). More essentially than organization charts and procedures, it is this trust that actually integrates the organization.

Egger (1965, p. 303) cautions us to be suspicious of the notion that an administrator can function "as a sort of ethical automaton." He argues, in effect, that the need for logic and consistency in our administrative behavior requires a developed subjective responsibility.

The range of administrative discretion that the objective sources of responsibility allow must be structured by "possession of some of the impediments of reflective morality" (p. 303). An administrator needs "some benchmarks for relating the various and frequently conflicting claims of competing values which enter into his official actions" (p. 303). These will not be provided by the law, the courts, or delegated authority; they are too general in nature. According to Egger, sources of subjective responsibility are the means for "the maintenance of a consistent and perhaps corrective ethical continuum to the administrative process" (p. 304).

Consequently, subjective responsibility is not only an unavoidable fact of human experience, growing out of our socialization and our other roles, but its conscious and systematic development is essential for carrying out objective responsibility in a consistent, rational, and dependable fashion. Consistent and powerful internal controls allow administrators to exercise discretion in a pattern that is relatively predictable and therefore engenders trust among associates. The ethical process is the means by which these internal sources of responsibility are related to external demands. Moral imagination is the requisite skill for meshing the two without a loss of integrity. The reflective decision-making approach ... outlines the steps for maintaining congruence between values and external obligations associated with the administrative role.

Now let us turn to another case situation and attempt to apply some of these concepts and distinctions related to subjective and objective responsibility.

"WHAT TO DO ABOUT MRS. CARMICHAEL"

The Municipal Redevelopment Agency (MRA) is involved in a project in Victoria, one of the older communities in Urbopolis. Because most of the turn-of-the-century housing is in a seriously dilapidated state, the Urbopolis City Council has declared Victoria an appropriate area for redevelopment.

You have been appointed assistant project director, with primary responsibility for determining which of the houses should be rehabilitated and which must be demolished. You have a staff that includes two specialists in municipal building codes and housing construction. You have assigned them to conduct on-site inspections of the residences in the first project area and prepare a draft report with their recommendations. They are nearing the completion of their fieldwork; another two or three weeks should do it.

Harmon, one of the two specialists, buzzes you on the intercom to say that he and Franklin, the other specialist, need to talk with you as soon as possible about Mrs. Carmichael, who lives in project area 1; in fact, she has lived there for thirty years. Mrs. Carmichael is now eighty-two years old, her husband is deceased, and her income has been so battered by inflation that it barely meets her basic living expenses. The mortgage has been paid off, but there have been taxes and maintenance costs. Some time ago Mrs. Carmichael began to neglect repairs on her home as her money shrank in value. "Now," Harmon says, "her house is in pretty bad shape." He sums up the condition of the house by admitting that according to the standards they have been applying elsewhere in the first project area, Mrs. Carmichael's home should be demolished.

However, Harmon cannot bring himself to recommend the destruction of the old woman's home. This is his fourth redevelopment project and he has seen it happen before: "Elderly people, whose homes cannot justify rehabilitation loans, are relocated into apartments, or board and care homes, only to lapse into senility and sometimes death." Harmon never felt very good about it before, and he just cannot stand to do it again. He tells you that he knows what the law requires and what the MRA project guidelines specify, but it seems wrong. He argues that "the government has no business treating decent people who have worked hard all their lives as though they were disposable trash."

You feel moved by Harmon's concern for Mrs. Carmichael, but you are unsure about what it means for you and the project. It occurs to you that Franklin has said nothing, so you ask if he agrees with Harmon.

No, Franklin does not agree. He feels as strongly as Harmon but not in the same way. "It is too bad about Mrs. Carmichael, and all the Mrs. Carmichaels who get caught in her predicament, but there is nothing *we* can do about it," says Franklin. He tells you that the MRA's job is to rehabilitate when it can and demolish when it cannot, and there are laws and rules and standards that must govern those decisions.

Franklin insists that you cannot go around making exceptions; you have to be fair with everyone, and that means treating everyone equally. There must be no special favors, or the entire project will be jeopardized. Everyone will demand an exception, and nothing will get done. The only way to deal with this case is to go by the book. "Let the relocation unit find her a satisfactory place to live—that's their problem," Franklin maintains. "Our problem is to make a decision about whether to fix up her place or tear it down." He knows that the house is beyond repair according to the standards employed by the MRA for all other similar projects.

The tension has been rising between Harmon and Franklin, and at this point a heated argument breaks out between the two men. You try to calm their tempers, and as they settle back into their seats, you express appreciation for both men's concerns. You assure them that you respect their judgment and indicate that you would like to give the matter some thought and discuss it again later. Harmon and Franklin thank you for hearing them out and then leave your office.

It is not our intention to attempt to resolve the issue of Mrs. Carmichael's house, but to use this case to illustrate some of the concepts just discussed in this chapter and indicate ways of clarifying the situation that will be helpful in arriving at a decision.

First, consider the facts concerning your objective responsibility. You know, for example:

1. The laws related to this redevelopment project clearly authorize the condemnation and demolition of substandard structures. If the owner cannot or will not make the necessary repairs, the building may be torn down.

2. A long series of court cases have upheld this kind of action.

3. The criteria for determining substandard buildings are well defined in the agency guidelines for such projects and in the Urbopolis building and safety code.

4. You are responsible to Bronson, the Victoria Redevelopment Project director, for recommending which buildings should be demolished and which rehabilitated. If it looks as though this case will be a matter of dispute or if you cannot resolve the issue in your own mind, you may have to discuss it with him.

5. You are not sure what your responsibility for upholding the public interest requires of you in this case. You need to ascertain how the public, at least in the Victoria area, feels about it.

Then you review in your mind what you know about Mrs. Carmichael's case and what essential information you need to obtain. You feel reasonably confident about the following:

1. From Harmon's description, the house probably falls into the demolition category. Harmon did not try to soften the hard realities of its condition, and Franklin concurred.

2. Because the house is in such bad shape, it will not qualify for a federal grant or loan large enough to do the work required to avoid condemnation.

3. Mrs. Carmichael could not qualify for a loan from a private lending institution, and she would be unable to make the payments if she did.

4. If demolition takes place, Mrs. Carmichael could not afford to rebuild on the present site.

5. If the agency condemns the house for demolition, Mrs. Carmichael will receive market value for it.

You feel much less certain about several other aspects of the case. You believe that you need to clarify the following:

1. How does Mrs. Carmichael feel about the situation? Harmon is deeply concerned about saving her house, but not once in his presentation of the problem did he report *her* viewpoint. It would be a good idea to stop by and hear her reactions first-hand. Maybe she would like to move into a place that she could manage better.

2. Can she handle a change in residence? What are her mental, emotional, and physical states? Is she in reasonably good health? You know that Harmon is right about the serious negative impact of moving on some older people.

3. What are some options if her house is demolished? Will she have enough money from the agency's purchase of her house to buy another house elsewhere, or perhaps a condominium? Maybe she could invest the proceeds and produce enough additional income to afford a nice apartment.

4. Is Mrs. Carmichael truly an exceptional case? Are there other elderly people in the project area who face the same threat? Maybe they should be considered as a group.

5. How do people in the community feel about Mrs. Carmichael's case? Without violating her privacy, is it possible to assess how others believe their interests might be served or subverted by the way her case is handled?

Finally, you reflect on your own personal inclinations. You attempt to clarify in our own mind what your subjective responsibility is with respect to Mrs. Carmichael. After mulling it over for a while, you realize the following:

1. Your general *attitude* toward older people is one of deep respect. Since your boyhood days with your grandparents, you have felt almost a reverence for those who have survived the vicissitudes of the modern world. They evoke within you a deferential feeling.

2. This attitude is composed of a number of *beliefs*. You view them as having "paid their dues," as having worked hard and deserving our esteem for having done so. You believe young people often do not recognize the valuable knowledge and experience that older people have accumulated. You believe that the elderly are often ignored and mistreated. They generally do not receive what is coming to them.

3. Behind these beliefs are some *values* you have long recognized within yourself. Wisdom about life in the world, based on knowledge and experience, is important to you. Getting the most out of the time allotted to you is something about which you feel deeply. Perseverance in the face of hardship is a significant virtue in your value system. Fairness, or equity, is one of the most essential principles of all. Sensitivity to the feelings of others is another of your values.

On the basis of these reflections, you conclude that your strongest sense of subjective responsibility leads you in the direction of trying to resolve the problem without harming Mrs. Carmichael in any way. You do not want to disturb her life. However, you have other obligations too. You are the administrator responsible for making a recommendation about Mrs. Carmichael's house. You are paid to do that by MRA, and you made a commitment to carry out that responsibility when you accepted the job. It is your objective responsibility, and as long as you hold this position, you may not ignore it.

Also, you have other subjective responsibilities associated with your administrative role. You feel responsible for maintaining morale and a cooperative team spirit among staff members. You value efficiency, and you believe these qualities are essential for an efficient organization. You also feel responsible for avoiding conflict with the residents of Victoria, both because that would upset the orderly schedule of work and lead to reduced efficiency and because you value the esteem of others. You want the residents to feel that you have been fair with them. Furthermore, you feel responsible to Bronson, the Victoria Project director, and Markham, the executive director of MRA, for maintaining the image of the agency. Loyalty to the organization is important to you.

In determining the best course of action, you may simply respond to the strongest and most definitive sources of objective responsibility—perhaps your superior, the law, or both if they coalesce. Or you may allow deep-seated feelings to function as the decisive factors.

References

Appleby, P. H. *Morality and Administration in Democratic Government.* Baton Rouge: Louisiana State University Press, 1952.

Bailey, S. K. "The Relationship Between Ethics and Public Service." In R. C. Martin (Ed.), *Public Administration and Democracy: Essays in Honor of Paul Appleby.* Syracuse, NY: Syracuse University Press, 1965.

Barnard, C. I. "A Definition of Authority." In R. K. Merton and others (Eds.), *Reader in Bureaucracy.* New York: The Free Press, 1952.

Barnard, C. I. *The Functions of the Executive.* Cambridge, MA: Harvard University Press, 1964.

De George, R. T. "Agency Theory and the Ethics of Agency." In N. E. Bowie and R. E. Freeman (Eds.), *Ethics and Agency Theory.* New York: Oxford University Press, 1992.

Dees, J. G. "Principals, Agents, and Ethics." In N. E. Bowie and R. E. Freeman (Eds.), *Ethics and Agency Theory.* New York: Oxford University Press, 1992.

Drews, E. M., and Lipson, L. *Values and Humanity.* New York: St. Martin's, 1971.

Egger, R. "Responsibility in Administration: An Exploratory Essay." In R. C. Martin (Ed.), *Public Administration and Democracy: Essays in Honor of Paul Appleby.* Syracuse, NY: Syracuse University Press, 1965.

Flathman, R. E. *The Public Interest: An Essay Concerning the Normative Discourse of Politics.* Hoboken, NJ: John Wiley & Sons, 1966.

Friedrich, C. J. "Some Observations on Weber's Analysis of Bureaucracy." In R. Merton (Ed.), *Reader in Bureaucracy.* New York: The Free Press, 1952.

Friedrich, C. J. (Ed.). *The Public Interest.* New York: Atherton Press, 1962.

Harmon, M. "Administrative Policy Formulation and the Public Interest." *Public Administration Review,* 1969, *29*(5), 483–491.

Heclo, H. "OMB and the Presidency: The Problem of Neutral Competence." *Public Interest,* 1975, *38*(2), 80–98.

Held, V. *The Public Interest and Individual Interests.* New York: Basic Books, 1970.

Jaques, E. *A General Theory of Bureaucracy.* New York: Halsted Press, 1976.

Lippmann, W. *Public Opinion.* Orlando, FL: Harcourt, 1922.

Merton, R. K. "Bureaucratic Structure and Personality." In R. K. Merton (Ed.), *Reader on Bureaucracy.* New York: The Free Press, 1952.

Morgan, D. F. "The Public Interest." In T. L. Cooper (Ed.), *Handbook of Administrative Ethics.*(2nd ed.). New York: Marcel Dekker, 2001.

Mosher, F. *Democracy and the Public Service.* New York: Oxford University Press, 1968.

Perrow, C. *Complex Organizations: A Critical Essay.* Glenview, IL: Scott, Foresman, 1972.

Rawls, J. *A Theory of Justice.* Cambridge, MA: Belknap Press of Harvard University Press, 1971.

Rokeach, M. *Beliefs, Attitudes and Values.* San Francisco: Jossey-Bass, 1970.

Sappington, D.E.M. "Incentives in Principal-Agent Relationships." *Journal of Economic Perspectives,* 1991, *5*(2), 45–66.

Srivastva, S., and Cooperrider, D. L. "The Urgency for Executive Integrity." In S. Srivastva and Associates, *Executive Integrity: The Search for High Human Values in Organizational Life.* San Francisco: Jossey-Bass, 1988.

Tullock, G. *The Politics of Bureaucracy.* Washington, DC: Public Affairs Press, 1965.

Waldo, D. "Reflections on Public Morality." *Administration and Society,* 1974, *6*(3), 267–282.

Weber, M. *From Max Weber: Essays in Sociology.* (H. H. Gerth and C. W. Mills, Eds.) New York: Oxford University Press, 1946.

Wilensky, H. *Organizational Intelligence.* New York: Basic Books, 1967.

Winter, G. *Elements for a Social Ethic.* New York: Macmillan, 1966.

Wright, D. *The Psychology of Moral Behavior.* Baltimore, MD: Penguin, 1971.

At time of original publishing Terry L. Cooper was the Maria B. Crutcher Professor in Citizenship and Democratic Values (Social Ethics) at the School of Policy, Planning, and Development, University of Southern California.

CHAPTER SEVENTEEN

Empowering People to Lead

Bill George

I get things done by identifying with the people in the company and by trusting them. I care most about building a good team to lead the company.

—*Anne Mulcahy, Chair and CEO, Xerox.*

W atching the brilliant young Norwegian con--ductor Arild Remmereit lead the Dallas Symphony Orchestra, I realized that an entirely new version of the "conductor as metaphor for leadership" has emerged, one that is consistent with our vision of how the new breed of authentic leaders empowers others to step up and lead.

Remmereit's style was in sharp contrast to the great showmen who led major orchestras in years past, when the conductor was out front taking all the credit. As he prepared to conduct Mendelssohn's Scottish Symphony, Remmereit spoke to the audience in his Norwegian accent. "The musicians know within five minutes whether a

---

Originally published as "Empowering People to Lead" in Bill George, *True North*. (San Francisco: Jossey-Bass, 2007).

new conductor is any good or not," he said, "and soon you will learn what they think of me as their leader."

For the next forty-seven minutes he demonstrated that his quiet confidence was well placed. Without using a single sheet of music to conduct the complex work, he knew every bar of the symphony as well as the parts for each instrument and how he wanted them played. His demeanor on the podium was engaged and inspiring.

When the orchestra finished the finale, the audience rose in unison for a standing ovation. Unwilling to take credit, Remmereit insisted that the entire orchestra rise to take their bows and hurried from the stage. Returning to the audience's rhythmic applause, he wandered through the rear of the orchestra, asking the musicians to stand and take the credit, instead of mounting the podium as other conductors do. Eventually making his way to the podium, he again refused the solo bow and would only be recognized with the entire orchestra.

Remmereit's leadership is a metaphor for the best of today's business leaders:

- He knew his True North: being true to the music as originally intended.
- He knew his purpose: producing beautiful and inspiring music.
- He knew his subject in amazing detail.
- He was highly authentic and humble in a confident way.
- He knew how to get the best out of his musicians by empowering them.
- Finally, he was challenging, inspiring, respectful, and willing to share the credit.

ANNE MULCAHY: EMPOWERING PEOPLE THROUGH A CRISIS

Xerox CEO Anne Mulcahy is an exceptional leader who has demonstrated a remarkable ability to empower a large, diverse organization around a common mission. Back in 2000, becoming CEO of Xerox was the furthest thing from her mind. One day, as she was preparing for a business trip to Japan, chairman Paul Allaire came to her office and told her he planned to recommend that the Xerox board terminate its current CEO and promote her to COO and eventually CEO. She was so shocked that she asked for the evening to discuss it with her family. The next day she accepted the job.

The board's decision surprised Mulcahy as well as everyone else. Since joining Xerox twenty-five years before, she had worked in field sales and on the corporate staff but not in finance, R&D, or manufacturing. At the time she was enjoying her first general management assignment, running a relatively small business outside the Xerox mainstream. "It was like going to war," she recalled, "knowing it was the right thing for the company and there was so much at stake."

> "This was a job that would dramatically change my life, requiring every ounce of energy that I had. I never expected to be CEO, nor was I groomed for it."

What no one understood was that Xerox was facing a massive liquidity crisis and was on the verge of bankruptcy. Its revenues were declining, its sales force was unraveling, and its new-product pipelines were depleted. The company had $18 billion in debt, and all lines of credit were exhausted. With the share price in free fall, morale inside the company was in disarray. Xerox had just one week of cash on hand as key advisers recommended that the company consider bankruptcy. To make matters worse, Xerox's chief financial officer was preoccupied with an SEC investigation into the company's revenue recognition practices.

As the situation went from bad to worse, Mulcahy recognized just how great the risks of bankruptcy were.

> "My greatest fear was that I was sitting on the deck of the Titanic and I'd get to drive it to the bottom of the ocean—not exactly a moment to be proud of.
>
> "Nothing spooked me so much as waking up in the middle of the night and thinking about 96,000 employees and retirees and what would happen if things went south."

How could Mulcahy cope with this crisis when she had had no financial experience? She brought to the CEO's role relationships built over twenty-five years and an impeccable understanding of the organization. She bled for Xerox and everyone knew it. To ameliorate the gaps in her experience, she was tutored on finance by the treasurer's office and surrounded herself with a diverse set of leaders.

As Mulcahy recognized the depth of the company's problems, her purpose became crystal clear: to save the company from bankruptcy and restore Xerox to its former greatness. Her challenge was to unite the disheartened organization and to get leaders throughout the company to step up to the challenge.

"I get things done by identifying with the people in the company and by trusting them," she said. "I care most about building a good team to lead the company." She met personally with the top one hundred executives to ask them if they would stay with the company despite the challenges ahead. "I knew there were people who weren't supportive of me," she said.

> "So I confronted a couple of them and said, 'Hey, no games. Let's just talk. You can't be thrilled. If you choose to stay, either we're totally in synch or when you go, it won't be pleasant, because I have no appetite for managing right now. This is about the company.'"

The first two people she talked to, both of whom ran big operating units, decided to leave, but the remaining ninety-eight committed to stay. They did so because Mulcahy appealed to their character and to the purpose of saving the company they loved. One of them, Ursula Burns, noted, "I have a wonderful life and great friends because of my partnership with this company. What do you say when times are tough? 'Thank you very much, I'll see you later?' That's not what my mother taught me."

In spite of the pressures and endless rounds of meetings at headquarters, Mulcahy decided to get into customers' offices and ride with field salespeople to see whether she could help stem the tide of customer defections and field-sales resignations. She told her sales force, "I will go anywhere, anytime, to save a Xerox customer." Her customer-engagement contrasted sharply with her predecessor, who had rarely been seen outside the headquarters building. It sent an important signal that solidified the Xerox field organization and restored customer confidence.

Yet Mulcahy was both challenging and demanding, as she held people publicly accountable for their results. Despite the tremendous pressures the company was under, she set realistic expectations. "You can't wish your way to good performance," she said. "If you set the bar someplace that buys you ninety days of stock-market esteem, you will eventually get killed. Boy, is it ugly."

She encouraged senior managers to engage each other directly. "We talk about everything," said Burns. "Anne is really clear: 'Make sure you get it.'" Mulcahy did not take the lead in every discussion, playing instead what Burns described as an orchestrating role. "She's very good at reading people," Burns explained, "and getting us to work together."

The bankruptcy question came to a head in the third week of October 2001. Earlier in the month, Mulcahy candidly told the company's shareholders that Xerox's business model was unsustainable. The next day the stock dropped 26 percent. Mulcahy noted, "This was my baptism by fire."

Mulcahy had traditionally drawn support by interacting with her peers, but in her new role she had to provide her team with confidence that the company could survive—in spite of any personal doubts she had. "As a touchy-feely people person, the hardest thing was that my new role required some distance I wasn't prepared for."

Yet Mulcahy was not immune from uncertainty and stress. "One day I came back to the office from Japan and found it had been a dismal day," she explained.

> "Around 8:30 p.m. on my way home, I pulled over to the side of the Merritt Parkway and said to myself, 'I don't know where to go. I don't want to go home. There's just no place to go.'"

Have you ever felt like that? In my experience, feelings of despair among leaders are quite common, but most do not have the courage to admit it. In times like these, you need the support of your colleagues. Mulcahy explained, "I picked up my voice mail and listened to a message from chief strategist Jim Firestone: 'This may seem like the worst day, but we believe in you. This company will have a great future.'" That was all Mulcahy needed to drive home and get up the next day. "The team gave me incredible supportive strength. We fight, we debate, but at the end of the day, they've been extremely loyal and supportive."

When the company's external advisers argued that Xerox should prepare for a bankruptcy filing to relieve the $18 billion debt burden, Mulcahy exploded.

> "I told them, 'You don't understand what it's like to be an employee in this company—to fight and win. Bankruptcy's never a win. I'm

not going there until there's no other decision to be made. There are a lot more cards to play.' I was so angry because they could not comprehend the passion and drive that's required to succeed and the impact of bankruptcy on the company's employees. Our people believed we were in a war we could win."

Anne Mulcahy did win in the end. She staved off bankruptcy by cutting billions in operating expenses without touching R&D or field sales and by reducing debt by 60 percent. In launching sixty new products with new color and digital technology, she restored revenue and profit growth. What distinguished her leadership throughout this crisis was her ability to empower people to rise to the challenge and to keep them focused on the shared mission of saving and restoring Xerox.

MUTUAL RESPECT: THE BASIS FOR EMPOWERMENT

To bring out the best from teammates, authentic leaders must develop trusting relationships based on mutual respect. There is no substitute. Like loyalty, respect provides a basis for empowerment, but it must be earned. Here are some of the things leaders do to gain the respect of their colleagues:

- Treating others as equals.
- Being a good listener.
- Learning from people.
- Sharing life stories.

Treating Others as Equals

We respect people who treat us like equals, especially when they are successful investors like Warren Buffett. Buffett has the same sandwich and cherry Coke combination with a group of wide-eyed students as he does with his close friend Bill Gates. He does not rely upon his image to make people feel he is important or powerful. He genuinely respects others, and they respect him as much for those qualities as for his investment prowess. Although Anne Mulcahy had never met Buffett, she felt able to fly to Omaha to get his advice over his traditional steak dinner. By being authentic in his interactions, Buffett empowers people to lead in their own authentic ways.

Being a Good Listener

We are grateful when people genuinely listen to us. Active listening is one of the most important abilities of empowering leaders, because people sense such individuals are genuinely interested in them and not just trying to get something from them.

Learning from People

We feel respected when others believe they can learn from us or ask for our advice. When Warren Bennis, now in his eighties, meets with his incoming class of USC undergraduate students each year, he tells them, "I know I have a lot to learn from you." The students find that hard to believe at first, but they soon see how their feedback helps him understand how younger generations think.

Sharing Life Stories

When leaders are willing to be open and share their personal stories and vulnerabilities, people feel empowered to share their own stories and uncertainties in return. On Thanksgiving eve in 1996, I sent an e-mail to all Medtronic employees expressing my gratitude for the support Penny and I received following her ordeal with breast cancer and chemotherapy. We were overwhelmed by the number of people who spontaneously shared their stories with us.

Sharing our life stories can free us from our defenses and open us to authentic relationships. Safeco CEO Paula Rosput Reynolds described a prior experience in leading a team that had very low trust. One person in particular was viewed as too opinionated and unable to work well with colleagues until she asked him to share his story with the team. He explained that his older brother and father died during his preteen years, and he felt obligated to carry on for them, including working for the same company his father had worked for. "All of a sudden, everyone understood and was willing to work with him," Reynolds explained. "That is why leadership must be personal."

EMPOWERING PEOPLE TO LEAD

If mutual respect provides the foundation for bringing out the best from people, what are the steps needed to empower them? The skills of empowerment take many forms, from simply showing up to engaging people, helping them, challenging them, stretching them, and aligning them with the mission. Effective leaders use all of these approaches at different times, depending on the capabilities of the people involved and the situation they are facing.

- Showing up.
- Engaging people.
- Helping teammates.
- Challenging leaders.
- Stretching people.
- Aligning everyone around a mission.

Showing Up

Woody Allen once remarked, "Eighty percent of success is showing up." Surprisingly, many leaders get so busy they don't take the time to be there for people. They don't bother to attend award ceremonies, company picnics, sales meetings, and even business and project reviews. Nor do they show up around the offices, factories, labs, and field sales and service locations. Often they are too busy to come to important customer meetings or trade shows. As a result, their teammates never get to know them on a personal basis. Their only contact with their leaders is through impersonal media like speeches, voice mail, videotapes, and web-streaming of company events.

Howard Schultz told of visiting a Starbucks store one Saturday morning:

> "I walked in, dressed so that nobody would recognize me. As soon as I sat down, the manager came up and said, 'Howard, is that you?' I said, 'Yes, it is.' She was telling me about receiving Starbucks stock, and what it did for her and her family. Then she started crying and said, 'I'm so moved that you're in my store.' Later I got voice mail from her, saying what that moment was like for her. I immediately called her back and thanked her for sharing with me."

Stories of basic human interactions like this one are very powerful. All Schultz had to do was show up. Showing up at important events or at unexpected times means a great deal to people and enables them to take their leaders off their proverbial pedestals and see them as real people.

Engaging People

The most empowering leaders are those who engage a wide range of people. That means being with them face-to-face; inquiring about their work, their families, their personal lives, and their careers; and being open and vulnerable with them. This degree of intimacy with people they don't know well makes some leaders uncomfortable, but it is a powerful means of establishing deeper connections.

One of my MBA students shared a story about working for Procter & Gamble in Chile:

> "We had the first visit ever from CEO A.G. Lafley. Lafley asked in advance to visit the homes of poor people the day before our meeting. This surprised all of us, since we generally do not go into the homes of poor people. The next morning I was at my desk at 7:30 a.m. when Mr. Lafley came walking down the hall. He stopped at my desk, put out his hand, and said, 'My name's A.G. Please tell me about your work.' When I nervously concluded explaining how we were expanding the market for P&G products in Chile, again he shook my hand and said, 'Thank you. Your work is vital to the future of P&G and our ability to grow in countries like Chile. I came here to see first-hand how we can expand our business in developing markets and reach a broader range of consumers.'"

That is empowerment. Your first reaction may be that Lafley reached only one of the hundred thousand P&G employees, but the reality is that my student and his colleagues told that story to hundreds of people inside and outside the company to illustrate the personal qualities of their leader.

Helping Teammates

Authentic leaders help their teammates, whether it is with a personal problem or a career problem, by counseling with them, offering suggestions, or assisting them in making vital contacts. That in turn is highly empowering.

Merck CEO Roy Vagelos ate regularly in the company cafeteria, where he asked people about their work and the challenges they were facing. He took notes about the conversations and then thought about the specific problems for a few days before calling the employees back with his ideas.

Imagine how Merck researchers must have felt when they picked up the phone to hear Vagelos getting back to them. "I'd call them up and say, 'That's a tough problem, but here are a couple things you might try,'" Vagelos said. "People love to have involvement of the leader. They feel you want to help them and are part of the solution." These interactions reinforced the importance of the researchers' work and had a multiplier effect upon employees.

Challenging Leaders

Empowering people is much more than a series of positive interactions. Often, the most empowering response is to challenge people's ideas, to ask why they are doing something a particular way, and to help them sharpen their ideas through dialogue. Although people may feel uncomfortable in being challenged at first, they are usually engaged with their leaders and anxious to respond.

Jack Welch was a master at asking challenging questions that caused GE leaders to set higher standards for themselves and their teams and to think more deeply about important issues of their business. He wouldn't hesitate to get on the phone and challenge managers who were several levels below him.

Stretching People

Most people want to be stretched in assignments that enable them to develop. The leader's key is to sense when people are ready for such challenging experiences, of the sort Jeff Immelt had in GE's plastics division.

Yet it is also important for your team to know that you will be there to support them if necessary. Medtronic's Martha Goldberg Aronson tells the story of a boss who was willing to bet on her in stretch roles while supporting her. On taking a new position, Aronson said, her new boss advised her:

> "On certain days you will feel that you're way out on this limb. The wind is going to start to blow, and you're going to feel like the limb is going up and down. You're going to hear it crack, and you're going to come crashing down. That's when I'll be there to catch you."

It wasn't long before Aronson encountered a quality problem with her new line of catheters. She noted, "The branch cracked a few times, and my boss was really there." Just knowing you have support from your leaders if things go wrong is very empowering. It enables you to recognize that you will not be hung out to dry, so you can take on stretch goals and significant challenges without fear of someone sawing off the limb behind you.

Aligning Around a Mission

The most empowering condition of all is when the entire organization is aligned with its mission, and people's passions and purpose are in synch with each other. It is not easy to get to this position, especially if the organization has a significant number of cynics or disgruntled people. Nonetheless, it is worth whatever effort it takes to create an aligned environment.

Individuals usually have their own passions that drive them. If the organization's leaders can demonstrate how they can fulfill their purpose while achieving the organization's mission, then alignment can occur.

Several years ago I visited Medtronic's heart-valve factory in southern California, where employees reconfigure valves from pig hearts to replace human heart valves. Because the process is more art than science, it requires extremely skilled workers. On the factory floor I met the top producer, a Laotian immigrant who made a thousand valves a year. When I asked her the key to her process, she looked at me with passion in her eyes and said, "Mr. George, my job is to make heart valves that save lives."

> "Before I sign my name to a completed valve, I decide whether it is good enough to put in my mother or my son. Unless it meets that standard, it does not pass. If just one of the valves I make is defective, someone may die. To the company 99.9 percent quality may be acceptable, but I could not live with myself if I caused someone's death. But when I go home at night, I fall asleep thinking about the five thousand people who are alive today because of heart valves I made."

Can there be any question that she is a leader among her peers? She has a passion for her work that is tied directly to the company's mission; she sets high standards for herself, and she sets the example for everyone else to emulate.

MARILYN CARLSON NELSON: BUILDING AN EMPOWERED CULTURE

Marilyn Carlson Nelson, CEO of travel-and-leisure conglomerate Carlson Companies, has dramatically transformed the company founded by her father, Curtis Carlson. Carlson was a consummate salesman and a tough, demanding boss. Seeing an employee leaving the office at 7:30 p.m. one night, Carlson asked if he had lost his enthusiasm for the business. "Monday through Friday are about staying even with the competition," he often said. "Saturday is when you get ahead."

The elder Carlson taught his daughter about business but never encouraged her to join his company, believing that women were not meant for the workplace. After giving birth to her first child, Nelson worked from her home as publisher of Carlson's employee newspaper. After she produced a catalog of the company's products, she was promoted to department head. When she reported this news to her father, his response was blunt: "You're getting too involved in the business. You should be at home with your children." Added Nelson, "My father fired me on the spot. I left the building with tears running down my face."

While raising her family, Nelson became deeply involved in the Minneapolis community, chairing the Minnesota Orchestral Association, creating "Scandinavia Today," and bringing the 1992 Super Bowl to Minnesota on the coldest weekend of the year. She also became the first woman to serve on the boards of major local corporations and was co-owner of a rural bank. As her business profile continued to rise, her father repeatedly rebuffed her interest in his company.

When her last child went off to college, Nelson finally rejoined Carlson—at age forty-eight. In her first month she accompanied her father to a presentation by MBA students at Minnesota's Carlson School about their research into Carlson Companies' corporate culture. Nelson recalled asking, "How do the students see Carlson?" No one dared to answer. Finally, one student said, "Carlson is perceived as a sweatshop that does not care about people. Our professors don't recommend that we work for Carlson." Nelson was stunned. "That meeting lit a fire under me," she said. She realized then she needed to change the corporate culture away from her father's top-down, autocratic style.

When her brother-in-law abruptly departed as CEO two years later, her eighty-year-old father returned to active management, and Nelson took on more prominent operational roles but still was not designated as successor. Meanwhile, the management turmoil continued as key executives left the company, frustrated by Carlson's command-and-control management style. Eventually, Nelson assumed responsibility for key Carlson divisions and began to reshape the company's leadership and strategy. At the celebration for her father on the company's sixtieth anniversary, she was named CEO.

Undaunted, Carlson cautioned his daughter against relying on others. "Be very careful," he told her. "You can't trust anyone besides yourself." Nelson had just the opposite point of view, feeling that trust would work in a caring environment. "If you create a supportive environment, you can attract people who are trustworthy, so long as you trust them and you are trustworthy yourself," she explained.

In place of the company's founder-driven culture, Nelson focused on employees and customers. "In the command-and-control environment," she explained, "my dad robbed himself of the opportunity to hear contrarian views."

> "The contrarian view forces you to either understand or change your position. I moved to a collaborative mode of management. Now we rely on everybody to bring their wisdom and experience to bear on decisions. I believe that collective wisdom has great value when it comes from solid thinking. Ultimately, the leader still has to make the final decision."

Nelson decided to reinvent Carlson as a company that cared for customers by creating the most caring environment for its employees. She shifted emphasis away from stewardship of financial capital toward acquiring and cultivating human capital with experience, wisdom, and collective-thinking skills. She looked for three characteristics in employees: character, competence, and caring. "The need for character as absolute trustworthiness, and competence in the form of global experience, expertise, and judgment, are not surprising," Nelson explained, "but the characteristic of caring was not self-evident."

> "I looked for people who had 'a servant's heart.' Servant leadership is an important driver of the culture we want to create. A satisfied employee delivers a satisfied customer. In the service business,

customers understand very quickly whether you legitimately care about serving them."

Recognizing that these values had to be embraced by Carlson locations worldwide if they were to become key behaviors for every Carlson employee, Nelson traveled tirelessly to meet with company employees and customers around the world. "We can build relationships only if an employee is affirmed and empowered, enjoys clarity of direction, and understands the vision and mission of the company," she said.

> "We cannot just teach restaurant employees to put a meal on the table. In a restaurant you can customize the experience if you know when customers want privacy or when they want fun."

Reflecting on the changes she had wrought over the course of nine years, Nelson said that these days no follow-up study by MBAs could conclude that Carlson does not care about people. "You cannot change a culture in six months," she explained. "If you change the business model and build transparency and collaborative discussion into the culture, it will eventually take hold, but it takes time."

Having suffered from her own daughter's death twenty years before, Nelson never lost sight of her personal mission "to use every tool at hand as an opportunity to give back or make life better for people." Her transformation of Carlson to a collaborative culture is a remarkable example of how a leader can inspire employees around a common vision and empower them to lead.

Leaders like Mulcahy and Nelson have discovered that the results achieved by empowering people throughout their organizations with passion and purpose are far superior to what can be accomplished by getting them to be loyal followers. By giving others the latitude to lead within the organization's broad purpose, they are able to delegate more of their leadership responsibilities and still expand the scope and reach of their leadership through more people.

Bill George was chief executive of Medtronic, the world's leading medical technology company, from 1991 until 2001 and chairman of the board from 1996 to 2002. He has been named one of the Top 25 Business Leaders of the Past 25 Years by PBS.

CHAPTER EIGHTEEN

Enlist Others
Attracting People to Common Purposes

James M. Kouzes
Barry Z. Posner

"You have to paint a powerfully compelling picture of the future for people to want to align with the vision."

Vicky Ngo-Roberti, VMware, Inc.

"Whhat really drives performance," Keith Sonberg told us, "is not metrics. It's passion plus pride equals performance. I call it the three P's. The leader's job is to create an environment where people are passionate about what they're doing and take pride in what they're doing. The end result will always be performance." For Keith, director of site operations for Roche in Palo Alto, California, and his team, the three P's are all about sustainability, a vision of a company that delivers a triple bottom line. "We want to be environmentally sound, economically viable, and socially just," Keith explained.

Originally published as "Enlist Others: Attracting People to Common Purposes" in James M. Kouzes and Barry Z. Posner, *The Leadership Challenge* (2nd ed.). (San Francisco: Jossey-Bass, 2007).

This new vision of sustainability began in 2002 when Keith was delivering his annual "state-of the-union" speech to the seventy-five employees in site operations. That year he asked everyone—the mechanics, engineers, security people, folks from shipping and receiving, and the service groups—to reflect on a question Keith felt passionate about. "What's the legacy that you're leaving behind?" he asked. "When you're no longer here, no longer at Roche, or no longer on this earth, what is it that people will remember you for? What would you like them to remember you for?"

This is not exactly the kind of thing you expect to hear at an operations review, but that year Keith wanted to infuse renewed energy into the organization and more fully engage people. "With that in mind," he asked, "how are you going to approach your job and your life so that you are creating a legacy you can be proud of?"

For Keith, the answer was clear. "There's no greater legacy," he said, "than a positive environmental legacy. There was a great opportunity for people to really feel a passion for creating this legacy." So he met with his management team and they talked about a new vision for the organization, one that would engage everyone and inspire great pride and passion every day they came to work—and went home from work. "It was my vision of a legacy, and I wanted to make sure it was a compelling vision.... I absolutely felt that this was something that would benefit everyone, that would have an impact on people, and that at the end of the day would change people."

So Keith told his team, "Sustainability is about more than just daily operations that are environmentally friendly. This is something bigger. This is our responsibility, and that responsibility is something that we can't turn our backs on. We've got all these fantastic skills that we've developed over the years to make our business great. Now we have to take those same skills and focus them on sustainability in a way that really makes an impact. That's our responsibility." Then Keith popped the question. "Do you accept that responsibility?"

Indeed they did. "Once we talked about it," Keith told us, "it was a challenge that they could embrace and get behind as well." Then they took it a step further. "We wanted to be completely transformed," Keith said. "We wanted to do something that you go home and talk about." Beyond the vision and mission statements, Keith and his team developed a program with seven categories of projects—including energy conservation, natural resources conservation, recycling, green engineering and construction, and employee and community growth and development. They started to document everything, including developing manuals so they could share their successes with others. They wanted to become a model for what an organization could do to create sustainability.

When you listen to Keith you can't help but get caught up in his enthusiasm and excitement. He inspires you to accept your own responsibility for the future of the planet, and he enables you to see how that makes for good business. And for Keith, as for all the leaders who enlist others in a common vision, it all comes down to something fairly simple and straightforward. "Have a passion for making a difference in people's lives," he said, "and at the end of the day that's what it's all about."

In the personal-best cases that we collected, people frequently talked about the need to get everyone on board with a vision and to enlist others in a dream. People talked about how they had to communicate and build support for the direction in which the organization was headed. These leaders knew that in order to get extraordinary things done everyone had to fervently believe in and commit to a common purpose.

We've also learned from our research that constituents expect their leaders to be inspiring. A shared vision of the future is necessary, but insufficient, to achieve extraordinary results. We all need vast reserves of energy and excitement to sustain our commitment to a distant dream, and leaders are expected to be a major source of that energy. We're not going to follow someone who's only mildly enthusiastic about something. They have to be wildly enthusiastic for us to give it our all.

Whether they're trying to mobilize a crowd in the grandstand or one person in the office, to Enlist Others leaders must improve their capacities to act on these two essentials:

- Appeal to common ideals
- Animate the vision

Successfully engaging in these two essentials can produce very powerful results. In our research we found that when leaders effectively communicate a vision—whether it's to one person, a small group, or a large organization—constituents report significantly higher levels of job satisfaction, motivation, commitment, loyalty, team spirit, productivity, and profitability. Clearly there's a big payoff to bringing the vision to life.

APPEAL TO COMMON IDEALS

In every personal-best case leaders talked about ideals. They expressed a desire to make dramatic changes in the business-as-usual environment. They reached for something grand, something majestic, something magnificent, something that had never been done before.

Visions are about ideals—hopes, dreams, and aspirations.

They're about our strong desire to achieve something great. They're ambitious. They're expressions of optimism. Can you imagine a leader enlisting others in a cause by saying, "I'd like you to join me in doing the ordinary better"? Not likely. Visions necessarily stretch us to imagine exciting possibilities, breakthrough technologies, or revolutionary social change.

Ideals reveal our higher-order value preferences. They represent our ultimate economic, technological, political, social, and aesthetic priorities. The ideals of world peace, freedom, justice, a comfortable life, happiness, and self-respect are among the ultimate strivings of our existence—the ones that we seek to attain over the long term. They're statements of the idealized purpose that we hope all our practical actions will enable us to attain.

By focusing on the ideal, we gain a sense of meaning and purpose from what we undertake. When leaders communicate visions, they should be talking to people about how they are going to make a difference in the world, how they are going to have an impact.

Connect to What's Meaningful to Others

It's essential for leaders to understand what's meaningful to others. In communicating a shared vision, leaders have to bring these ideals into the conversation. Remember, exemplary leaders don't impose their visions of the future on people—as if one could in this day and age—they liberate the vision that's already in their constituents. They awaken dreams, breathe life into them, and arouse the belief that we can achieve something grand.

When leaders talk about visions of the future, it's not all about the numbers, about revenue earned, growth rates, or returns to shareholders. Those things are certainly extremely important concerns for leaders and constituents, but they don't get people enthused and energized over the long haul. What truly pulls people forward, especially in the more difficult times, is the exciting possibility that what they are doing can make a profound difference to the future of their families, friends, colleagues, customers, and communities. They want to know that what they do matters.

When Preethi Chandrasekhar was put in charge of a newly developed technical support center for a VoIP company, she understood that others would be looking to her for direction and for setting standards. However, she quickly realized that in order to make the vision exciting and relevant to her team, she needed to make it meaningful. So she started out by having informational sessions in which she and the team members talked about the "big picture" and why their work matters: What difference do we make for this company and for our customers? How will our working together make a difference?

She proceeded to ask the team to continue thinking about a vision and a set of objectives. She conducted a follow-up brainstorming session in which everyone shared their ideas and suggestions on what they needed to do to reduce call volume, improve customer wait times, and reduce the time reps spent on the telephone. Preethi recalled, "I could see the team was motivated, and individuals took it upon themselves to provide thoughtful insights on how we could improve the call center." But it was always important, she told us, "to keep focusing on the big picture, while still concentrating on the details that would enable us to realize these aspirations."

While Preethi searched for a unique way to communicate to her team the meaning and significance of their work, what she discovered was that she could do something each and every day to keep people focused and excited about their vision. "All of us have the power within ourselves to accomplish whatever we desire," she told us, and, more important, she found ways each and every day to repeat this statement to the members of the call center in the context of achieving their shared vision. She made sure that each team member could repeat the vision, not just by rote but from the heart, and she showed how their individual and collective efforts could make a positive difference.

"We put pride back in the workplace," Preethi observed. "We would be the envy of the company when it came to enjoying our work, basking in one another's accomplishments, and making our customers' lives not just easier but more productive. After all, what's better than being the geniuses who can answer other people's questions?"

In time, Preethi's message became a march. Everyone could connect with these ideas and aspirations. Each member of the team could easily see how they would answer a friend's question, "So, why do you work there?" Preethi lifted them up from the humdrum mechanics associated with the call center—or any workplace for that matter—and reminded them about the nobility of what they accomplish.

Leaders help people see that what they are doing is bigger than themselves and bigger, even, than the business. It's something noble. It's something that lifts their moral and motivational levels. When people go to bed at night they can sleep a little easier knowing that others are able to live a better life because of what they did that day.

Take Pride in Being Unique

Exemplary leaders also communicate what makes us—our work group or organization—and our product or service singular and unequaled. Compelling visions set us apart from everyone else. Visions must differentiate us from others if we're to attract and retain employees, volunteers, customers, clients, donors, or investors.[1] There's no advantage in working for, buying from, or investing in an organization that does exactly the same thing as the one across the street or down the hall. Saying, "Welcome to our company. We're just like everyone else," doesn't exactly make the spine tingle with excitement. When people understand how we're truly distinctive and how we stand out in the crowd they're a lot more eager to voluntarily sign up and invest their energies.

Uniqueness fosters pride. It boosts the self-respect and self-esteem of everyone associated with the organization. The prouder all of us are of the places we shop, the products or services we buy, the school we (or our children) attend, the community in which we live, or the place we work, the more loyal we're likely to be.

Answer this question: Why should your customers or clients want to buy your service or product, attend your school, enroll in your program, or listen to your sermon?

The late Edward Goeppner, former managing partner of the Podesta Baldocchi flower shop, one of the oldest businesses in San Francisco and one of the oldest, continuously operating floral-design businesses in the United States, offered a simple yet eloquent response to the question of "Why should people want to buy from you?" He said, "We don't sell flowers, we sell beauty."

Customers of a florist do exchange money for a dozen roses, but what they're really buying is something more than that; they want to beautify their homes, or express their love for others, or brighten the day. It doesn't take vision to sell a flower on a street corner, but it does take vision to sell beauty.

Uniqueness also makes it possible for smaller units within large organizations, or neighborhoods within large cities, to have their own visions while still encompassed by the collective vision. While every unit within a corporation, public agency, religious institution, school, or volunteer association must be aligned with the overall organizational vision, it can express its distinctive purpose within the larger whole. Every function and every department can differentiate itself by finding its most distinctive qualities. Each can be proud of its ideal and unique image of its future as it works toward the common future of the larger organization.

These days, though, with the latest and greatest available in a nanosecond at the touch of a key, it's become increasingly difficult to differentiate yourself from others. Log on to any Internet search engine, type in a key word, and up come thousands, sometimes tens of thousands, of sites and offerings. And it's not just the speed and volume of information that create problems. It's a sea of sameness out there. Towns around the world are looking the same. Whether you're in the United Kingdom or the United States, Germany or Greece, you're likely to find establishments like Levi's, Starbucks, Citibank, and Wal-Mart. Everything begins to look and sound alike, and eventually it gets awfully boring. Businesses, new and old, must work harder and harder to differentiate themselves (and their products) from others around them. Business consolidations, the Internet, the information overload, the 24/7/365 always-on, everyone's-connected world means leaders must be even more attentive to ways in which they can be the beacon that cuts through the dense fog and steers people in the right direction.

Align Your Dream with the People's Dream

In learning how to appeal to people's ideals, move their souls, and uplift their spirits—and your own—there is no better place to look than to a master of this art: the Reverend Dr. Martin Luther King Jr. He certainly did offer people a brilliant beacon of light that cut through the fog of his troubled times to offer guidance to a more promising future. His "I Have a Dream" speech tops the list of the best American public addresses of the twentieth century (University of Wisconsin, 1999).

On August 28, 1963, on the steps of the Lincoln Memorial in Washington, D.C., before a throng of 250,000, Martin Luther King Jr. proclaimed his dream to the world. As he spoke, and as thousands clapped and shouted, a nation was moved. Imagine that you're a communication researcher studying how leaders enlist others in a dream. Imagine that you're there in the audience on that August day, listening to King. Imagine that you're there to better understand how King is so capable of moving people. As you read this text, pay attention not just to the content but imagine how he expressed these words and phrases. Think about the rhythm, the cadence, and the pauses. Place yourself on the steps of the Lincoln Memorial and attempt to get a feel for how the audience reacted as they listened to these words:

> "I say to you today, my friends, so even though we face the difficulties of today and tomorrow, I still have a dream. It is a dream deeply rooted in the American dream.
>
> "I have a dream that one day this nation will rise up and live out the true meaning of its creed: 'We hold these truths to be self-evident: that all men are created equal.'
>
> "I have a dream that one day on the red hills of Georgia the sons of former slaves and the sons of former slave owners will be able to sit down together at the table of brotherhood.
>
> "I have a dream that one day even the state of Mississippi, a state sweltering with the heat of injustice, sweltering with the heat of oppression, will be transformed into an oasis of freedom and justice.
>
> "I have a dream that my four little children will one day live in a nation where they will not be judged by the color of their skin but by the content of their character.
>
> "I have a dream today.

"I have a dream that one day, down in Alabama, with its vicious racists, with its governor having his lips dripping with the words of interposition and nullification, one day right there in Alabama, little black boys and black girls will be able to join hands with little white boys and white girls as sisters and brothers.

"I have a dream today.

"I have a dream that one day every valley shall be exalted, every hill and mountain shall be made low, the rough places will be made plain, and the crooked places will be made straight, and the glory of the Lord shall be revealed, and all flesh shall see it together.

"This is our hope. This is the faith that I go back to the South with. With this faith we will be able to transform the jangling discords of our nation into a beautiful symphony of brotherhood. With this faith we will be able to work together, to pray together, to struggle together, to go to jail together, to stand up for freedom together, knowing that we will be free one day.

"This will be the day, this will be the day when all of God's children will be able to sing with a new meaning, 'My country 'tis of thee, sweet land of liberty, of thee I sing. Land where my fathers died, land of the pilgrim's pride, from every mountainside, let freedom ring.'

"And if America is to be a great nation this must become true. So let freedom ring from the prodigious hilltops of New Hampshire. Let freedom ring from the mighty mountains of New York. Let freedom ring from the heightening Alleghenies of Pennsylvania!

"Let freedom ring from the snowcapped Rockies of Colorado!

"Let freedom ring from the curvaceous slopes of California!

"But not only that; let freedom ring from Stone Mountain of Georgia!

"Let freedom ring from Lookout Mountain of Tennessee!

"Let freedom ring from every hill and molehill of Mississippi. From every mountainside, let freedom ring.

"And when this happens, and when we allow freedom to ring, when we let it ring from every village and every hamlet, from every state and every city, we will be able to speed up that day when all of God's children, black men and white men, Jews and Gentiles, Protestants and Catholics, will be able to join hands and sing in the words of the old Negro spiritual, 'Free at last! Free at last! Thank God Almighty, we are free at last!'" (King, 1983)

What do you observe? What do you hear? What do you notice about this speech? How was he able to move so many, what makes it so powerful, and why has this speech survived the test of time? Here are some of the observations that participants in our workshops and classes have made in reflecting on King's speech:

"He appealed to common bonds."

"He talked about traditional values of family, church, country."

"It was vivid. He used a lot of images and word pictures. You could see the examples."

"People could relate to the examples. They were familiar."

"His references were credible. It's hard to argue against the Constitution and the Bible."

"He mentioned children—something we can all relate to."

"He knew his audience."

"He made geographical references to places the people in the audience could relate to."

"He included everybody: different parts of the country, all ages, both sexes, major religions."

"He used a lot of repetition: for example, 'I have a dream,' 'Let freedom ring.'"

"He said the same thing in different ways."

"He began with a statement of the difficulties and then stated his dream."

"He was positive and hopeful."

"Although positive, he also said people might have to suffer in order to get there. He didn't promise it would be easy."

"There was a cadence and a rhythm to his voice."

"He shifted from 'I' to 'we' halfway through."

"He spoke with emotion and passion. It was deeply felt."

Dr. King's "I Have a Dream" speech illustrates how the ability to exert an enlivening influence is rooted in fundamental values, cultural traditions, personal conviction, and a capacity to use words to create positive images of the future. To enlist others, leaders need to bring the vision to life. Leaders have to animate the vision and make manifest the purpose so that others can see it, hear it, taste it, touch it, feel it.

In making the intangible vision tangible, leaders ignite constituents' flames of passion.

And there is something else you can learn when you actually listen to King's speech. What you'll hear is an audience that was participating. The people in the crowd that day were clapping and shouting back, "Yes," and "Oh, yes," and "Um-hmm," and "Hear, hear." They were fully engaged. It wasn't a one-way street. King was in a conversation with them about their lives and about their dreams. They could see the dream he was envisioning, and they were affirming it. They were telling him with their shouts and nods and claps and responses, "You have heard me, and you are talking to me about what I long for. You are saying what I am feeling." Their shouts and claps prove that Dr. King's dream was not his dream alone. It was the people's vision. It was a shared vision.

ANIMATE THE VISION

Leaders have to arouse others to join in a cause and to want to move decisively and boldly forward. Part of arousing others is appealing to their ideals. Another part, as we see in Dr. King's "I Have a Dream" speech, is animating the vision, breathing life into it. To enlist others you have to help them *see* and *feel* how their own interests and aspirations are aligned with the vision.

You have to paint a compelling picture of the future, one that enables constituents to experience viscerally what it would be like to actually live and work in an exciting and uplifting future. That's the only way they'll become internally motivated to commit their individual energies to its realization.

"But I'm not like Dr. King," you say. "I can't possibly do what he did. Besides, he was a preacher, and I'm a businessperson. His constituents were on a protest march, and mine are here to get a job done." Most people initially respond this way. Most people don't see themselves as personally uplifting, and certainly don't get much encouragement for behaving this way in most organizations. Despite the potency of clearly communicated and compelling visions, the people we studied feel more uncomfortable with inspiring a shared vision than with any of the other leadership practices. And, more specifically, their discomfort comes less from envisioning the exciting possibilities of the future and more from having to express their emotions. That's not easy for working adults to do; it becomes a lot tougher as people get older to express naked enthusiasm for the work that they're doing and the ends they're striving to achieve. But we all underestimate ourselves. We sell ourselves short. We're too quick to discount our capacity to communicate with passion and enthusiasm.

People's perception of themselves as uninspiring is in sharp contrast to their performance when they talk about their personal-best leadership experiences or when they talk about their ideal futures. When relating hopes, dreams, and successes, people are almost always emotionally expressive. Expressiveness comes naturally when talking about deep desires for the something that could be better in the future than it is today. People lean forward in their chairs, they move their arms about, their eyes light up, their voices sing with emotion, and smiles appear on their faces. They're enthusiastic, articulate, optimistic, and uplifting. In short, they are inspiring!

This contradiction is most intriguing. Why is it that people seem to see no connection between the animated, enthusiastic behavior they use in describing their personal bests and their ability to be inspiring? This is because most people have attributed something mystical to the process of being inspirational. They seem to see it as supernatural, as a grace or charm that comes from the gods. This assumption inhibits people far more than any lack of natural talent for being inspirational. It's not necessary to be a famous, charismatic person to inspire a shared vision. It is necessary to believe, however—and to develop the skills to transmit that belief. A deeply felt belief, along with commitment and enthusiasm for it—genuinely displayed—brings the vision to life for all of us.

If you're going to lead, you have to recognize that your enthusiasm and expressiveness are among your strongest allies in your efforts to generate commitment in your constituents. By using symbolic language, creating word images of the future, practicing a positive communication style, tapping into verbal and nonverbal expressiveness, and speaking from the heart, you breathe life (the literal definition of the word *inspire*) into a vision.

Use Symbolic Language

Leaders make full use of the power of symbolic language to communicate a shared identity and give life to visions. They use metaphors and other figures of speech; they give examples, tell stories, and relate anecdotes; they draw word pictures; and they offer quotations and recite slogans. They enable constituents to picture the future, to hear it, to sense it, to recognize it.

Ricardo Semler (2004) is the chief executive of the Brazil-based company Semco, but he uses the CEO title in a very unusual way. "I'm a catalyst," he writes. "By definition a catalyst, usually an enzyme, initiates a reaction. The way I handle the role is by broaching weird ideas and asking dumb questions. Strictly speaking, I'm a highly evolved CEO, as in 'Chief Enzyme Officer.'" Now Semler is not literally an "enzyme," but figuratively he is. This simple metaphor says more about how Semler sees his job than any lengthy job description could. And Semler is full of them. In a clear and clever contrast to the notion of work being 24/7 or a seven-day work week, he says, "I've got a much better idea, though, one that I've been testing now for many years: the seven-day weekend." In reference to how Semco develops people, he says, "Planting seeds is more effective than pulling weeds." And in discussing his approach to business planning, he comments, "Money doesn't grow on decision trees" (p. 217).

"Leaders can use metaphors explicitly and deliberately to influence others, give shape to the world, and even manipulate listeners," write Thomas Oberlechner and Viktor Mayer-Schönberger (2003) of the John F. Kennedy School of Government at Harvard University. There are war metaphors, game and sports metaphors, art metaphors, machine metaphors, and religious or spiritual metaphors. "Paying attention to metaphors and to their implications helps us recognize such influences more quickly and react to them in more informed and reflective ways" (p. 170). When Amy Cole, then director of sales training and services at Intraware, was just assembling her team, she spoke about "painting a picture" and about "getting everyone on the bus." "I used the metaphor that we are a team traveling in a bus," she explained, "and it is important that we all travel in the same direction." All leaders need to be more conscious about the powerful effect that these tools of language can have in shaping the way people envision their work—and in shaping the ethics of a firm.

Andrew Coven, when taking over leadership of a technology design team for Adobe Systems, used another variation of symbolic language. He reframed the existing work of his team in terms of "telling a story"—this was a novel, engaging, and unique way of training third-party developers, who were used to just straight reference documentation.

We created a fictional company that became our example third-party developer company in our documentation. The company was called "Code-Hawgs" (a play on words, to hog all the code). Code-Hawgs was a systems integrator that was creating plug-ins to integrate our product with their own database and workflow management system. We even created a mascot (the Code-Hawg), which then appeared everywhere—like shirts, flyers, walls, etc.—to remind folks what we were about.

"Code-Hawg" was just one way that Andrew painted a word picture that portrayed the meaning behind their vision. Andrew went so far as to invent new words and phrases (such as "training-centric"), and then he would listen carefully to see who had read various documents by noting who was using these new catchphrases.

Leaders such as Andrew appreciate the way using symbolic language not only sparks people's imaginations but makes them feel part of a very special team. They learn to master the richness of figurative speech so that they can paint the word pictures that best portray the meaning of their visions.

Make Images of the Future

Visions are images in the mind, impressions and representations. They become real as leaders express those images in concrete terms to their constituents.

Just as architects make drawings and engineers build models, leaders find ways of giving expression to our collective hopes for the future. When talking about the future we all talk in terms of foresight, focus, forecasts, future scenarios, points of view, and perspectives. The thing that each of these words has in common is that they are visual references. The word *vision* itself has at its root the verb "to see." Statements of vision, then, should not be statements at all. They should be pictures—word pictures. They're more image than words. For a vision to be shared it needs to be *seen* in the mind's eye.

In our workshops and classes we often illustrate the power of images with this simple exercise. We ask people to shout out the first thing that comes to mind when they hear the words, *Paris, France*. The replies that pop out—the Eiffel Tower, the Louvre, the Arc de Triomphe, the Seine, Notre Dame, good food, wine, romance—are all images of real places and real sensations. No one calls out the square kilometers, population, or gross domestic product of Paris.

Why? Human memory is stored in images and sensory impressions, not in numbers.

So what does this mean for leaders? It means that to enlist others and inspire a shared vision, you must be able to draw upon that very natural mental process of creating images. When you speak about the future, you need to paint word pictures so that others get a mental image of what things will be like when you are at the end of your journey. Images are windows on the world of tomorrow. When talking about going places you've never been—whether to the top of an unclimbed mountain or to the pinnacle of an entirely new industry—you have to be able to imagine what they'll look like.

You have to picture the possibilities. Those who are more auditory by nature talk about it as a "calling." While Martin Luther King's underlying vision (and message) was about freedom, he called upon us to see by imagining a situation in which "little black boys and black girls will be able to join hands with little white boys and white girls as sisters and brothers."

The ability to enable others to see into the future is not some supernatural power. Every one of us possesses it. We do it every time we return from a vacation and show the photos to our friends. If you doubt your own ability, try this exercise. Sit down with a few close friends and tell them about one of your favorite vacations. Describe the people you saw and met, the sights and sounds of the places you went, the smells and tastes of the food you ate.

Show them the photos or videos if you have them. Observe their reactions—and your own. What's that experience like? We've done this activity many times, and people always report feeling energized and passionate. Those hearing about a place for the first time usually say something like, "After listening to you, I'd like to go there someday myself."

Although some people may have a more creative imagination than others, all of us have the capacity to get other people to see places they've never been to before. The first challenge is to vividly imagine the destination in your mind's eye, and the second part is to describe it so colorfully that others will see it and want to visit it themselves.

Practice Positive Communication

To foster team spirit, breed optimism, promote resilience, and renew faith and confidence, leaders must learn to look at the bright side.

They must keep hope alive. They must strengthen their constituents' belief that life's struggle will produce a more promising future. Such faith results from an intimate and supportive relationship, a relationship based on mutual participation in the process of renewal.

Constituents look for leaders who demonstrate an enthusiastic and genuine belief in the capacity of others, who strengthen people's will, who supply the means to achieve, and who express optimism for the future. Constituents want leaders who remain passionate despite obstacles and setbacks. In today's uncertain times, leaders with a positive, confident, can-do approach to life and business are desperately needed.

We all want leaders with enthusiasm, with a bounce in their step, with a positive attitude. We want to believe that we'll be part of an invigorating journey. We follow people with a can-do attitude, not those who give sixty-seven reasons why something can't be done. Researchers working with neural networks have found that, when people feel rebuffed or left out, the brain activates a site for registering physical pain (Goleman, 2006). People actually remember downbeat comments far more often, in greater detail, and with more intensity, than they do encouraging words. When negative remarks become a preoccupation, an employee's brain loses mental efficiency. In light of the impact their words have on other people's brains it is even more critical for leaders to be positive.

Consider the positive attitude and communication style that Joan Carter exhibited when she took over as general manager and executive chef of the Faculty Club at Santa Clara University. Before Joan's arrival, both membership and sales had been seriously declining for several years, the restaurant's remaining customers were unhappy, its balance sheet was "scary," and the staff was divided into factions.

Joan took all this in, and what she saw was a dusty diamond. "I saw a beautiful and historic building full of mission-era flavor and character that should be, could be, would be *the* place on campus." In her mind's eye, she saw the club bustling. She saw professors and university staff chatting on the lovely enclosed patio and enjoying high-quality, appealing yet inexpensive meals. She envisioned the club assisting alumni in planning wonderful, personal, and professionally catered wedding receptions and anniversary celebrations.

Joan could see a happy staff whose primary concern was customer satisfaction, a kitchen that produced a product far superior to "banquet food," and a catering staff that did whatever it took to make an event exceptional. She wasn't quite sure how the club had deteriorated to the extent it had, but that really didn't matter. She decided to ignore the quick fix and set out to teach everyone how unique and wonderful the club could be.

Over the next two years, as she talked with customers and worked with her staff, she instilled a vision of the club as a restaurant that celebrated good food and good company. As food and service quality began to improve, smiles became more prevalent among customers and staff and sales began to rise: 20 percent the first year and 30 percent the next. When a top financial manager of the university asked how she had managed to turn the finances around so quickly and dramatically, Joan responded, "You can't turn around numbers. The balance sheet is just a reflection of what's happening here, every day, in the restaurant. I just helped the staff realize what we're really all about. It was always here," she said, "only perhaps a little dusty, a little ignored, and a little unloved. I just helped them see it."

Express Your Emotions

In explaining why particular leaders have a magnetic effect, people often describe them as charismatic. But *charisma* has become such an overused and misused term that it's almost useless as a descriptor of leaders. "In the popular media," notes leadership scholar Bernard Bass (2005), "charisma has come to mean anything ranging from chutzpah to Pied Piperism, from celebrity to superman status. It has become an overworked cliché for a strong, attractive, and inspiring personality."

Social scientists have attempted to investigate this elusive quality in terms of observable behavior. What they've found is that people who are perceived to be charismatic are simply more animated than others. They smile more, speak faster, pronounce words more clearly, and move their heads and bodies more often. What we call charisma, then, can better be understood as energy and expressiveness. The old saying that "Enthusiasm is infectious" is certainly true for leaders.

"You, as leader, are responsible for the energy level—the level of authentic excitement—in your organization," write leadership developers Belle Linda Halpren and Kathy Lubar (2003). "Emotion drives expressiveness," they tell us, and leaders must communicate their emotions using all means of expression—verbal and nonverbal—if they are to generate the intense enthusiasm that's required to mobilize people to struggle for shared aspirations.

There's another thing that emotion drives. It makes things more memorable. And since leaders want their messages to be remembered, they need to add more emotion to their words and their behavior. James L. McGaugh (2003), professor of neurobiology at the University of California, Irvine, and a leading expert on creation of memory, has reported that "emotionally significant events create stronger, longer-lasting memories." No doubt you've experienced this yourself when something emotionally significant has happened to you—a serious trauma, such as an accident, or a joyful surprise, such as winning a contest. But the events don't have to be real to be memorable. They can simply be stories. For example, in one experiment researchers showed subjects in two groups a series of twelve slides. The slide presentation was accompanied by a story, one line for each slide. For one group in the study the narrative was quite boring, for the other the narrative was emotionally moving.

Two weeks later the two groups returned and took a test of how well they remembered the details of each slide. (They didn't know when they watched the slides that they would be tested.) While neither group differed in its memory of the first few or last few slides, they did differ significantly in the recollection of the slides in the middle. "The subjects who had listened to the emotionally arousing narrative remembered details in those particular slides better" than the group that listened to the neutral story. "Stronger emotional arousal," says McGaugh (2003), "is associated with better memory; emotional arousal appears to create strong memories."

It doesn't even have to be a complete narrative to make strong memories. It can be just the words themselves. In another laboratory experiment, researchers asked subjects to learn to associate pairs of words. "Some of the words in the pairs ... were used because they elicited strong emotional responses, as indicated by changes in the subjects' galvanic skin response.... On a retention test a week later the subjects remembered the emotionally arousing words better than they remembered less arousing words" (McGaugh, 2003). Whether it's a story or a word, we're more likely to remember the key messages when they're attached to something that triggers an emotional response. The reasons for this have to do with our physiology. We're just wired to pay more attention to stuff that excites us or scares us. Keep all this in mind the next time you deliver a PowerPoint presentation. It's not just the content that will make it stick; it's also how well you tap into people's emotions.

The dramatic increase in the use of electronic technology also has an impact on the way people deliver messages. From podcasts to webcasts, MySpace to YouTube, more and more people are turning to their digital devices for information. This trend only lends support to what researchers are discovering about memory. Entertainment is playing a bigger and bigger role in our lives. Leadership is a performing art, and this has become even truer as new technologies hit the market. It's no longer enough to write a good script—you've also got to put on a good show. And you've got to make it a show that people will remember.

Speak from the Heart

None of these suggestions will be of any value whatsoever if you don't believe in what you're saying. If the vision is someone else's, and you don't own it, it will be very difficult for you to enlist others in it. If you have trouble imagining yourself actually living the future described in the vision, you'll certainly not be able to convince others that they ought to enlist in making it a reality. If you're not excited about the possibilities, how can you expect others to be? *The prerequisite to enlisting others in a shared vision is genuineness.* The first place to look before talking to others about the vision of the future is in your heart.

When asked how she was able to lead the development team for the PCNet family of Advanced Micro Devices, breaking all barriers and launching this extremely successful family of products, Laila Razouk replied simply, "I believed. Believing is a very important part of the action. You have to have faith. If you don't have that, then you're lost even before you get started." It's easy to understand why people were eager to follow Laila: "If I believe in something badly enough, and if I have the conviction, then I start picturing and envisioning how it will look if we did this or if we did that. By sharing these thoughts with other people, the excitement grows and people become part of that picture. Without much effort—with energy, but not much effort—the magic starts to happen. People start to bounce ideas back and forth, they get involved, brainstorm, and share ideas. Then I know I don't have to worry about it."

How successful would the project have been if instead Laila had thought, "This project will never work. The person who thought this up doesn't understand the details. I'm doing this because I'm forced to, but I really think this project is a stupid idea!" For Laila, the net effect of speaking from the heart, as she explained, is that "by openly sharing what I saw, what I knew, and what I believed—not by dictating it, but by being willing to iterate and adjust things— I got other people involved."

There's no one more believable than a person with a deep passion for something. There's no one more fun to be around than someone who is openly excited about the magic that can happen. There's no one more determined than someone who believes fervently in an ideal. People want leaders who are upbeat, optimistic, and positive about the future. It's really the only way we can get people to want to struggle for shared aspirations.

REFLECTION AND ACTION: ENLISTING OTHERS

Leaders appeal to common ideals. They connect others to what is most meaningful in the shared vision. They lift people to higher levels of motivation and morality, and continuously reinforce that they can make a difference in the world. Exemplary leaders speak to what is unique and singular about the organization, making others feel proud to be a part of something extraordinary. And the best leaders understand that it's not their personal idiosyncratic view of the future that's important, it's the aspirations of all their constituents that matter most.

To be sustained over time, visions must be compelling and memorable. Leaders must breathe life into visions, they must animate them so that others can experience what it would be like to live and work in that ideal and unique future. They use a variety of modes of expression to make their abstract visions concrete. Through skillful use of metaphors, symbols, word pictures, positive language, and personal energy, leaders generate enthusiasm and excitement for the common vision. But above all, leaders must be convinced of the value of the shared vision and share that genuine belief with others. They must believe in what they are saying. Authenticity is the true test of conviction, and constituents will only follow willingly if they sense that the vision is genuine.

Here are three action steps you can take to increase your ability to Enlist Others.

Record Your Shared Vision

You need to practice expressing your hopes, dreams, and aspirations fully. In Chapter Five [of *The Leadership Challenge*] we asked you to do a few things to envision the future. Now we'd like you to take all the information you've just gathered and write your *ideal and unique image of the future for yourself and for your organization*. We recommend that this statement be brief but not a one-liner. The one-liners come later. Martin Luther King Jr.'s "I Have a Dream" speech was five minutes and a few seconds in length, so we suggest you aim for something in the three- to five-minute range. Any longer, and people are likely to lose interest. Much shorter, and you won't be providing enough vivid detail for people to know where you really want to be ten or so years from now—what it truly feels like to really be there. Using your notes from your responses to the questions about the "something" you want to do, expand your vision by answering these questions:

- What is your *ideal* work community? What do you personally aspire to create?

- What is *unique* about your hopes, dreams, and aspirations? How are they distinctive compared to all the other visions of the future?

- When you project this vision into the *future* ten to fifteen years, what does it look like? What innovations and trends will influence that future? What vision will carry us forward into the future?

- What *images* come to mind when thinking of the future? What does it look like, sound like, taste like, and feel like?

- How does this vision serve the *common good*? What are the shared aspirations among all the constituents? How does the vision fulfill others' ideal and unique images of their futures?

Don't censor yourself. This is about aspirations; it needs to be uplifting. Give voice to your dreams. Once you've written your vision, try drawing it, finding a picture that resembles it, or creating a symbol that represents it. Finally, create a short slogan of five to nine words that captures the essence of your vision. Something similar to Edward Goeppner's "We don't sell flowers, we sell beauty" is what we have in mind. A brief slogan is no substitute for a complete statement, but it does help others remember the essential message, and it can evoke images of a shared destiny.

After you've crafted your vision statement, revisit it periodically. Refine it and update it. The world changes, so be sure to adapt your statement and slogan to the changing times. Also keep in mind that, while we're talking about your vision statement, we are definitely not suggesting that you impose your will on your constituents. Successful visions are shared. Much as we strongly encourage you to write and rehearse a consistent message to deliver to others, communicating a vision should be a conversation—not just a speech.

What you articulate should provide others with the opportunity for dialogue.

Breathe Life into Your Vision

Remember earlier in this chapter when we related the images people had when they heard the words *Paris, France*? People recalled sights, feelings, tastes, and smells. When Martin Luther King Jr. spoke he used historical events, Biblical texts, patriotic songs, important documents, significant places, and patriotic symbols to give his speech a unique narrative quality. You have to be able to do the same thing. You have to make the future come alive in people's minds. You have to stir their hearts. Recall that study about the slides? It was the strong emotions that made each slide more memorable. You have to evoke strong emotions if you want people to remember where it is you want them to go.

Values such as quality, service, respect, freedom, creativity, and responsiveness don't exist in nature. They must be defined in concrete terms. Your job is to make these intangible values tangible by using the richness of language to transport people to a place they've never been. Use as many forms of expression as you can to transform the vision's intangibles into tangibles.

- If your vision speech were to have a sound track, what songs would be in it?
- What poem best expresses the shared vision of the future?
- What short stories express what you are trying to communicate?
- What memorable quotations enrich the delivery?

- What symbols best represent the shared vision?
- What metaphors and similes express the vision and achieve the effect you are seeking?
- What geographical locations come to mind when you think about the vision?

When it comes to making visions memorable you have to be evocative, even provocative. It's the figures of speech, not the figures on the balance sheet, that create that memory.

Expand Your Communication and Expressiveness Skills

In our research we found that expressing a vision is *the* most difficult of all the leadership skills. People find it easier to imagine an ideal and unique future than they do painting a compelling picture for others. When it comes to inspiring a shared vision, we all could use some help in articulating it.

A course in presentation skills will benefit you greatly. If you haven't taken one yet, sign up for the next available class. Join Toastmasters. More than likely there's a chapter in your town. Having to give a short speech once a week is great practice. Presentation skills workshops and meetings not only help you learn effective techniques for getting your ideas across, they also help you gain confidence in yourself. Whenever possible, volunteer to stand up in front of a group and speak, even if it's just to introduce someone or make an announcement. The more practice in public speaking you have, the more comfortable you will become.

Put on a DVD collection—or connect to a website—of famous speeches. Listen and watch. Notice what the speaker does to move the audience. Do the same thing when you are in the audience and someone is speaking. If the speaker doesn't connect, notice what he or she does that fails to arouse emotion and interest. And it's not too much of a stretch to suggest that you take an acting class. After all, the "Great Communicator," the late President Ronald Reagan, managed to use to great effect the skills he learned in the movies.

And be sure to put more energy and enthusiasm into your vision presentations. Let your emotions show. Smile. Use gestures and move your body. Speak clearly and quickly. Make eye contact. All of these signals are cues to others that you're personally excited about what you're saying. If you don't perceive yourself as an expressive person, begin to practice expressiveness by talking to a favorite friend about what most excites you in life. As you do this, pay attention to your verbal and nonverbal behavior. If possible, turn on a video camera so that you can watch yourself later. We bet that you'll discover that when you talk about things that excite you, you do a lot of the things we've just described.

And finally, practice, practice, practice. None of history's greatest speeches were delivered extemporaneously. They had been rehearsed and tested in other events and in other conversations. Be prepared to take your first draft (or latest draft, whatever its number) and continue to revise, hone, edit, and revise again until you think it expresses your ideas just right. Try it out in front of others, obtain feedback, and determine the words, phrases, and thoughts that most resonate (and which ones don't). You just never know when someone might ask you, "Tell me about your dreams for this organization." When that opportunity knocks you want to be ready to answer the door.

Note

1. Market researcher and author Doug Hall (2001) has found that "dramatically different" levels in a new product or service increase the idea's probability of success in the marketplace from 15 percent to 53 percent. That's a 253 percent greater chance of success. The same is true for a vision; the more unique it is the higher the probability of success in getting people to buy in.

References

Bass, B. M. *Leadership and Performance Beyond Expectations.* New York: The Free Press, 1985.

Goleman, D. *Social Intelligence: The New Science of Human Relationships.* New York: Bantam, 2006.

Hall, D. *Jump Start Your Business Brain: Win More, Lose Less, and Make More Money with Your New Products, Services, Sales and Advertising.* Cincinnati, OH: Brain Brew Books, 2001.

Halpren, B. L., and Lubar, K. *Leadership Presence: Dramatic Techniques to Reach Out, Motivate, and Inspire.* New York: Gotham Books, 2003.

King, M. L. Jr. "I Have a Dream." In C. S. King (Ed.), *The Words of Martin Luther King, Jr.* New York: Newmarket Press, 1983.

McGaugh, J. L. *Memory and Emotion.* New York: Columbia University Press, 2003.

Oberlechner, T., and Mayer-Schönberger, V. "Through Their Own Words: Towards a New Understanding of Leadership Through Metaphors." *Working Papers.* Boston: Center for Public Leadership, John F. Kennedy School of Government, Harvard University, 2003. [www. ksg.harvard.edu/leadership/pubs/papers/index.php?year=2003] September 24, 2006.

Semler, R. *The Seven-Day Weekend: Changing the Way Work Works.* New York: Penguin, 2004.

"'I Have a Dream' Leads Top 100 Speeches of the Century." Press release from the University of Wisconsin, December 15, 1999. [www.news .wisc.edu/releases/3504.html], June 13, 2006.

James M. Kouzes and Barry Z. Posner are preeminent researchers, award-winning writers, and highly sought after teachers in the field of leadership. Their groundbreaking studies, pioneered in 1983, led them to create a model of leadership that has been embraced by more than one million people around the world.

CHAPTER NINETEEN

Diversity Management
An Essential Craft for Leaders

R. Roosevelt Thomas, Jr.

—◁◁◁▷▷▷—

For twenty years I have worked as a diversity consultant, researcher, and author. Now as never before I see the need to broaden and redefine our ideas and behaviors around diversity. Indeed, what happens in the next decade will be crucial in determining whether America's leaders move forward in their efforts to create cohesive, effective organizations—or simply muddle through. In turn, what happens in the area of diversity management will have enormous impact on the success of future leaders.

WHY CHANGE NOW?

A number of factors conspire to encourage a reconsideration of diversity—and its management. One such factor is that both organizational leaders and diversity professionals are increasingly aware that the field is stuck in the mid-1960s, focusing on "representation"

Originally published as "Diversity Management: An Essential Craft for Leaders," *Leader to Leader, 41.* (Summer 2006).

and "relationships." Leaders ask, "Isn't there more to diversity than 'counting' and 'getting along'?"

The evidence clearly shows that there must be. Although some people have little faith in organizational diversity efforts—growing increasingly cynical in their outlook—I do not believe that America's leaders will remain content with paradigms and programs that foster cynicism and discontent. They have always risen to important challenges, and I am convinced they will do so now.

TEN EXPECTATIONS FOR THE FUTURE

I have identified ten expectations for the future of diversity management. I cannot predict precisely the rate of evolution, but I am confident that these trends will become a reality for tomorrow's leaders.

One. Future leaders will differentiate between representation and diversity. *Representation* will refer to the presence of multiple races and both genders in the workplace, while *diversity* will refer to the behavioral differences, similarities, and tensions that can exist among people when representation has been achieved. This will be quite different from current practice, where discussions about diversity are really about representation.

Today's emphasis on representation is evident in most diversity best practices lists, where the selection criteria center on representation (the numbers) and relationships (awareness and sensitivity). Leaders will be forced to make this differentiation because those who fail to address these behavioral differences and similarities will lose their representation gains. Leaders who recognize that they must manage representation *and* diversity will gain a competitive edge in fully accessing the potential of their associates.

Two. Future leaders will not think in terms of diversity, nor will they view it only as an extension of the civil rights movement. Leaders will concern themselves with diversity management and view it as a craft—one that can complement traditional civil rights initiatives that focus efforts solely on issues of race and gender. They will see this craft of diversity management as one that is applicable to *any* diverse mixture of people in the workplace.

While some might see this as a radical shift in thinking, it is not. In fact, this change will be more congruent with the historic reality that diversity per se can be traced back to applications beyond that of civil rights. My introduction to the topic, for example, was as a doctoral student studying functional diversity in corporate settings. The key question was, "How can you have functions appropriately differentiated to match their different task environments, yet also effectively integrated as a cohesive, purpose driven whole?"

The focus is on achieving cohesiveness in the midst of differences, similarities, and tensions.

Three. Future leaders will define diversity management as "making quality decisions in the midst of differences, similarities, and tensions." This definition will allow them to deal with *all* kinds of discussions involving differences, similarities, and tensions and to see themselves as engaged in diversity management.

Leaders cannot help becoming aware of the craft's ability to assist in unraveling and creatively conceptualizing complex situations. As a result, they will count on the craft when approaching any situation where diverse perceptions, purposes, people, or other differences create substantial complexity. This will be true not only when the issue is race and gender complexity, but also when the complexity is created by diversity mixtures such as customers, mergers and acquisitions, and differing geographic business locations.

Four. Future leaders will not automatically assume that all racially inappropriate behavior is caused by racism. They will recognize that people can have difficulty making quality decisions in the midst of differences, similarities, and tensions for reasons other than bias.

Five. In contrast to today, future leaders will be more willing to admit having difficulty making decisions in the midst of diversity. They will also be more comfortable discussing specific ways in which they are challenged by particular types of diversity. In part, this will be because they can distinguish between diversity in the broader sense and the race and gender focus of the civil rights movement. As a result, difficulty with diversity is less likely to be seen as a moral offense and more likely to be seen as managerial uncertainty or ineffectiveness—particularly in those instances where the "isms" are not the undergirding factors.

Six. As these trends emerge, future leaders will grow in their understanding of diversity management as a craft. They will understand the core craft capability to be "making quality decisions in the midst of differences, similarities, and related tensions." As a result, they will be motivated to master this craft. Leaders will understand that the craft of diversity management has the following components:

- *Concepts:* The definitions that provide the craft's foundation;
- *Fundamental dynamics:* The principles that along with the concepts constitute the craft's basics; and
- *Prerequisites for mastery:* Acquisition of diversity management skills, achievement of diversity maturity, and practice in applying the craft.

Diversity management concepts and fundamental dynamics, while unfamiliar to many, are not that difficult to learn. More difficult are the tasks of achieving diversity maturity and acquiring and practicing the requisite skills.

Neither diversity skills nor diversity maturity can be achieved without practice. In accepting the need for such practice, future leaders will of necessity depart from current thinking. They will understand that a single training session ranging from two to eight hours in length cannot provide the necessary capability.

A look at the necessary diversity management skills will demonstrate why this is true. These skills include:

- The ability to recognize and analyze diversity mixtures;
- The ability to determine if action is required with respect to a particular mixture; and
- The ability to respond appropriately to the issue in question.

The vast majority of individuals must work long and hard to develop the skills and maturity needed to practice the craft effectively.

Seven. Leaders armed with the diversity management craft will become more comfortable with tension and complexity. We all have witnessed the ineffectiveness of individuals who are uncomfortable with diversity tensions, and most of us have yet to say, "I just cannot get enough complexity." Instead, we struggle to "keep it simple" and indeed to avoid complexity. This may appear to reduce tensions, but it does so at the risk of distortion and ineffectiveness.

Diversity management can address this problem. The craft provides a methodology for making quality decisions in spite of the presence of tension and complexity. While diversity management will not necessarily increase the comfort level with tension and complexity, it will help leaders become more comfortable with being uncomfortable. For them, manifestations of tension and complexity will not mean that progress toward mission and vision is impossible.

Eight. Given the universality of diversity management, leaders across the globe will make it a global craft, as opposed to one confined to the United States. Leaders will use the craft both within and across borders as globalization becomes ever more the norm.

At present, leaders outside the United States often see diversity management as a phenomenon related to this country's unique struggle with race and slavery. As a result, they believe it is irrelevant to their own national circumstances. As recent clashes between police and ethnic minorities in European countries have shown, however, diversity management is more relevant to these foreign leaders than ever before. Decoupling diversity from the civil rights movement's agenda will help to generate clarity about the true nature of diversity and diversity management.

Nine. Future leaders will be more strategic in their approach to diversity and diversity management. Decisions as to where to focus attention and how to respond to issues will be guided by an organization's mission, vision, and strategy. Accordingly, what will be appropriate in one setting may not be appropriate in another if differences exist with respect to mission, vision, and strategy. Strategic context will be defining.

Ten. As future leaders master the application of the craft in their workplaces, inevitably and eventually they will turn their attention to diversity issues within their countries and communities. In the United States, for example, this will mean addressing the various divides we experience along at least the following lines: race, class, ethnicity, gender, politics, geography, and religion.

An understanding of the diversity management craft will provide an approach that leaders and the rank-and file citizenry can use to work through diversity challenges. Use of the craft won't eliminate the divides, but it will provide the capability for addressing them whenever and wherever they threaten the ability to achieve local or national goals. This capability will enhance the likelihood of achieving a naturally cohesive, purpose-driven unity in spite of our divisions. For the United States and indeed for all countries, such a contribution would be enormous.

EVIDENCE OF CHANGE

What makes me think that our approach to diversity and its management will change? The fact that it is changing now. The future is surfacing as I write. Diversity professionals who historically have relied primarily on benchmarking to determine what to do next are backing away from this practice. Instead, they are less likely to assume that the answers already exist and are simply waiting to be discovered. Instead, they are more inclined to rethink the basic assumptions that have guided their efforts in hopes that doing so will lead to different and more effective alternatives. Stated differently, they are more willing to pioneer and less inclined to play follow the leader.

Still another example of change is evident in one corporation's approach to global diversity training. When discussing an upcoming training session for managers from a variety of countries, company leaders asked that my colleagues and I not use the word *diversity*. They felt it did not work for individuals outside the United States. We offered *complexity* as an alternative. They agreed. We then went through our materials and systematically replaced "diversity" with "complexity." The result was a rich experience that highlighted the depth of the notion of diversity even more so than if we had used the word. I suspect that this interchanging of diversity and complexity eventually will become routine.

The example of another global enterprise demonstrates a growing awareness of diversity independent of the civil rights movement. A European subsidiary requested my appearance for a presentation and asked that I arrive a day early to receive an orientation to their particular issues. They were concerned that I would bring a U.S. civil rights perspective based on race. I agreed to their request. Our orientation session started with my comments about diversity and diversity management. I provided a definition of diversity mixtures and cited as examples of diversity issues those related to nationalism, mergers and acquisitions, functional integration, headquarters field relationships, customers, products, and brands. I then asked them what they thought I should keep in mind for my presentation on the next day. They responded, "You've got it! We are comfortable with your approach."

This confirmed my own view that diversity management has enormous potential as a global craft for making quality decisions across national boundaries in the midst of differences, similarities, and tensions.

IN SUMMARY

We are not there yet. Clearly, much needs to be done if my expectations for the future are to be realized. And there will be opposition, particularly when it comes to uncoupling diversity management from the civil rights movement and social justice agenda.

Yet I believe this uncoupling will occur. The diversity focus will shift from a concept centered around race and gender, the civil rights movement, and social justice to a craft for making quality decisions in the midst of differences, similarities, tensions, and complexities.

What must be kept in mind is that many if not most social justice issues can be conceptualized as challenges in making quality decisions in the midst of differences, similarities, and tensions. Adoption of a craft that facilitates such decision making would enhance the probability of achieving social justice goals. I therefore anticipate that diversity management will become a valued complement to traditional civil rights initiatives as opposed to compromising or replacing them, enhancing the effectiveness and efficiency of organizations in the process.

—◆◆◆—

At time of original publishing R. Roosevelt Thomas, Jr., was president of the American Institute for Managing Diversity and CEO of Roosevelt Thomas Consulting & Training, Inc.

CHAPTER TWENTY

Negotiating for the Public Good

Lisa Blomgren Bingham

───∿∿∿───

Suppose you have a limited budget. You have certain authority, but you cannot force someone to comply with a regulation without invoking other agency resources. Or perhaps you are trying to get more resources allocated to your department, division, or bureau. Maybe you have worked long and hard in a rule-making proceeding, and want to get the rule implemented, but are concerned that affected parties may challenge it. Perhaps a contractor feels you have violated the terms of a supply agreement or that your demands are not within the scope of the original construction agreement. And to round out a perfect day, one of your employees has just filed an EEO complaint against the agency. How do you handle the daily conflict that is a part of any public administrator's job? You negotiate, every day and in a wide variety of contexts. This chapter will address the emerging literature on negotiation, from the perspective of when,

Originally published as "Negotiating for the Public Good." In James L. Perry (Ed.), *Handbook of Public Administration* (2nd ed.). (San Francisco: Jossey-Bass, 1996).

why, and how you should negotiate. It will give you an overview of techniques so that you can recognize an unprincipled negotiator and respond with principled negotiation. Conflict can be a creative force for good, if you use it constructively.

WHEN TO NEGOTIATE

Public administrators have always resolved a variety of disputes voluntarily through negotiation (Harter, 1987), but only recently have legislatures and commentators come to acknowledge the role negotiation can play in making an agency more effective and efficient. In part to codify existing practice (and encourage its expansion), Congress enacted the Administrative Dispute Resolution Act (ADRA) of 1990 and the Negotiated Rulemaking Act (NRA) of 1990 (Susskind, Babbitt, and Segal, 1993). In addition, state legislatures have begun to make changes to their versions of the Uniform Administrative Procedure Act (UAPA) to encourage expanded use of negotiation in state agencies. These acts and amendments are intended to eliminate any concern that administrators who engage in negotiation and settlement are acting outside the scope of their authority. Specifically, the ADRA defines alternative means of dispute resolution as any procedure followed in lieu of adjudication, including but not limited to settlement negotiations, conciliation, facilitation, mediation, fact-finding, and "mini trials" (*Administrative Dispute Resolution Act,* 1995). It encourages federal-level administrators to use these techniques, all of which entail negotiation at some stage in the proceeding (Harter, 1987). The NRA encourages agencies to consider using negotiation in rule making. Federal agencies may consider whether negotiation is appropriate in light of the number of parties who may be affected by a rule, the likelihood that they will reach an agreement with the aid of a facilitator, and the feasibility of negotiating such an agreement within a reasonable time frame (*Negotiated Rulemaking Act,* 1995; Harter, 1987). A variety of federal, state, and local agencies have specific statutory authorization to mediate or use other means of alternative dispute resolution.

The purpose of all these changes is to authorize public administrators to explore various means—including principled negotiation and mediation or facilitation—to achieve public objectives without fear that they will be accused of ad hoc decision making. Specifically, the ADRA recognizes that some disputes may not be suitable for negotiation. Just as a prosecutor will seek the maximum sentence for a serial killer, a public administrator considering an enforcement action may choose to make an example of an open or egregious violator. Similarly, agencies may choose not to settle a case because there is an important legal principle or precedent at stake (for a detailed discussion of cases that are inappropriate for settlement, see Edwards, 1986; Fiss, 1984). The statutes cited above give administrators the discretion to make these choices. The ADRA (sec. 572) specifically cautions administrators that alternative dispute resolution may not be appropriate in every case. For example, it directs administrators not to use negotiation or other means of settlement if a definitive or authoritative resolution is required for a legal precedent or if the matter may significantly affect the rights of parties other than the disputants. If administrators exercise this discretion appropriately, they can resolve most disputes and at the same time achieve greater public participation in the decision-making processes of government (Manring, 1994; Stephenson and Pops, 1991).

WHY TO NEGOTIATE

Although systematic evaluation of alternative dispute resolution is difficult and is still in its earliest stages (Esser, 1989; Galanter, 1988), the evidence tends to show that administrators can save time and money by using direct or assisted negotiation. Most studies of procedures using negotiation have concerned procedures that state or federal courts supervise; commentators have recognized the applicability of this experience for agencies that have heavy case loads (Harter, 1987). It is certainly clear that parties are better satisfied with dispute resolution processes they have more control over (Wall and Lynn, 1993). Moreover, the evidence shows that negotiated settlements are implemented at higher rates; that is, they stick (McEwen and Maiman, 1984). There is some evidence that *mandatory* mediation or arbitration may actually slow down case processing, by diverting disputants who would otherwise settle directly, without the assistance of a mediator (MacCoun, 1991). However, if the parties do not automatically plan on using a mediator and resort to mediation only when it is clear that direct negotiation will be inefficient or ineffective, there is no evidence of additional delay. It is certainly true for any given case that it is cheaper to negotiate an acceptable settlement than to face protracted litigation.

HOW TO NEGOTIATE

Books describing how to become an ace negotiator are legion. They fall into two main categories, however: those discussing traditional negotiating techniques and those advocating principled, collaborative, or "win-win" bargaining. They all agree on the importance of preparing oneself before sitting down at the bargaining table. This section will discuss preparation, the basics of principled negotiation, and a catalogue of hard-bargaining techniques.

Preparing to Negotiate

Before you sit down at the negotiating table, you need to know what issues you will discuss, with whom you will discuss them, and what each of you can do if negotiations are fruitless. Armed with this information, you can then negotiate the rules of the game.

IDENTIFY THE SUBJECT AND SCOPE OF THE NEGOTIATION. There are different conventions for negotiating different issues. First, you should determine whether the negotiation is for the purpose of dispute resolution or planning (see Boskey, 1993, p. 9). Dispute resolution negotiations address an existing claim, case, or problem, often one that can end up in litigation (for examples relating to harassment claims, see Rowe, 1990). There may or may not be a continuing relationship between the parties, and the negotiation focuses on past events. Planning negotiations include zoning and site issues (Susskind, 1990), establishing long-term contractual relationships, and rule making. They generally involve defining a continuing or future relationship between parties. Second, you may wish to determine whether you are facing a zero-sum or non-zero-sum negotiation (see Boskey, 1993, p. 9). A zero-sum negotiation is where your gain is of necessity the other party's loss. It is also referred to as a fixed-pie negotiation, although it is possible to enlarge the pie in most zero-sum negotiations with the use of creative bargaining (see Susskind and Cruikshank, 1987, pp. 178–184). These first steps will help you begin to identify how the other party will approach the negotiation and what conventions that party may expect you to follow. For example, it is conventional in labor negotiations for the parties to exchange a long laundry list of initial proposals when it is time to renegotiate a contract. This is not the convention with business agreements that have generally worked well during the term, however. In the latter case, you can anticipate far fewer proposals for change.

DECIDE WHO HAS AUTHORITY TO BARGAIN. This step can be more problematic in the public sector than in the private sector. For example, is the other party a corporate entity, so that you can deal with top executives? In order to negotiate a settlement using a mini trial, parties must bring their chief executives to the table. Is the other party a manufacturers' association, which will have to go back to its membership for approval of any deal? Are you dealing with an individual or with a lawyer who may or may not have the authority to bind his or her client to a settlement? In order to avoid these problems, clarify your bargaining authority before you sit down to negotiate. Are you the appropriate person to sit at the bargaining table, or should your superior be there instead? Recent ADRA-related amendments address this issue and increase federal-level administrators' authority to settle monetary claims. At the table, make your bargaining authority explicit, and determine the extent of the other party's authority. You do not want to reach an agreement only to find it must be approved by someone you could have dealt with directly. A classic bargaining ploy is for a lawyer to negotiate his or her best deal and only then explain that the client must approve it. This tactic often provides an opening for a hard bargainer to make new demands.

IDENTIFY YOUR BATNA. Before you sit down to negotiate, you need to have certain information. First and foremost, you need to know your "best alternative to a negotiated agreement," or BATNA (see Fisher and Ury, 1991, pp. 97–106). If negotiation fails, what might happen? If you do not have a strong sense of where you could go from the table, you cannot recognize a good settlement when you have one. To identify your BATNA and that of the other party, you should take into account three crucial variables that affect any negotiation: power, time, and information (see Cohen, 1991, p. 50). As possible sources of power, Cohen identifies competition (that is, economic demand for your product or service), legitimacy (for example, a government stamp of approval), risk taking (willingness to risk losing), commitment (the ability to get other relevant people or parties committed to your interests), expertise (on the subject matter in dispute), knowledge (of each side's true needs), investment (in time, money, and energy), rewards and punishments (in regard to future dealings with the same parties), identification (getting others to identify with you), morality (perceived fairness), precedent, persistence, persuasive capacity, and attitude.

For an example of the power of precedent, if the case involves differing interpretations of a statute or contract, do you know whether the courts will support you? Is the law or contract language clear, or is it uncertain? If it is clear and in your favor, you are negotiating from a position of strength. Your BATNA may be to litigate. If it is uncertain, is this the best case to use to make a precedent? It is often said that "hard cases make bad law." For an example of the power of investment, consider what resources you have and how much you have invested in resolving this dispute. If you litigate, do you exhaust a limited fund, putting yourself in a worse position to negotiate the next case? For example, if your agency does not have the resources to litigate every employee grievance, you must consider for each particular case whether litigation is wise. You need to keep your resources in perspective; if a proffered settlement exceeds them, you will know to walk away from the bargaining table (that is, to exercise your BATNA).

The second crucial variable, time, may affect a negotiation in a number of ways. As Cohen (1991) observes and any mediator knows, most deal making occurs at or shortly before the deadline for completing a negotiation, if there is a deadline. This explains why international mediators go out of their way to create a series of deadlines, fictitious though they may be. If you have a deadline by which you must accomplish your goal, it will help define your BATNA (and that of the other party). For example, is there a statutory time limit for instituting enforcement proceedings? Is there a statute of limitations for litigation? The federal government adopted a sixty-day deferral policy for equal employment opportunity complaints for all agencies that have an alternative dispute resolution procedure in place, including negotiation. This sixty-day limit creates a deadline.

In addition, because it is a process, negotiation takes time. Agency personnel may become frustrated with the seeming inefficiency of spending hours in discussions, particularly when their performance appraisals measure productivity in terms of cases processed or penalties assessed. Negotiated rule making, for example, takes significantly longer to produce a published rule than traditional rule making; the advantage comes when no one contests the rule in court. If you cannot devote the time the process demands, this can also affect your BATNA.

Information is the third (and most key) variable. Information will help you put an agreement together, and the lack of it can frustrate settlement. It is important to gather as much information as you can in the preparatory stage of negotiation. After talks become formal, sources of information previously available to you will dry up (see Cohen, 1991, p. 102). For example, if your agency conducts inspections at a plant or workplace, the investigator has a perfect opportunity to collect information by holding informal discussions with employees; this information may later be relevant to negotiations over a civil fine. Once the facility calls in its counsel, all communication will occur through that third party. Thus, it is wise to collect as much information as you can about the other party's financial situation, priorities, deadlines, costs, interests, needs, and organizational or political pressures (see Cohen, 1991, p. 104). In addition, you should collect and share with your negotiating team the same information about your agency.

IDENTIFY THE OTHER PARTY'S BATNA. Is the other party a small supplier whose primary contracts are with your agency? If the supplier desires a continuing relationship with the agency, its BATNA is not going to be as desirable as negotiating. However, if the other party is a member of a major regulated industry and has substantial financial resources, it may conclude that its BATNA (for example, to delay implementation of a new environmental or safety technology through protracted litigation) is more desirable than negotiating to comply now. Collect as much information as you can on the cost of compliance, the cost of litigation, and the resources of the party you are dealing with. Also, determine whether you can worsen the party's BATNA through punitive sanctions or criminal prosecution of responsible executives. Sometimes a party's BATNA is so undesirable that it really has no choice but to negotiate. For example, a felon caught red-handed can either face prosecution or plea-bargain and turn state's evidence. If the felon's BATNA is a long prison sentence, bargaining may be the only reasonable choice.

SET GROUND RULES. For more formal negotiations—that is, when you anticipate sitting down at the bargaining table for more than one session—it is wise to agree upon ground rules in advance or at the beginning of the first session. Sometimes, in multiparty public policy disputes, a facilitator will refer to ground rules as the protocol for negotiation (Cormick, 1989). A wise bargainer will agree to the ground rules in writing. By negotiating first over the procedure for negotiation, you can set a firm but fair tone for later, substantive issues. You can also use these preliminaries to develop trust and rapport. The following four key ground rules from labor negotiations translate well to other settings.

- *No Press Releases.* Negotiation should be conducted confidentially, not in the press. Recent statutory changes make this ground rule more compatible with the Freedom of Information Act and sunshine laws than it was previously. Check with your counsel first. If there are to be press releases, they should be by mutual agreement and committed to writing before the end of a bargaining session.

- *All Meeting Times, Dates, and Locations Must Be Set by Mutual Agreement.* Ordinarily, negotiation takes place on an agency's own turf. Even in public sector labor relations, bargaining usually takes place at a town hall or on public property, such as a school building. Of course, there will be instances of negotiation that occur at the other party's place of business (for example, when an investigator conducts an inspection or audit of an employer's books and discusses the scope of the inspection or audit with the employer's representatives). Unlike labor negotiation, which usually occurs at night, most public sector negotiation occurs during regular working hours. On occasion, it may be appropriate to keep negotiating around the clock until you have reached an agreement, however. Labor mediators have long recognized that locking parties who are motivated to reach an agreement into one building for a prolonged period can often break through an impasse. Clearly, if the other party's BATNA is strong, this stratagem is ill advised for you.

- *Substantive Issues Must Be Raised by a Given Deadline.* This rule essentially requires that you agree in advance on the agenda and scope of the negotiation. A party who has negotiated long and hard over how to comply with certain regulations for one of its facilities will not be happy if a second facility is added into the mix after an agreement has been reached on the first.

This rule does not prevent an agency from initiating a separate enforcement proceeding. It simply means that if you are considering including multiple facilities in a given negotiation (or any analogous expansion of the scope of the negotiation), put it on the table up-front.

• *Tentative Agreements Are Binding Pending Agreement on All Issues.* Once the parties reach agreement on a distinct issue, they should initial the agreement and take that issue off the table pending agreement on the rest of the issues in dispute. These "tentative agreements" are conditionally binding; that is, they are binding on the condition that a final complete agreement on all issues is approved by both parties. If the parties fail to reach a complete agreement, they are no longer bound by these partial tentative agreements. This ground rule keeps a party from revisiting old ground and reneging on previously settled points. Backtracking on agreements and escalating demands are hallmarks of the hard or bad-faith bargainer. If you will have to submit the completed agreement to a higher authority for approval, make it clear in the ground rules that tentative agreements are conditionally binding pending final approval of the whole settlement. Otherwise, some members of the public may become quite frustrated with agency approval processes and the limited negotiating authority most public administrators possess. Also, if your superior refuses to approve the agreement and sends you back to renegotiate, the other party may perceive it as a bargaining stratagem.

Practicing Principled Negotiation

This term has come to encompass an approach to bargaining advocated by the Harvard Negotiation Project (Fisher and Brown, 1988; Fisher and Ury, 1991; Ury, 1991; Ury, Brett, and Goldberg, 1989) and includes collaborative, or win-win, bargaining (Cohen, 1991) as well. It is at the opposite end of the negotiation continuum from positional, confrontational, competitive, or adversarial bargaining (Koren and Goodman, 1991). Cohen (1991) characterizes adversarial bargaining as "winning at all costs.... Soviet style" (p. 119). In positional negotiation, parties often get caught up negotiating over a series of artificial positions instead of addressing their true needs and interests and the real issues behind the dispute. They hoard information because they see it as a source of bargaining power. The classic example of positional negotiation is the bargaining typically employed in the purchase of a new car (or anything you might purchase for your agency). The dealer starts with some fanciful "sticker price," and the buyer starts somewhere lower, depending on the quality of his or her research. The parties then take turns taking positions that move incrementally toward each other's stance. This negotiation style assumes a fixed pie (in this case, the parties are negotiating over how much the dealer will profit from the sale). One party's concession is the other party's gain. Each party's BATNA is to walk away from the deal. The buyer can go to a different dealer; the seller can sell to a different buyer.

If these same parties were to engage in principled bargaining, they would discuss issues such as the dealer's cost, the salesperson's interest in meeting a particular monthly quota or commission target, the buyer's ability to pay, the fact that there is a profit built into the so-called dealer invoice, the question of what is a fair or reasonable profit in light of the time of the year or the demand for the particular model, and a variety of other objective criteria that relate to the parties' respective interests in sealing the deal. The parties would focus on interests, not positions. They would try to identify ways to enlarge the pie. Will the customer refer friends? Will the customer be purchasing another car anytime soon? (Agencies can provide a continuing source of business for many vendors.) How will the customer's experience affect the dealer's reputation in the community? Can the customer provide the dealer with some free advertising? Principled negotiation is most easily applied when the parties have an ongoing relationship—for example, a manufacturer (or, analogously, an agency) and its supplier, the divorcing parents of two children, international allies, or a labor union and an employer. However, a negotiator can also use principled negotiation effectively in a one-shot deal, with certain caveats (for example, beware of the hard-bargaining tactics described later).

There are a number of reasons why public administrators should make every effort to use principled rather than positional negotiation. First, public agencies potentially face a continuing relationship with every regulated entity and every former employee; each is a member of the public the agency serves. In public service, very often the "how" of what you do is as important as what you accomplish. Unfortunately, most press coverage these days seems to focus on the how, and not the what, of agency business. In other words, principled negotiation is good public relations. Second, principled negotiation is ethical practice. A reputation for integrity is a negotiator's greatest asset. Principled negotiation is a step-by-step recipe for negotiating integrity. Third, public administrators hold a position of public trust. The public has high expectations, and it holds public administrators to higher standards of personal conduct. It would violate that trust to knowingly mislead a party in a negotiation—and a member of the public might construe many of the standard hard-bargaining ploys as intentional deception. There is no hard evidence that a competitive negotiating style is any more effective than principled negotiating, so you need not feel that you will sacrifice the public interest if you pursue the principled approach (Williams, 1983).

The Harvard Negotiation Project concept of principled negotiation entails four steps: (1) separate people from the problem; (2) focus on interests, not positions; (3) invent options for mutual gain; and (4) use objective criteria (Fisher and Ury, 1991, p. 13). The win-win concept suggests seven analogous steps: (1) establish trust, (2) obtain information, (3) meet parties' needs, (4) use their ideas, (5) transform relationship to collaboration, (6) take moderate risks, and (7) get their help (Cohen, 1991, pp. 176–177). Generally these steps provide a shorthand for describing and structuring a process that—because it takes place among a group of people—is part of an evolving interpersonal dynamic. No one step exists in isolation.

Any attempt to label points of the process as discrete stages is somewhat artificial because at each stage you collect ideas that may be useful in the next one. It does help you recognize where you are in the process, however. With this qualification in mind, then, we might identify five stages in the process. The first stage entails establishing a mode of discussion and identifying any interpersonal dynamics that may help or hamper subsequent discussions. The second stage essentially consists of extended information gathering by both sides. The third stage entails creating possible elements of a settlement. The fourth is packaging these elements. The final stage is bringing people to the point of closure on a complete agreement. The following sections discuss each stage in detail.

IDENTIFY THE INTERPERSONAL DYNAMICS INVOLVED. Everyone has stories about having run into a "communication problem." In order to negotiate effectively, you need to determine whether personality clashes might cast shadows over the discussions. For example, a labor mediator often spends time in the hallway, listening to one advocate's extended descriptions of the other team's makeup. The advocate might point out who is constructive, who tends to fly off the handle, who has a long history of animosity with the human resource manager, and whom the others turn to for guidance and good judgment. You may perform this function for a subordinate who has handled a dispute up to this point, or you may do it for yourself. Have you formed a visceral dislike for the person you are dealing with? If so, you need to leave it behind. The negotiation is not about that person's character; it is about solving a problem. Detach yourself from your dislike. Remember that in five years you will laugh about this experience, if you even remember it at all. Ury (1991) calls this state of detachment "going to the balcony" to watch the negotiation as if from a great distance (p. 17).

Moreover, if there are feelings of dislike, they are probably mutual. Thus, Fisher and Ury (1991, p. 36) urge you to separate people from the problem you are negotiating. They suggest you deal directly with any people problems; that is, bring them up at the table and discuss them. To help identify people problems, they suggest that you

- Try to understand how the other party perceives the dispute and how that party might feel about it.
- Suspend judgment.
- Recognize and legitimate the emotions at work.
- Allow people to let off steam (but not react to their outbursts).
- Build a relationship with any adversary by talking directly to that party, listening actively, speaking about yourself using "I statements," and not characterizing the other party.

One might call this the Zen of negotiating. Fisher and Brown (1988) suggest that having a good bargaining relationship is not the same as approving of the other side, sharing the same values, avoiding disagreement, or demonstrating perfect trust. Instead, it consists of establishing an attitude that is unconditionally constructive—using rationality in response to emotion, understanding others when they misunderstand you, consulting them even if they appear not to listen, not trying to deceive them, being noncoercive (and not yielding to coercion), and accepting them and their concerns as worthy of consideration. Fisher and Brown's comments refer to long-term continuing bargaining relationships; thus, they may not appear to apply to all public-sector negotiation situations. But public administrators can be said to have a long-term bargaining relationship with the public—the public is represented by all the various people who do business or otherwise interact with public agencies. In this context, Fisher and Brown's advice is readily transferable to public administration.

DISCOVER THE OTHER PARTY'S NEEDS AND INTERESTS. You have already gathered a substantial amount of information in preparation for negotiating. It will most likely be objective information, not information about the other party's perceptions. Perhaps the Harvard Negotiation Project's most useful contribution was the language it gave us for talking about the most important information in a negotiation. This is the language of interests. The adversarial negotiator will speak the language of positions, as in "Well, that is our position." The principled negotiator will attempt to identify the other party's interests by asking questions to determine what the other party truly needs in terms of security; economic well-being; sense of belonging to an organization, community, or profession; recognition of that party's contribution or efforts; and autonomy or control over that party's own decisions or business (Fisher and Ury, 1991, p. 48).

To elicit responses that will identify these interests, the principled negotiator uses a powerful problem-solving tool—questions, particularly "why?" and "why not?" Other problem-solving questions are the same questions lawyers use on direct examination: questions beginning with who, what, where, when, and how. Leading questions, particularly those with an implicit accusation ("When did you stop abusing your spouse?"), are not helpful. The principled negotiator may also identify interests by considering the consequences for the other party of a particular negotiating outcome—for example, by looking at the short- or long-term economic impact, legal implications, psychological effects, precedential effect, impact on political support, or impact on the larger affected group's interests (Fisher and Ury, 1991, p. 47). An essential part of this process is to listen actively to the answers you get. You ask questions to get information; let the other side know you have heard and understood the response. For example, you can respond by paraphrasing back to the other party the concerns that party articulates. You can use phrases like, "Let me make sure I understand you correctly," followed by a repetition of the key aspects of the other party's statement.

In addition to eliciting information about the other party's interests, you need to communicate information about yours. You can do this by expressing your agency's concerns and interests in connection with certain outcomes, by being specific, and by using concrete examples to explain why you believe a particular outcome is fair or appropriate or necessary for the agency or for the public interest. Before suggesting a solution to a problem, you should acknowledge and recognize the other party's interests and then describe the problem as you see it.

The interests you identify may be separate but reconcilable, conflicting, or shared (Fisher and Ury, 1991, p. 40). By identifying where these interests overlap or are compatible, you can begin to move to the next stage of the negotiation process—identifying the pieces of the settlement puzzle.

CREATE POSSIBLE ELEMENTS OF A SETTLEMENT. Some have said that the essence of creativity is the ability to keep an open mind and suspend judgment. In labor relations, a contract settlement will address many issues, from wages to working conditions to job security. During negotiations, the parties begin to get a sense of what the possibilities are in each area—the possible elements of a settlement—without prejudging precisely which puzzle pieces will fall into place in the final package. Almost any fixed-pie negotiation can be viewed as a deal with a variety of elements. For example, a simple sale can become a public relations asset if the buyer is someone with standing in the community who endorses the product. The ability to use information about the other party's interests to enlarge the pie into a multifaceted, mutually beneficial deal is the key to brainstorming, or what the Harvard Negotiation Project terms "inventing options for mutual gain" (Fisher and Ury, 1991, p. 56) and Cohen (1991) calls the "win-win technique."

Many public sector managers have already received some training in brainstorming techniques in the course of planning total quality management (TQM) efforts. Facilitators have begun using similar techniques to work with city councils on visioning, as a method of planning their community's future. The participants face a flip chart, blackboard, or overhead projection; whether they are on separate negotiating teams or not, all should be facing the same direction to work on their common problem. They designate a facilitator or scribe to write down ideas. The facilitator should place the list so that everyone in the room can see it. The participants then proceed to list every single idea they can think of to meet their respective interests and solve the problem they have identified. As the facilitator or scribe writes down the ideas, there should be no discussion or commentary on their relative merits. Discussing the ideas at this stage might inhibit people from making further suggestions for fear of criticism. Also, discussing every entry on the list would bog down the creative process. It may not be necessary ever to discuss some of the ideas if clearly superior ones have emerged by the time the list is complete. The facilitator or scribe should not attribute specific ideas to either party. It may make for easier reading if the facilitator alternates pen or chalk colors with each idea. The parties should make as long a list as they possibly can. They should not self-censor suggestions as too crazy or impossible, but they should try to come up with suggestions that meet both parties' needs and interests.

When no one has any more ideas, it is time to consider which ones are best. There are various techniques for doing this. Some facilitators will give each person in the room three or four stickers, sometimes with different colors and point values, and direct them to place one sticker by each of their top three or four ideas. Others will go through the entire list and ask the group to rank each idea as a 1 ("warrants further discussion"), a 2 ("maybe we'll consider it later"), or a 3 ("let's forget it"). After the ideas are ranked, the group proceeds to discuss the top-rated ideas and determine whether elements of these, or some combination of them, might resolve the problem or dispute. This is a highly efficient way for a group to consider solutions to a problem. Obviously, in a negotiation between two people, the parties could do the same thing with a pad and paper. No suggestion should be viewed as a concession or an agreement, but only as an idea to discuss.

The advantage to this process is that, as the parties discuss the various ideas, they will of necessity learn more about each other's interests and concerns, which in turn will facilitate the invention of ideas that are more tailored to meeting those interests or concerns. You can then convert the ideas into concrete options to implement. Fisher and Ury (1991, p. 70) suggest that you can convert ideas into options by using different perspectives or forging agreements of different strengths. An agreement may be permanent or provisional, substantive or procedural, comprehensive or partial, unconditional or contingent.

For example, consider the following case of a public agency engaged in collective bargaining with a newly elected union for the first time. While the negotiations are under way, an agency manager disciplines a union member (an agency employee) for poor job performance. The union demands that management withdraw the disciplinary action. The manager insists that the action must stand; she wants to demonstrate that performance standards will be the same under a union contract and that she is not intimidated by the union. The parties have not yet agreed on disciplinary procedures or a grievance process for the agency. The union's interests lie in demonstrating to the employees that it is an effective representative. It also wants to ensure that the manager is not disciplining the employee in part because of that employee's union affiliation. Management's interests lie in enforcing performance standards evenhandedly. Both parties detail these interests for the other side, and in a brainstorming exercise they come up with the idea of turning this one case over to a third party—an arbitrator. The arbitrator can settle the matter without prejudicing the ongoing negotiation over the terms of the contract. The decision to go to arbitration represents a procedural agreement, not a substantive one. It is also provisional—for this case only—not a permanent part of the contract. However, it does meet everyone's interests in maintaining fair, evenhanded administration of discipline. If the parties had only discussed their positions and not their underlying interests and ideas for how to satisfy them, they might never have reached this agreement. The beauty of brainstorming is its ability to create value—you leave the process with a much better sense of all the pieces of the settlement puzzle (for a more detailed discussion on creating value, see Lax and Sebenius, 1986).

PACKAGE A MUTUALLY ADVANTAGEOUS AGREEMENT. Some mediators say that the way to recognize a good settlement is that both parties leave the negotiations equally unhappy. Often the unhappiness is a pose, however—they do not want those representing the other party to think they got away with something. In fact, it is possible to come up with mutually advantageous, win-win agreements. After the parties have generated their list of ideas, discussed it, and converted some of the ideas into options, the key is to put together a combination of options or elements that meets everyone's needs and interests to some reasonable extent. Examples include agreements to pay a civil fine without admitting liability or wrongdoing, employee grievance settlements that both sides agree will not constitute a precedent, and paying compensatory damages over a period of time so that they do not impact too heavily on the penalized party's cash flow.

Sometimes parties are reluctant or unable to communicate their interests directly to the extent necessary to construct a settlement. In these circumstances, a mediator's assistance may prove invaluable. Mediation is simply negotiation with some assistance: each party tells the mediator which elements of an agreement might meet the party's needs, and the mediator uses each party's confidential communications to put together a package for settling the dispute. By presenting a solution as the mediator's package instead of one party's proposal, the mediator can take the onus off both sides of possibly losing face before their constituencies. This principle works equally well for labor negotiators with their respective constituencies of union members and managers, lawyers with their respective clients, and elected officials serving diverse groups of citizens. Federal agencies are training their own employees as mediators so that they can exchange these employees with other agencies to fill this impartial mediator role. Agencies are also appointing ombudsmen to serve this purpose, both internally (for personnel issues) and externally (to resolve specific complaints from the public).

COMPLETE THE AGREEMENT. A negotiation is not successful until all the pieces fit and the parties have reduced their preliminary agreement to some form of written memorandum. If there is an impasse over a particular point, now is the time to use objective criteria to resolve it. Principled negotiation does not use power or coercion to resolve an impasse (Fisher and Ury, 1991, p. 81). Instead, you might look to law, precedent, tradition, market value, professional standards, efficiency, costs, scientific data, or what a court or arbitrator might do. You can also resort to notions of equal treatment, fair procedures, reciprocity, and moral standards. Speak to the merits of the dispute; do not resort to personal attacks or threats. If all else fails, you can do what Ury (1991) refers to as "deploying" your BATNA (without actually exercising it—yet). There is a difference between trying to coerce the other party and warning them that you have a BATNA that is a more desirable option than anything currently on the table. You are not threatening them; you are merely conveying information about your interests and needs and letting the other party know you might be better served by walking out of the negotiation than by agreeing to the option they have proposed. This is not coercion; it is reality.

Disarming the Hard Bargainer

Although you may be committed to principled bargaining, others may not be. It is important to be able to recognize classic hard-bargaining tactics. If you can name these tactics, then you can confront the other party's use of them: "Why are you setting preconditions? I want to discuss the merits." Ury suggests that naming a tactic and letting the other party know you recognize it robs it of its effectiveness (Ury, 1991, p. 22). So here is a list—by no means exhaustive—of classic hard-bargaining tactics (Ury, 1991; Meltsner and Schrag, [1973] 1992).

1. Stonewalling.

2. Making a first, firm, fair, final, nonnegotiable offer (known in labor relations as Boulwarism; for a discussion of its use in politics and foreign policy, see Jacobs, 1989).

3. Using "good cop–bad cop" routines, where one member of the negotiating team appears reasonable while the other makes irrational threats.

4. Setting preconditions to bargaining (that is, designating a demand as a precondition to any negotiation).

5. Making personal attacks or using ethnic or racial slurs.

6. Manipulating data, using false figures.

7. Locking yourself in with a public or press announcement.

8. Making extreme demands.

9. Placing major demands at the beginning of the agenda.

10. Escalating demands or backtracking during negotiations.

11. Acting irrational.

12. Claiming to have no authority to compromise.

13. Having your constituency reject the final agreement and then raising your demands.

If you find yourself facing one of these tactics, the key is not to react. Tactics such as these are only effective if you let them be. Ury suggests that you will be tempted to strike back, give in, or break off negotiations in the face of hard bargaining (Ury, 1991, p. 12). He suggests that you instead take a break, hold a caucus, examine your BATNA, identify the tactic, ask the other side to restate its position, and then direct the other side back to a principled, substantive discussion by asking problem-based questions. You should largely ignore personal attacks. You can willfully misunderstand a first, firm, fair, final offer as the other party's negotiation goal instead of recognizing it as nonnegotiable (p. 72). By continuing to approach the negotiation constructively, you may disarm the other party. As a last resort, you can deploy your BATNA to test the other party's resolve. Meeting tricks with tricks will only escalate the adversarial atmosphere, perhaps to the point of a breakdown in talks. This is not to say that you should follow a policy of appeasement. If there are compatible or reconcilable interests leading to points you can agree with, then by all means agree where you can. However, do not yield in the hope that the other side will reciprocate. Maintain a principled approach to the negotiation. If all else fails, you may propose to bring in a third party, such as a mediator, to break through the deadlock.

SUMMARY

The purpose of this chapter has been to introduce you to various negotiation skills. These are skills you can bring to bear upon any conflict you face as a public administrator. With preparation, appropriate ground rules, and principled negotiation where appropriate, you can better achieve public objectives than you can through costly and time-consuming adversarial processes. To prepare for negotiating, first identify the subject and scope of the negotiation, and then determine who has the authority to bargain. Carefully determine your BATNA and that of the other party by considering each side's relative power, the time available to reach an agreement, and any information you can gather regarding each party's costs, interests, needs, priorities, deadlines, finances, and political pressures. Set ground rules or protocols for the negotiation that can be changed only by mutual agreement, including a limit on press releases; a schedule of meeting times, dates, and locations; a deadline for raising substantive issues; and an understanding that tentative agreements are conditionally binding pending final agreement on all the issues on the table.

Use principled negotiation to achieve your objectives. Public administrators have a continuing relationship with the public and with those they regulate. Principled negotiation is good ethical practice, and it is consistent with honoring the public trust. Thus, it is also good public relations.

Use the language of interests, not positions, during bargaining. Identify interpersonal dynamics that may help or hamper discussions. Gather as much information as you can about the other parties' needs and interests by using problem-based questions and active-listening techniques. Create possible elements of a settlement using brainstorming techniques. List all the alternatives, without attribution or criticism, before determining which you should discuss first. Use meeting both parties' interests as the basis for prioritizing your alternatives, and combine elements of the best ideas to create options for an agreement. Package a mutually advantageous agreement, and use objective criteria—not threats or power—to resolve sticking points. Last, do not react or yield to hard-bargaining ploys, but take a caucus, name and raise the tactic, ask the other party to restate the concern, and then direct the discussion back to principled bargaining by asking problem-based questions. If you reach an impasse, inform the other party that your BATNA is better than the proposed agreement, and bring in a mediator if necessary. You may not resolve every dispute by negotiating, but you will resolve many of them—and conserve public resources in the process.

References

Administrative Dispute Resolution Act. U.S. Code. Vol. 5, secs. 571–572 (1995).

Boskey, J. B. "Blueprint for Negotiations." *Dispute Resolution Journal*, 1993, *48*(4), 8–19.

Cohen, H. *You Can Negotiate Anything: How to Get What You Want.* New York: Citadel Press, 1991.

Cormick, G. W. "Strategic Issues in Structuring Multi-Party Public Policy Negotiations." *Negotiation Journal*, 1989, *5*(2), 125–132.

Edwards, H. T. "Alternative Dispute Resolution: Panacea or Anathema?" *Harvard Law Review*, 1986, *99*(3), 668–684.

Esser, J. P. "Evaluations of Dispute Processing: We Do Not Know What We Think and We Do Not Think What We Know." *Denver University Law Review*, 1989, *66*(3), 499–562.

Fisher, R., and Brown, S. *Getting Together: Building Relationships as We Negotiate.* New York: Viking Penguin, 1988.

Fisher, R., and Ury, W. *Getting to Yes: Negotiating Agreement Without Giving In.* New York: Viking Penguin, 1991.

Fiss, O. M. "Against Settlement." *Yale Law Journal,* 1984, *93*(6), 1073–1090.

Galanter, M. "The Quality of Settlements." *Journal of Dispute Resolution,* 1988, 55–84.

Harter, P. "Points on a Continuum: Dispute Resolution Procedures and the Administrative Process." *Administrative Law Journal,* 1987, *1,* 141–211.

Jacobs, D. C. "Political Boulwarism: Bargaining During the Reagan Years." *Negotiation Journal,* 1989, *5*(4), 349–353.

Koren, L., and Goodman, P. *The Haggler's Handbook: One Hour to Negotiating Power.* New York: W.W. Norton, 1991.

Lax, D. A., and Sebenius, J. K. *The Manager as Negotiator: Bargaining for Cooperation and Competitive Gain.* New York: The Free Press, 1986.

MacCoun, R. J. "Unintended Consequences of Court Arbitration: A Cautionary Tale from New Jersey." *The Justice System Journal,* 1991, *14*(2), 229–243.

McEwen, C., and Maiman, R. "Mediation in Small Claims Court: Achieving Compliance Through Consent." *Law and Society Review,* 1984, *18,* 11–50.

Manring, N. J. "ADR and Administrative Responsiveness: Challenges for Public Administrators." *Public Administration Review,* 1994, *54*(2), 197–202.

Meltsner, M., and Schrag, P. "Negotiating Tactics for Legal Services Lawyers." Reprinted in part in S. Goldberg, F.E.A. Sander, and N. Rogers, *Dispute Resolution: Negotiation, Mediation, and Other Processes* (2nd ed.). Boston: Little, Brown, 1992. (Originally published 1973.)

Negotiated Rulemaking Act. U.S. Code. Vol. 5, sec. 563 (1995).

Rowe, M. P. "People Who Feel Harassed Need a Complaint System with Both Formal and Informal Options." *Negotiation Journal,* 1990, *6*(2), 161–172.

Stephenson, M. A., Jr., and Pops, G. M. "Public Administrators and Conflict Resolution: Democratic Theory, Administrative Capacity, and the Case of Negotiated Rule-Making." In M. K. Mills (Ed.), *Alternative Dispute Resolution in the Public Sector.* Chicago: Nelson-Hall, 1991.

Susskind, L. E. "A Negotiation Credo for Controversial Sitting Disputes." *Negotiation Journal,* 1990, *6*(4), 309–314.

Susskind, L. E., Babbitt, E. F., and Segal, P. N. "When ADR Becomes the Law: A Review of Federal Practice." *Negotiation Journal*, 1993, 9(1), 59–75.

Susskind, L. E., and Cruikshank, J. *Breaking the Impasse: Consensual Approaches to Resolving Public Disputes*. New York: Basic Books, 1987.

Ury, W. *Getting Past No: Negotiating with Difficult People*. New York: Bantam Books, 1991.

Ury, W. L., Brett, J. M., and Goldberg, S. B. *Getting Disputes Resolved: Designing Systems to Cut the Costs of Conflict*. San Francisco: Jossey-Bass, 1989.

Wall, J. A., Jr., and Lynn, A. "Mediation: A Current Review." *Journal of Conflict Resolution*, 1993, 37(1), 160–194.

Williams, G. R. *Legal Negotiation and Settlement*. St. Paul, MN: West, 1983.

—◁⌁▷—

Lisa Blomgren Bingham is the Keller-Runden Professor of Public Service at Indiana University's School of Public and Environmental Affairs, Bloomington, Indiana.

CHAPTER TWENTY ONE

Seeing Your Way

Why Leaders Must Communicate
Their Visions

Talula Cartwright
David Baldwin

A vision has to be shared in order to do what it is meant to do: inspire, clarify, and focus the work of the organization. One part of a leader's job is to create commitment to the organization's vision. To do this, leaders must communicate the vision effectively in ways that will help others understand it, remember it, and share it.

Leaders in today's organizations face issues of growth, change, customization, globalization, and technology that force them to create new pathways toward success and sustainability. But a newly blazed strategic trail cannot itself create the focus, the underlying tactics, and the foresight necessary for long-term growth and deep impact. Many organizations that falter have failed to effectively communicate their strategies. As a result, employees do not understand their role in implementing the organization's mission and strategy.

Originally published as "Seeing Your Way: Why Leaders Must Communicate Their Visions," *Leadership in Action* (pp. 15–24). (July/August, 2007).

Leaders can adopt many tactics for coordinating messages and creating alignment among employees, whether at the unit, team, or organizational level. One effective tactic is to transmit strategic intent through a vision—an imagined or discerned future state that clearly captures the organization's direction and defines its destination.

What is a vision? It describes some achievement or future state that the organization will accomplish or realize. It inspires, clarifies, and focuses the work of an organization for a specific time. A vision differs from goals, which express the steps of a plan for accomplishing an objective. A vision differs from a mission statement, which explains an organization's reasons for existence or for seeking its objectives.

Whatever your organization's vision may be, communicating it is a unique challenge. Employees may disagree about organizational values or may be unwilling to change or to be influenced in a particular direction. They may misunderstand the leader's intent or have trouble imagining the future state expressed in the vision. Effective communication of the vision is vital.

Although there are distinctions to be made between vision, mission, and goals, the same strategies and techniques for communication are applicable to all three. One part of a leader's job is to create commitment to and alignment with the organization's picture of future success. Communicating this vision throughout the organization is essential to moving the organization forward.

To inspire commitment to a vision, a leader needs to have an effective way to communicate it. Presumably, the leader supports the vision and can draw on his or her personal passion and professional commitment to be dynamic in presenting it to others. Leaders who are perceived to be dynamic have a passion about something and speak about it often. Leaders should be this dynamic about the vision. Many people attribute their organization's vision to the people in leadership roles. If leaders stop talking about the vision, it becomes more difficult to see.

Leaders can never communicate too much. They should treat every communication effort as though it is their most important attempt at getting the message out. People may not hear the message the first time around, so when they finally do hear it, they are likely to think that's the first time the leader has said anything about it. This is especially true when a leader introduces a new vision. People need time and multiple opportunities to hear the message and to separate it from the noise of change. It takes more than one memo or speech to capture attention and build support. Intersperse the vision throughout regular conversations, be dynamic, and communicate continuously.

STORY TIME

Stories give life to a vision and help people see and remember it. They give integrity to the vision by grounding it in common values and truths. Telling stories creates trust and captures the hearts and minds of the audience. Stories establish common ground between the teller (the leader with a vision, in this case) and the audience (managers, employees, stakeholders, customers, other leaders, and anyone else associated with the organization). A story is a powerful tool for disseminating a vision; people share the story with others, creating a ripple effect.

Stories galvanize people around a cause and give them confidence as they move forward in the face of uncertainty. Stories are powerful, dynamic, and necessary for communicating a vision. Leaders do not always have the time or opportunity to tell them as often as they might like or need to, but that doesn't mean they shouldn't try to communicate the vision briefly, clearly, and with conviction at every opportunity.

Leaders have many informal opportunities to communicate their visions: a few minutes at the water cooler or in line at the cafeteria, a quick visit to the mailroom or customer service department, a company celebration, even a walk through the parking lot at the end of the workday. The message may be short, but the impact over time and through repetition can be powerful.

CONSTANT REMINDERS

In an instant-access, always-on world of cell phones and personal digital assistants, tried-and-true communication channels and tactics such as posters and business card reminders may sound quaint. But the more channels you open, the better your chances of communicating.

Put pithy reminders wherever you can—coffee mugs, T-shirts, letterheads, computer screen savers, luggage tags, pencils, file cabinet magnets, suggestion box prizes, notepads—anywhere that will keep the message first and foremost in the minds of your employees, stakeholders, and customers. You can even embed the vision in your organization's performance and leadership development activities so that employees can associate their personal goals with the organization's future success.

To use all these media effectively, state the vision briefly. People remember small phrases. Communicating a vision is like making a sales pitch. You want people in the organization to believe in the vision and pass it on to others. You want it to be infectious.

Some leaders feel embarrassed or uneasy about the selling required to communicate a vision. Even when it comes to their personal visions for success, some leaders feel uncomfortable promoting ideas because they are uncomfortable promoting themselves. But as a leader representing a vision, you are at the front of the curve. You are an early adopter. You already support the vision, but others may not know enough about it even to see it, much less support it. It is part of the leader's job to inform and persuade.

PERSONAL TOUCH

Another effective strategy for communicating your vision is to make it personal, to engage others in one-on-one conversations. Personal connections are extraordinarily effective conduits for communication. They give leaders opportunities to transmit information, receive feedback, build support, and create energy around the vision. Developing these relationships requires skill at communicating a compelling and clear vision of the future. When individuals gain a personal understanding of where the organization is and where it wants to go, they are more apt to join in on the journey and champion the cause.

Leaders can inspire themselves and others by tapping into their personal visions. For example, someone with a personal vision of leadership that includes serving others so that more caring and appreciation can be brought into the world can inject the core of that vision into conversations about conflict, influence, power, strategy, empowerment, and many other leadership topics. Just a mention in the context of personal relationships can inform others and inspire them to think of the purpose and vision for their own leadership. It can keep them inspired, inviting their rededication to their own vision.

OTHER WAYS

Here are some other suggestions for continuously and dynamically painting a picture of the future:

> *Draw a crowd.* Identify key players, communicators, stakeholders, and supporters throughout the organization who will motivate others to listen to, reflect on, and be engaged with the vision.
>
> *Map your ground.* Create a formal communication strategy, and give a team the power and resources to implement it. Put a team in place to educate new staff members about the vision.
>
> *Stay on the sunny side.* Remain positive about the vision. Pass along positive gossip; correct misinterpretations. People are going to talk; you have to decide what you want them to talk about.
>
> *Be everywhere your message can be.* Visit different locations in your organization, whether that means a trip to the mailroom or a flight to the other side of the world. Make your presence known on your organization's intranet. Create a blog. Be the visible ambassador of your organization's vision—the champion of its success.
>
> *Make it meaningful.* Sponsor contests and celebrations that encourage employees to own a part of the vision. Help them create the future, not wait for it.
>
> *Make memories.* Create metaphors, figures of speech, and slogans, and find creative ways to use them. Write a theme song or a memorable motto.
>
> *Mind the gap.* Explicitly and quickly address vision inconsistencies. Resistance to change may not be the issue—it may be that people have not heard the message or have misunderstood it. Be patient, move forward, and bring them along.
>
> *Notice the good deed.* Reward behavior and actions that demonstrate and reflect the vision. Create curiosity and reward involvement.
>
> *See how the other half lives.* Imagine that your employees are customers. Give them the message you want them to hear. Help them see the vision so they can join in the journey.

Open a joint account. Connect the vision to real business outcomes if you lead a commercial enterprise or to tangible results and impact if you lead a nonprofit.

Keep to the FAQs. Employ technology, such as a knowledge base accessible through the web or your organization's intranet, to answer questions from employees, customers, and stakeholders. Assign responsibility for responding.

Talk it up. Communicate, communicate, communicate. You cannot put your message out too often.

Back it up. If the message is out there, make sure people can see that it reflects real change. If they see one thing and hear another, your credibility is shot and your vision is dead.

FOLLOW THE LEAD

Effective leaders learn from example and experience. The following instances provide lessons and ideas for action:

Keep the vision simple and easy to remember. When Nike coined the phrase "just do it," these three words motivated the company's own staff even as they challenged the world to engage.

Tie the vision to specific and obvious organizational values. In 1939, Bill Hewlett and Dave Packard started a business in a garage. Over time they created a way of doing business that came to be called the HP Way. It was an ideology of respect for the individual, affordable quality and reliability, and commitment to community responsibility.

> One of the most important things any communicator ever learns is to design a message for the intended audience.

Build meaning by giving individuals a personal connection to the vision. Mary Kay saw a way to enrich the lives of women not just through offering women cosmetic products but also by making it possible for them to become entrepreneurs themselves.

Customize the benefits of the vision to each stakeholder group. Acknowledge the differences between groups while making connections that show how all the pieces of the organization allow the vision to become reality. The U.S. Army's former slogan,

"Army of One," appealed to the individual soldier's needs and desires, highlighting individual strengths while connecting the soldier to the larger army organization.

Make the vision attractive and motivating. Consider Google's mission of organizing the world's information and making it universally accessible and useful.

Walk the talk. CEO Herb Kelleher of Southwest Airlines took on the role of baggage carrier, flight attendant, and customer service agent a few times each year to stay abreast of the challenges his employees faced.

Make certain you demonstrate your belief in the vision. When former Chrysler chairman Lee Iacocca approached the U.S. government seeking loans for a bailout, Congress was not impressed. But Iacocca had done his homework, and he argued that Chrysler's collapse would cost the country $2.75 billion in unemployment benefits alone. His speech persuaded Congress to lend the money. Iacocca cut his own salary to $1 a year as a testament to his vision that Chrysler could turn around.

OPPOSING FORCES

In your efforts to communicate a vision, you may encounter resistance from your audience. Such circumstances increase the difficulty of your task, but there are positive ways to work through them.

One of the most important things any communicator ever learns is to design a message for the intended audience. It's natural to wish that your audience would be supportive, but if it is not, there's no point in pretending that it is. You must prepare your message for the audience you have. When listeners are resistant, it is often because there is a competing priority. Consider the following example:

In response to a written survey a college's faculty members over-whelmingly said that they would be willing to give up their reserved parking places next to the building in order to be more egalitarian and less elitist. The idea was to give the best spaces to the students, in an effort to be student-centered. When faculty members continued using these spaces, the college president was frustrated. Even when he gave up his own parking space, the faculty continued to resist. Finally, after conducting some additional informal surveys on the golf course and in the cafeteria, the president realized that taking away the parking spaces would be taking away the only visible symbol the faculty members had of their importance and value to the college.

A person who is leading a change must over-communicate—that is, communicate patiently again and again, on different levels, using different media. It is difficult and time consuming to lead people out of their resistance. The vision is distant and indistinct. The resistance is here and now. Over-communication is one of the answers. It takes a stalwart leader to demonstrate the continuing patience needed to deal with resistance, and it takes a dynamic leader to engender the enthusiasm needed to lead people into the new vision. At the same time that the leader is patiently over-communicating, he or she must start building the concrete part of the vision that the resistant audience can finally claim as its own.

> The college president put numbered spaces at the far end of the parking lot and put up signs forbidding anyone except the owner of a space from parking there before 9:00 a.m. He had the "reserved" label on the spaces near the building painted over, and he sent out a list of space assignments in the distant lot, based on seniority. The number one space (also the farthest from the building) was for the person who had been with the college the longest. Deans and directors got no additional consideration.

A dynamic leader is one who has a passion and talks about it frequently. In communicating a vision, this means not only talking about the intended result but also speaking passionately about the process of getting there. It may be a long time before some of the audience members get to the vision, but if they can buy into the process in the meantime, that will help move them along.

> The college president and his executive staff came up with a mission statement about students being the top priority, the maintenance team put up banners with the mission statement on them, and the student government started a nomination program to honor people who had gone "above and beyond." The president didn't talk about the parking issue any more. He got the newspaper to run a big ad about the new mission, and the paper followed up with a feature article. People continued to joke about the parking, and some faculty members

continued to come to work at 7:00 a.m. so they could get a space next to the building, but slowly the problem diminished. And as it did, the enthusiasm for and pride in the new mission and vision increased.

Resistance shows up in unexpected ways. It's important to remember that it usually represents a competing priority and to figure out a way to address that priority. It's critical to keep communicating in as many ways as possible and to be patient. Some people won't buy in until you've said your message over and over, and when they finally do buy in, as far as they're concerned, that's the first time you've said it. So keep talking, patiently and passionately.

LIGHTING THE WAY

Having a vision but not communicating it isn't much of an improvement over not having a vision at all. A vision has to be shared in order to do the things it is meant to do: inspire, clarify, and focus the work of your organization. Remember that as a leader you're in the role of an early adopter. Your job is to communicate the vision to others in ways that will help them understand it, remember it, and then go on to share it themselves. In this way the vision can become a bright lantern leading your organization toward its future.

―〰〰―

At time of original printing Talula Cartwright was an enterprise associate and senior faculty member at the Center for Creative Leadership.

At time of original printing David Baldwin was a former faculty member at the Center for Creative Leadership in San Diego.

CHAPTER TWENTY-TWO

Seven Communication Tips an Effective Leader Must Have

William F. Kumuyi

I f persuasion is what you want, the email, voice mail, telephone, and telefax are "poor" channels. If you want to put your workers on the vision trip, look into their eyes and tell them your mission.

Small things have great effects. For example, communication is something every Dick and Harry does. Yet, it carries such a great deterministic power that the success or failure of any union depends on its proper use! Bad or no communication trips collective balance and unleashes disintegration. For example, communication failure among European powers was essentially responsible for the outbreak of World War I, some historians say. And in an organization, it's easy to see how a communication failure can wreck things up. It

---

Originally published as "Seven Communication Tips an Effective Leader Must Have," *New African* (July/August/September 2007).
Copyright International Communications, August/September 2007.
Provided by ProQuest Information and Learning Company. All Rights Reserved.

taxes the organization along the path of division for a sorry flight to workers' disloyalty, apathy, and aloofness. The organization's fibers wouldn't cohere; and the lack of cohesion would hinder motivation for progress, workers would work for the pay: but they would be unwilling to go the extra mile to achieve anything extraordinary for the organization. The vision trip then would have on board a bunch of grumbling, petty, uncommitted men. Men ever ready to jump ship at the least tolling of billows!

Conversely, good communication ensures corporate home stasis and helps move things up. It gives rise to a bond of peace, a pervasive sense of fraternity, unity and mutualism. The effect of all this is internal cohesion; which helps inject workers with motivation for progress. This make the vision trip a jolly ride of one happy throng. The end is all-round growth for the organization. Leadership communications, therefore, passing a message to an audience by any appropriate means such that the audience understands the message, accepts it and reacts to it according to the sender's expectation! I admit this is a rather stringent view of effective communication in that it includes persuasion and attitude change in the effects.

Many leaders may agree that good communication results in suc-cessful transmission, acceptance, and understanding of information or a message. But some may frown at the idea that it must result in persuasion. Their experience won't agree with this prediction. For many a leader can remember various instances when communication fails to move people to any action leading to change. I won't deny such a failure occurs. But while some of the people may choose to shrug off the charm of effective communication, the majority often succumbs to it. The *Bullet Theory* of communication doesn't always hold. But that doesn't mean its claims are totally false. Other things being equal, when messages are communicated effectively, they catch.

It isn't, however, my purpose to explore rare cases of communi-cation failure. I'm out to share with you the factors of good commu-nication that enhance organizational growth and stability—factors that most leaders can testify play a crucial workplace role in calming storms, fueling zeal, and making the workforce go marching as to war.

Now effective communication isn't necessarily a function of elo-quence or oratory. You don't need to be a Cicero in order to be a good communicator-leader. Fluency does help: and eloquence can play the catalyst. But the effective communicator requires more than gift of gab. A lot of wordsmiths with feline tongue and nimble pen are bad communicators. Figurative language, good phrasing, and flawless grammar may count as inputs of good communication, but they are not the hub. To get anticipated results through communication in leadership, here are seven things you must do.

EXAMINE THE MESSAGE

Ensure that you prepare your message well. By this I mean: make it right in both content and context. Simple, it seems! But I'm not sure all leaders take all pains to tidy the content and context of their messages before sending them. By context I mean the human factors controlling delivery of the message. Certainly not all leaders possess and apply the diligence of Winston Churchill that helps ensure an oral or written communication is strong, deep, sensible, and credible enough to galvanize its audience. Churchill spent hours rewriting and rehearsing his speeches. No wonder they contributed to Britain's resilience and victory in World War II.

I guess every leader knows what he wants to say and gets the content right either on paper or in oral speech. But how many of us worry about how our messages may impact the sensibilities of our audience? In delivering his or her message, the leader should consider the emotional intelligence of the audience, their capacity to receive, understand, and react to dissonant messages without feeling dehumanized. Naturally, nobody suffers criticisms gladly. And everybody wants to hear what they like to hear. If you're always hitting the people with the bullets of brutal facts, you can't convince them to buy into your plans. Yes, you're the boss and you can fire dissenters. But dissenters know they can be fired, so they hide. The upshot of this is the emergence of a hibernating, discontent, disloyal workforce. This is one reason why many change efforts fail. The workforce kills the dream.

It isn't easy to inspire the workforce with a barrage of bare facts lampooning their shortcomings. You would only succeed in whipping up self-pity, anger, despair, and forlorn. Imagine a leader seeking to increase employees' productivity in order to trigger growth. Here is a part of this address to his line officers. (Let's call him Mr. Frank.)

MR. FRANK: "I must say I'm not impressed one bit about your performances. The last quarter has witnessed rapid reduction in turnover and actual sales, and you line officers show no concern. The workforce is docile and wrapped up in slothfulness—and you line officers don't bother. Now, I won't stay here as CEO fiddle-playing while this great organization drowns in red. Some of you will be laid off.... At least, that will proved to the lazy drones that we mean business...."

Not even in the military will such bare facts inspire or motivate anyone to give his or her total best. Mr. Frank spoke with tongue dipped in gall. He was unmindful of the human context of his message. I bet those officers would leave the meeting with one idea: It's time to look elsewhere for a job. Hard facts need to be delivered with understanding of human sensibilities and frailty.

The right context would demand that Mr. Frank reword his message and "cool" the tone and mood of its delivery. With graceful tone and concerned but non-vindictive mood, he could make his message more persuasive and less scathing, thus:

MR. FRANK: "Our performances haven't been too encouraging. See, the last quarter has witnessed rapid reduction in turnover and actual sales—and I suppose all of us are worried by the sharp decline. Our workforce can perform better so I would want to know what else the organization can do to increase productivity. This is my duty as CEO. Let's act fast. For a continuous decline in a company's fortunes will in the end result in downsizing. However, I believe we can move things up and avoid the pain of lay-offs...."

Whether in writing or speaking, effective communicator-leaders weigh their words and put them in context. Of course, effective communication doesn't foreclose rebuke and reprimands. But an effective leader would rein in deviants in plain words shorn of insults.

ESTABLISH THE RIGHT WORKING CLIMATE

Working climate relates to how the workers are treated and valued. It shows in the quality and type of relationship that exists between the leader and the workforce. Dr. John A. Kline, the academic provost of Air University, has identified three basic climates: (1) dehumanized, (2) over-humanized, and (3) situational.

The first climate treats workers as machines, discourages initiatives and creativity, and thrives on command-and-control structures. The second climate places workers' personal welfare above organizational goals. It advocates promotion of workers' self-worth, avoids schism, and favors decision-making by consensus. The third climate combines features of dehumanized and over-humanized climates. It's an approach that harmonizes individual and organizational goals. I call it "fair deal" climate. This approach ensures workers are "whipped" into line when the situation demands maximum control. And when it's necessary to adjust the organization's policy to boost workers' satisfaction, it's done. Each climate has its own catalytic effect on effective communication in the workplace. I won't dwell on the effects here; but will tell you the best approach leaders seeking success should use.

If you seek to excel in using communication as a human influence strategy, I recommend the "situational climate." It confers credibility on the leadership because of the fair-deal equitable symbiotic relationship it fosters. Owing to the leader's sincerity and fairness, the audience is more positively exposed and responsive to his messages. For this reason, strategic communication under "situational climate" probably is the most effective for real organizational change.

ENGAGE THE RIGHT CHANNEL

In this modern time of a vast array of communication technology, leaders are tempted to adopt the cheapest, fastest, and safest technology to send their messages. Writing in *The Technology Management Handbook* (1998), Dr. Terry Pearce, the leadership communication scholar, noted that: "There seems to be general agreement that some messages just do not lend themselves to technology." Such messages are communications intended to inspire people to go for change. Studies have shown that no medium has the power of human speech delivered face-to-face with the audience.

Research by Albert Mehrabian (of the University of California, Los Angeles) in the 1970s on how people understand and draw conclusions about what they hear showed that people rely on the words only for 7 percent of their judgment, 38 percent on voice quality, and 55 percent from other physical cues such as gestures, body movements, space, etc. Thus, in regard to persuasion, the email, voice mail, telephone and telefax are "poor" channels. If you want to put your workers on the vision trip, look into their eyes and tell them your mission.

EMPATHIZE WITH THE AUDIENCE

Leaders who operate aloof of the people, pass the buck but keep the bucks and look for scapegoats, can't use communication for persuasive end. If you didn't identify with the problem, the workforce would perceive your motivation as condemnation and seek defense.

Walter Dill Scott, the former president of Northwestern University, observed that: "Every idea, concept, or conclusion which enters the mind is held as true unless hindered by some contradictory idea." Thus, if one grain of a contradictory idea is allowed in the gambit of a message, the chance of its acceptance dips.

For example, if your audience is moved to say: "No Sir, we aren't totally at fault" at the beginning of your talk, you have moved them into a condition of rejection. That is why the world's famous master of oratory. Dale Carnegie, in his best-selling book, *Effective Public Speaking*, advised communicators to keep their audience yes-minded. One way of doing this is to launch your message with a common point of view. This is the wisdom America's celebrated president, Abraham Lincoln, often adopted. "My way of opening and winning an argument," revealed Lincoln, "is to first find a common ground of agreement."

Be wary of buck-passing when discussing a problem or sharing a challenge. Tactical collectivism in communication helps galvanize group cooperation by neutralizing opposition. Don't look for scapegoats if you want to turn your workforce into change agents.

EXPRESS YOURSELF TO IMPRESS YOUR AUDIENCE

You must express your mind in such a way that your audience is impressed and moved to do your bidding. To do this, you must demonstrate conviction and faith by your tone and flaunt enthusiasm by your manner. You must sound sure before you can assure your audience. Let your voice ring with contagious enthusiasm.

Dale Carnegie advised that: "If you would impress an audience, be impressed yourself." Your attitude to your own message will determine your audience's attitude to it. Unless you are sufficiently motivated and can show it, you will never be able to motivate others. So, as you speak or write, be earnest. Stir up yourself. Keep your hairs up.

EMPLOY THE APPROPRIATE LANGUAGE

Clarity is the first law in leadership communication. Choose words that say exactly what you mean and can appeal to your audience's emotions without throwing up a semantic blur. Often, when communication fails to catch, it's because the audience members don't comprehend the message or they aren't pinched by it owing to inappropriate diction.

Carnegie's book, *Effective Public Speaking*, suggests using concrete, familiar words that create pictures. People are soon put off by colorless phraseology and bland abstract expressions that feed listeners' souls with boredom.

Let your words conjure images. Send your audience into dreaming. Massage their imagination. Abraham Lincoln was a master at this. Hear his objection to the long, complicated reports he received daily at the White House: "When I send a man to buy a horse, I don't want to be told how many hairs the horse has in his tail. I wish only to know the points." How visual! His words call up pictures and stick up like glue.

William Strunk, Jr., in his book, *The Elements of Style*, wrote: "The greatest writers ... are effective largely because they deal in particulars.... Their words call up pictures." The French philosopher Alain, said: "An abstract style is always bad. Your sentences should be full of stones, metals, chairs, tables, animals, men and women." Effective communication calls for painstaking search, selection, and stringing of picture-building words.

EXPECT FEEDBACK

Communication is an exchange, not a monologue. As a process, it isn't complete and fulfilling until the receiver has given his response to the message of the sender. You can't be sure that your message has been received and understood if you received no response. Many times, however, leaders don't pause for their subordinates to respond to their communications before they close the talk. Later, they wonder why the workforce doesn't behave as envisaged.

Without feedback, communication is reduced to a give; but the giver may never know what impact his "gift" has made on the receiver. "The link of feedback," writes Professor Anthony D'souza of the Haggai Institute, "completes the chain of communication."

One of the major factors of communication failure is the neglect of feedback. The boss issues an instruction, growls at the end, "Have you got that?" and ends the talk without waiting for the addressee's reply and reaction!

Such communication only results in frustration as staff scoot off to do what they feel is the leader's directive—only to end up making painful mistakes.

I agree we all do this and seem to get by, especially in minor daily leadership routines. But when a specific far-reaching change is our goal, there must be plentiful interactive communication. Leadership communication for change thrives on negotiation. The leader must lay out his or her vision, allow some haggling, and close the deal with the people's "aye."

Feedback, however, may be misleading. Subordinates may hide their feelings and give the impression that they are in agreement with the leader's views, especially if they fear a different opinion might offend the leader.

Therefore, to receive accurate feedback you must do three things. One, you must desire it. Let the workforce know you sincerely cherish their feelings and views about any communications they receive from you.

Two, you must demand it. Don't just speak to or speak with. Ask the group or person what he or she thinks about what you're saying. Or build feedback promptings into the message. For example, in sharing a vision for the organization's expansion, you might share your plans, inviting your employees' contributions.

You might say: "I can see it's time we re-invented our organization to maintain our share of the market. I'm looking at our brands and sales outlets, our marketing and customer retention strategies. All seem out of tune with the changing landscape and are crying for overhauling . . . . Or what do you think?"

But if your staff know that you're averse to contrary opinions, they would shy from giving any. Therefore, the third thing you must do is demonstrate your sincerity about listening to opinions of others.

To listen effectively, however, you must keep an open mind, avoid prejudice, separate ideas from factual details, keep the man and the message separately, and avoid speculative cut-ins. When listening to your subordinates, just listen.

EXPEL THE BARRIERS

No matter how skilful a leader is in communication, he wouldn't influence many people by it unless he removes certain barriers. These are inhibitions that limit the power of communication as a weapon of organizational influence. The barriers are associated with the sender, the channel, and the audience, respectively. Details on these barriers can be found in the relevant literature; only an outline of them will be attempted here.

The sender (the leaders) must avoid the wrong attitude. Don't be judgmental, hostile, touchy, impatient, rash, proud, domineering, and vindictive. Otherwise, your audience may accept and treat your message with deception, pessimism, and disbelief.

Argument is another barrier. Avoid it with your subordinates as much as possible. For you may win the points but lose the person. Also, watch against information overload, illogical presentation, abstract language, and ambiguous diction. Above all, in cases of interpersonal communication, ensure that your verbal and non-verbal cues rhyme.

For example, don't say "Well done" with a frown or "Is there any way I can help?" in a sarcastic tone. For channel-related barriers, the leader should ensure that the medium is functioning well.

A malfunctioning system not only hinders smooth passage of the message, but may also distort meaning. Moreover, the channel and the message should match. Inappropriate channels can diminish the intrinsic power of a message.

Finally, the audience-related barriers: these are barriers the receiver may deliberately or inadvertently erect. Three of such barriers are explained by what is called the "selectivity theory."

First, there is selective exposure by which people choose which communication they would receive or reject. Second, there is selective perception by which people choose to understand some communication and misunderstand others. Your workers may adopt selective perception if they see they can't practice selective exposure.

The third is selective retention by which people choose to retain in their memory certain messages they like, and wipe off their minds those they detest. If your workers choose to forget your message, the chance of influencing them in any way is nil.

However, audience-related barriers can be removed by creating and adopting appropriate working climate and applying the basic communication rules we have been discussing.

The road to effective communication has no shortcut. But those who keep learning and practicing will get there.

———

On the completion of his post-graduate study program, Pastor Kumuyi became a lecturer in the Department of Mathematics at the University of Lagos in 1973.

CHAPTER TWENTY-THREE

Nonprofits and Evaluation
Managing Expectations
from the Leader's Perspective

Salavatore P. Alaimo

he late Peter Drucker stated that "every knowledge worker in a modern organization is an 'executive' if, by virtue of his position of knowledge, he is responsible for a contribution that materially affects the capacity of the organization to perform and obtain results" (1967, p. 5). This definition aptly fits an executive director (ED) who assumes the top hierarchical position and is typically the highest-paid staff in a nonprofit 501(c)(3) organization. The ED plays an important role in shaping the organization's vision (Lynch, 1993), leading their organization's strategic planning process (Dym and Hutson, 2005) and ensuring the organization has the necessary financial resources to operate in an ever-changing environment (Herman and Heimovics, 1991). The ED is ultimately responsible for management of the financial, human, and capital resources the organization requires to deliver programs and work toward satisfying its mission.

Originally published as "Nonprofits and Evaluation: Managing Expectations from the Leader's Perspective. In J. G. Carman and K. A. Fredericks (Eds.), *Nonprofits and Evaluation. New Directions for Evaluation, 119.* (Fall 2008).

EDs face the challenge of managing the political environment, which has them accountable to myriad stakeholders (Tschirhart, 1996), including their board, staff, volunteers, consumers, community, funding organizations, accreditation organizations, government agencies, and others, some of whom may have competing demands for the ED and the organization. In theory, the ED balances these accountabilities while integrating the organization's mission, acquiring adequate financial resources, and managing the strategic direction for the future of the organization (Herman and Heimovics, 2005). EDs of nonprofit organizations ideally would also effectively lead their organizations by influencing members to achieve a common goal (Northouse, 2004), remain competitive, and reach their full potential. Some desirable leadership traits include being proactive (Lynch, 1993), communicating effectively (Denhardt, Denhardt, and Aristigueta, 2002), and aligning personality and behavior with the organization's culture (Dym and Hutson, 2005).

One specific challenge EDs of nonprofit human service organizations face is demonstrating the effectiveness of their programs. The capacity to evaluate such programs requires, first, an understanding of the internal and external organizational context with regard to the political environment, organizational culture, and processes for making decisions. Second, it requires organizational structures such as documentation, reporting and communications systems, and learning structures that enable evaluation capacity building (ECB). Third, it requires resources such as funding, personnel, and information (Volkov and King, 2005).[1] This study examines the role forty-two EDs have played in building capacity for having their organizations' programs evaluated. Also, Volkov and King's (2005) evaluation capacity building checklist is used as the basis for analyzing two cases of organizations that have been successful at building evaluation capacity.

LEADERSHIP AND ORGANIZATIONAL CULTURE

Organizational culture comprises shared values, ideas, beliefs, assumptions, norms, artifacts, and patterns of behavior (Ivancevich, Szilagyi, and Wallace, 1977; Ott, 1989; Schein, 1992). Such culture is defined as

"... the importance for people of symbolism—rituals, myths, stories, and legends—and about the interpretation of events, ideas, and experiences that are influenced and shaped by the groups within which they live" (Frost, Moore, Louis, Lundberg, and Martin, 1985, p. 17). Schein's definition noticeably includes references to internal and external environments, "a pattern of shared basic assumptions that the group has learned as it solved problems of external adaptation and internal integration . . . ." (1992, p. 12)

The culture of a nonprofit organization is largely built on the ED's values, activities, and tasks, which are inculcated in staff and other stakeholders (Hay, 1990). Congruence should exist between values and operating norms for an organization to be successful (Anthes, 1987). Culture and strategy are linked; affecting an organization's culture will likely influence the strategic direction and the ability to achieve its goals (Davis, 1984; Hay, 1990). Therefore leaders must align the organizational values and culture to support that strategy (Kaplan and Norton, 2006). Alignment can help leaders overcome such constraints as resistance from stakeholders, organizational life cycles, poor communication, lack of stakeholder development, subjective interpretation of issues, and bad timing due to an organizational crisis (Nord, 1985). Leaders must be able to handle the personal and professional discomfort that typically comes with the reflection and introspection necessary for effective cultural change (Block, 2004). Then they can be the catalyst for change through symbolism and modeling behavior that has an impact on their organization's vision, strategy, operations, and performance.

COURSES OF ACTION FOR PROGRAM EVALUATION

EDs face the challenge of conforming to environmental constraints while attempting to develop a more favorable environment for their organization (Pfeffer and Salancik, 2003). This leadership and management challenge suggests that leaders of organizations must constantly measure their organization's performance (Nanus and Dobbs, 1999). Program effectiveness is increasingly factored into funding decisions, and it requires balancing with fiscal responsibility for overall organizational accountability (Brinkerhoff, 2000; Carlson and Donohoe, 2003; Gray and Stockdill, 1995; Mesch and McClelland, 2006; Werther and Berman, 2001).

There are four primary courses of action EDs can choose to meet the challenge for program evaluation. First, they may choose to do nothing. If their organization is financially sound, and they view program evaluation solely as a means to satisfy external stakeholders and acquire financial resources, they may not recognize the need for it. This also can be a choice if the expense of evaluation is greater than, or a large percentage of, the potential revenue associated with it. EDs might desire to have their programs evaluated but may feel forced to do nothing because their organizations do not have the capacity.

Second, they may choose to engage in evaluating programs for the sole purpose of meeting the demands of external stakeholders such as funding organizations, government agencies, and accreditation organizations. This is characterized as an *external pull.* EDs will likely allow these demands to drive the evaluation process. Resource dependency is a powerful influence on nonprofit leaders because their organizations are open systems that rely on external resources.

Third, EDs may decide to develop an intrinsically motivated effort for program evaluation focused on organizational learning and a culture of continuous improvement and driven by the organization's mission. This is characterized as an *internal push.* EDs typically already are engaged in the first step toward building intrinsic motivation among their internal stakeholders by communicating their organization's vision, mission, and strategy (Kaplan and Norton, 2006). The key to embedding program evaluation in this effort is for the ED to communicate that it is an effective tool for determining the organization's progress toward accomplishing the vision, mission, and strategy.

Last, EDs may choose to integrate the demands from the external pull into the efforts of the internal push in an attempt to manage and balance both. The ED choosing this course balances the importance of satisfying external stakeholders and acquiring resources with retaining autonomy and the direction of the organization's mission. Balancing the external and internal organizational contexts is important for effective evaluation capacity building. Integration of external demands and support from the organization's leadership are both critical for successful ECB (Volkov and King, 2005).

Inclusion of the internal push also enables an organization to work toward mainstreaming evaluation, " . . . the process of making evaluation an integral part of an organization's everyday operations" and " . . . part of the organization's work ethic, its culture, and job responsibilities at all levels" (Sanders, 2003, p. 3).

MEETING THE CHALLENGES FOR PROGRAM EVALUATION

Organizations desiring to engage in program evaluation face the challenge of building evaluation capacity. Evaluation capacity is defined as "human capital (skills, knowledge, experience, etc.) and financial/material resources" that are necessary for the practice of evaluation (Boyle, Lemaire, and Rist, 1999, p. 5). ECB is defined as "the intentional work to continuously create and sustain overall organizational processes that make quality evaluation and its uses routine" (Stockdill, Baizerman, and Compton, 2002, p. 1). Volkov and King (2005) offer three main elements for ECB: *organizational context, structures,* and *resources.* EDs can face the typical challenge of lack of stakeholder skills or expertise, funding, or other resources (Dym and Hutson, 2005; Paddock, 2001) and play an important role in ECB by allocating the necessary *resources* for the evaluation process, including personnel, facilities, funds, equipment, software, and time (Mesch and McClelland, 2006; Sonnichsen, 1999; Stufflebeam, 2002; United Way of America, 1996; Volkov and King, 2005; Werther and Berman, 2001). They can also develop *structures* conducive for ECB, such as an ECB plan, inclusion of evaluation in organizational policies and procedures, a system for reporting and monitoring, and incorporation of a feedback mechanism and effective communication system (Stufflebeam, 2002; Volkov and King, 2005). Organizational culture is an important factor for ECB and for participation in program evaluation (Grudens-Schuck, 2003; Marais, 1998; Mesch and McClelland, 2006; Poole, Davis, Reisman, and Nelson, 2001). EDs can recognize their internal and external *organizational contexts* by building an internal supportive culture for ECB while integrating the demands from external stakeholders (Volkov and King, 2005).

One example of a cultural challenge may be political tension between evaluation stakeholders (Murray, 2005; Oster, 1995; Paddock, 2001; Thomas, 2005) and potential stakeholder incongruence on what composes effectiveness (Herman and Renz, 1997). Evaluation involves making value judgments, which is inherently political (Palumbo, 1987; Weiss, 1998).

Programs are developed through political decisions (Weiss, 1987), and thus the reasons programs are evaluated are also political (Weiss, 1998).

Another potential political tension involves whose interests are served by having the programs evaluated, which is inherently a component of any process seeking to measure effectiveness (Pfeffer and Salancik, 2003). Program evaluation is therefore contained within a political environment that should be recognized and effectively managed. EDs can do so by using evaluation as the means for assessing their organization's work toward accomplishing the mission, which can help diffuse personal agendas; fear of evaluation; and fear of a negative reflection on programs, the organization, or the stakeholders' work. An ED can help develop a culture for continuous improvement by ensuring stakeholders understand that perceived "negative" information about programs represents an opportunity for improvement and learning.

ORGANIZATIONAL LEARNING

Program evaluation can be used as the means for organizational learning (Gray and Stockdill, 1995; Preskill and Catsambas, 2006). Organizational learning involves learning from successes and failures and changing behavior due to encountering situations within an organization's environment. It involves individuals learning new ways to achieve their goals and sometimes involves individuals learning to change goals (Denhardt, Denhardt, and Aristigueta, 2002). Some scholars suggest that becoming a learning organization is necessary for adapting and being successful in the twenty-first century (Green, 2004; Senge, 1996). Evaluation becomes a part of organizational learning when it is institutionalized as part of the organization's information, power structure, processes, and systems that influence decision making and action (Boyle, Lemaire, and Rist, 1999).

Institutionalization of program evaluation within a learning framework requires that EDs ensure individual members learn, grow, and adapt in an encouraging and rewarding environment (Ott, 1989). Members should have access to information, an available feedback loop, and a learning process that contributes to improved performance (Mesch and McClelland, 2006).

Information must flow in both hierarchical directions for a nonprofit to be a learning organization (Drucker, 1990). Patton reminds us that "participation and collaboration can lead to ongoing, longer-term commitment to using evaluation logic and building a culture of learning in a program or organization" (1997, p. 100). Organizational learning is a socialization process driven by structures, systems, and culture. EDs should focus on building an infrastructure for learning that includes recording the organization's history; reflecting on successes, failures, and innovation; and incorporating learning into the organization's planning process (Senge, 1996).

This research proposes that an executive director as a leader and a manager is fundamental to investment in the organization's capacity for program evaluation. Several questions are investigated to support this proposition. What factors influence EDs' decisions with regard to program evaluation? How do they see their role in evaluation capacity building? Ultimately, what steps do EDs take to successfully build evaluation capacity for their organizations?

METHODOLOGY

This exploratory, qualitative study comprised forty-two one-on-one, face-to-face interviews with EDs of nonprofit human service organizations (NHSOs). They were conducted with twenty-one EDs each from the twenty-county Atlanta (Georgia) and nine-county Indianapolis (Indiana) metropolitan statistical areas (MSAs).

GuideStar, an online database (http://www.guidestar.org) containing information on public charities including their Internal Revenue Service (IRS) 990 forms, was used to develop the database from which the samples were drawn. Human services is the largest subsector in the United States classified by the National Taxonomy of Exempt Entities (NTEE); it comprises 31 percent of the 664,120 known nonprofits registered with the IRS.[2] This subsector was selected because of its policy and service domain for which there is substantial external pull for program evaluation from foundations, the United Way, government agencies, and accreditation organizations. The devolution of the federal government's provision of social services to the state level has increased reliance on NHSOs (Fredericks, Carman, and Birkland, 2002). The overall increasing competition for funding and demands for accountability present challenges to leaders who seek strategies to meet these demands and possibly build capacity to evaluate their programs.

A twenty-question, semi-structured, pre-tested questionnaire containing nondirective probes was used for the face-to-face interviews in both MSA samples. The forty-two interviews averaged approximately one hour, were recorded, transcribed, and analyzed using NVIVO7 software. In addition, two case studies of NHSOs were conducted to analyze their successful efforts to build evaluation capacity. These case studies are situation analyses involving interviews with key stakeholders, a review of organizational documentation, and attendance at evaluation-related committee meetings. The two organizations analyzed were intentionally chosen as potential models for ECB that other NHSOs may learn from.

SAMPLE CHARACTERISTICS

The forty-two NHSOs represent the great diversity of service delivery categories within human services, including those that serve senior citizens, youth, people with disabilities, and rape victims, and that deal with housing issues and adoption among others. Approximately 17 percent of the organizations are faith-based. The mean organizational income is $10,695,636, the median income is $2,148,380, and the range is from $136,962,789 to $284,634. All but one of the forty-two organizations (98 percent) have engaged in some effort to evaluate their program(s), ranging from acquiring informal consumer feedback to longitudinal studies that track consumer progress using internal and external benchmarks. Approximately 71 percent of the organizations have one or more government contracts with various federal, state, and county agencies.

The tenure of EDs ranges from just under one year to thirty-six years and averages eleven and a half years. More than half (52 percent) have a master's degree, while 40 percent have a bachelor's degree and the remaining 8 percent are high school graduates. The major concentration of studies for those with college degrees varies across thirteen areas, the two most frequent being social work (19 percent) and business (12 percent). Only one executive director has a master's degree in nonprofit management. More than three-quarters (76 percent) of the EDs have some previous instruction in evaluation, with 55 percent attending workshops or seminars, 10 percent taking college courses, and 11 percent experiencing both.

DATA AND FINDINGS: EXECUTIVE DIRECTOR INTERVIEWS

The results of the forty-two interviews begin with observations of the external pull versus internal push. This is followed by analysis of eight action steps taken by the EDs in varying degrees that contribute to evaluation capacity building.

External Pull Versus Internal Push

The challenge of balancing and managing the external pull with the internal push for program evaluation is a pervasive theme throughout the interviews. Some EDs suggest it is "what funders require" and that "the days of not evaluating programs are over." Others indicate they work hard to be driven by their organizational mission and goals rather than exclusively by the objectives of funders. A few discuss how they seek to improve and evolve their evaluation process, with some citing internal motivations, some external, and some both.

Approximately 60 percent of the EDs whose organizations receive government funding report that their government agencies require only output information such as dollars and the number of people served. Some discuss gaps between what their government agencies require for program evaluation and what they deem important to evaluate for their programs. One states that he tried unsuccessfully to get a state agency his organization contracts with, to be interested in program outcomes. Still others assert that there are other external pull mechanisms, such as state requirements for organizational accreditation, specific to their program areas.

Executive Director Actions for Program Evaluation

The extent to which these EDs managed the balancing of the external pull with the internal push for program evaluation resulted in eight possible primary action steps EDs take for meeting the challenge for program evaluation. Figure 23.1 illustrates these steps as a continuous process that contributes to building capacity for program evaluation.

The forty-two organizations are separated into three categories—Type I, II, and III—on the basis of the characteristics they demonstrate for program evaluation, as shown in Table 23.1.

For example, EDs who take all eight action steps lead Type I organizations, which make up 29 percent of the sample, while EDs who took fewer than eight lead Type II organizations, composing 69 percent of the sample. One Type III organization (2 percent of the sample) did not report an effort to have its programs evaluated. This typology is used to simplify the divisions among the program evaluation characteristics in the participating organizations, because some organizations arguably overlapped a bit between Type I and Type II. It is important to note that approximately half of the EDs of Type II organizations explicitly desire to expand or improve their

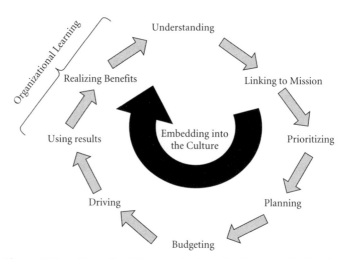

Figure 23.1.   Executive Director Actions for Program Evaluation

Organization Type	Program Evaluation Characteristics
Type I	Comprehensive and usually mixed evaluation methods reflecting a balanced approach Program-driven and outcome-focused rather than externally driven evaluation Staff dedicated to evaluation or external evaluators conduct the evaluation Evaluation results used primarily to improve programs Demonstration of long-term commitment for and activity in program evaluation Efforts to ensure the evaluation process improves and evolves
Type II	Primarily a single evaluation method, usually comprising a consumer survey Focus on consumer satisfaction and external stakeholder requirements Staff conduct the evaluation on an ad hoc, as-needed basis Evaluation results used primarily for program evaluation limited by lacking capacity or driven by changes in external stakeholder demands Evaluation process changes little or not at all
Type III	Evaluation process changes little or not at all

Table 23.1.   Program Evaluation Characteristics for Three Organization Types

program evaluation efforts. They cite limited capacity, with lacking financial resources as the primary limiting factor. Further contrasts between Type I and Type II organizations are seen in the majority of the eight steps that EDs of each type took with regard to meeting the challenge for program evaluation. These contrasts within each of these steps are described next.

Understanding of Program Evaluation

There is variance in how leaders describe their understanding of program evaluation. The EDs who characterize program evaluation within the context of measuring the effectiveness of program(s) tend to lead Type I organizations. Those who characterize program evaluation as more of a management or administrative task typically lead Type II organizations. This is indicative of the external pull's influence and the narrower perspective of program evaluation as a task to satisfy external stakeholders or internal reporting requirements rather than a systematic process to determine the effectiveness of programs.

Alignment with Mission

When asked whether program evaluation is related to their organization's mission, 93 percent of the EDs in the study sample confirm that it is. The majority explain why this relationship exists. Here are two example responses:

> "I think in order to be able to accomplish our mission we have to evaluate what we're doing. It is sort of like the roadmap to get us to continually fulfill our mission."
>
> "Yes because the fact that our mission is to put people to work, and we have to know how many people went to work and where they went to work, was the training and/or the placement service and/or the job successful in getting to that outcome, to fulfilling our mission."

The EDs who report cascading this value orientation about performance and alignment with their mission throughout their organizations lead Type I organizations. They characterize program evaluation as a process to be integrated with other important tools and systems for performance, such as strategic planning, performance budgeting, and resource allocation. Those who describe this relationship but do not use the mission as a value orientation lead Type II organizations.

Prioritization

The EDs' top three priorities fall primarily into the categories of financial stability, program effectiveness, and staffing.[3] The top priority receiving the most responses, identified by 40 percent of the respondents, is financial stability. The second priority receiving the most responses, identified by 31 percent of the respondents, is program effectiveness. Of the 48 percent of the EDs who choose program effectiveness as a top-three priority, 33 percent rank it as their first priority, 54 percent as their second and 13 percent as their third. EDs who choose program effectiveness as one of their top two priorities tend to lead Type I organizations. The most commonly reported third priority, identified by 21 percent of the respondents, relates to staffing issues such as hiring, training, and professional development.

Program Evaluation's Role in Planning

Of the thirty-four organizations (81 percent) having a current strategic plan, 73 percent of the EDs state that program evaluation is included in those plans. Slightly less than half of these EDs (43 percent) play a part, either by themselves or in conjunction with other stakeholders such as their board of directors, in ensuring program evaluation is included in the organization's strategic plan. These EDs typically lead Type I organizations. One ED indicates that annual program evaluation results drive the organization's strategic plan through recommendations for improving the program and operationalizing their implementation.

Financial Commitment for Program Evaluation

Approximately 60 percent of the EDs play a part in ensuring their organizations' evaluation efforts are budgeted. Of the forty-one organizations engaging in program evaluation, 88 percent fund their evaluation efforts solely out of operating budgets, while 10 percent fund their efforts through a combination of operating budgets and external sources such as grants, and 2 percent fund their efforts solely through grants. Variance exists between how Type I and II organizations allocate, budget, and manage financial resources for program evaluation, yielding no clear trend.

The Role of the Leader

EDs describing themselves as "drivers" of the evaluation process characterize their role as "making sure the organization participates in evaluation because it is important," "making sure it gets done," "making sure it continues to happen," and "deciding who's on point for program evaluation and how much time is spent on it." These EDs lead Type I organizations, while those characterizing themselves more passively as "overseers" of the evaluation process lead Type II organizations.

USING RESULTS AND REALIZING BENEFITS: AN OPPORTUNITY FOR ORGANIZATIONAL LEARNING

Approximately 67 percent of the EDs state their organizations use evaluation information to alter program(s). The next two most frequent responses are fund raising at 17 percent and staffing at 11 percent. Of those leaders who indicate they alter the program(s), 18 percent who specifically reference "improving their programs" all lead Type I organizations. Of the forty-one organizations engaging in program evaluation, 100 percent of them state their organization benefited from it. The majority of the EDs reference several benefits; however, 24 percent of them indicate that having information to demonstrate program effectiveness is their most important benefit.

The EDs who reference program evaluation as a learning opportunity for their organizations lead Type I organizations. They indicate that organizational learning takes place when results are used and stakeholders realize the benefits of program evaluation. They explain how this is the turning point for stakeholders, especially staff and the board, when they realize how evaluation can be used to improve the program(s), the organization's work toward the mission, and their individual work performance.

Two examples of Type I organizations, one from the forty-two organizations in the sample and one not, follow in case studies. These cases serve to illustrate the determining factors behind the organizations' success in evaluation capacity building, and more specifically what their EDs' role was in such efforts.

DATA AND FINDINGS: CASE STUDIES OF NHSOs

Two case studies examine Families First and Decatur Cooperative Ministry, using Volkov and King's Evaluation Capacity Building Checklist (2005) as a framework for analyzing their ECB efforts. (Those ECB guidelines from this checklist that are italicized are exemplified by these organizations.) Particular emphasis is given to the role of the ED and the impact of his or her efforts in the ECB process. In addition to using the checklist as a framework, specific aspects of the leader's role in building evaluation capacity contained in the literature are highlighted when discovered.

One example is *managing the political environment* in which evaluation resides by driving an organization's culture to be conducive for evaluation as well as managing the political nature of various and sometimes competing demands of stakeholders. Another example is *organizational learning,* where behavior is changed through documentation of what has worked and what has not; evaluation is the means for this continuous learning process. Last, once evaluation is embedded into the operations and culture of an organization to the point where it is an integral part of what the organization does, it becomes a *basic assumption.*

Families First

The mission of Families First, located in Atlanta, is "to strengthen and preserve families in partnership with them and their communities" (Families First, 2007). The organization works toward achieving this mission through seven program areas: adoption, foster care, residential services, employee assistance, counseling services, divorce education, and child visitation. In 1988, the organization was experiencing its 100th anniversary, and with an annual budget of about $1.5 million they decided to conduct their very first capital campaign to fund new programs. The organization also began to formally build capacity for and engage in program evaluation, eight years before the United Way's outcome measurement movement and about eleven years before literature on ECB appeared in publications.

Bert Weaver, the executive director of Families First in 1988, realized the time had come for the organization to formalize its approach to program evaluation. Weaver reflects, "I knew that we needed to get very serious about outcomes in saying this program works or it doesn't work. That's really what kind of got us going in that direction." Weaver decided to personally *support and share responsibility for* ECB, and he had another *evaluation champion in the organization* in Chris Valley, who was then the organization's director of program development and research. Valley sent a memo to Weaver on October 18, 1988, calling for a "professional approach to program evaluation" and a new, full-time program evaluation director position. Valley reasoned that this person "would add a new dimension to agency efforts in monitoring program performance, marketing services to funders, and the possible redesign of services. It would be an invaluable support to agency program development."

Weaver recognized both the *internal and external organizational contexts* for program evaluation. Funders were beginning to ask critical questions about programs and their effectiveness, so he presented the organization's intended new direction and Valley's proposal to the board of directors. Weaver set out to *increase the organization's interest in and demand for evaluation information.* However, beyond the explicit support from Valley and Pat Showell, then vice president for programs (and the current ED), he had to *determine if and to what extent the internal environment was supportive of change.* The board "reacted very positively" to this new direction and voted to extract funds from the capital campaign to support the new position.

The new position was occupied by Hugh Potter. The campaign also established an endowment that funded, among other things, evaluation expenses from its interest and investment earnings. The endowment currently is valued at more than $1 million, and it has enabled the organization to internally fund myriad evaluation projects, including some longitudinal studies, over the past twenty years. Weaver, along with board support, *built up organizational and individual ability, and readiness to implement evaluation activities* by *coming up with a revenue-generating strategy to support ECB,* and *assuring long-term fiscal support* and *explicit, dedicated funding for program evaluation activities.*

Weaver, Valley, and Showell all noted initial apprehension on the part of program staff. But all played roles in changing apprehension into interest and excitement in a relatively short time by *emphasizing and implementing purposeful trust building.* Weaver recalls, "I wasn't preaching and I wasn't dictatorial about it, but I was convinced we needed to know if these programs were making a difference or not. We worked with the management team for months, years, and we did it in steps. I think all that was convincing and reassuring, and the staff was seeing this as a new direction we were going in." Potter comments on Weaver's role in this culture change: "I think Bert was visionary and he was doing things at Families First in the late eighties that we're still not doing in the federal government. It was Bert's vision and his ability to really translate some of the business practice stuff into the nonprofit human service environment."

Weaver strongly encouraged access to and involvement from the board of directors. As a result, Families First *established a capable evaluation oversight group* in their Evaluation Advisory Committee in 1988, which consists of the executive director, director of programs, director of evaluation, three board members, and outside evaluation experts, usually from local universities. The committee's purpose is "to review, critique, comment, and recommend necessary changes in evaluation designs, procedures, and reports." Potter, Robert Fischer (who came after him as the director of evaluation), and Peter Lyons (their current external evaluator and a professor from Georgia State University) all indicate the committee has significantly helped their work. The collaborative efforts of these evaluators with the committee demonstrate the effort by Families First to *make the most of evaluation personnel (internal professionals and/or external consultants).* Fischer *developed and used an internal reporting, monitoring, and tracking system* and *developed an effective communication and public relations capability to relay evaluation findings to evaluation stakeholders.* Weaver and Valley encouraged and supported Fischer's efforts to publish journal articles; evaluations are featured in *Research on Social Work Practice, Journal of Divorce and Remarriage, Child Welfare,* and *Family and Conciliation Courts Review,* among other publications. Fischer cites Weaver's leadership as the driving force behind enabling him to advance program evaluation in Families First: "He was vitally interested in evaluation, a real champion of it, and he asked tough questions."

MANAGING THE POLITICAL ENVIRONMENT. Managing the political environment for program evaluation in Families First remained a priority for Bert Weaver and Pat Showell, the organization's last two EDs. Weaver reflects on having an internal evaluator during his tenure: "The danger for an in-house person is that they are a colleague, they are a staff member, and they are a friend. And if they're not really professional, that sharpness can begin to be co-opted. So you want to be careful about that." The issue of the objectivity of internal evaluators invoked *organizational learning* from Valley: "All of our evaluation is a point of departure for debate, and it's about what can we learn about our programs." Lyons discusses what made him decide to become the next evaluator after Fischer: "I was only interested in doing it if they were really interested in genuine program evaluation. I didn't want to do something that says this was just a snow job. Chris's response was that I would report whatever comes out. And I've been able to say, 'You know, it isn't working.'"

ORGANIZATIONAL LEARNING. Showell describes how program evaluation is driving *organizational learning* at Families First:

> "I think we are more of a data-driven organization. We come to issues, problems, and opportunities out of that data, that knowledge, rather than our emotions. That's a good thing. We're a social work organization, so we all have our opinions and emotions. Evaluation provides a framework that we wouldn't have otherwise. It was also validating. I really do think our staff is proud of the evaluation reports and information, and they take pride in them."

Valley adds: "The staff began to look forward to these meetings with the program evaluation person. It was almost as if they were learning about what they did. It was tremendously engaging intellectually ... organizationally, we learn as program evaluation is conducted."

PROGRAM EVALUATION AS A BASIC ASSUMPTION. Program evaluation is embedded in the culture of Families First. Potter, Fischer, and Lyons all indicate they have received the proper support and resources to effectively do their job. Lyons calls it "such an integral part of what they do," and the current board chair, Mary Yates, calls it "a tradition at Families First." One of the biggest threats to organizational culture is leadership transition, but not in the case of Showell succeeding Weaver as ED. Weaver comments: "She certainly was her own person and had all the background for the last sixteen years and could use it in her own style. I think it was helpful for her to have that kind of experience with program evaluation and develop that kind of conviction."

Showell confirms her intent on advancing this strong foundation:

> "There was a belief and vision that it was important not only for the stakeholders and funders, but it was also important for us. So, I see my role as picking up on the prior CEO's belief that if we're going to make a difference and have impact, we need to be able to know beyond the warm and fuzzy stories we have."

She describes the role of program evaluation as "integral to our ability to provide the kinds of services that our constituents need as well as the quality of services." Showell also describes her role in ECB in similar fashion:

> "It means an organizational focus to look at ... a standpoint in terms of the efficiency and effectiveness of your programs, and that you have the knowledge and the resources to do that. I tend to think that leadership sets the tone. If I don't see it as important and really an integral part of what we do and how we do it, then I think it either doesn't happen or doesn't happen in a concerted way. So I see myself as having a very significant role in keeping it on the front burner, communicating its importance, and in our being able to do the quality of service that we do."

Pat Pillow, the current vice president for programs, sums up Showell's role in the process:

> "I think the culture here understands that it's part of doing business and it's a necessary part of what we do. I think she's the driving force behind all of that initiative. I think when she's having the agency value it and creating the resources to have it, it comes from her as the top-down commitment."

Decatur Cooperative Ministry

Decatur Cooperative Ministry (DCM), located in Decatur, Georgia, offers a continuum of services to at-risk and homeless families. Their mission reads: "Decatur Cooperative Ministry serves our neighbors in need. Together, we strive to end homelessness, empower our community through education, and celebrate our faith-based diversity" (DCM, 2007). The organization, founded in 1969, has an annual budget of approximately $500,000. The organization's strategic plan for the period 2003–2006 contained four primary goals, one concerning effective and efficient program services, so DCM embarked on evaluating all three of its programs: Project Take Charge, Hagar's House, and Family Transitional Housing.

Beth Vann became DCM's executive director in 2001. The organization already had a *capable evaluation oversight group* in place with the Organizational and Program Assessment work group made up of board members and volunteers. The charge for the group is to "conduct comprehensive assessments and evaluations of DCM programs, services and organizational effectiveness; develop a process and a schedule to evaluate various programs; present written reports and recommendations to the board and staff for proposed areas of improvement." The committee was developed by board member Sarah Gill, who worked for a large evaluation consulting firm in the Atlanta area. Sarah was also responsible for recruiting professional evaluators, one of whom is a former supervisor at the firm and now works at the Centers for Disease Control and Prevention (CDC) to volunteer time and evaluate DCM's programs.

Vann notes that Sarah "was willing to really drive the process where I could be part of the process, but it wasn't that I had to drive it." Vann admits if she had to be the driver of the program evaluation process, it likely would not have happened because of her responsibilities of managing crises and keeping the organization financially healthy. She also attributes the board's interest in critically looking at the programs as a driving force, allowing her "to want to look at the programs harder, as well as look at the whole organization and its structure." Vann did, however, *support and share the responsibility for ECB* by telling the staff, "'This is what we're going to be doing. They're going to be interviewing your clients and volunteers." So it was just getting everybody on board ... and making the time and allowing the time for that." Vann attended the program evaluation stakeholder meetings, led by the evaluators, that involved the program manager, key volunteers, and a board member to *determine the extent the internal environment was supportive of change*. "It was really just letting the staff know, getting buy-in, hearing what their thoughts were, and creating the time, access, and space to do it."

Vann ensured program evaluation was, and continues to be, a staff priority. They dedicate a portion of their time for it, which also ensures they have *opportunities for sufficient input in decision making* for the programs. Staff sat in on the initial planning meeting and were interviewed by the evaluation team. They gave the team access to files, briefed their program participants on the project, and let them know evaluators would be contacting them. They also played primary roles in implementing the evaluation recommendations, some that have been completed and some that are still in progress. Vann's support and the evaluation's team framework both enabled the *incorporation of a feedback mechanism in the decision-making process and an effective communication system.* Vann recognizes *the external and internal organizational contexts* for program evaluation:

> "We invested a lot of time . . . in doing the evaluations and we also had a work group that invested time implementing the recommendations. It has given us things to really help bring our programs up a level, run better, more smoothly. You know, everybody wants a logic model these days and [everybody] has their format. But the thing is they did these really great logic models. So I feel like we know a lot about that and have the capacity to create that kind of thing now. When they ask about evaluation in grant applications or in a site visit, we can really clearly point out what we've done. I think it gives us really strong positioning to talk to grantors that we really do take all this seriously. And that we do really look at ourselves and want to do the best we can."

DCM has been able to have their three programs evaluated by a team of professional evaluators at very little cost, thanks to the team's willingness to volunteer their time. Vann and the organization *made the most of evaluation personnel* through a collaborative and participatory framework involving staff, board, and volunteers. This process has contributed to *organizational learning*, and Vann reflects on some examples:

> "As I think of Project Take Charge, it really changed the way that the program manager thought about the financial management classes, for example, with the materials and the curriculum. Some of what came out in that evaluation for Family Transitional Housing is the need for better training of, and more involvement from, the

volunteers so they feel more connected. And so now that's something we're working on for that particular program. I think overall, it just reinforced the importance of their work and the program."

DCM with Vann's leadership, board involvement, and the efforts of the evaluation team have all contributed to ECB within the organization. However, if volunteer evaluators are not available in the future, will the organization *assure long-term fiscal support* and/or *come up with revenue-generating strategies to support ECB*? Strong commitment exists from Vann, her board, and her staff for ongoing program evaluation, which challenges DCM to ensure that commitment can be realized in the future.

CONCLUSIONS AND IMPLICATIONS

The executive director of a nonprofit human services organization can play a primary role in the organization's efforts and activities for program evaluation. EDs in this study who recognize the external and internal organizational contexts for program evaluation, and who effectively balance the external pull with the internal push, are more likely to build long-term capacity for program evaluation. This involves various aspects of leadership commitment, notably prioritizing, driving the process, managing the political environment, and incorporating organizational learning.

Long-term capacity is evident when program evaluation is embedded in the organization's culture as a basic assumption. Leadership is therefore fundamental to investing in the organization's capacity for and utilization of program evaluation. This has implications for EDs who desire to develop a culture for continuous improvement for their organizations and help create a service delivery model of excellence. Such demonstration can strengthen existing and develop new relationships, as well as enhance public perception for the organization.

Evaluators, as indicated by the existing ECB literature, play an important role in helping an organization build capacity for program evaluation. However, this role may be limited; the evaluator does not control resources or influence the organization's culture to the extent of an executive director, and she or he may ultimately be perceived as an outsider (even in the case of an internal evaluator). Evaluators have an opportunity to better understand the implications of a leader's influence on the evaluation process and incorporate it into ECB. This opportunity may involve educating, assisting, affirming, empathizing, and enabling EDs in ECB, in a way that enhances the value of the evaluator's work by minimizing this outsider perception. ECB is ultimately driven from within an organization. Evaluators should seek—with caution about being co-opted—opportunities to work together with EDs for ECB. Such collaborative work has the potential to ensure that EDs and their organizations will gain a better understanding of, and build long-term commitment and capacity for, program evaluation.

Notes

1. Volov and King's "A Checklist for Building Organizational Evaluation Capacity" is available at http://wmich.edu/evalctr/checklists/ecb.pdf.
2. Calculated from the National Center for Charitable Statistics, http://nccsdataweb. urban.org/NCCS/Public/index.php, as of November 2005. The subcategories of Crime, Legal; Employment, Job Related; Food Agriculture and Nutrition; Housing, Shelter; Public Safety; Recreation, Sports, Leisure, Athletics; Youth Development; and Human Services, Multipurpose and Other were combined to make up the overall Human Services category. Other major NTEE categories include Art, Culture and Humanities, Education, Environment and Animals, Health, International, Mutual Benefit, Public and Societal Benefit, and Religion.
3. *Financial stability* comprised responses such as "fiscal stability," "money," "financial security," "resource development," "be financially solvent," "diversify funding," "fund raising," "funding," etc. *Program effectiveness* responses included "ensuring our programs have an impact," "helping teenagers succeed," "ensuring families' needs are met," "make programs efficient and effective," etc. Some *Staffing* issues were "training," "hiring good people," "staff," "keep a stable, loving staff," "quality staff," "have the right staff," "encourage staff to grow and develop," "stabilize and enhance workforce."

References

Anthes, E. W. "Organizational Issues in Nonprofit Personnel Administration and Management." *Personnel Matters in the Nonprofit Organization.* Hampton, AR: Independent Community Consultants, 1987.

Block, S. R. *Why Nonprofits Fail.* San Francisco: Jossey-Bass, 2004.

Boyle, R., Lemaire, D., and Rist, R. C. "Introduction: Building Evaluation Capacity." In R. Boyle and D. Lemaire (Eds.), *Building Effective Evaluation Capacity: Lessons from Practice.* New Brunswick, NJ: Transaction, 1999.

Brinkerhoff, P. *Mission-Based Management.* Hoboken, NJ: John Wiley & Sons, 2000.

Carlson, M., and Donohoe, M. *The Executive Director's Survival Guide.* San Francisco: Jossey-Bass, 2003.

Davis, S. *Managing Corporate Culture.* Cambridge, MA: Ballinger. Decatur Cooperative Ministry (DCM), 2007. (Originally published 1984.) "Mission and Vision." [http://www.decaturcooperativeministry.org/missionvision2.htm] April 2007.

Denhardt, R. B., Denhardt, J. V., and Aristigueta, M. P. *Managing Human Behavior in Public and Nonprofit Organizations.* Thousand Oaks, CA: Sage, 2002.

Drucker, P. F. *The Effective Executive.* New York: Harper & Row, 1967.

Drucker, P. F. *Managing the Nonprofit Organization.* New York: Harper-Collins, 1990.

Dym, B., and Hutson, H. *Leadership in Nonprofit Organizations.* Thousand Oaks, CA: Sage, 2005.

Families First. "Welcome to Families First." [http://www.familiesfirst.org/index.html] April 2007.

Fredericks, K. A., Carman, J. G., and Birkland, T. A. "Program Evaluation in a Challenging Authorizing Environment: Intergovernmental and Interorganizational Factors." In R. Mohen, D. J. Bernstein, and M. D. Whitsett (Eds.), *Responding to Sponsors and Stakeholders in Complex Evaluation Environments: New Directions for Evaluation.* San Francisco: Jossey-Bass, 2002.

Frost, P. J., Moore, L. F., Louis, M. R., Lundberg, C. C., and Martin, J. "An Allegorical View of Organizational Culture." In P. J. Frost, L. F. Moore, M. R. Louis, C. C. Lundberg, and J. Martin (Eds.), *Organizational Culture.* Thousand Oaks, CA: Sage, 1985.

Gray, S. T., and Stockdill, S. H. *Leadership Is Evaluation with Power.* Washington, DC: Independent Sector, 1995.

Green, F. L. "Ten Things Nonprofits Must Do in the Twenty-First Century." In R. E. Riggio and S. Smith Orr (Eds.), *Improving Leadership in Nonprofit Organizations.* San Francisco: Jossey-Bass, 2004.

Grudens-Schuck, N. "The Rigidity and Comfort of Habits: A Cultural and Philosophical Analysis of the Ups and Downs of Mainstreaming Evaluation." In J. J. Barnette and J. R Sanders (Eds.), *The Mainstreaming of Evaluation: New Directions for Evaluation.* San Francisco: Jossey-Bass, 2003.

Hay, R. D. *Strategic Management in Nonprofit Organizations.* Westport, CT: Greenwood Press, 1990.

Herman, R. D., and Heimovics, D. *Executive Leadership in Nonprofit Organizations: New Strategies for Shaping Executive-Board Dynamics.* San Francisco: Jossey-Bass, 1991.

Herman, R. D., and Heimovics, D. "Executive Leadership." In R. D. Herman and Associates (Eds.), *The Jossey-Bass Handbook of Nonprofit Leadership and Management.* San Francisco: Jossey-Bass, 2005.

Herman, R. D., and Renz, D. O. "Multiple Constituencies and the Social Construction of Nonprofit Organization Effectiveness." *Nonprofit and Voluntary Sector Quarterly,* 1997, *26*(6), 185–206.

Ivancevich, J. M., Szilagyi, A. D., Jr., and Wallace, M. J., Jr. *Organizational Behavior and Performance.* Santa Monica, CA: Goodyear, 1977.

Kaplan, R. S., and Norton, D. P. *Alignment: Using the Balanced Scorecard to Create Corporate Strategies.* Boston: Harvard Business School Press, 2006.

Lynch, R. *Lead! How Public and Nonprofit Managers Can Bring Out the Best in Themselves and Their Organizations.* San Francisco: Jossey-Bass, 1993.

Marais, L. C. The Relationship Between Organizational Culture and the Practice of Program Evaluation in Human Service Organizations. Unpublished dissertation, Western Michigan University, UMI Dissertation Services, 1998.

Mesch, D. J., and McClelland, J. "Managing for Performance and Integrity." In D. Young (Ed.), *Wise Decision Making in Uncertain Times: Using Nonprofit Resources Effectively.* New York: Foundation Center, 2006.

Murray, V. "Evaluating the Effectiveness of Nonprofit Organizations." In R. D. Herman and Associates (Eds.), *The Jossey-Bass Handbook of Nonprofit Leadership and Management.* San Francisco: Jossey-Bass, 2005.

Nanus, B., and Dobbs, S. M. *Leaders Who Make a Difference: Essential Strategies for Meeting the Nonprofit Challenge.* San Francisco: Jossey-Bass, 1999.

Nord, W. R. "Can Organizational Culture Be Managed?" In P. J. Frost, L. F. Moore, M. R. Louis, C. C. Lundberg, and J. Martin (Eds.),

Organizational Culture (pp. 187–196). Thousand Oaks, CA: Sage, 1985.

Northouse, P. G. *Leadership: Theory and Practice.* Thousand Oaks, CA: Sage, 2004.

Oster, S. M. *Strategic Management for Nonprofit Organizations: Theory and Cases.* New York: Oxford University Press, 1995.

Ott, J. S. *The Organizational Culture Perspective.* Chicago: Dorsey Press, 1989.

Paddock, S. C. "Evaluation." In J. S. Ott (Ed.), *Understanding Nonprofit Organizations: Governance, Leadership, and Management.* Boulder, CO: Westview Press, 2001.

Palumbo, D. J. "Politics and Evaluation." In D. J. Palumbo (Ed.), *The Politics of Program Evaluation.* Thousand Oaks, CA: Sage, 1987.

Patton, M. Q. *Utilization-Focused Evaluation: The New Century Text.* Thousand Oaks, CA: Sage, 1997.

Pfeffer, J., and Salancik, G. R. *The External Control of Organizations: A Resource Dependence Perspective.* Palo Alto, CA: Stanford University Press, 2003.

Poole, D. L., Davis, J. K., Reisman, J., and Nelson, J. E. "Improving the Quality of Outcome Evaluation Plans." *Nonprofit Management and Leadership,* 2001 *11*(4), 405–421.

Preskill, H., and Catsambas, T. T. *Reframing Evaluation Through Appreciative Inquiry.* Thousand Oaks, CA: Sage, 2006.

Sanders, J. R. "Mainstreaming Evaluation." In J. J. Barnette and J. R. Sanders (Eds.), *The Mainstreaming of Evaluation: New Directions for Evaluation.* San Francisco: Jossey-Bass, 2003.

Schein, E. *Organizational Culture and Leadership.* San Francisco: Jossey-Bass, 1992.

Senge, P. "Leading Learning Organizations." In F. Hesselbein, M. Goldsmith, and R. Beckhard (Eds.), *The Leader of the Future.* San Francisco: Jossey-Bass, 1996.

Sonnichsen, R. C. "Building Evaluation Capacity Within Organizations." In R. Boyle and D. Lemaire (Eds.), *Building Effective Evaluation Capacity: Lessons from Practice.* New Brunswick, NJ: Transaction, 1999.

Stockdill, S. H., Baizerman, M., and Compton, D. W. "Toward a Definition of the ECB Process: A Conversation with the ECB Literature." In D. W. Compton, M. Baizerman, and S. H. Stockdill (Eds.), *The Art, Craft, and Science of Evaluation Capacity Building: New Directions for Evaluation.* San Francisco: Jossey-Bass, 2002.

Stufflebeam, D. *Institutionalizing Evaluation Checklist*. Evaluation Center, Western Michigan University, 2002. [http://www.wmich.edu/evalctr/checklists/institutionalizingeval.pdf] March 2007.

Thomas, J. C. "Outcome Assessment and Program Evaluation." In R. D. Herman and Associates (Eds.), *The Jossey-Bass Handbook of Nonprofit Leadership and Management*. San Francisco: Jossey-Bass, 2005.

Tschirhart, M. *Artful Leadership: Managing Stakeholder Problems in Nonprofit Arts Organizations*. Bloomington: Indiana University Press, 1996.

United Way of America. *Measuring Program Outcomes: A Practical Approach*. Alexandria, VA: United Way of America, 1996.

Volkov, B., and King, J. "A Grounded Checklist for Implementing Evaluation Capacity Building in Organizations." Presented at the Joint Meeting of the American Evaluation Association and the Canadian Evaluation Society, Toronto, Canada, October 2005.

Weiss, C. "Where Politics and Evaluation Research Meet." In D. J. Palumbo (Ed.), *The Politics of Program Evaluation*. Thousand Oaks, CA: Sage, 1987.

Weiss, C. *Evaluation* (2nd ed.). Upper Saddle River, NJ: Prentice Hall, 1998.

Werther, W. B., Jr., and Berman, E. M. *Third-Sector Management: The Art of Managing Nonprofit Organizations*. Washington, DC: Georgetown University Press, 2001.

—⟡—

At time of original publishing Salavatore P. Alaimo was an adjunct professor in the School of Public and Environmental Affairs at Indiana University-Purdue University Indianapolis (IUPUI).

PART FOUR

The Next Generation of Leaders and Leadership

Editor's Introduction

The concluding part of this reader looks to the future of the leadership function in the nonprofit and public sectors and the leaders who will invigorate the sectors with their vision, energy, and wisdom. As Crutchfield and Grant noted in "Share Leadership" in Part II, the business literature exalts the individual heroic leader, but nonprofit and public organizations, by the very nature of their public-benefit charters, often rely on collective models of leadership to realize the public good. Thus, the readings in Part IV are distributed across questions of the what, who, and how of the next generation of leaders and leadership.

In Part I, I noted the convergence of Max DePree and John Gardner's exhortation that leaders establish institutions. You will recall that institutionalization refers to how leaders can make their contributions permanent by establishing a legacy for their successors. Creating institutions is the focus of the first article in Part IV. In "Sustaining Impact," Leslie Crutchfield and Heather McLeod Grant report how leaders in twelve large, successful national nonprofits have secured their futures. The authors contend that three elements allow the nonprofits they studied to maintain and deepen their impact in the future. The three elements are

- *People*: develop a people strategy and invest heavily in top performers;
- *Capital*: find the *right* sources of funding; and
- *Infrastructure*: invest in overhead, despite the pressure to look lean.

Although the element of capital may play out differently in government, I suspect that an empirical study of government would turn up similar elements and that people, capital, and infrastructure would make the short list.

The next generation of nonprofit and public leaders will be confronted not only by a need to institutionalize the best in their organizations, but they must also prepare to change and innovate. Public perceptions about innovativeness vary across the nonprofit and public sectors so two chapters, one focusing explicitly on the public sector, present perspectives about how the next generation of leaders can drive change and innovation. In the first of the two chapters, "Characteristics of Leadership Effectiveness: Implementing Change and Driving Innovation in Organizations," Ann Gilley, Pamela Dixon, and Jerry W. Gilley investigate empirically the skills associated with effective leadership of innovation. These authors identify six leadership skills from the general literature on organizational change and innovation. They test the associations between these skills and the perceived effectiveness of leaders in implementing change using convenience samples of MBA and organizational development master students. They find that four skills, communications, motivation, involving others, and coaching, are perceived by their sample as significantly related to leadership effectiveness in implementing innovation. Two of the skills, communications and motivation, which were covered in depth in Part III, were highly significant. The implication is that leaders who possess strong skills to communicate and motivate have a better chance of making the challenge of innovation more manageable.

Sandford Borins analyzes three specific types of innovation situations in public organizations. The situations range from politically led responses to crises, to organizational turnarounds led by new agency heads, to bottom-up innovations led by middle managers. The sample of innovations Borins studies in "Leadership and Innovation in the Public Sector" are drawn from both case studies and quantitative analysis of innovation-award winners. Borins finds that innovation in politically led responses to crises depends on breadth in the search for information and consultation with stakeholders and healthy skepticism when assessing options. Regarding bottom-up innovations, Borins concludes that they occur more frequently than generally believed. He finds that leaders at all levels of public organizations are important for nurturing bottom-up innovations. Turnaround situations impose three simultaneous demands on leaders. The agency head must restore political confidence, reconnect with external stakeholders, and reinvigorate the morale and efficacy of staff. One commonality of all three situations is that the relationship between political and bureaucratic leaders is a key to innovation.

The next four readings in Part IV take us from the what of the next generation of leadership to whom. Who will be the next generation of leaders? Frances Kunreuther sheds light on this question in "The Changing of the Guard: What Generational Differences Tell Us About Social-Change Organizations." As those of us who are Baby Boomers know, our generation will soon be retiring in large numbers, setting off a succession chain reaction in the organizations we inhabit. The federal government, for example, is nearing the point at which almost half of its workforce will be retirement eligible. In his introductory paragraph, Kunreuther crystallizes Baby Boomer concerns about what some have called a pending retirement tsunami: "Young people entering the sector are not as visionary, competent, committed, or well trained as those who are leaving. What will happen to these organizations?" Drawing upon interviews with executive directors and staff stratified by age, Kunreuther devotes the remainder of the article to answering the important question he poses. Kunreuther offers reassurance that the next generation of leaders will be much like the group that preceded them, but he also acknowledges differences that organizations must confront.

Regardless of how the demographics of generational change will affect them, nonprofit and public organizations must engage in not only finding enough leaders, but finding the right kind of leaders. The quality of the next generation of leaders will depend on processes of leadership succession, which confront nonprofit and public organizations alike. In many government organizations, leadership transitions at the very top of the organization are institutionalized through the electoral process whereby mayors, governors, and a variety of political appointees transition out routinely. The departure of city managers in council-manager cities is another setting in which such transitions are common. The demographics of Baby Boomers will vastly magnify leadership transitions in non-routine ways during the coming decade. Michael Allison's "Into the Fire: Boards and Executive Transitions" reports on leadership transitions in twenty-eight nonprofit organizations and identifies three threats to successful transition that may be generalizable to many other nonprofit and public organizations.

Two experienced professionals offer their perspectives about the quality of the next generation of leaders based upon their recent experiences with the nonprofit and public sectors. Marcia Marsh, senior VP for operations at the World Wildlife Fund, affirms results from a recent survey of leaders by the Corporate Leadership Council. In "Leadership and Leading: Leadership Challenges," Marsh contends that stretch assignments, personal development plans, and mentoring are likely to make the strongest contributions to cultivating new leaders.

The second experienced professional, Thomas J. Tierney, is chairman and cofounder of The Bridgespan Group, a nonprofit organization created to provide consultancy services to nonprofits. Tierney presents two primary arguments in "Understanding the Nonprofit Sector's Leadership Deficit." The first is that the demand for new leaders in nonprofits, such as the federal government, is likely to be staggering. Based on a recent study by Bridgespan, Tierney estimates that by 2016 nonprofits will need 2.4 times the number of senior leaders who are now employed by the sector. As daunting as is the predicted demand for senior leaders in nonprofits, Tierney suggests some responses by the nonprofit sector that can help to narrow the projected gap.

The next chapter in Part IV focuses on another phenomenon of twenty-first-century organizations—leaders who are continuously spanning organizational boundaries. In "The Nexus Effect: When Leaders Span Group Boundaries," Jeffrey Yip, Serena Wong, and Christopher Ernst argue that leaders are called on increasingly to bridge boundaries across nonprofit, public, and the commercial sectors. What sets their perspective apart is that many of the examples they provide are grounded in situations in which mutual gains were not envisioned and parties are not engaged in ongoing collaborations. In fact, Yip and his co-authors contend that organizations are nodes in resource networks and must increasingly reach out to groups with which they have not interacted or with whom they may have differences. The need to work outside one's in-group comfort zone could pay dividends for finding collective solutions to thorny problems.

The final three articles in this book return to the big picture with which we started in Part I. They represent closing reflections about the future of leadership in the public, nonprofit, and for-profit sectors. The theme of institutions—their design and maintenance—is again prominent. A related theme, one that is contested across the readings, is that public- and private-sector leadership is converging.

Leslie Lenkowsky puts the future of leadership in the philanthropic sector in the context of recent Congressional hearings and high-profile misbehaviors in the sector. Lenkowsky takes the critics of philanthropy head on in "The Politics of Doing Good: Philanthropic Leadership for the Twenty-First Century." His general thesis is that the criticism leveled at philanthropy is part of the politics of doing good through private means. The philanthropic sector has grown in size and probably influence. The growth of influence has brought greater scrutiny and even higher expectations. Philanthropic leaders, Lenkowsky concludes, need to be more attentive to how their organizations are perceived by the public and whether their actions are justifiable in terms of the charitable missions of their organizations. The delicate balance philanthropic leaders must maintain, Lenkowsky suggests, requires continuous assessment.

Joseph S. Nye, Jr., reflects on the evolving nature of public leadership in "New Models of Public Leadership." Nye begins by observing that markets and nonprofit organizations are agents of public action, often replacing government, a theme that echoes Lenkowsky. The devolution of government's responsibilities to market and nonprofit organizations is but one of the changes that Nye identifies as being in store for the next generation of leaders in public service. The waves of change that are breaking over the public sector lead Nye to address the issue of what good leadership will mean for the next generation of leaders and how public policy and administration schools can best prepare students for the future.

In the concluding chapter in the reader, Barbara Kellerman argues that public- and private-sector leadership are converging. Her argument in "Ties That Bind" is novel because she does not reject the view that fundamental differences exist between business, government, and nonprofit institutions. She instead argues that several overarching dynamics are contributing to convergence *and* leaders in different sectors must join forces to solve intractable problems that will confront future generations. Two of most influential drivers of convergence are the information revolution and globalization. Kellerman presents seven summary conclusions that follow from her contention that public- and private-sector leadership are converging. Whether or not you agree with Kellerman, her chapter brings us full circle from where we started in Part I. To what *should* the next generation of leaders aspire? And are they prepared to measure up to the public's expectations?

CHAPTER TWENTY-FOUR

Sustaining Impact

Leslie Crutchfield
Heather McLeod Grant

T each For America was only a few years old when its founder and president, Wendy Kopp, found herself facing a mutinous staff. The entire organization had convened in August 1992 in Los Angeles for its second summer training institute, an annual program designed to train new teachers before sending them out into classrooms. But after more than two chaotic years in startup mode, staff members were fed up with the long hours and low pay, the absence of organizational systems, and the unclear decision-making authority. Staff members told Kopp they would jump ship if things didn't change. The episode became known as the "coup de Kopp."[1] To make matters worse, the mutiny dovetailed with a major funding crisis: Kopp needed to raise $700,000 within four weeks to avoid shutting the doors. It was the perfect storm. At that moment, Teach For America was on the brink—not of breakthrough impact, but of implosion.

Originally published as "Sustaining Impact" in Leslie Crutchfield and Heather McLeod Grant, *Forces for Good: The Six Practices of High-Impact Nonprofits.* (San Francisco: Jossey-Bass, 2008).

Kopp had launched the ambitious group in 1989, based on an idea she developed in her senior thesis at Princeton University. Teach For America would be a national teaching corps, placing young college graduates in America's neediest schools, while working simultaneously to reform the larger educational system. From the outset, Kopp's vision was grand. She disregarded early advice to start with a single pilot site and scale up slowly, insisting that her idea would require an immediate national presence and a corps of five hundred teachers.

"Almost everyone advised me to start smaller," she recounts in her book, *One Day, All Children . . .* "I should recruit fifty people for one site, learn from that experience, and then expand from there. But this perspective was counter to my very conception of what Teach For America would be. This was not going to be a little nonprofit organization or a model teacher-training program. This was going to be a movement."

Kopp nearly killed herself to launch this movement. She worked twenty-hour days for the first year, at times only sleeping "every other night," she says. Passionate and persistent, she obtained donated office space in New York, scrounged up borrowed furniture, and sent out thousands of fund-raising letters. She also recruited a small staff of young education advocates to join her crusade.

They traveled around the country, recruiting the first class of corps members from college campuses, without yet knowing where the teachers would be placed, how they would be paid, or what support they might need. They were making it up as they went along.

Like most start-ups, the organization was in constant crisis mode those first few years. Meetings regularly ran until three in the morning; few management systems were in place; everyone was paid the same meager $25,000 salary; and the entire staff reported to Kopp. To make matters worse, most of the recent college grads Kopp hired had never held a real job before, let alone operated a national nonprofit. The organization ran on idealism, caffeine, and the largesse of foundations and individual donors who dared to take a risk on her dream.

Although she was able to persuade her staff to stay after the "coup," Kopp realized she was in over her head. So when she received a lucrative job offer to join Edison Schools, an education start-up run by entrepreneur Chris Whittle, she was sorely tempted to abandon Teach For America in exchange for less overwhelming responsibility. Ultimately, Kopp declined his offer, but not before a concerned Whittle loaned her a top executive, vice chairman Nick Glover, to help her sort out her financial and organizational crisis.

Glover convened a three-day retreat at the Waldorf-Astoria Hotel in New York with Kopp and a handful of her most trusted staff members. He told the group to put more time, energy, and resources into fund raising and to balance out its large program staff with more development employees. (At the time, Kopp and one other colleague were the only ones raising funds, while sixty staff members worked on the program side.) He also advised Kopp to put together a senior management team and to delegate more responsibility. Glover convinced her to let go of the egalitarian pay structure, and he helped implement some basic management and decision-making systems to help things run more smoothly.

"It worked," writes Kopp. "Within weeks Teach For America felt like a different place. [The] organizational difficulties had taken their toll.... But we had refined our approach to selecting and training corps members. We had beefed up our systems for providing them with ongoing support. We had raised the funding we needed to cover our costs. And Nick Glover had restored my sense of possibility. With the lessons he taught us, I figured we could accomplish anything."

Teach For America wasn't out of the woods just yet. Following the coup were what Kopp now calls the "dark years," a lean time in which many of the group's initial grants expired. The nonprofit was also stretched thin, with too few staff members running too many programs and a lack of the organizational resources needed to sustain rapid growth.

But that first crisis marked a real turning point. It was the moment when Teach For America, at the brink of failure, realized that it needed to build an *organization* to sustain its *movement*. Over the next few years, Kopp and her senior team cut less critical programs, reduced costs to meet their actual budget (rather than continuously raising more money to support too many programs), created a long-term fund-raising plan, developed management systems, and invested in organizational capacity and people. With this stable foundation, Teach For America finally began to take off. Today, the organization is widely considered to be one of the great success stories of the last decade. With a staff of 650, a budget of $70 million (and growing), strong leadership, and an increasingly recognized brand, Teach For America—and its influential alumni—are now a force to be reckoned with in the education field. But had a few things gone differently back in the early 1990s, we might not be writing about it in this book. Indeed, the group might have been yet another nonprofit to fall into the chasm between high expectations and insufficient organizational capacity.

CROSSING THE CHASM

Like Teach For America, many of the organizations we've written about have faced difficult times. Although they are truly great in terms of what they have achieved, their impact hasn't come easily—even though it may look that way in hindsight or from a distance. For the majority, success has been a bumpy road rather than a smooth path. Several of the organizations we studied faced near-death experiences, when they almost imploded or ran out of money, or when their operations couldn't keep up with their ambitious goals.

For the National Council of La Raza, the moment of reckoning came early in its history, not long after Raul Yzaguirre had stepped in as president in the late 1970s. At the time, NCLR received more than half of its funding from government grants, which were slashed after Ronald Reagan was elected president in 1980. The nonprofit's budget went from $5 million to less than $2 million almost overnight, and NCLR was forced to lay off 70 percent of its staff. It wasn't clear that the group would survive, until Yzaguirre formed a corporate council and aggressively pursued alternative sources of funding.

Many of the other organizations in our sample have faced their own crises of funding or capacity, times when it looked like they might not pull through or when their organization was stretched too thin. And the social sector is littered with has-beens and also-rans— nonprofits that have a good idea but never achieve significant impact, or those that are unable to sustain impact because they haven't been able to secure the basics. "The gap between the capacity of nonprofits and the size of the problems they are attempting to address often looks more like a chasm," writes William Foster (2007), a partner at the Bridgespan Group, a nonprofit consulting firm.

Despite the desire among many groups to get to a certain scale—or even just to maintain steady state—it is incredibly difficult to do so. All nonprofits face barriers to finding ongoing funding and to investing in their own infrastructure and organizations. For one thing, most nonprofits don't have a revenue stream to cover their costs, as successful for-profit companies do. They can't depend on profit margins—they exist to correct market imperfections and to provide for those people who can't always pay. Instead, they must ask third parties (foundations, government, individuals) to donate more money each year to deliver on their mission. "Most companies eventually become self-funding," says Eileen Jacobs, a City Year board member and former business executive. "But nonprofits don't have that luxury. Most nonprofits do not have huge endowment funds; they have to sell their story year after year. Having to raise money to live day-by-day is tough."

Businesses also have access to sophisticated capital markets to raise additional money as they expand. Corporations can issue stocks or bonds to invest in their organizations as they grow, and they can tap into an impressive array of financial institutions designed to meet their needs at each stage of development, including "angel" investors, venture capitalists, investment bankers, and various lending firms. But the social sector's capital markets are not as developed, a topic that scholars and practitioners have recently begun to study and discuss.

There is also a *disincentive* for nonprofits to invest in the critical organizational elements—people, infrastructure, and systems—that make success sustainable. In the private sector, investors recognize the importance of not just investing in a product, but also supporting the company behind that product. As Christine Letts, William Ryan, and Allen Grossman argued in their influential 1997 *Harvard Business Review* article, "Virtuous Capital," nonprofit investors have a great deal to learn from their for-profit counterparts (Letts, Ryan, and Grossman, 1999). The social sector has inherited an erroneous belief that every penny should go directly to programs rather than overhead, as if programs could deliver themselves.

As a result of these dynamics, most nonprofits have a more difficult time reaching the minimum scale that they need to achieve their goals, let alone maintaining the same size or even building a broader platform for future impact. Our point is not that these organizations need to be *huge* to have big impact. On the contrary: the Center on Budget and Policy Priorities achieves significant impact with its $13 million budget, as does Habitat with its $1 billion global budget (see Figure 24.1). These two groups have very different missions and goals, which lead to very different business models and funding strategies, as we'll see later. But once a nonprofit gets to the size it deems effective to support its strategy, it can have difficulty *sustaining* its organization and its impact.

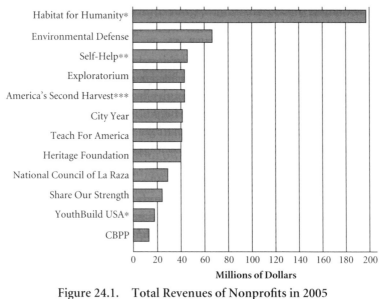

Figure 24.1.   Total Revenues of Nonprofits in 2005
*Headquarters only—does not include affiliate budgets
**Net revenue spread
***Does not include value of in-kind donations

Herein lies the challenge: most social entrepreneurs want to scale up, or at least sustain their current levels of impact, but they face a powerful countervailing force. All the leaders discussed in our book [*Forces for Good*] grappled with how to get more bang for their buck, how to maximize their results without increasing their costs, and how to raise enough capital to build their organizations. Great nonprofits know that they must continually close the gap between their outward-looking vision—their constant desire for greater impact—and their need to invest in themselves.

THREE CRITICAL ELEMENTS TO SUSTAIN IMPACT

In the previous chapters [of *Forces for Good*] we've illustrated how these twelve great nonprofits leverage forces outside their organizational boundaries in order to achieve more impact. In addition to focusing externally, however, they also need to be able to deliver on their promises. Although we recognize that not all the groups are perfectly managed, neither can they afford to neglect the basics, such as keeping good people, raising money, and building the right infrastructure. At the same time that they work externally to *increase* their impact by applying the six practices, they must also invest internally to *sustain* their impact. It's not "either-or"—it's "both-and."

Reaching for ambitious goals and building organizational capacity can be mutually reinforcing: by working with and through other sectors, nonprofits can also find the financial resources necessary to sustain themselves. External partners—government, business, individuals—often provide money, in-kind donations, credibility, volunteer labor, and other critical resources. As we've seen in the preceding chapters [of *Forces for Good*], successful groups can influence government as both a *means* to funding and as an *end* in itself— to achieve policy change. Similarly, they can work with businesses to obtain resources for their cause and to influence business practices. They can engage individuals and work through nonprofit networks to raise funds; they can also mobilize these networks to achieve grassroots or cultural change.

High-impact nonprofits recognize that there are three critical elements needed in order to maintain and deepen their impact over time: *people, capital,* and *infrastructure.* These are the "necessary but not sufficient" ingredients that enable them to build "good enough" organizations. In our view, none of these elements really constitutes a practice, but they are nonetheless essential to these organizations' ability to sustain their impact.

PEOPLE: DEVELOP A PEOPLE STRATEGY AND INVEST HEAVILY IN TOP PER-FORMERS. Every one of these organizations cited staff as a critical success factor. Although all nonprofits rely heavily on employees, we discovered that great nonprofits have developed particular capacities for hiring, developing, and retaining top talent that can serve as examples for other organizations.

CAPITAL: FIND THE *RIGHT* SOURCES OF FUNDING. None of these groups could keep going without having one or more sustainable funding mechanisms—the critical input that fuels their outputs or impact. Their sources of support may vary, but successful groups integrate fund raising with their strategy, and they find ways to diversify these sources over time to reduce their financial risks.

INFRASTRUCTURE: INVEST IN OVERHEAD, DESPITE THE PRESSURE TO LOOK LEAN. All the groups have reached a point in their growth at which they needed to invest heavily in information technology, buildings, or management systems and build their own organizational capacity. They've found creative ways to raise capital for these needs.

People: Invest in Top Talent

We have seen how great nonprofits retain their senior leaders over time, first and foremost because they empower their top teams. When asked what keeps them at their jobs, many top managers cite a passion for the mission, the ability to make a difference, and the other committed people with whom they work.

The same goes for mid-level and junior staff. Most often, people initially gravitate toward nonprofit work for purpose and passion. But intrinsic motivation is not always enough to retain people, particularly over long periods of time. Successful nonprofits have learned that they need a *people strategy* to keep the best and brightest talent on their teams. Surprisingly, only about half of the organizations we examined have a formal human resources director or department. However, all of them have learned to do a few things right with respect to their senior staff, and these policies tend to trickle down to midlevel managers and entry-level positions as well.

FOCUS FIRST ON WHAT, THEN WHO. Many of the nonprofits we studied said that it's important to "get the right people on the bus," and a few even quoted Jim Collins's (2001) book *Good to Great,* which included a chapter on that topic.[5] Collins claims that successful businesses need to focus on "first who, then what." That is, if they first get the right people on board, they can then figure out where and how to steer the bus, in terms of their strategy and tactics.

But in the nonprofit world, it's actually "first what, then who." All the organizations we studied are guided first and foremost by their *mission,* and this purpose is the primary reason a person will take the job. These groups look for new hires with a passion for their mission and a strong cultural fit. In other words, they already know where the bus is headed; they're looking for good people who are going in the same direction. Although the strategy or tactics may change over time, their overall cause is unlikely to change.

"For us it's mission first," says Martin Eakes, founder of Self-Help. "You can't work at Self-Help longer than a week and not have someone raise the question, 'Is this in line with our mission?' This is not a place where people come for a paycheck. If this is not a calling, and you're not primarily motivated by the mission, get off the bus and leave us a seat." Some of the nonprofits go so far as to say that a person's fit with the organization's mission matters even more than basic skills. "The skills matter, but they matter less than the passion, because you can learn the skills," says Cecilia Muñoz from National Council of La Raza. "The focus and commitment you can't learn—that's what makes good advocates."

PAY TO PLAY. Although nonprofit leaders don't take their jobs *because* of the money, in order for them to stay (particularly those raising families or those without a second income or independent wealth), it is important to establish a base salary that at least makes the financial equation palatable. It is one thing to take a low-paying job just out of college to follow your bliss, and another thing entirely to support a family or face retirement on a $40,000 salary, particularly in major urban areas. Unlike the stereotypical nonprofit, these organizations don't burn out their talent with entry-level wages. *It's both mission and then money that matter, in that order.* Indeed, a recent study confirmed that nonprofit executives who are very dissatisfied with their compensation are twice as likely to leave within a year as executives who are satisfied (Bell, Moyers, and Wolfred, 2006).

We discovered that successful groups are willing to compensate generously to attract and retain top talent. They "pay to play." Ten out of the twelve organizations discussed in this book [*Forces for Good*] aim to compensate at the higher end of the nonprofit pay scale, relative to other organizations of the same size and in similar fields and regions (see Figure 24.2). They didn't all start out that way—most paid the paltry salaries that characterize any start-up—but over time, they have moved to the top tier. These nonprofits also offer competitive benefits, which enables them to keep their best performers. They don't constantly rely on young people who are willing to work for lower wages but who don't have the experience or expertise necessary to generate substantial impact.

Environmental Defense came to this conclusion about fifteen years into its growth. "In the early 1980s, the board didn't have a pension or benefits plan," recalls Michael Bean, a senior attorney who has

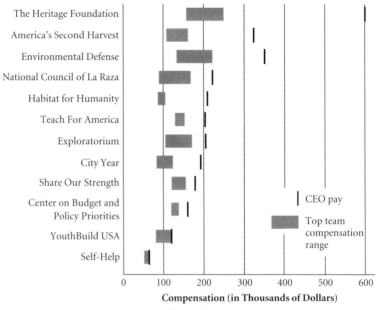

Figure 24.2.   Well-Paid Executives (2005)

Note: This figure includes data from 2005 or the most recently available year before 2005. Data were provided by the organization or were taken from the organization's 990 form, published by GuideStar, and include salary and bonuses where applicable, but not benefits.

been with the organization twenty-four years. "They had to ask, 'Do we want to keep the good people we've hired, or … have a staff constantly in their twenties with new ideas?'" The board voted for the former, and increased compensation and benefits to keep senior people, many of whom joined the organization in the 1970s.

Although senior-level salaries are still lower than in the private sector, compensation at these organizations is competitive among their peers. Some are even able to entice talented leaders from business, who take pay cuts to work on issues they care about. Offering respectable salaries makes a difference. For example, vice presidents at many of the groups earn $130,000 or more per year. In addition, many of the organizations provide high-quality health care and retirement benefits.

Only two organizations in our sample did not compensate at the top of the nonprofit pay scale at the time we studied them. Under newly appointed CEO Jonathan Reckford, Habitat for Humanity is now moving from paying 20 percent lower than other Christian nonprofits to compensating at the median level. But for years founder Millard Fuller relied heavily on unpaid staff, who worked full-time in return for "pig-checks," or certificates that could be redeemed at the local Piggly Wiggly grocery store. These volunteers didn't necessarily have the skills required for their jobs as the organization grew.

Self-Help has a similarly ideological view, based on a philosophy that the spread between the highest- and lowest-paid positions should be small and that external markets should not determine the value of an employee. Under founder Martin Eakes's formula, top salaries at Self-Help in 2005 were capped at around $63,000 (much lower than the other organizations we examined). However, the nonprofit has raised entry-level salaries, so that the lowest-paid staff members make relatively more than their peers at other nonprofits. In this sense, Self-Help also takes compensation off the table. It doesn't even attempt to compete in the talent marketplace—it has made an ethical, not an economic, choice about compensation. You join Self-Help for the mission, not the money. (Whether this compensation approach is sustainable remains to be seen; several staff members questioned it in our interviews with them.)

In addition to paying well, some of the groups have moved to performance-based pay. The Heritage Foundation was an early pioneer of the approach. "We are one of the first think tanks to set up a goal system in the 1980s," says Philip Truluck, executive vice president. "Other groups come out and ask how they can be as great as we are. Well, goals are set and goals are measured. We are still one of the few [nonprofits] that set up a bonus system."

CREATE NON-MANAGEMENT CAREER PATHS. People often come to work in the social sector because they are passionate about an issue like education or the environment, and they have skills or deep knowledge in the area. But in many nonprofits, the only way to move up is to take on more management and administrative responsibilities. The move often takes leaders away from their core competencies, such as advocacy, research, writing, or running programs.

Although all the organizations we examined have promoted internal people into management, many have also created non-management career paths for star senior staff: economists, scientists, policy researchers, analysts, or other experts. "There was a view that moving up into management meant success. But we tried to create career paths that weren't automatically management. If you are a great researcher, then you can stay here. I wish I had pinpointed that beforehand," says Truluck of The Heritage Foundation.

In many ways, these groups are structured more like a university—with a division between administration (management) and faculty (subject experts)—than like a typical business. In fact, a number of them, particularly those that have a strong research, analysis, and advocacy component, have Ph.D.s on staff, including the Center on Budget and Policy Priorities, the Exploratorium, Environmental Defense, and The Heritage Foundation. Their ability to keep subject experts, along with talented managers, means that they have high retention rates in the senior ranks. We believe that this is a fundamental factor for sustaining impact at extraordinarily high levels.

"The other day I calculated that around thirty people are here today who started during [founder Frank Oppenheimer's] time," says Robert Semper, director of the Center for Learning and Teaching at the Exploratorium. "In my case, it's because I've been able to get involved and have had enough learning opportunities that have allowed me to maintain my engagement."

LET GO OF UNDERPERFORMERS. "You never wish you'd waited longer to fire an employee who wasn't working out," says Billy Shore, founder of Share Our Strength. He and the other CEOs we met have had plenty of hiring successes, but they've also made some blunders along the way. It is hard for any manager to let go of a committed individual who has a passion for the cause but who is underperforming or isn't a good fit.

Because nonprofits are mission based and tend to be more "touchy-feely" than businesses, they can often fall into the trap of hanging on too long to people who aren't working out. Organizational effectiveness suffers: efficiency remains lower than it could be, and talented staff members can become demoralized when they see underperformers being indulged. More important, with limited resources and ambitious goals, these groups need strong staff to achieve the level of impact to which they aspire. Anything else just won't cut it. Although not every organization we studied has learned this, many have mastered the art of firing.

"You perform or you're out," says Kevin Huffman, vice president for strategy at Teach For America. "People who don't hit their fund-raising goals here don't last long in their roles. If a regional director is not performing, or he is not a good fit, he is counseled out.... Every person at Teach For America has defined goals and a sense of accountability."

Fred Krupp at Environmental Defense echoes the tough-love approach. "We have a philosophical commitment to firing people," he says. "When I see program managers or departments that are not letting people go, that is when I know to meet with the managers. We have 280 people, and we imagine that we are changing the world. If we do not have the very best people we can find, if we view ourselves as coddling, then we're done."

All these organizations have achieved a virtuous cycle of talent management, and it can be hard to tease out cause and effect. Are these nonprofits successful because they've figured out how to develop leaders and keep top talent over time? Or do people stay mainly because the organizations are so successful and have reached a certain size and stability? Studies show a correlation between the size of an organization and its ability to retain talent. Ultimately, it's probably a bit of both. People like working for a successful organization that is having real impact. They feel they are making a difference, they are surrounded by interesting and motivated colleagues, they are likely to be paid well and find new challenges as the organization grows, and hence they are more likely to stay. Because good people stick around, the organization continues to do well. It's a self-reinforcing cycle.

Capital: Find the *Right* Sources of Funding

There is no magic formula for raising the money needed to fuel your work—every organization has had to blaze its own trail. Initially we found stark differences in capital structures and a diversity of funding sources among these nonprofits. But as we looked closer, we realized that there were a few interesting insights that can be helpful to any group seeking to raise funds to sustain its impact.

We observed that high-impact nonprofits don't treat fund raising as a stand-alone function of management; it is highly integrated with their programs, their mission, and their strategy. In some cases, fund raising is actually part of their "theory of change." The best organizations have a financial strategy that is aligned with their larger vision for creating social impact. These nonprofits choose to pursue funding from the government, the private sector, or individuals not just because they are good sources of revenue, but because they can help solve the problems these nonprofits are trying to address.

For example, Dorothy Stoneman lobbied the federal government to create a national YouthBuild program, in part because she knew that's where she could find a large infusion of cash to expand quickly. But Stoneman also pursued federal appropriations because, as a former civil rights activist, she had a deeply held belief that government *should* help low-income youth. Working with government was part of her larger strategy for delivering impact. "We believe the federal government has a responsibility to address these issues and offer a solution," she says. "It was my political conviction that we had a responsibility to work with the government."

Likewise, when The Heritage Foundation set out to "win the war of ideas," it realized that the traditional think-tank approach was insufficient for promoting policy ideas to the general public. Heritage built a conservative *movement,* working with a network of other nonprofits and engaging 275,000 donor-members in the process. Its theory of change supported, and was supported by, its fund-raising strategy.

Michael Brown and Alan Khazei of City Year pursued corporate support—along with federal AmeriCorps funding—from the outset. They were part of a new generation of social entrepreneurs who believed it was critical to involve the business community in their vision for national service. The first pilot program was funded with $250,000 from five corporations, and today the group generates a large percentage of revenues from a wide range of corporate sponsors, in addition to receiving significant funding from government and foundations.

Like City Year, many high-impact nonprofits realized that they needed to diversify their revenue base if they wanted to sustain their impact. Indeed, as might be expected of organizations of this age (fifteen to forty years) and size (over $10 million), the majority have diversified their funding sources to varying degrees to decrease their risk (see Figure 24.3). But simultaneously, many have continued to pursue a dominant source of support, with more than 50 percent of their revenues coming from one of the following places: government, individuals, corporations, earned income, or foundations.[2] We explore each of these sources in the next sections.

GOVERNMENT: MOBILIZING PUBLIC FUNDS FOR SOCIAL IMPACT. Almost half the organizations we examined lobby the government—at the federal, state, and local levels—for appropriations and contracts. They pursue policy change because they believe that their programs are important enough to receive broad public support. In this way, changing public policy can be both a means of obtaining funding and an end in itself. (It is important to note that some nonprofits engage in policy advocacy but do not accept government funding because to do so would represent a conflict of interest.)

For organizations that have pursued government funding, many experienced rapid growth once they received the money. Government funding probably gives the quickest bang for the buck, as it requires less of an initial investment to obtain than other sources. Government grants or contracts also are often substantially larger than any other single funding source. "That's where the big money is," says YouthBuild USA COO Tim Cross. "You're never going to find an annual outlay of $65 million from any single corporation or foundation. To even begin to meet the need, the feds have to be in the picture."

For YouthBuild USA, pursuing significant government funding was essential. Not only did it provide a lot of money and fulfill Stoneman's belief in the role of taxpayers, but government also provided the distribution muscle that YouthBuild needed to spread its model quickly throughout the country.

Relying heavily on government funding also has its risks, however. YouthBuild USA learned this lesson in the mid-1990s, when a change in administration and subsequent budget cuts briefly reversed its steep growth curve. In just a few years, YouthBuild had gone from a small local program in one city to a national network of 226 local programs with combined annual revenues of $180 million, fueled by federal grants of $40 million to $65 million per year. But when Congress changed hands in 1996, major cuts forced the program to scale back. Today, YouthBuild USA still depends on federal contracts for 70 percent of its budget, but the organization is working hard to diversify its funding base *within* federal sources, as well as through individual and corporate support.

YouthBuild USA made other tradeoffs in pursuing federal funding: it relinquished a great deal of control over its network to the federal agency, HUD. The organization decided not to control the total

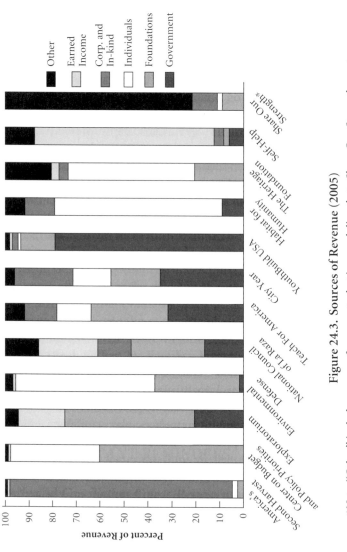

Figure 24.3. Sources of Revenue (2005)

Note: "Other" includes revenue from events that is passed directly to Share Our Strength grantees.

appropriation and "own" its affiliate programs—sacrificing some control over the members in its network. Instead, it chose to scale out the Youth-Build model more quickly and to allow other non-profits to apply for federal grants. Achieving widespread impact as rapidly as possible was a fundamental part of YouthBuild USA's social change strategy, and government funds were the primary mechanism for scaling its impact. For YouthBuild, the tradeoff was worthwhile.

INDIVIDUAL DONORS: CAPITALIZING ON CITIZEN SUPPORT. A number of the nonprofits we examined have built large individual donor bases and rely primarily on that source to sustain their organization and impact. Groups that receive substantial funding from individual donors include Share Our Strength (from fund-raising events), America's Second Harvest (from individual donors), Environmental Defense and The Heritage Foundation (from membership bases), and Habitat for Humanity (from direct marketing and events). For these organizations, engaging volunteers, members, and individual donors in their mission has been critical to their strategies for increased impact. Not surprisingly, a number of these groups also excel at engaging individuals in experiential activities and at inspiring evangelists.

The most dramatic—and counterintuitive—example of an organization effectively raising big money from individual citizens is The Heritage Foundation, with its 275,000 donor-members. Its broad, diverse individual funding base has resulted in large part from Heritage's ability to build a highly influential conservative movement and to engage individuals in its cause. Moreover, its funding base has allowed Heritage to turn down money that comes with strings attached and has given the organization enormous strategic freedom. CEO Ed Feulner recounts a story about the time when a high-profile corporate leader disagreed with Heritage's view on trade: "He asked if we would change our position." Feulner says he pulled out the man's check and ripped it up.

Individual engagement is also a significant part of Habitat for Humanity's theory of change. Habitat did not choose the most efficient or cost-effective way to build houses for the poor. But its vision was always much larger than just building homes; it wanted to mobilize volunteers to work alongside the recipients of the home, and in the process, build an antipoverty housing *movement*.

Since its inception, Habitat has engaged more than a million volunteers in its movement, and as a result, the organization also has one of the strongest brands in the world. This in turn bolsters its ability to raise significant dollars from the individuals who volunteer and from ever-widening circles of their friends and colleagues.

Although building a large, renewable individual donor base certainly has its rewards, doing so requires a significant investment of resources. Most of the nonprofits that rely on individual donations have larger development staffs, with larger budgets, than those organizations that rely on government or foundation support. For example, Environmental Defense has forty development staff members, who collectively manage thousands of relationships.

CORPORATIONS: APPLYING PRIVATE DOLLARS TO SOCIAL CHANGE. Corporations have been a source of both funding and in-kind support for a number of organizations. Many of the high-impact nonprofits we studied find ways to work with business. Although only one of them is predominantly reliant on corporate funding (America's Second Harvest, which receives nearly $500 million in donations of food and related products from corporate partners), many use corporate funding to supplement their income.

For instance, City Year creates engaged partnerships with companies. "Our goal was never to just get a check," says Michael Brown. "From the beginning, we asked sponsors to get involved, come out and do service, and begin seeing service as a vehicle to bring people together." These corporate relationships not only provide City Year with much-needed funding but also create mutual benefits for the companies and the nonprofit, spread City Year's message of national service to an important audience, and hold it accountable to a wide constituency. Corporate dollars are the *right* dollars for supporting City Year's theory of change.

The National Council of La Raza is another nonprofit we studied that moved away from reliance on government funding after significant cuts were made in the early 1980s. Instead, NCLR began to cultivate a large number of corporate supporters. "I think traditionally, a lot of nonprofits relied on federal funding," says CEO Janet Murguia. "Raul learned some hard lessons about diversifying. He understood that a little earlier than others, and put it into practice—looking at foundations and also the business community, and growing those relationships."

EARNED INCOME: DRIVING A DOUBLE BOTTOM LINE. Self-Help is perhaps the most financially sustainable of all the organizations we studied, because it generates a large portion of its revenues through earned income. But it is the exception, not the rule. Earned income is such a powerful source of revenues for Self-Help because its business model for economic development is completely aligned with its mission and social impact goals. It is truly a double-bottom-line business. Self-Help generates earned income from capital instruments, such as mortgage-backed securities and low-interest loans, which involve the core products it offers customers. These revenues give the organization incredible freedom and financial stability. The metaphor that Self-Help staff members often use is "two wheels of the bicycle": the front wheel is the mission of the organization, and the back wheel is the financial engine that propels its growth. "Our bicycle [is] a consistent financial base that allows us to innovate and take risks," says Bob Schall, president of Self-Help Ventures Fund. "We're not held hostage by funders to do certain things or not do certain things."

Although Self-Help's financial success is impressive, it should not come as a surprise that none of the other organizations has attained the same level of financial independence. Their strategies for achieving social impact are less aligned with a profitable business model. Still, some are making real efforts to increase their sources of earned income in ways that are clearly in sync with their mission and strategy for impact. For example, the Exploratorium receives 15 percent of its revenues from admission fees, which is actually a smaller percentage than many museums. But it has also developed other income through the sale of publications and the rental of exhibits, both of which extend its social impact as well.

FOUNDATIONS: A MAINSTAY FOR MANY NONPROFITS. Some organizations' missions lend themselves to relying more heavily on foundations, particularly those with strategies that preclude them from accepting funding from the government or the private sector for conflict-of-interest reasons, such as Environmental Defense, Heritage, and the Center on Budget and Policy Priorities. Foundation support can be useful for a variety of purposes, including research, launching new ideas, and evaluation of existing programs. And although the groups we studied received concentrated funding from other sources, they all have received additional support from foundations.

Of the nonprofits we studied, the Center on Budget and Policy Priorities has been the most reliant on foundation support, with 90 percent or more of its funding coming from major foundation grants throughout most of its history. Since 2000, it has received grants totaling $34.4 million from nearly thirty foundations; its largest foundation funder provides 13 percent of the total grants awarded. Because the Center lobbies the government on budget issues, it would be a conflict of interest to take taxpayer dollars. And historically the group has not diversified into individual support, although it is just beginning to do so. By 2006, the Center received 35 percent of its funds from smaller donors.

Although these days it is popular to critique "traditional" philanthropists for making short-term, relatively small grants, notably a number of the nonprofits we studied have long-term relationships with foundation funders, who have stuck with them over *decades*. The Ford Foundation and the Surdna Foundation, in particular, have played a critical role in funding many of these groups over time. If your organization has a clear strategy, a strong track record of success, and a mission compatible with the goals of the foundation, at least a few institutional funders seem willing to invest for the long haul. "We do have these long-standing relationships with our funders, and they have seen a return on their investment," says Kathryn Greenberg, the Center's director of development.

Infrastructure: Invest in Overhead

Finding great people and raising ongoing funding are two significant challenges facing all nonprofits, but there is a third challenge as well. Within the social sector, organizations are discouraged from investing in the very things they need in order to build their own capacity and sustain their impact: systems and infrastructure.

Unfortunately, individual donors often do not want to pay for organizational overhead, preferring that their dollars go directly to programs. In the business world, it is widely recognized that having a superior company enables success. It takes money to make money. But in the social sector, the idea still remains difficult for donors to grasp. "This is the real challenge for many nonprofits—how do you get the funding to match the work that you need done, knowing that you need some flexibility?" says Janet Murguia, CEO of National Council of La Raza. "It's very difficult to get unrestricted dollars."

At some point in their evolution, almost all the groups we studied needed to raise substantial capital, above and beyond their annual operating costs, to invest in the development of their organizations. And they've been both persistent and creative about funding necessary things like buildings, computers, and additional staff to manage their rapidly expanding programs. In fact, many ran "growth campaigns" to invest in the critical systems and teams they needed to keep up with program growth. They often structured campaigns as one-time events rather than folding them into annual operating costs, which helped to keep their overhead ratio low as well as generate momentum and excitement among funders.

Teach For America and City Year both conducted growth campaigns not unlike the more familiar capital campaign that nonprofits hold when raising funds to purchase a building. Both organizations had reached a point at which they could no longer sustain their growth with the systems and infrastructure they had. They needed to invest in the basics to shore up day-to-day operations and close the chasm between their ambitious goals and their ability to deliver.

City Year's campaign raised $30 million for organizational capacity from 1999 to 2004, with the goals of "maximizing impact, growing to scale, building sustainable resources, and increasing leverage." City Year was incredibly strategic about linking these critical capacities with its ability to both sustain the current level of impact and have greater impact in the future.

It worked with a formerly anonymous funder, Atlantic Philanthropies, to provide the lead grant of $10 million, and raised a total of $30 million over five years. The funding was invested in twelve critical areas of "enterprise-wide business processes, management systems, and organizational capacities," which included things like recruiting software, systems to engage and mobilize the alumni network, a public policy "Action Tank," information technology, staff development, and strategic planning.[3]

"It was [cofounder] Michael Brown's idea for a capital campaign to build the capacities we needed to grow," says board member Eilene Jacobs. "We had not seen this approach before, but it made a huge amount of sense. With every new site, it felt like we were reinventing the wheel. We realized we needed to have the systems—finance, training, and development tools—to run the organization much better. There has been a high return on that investment. Now we are well positioned to grow and run the organization much better."

Teach For America's goal was to double its budget from $20 million to $40 million in the five years ending in 2005, and now it is seeking to double it again by 2010. To achieve this, the group deliberately identified individual and foundation donors for the campaign and approached them for growth funds separate from ongoing needs. With a campaign mentality and a rigorously constructed plan in place, Teach For America met its revenue goals, despite the fact that the years following the 9/11 terrorist attacks were one of the most challenging fund-raising periods in recent American history for many nonprofits.

The organization also used some of this funding to build a robust operating reserve, so that it had enough cash on hand to cover six months' of operating costs. The strategy allowed it to resist dipping into growth funds to support annual expenses when setbacks occurred. When Congress threatened to cut AmeriCorps in 2003, Teach For America's teacher education awards were cut. Still, the organization covered the cost of the awards with funds from its operating reserve, while keeping its programs running. A key to the success of both Teach For America and City Year was the deliberateness and discipline with which they approached growth campaigns. Their leaders realized that they needed to step out of the day-to-day fund-raising grind and focus on the bigger picture in order to build a sustainable organization. They couldn't keep living from grant to grant, without being more strategic about how their funding and their organization supported their long-term aspirations. This took conviction and leadership at all levels of the organization. "Michael brought the board along with him," explains Jacobs.

At America's Second Harvest, the challenge was to raise funds for the major technology upgrades needed to support its complex food transportation systems. Initially, large funders were reluctant to invest in such mundane things. "ConAgra was the first big donor to the technology campaign—and they initially didn't want to fund it," says David Prendergast, senior vice president for technology and planning. "They wanted to fund the Kids Cafe program. But our development department said, 'We can't do these things unless we improve our infrastructure.' So they made an initial, multimillion-dollar, multiyear grant."

Prendergast says the nonprofit had to be strategic and persistent about its fund-raising plan. "We were successful in putting together a technology plan," he says. "We then went out and got significant funding of $12 million over a five-year period to do the things we needed to do." Although it does cost money to maintain technology, the ongoing costs are much less than the initial investment and can be manageably folded into the operating budget.

Other nonprofits conducted more traditional capital campaigns, for a building or for an endowment used to increase their financial sustainability. National Council of La Raza raised $35 million in the last few years of Raul Yzaguirre's tenure, using the funds to buy a building, invest heavily in infrastructure, and set aside a financial cushion to subsidize ongoing operations. "There is no question that we will be able to raise much more money once we put these systems in place," says CEO Janet Murguia, underscoring the adage that it takes money to make (or raise) money. "It's going to be a lot easier—our plans will allow us to demonstrate how we can be credible and effective."

Of course, because of their investment in infrastructure, these organizations don't always meet traditional measures of nonprofit success—despite some groups' efforts to structure campaigns as separate from annual operating budgets. The most common measure used to evaluate nonprofit performance is the ubiquitous overhead ratio, which shows how much money a group spends on its programs (or services) versus how much it spends to maintain its own operations (administration, fund raising, and so on). Not all of the nonprofits we studied score well on these conventional measures, as Table 24.1 illustrates.[4]

The problem with using these metrics is that they fall into the trap of measuring financial inputs or ratios as a proxy for success, rather than measuring *impact,* or the amount of change accomplished with that investment (Lowell, Trelstad, and Meehan, 2005). Worse yet, they assume that nonprofits can implement programs without any infrastructure or support. They may encourage donors to support groups that spend too little on people, IT systems, or management, which can lead to weak organizations at best, or accounting trickery at worst.

The nonprofits we identified, however, don't spend too much time worrying about these metrics. They spend what they need to sustain their impact.

Organization	GuideStar Rating
America's Second Harvest	★ ★ ★
Center on Budget and Policy Priorities	★ ★ ★ ★
City Year	★ ★ ★ ★
Environmental Defense	★ ★ ★
Exploratorium	★ ★
Habitat for Humanity	★
The Heritage Foundation	★ ★ ★
National Council of La Raza	★ ★
Share Our Strength	★ ★
Teach For America	★ ★ ★
YouthBuild USA	★ ★

Table 24.1.   Conventional Ratings Don't Account for Impact
Note: Self-help is not rated.

A PLATFORM FOR FUTURE IMPACT

As these groups have learned, it's not enough only to focus externally—they must also build strong organizations. For some, particularly those that are still growing rapidly, it is like playing a never-ending game of catch-up. As they grow and expand, they must build their organizational capacity to fill in the gap between their expectations and their effectiveness. Other nonprofits we studied have already reached their own "steady state" and are content to remain about the same size as they are today. Figure 24.4 gives an overview of the growth trajectory of these nonprofits over the past thirty-five years.

As Figure 24.4 illustrates, these nonprofits have taken many different paths to growth. A few scaled up their operations relatively quickly. Teach For America and City Year were both founded around 1990, and within fifteen years were raising annual revenues on par with more mature organizations like Environmental Defense and The Heritage Foundation. Others grew at a moderate pace and then shot up in a moment of breakthrough impact, such as when Self-Help received a $50 million Ford Foundation grant and combined it with investment capital from Fannie Mae.

And although some organizations have begun to intentionally level off their growth, several are in the midst of major expansion campaigns: Teach For America and Environmental Defense each looks to double its budget in the next few years. Environmental Defense is undertaking a growth campaign to reach a budget of $100 million in the next five years. "We're at a real tipping point,"

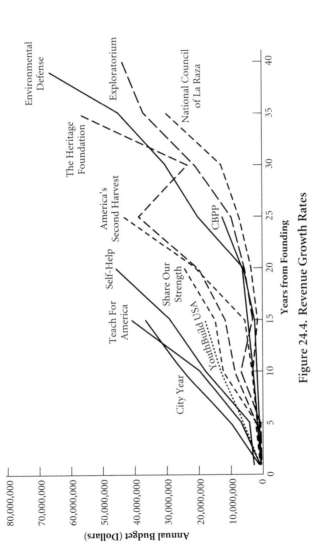

Figure 24.4. Revenue Growth Rates

Note: Historical data for Habitat for Humanity were not available. America's Second Harvest revenue does not include value of in-kind donations.

says David Yarnold, executive vice president. "We're poised at this place where our success going forward will be all about our ability to execute. It's not about having enough money—we have a network of allies and donors, and just need to figure out how to activate them. It's all about execution. We're building the airplane while flying it."

Teach For America was almost midway through its five-year growth campaign to double in size as this was written. The goal was to take the budget from $50 million to $100 million, and the campaign was showing every promise of succeeding. "Scale is critical to our success," says founder Wendy Kopp. "We have to play such a numbers game. We have to have a critical mass of corps members within communities to make them feel part of something larger, and influence the consciousness of the country." The group has worked with the Monitor Institute, a consulting group, to identify the critical capacities needed to expand the organization and increase its impact exponentially.

On the flip side are organizations like Heritage and the Center on Budget and Policy Priorities, which believe they have reached an efficient scale and are not interested in growing much more. Because they focus mainly on advocacy, and work through informal networks at the state and local levels, they don't actually need to grow to have more impact. "I'm very skeptical of growth," says Stuart Butler, vice president of Heritage. "I think there's a danger of inefficiency with size. I already spend a significant amount of time navigating Heritage—I think that is a cost. We've tried to keep it to around two hundred staff for a while."

For others, the challenge isn't necessarily to raise more money to grow, as much as it is to focus on shoring up the organization. For Habitat, which already has twenty-one hundred affiliates globally, the new emphasis is not on growth but on sustainability and on deepening the quality and impact of participants in the network. With a new CEO in place, Habitat is finally building the organization needed to support its global movement.

Share Our Strength is similarly focused on building its internal capacity. "We're really good at raising money for others, not ourselves," says Pat Nicklin, managing director. "We've been good at coming up with corporate partnerships and events that raise money for hunger. But we're not as good at raising working capital for the organization. We keep putting our oxygen mask on other people, not ourselves. It's ironic—everyone else is trying to diversify into what we are doing, and we're going the other way."

Regardless of which choice these nonprofits make, it's clear that most of them have demonstrated that they can sustain their current levels of impact, if not increase them over time. They recognize that they have to attract talented people, empower them, and compensate them adequately; that they have to invest money to raise money; and that they must build sufficient organizational systems to remain effective. And they do all these things despite powerful countervailing forces.

Although the challenges to building nonprofit capacity are real, they are not insurmountable. These groups have already proved themselves to the world, and they hold more power over their futures than most people realize. "It becomes a self-fulfilling prophecy, whether you operate with fear or you operate from the place of, 'This is our plan, and we are going to execute against it,'" says Kopp of Teach For America. "You really can control your own destiny."

Notes

1. This story and most narrative background were taken from W. Kopp, *One Day, All Children. . .: The Unlikely Triumph of Teach For America, and What I Learned Along the Way.* New York: Perseus Books, 2001.

2. Based on our analysis of organizations' current sources of revenue. The idea of looking at concentration of funding in one source came from William Foster's paper, cited below.

3. *The City Year Challenge: Strengthening Our Capacities to Serve.* [Internal document].

4. GuideStar ratings were taken from GuideStar reports on the organizations in our sample. Stars are assigned on the basis of organizational "efficiency," with 4 being the highest rating and 0 the lowest, determined by such measures as the ratio of spending on administration versus spending on programs. For more details, see www.guidestar.org. Charity Navigator uses a similar rating system. Nonprofit data analyzed by these sites are taken from IRS form 990s, which nonprofits are required to file for tax purposes.

References

Bell, J., Moyers, R., and Wolfred, T. *Daring to Lead 2006: A National Study of Nonprofit Executive Leadership.* San Francisco: CompassPoint, 2006.

Collins, J. *Good to Great: Why Some Companies Make the Leap . . . and Others Don't.* New York: HarperBusiness, 2001.

Foster, W. "How Nonprofits Get Really Big." *Stanford Social Innovation Review*, 2007, 5(2), 46–55. (*Note:* This exact quotation was taken from an earlier internal draft of the paper and does not appear in the published version.)

Letts, C. W., Ryan, W. P., and Grossman, A. "Virtuous Capital: What Foundations Can Learn from Venture Capitalists." *Harvard Business Review on Nonprofits.* Boston: Harvard Business Review Press, 1999.

Lowell, S., Trelstad, B., and Meehan, B. "The Ratings Game." *Stanford Social Innovation Review*, 2005, 3(2), 39–45.

At time of original publishing Leslie R. Crutchfield was a managing director of Ashoka and a research grantee of the Aspen Institute's Nonprofit Sector and Philanthropy Program. Heather McLeod Grant was an adviser to the Stanford Center for Social Innovation and research fellow with Duke University's Center for the Advancement of Social Entrepreneurship (CASE).

CHAPTER TWENTY-FIVE

Characteristics of Leadership Effectiveness

Implementing Change and

Driving Innovation in Organizations

Ann Gilley

Pamela Dixon

Jerry W. Gilley

R esearch indicates that numerous variables impact a leader's effectiveness. In this study, the authors explore leadership effectiveness in driving change and innovation, along with the precursory skills necessary to do so. The findings confirm previously identified low rates of organizational success with change and point to skill deficiencies as a cause. Specifically, the abilities to communicate appropriately and motivate others significantly influence a leader's ability to effectively implement change and drive innovation.

It is said that organizations remain competitive because they are able to support and implement continuous and transformational change (Cohen, 1999). Given this fact, it is no wonder that organizational change has been the subject of much research. Many have sought to explain the principles of change, how to manage it, and why it is so difficult to achieve. Theories, models, and multi-step

Originally published as "Characteristics of Leadership Effectiveness: Implementing Change and Driving Innovation in Organizations," *Human Resource Development Quarterly*, 19. (February 2008).

approaches to change abound, but successfully implementing it often proves elusive (Senge, Kleiner, Roberts, Ross, Roth, and Smith, 1999). Research indicates that one-third to two-thirds of major change initiatives are deemed failures (Beer and Nohria, 2000; Bibler, 1989) or have made the situation worse (Beer, Eisenstat, and Spector, 1990). It has been suggested that the rate of failure to deliver sustainable change at times reaches 80 to 90 percent (Cope, 2003).

Why is this? According to literature from the past two decades, unsuccessful implementation of change efforts stems from an organization's inability to remain flexible and adaptive to a dynamic business environment (Bossidy and Charan, 2002; Drucker, 1999; Finkelstein, 2003). These unsuccessful attempts have caused operational and financial difficulties for organizations. Those organizations that are able to anticipate, adapt to, and execute change successfully experience increased long-term viability (Conner, 1992; Cummings and Worley, 2005; Pfeffer, 2005). The critical factor in enabling and driving change efforts is the leadership within the organization (Gilley, 2005; Gilley, Quatro, Hoekstra, Whittle, and Maycunich, 2001; Pfeffer, 2005).

We contribute to the literature on leadership and organizational change and innovation by answering our two research questions: (1) What is the level of leadership effectiveness in implementing change, and, subsequently, driving innovation within organizations? (2) Which specific leadership skills are perceived as necessary to execute change initiatives and drive innovation? Throughout this chapter, our reference to "leaders" implies all levels of leaders and managers within an organization.

CHANGE AND INNOVATION

Emerging as a market leader or remaining competitive is dependent on change efforts that drive organizational innovation (Denning, 2005). For more than two decades, there has been increasing emphasis on change and innovation as primary determinants of organizational success (Drucker, 1999; Ford and Gioia, 2000; Friedman, 2005; Johansson, 2004). This in turn has resulted in research focused on how to harness change and innovation in ways that best yield a competitive advantage (Florida, 2005; Friedman, 2005; Howkins, 2001).

Early on, Kuhn (1970) argued that change efforts that reject current paradigms or question fundamental assumptions—also known as double loop learning (Argyris and Schön, 1996)—are considered transformational. Change can also be viewed as incremental, working within a current organizational paradigm. The latter is suggestive of single loop learning occurring in the organization (Argyris and Schön, 1996). Although continuous and incremental change is important for organizational sustainability, transformational change is the key to realizing innovation in an organization (Kuhn, 1970).

Change initiatives that ostensibly lead to innovation have been applied to products and services, as well as to technology, organizational structure, and processes (Lewis, 1994) and organizational business models (IBM, 2006). Regardless of where efforts are focused, innovation necessitates disruptive change—not just getting better at what the organization currently does (incremental) but changing to the extent of clearly differentiating itself in the market (Denning, 2005).

Successful execution of transformational change has been identified as leading to innovation, and subsequently increased competitiveness. However, the literature abounds with accounts of failed attempts and the rarity with which organizations demonstrate the ability to achieve transformational change (Beer and Nohria, 2000; Cope, 2003; Senge, Kleiner, Roberts, Ross, Roth, and Smith, 1999). It has been suggested that a primary reason for an organization's inability to change and innovate lies with its leaders—the individuals who are responsible for leading change efforts—and their lack of skill or will, impeding successful implementation. Although many organizations and their leaders desire lasting, meaningful change, few are capable of achieving it. Organizations often go through the motions necessary to bring about change while simultaneously hoping that its catalyst disappears (Conner, 1992).

The apparent chasm that exists between an organization's intentions to implement change initiatives and the ability of the leadership to successfully execute and realize transformational change is deserving of critical investigation. The literature reviewed in these pages explains change, innovation, and the leadership skills that enable both. The end results lead to a view of change and innovation as an integrated whole, offering insight into how leadership skills and abilities influence one's effectiveness at implementing change, which in turn nurtures and cultivates creativity, enabling innovation and ultimately transformative change.

Organizational Change

Organizational inability to embrace change is nothing new (Ulrich, 1998). Although individuals within organizations recognize the need for change, few are able to sustain successful change efforts. People are inherently resistant to change; avoiding or resisting it is human nature (Bovey and Hede, 2001). Although resisting change is natural, failing to change can be deadly. Businesses that don't change disappear (Lewis, Goodman, and Fandt, 2001). Thus the importance of the leader's role and skills in driving change is clear.

Large-scale, transformational change significantly affects how organizations are managed, how they function, and their ability to remain competitive (Gilley, Quatro, Hoekstra, Whittle, and Maycunich, 2001; Preskill and Torres, 1999). Changing how one manages and/or how the organization functions is an essential step in successful execution; however, more often than not, lack of these abilities is cited as a barrier (Bossidy and Charan, 2002; Gilley, 2005). Other barriers are failure to understand effective change implementation techniques, lack of management recognition or rewards for those who change, and inability to motivate others to change (Burke, 1992; Kotter, 1996; Patterson, 1997; Ulrich, 1998).

In all cases, the leadership in an organization can influence and remove these barriers. Specifically, it has been suggested that organizational leadership has a direct influence on behavior in the work environment that enables change and innovative thinking and actions (Drucker, 1999; Gilley, 2005; Howkins, 2001) that overcome individual resistance and obstacles.

Innovation

Creativity has been described as the emergence of novel ideas; innovation can be described as implementation of those ideas (Zornada, 2006). There are multiple elements within the organizational culture and work environment that serve to enhance or inhibit innovation. According to a study conducted by Birdi (2005), poor leadership support and an inadequate work environment limit the impact of creativity in terms of influencing idea implementation leading to innovation. Leaders influence the culture and environment by focusing on different ways of thinking, as well as ways of "being" or taking action.

As complex adaptive systems (Wheatley, 1992), organizations need to generate new ideas, grow, renew, and change; this requires the capacity to quickly respond to novel problems or situations in the environment (Berkes, Colding, and Folke, 2000). To support adaptability and capacity building, organizations rely on innovation, typically by implementing initiatives that support continuous learning and performance improvement (change). Further, organizations demonstrate agility by changing structure or processes. Underlying patterns of thinking regarding relationships, information sharing, and behaviors manifest structures and processes (Wheatley and Kellner-Rogers, 1999). Therefore it can be inferred that approaches to ensuring innovation consist of changing both how we think and how we behave (action). Literature on creativity offers insight into thinking differently through creative problem solving (John-Steiner, 2000; Zornada, 2006) and the role of environmental support, such as leadership practices and actions. Hence, the linkage between leadership skills and abilities and effectiveness at implementing change and driving innovation is clear. Rogers (2003) explains human reactions to change and innovation in his research into adoption of innovation. An innovation is the direct result of any idea, practice, procedure, or object perceived as new by an individual. The degree of newness for the individual determines his or her reaction to the change. Adoption of the new idea or practice is influenced by how the change is communicated via certain channels, over time, among members of a system.

Rogers' stages of adoption (2003) are *awareness* of the innovation, *interest* in the change, *trial*, the *decision* to continue or quit, and *adoption* of the innovation into one's lifestyle. Individuals are categorized on the basis of their general acceptance of change as *innovators, early adopters, early majority, late majority,* and *laggards.* Innovators are venturesome, information seekers; early adopters are opinion leaders who are generally respected members of the social group; the early majority are deliberate accepters of change; the late majority are skeptical and occasionally succumb to peer pressure in order to change; and laggards are traditional, steadfast individuals who often attempt to hold on to the past. Clearly, members of the late majority and laggards are most resistant to change. Effective management of change (managing individual resistance through communications) has proven to be an essential contributor to the success of a change initiative.

LEADERSHIP SKILLS AND ABILITIES

According to Miles (2001), any change, no matter its size, has a cascading effect on an organization. Consequently, leaders at all levels in organizations will routinely confront the challenges of change while concurrently facing opportunities to create a work environment that supports change readiness and innovation. The six skill sets discussed next have been found to positively influence the organizational success rate and have therefore been incorporated as targeted elements into numerous change models (Gilley, 2005; Kotter, 1996; Ulrich, 1998).

Ability to Coach

Hudson (1999) suggests that the primary role in coaching is that of an agent of change, which he argues is a constant in today's organizations. Moreover, he believes that leaders who coach help employees improve their renewal capacity and resilience, which positively influences organizational success. Accordingly, Hudson suggests that coaching entails the ability to question the status quo, approach situations from a new perspective, and allow others to make mistakes and learn from them. Coaching inspires others to be their best, remain future-oriented and cautiously optimistic, and pursue useful alliances and networks that enhance cooperation and results.

Research reveals that coaching involves establishing a collegial partnership between leaders and their employees, one based on two-way communication that is nonjudgmental, free of fear, personal, and professional (Gilley and Gilley, 2007). Coaching allows managers the opportunity to better serve their employees in implementing change and innovation activities. Coaching surfaces creative approaches to solving conflicts that often arise during change, and it enables organizations to identify and incorporate new ideas, processes, or procedures that drive innovation (Gilley and Boughton, 1996).

Whitmore (1997) suggests that the first key element of coaching is *awareness*. The *Concise Oxford Dictionary* defines awareness as "conscious, not ignorant, having knowledge." *Webster's New World Dictionary* adds: "Awareness implies having knowledge of something through alertness in observing or in interpreting what one sees, hears, feels, etc." Whitmore suggests that awareness can be raised or heightened considerably through focused attention and practice.

Ability to Reward

LeBoeuf's research (1985) revealed that a compensation and reward philosophy should be based on rewarding employees for the "right" performance. Organizations encourage change and innovation by demonstrating their understanding that "the things that get rewarded get done" (p. 9). This approach ensures that the organization will secure its desired outcomes. By contrast, failure to reward the right behaviors leads to unsatisfactory outcomes.

A compensation and reward philosophy should be flexible enough to take into account the dynamic nature of the organization's change initiatives, along with other important system-wide activities (Flannery, Hofrichter, and Platten, 1996). Consequently, compensation and rewards are to be fluid and subject to review, alteration, or redesign.

An effective reward philosophy takes into account each step of the organization's change process. Employees respond favorably to celebrating milestones and being rewarded for incremental change by leaders who create win-win situations related to change and innovation (Lussier, 2006). Reward programs should be designed to help an organization achieve specific change outcomes, such as creativity and innovation, leadership, teamwork and cooperation, commitment and loyalty, long-term solutions, and learning and applying new skills (Ulrich, Zenger, and Smallwood, 1999).

Ability to Communicate

Denning (2005) argues that innovation requires leadership to move beyond the command-and-control mode of managing, which ultimately maintains the status quo. Specifically, innovation requires an array of communication techniques—for example, "communicating to the organization the risks in clinging to the status quo and the potential rewards of embracing a radically different future" (p. 12). Communication such as this creates a sense of urgency that motivates individuals to act. Specifically, leaders are advised to provide abundant information to employees about proposed changes and innovation, inform employees about the rationale for change, hold meetings to address employees' questions and concerns, and give those who feel the impact of the change opportunities to discuss how change might affect them (Rousseau and Tijoriwala, 1999).

According to work by Luecke (2003), communication is an effective tool for motivating employees involved in change. It is essential in overcoming resistance to change initiatives, for preparing employees for the pluses and minuses of change, and for giving employees a personal stake in the change process. Saunders (1999) identified eleven recommendations for communicating during a change initiative:

1. Specify the nature of change.
2. Explain why.
3. Explain the scope of the change.
4. Develop a graphic representation of the change initiative that employees can understand.
5. Predict negative aspects of implementation.
6. Explain the criteria for success and how it will be measured.
7. Explain how people will be rewarded for success.
8. Repeat, repeat, and repeat the purpose of change and actions planned.
9. Use a diverse set of communication styles that are appropriate for employees.
10. Make communication a two-way proposition.
11. Be a model for the change initiative.

Communication includes giving employees feedback and reinforcement to guarantee their motivation to implement and manage change (Peterson and Hicks, 1996). Positive feedback and reinforcement powerfully encourage employee participation and involvement. Absent feedback, employees make uninformed decisions regarding their performance, resulting in mistakes that can lead to disastrous results. Without feedback, employees do not know where they are, how they are doing, or whether they are applying new skills and knowledge appropriately. Feedback informs employees as to whether they are producing results on time, at the correct level of quality, and in the correct form.

Ability to Motivate

Webster's Dictionary defines motivation as "influence, incentive, or drive; that which causes us to act." Understanding *why* people do the things they do is not an easy task; predicting *how* individuals will respond to a situation may be tougher yet. Motivation is a unique, very personal concept. In an organizational context, a leader's ability to persuade and influence others to work in a common direction is imperative. A leader's ability to influence is based partly on his or her skill and partly on the motivation level of the individual employee. It has been shown that predictors of motivation include job satisfaction, perceived equity, and organizational commitment (Schnake, 2007). In other words, motivation is either positively or negatively affected by the experience an employee has within a given work environment and with the leadership.

Carlisle and Murphy (1996) contend that motivating others requires skilled managers who can organize and foster a motivating environment, communicate effectively, address employees' questions, generate creative ideas, prioritize ideas, direct personnel practices, plan employees' actions, commit employees to action, and provide follow-up to overcome motivational problems. In a recent study involving highly creative technical professionals, it was identified that *how* these employees were managed was a significant motivating factor (Hebda, Vojak, Griffin, and Price, 2007). Specifically, 23 percent of respondents indicated that having freedom, flexibility, and resources was viewed as a significant motivator; and 25 percent indicated that the most important motivator was the time provided by their management—a long stretch of time to focus on solving complex problems (Hebda, Vojak, Griffin, and Price, 2007). Leifer, McDermott, Colarelli-O'Conner, Peters, Rice, and Veryzer (2000) support this contention and state that innovation is most common in organizations with leaders who support and reward new ideas.

Additionally, a valuable management skill is the ability to attract and retain individuals who are passionate about their work and intrinsically motivated. Incentive and motivation problems are largely management problems—the manifestation of action or lack thereof by poorly skilled leaders, administrators, or supervisors. Organizations that make it a practice to hire or promote talented leaders—those who understand human behavior—are well on the way to motivating their employees (Gilley, Boughton, and Maycunich, 1999).

Today leaders are planning, organizing, and executing work processes in complex organizations. The complexity reflects continuous changes in technology, shifts in workforce demographics, and the need for faster decision making and development of the capability to continuously adapt and change. It is within this organizational context that leaders must create a work environment that elicits employee motivation. Incentive and motivation problems are largely management problems, a manifestation of action or lack thereof on the part of poorly skilled leaders, administrators, or supervisors.

Ability to Involve and Support Others

Sims' research (2002) reveals that employee involvement and support prove critical to successfully implementing change. Showing confidence in the employee's ability to be successful on the job and valuing contributions also demonstrate support. The ability to connect with employees and offer a high level of support has been positively related to innovation and creativity (Williams, 2001). Kotter and Schlesinger (1979) assert that those allowed to meaningfully participate in change are more committed to its success as their relevant contributions are integrated into the change plan.

Research by Birdi (2005) shows that management support (involving employees, soliciting feedback) greatly influenced the extent to which action was taken on creative ideas. Pfeffer and Sutton (2000), however, suggest that actually taking action (versus talking about being innovative) rarely occurs. Other authors give examples of overcoming barriers to taking action and realizing success through innovation. Specifically, successfully driving change and innovation requires a facilitative management style ensuring that communication (including coaching, information sharing, and appropriate feedback) mechanisms are in place, worker involvement flourishes, and social networks (teams and collaboration) are supported (Denning, 2005; Drucker, 1999; Williams, 2001).

Ability to Promote Teamwork and Collaboration

Effectively managing teams and structuring work groups so as to support collaboration are two leadership abilities critical for achieving organizational goals. Early in the twentieth century, management scholars made an empirical case for collaborative approaches to managing (Follett, 1924). More recently, Williams (2001) and Fuqua and Kurpius (1993) found significant influence on change and innovation flows from teamwork and collaboration in the form of work group design.

Interpersonal skill combines with group processes and structure to promote or inhibit teamwork and collaboration, which ultimately have an impact on desired outputs (Fuqua and Kurpius, 1993; Nadler and Tushman, 1989). Also, work groups can be designed so that members who have diverse skills and backgrounds can communicate and interact such that members are able to constructively challenge each other's ideas (Williams, 2001). Further, it has been evidenced that social networks have important effects on team performance and viability (Balkundi and Harrison, 2006). Specifically, the results of a meta-analysis indicate that teams with a dense configuration of connections within their social network tended to attain their goals more frequently and remained intact as a group for a longer period of time (Balkundi and Harrison, 2006).

Leaders sabotage teamwork and collaboration by creating a hostile environment, setting unrealistic expectations, communicating poorly, failing to furnish skills training, and using coercive control rather than coactive control (Follett, 1924; Longenecker and Neubert, 2000; Rayner, 1996; Zhou and George, 2003). Conversely, those who establish open communications, share leadership, define clear roles and work assignments, value diverse styles, and maintain a sense of informality promote effectiveness in teamwork and collaboration (Parker, 1990).

Review of the literature has presented scholarship and perspectives over the past few decades that suggest a lack of results and unrealized potential in terms of managing change and bringing about innovation. Further, it has been shown that certain managerial practices and skills positively influence organizational results through successful execution of change initiatives. It is clear that the potential to increase market competitiveness and growth is within the control of an organization's leadership. It is through the deliberate and disciplined action of management that organizations effectively implement change initiatives and cultivate a work environment conducive to innovative achievements.

METHODS

This chapter draws from our study of leader effectiveness in implementing change within an organization. A host of research on change reveals that effective implementation often proves elusive, in spite of numerous models and theories for successful change facilitation (Kotter, 1996; Lewin, 1951; Ulrich, 1998). Offering another perspective, recent research revealed that nearly 55 percent of CEOs believe their past successes at implementing change were "quite" or "very" successful, with only 13 percent responding that previous change efforts were "unsuccessful" or only "a little successful" (IBM, 2006, p. 45). One consensus is clear: change is here to stay (Sims, 2007), and organizations have an opportunity to harness innovation as a way of remaining viable.

Research Questions

Our approach was to examine the skills and behaviors of leadership and management with respect to change and innovation as perceived by employees at all levels (including mid-level and upper-level management).

Specifically, we investigated whether leaders effectively implement change within their organization. Further, we asked about the frequency with which leaders display specific skills associated with effective change implementation. The results of this study will give leaders insight into employee perceptions of leader effectiveness in implementing change and innovation, and the specific skills required to be successful (examples being coaching, rewarding, communicating, motivating, building teams, and involving employees).

This project is based on results of our larger two-year study of leadership practices. Our initial overall interest was to explore the macro and micro processes of organizational leadership and management. Our desire to develop greater understanding of change and innovation within the broad spectrum of people and industries led us to pursue a quantitative research design for this specific focus.

Data Collection

This descriptive study consisted of collecting and analyzing employee perceptions of their management's effectiveness at implementing change. A written questionnaire solicited data that were largely perceptual.

Our desire was to examine a broad range of participants, industries, and companies. Participants in the convenience sample were students in MBA and OD master's degree classes at three four-year universities (two public and one private) over two years (four semesters). The two public institutions are in the Midwest and Mountain West; the private institution is in the South. All master's students in these particular degree programs were made aware of the study and voluntarily participated; thus respondents self-selected. Survey questions sought basic demographic data such as participant age, title or level within the organization, gender, and industry type. Of 362 students with access to the survey, 337 responded, yielding a 93 percent response rate.

Data Analysis

The dependent variable in this study was the frequency with which employees believe their leaders effectively implement change and innovation, ranging from "never" to "always" on a five-point scale. The independent variables explored by this study included specific leadership skills and abilities related to change (Burke, 1992; Conner, 1992; Gill, 2003; Gilley, 2005; Sims, 2002; Ulrich, 1998). Employees were asked to evaluate the frequency with which leaders:

1. Coach employees

2. Effectively reward or recognize employees

3. Appropriately communicate with employees

4. Motivate employees

5. Involve employees

6. Encourage teamwork and collaboration

7. Effectively implement change (dependent variable)

Associated frequencies and percentages were calculated for all questions and data. Correlations were run between and among all variables, while regression analysis further tested the independent variables' degree of influence on change.

FINDINGS

The respondent population was 48.4 percent male, 50.6 percent female, with 1 percent not reporting gender. Industry type was 10.42 percent manufacturing, 54.46 percent service, 15.77 percent education, 11.61 percent professional, 6.55 percent government, and 0.89 percent "other." When specified, the category "other" included medical, consultant, technician, doctoral candidate, and senior research specialist. Of the respondents, 62.09 percent indicated that their immediate supervisor was male, while 37.31 percent listed their direct manager as female.

Front-line employees made up 39.58 percent of the population, supervisors or team leaders were 23.81 percent, mid-level leaders represented 22.62 percent, senior and executive leaders were 11.61 percent, and 2.38 percent listed "other." When specified, the category "other" included owner, CEO, and self-employed.

Table 25.1 reports descriptive statistics, including frequencies and percentages, for the dependent variable (effectiveness at implementing change). Survey respondents indicated that leaders are "never" or "rarely" effective at implementing change with a frequency of 35.91 percent, "sometimes" effective 40.06 percent, and "usually" or "always" effective 24.03 percent, with a mean of 2.86.

Table 25.2 lists descriptive statistics and inter-correlations. All study variables showed high positive correlation (.50–1.0; Cohen, 1988). Leaders' skills in communications and motivation (variables 3 and 4) reflected the highest positive relationships with change implementation (.66 and .67, respectively).

	Never (1)	Rarely (2)	Sometimes (3)	Usually (4)	Always (5)
N	33	88	135	54	27
%	9.80	26.11	40.06	16.02	8.01
CUM		35.91	75.97	91.99	100.00

Table 25.1.   Leader Effectiveness in Implementing Change
Note: N = 337, Mean = 2.8635, *SD* = 1.0574.

M	SD		1	2	3	4	5	6	7
1. Coaching		2.84	1.08						
2. Rewarding		2.90	0.97	.56					
3. Communicating	3.02	0.99	.61	.55					
4. Motivating		2.80	1.01	.69	.65	.65			
5. Involving		3.08	1.15	.63	.58	.60	.69		
6. Teams		3.33	1.07	.60	.59	.58	.66	.69	
7. Implementing change		2.86	1.05	.59	.52	.66	.67	.59	.57

Table 25.2.   Descriptive Statistics and Inter-Correlations

Variables	Model 1			Model 2		
	b	s.e.	P-val	b	s.e.	P-val
1. Coaching	0.089	0.053	0.095	0.100	0.050*	0.046**
2. Rewarding	0.008	0.057	0.877			
3. Communicating	0.341	0.059	0.000	0.350	0.054	0.000***
4. Motivating	0.268	0.069	0.000***	0.295	0.061	0.000***
5. Involving	0.102	0.058	0.081	0.124	0.049	0.012**
6. Teams	0.089	0.057	0.123			
N		337			337	
R^2		0.554			0.550	
R^2_{adj}	0.542			0.545		

Table 25.3. Regression Analysis
Note: $^*p<.05$; $^{**}p<.01$; $^{***}p<.001$.

Table 25.3 reveals the results of regression analysis. Simultaneous regression is appropriate for detecting significant influences of several independent variables (e.g., motivation) on one dependent variable. Initial results indicated significant ($p = .05$) influence by variables 3 and 4 (communications and motivation), and potentially significant influence by variables 1 and 5 (coaching and involving). We removed the non-significant variables (2 and 6) and tested again. Multiple regressions distilled the six independent variables to a four-variable model reflecting significant impact on the dependent variable (effectiveness in change implementation). Specifically, significant ($p < .001$) influence on the dependent variable was exhibited by variables 3 and 4, leadership skill and ability in communications (.000) and motivation (.000); while lesser significance ($p < .05$) surfaced for variables 1 and 5, coaching (.046), and involving others (.012). In each regression, the independent variables explained 55 percent (R^2 adj = 54 percent) of the variance in leadership effectiveness in implementing change.

DISCUSSION

This study makes two contributions to the research on leaders' ability to drive change and innovation along with the skills necessary to do so. First, the findings indicate that employees at all organizational levels hold a somewhat negative perception of their leaders' ability to effectively implement change and innovation. Nearly 76 percent of respondents reported that their leaders never, rarely, or only sometimes effectively implement change. Leadership is often cited as a significant barrier to or resister of change (Gilley, 2005; Schiemann, 1992), despite their self-reports to the contrary (IBM, 2006).

Second, this research reveals a four-component model of skills necessary for leaders to master if they are to successfully drive change and innovation, and it identifies two skills as critical. Previous studies indicate that coaching, rewarding, communicating, motivating, involving others, and building teams, among others, are necessary for leading change and innovation (Burke, 1992; Conner, 1992; Gill, 2003; Gilley, 2005; Sims, 2002; Ulrich, 1998). The data from this study support past research with respect to linkages between these specific skills and leadership effectiveness. Leaders' ability with respect to each of these skills (variables) is highly and positively related to their overall ability to effectively implement change and drive innovation. However, our findings reveal that four specific talents (communications, motivation, involving others, and coaching) have a significant impact on a leader's ability to drive change and innovation, while two of them—communications and the ability to motivate—are critical for one's success.

Communicating appropriately and motivating employees are each highly and significantly associated with effective implementation of change and innovation. Predictors of individual motivation are job satisfaction, perceived equity, and organizational commitment (Schnake, 2007). These predictors are primarily realized through the work environment; therefore, a leader's ability to cultivate a work environment that is focused on employee motivation is critical (Hebda, Vojak, Griffin, and Price, 2007; Carlisle and Murphy, 1996). Unfortunately, little attention is paid to organizational communication strategies (Argenti, Howell, and Beck, 2005).

Additional skills that significantly and directly impact a leader's effectiveness with change and innovation include the willingness and ability to involve employees and coach them in the process of change. Employee involvement is a participative process that enables employees to offer input that increases their commitment to the firm's success. Involving employees in decisions that affect their work and increase their autonomy promotes worker motivation, commitment, productivity, and job satisfaction while lowering scrap rate and turnover (Bowen and Ostroff, 2004; Seibert, Silver, and Randolph, 2004). Similarly, coaching creates an environment that brings out the best in people (Gilley and Boughton, 1996).

The common thread among these four soft skills builds an environment of support for employees facing the challenges posed by impending change and demands for innovation. It is no surprise, then, that the inability to recognize or respond to the need for change and innovation contributes to leaders' failures (Shook, Priem, and McGee, 2003). This study confirms abundant research detailing current and past organizational lack of success with change and points to leadership skill deficiencies as a viable cause. Specifically, the inability to communicate and motivate explains many organizational change failures.

Limitations of the Study

Several caveats are appropriate to this research. The possibility that the facts may differ from perceptions for any individual or situation must be considered a limitation. This study relies on quantified perceptual, highly subjective data; therefore some bias may exist. Common rater biases are recency, stereotyping, and halo and horn effects.

Although we avoided concentrating on any single firm in favor of more generalizable data, there is a tradeoff between depth and breadth. Richness may have been sacrificed in favor of quantity. Our inclusion of industry type data attempted to focus and refine responses while maintaining a broad view.

The convenience sampling methodology that enabled us to draw on MBA and OD master's students at a small number of universities may limit the potential for generalization. Further, these master's students, themselves engaged in the process of self-change and development and the desire for growth, may be particularly critical of their leaders and organizations. Self-selection may yield skewed results (Podsakoff, MacKenzie, Lee, and Podsakoff, 2003), which we have attempted to mitigate by including multiple groups of people.

Recommendations for Future Research

A number of important issues emerged as a result of this study. First, employees have strong opinions regarding the ability of their leaders to successfully drive change and innovation within their firm. These perceptions are no doubt the result of first-hand experience with change initiatives, management, policies, and procedures within their organizations. Exploration of respondent characteristics may add value. For example, does respondent title or level, gender, age, or industry influence perceptions? Additional study of employee perceptions would also add valuable data and enhance reliability.

Next, just as employees have valuable insight and opinions regarding general managerial talent, so too do they have opinions regarding specific skills necessary for effective change management. This study highlights employees' opinions of *what* needs to improve with respect to leadership skills to implement change. Additional investigation may be warranted to explore needed management development and define *who* or which levels of management most need to improve, and in which areas. Additionally, why do leaders lack these skills? How can organizations enhance these skills within their management teams? Finally, research is needed that compares and contrasts employees' perception of the rate of success of change initiatives with documented organizational results (increased revenues, level of customer service, employee satisfaction). Future study should offer evidence of these relationships and support or refute whether employees' perceptions of their leadership are reality, along with the link between perception and expectations.

CONCLUSION

Organizations' difficulty with change and innovation is confirmed by the results of this study. Employees at all levels recognize their leaders' abilities, or lack thereof, to drive change and innovation. This study demonstrates the perceived importance of specific leadership skills and abilities necessary for successful change and innovation. Thus to enhance change effectiveness skills, organizations will be interested in assessing and improving change and innovation talent and abilities of leaders at all levels, including the executive. Given the critical nature of change in the global economy, leadership and management development should focus on change skills and abilities.

References

Argenti, P. A., Howell, R. A., and Beck, K. A. "The Strategic Communication Imperative." *MIT Sloan Management Review*, 2005, 46, 83–89.

Argyris, C., and Schön, D. *Organizational Learning II: A Theory of Action Perspective*. Reading, MA: Addison-Wesley, 1996.

Balkundi, P., and Harrison, D. A. "Ties, Leaders, and Time in Teams: Strong Inference About Network Structure's Effects on Team Viability and Performance." *Academy of Management Review*, 2006, *49*(1), 49–68.

Beer, M., Eisenstat, R. A., and Spector, B. "Why Change Programs Don't Produce Change." *Harvard Business Review*, 1990, *68*(6), 158–166.

Beer, M., and Nohria, N. *Breaking the Code of Change*. Cambridge, MA: Harvard Business School Press, 2000.

Berkes, F., Colding, J., and Folke, C. "Rediscovery of Traditional Ecological Knowledge as Adaptive Management." *Ecological Applications*, 2000, *10*(5), 1251–1262.

Bibler, R. S. *The Arthur Young Management Guide to Mergers and Acquisitions*. Hoboken, NJ: John Wiley & Sons, 1989.

Birdi, K. S. "No idea? Evaluating the Effectiveness of Creativity Training." *Journal of European Industrial Training*, 2005, *29*(2), 102–111.

Bossidy, L., and Charan, R. *Execution: The Discipline of Getting Things Done*. New York: Crown, 2002.

Bovey, W. H., and Hede, A. "Resistance to Organizational Change: The Role of Defense Mechanisms." *Journal of Managerial Psychology*, 2001, *16*(7), 534–549.

Bowen, D. E., and Ostroff, C. "Understanding HRM-Firm Performance Linkages: The Role of the 'Strength' of the HRM System." *Academy of Management Review*, 2004, *29*, 203–221.

Burke, W. W. *Organization Development: A Process of Learning and Changing*. Reading, MA: Addison-Wesley, 1992.

Carlisle, K. E., and Murphy, S. E. *Practical Motivation Handbook*. Hoboken, NJ: John Wiley & Sons, 1996.

Cohen, J. *Statistical Power Analysis for the Behavioral Sciences* (2nd ed.). Hillsdale, NJ: Lawrence Erlbaum Associates, 1988.

Cohen, M. "Commentary on the Organization Science Special Issue on Complexity." *Organization Science*, 1999, *10*, 373–376.

Conner, D. *Managing at the Speed of Change*. New York: Villard, 1992.

Cope, M. *The Seven C's of Consulting* (2nd ed.). London: Financial Times/Prentice-Hall, 2003.

Cummings, T. G., and Worley, C. G. *Organization Development and Change* (8th ed.). New York: Thomson, 2005.

Denning, S. "Transformational Innovation." *Strategy & Leadership*, 2005, *33*(3), 11–16.

Drucker, P. *Management Challenges for the 21st Century*. New York: Harper-Collins, 1999.

Finkelstein, S. *Why Smart Executives Fail and What You Can Learn from Their Mistakes.* New York: Portfolio, 2003.

Flannery, T. P., Hofrichter, D. A., and Platten, P. E. *People Performance and Pay: Dynamic Compensation for Changing Organizations.* New York: The Free Press, 1996.

Florida, R. *The Flight of the Creative Class.* New York: HarperBusiness, 2005.

Follett, M. P. *Creative Experience.* Mary Parker Follett Foundation, 1924. [http://www.follettfoundation.org/mpf.htm] October 2007.

Ford, C., and Gioia, D. "Factors Influencing Creativity in the Domain of Managerial Decision Making." *Journal of Management*, 2000, *26*(4), 705–732.

Friedman, T. L. *The World Is Flat.* New York: Farrar, Straus, & Giroux, 2005.

Fuqua, D. R., and Kurpius, D. J. "Conceptual Models in Organizational Consultation." *Journal of Counseling and Development*, 1993, 602–618.

Gill, R. "Change Management—or Change Leadership?" *Journal of Change Management*, 2003, *3*(4), 307–321.

Gilley, A. *The Manager as Change Leader.* Westport, CT: Praeger, 2005.

Gilley, J. W., and Boughton, N. W. *Stop Managing, Start Coaching!* New York: McGraw-Hill, 1996.

Gilley, J. W., Boughton, N. W., and Maycunich, A. *The Performance Challenge: Developing Management Systems to Make Employees Your Organization's Greatest Asset.* Cambridge, MA: Perseus, 1999.

Gilley, J. W., and Gilley, A. *The Manager as Coach.* Westport, CT: Praeger, 2007.

Gilley, J. W., Quatro, S., Hoekstra, E., Whittle, D. D., and Maycunich, A. *The Manager as Change Agent: A Practical Guide for High Performance Individuals and Organizations.* Cambridge, MA: Perseus, 2001.

Hebda, J. M., Vojak, B. A., Griffin, A., and Price, R. L. "Motivating Technical Visionaries in Large American Companies." *IEEE Transactions on Engineering Management*, 2007, *54*(3), 433–444.

Howkins, J. *The Creative Economy.* London: Penguin, 2001.

Hudson, F. M. *The Handbook of Coaching: A Comprehensive Resource Guide for Managers, Executives, Consultants, and Human Resource Professionals.* San Francisco: Jossey-Bass, 1999.

IBM. IBM Global CEO Study 2006. [http://www31.ibm.com/tela/servlet/asset/66859/The_Global_CEO_Study_2006.pdf] April 2007.

Johansson, F. *The Medici Effect.* Cambridge, MA: Harvard Business School Press, 2004.

John-Steiner, V. *Creative Collaboration.* New York: Oxford University Press, 2000.

Kotter, J. P. *Leading Change*. Cambridge, MA: Harvard Business School Press, 1996.

Kotter, J. P., and Schlesinger, L. A. "Choosing Strategies for Change." *Harvard Business Review*, 1979, 106–114.

Kuhn, T. S. *The Structure of Scientific Revolutions* (2nd ed.). Chicago: University of Chicago Press, 1970.

LeBoeuf, M. *Getting Results: The Secret to Motivating Yourself and Others*. New York: Berkeley Books, 1985.

Leifer, R., McDermott, C. M., Colarelli-O'Connor, G., Peters, L., Rice, M., and Veryzer, R. *Radical Innovation: How Mature Companies Can Outsmart Upstarts*. Cambridge, MA: Harvard Business School Press, 2000.

Lewin, K. *Field Theory in Social Science*. New York: Harper, 1951.

Lewis, R. "From Chaos to Complexity: Implications for Organizations." *Executive Development*, 1994, 7, 16–17.

Lewis, P. S., Goodman, S. H., and Fandt, P. M. (2001). *Management: Challenges in the 21st Century* (3rd ed.). Cincinnati, OH: South-Western.

Longenecker, C. O., and Neubert, M. "Barriers and Gateways to Management Cooperation and Teamwork." *Business Horizons*, 2000, 37–44.

Luecke, R. *Managing Change and Transition: Harvard Business Essentials Series*. Cambridge, MA: Harvard Business School Press, 2003.

Lussier, R. N. *Management Fundamentals: Concepts, Applications, Skill Development* (3rd ed.). Springfield, MA: Thomson South-Western, 2006.

Miles, R. M. "Accelerating Corporate Transformations by Rapidly Engaging All Employees." *Organizational Dynamics*, 2001, 313–321.

Nadler, D. A., and Tushman, M. L. "Organizational Framing Bending: Principles for Managing Reorientation." *Academy of Management Executive*, 1989, 194–203.

Parker, G. M. *Team Players and Teamwork: The New Competitive Business Strategy*. San Francisco: Jossey-Bass, 1990.

Patterson, J. *Coming Clean About Organizational Change*. Arlington, VA: American Association of School Administrators, 1997.

Peterson, D. B., and Hicks, M. D. *Leader as Coach: Strategies for Coaching and Developing Others*. Minneapolis: Personnel Decisions International, 1996.

Pfeffer, J. "Producing Sustainable Competitive Advantage Through the Effective Management of People." *Academy of Management Executive*, 2005, *19*(4), 95–108.

Pfeffer, J., and Sutton, R. I. *The Knowing-Doing Gap: How Smart Companies Turn Knowledge into Action.* Cambridge, MA: Harvard Business School Press, 2000.

Podsakoff, P. M., MacKenzie, S. B., Lee, J. Y., and Podsakoff, N. P. "Common Method Biases in Behavioral Research: A Critical Review of the Literature and Recommended Remedies." *Journal of Applied Psychology*, 2003, *88*, 879–903.

Preskill, H., and Torres, R. T. *Evaluative Inquiry for Learning in Organizations.* Thousand Oaks, CA: Sage, 1999.

Rayner, S. R. "Team Traps: What They Are, How to Avoid Them." *National Productivity Review*, 1996, 101–115.

Rogers, E. M. *Diffusion of Innovations* (4th ed.). New York: The Free Press, 2003.

Rousseau, D. M., and Tijoriwala, S. A. "What's a Good Reason to Change? Motivated Reasoning and Social Accounts in Promoting Organizational Change." *Journal of Applied Psychology*, 1999, 514–528.

Saunders, R. "Communicating Change." *Harvard Management Communication Letter*, 1999, *8*(1), 35–36.

Schiemann, W. "Why Change Fails." *Across the Board*, 1992, 53–54.

Schnake, M. "An Integrative Model of Effort Propensity." *Human Resource Management Review*, 2007, *17*, 274–289.

Seibert, S. E., Silver, S. R., and Randolph, W. A. "Taking Empowerment to the Next Level: A Multiple-Level Model of Empowerment, Performance, and Satisfaction." *Academy of Management Journal*, 2004, *47*(3), 332–349.

Senge, P. M., Kleiner, A., Roberts, C., Ross, R., Roth, G., and Smith, B. *The Dance of Change: The Challenges of Sustaining Momentum in Learning Organizations.* New York: Currency/Doubleday, 1999.

Shook, C. L., Priem, R. L., and McGee, J. E. "Venture Creation and the Enterprising Individual: A Review and Synthesis." *Journal of Management*, 2003, *29*, 379–399.

Sims, R. R. "Employee Involvement Is Still the Key to Successfully Managing Change." In S. J. Sims and R. R. Sims (Eds.), *Changing the Way We Manage Change.* Westport, CT: Quorum Books, 2002.

Sims, R. R. *Human Resource Management: Contemporary Issues, Challenges, and Opportunities.* Charlotte, NC: Information Age, 2007.

Ulrich, D. *Champions of Change: How CEOs and Their Companies Are Mastering the Skills of Radical Change.* San Francisco: Jossey-Bass, 1998.

Ulrich, D., Zenger, J., and Smallwood, N. *Results-Based Leadership: How Leaders Build the Business and Improve the Bottom Line.* Cambridge, MA: Harvard Business School Press, 1999.

Wheatley, M. J. *Leadership and the New Science.* San Francisco: Berrett-Koehler, 1992.

Wheatley, M. J., and Kellner-Rogers, M. *A Simpler Way.* San Francisco: Berrett-Kohler, 1999.

Whitmore, J. *Coaching for Performance: The New Edition of the Practical Guide.* London: Nicholas Brealey, 1997.

Williams, S. "Increasing Employees' Creativity by Training Their Managers." *Industrial and Commercial Training*, 2001, *33*(2), 63–68.

Zhou, J., and George, J. M. "Awakening Employee Creativity: The Role of Leader Emotional Intelligence." *Leadership Quarterly*, 2003, *14*, 545–568.

Zornada, M. "Stroke of Genius?" *Innovation*, November 2006 (pp. 28–29). [www.instam.org].

Ann Gilley is an associate professor in the Department of Management at Ferris State University, Big Rapids, Michigan, where she teaches strategy and management. Pamela Dixon is an assistant professor in the business and economics department at Wayne State College, Wayne, Nebraska. She teaches business ethics, organizational behavior, and strategic human resource management.

At time of original publishing Jerry W. Gilley was professor and chair of the Organizational Performance and Change and Human Resource Studies Programs at Colorado State University, Fort Collins.

CHAPTER TWENTY-SIX

Leadership and Innovation in the Public Sector*

Sandford Borins

—◁∿▷—

Innovation has become a topic of great interest to managers in both the public and private sectors.[1] In the private sector, the rapid development of technology has provided opportunities for firms to launch new products, transform their production processes, and do business in new ways. The Schumpeterian process of creative destruction has become particularly intense and, in many industries, the choice faced by managers is innovate or die.

The conventional wisdom regarding the public sector is that public-sector innovation is a virtual oxymoron. A number of explanations have been put forward as to why this would be the case. Public choice theory argues that public-sector agencies are usually monopolies, with no competitive pressure to innovate.

Originally published as "Leadership and Innovation in the Public Sector," *Leadership & Organization Development Journal, 23.* (2002).

*The author would like to acknowledge the research assistance of Li Zhou and the comments of Eleanor Glor, Beth Herst, Marie Mc Hugh, and two anonymous referees.

Political scientists have observed that the media's and opposition parties' interest in exposing public-sector failures (management in a fishbowl) forms a powerful impediment to innovation. Furthermore, stringent central agency constraints—to minimize corruption and ensure due process—raise barriers to note that public-sector organizations are usually large bureaucracies structured to perform their core tasks with stability and consistently, and resist change or disruption of these tasks (Wilson, 1989, pp. 218–226).

In recent years this conventional wisdom has been questioned. The public sector has faced challenges—such as driving down costs to reduce the debt burden—and opportunities—such as applying information technology—that have forced it to innovate. Non-governmental organizations in a number of countries have attempted to catalyze public-sector innovation by establishing public management innovation awards. These awards shared two key objectives: countering public criticism or hostility to the public service, in part because it is perceived as not being innovative, and encouraging the development and dissemination of innovations and best practices within the public sector.

Public management innovation has become a subject of considerable academic interest. One line of research involves detailed, and sometimes comparative, case studies. In some instances, the innovations were originally identified because they were among the winners of innovation awards. Case studies have dealt with innovations in particular policy areas, such as community policing (Sparrow, 1994), educational choice (Roberts and King, 1996), or civic environmentalism (John, 1994). Other case studies of innovation have dealt with overarching themes such as alternative service delivery (Goldsmith, 2001), the application of information technology (Fountain, 2001), and organizational transformation (Barzelay, 1992; Osborne and Plastrik, 2000). Another approach has involved using large samples of innovations identified by innovation awards to generate and test hypotheses about the process of innovation (Borins, 1998, 2001).

The objective of this chapter is to use the results of both case studies and quantitative analysis to explore the relationship between leadership and innovation in the public sector. That relationship can be probed by asking a number of questions. Who leads innovations? Do innovations create leadership capacity for the public sector? How do leaders exercising formal authority react to innovations? What climate do they create for potential innovators? This chapter starts with a fundamental distinction between bottom-up and top-down innovations and then examines the role that leadership plays in each.

THREE IDEAL TYPES OF PUBLIC-SECTOR INNOVATION

While students of business have found that strategic decisions regarding the adoption of innovations are often taken by CEOs and boards of directors, they have also discovered that many innovations emerge from the bottom up (Kanter, 1988, 2001). In technology-based firms in particular, many innovations result from scientists or other staff with technical expertise following their own research interests to develop new products or processes. Many firms have instituted the practice of giving their researchers one day per week, plus commensurate resources, to work on their own projects. Peters and Waterman (1982) took the argument further, pointing to innovations undertaken by mavericks working at "skunkworks" far from central offices, often operating without a clear mandate from above and using bootlegged resources. Hamel (2000) presented case studies showing that the inspiration for IBM's involvement with the Internet came from two middle managers, one a programmer and the other a marketer, that the idea for the development of Sony's PlayStation video game console came from a mid-level researcher, and that the impetus for Shell to become involved in the production of renewable energy came from a mid-level planner. Hesselbein, Goldsmith, and Somerville (2001), in a recent collection of articles, showed that there is a consensus among private-sector researchers and practitioners about the importance of such bottom-up innovations and provide suggestions for how organizations can support them.

In contrast, the conventional wisdom in the public sector is that whatever innovation occurs comes almost exclusively from the top (Wilson, 1989, pp. 227–232). In both parliamentary and presidential democracies, voters elect politicians to enact policies. While the United States makes a greater proportion of senior executive appointments on a political basis, in many parliamentary democracies the most senior appointments in the public service are made by the politicians. This would seem to place the responsibility—and motivation—for innovation outside the public service itself. (The rationale for the system, of course, is to make the bureaucracy indirectly responsive to the public through the politicians they elect.) Similarly, some public management academics have argued that innovation from within the public service could conflict with traditional values such as due process and accountability (Gawthrop, 1999; Goodsell, 1993; Terry, 1998). Furthermore, stability-seeking public-sector organizations having strong central controls and operating in hostile environments can be expected to have personnel systems that do not reward career public servants for successful innovation but that punish them for unsuccessful attempts. These asymmetric incentives may well lead to adverse selection, namely the avoidance by innovative individuals of public service.

That is the received wisdom. The results of extensive research using applications to several innovation awards tell a different story (Borins, 2001, pp. 27–29).[2] In the USA approximately 50 percent of the innovations originate from middle managers or front-line staff, 25 percent from agency heads, 21 percent from politicians, 13 percent from interest groups, and 10 percent from individuals outside government. In the sample from the economically advanced countries of the Commonwealth (Canada, Australia, New Zealand, Singapore, UK), the proportion from idle managers for front-line staff (82 percent) and agency heads (39 percent) was higher, while that of politicians (11 percent), interest groups (2 percent), and individuals outside government (5 percent) was lower. For the developing countries in the sample (Bangladesh, Ghana, India, Jamaica, Malaysia, Seychelles, South Africa, Zimbabwe), the results are also similar. Since some respondents gave multiple answers, these numbers sum to more than 100 percent (see Table 26.1).

In both Commonwealth samples and the 1995–1998 U.S. data, middle managers were separated from front-line staff. It was found that, in the U.S. sample, middle managers were involved in the initiation of 43 percent of the innovations, while front-line staff were involved in 27 percent, the same frequency as politicians (27 percent) and agency heads (28 percent). The commonwealth sample showed that in the economically advanced countries middle managers were involved in 75 percent of the innovations and front-line staff in 39 percent. In the developing countries, middle managers were involved in initiating 44 percent of the innovations, a figure comparable to the 43 percent in the USA, but front-line workers initiated only 7 percent of the innovations. The latter figure is attributable to the disinclination of developing countries to empower

Initiator	USA, 1999–1998	Commonwealth, Advanced	Commonwealth, Developing
Politician	21	11	15
Agency head	25	39	37
Middle manager	43a	75	44
Front line staff	27a	39	7
Middle manager or front-line staff	51	82	48
Interest Group	13	2	11
Citizen	7	0	11
Program client	3	5	0
Other	6	9	11
Total (percent)	126	148	133
N	321	56	27

Table 26.1.   Initiators of Innovation (Percent)

Notes: n = number of innovations. A indicates that the breakdown between innovations initiated by middle managers and innovations initiated by front-line staff for the U.S. data was based on the 104 cases front 1995 to 1998. In the 217 cases from 1990 to 1994, these groups were coded together.

Source: Borins, 2001, p. 28.

their front-line staff. This may result from pay that is too low to be a motivator, an unwillingness or inability to provide training, a lack of resources necessary to test innovations, and/or rigid hierarchies. All told, these data confirm, in a wide variety of national contexts, that a substantial proportion of public-sector innovation comes from middle management and the front lines. Similarly, Walters (2001, p. 9), based on a more qualitative look at the applications to the Innovations in American Government awards, concludes that "Innovation ideas spring up from all over the place—both inside and outside of organizations, and from the middle, bottom, and top layers of an organization. Innovation, it turns out, has little regard for title." Light (1998, p. 45) studied a sample of eighteen particularly innovative non-profit and eight small governmental organizations in Minnesota and found that "almost all of them harvested ideas up and down the organization regardless of who has the idea."

While the largest number of innovations are initiated by middle managers and front-line staff, substantial percentages of innovations are initiated by politicians—10 to 20 percent—and by agency heads—over 25 percent (Borins, 1998, 2001). Because organizations are pyramidal in shape, there are many more front-line staff and middle managers than agency heads and politicians, so that the propensity to innovate (that is, innovations per capita) on the part of middle managers and front-line staff. Borins (1998, pp. 48–49) explored for systematic differences in the circumstances of innovations initiated by politicians, agency heads, and middle managers and front-line staff (the latter two groups being pooled). Statistically, politicians tended to be the initiators when the innovation was a response to a crisis. Crisis was defined broadly as publicly visible failure, whether current or anticipated. This has an intuitive appeal because when there is a crisis in the public sector, citizens expect politicians to lead the response. Agency heads tended to be the initiators when they took over as the new leader. When a public-sector agency is performing poorly and its poor performance becomes publicly visible, citizens expect politicians to appoint a new agency head to lead turnaround. Finally, middle managers lead a turnaround. Finally, middle managers and front-line staff tended to initiate innovations that responded proactively to internal problems or took advantage of opportunities created by new technology. These can be thought of as three ideal types or polar cases.

Subsequent research regarding the process of gathering support for an innovation also showed that the three groups employed different strategies for building support. Applicants were asked who were the strongest supporters of their innovation. Innovations initiated by public servants had a positive correlation with the strongest support from immediate supervisors and a negative correlation with strongest support from the president or governor, the legislature, business lobbies and the general public. Innovations initiated by agency heads had a positive correlation with strongest support from the political head of the agency and business lobbies. Innovations initiated by politicians had a positive correlation with strongest support from the president or governor, the legislature, business lobbies, the media, and the general public. Public servants worked through bureaucratic channels, rather than going over the heads of their colleagues to appeal directly for political support, while politicians went through political channels and mobilized public support (Borins, 2000a, pp. 503–504).[3]

We will consider each of the three ideal types of public-sector innovation in more detail, providing several examples and exploring the role of leadership in it.

BOTTOM-UP INNOVATION

What is the relationship between bottom-up innovation and leadership? To begin with, bottom-up innovations require and create leadership. The innovative process is not simply a matter of someone coming up with a good idea, putting it in a suggestion box, and the organization implementing it through its normal channels. Innovations require advocates and often become the subject of debate within an organization. They are sometimes introduced as pilot programs which must be evaluated before being applied in the entire organization. Innovations also lead to new structures within a given organization. For example, innovations frequently involved inter-organizational collaboration (Bardach, 1998; Borins, 1998, pp. 19–23, 2001, pp. 11–13) and this collaboration is governed by creating coordinating structures, such as interdepartmental committees (Borins, 1998, pp. 96–101). The initiators of the innovation are likely to play a role in several of these aspects of the innovative process, such as advocacy or leading a pilot project. Because they are on the front lines or in middle management, they are creating an informal or alternative leadership structure. In one case the award applicant noted that "rebels, idea people, and employees involved in a leadership capacity outside came to the fore" (Borins, 2000b, p. 55). Innovation awards provide publicity for the winners, and initiators may develop visibility beyond their own organization, as they become involved in educating potential replicators. Individuals at lower ranks who distinguish themselves by initiating innovations are likely to be put on the fast track to senior positions.

A recent example supports these observations. A group of young officers in the Ontario public service had the idea of holding a national conference looking at human resource issues from their own perspective. They formed a planning committee, approached the federal and several provincial governments for funding, and invited practitioners and academics as speakers. This advocacy process put them in touch with a variety of people they would not normally have encountered in their daily work, such as senior public servants (including several cabinet secretaries and permanent secretaries) and senior academics. The conference, entitled "New Professionals Driving a New Public Service," turned out to be a great success, attracting 350 participants from all over Canada. After the downsizing of the last decade, public services are facing a need for renewal, particularly at the entry level, and this conference spoke to that concern. The conference organizers are maintaining their website (www.newpublicservice.ca), accepting speaking invitations, and planning to create a permanent organization.

A second aspect of the relationship between leadership and bottom-up innovation is the stance that the public sector's top leadership—ministers, permanent secretaries, and senior public servants—take toward these initiatives. It could range from negative, to neutral, to highly supportive. A negative stance could come from a permanent secretary and senior public servants whose approach to management is strictly hierarchical, or from a minster who, possibly for ideological reasons, has an antipathy to her department. An American instance of the latter is Republican administrations that are unsympathetic to the mandates of the Department of Labor and the Environmental Protection Agency and that choose political appointees who want these departments to do as little as possible, certainly not to develop new programs. We can expect some permanent staff to leave and those who remain to keep their heads down. The Republican appointees might be receptive to initiatives that improve efficiency, thereby reducing the cost of existing operations. The appointees would want to see savings employed in other public-sector priorities or used to reduce taxes. Because there is no possibility that any of the savings would be returned to the department, permanent staff would be unlikely to come forward with ideas to improve efficiency.

A supportive stance requires politicians and senior managers creating a climate favorable for innovation. Robert Reich, Secretary of Labor in the Clinton administration from 1993 to 1997, excelled at this. First, he made clear the department's priorities, which included initiatives to improve wages and working conditions for America's lowest paid and most vulnerable workers. Second, he made a habit of consulting career civil servants, for example in quarterly departmental town hall meetings. Third, he took every possible opportunity to recognize staff initiatives (Glynn, 1999). Some forms of recognition included establishing a departmental innovation award, bringing his career public servants to meetings with politicians and political appointees, and inviting careerists whose ideas had been incorporated into legislation to White House signing ceremonies to meet President Clinton (Reich, 1997, pp. 129–134). The department's roof is an ideal vantage point to watch the fourth of July fireworks.

Previous secretaries always invited political appointees and friends; Reich used these coveted invitations to reward innovative careerists (Glynn, 1999).

Reich's support helped put in place a number of innovations initiated by front-line staff or middle managers that were subsequently recognized as finalists and winners of the Innovations in America Government Award. These included an initiative to eradicate sweatshops by putting pressure on retailers to ensure that the products they were selling were not made in sweatshops (Donahue, 1999, pp. 47–58), the Pension Benefit Guaranty Corporation's early warning program for large corporate pension plans at risk of default (Donahue, 1999, pp. 187–204), and a program in the Occupational Safety and Health Administration to identify proactively workplace health hazards among large employers (Donahue, 1999, pp. 114–127).

William Bratton, New York City's Chief of Police during the mid-1990s, led his department in the implementation of programs that led to a marked decline in the city's crime rate. He espouses a similar philosophy:

> "I know perfectly well that most police departments don't encourage or value innovation, cultivating instead conformity, complacency, and even timidity among police managers. But I also have met countless police officers and managers in my career who are bold, inventive, decisive, and eager for the big challenges of restoring order and safety to urban communities. My job as a police executive was to bring these people to the fore and let them run.... Every organization has a core group of people with original ideas and untapped talents. Some are in leadership positions, and some are not. A successful leader reaches deeply into the organization to find these people.... To propel a large organization forward, the leader has to enlist literally hundreds of co-leaders at every level.... When people show initiative, perseverance, and competence in the field, reward them. I found my best managers in the middle and bottom of the vast management cadre at the NYPD. Their promotions sent a signal of opportunities to their fellow managers." (Bratton and Andrews, 2001, pp. 252–257)

The Clinton administration's reinvention labs are another case of political support for innovation. These were pilot projects, many proposed by front-line staff and middle managers; Vice President Gore, who was in charge of the reinvention effort, tried to ensure that these projects would be granted waivers from regulations to facilitate experimentation, and let it be known that his office would advocate on behalf of the labs within their own departments or in their relationships with central agencies (Osborne and Plastrik, 2000, pp. 444–450, 564, 569).

To turn to a Canadian example: the Export Development Corporation (EDC) is a federal state-owned enterprise which finances purchasers of Canadian exports. In the late 1980s it established a capital markets group with the responsibility for finding new ways to raise money, rather than attempting to borrow under the aegis of the federal government, which itself had to finance huge deficits. The EDC capital markets group developed several sophisticated derivative-based financial instruments that were marketed to both large and small lenders. Staff in the federal Department of Finance were concerned and wanted to oversee the capital markets group closely. The deputy minister of finance at the time took the view that the group should be given autonomy; he also felt that if his department tried to rein them in, they would leave for lucrative private-sector jobs (Gorbet, 2001). His support gave the group the freedom it needed.

Not only can bottom-up innovations advance the goals set by politicians and senior public servants, but they can be the genesis of initiatives that politicians are willing to embrace as their own. Canada's SchoolNet program (www.schoolnet.ca) demonstrates this. In the early 1990s, one particularly innovative middle manager in Industry Canada was thinking about how the federal government could gain a presence on the rapidly evolving Internet. An undergraduate student on a work term in the government proposed an interactive website to which primary and secondary school educators would send educational materials and SchoolNet was launched (Dubeau, 2002; Hull, 2002). The program led to a federal-provincial initiative to connect all 16,500 Canadian elementary and secondary schools to the Internet by 2000. Federal and provincial politicians have become enthusiastic and highly visible supporters of these programs and have launched other initiatives to increase Internet access throughout Canada.

To summarize: this section illustrates a number of types of high-level support for innovation. These include establishing clear organizational goals that encourage staff to achieve in innovative ways, consultation with staff, establishing innovation awards and providing informal recognition for innovators, relaxing constraints upon innovators, protecting innovators by ensuring that their projects have a fair chance to demonstrate whether they work, and providing resources for innovators. The last, providing resources, is implicit in many of the above examples. The main resources include giving the initiators time to work on their projects, which might involve a reduction in their other responsibilities, and giving them the budget to pay for the running costs of their projects. While some organizations have formally established funds to support innovations (Borins, 2001, p. 32), the more likely case is that innovations are funded out of organizational slack that senior managers can identify. Finally, innovation is a two-way street, in that successful innovations provide opportunities for politicians to take public credit for wise policies and effective programs.

POLITICALLY DIRECTED INNOVATION IN RESPONSE TO CRISIS

The most clear-cut crises, and those that have received the most academic attention, involve the physical security of a nation. An immediate example is the terrorist attack on the United States on September 11, 2001. Leading the response has consumed most of the time and attention of President Bush, his cabinet, and their most senior advisors. The following crises, of varying magnitudes, have in common politically led and innovative responses:

- *City of Seattle Recycling Program.* The City's two landfills reached capacity in 1983 and 1986 and ceased operation. The federal government then designated these landfills as Superfund sites, thus raising closure costs to about $100 million. The city's reliance on more distant landfills, together with closure costs, had already doubled disposal assessment rates. The mayor and city council responded to the crisis by directing the city's solid waste utility to undertake an in-depth study of a wide range of options, including recycling, landfill, and incineration. The ultimate outcome was a greatly expanded recycling program, reinforced by pricing incentives and public attitudes, that became a global leader (Borins, 1998, pp. 196, 201, 204).

- *Environment Canada Ultraviolet Index Program.* This program was initiated in response to NASA's February 1992 prediction of a severe thinning of the ozone layer over North America that spring. Environment Minister Jean Charest gave his department four months to implement a program to inform the public of ultra-violet risk. They developed a daily index of the intensity of ultraviolet exposure that has been adopted internationally (Borins, 2000a, pp. 55, 68).

- *Cuban Missile Crisis.* In response to the secretive placement of Russian missiles in Cuba, the Kennedy administration implemented a naval blockade of Cuba that put sufficient pressure on the Russians to remove the missiles, without resorting to war (Allison, 1971).

- *Six-Day War.* In response to an Egyptian navel blockade of the Red Sea and invasion by Egypt, Syria, and Jordan, the Israeli cabinet initiated a war by directing its air force to launch a surprise attack that destroyed the entire Egyptian air force on the ground, clearing the way for a quick and massive victory over the Arab alliance (Brecher and Geist, 1980).

As a set, these four examples present a paradox. The first two are not well-known outside of their particular policy communities, but have been recognized by innovation awards in their respective countries. The last two are very well-known historically, but have not been thought of in terms of innovation. Detailed historical study, however, makes clear that the American and Israeli responses were both effective and innovative. In the American case, the alternative to a naval blockade was an air strike and/or an invasion, both of which were strongly favored by the military, but would likely have led to nuclear war between the USA and USSR. The blockade signaled the seriousness of American intentions, but gave the Russians time to make an orderly retreat. In the Israeli case, the air force attack relied on intelligence information that the Egyptian planes sat wingtip-to-wingtip at their bases. Since then, no combat-ready air force would ever again expose itself in a similar way.

The two famous crises have been of particular interest to students of decision making and crisis management. In his study of Israeli decisions in the Six-Day and Yom Kippur Wars, Brecher concluded that a tension mounted, the Israeli Cabinet's search for information and receptivity to it increased, the Cabinet broadened its consultative circle, and increased its search for, and care in the evaluation of, alternatives (Brecher and Geist, 1980, pp. 403–404). The decision-making process followed by the Excom (the ad hoc group chosen to advise President Kennedy) has been characterized as one based on inquiry, rather than advocacy (Garvin and Roberto, 2001). A wide range of options was proposed and studied carefully. The assumptions process was characterized by the same hunger for information, creative generation and testing of alternatives, and widespread consultation (at least subject to the constraints of secrecy) as the Israeli situation. These processes have been set forth as best practices for collaborative decision making under the high stakes and time pressures that typify crises.

These cases also demonstrate two patterns of political-bureaucratic interaction. In each case, politicians defined the problem and took responsibility for choosing the solution. They instructed the bureaucracy to provide information to inform their choices among alternatives and then to implement their decisions. In three of the four cases, the politicians were confident in the analytic and implementation capability of the bureaucracy. Seattle's politicians were sure the waste utility managers could analyze the disposal alternatives in terms of economic and environmental impacts; Environment Minister Charest relied upon his scientists to develop quickly a valid way of measuring ultraviolet exposure; the Israeli Cabinet trusted the air force to work out procedures for a sudden attack (time of day, altitude, route, etc.).

The exception was the Cuban Missile Crisis. As Allison (1971) made clear, and the recent movie *Thirteen Days* illustrates, there was considerable antipathy between the Kennedy administration and the armed forces, manifested at both the analysis and implementation stages. The politicians felt the generals were trigger-happy, and the generals thought the politicians (especially after refusing air support for the abortive Bay of Pigs invasion a year previously) were cowards. One political-bureaucratic confrontation described in Allison (1971, pp. 127–132) and depicted in *Thirteen Days* involved Secretary of Defense Robert McNamara giving explicit directions to captains of ships involved in the blockade, rather than going through the normal chain of command. The discussion of bottom-up innovation noted the difference between situations in which politicians trust the bureaucracy and those in which they are suspicious of its objectives. In a crisis context, suspicion gives rise to politicians seeking alternative sources of information at the analysis stage and monitoring closely at the implementation stage. In the instance in which politicians were suspicious of the bureaucracy, the politicians took full credit for the innovation. In the other cases, while the crisis response was politically initiated, credit for the innovation was shared with public servants.

ORGANIZATIONAL TURNAROUNDS LED BY AGENCY HEADS

The genesis of organization turnarounds is quite different from that of crises. Crises are a result of factors that are unprecedented, unpredictable, external, or environmental. In contrast, a turnaround is response to a public-sector organization that is simply not meeting normal expectations for service delivery. For example, some of the turnaround cases mentioned below involve failures to pick up garbage, provide swift emergency assistance to victims of natural disasters, regulate parking, pay workers' compensation claims in a timely manner, and maintain safety in public housing. Each involves an implicit comparison with normal practice in other jurisdictions, and each was found to be failing to meet minimum standards. The similarity between crises and organizational performance failures is that both are publicly visible, leading to public demands on politicians for quick and effective actions.

The first step in a turnaround is invariably the appointment by politicians of a new agency head (Borins, 1998, p. 157). The agency head who presided over the failing organization is fired or reassigned, and often other members of the senior management team who identified closely with the discredited agency head, or who are unable to adapt to the new head, are also let go. Turnaround leaders are generally energetic, dynamic, and relatively young for the post. They come from outside the organization, but are not neophytes. They know the type of operation well and/or are well acquainted with one or more of the major stakeholders. Knowing the operation is important because immediate action is necessary, and the turnaround leader cannot spend the first six months learning on the job. Knowing the stakeholders is also important because gaining their support is often a critical early step in the reform process. Turnaround leaders are not classic charismatic leaders, who can inspire their followers in any setting. Much of their success comes from their expertise about the operation and their knowledge of key stakeholders.

Agency turnarounds are not seen very frequently among the applications to innovation awards. Less than 5 percent of the applications to the innovation awards studied were classified as turnarounds. In a typical government, there are very few agencies that are total disasters. Most are performing relatively closely to the mean across jurisdictions, while a few may be best in their class. Most innovations are, therefore, attempts to move adequate performers to best in class, or initiatives by the best performers to push the frontiers forward (Borins, 1998, p. 154).

Agency heads attempting turnarounds face two leadership challenges, one involving the politicians to whom they are responsible, and the other involving their staff. The challenge at the political level is to regain confidence. Tactics for doing this include emphasizing political accountability to raise performance expectations of the organization, undertaking new initiatives that will demonstrate the organization's new vision and priorities, and using initial successes to convince politicians to provide additional resources for the organization (Borins, 1998, p. 156). A recent case that illustrates the importance of political support is the turnaround of the Federal Emergency Management Agency (FEMA) led by James Lee Witt during the Clinton administration (Daniels and Clark-Daniels, 2000). After FEMA experienced some dramatic failures during the (George H. W.) Bush administration, Clinton appointed Witt, who had served him previously as director of the Arkansas Office of Emergency Services. Clinton supported Witt in several ways, including designating FEMA as the lead federal disaster agency and elevating Witt's position to Cabinet status (Daniels and Clark-Daniels, 2000, p. 8).

The leadership challenge involving staff is to convince dispirited people that change is possible and that their efforts to do better will be supported. One essential tactic is scapegoating, namely, arguing that the agency's problems are not the fault of the staff who remain, but rather the fault of the discredited leadership. With the failed and discredited leaders removed, anything is possible. Many turnarounds involve reengineering the basic processes of the organization, for example, replacing a centralized functional structure with geographically decentralized structures that give front-line workers more autonomy but also demand accountability for results. This can be facilitated through the increased use of information technology. In addition, the agencies will reach out to their clients and stakeholders getting them more involved in both policy-setting and operations (Borins, 1998, pp. 156–158).

It might be asked whether turnarounds are necessarily innovative. Is it especially innovative if an organization moves from being worst in class to average in class or even better than average, if what it is doing is simply replicating those that are best in class? Turnarounds may become innovative because the process of scapegoating the discredited leadership, reorganization, and providing more autonomy for front-line staff makes it clear that the organization is truly open to new ideas and new ways of doing things. It is legitimate to question all the old ways and propose better alternatives. An organization in the process of a turnaround may therefore take advantage of the receptiveness to new ideas that its new leaders display to go from being worst in class to best, thus producing many innovations.

Even though turnarounds are relatively infrequent, there is no shortage of turnaround cases in the literature, in part because the actions of the turnaround leaders are often heroic—at least among bureaucrats—and in part because turnaround stories share the same mythic structure as biblical or literary tales of redemption or deliverance (Frye, 1982). Some recent examples include Witt's turnaround at FEMA and two turnaround cases presented in fine-grained detail in Mark Moore's (1995) well-known book *Creating Public Value: Strategic Management in Government*, one involving the Boston Housing Authority and the other the Houston Police Department. The discussion of turnarounds in Borins (1998, pp. 153–164) was based on four cases: New York City's child health care clinics and vehicle (sanitation and snow removal fleets) maintenance facility, the City of Chicago's parking enforcement program, and Washington State's workers' compensation system.

CONCLUSION

This chapter has made the case that there exists the strong link between innovation and leadership in the public sector. The two ideal types of top-down innovation, responses to crises and agency turnarounds, are led by politicians and agency heads, respectively. Politicians determine the strategic shape of responses to crises and agency heads the new vision and priorities for the organizations they are attempting to turn around. The best advice one could give to politicians responding to crises is to search widely for information, consult widely, and investigate a comprehensive set of options. Assumptions must be tested, and politicians and their advisers should act as skeptical generalists in evaluating information and options. Based on a substantial number of case studies, proven advice for agency heads leading turnarounds is to work simultaneously at regaining confidence at the political level and convincing dispirited staff that change is possible and their effort to do better will be supported. Tactics to regain political confidence include emphasizing political accountability to raise performance expectations, undertaking new initiatives that will demonstrate a new vision and priorities, reaching out to clients and stakeholders, and using initial successes to leverage additional resources. At the staff level, tactics involve scapegoating previous discredited leaders and reengineering basic work processes, often through information technology.

The quantitative evidence shows that bottom-up innovations occur more frequently in the public sector than received wisdom would have us believe. The individuals who initiate and drive these innovations are acting as informal leaders. The visibility these individuals gain and the results they achieve lead them to be promoted rapidly to positions of formal leadership. Politicians and senior public servants create organizational climates that will either support or stifle innovations from below. Creating a supportive climate would entail consulting staff, instituting formal awards and informal recognition for innovators, promoting innovators, protecting innovators from control-oriented central agencies, and publicly championing bottom-up innovations that have proven successful and have popular appeal.

A key thread running through this analysis is that the nature of the relationship between the political leadership, on the one hand, and the bureaucracy, on the other, has an impact on the nature and extent of innovation. If the political leadership distrusts the bureaucracy, it will attempt to stifle bottom-up innovation and make the bureaucracy a partner in both crisis response and agency turnarounds. Politicians have a sense of the magnitude of the tasks they face and the capability of the public service that supports them, and it is this that would drive their stance toward bureaucracy. The public good requires a bureaucracy that is loyal and professional and that can be a willing and capable partner in innovation.

Notes

1. The standard definition of innovation in the academic literature is the adoption of an existing idea for the first time by a given organization, as distinct from invention, the creation of a new idea (Rogers, 1995). In practice, innovation has come to refer to both. The reason appears to be that, in a period of rapid change, the line has blurred, and innovation organizations are both inventing and adopting. Sometimes adopted technology (VHS) turns out to be more popular than invented technology (Beta). Public-sector innovation awards, the source of data for this chapter, also blur the distinction and recognize both inventions and effective adoptions.

2. Applications to three innovation awards have served as the basis of this research: 321 applications to the Innovations in American Government award between 1990 and 1998, thirty-seven applications to the Institute of Public Administration of Canada (IPAC) public management innovation award between 1990 and 1994, and eighty-three applications to the Commonwealth Association for Public Administration and Management (CAPAM) international innovations award in 1998 and 2000. The American award was restricted to state and local government from 1990 to 1994 and broadened to include the federal government in 1995. The American award required semifinalists to complete a detailed questionnaire that dealt at length with the process of innovation, and responses were coded and analyzed. A questionnaire modeled very closely on the American award questionnaire was sent to the applicants to the IPAC and CAPAM awards, and responses were also coded and analyzed. For a discussion of methodological issues, see Borins (1998, pp. 12–18).

3. The next section discusses the importance of an organization's top leaders creating a climate favorable to innovation. This can be done without their being directly involved in deciding the fate of many, or even any, particular innovations. Thus, front-line innovators would work through bureaucratic channels, rather than appealing directly to the political level or outside the organization.

References

Allison, G. *Essence of Decision: Explaining the Cuban Missile Crisis.* Boston, MA: Little Brown, 1997.

Bardach, E. *Managerial Craftsmanship: Getting Agencies to Work Together.* Washington, DC: Brookings Institution, 1998.

Barzelay, M. *Breaking Through Bureaucracy: A New Vision for Managing in Government.* Berkeley, CA: University of California Press, 1992.

Borins, S. *Innovating with Integrity: How Local Heroes Are Transforming American Government.* Washington, DC: Georgetown University Press, 1998.

Borins, S. "Loose Cannons and Rule Breakers, or Enterprising Leaders? Some Evidence About Innovative Public Managers." *Public Administration Review*, 2000a, *60*(6), 498–507.

Borins, S. "What Border? Public Management Innovation in the United States and Canada." *Journal of Policy Analysis and Management*, 2000b, *19*(1), 46–74.

Borins, S. *The Challenge of Innovating in Government.* Arlington, VA: PricewaterhouseCoopers Endowment for the Business of Government, 2001.

Bratton, W., and Andrews, W. "Leading for Innovation and Results in Police Departments." In F. Hesselbein, M. Goldsmith, and I. Somerville (Eds.), *Leading for Innovation.* San Francisco: Jossey-Bass, 2001.

Brecher, M., and Geist, B. *Decisions in Crisis: Israel, 1967 and 1973.* Berkeley, CA: University of California Press, 1980.

Daniels, R., and Clark-Daniels, C. *Transforming Government: The Renewal and Revitalization of the Federal Emergency Management Agency.* Arlington, VA: PricewaterhouseCoopers Endowment for the Business of Government, 2000.

Donahue, J. (Ed.). *Making Washington Work: Tales of Innovation in America's Federal Government.* Washington, DC: Brookings Institution, 1999.

Dubeau, K. Private e-mail to the author, March 19, 2002.

Fountain, J. *Building the Virtual State: Information Technology and Institutional Change.* Washington, DC: Brookings Institution, 2001.

Frye, N. *The Great Code: The Bible and Literature.* Toronto: Academic Press, 1982.

Garvin, D., and Roberto, M. "What You Don't Know About Making Decisions." *Harvard Business Review*, 2001, *79*(8), 108–116.

Gawthrop, L. "Public Entrepreneurship in the Lands of Oz and Uz." *Public Integrity*, 1999, *1*(1), 75–86.

Glynn, T. U.S. Deputy Secretary of Labor, 1992–1996. Interview, November 8 1999.

Goldsmith, S. "Innovation in Government." In F. Hesselbein, M. Goldsmith, and I. Somerville (Eds.), *Leading for Innovation.* San Francisco: Jossey-Bass, 2001.

Goodsell, C. "Reinvent Government or Rediscover It?" *Public Administration Review*, 1993, *53*(1), 85–87.

Gorbet, F. Deputy Minister of Finance, Government of Canada, 1988–1992. Interview, October 10, 2001.

Hamel, G. *Leading the Revolution*. Boston: Harvard Business School Press, 2000.

Hesselbein, F., Goldsmith, M., and Somerville, I. (Eds.). *Leading for Innovation*. San Francisco: Jossey-Bass, 2001.

Hull, D. Speech to the Innovation Salon, Ottawa, March 18, 2002.

John, D. *Civic Environmentalism: Alternatives to Regulation in States and Communities*. Washington, DC: Congressional Quarterly Press, 1994.

Kanter, R. "Creating the Culture for Innovation in Organizations." *Research in Organizational Behavior*, 2001, *10*, 169–211.

Kanter, R. "Creating the Culture for Innovation." In F. Hesselbein, M. Goldsmith, and I. Somerville (Eds.), *Leading for Innovation*. San Francisco: Jossey-Bass, 2001.

Light, P. *Sustaining Innovation: Creating Nonprofit and Government Organizations That Innovate Naturally*. San Francisco: Jossey-Bass, 1998.

Moore, M. *Creating Public Value: Strategic Management in Government*. Cambridge, MA: Harvard University Press, 1995.

Osborne, D., and Plastrik, P. *The Reinventor's Fieldbook: Tools for Transforming Your Government*. San Francisco: Jossey-Bass, 2000.

Peters, T., and Waterman, R. *In Search of Excellence: Lessons from America's Best-Run Companies*. New York: Harper and Row, 1982.

Reich, R. *Locked in the Cabinet*. New York: Knopf, 1997.

Roberts, N., and King, P. *Transforming Public Policy: Dynamics of Policy Entrepreneurship and Innovation*. San Francisco: Jossey-Bass, 1996.

Rogers, E. *Diffusion of Innovations* (4th ed). New York: The Free Press, 1995.

Sparrow, M. *Imposing Duties: Government's Changing Approach to Compliance*. Westport, CT: Praeger, 1994.

Terry, L. "Administrative Leadership New-Managerialism, and the Public Management Movement." *Public Administration Review*, 1998, *58*(3), 194–200.

Walters, J. *Understanding Innovation: What Inspires It? What Makes It Successful?* Arlington, VA: PricewaterhouseCoopers Endowment for the Business of Government, 2001.

Wilson, J. *Bureaucracy: What Government Agencies Do and Why They Do It*. New York: Basic Books, 1989.

Sandford Borins is professor of public management at the University of Toronto.

CHAPTER TWENTY-SEVEN

The Changing of the Guard

What Generational Differences Tell Us About Social-Change Organizations

Frances Kunreuther

Accounts by executive directors and staff working in progressive social change organizations allude to generation-gap problems in the nonprofit sector that threaten the future work of these groups as they attempt to change "the system." To see how generational issues might be affecting social-change nonprofits, we conducted a series of in-depth interviews with executive directors (falling into two age groups) and with young staff (under forty years old). The findings of the study refute the notion of large generational differences.

Both older and younger people involved in these organizations have many of the same qualities: commitment, concern, energy, interest, and a strong belief in justice. However, differences are evident between those born in the Baby Boom generation and those who identify with Generation X in respect to their motivations to enter social change work, their concerns about the work/personal life divide, and their views of the future. Understanding these differences can help build strong leadership for the future.

Originally published as "The Changing of the Guard: What Generational Differences Tell Us About Social-Change Organizations," *Nonprofit and Voluntary Sector Quarterly, 32.* (2003).

B oth executive directors and staff frequently allude to generation-gap problems at social-change nonprofits—those organizations that are trying to change "the system" rather than simply work within it. It is not surprising that their accounts differ along generational lines. One story, usually narrated by someone in or near the "Baby Boomer" generation, is about the impending crisis. Baby Boomers heading nonprofit organizations will soon be retiring and there is nobody to take their places. Young people entering the sector are not as visionary, competent, committed, or well trained as those who are leaving. What will happen to these organizations? A flurry of activity has taken place to address this problem, including the emergence of initiatives to prepare the new generation for leadership roles.

There is a counter narrative, though, told by those from the younger generations. Older leaders running nonprofits have been sitting too long at the top of their organizations. They have ignored younger employees who bring new blood and new ideas. The crisis is that the Baby Boomer generation is *not* leaving, preventing a new generation from taking the reins. In this story, young people in nonprofits receive little respect, opportunity, or support. To them, it is no wonder that so many of their peers choose to enter the for-profit arena in which they have the chance to learn and grow.

As part of a larger project on the future of social-change organizations,[1] we probed deeper into this conflict. Is there in fact a generation gap? If there is, can we address it? Our inquiry suggests a complicated but hopeful situation. Although older and younger generations share many of the same values and commitments—more than some in the field might expect—they differ in their approaches to organizational life and the needs they bring to it. In fact, the social-change sector might do better to think of its challenge more as an organizational problem than a generational one. And although difficult, changing social-change organizations, and building better ones, is something to which the field can reasonably aspire.

THE GENERATION GAP: IN THE LITERATURE

If the popular literature is a reliable guide, it shouldn't be surprising that generational differences are on everyone's radar screen. In 1991, Douglas Coupland coined the term *Generation X* in a book that describes a new generation with different values and aspirations from those of the Baby Boomers who precede them.[2] The concept of Generation X rapidly spread through the 1990s, spawning a body of popular literature that described this new generation and the next, Generation Y, and the problems they have with the Baby Boom generation. These books, articles, and websites are for the most part written by, for, and about Gen Xers, especially educated professionals working in the for-profit sector. So it is not surprising that titles that dominate the field are *Managing Generation X* (Tulgan, 1996), *Generations at Work* (Filipczak, Raines, and Zemke, 2000), *Great Xpectations* (Hornblower, 1997), *A Politics for Generation X* (Halstead, 1999), and *13th Gen: Abort, Retry, Ignore, Fail?* (Strauss and Howe, 1993).

Each piece makes claims about the misunderstandings between the old guard and the new, frequently referencing each other as evidence. Gen Xers are characterized as "slackers" who are less invested in their work than Baby Boomers. Those Gen Xers who aren't slackers are said to "work to live," valuing their time away from the job. Baby Boomers "live to work" and tend to over identify with their job. Gen Xers who are dedicated to their work are not likely to be loyal to any one organization, whereas Baby Boomers tend to stay in one place and expect loyalty to the firm.

Gen Xers work better in an informal environment where they can consult with their peers; Baby Boomers are more comfortable in hierarchical settings. Whereas Gen Xers are more results-oriented, Baby Boomers are more process-oriented. Gen Xers are more technologically savvy and like to get things done quickly. In contrast, Baby Boomers—who rely less on technology—are slower and tend to look at issues more in-depth. Gen Xers are impatient to show what they can do; they want less oversight and more responsibility. Baby Boomers want to supervise/micromanage Gen X and expect them to "pay their dues" before giving them real authority.

In their social attitudes, Generation X is more comfortable than Baby Boomers working across race, gender, and sexual orientation. Both Gen X and Baby Boomers think the other generation is materialistic.

This litany of generalizations, of course, is so sweeping that it raises doubts about the generation-gap phenomenon. The academic literature presents a more tempered view. For one, it reminds us that there are always generational differences (Mannheim, 1952), and the current gap, although perhaps unique in its nuances, is nothing new. Moreover, suggest some, the Generation X and Y phenomenon doesn't describe an entire generation but rather a relatively narrow slice—of white professionals. The current crop of generational analyses never addresses issues of race and class differences, which might be more significant than generational issues alone (Kitwana, 2002; Levy, 1994). Finally, some scholars claim that Generation X is a self-fulfilling prophecy: those who identify with the claims of Gen X *are* Gen X (Kaminow, 1999).

Yet, as dubious as the popular literature may be in describing social-change organizations (or any organizations), most practitioners in the field do sense an issue here. In fact, at one of the first meetings we convened of leaders as part of our project on social-change organizations, generational conflict emerged as a major and heated theme.

THE GENERATION GAP: IN THE SOCIAL-CHANGE WORKPLACE

To see how generational issues might be affecting social-change nonprofits, we conducted a series of in-depth interviews with executive directors (including an older cohort, older than age forty-five, and one younger than forty) and with young staff (younger than forty). The interviews paint a mixed picture. Although they have much more in common than the popular literature suggests, the younger and older generations do differ from each other.

Our interviewees flatly contradicted the popular literature, and the assumptions of some social-change leaders, on the question of Gen X commitment. Across age, position in the organization, and type of organization, respondents talked about their commitment to their work, their drive to have an effect on the lives of the constituents they served, and the importance of their job in their life. Younger people were actually more likely than their older counterparts—whether they were directors or staff—to talk about how much they loved their jobs. Most were putting in long hours, and those who worked a 9-to-5 schedule were as likely to be older directors as young staff. Across generations, they talked about how they were compelled by the mission of the organization and its constituents. Several younger staff openly discussed their aspirations to run either the organization where they worked or a similar group in the future. As one younger respondent who had already worked in his organization for nine years put it, "There has honestly not been a day I've not loved my job."

Despite this startling similarity, we did recognize important differences between Baby Boomers and Gen X/Y in three areas.

1. *Baby Boomers and Generations X/Y were motivated to enter social-change work in different ways.* Younger participants—directors and staff alike—had come to social-change work through some significant personal experience. Several talked about how they had themselves been in situations that were similar to their constituents,' for example, as victims of violence or discrimination. One young director explained how he had "experienced a significant amount of violence growing up," which he eventually directed toward organizing to build an organization aimed at reducing violence among youth.

Others mentioned a significant personal moment. A staff member in her mid-30s described how she had nursed her mother through a long and painful death. The experience motivated her to leave her corporate job to find a position where she could work with women and children. As she describes it, she was looking for a place where she could express her spiritual side.

These personal accounts differed significantly from the responses of Baby Boomers. They talked more about a transformation they experienced through a more political awakening, an event or series of events that made them view the world in a different way. Older respondents described joining a social-change organization as the result of an educational process, learning an analysis or framework within a larger context of change. Their responses referenced having exposure to liberation theology, watching and learning about civil rights struggles, or joining the antiwar movement.

So despite their comparable levels of commitment, what motivates and animates younger and older people in the same social-change organization may be entirely different. Younger people are highly motivated based on their own personal experiences but often lack a framework for the change they seek, whereas older people have a framework but may not identify with those they work to serve.

2. *Younger people were just as likely as their older peers to spend long hours at work, but were far more anxious about conflicts between work and family life.* Several of the younger people we interviewed, especially the young men, were locked in a struggle between their work, which they felt required enormous time and commitment,

and their desire to have and be involved with their children in ways that meant spending fewer hours on the job. One young staffer who talked about starting a family explained, "I can't keep twelve-hour days forever.... I would love to have this job for the rest of my life. I don't know if that's possible."

The importance of time off then was generational in relation to the lifecycle. None of the older people we interviewed, including those who had raised families, mentioned this conflict. Maybe they had gone through a similar struggle when they were young. If so, it now seemed completely out of their consciousness. The fact that they appeared unaware of the depth of this conflict among younger staff was surprising, and it is easy to see how these differences could result in unspoken expectations and conflicts.

3. *Younger directors were far more likely to be experimenting with different organizational forms.* Older directors may at one time have used or had ambitions to create a different type of organizational structure. Over time, however, despite differences in size and function, the organizations under their leadership all seemed to take on a similar form, a kind of modified corporate structure, often with many mechanisms to solicit input from staff but fairly uniform in style.[3] Younger directors either talked about or were trying to run organizations in different ways—with leadership circles, leadership teams, co-directors, staff collectives, and significantly flattened hierarchies. In some organizations, new structures were designed to spread the responsibility of the director among a small group, allowing those in leadership to take time off without jeopardizing the vision and direction of the organization. Others developed teams that had power and authority to make decisions as a way to involve staff in running the organization. In still others, structures that involved constituents were designed as part of their social-change agenda—a way to spread authority and influence within the organization.

What should we make of these findings? Despite what some older social change leaders might fear, the challenge with the younger generations is not one of how to recruit them to social-change work. Young people in our interviews articulated the same values, dedication, and commitment as older social-change leaders. Rather than how to attract young people to social-change organizations, the challenge is how to support and develop them so they can sustain the work they love and do well. And here is where the generational gap shows up. Especially on the question of work-family balance, but also in their desire for more participatory organizations, younger people in all the organizations tended to express a good deal of anxiety, if not frustration.

We saw two different responses to these gap issues. In organizations founded and/or run by Baby Boomers, it seems these dilemmas of younger people are barely acknowledged, much less addressed successfully. In organizations run by Gen X/Y leaders, younger people were at least attempting to find new ways to organize their work. The generational differences, then, speak more to the need to change how we build and operate social-change nonprofits than how to convince a new generation of the importance of the cause.

THE PROSPECTS OF CHANGE

What can we do? We see at least four starting points:

1. *Older and younger generations both need to guard against history repeating itself*. In many ways, the study showed how easy it would be to repeat the past. The Baby Boom leaders we interviewed had often been at their jobs for much longer than a decade and for the most part had no intention of moving on. The younger directors, especially those who founded their organizations, were already headed in a similar direction. Although many talked about the need to not stay too long in their current positions, they often spun out scenarios that made it clear that they might need to stay in their current positions for years to come. It seemed unlikely they would leave their organizations any time soon. These directors were also trying to fashion an organizational structure, as had their predecessors, that fit their needs but that could lead to the exclusion of a new generation of younger staff as the years progress. Although they struggled with how to develop new structures, younger directors need support for thinking about how to implement these models effectively.

It is not only the organizational form that younger people have inherited. The culture of social-change work—never being able to do or give enough—seems to be effectively passed on from one generation to the next. And although this did not cause a problem for everyone, it was painful to see how some young people, so dedicated to social justice, were left without guidance or tools to solve this very basic dilemma. There seemed to be no serious consideration of how to create manageable jobs that allowed time for other types of civic engagement, family life, and relaxation for those who did not want to dedicate themselves entirely to their work. The unspoken question was how social-change work could be more than "just a job" while limiting the reach the work often had into every aspect of the staff members' and directors' lives.

2. *Directors need to develop a management and organizational development philosophy that reflects their values while supporting younger workers.* Baby Boomer directors were quick to confess that they had little or no interest in the management of their organizations. They were in it for the work, not for what they saw as the administrative tasks that came with building an organization. That indifference to management may account for some of the challenges younger workers face working in these organizations. The disdain by Baby Boomer directors for the work of managing the organization led to the creation of chief operating officer positions in several relatively small groups. However, the separation of the structure from the content of the work rarely seemed to solve the structural problems that faced younger staff.

Our interviews also suggest that it made more sense for management to be integrated into the social-change work and values of the organizations. We saw that Generation X is making significant strides in grappling with the challenges of management and mission and how both could operate hand in hand. This trend—for innovation and experimentation—should be encouraged and supported. The younger directors we talked with were enormously thoughtful about their management style and the structure of their organizations. Their emerging ideas about structure and management are just what we need now in a sector that often is confused by the dominance of either for-profit business practices or outdated nonprofit structures.

3. *Baby Boomers need to make active development of younger staff a priority.* Older directors have much to pass on to a new generation. However, they need to have ongoing, consistent, and productive contact with younger people, both to share what they have learned and to learn about what Generation X has to offer. A few of the older directors we interviewed were true models on how this could be accomplished. For example, a young staff member reported that her director repeatedly gave her opportunities to attend important meetings, spending an enormous amount of time both before and after discussing strategy and processing the outcome. The staff member felt her ideas were valued, she was trusted to take on real

responsibility, and she received the support she needed to do the job. She not only learned how to manage challenging situations but she also began building her own relationships outside the organization, a crucial element for successful leadership. In describing the director of her organization, she told the interviewer, "He's all about building new leadership." Unfortunately, this active leadership development of younger staff was exceptional.

4. *Changing of the guard: Recognizing the contributions of Generations X and Y.* Finally, it is important to recognize the similarity of commitment between Generation X/Y and Baby Boomers. But that means that it is time to place the movements of the 1960s and 1970s in their historical context, as important events that shaped many of our lives and as crucial lessons for learning. Baby Boomers are not the only ones who care about social change or who know how to make it happen. Older leaders have often worked hard to build a first generation of organizations that has had a tremendous effect on the lives of many people. Now they need to use the creativity, will, and imagination it took to start and run these organizations to determine how they can make it possible for the next generation to take on the future social-change work. Rather than yearn for the movements they were part of when they were young, older directors need to look for, listen to, and support the new emerging ideas for social change. These older directors can learn from the personal motivations of the next generation and they can help Generations X and Y to develop their own frameworks for creating change.

Younger people are bringing energy, ideas, and hope to their work in social-change nonprofits. It is now up to the older leaders to fan these young flames, work in partnership, or move aside so that the next generation of social-change organizations and their leaders can succeed.

Notes

1. The Building Movement project is funded in part by the Annie E. Casey Foundation and the Ford Foundation. For more information about the project or a full copy of the generational change report, e-mail frances _kunreuther@harvard.edu.

2. There are many different definitions of Baby Boomers, Generation X, and Generation Y, usually spanning huge time periods. The most common age references (give or take five years) are as follows: Baby Boomers, born 1945

to 1964; Generation X, born 1965 to 1980; and Generation Y, 1981 to 2000. When someone is born may be less important than the generation he or she identifies with.

3. The one exception was a collective that had no paid, full-time staff.

References

Filipczak, B., Raines, C., and Zemke, R. *Generations at Work*. New York: AMACOM, 2000.

Halstead, T. "A Politics for Generation X." *The Atlantic Monthly*, 1999, *284*(2), 33–42.

Hornblower, M. "Great Xpectations." *Time*, June 9, 1997, p. 58.

Kaminow, B. "X, Lies, and Social Signs: Defining Generation X." In L. L. Naylor (Ed.), *Problems and Issues of Diversity in the United States*. Westport, CT: Bergin and Garvey, 1999.

Kitwana, B. *The Hip Hop Generation: Young Blacks and the Crisis in African American Culture*. New York: Basic Books, 2002.

Levy, A. "Looking for Generation X." *Division and Diversity*, 1994, *3*(3), 24–26.

Mannheim, K. "The Problem of Generations." In K. Mannheim (Ed.), *Essays on the Sociology of Knowledge*. New York: Oxford University Press, 1952.

Strauss, W., & Howe, N. *13th Gen: Abort, Retry, Ignore, Fail?* New York: Vintage Books, 1993.

Tulgan, B. *Managing Generation X*. New York: Norton, 1996.

—*∿*—

At time of original publishing Frances Kunreuther, a Baby Boomer, was the former executive director of a social-change nonprofit and was a fellow at the Hauser Center for Nonprofit Organizations at Harvard University.

CHAPTER TWENTY-EIGHT

Into the Fire

Boards and Executive Transitions

Michael Allison

The process of firing pottery is an apt metaphor for human transformational events. If we pass the fiery test, we emerge transformed, stronger. If we can't take the heat, we end up broken—and must begin again creating the desired change.

When one executive director leaves and another takes over, the transition is analogous to taking a nonprofit organization into the kiln. For nearly all nonprofits, the board of directors is the leader of this process, as the sole body with authority for hiring and firing the chief executive. If the board is prepared, has an appropriate composition in its membership and supporting players, and uses a process that is well designed, the organization actually can become stronger through the transition. It can emerge with renewed clarity of purpose and an energized team poised for achieving success. Failure typically results in a poor choice of a new leader and a fragmented, exhausted group of people.

Originally published as "Boards and Executive Transitions," *Nonprofit Management and Leadership, 12.* (April 2002).

The Executive Transitions program of CompassPoint Nonprofit Services contracted with twenty-eight nonprofit organizations during its first two years (1998–1999). Our experience in consulting to these organizations revealed a pattern of three threats that boards face in leading such transitions. Our experience also offers hope that suitable assistance can help boards meet these threats successfully.

This chapter describes steps leading to the development of the services, the consulting model, and experience with its application. The chapter concludes with suggestions for practice that we have drawn from this experience and ideas for further research.

GENESIS OF EXECUTIVE TRANSITIONS SERVICES

Our consulting work with boards in this area grew out of our consulting experience and the exploratory research we did with 137 executive directors in the San Francisco Bay Area, whose results we published as a study titled *Leadership Lost: A Study on Executive Director Tenure and Experience* (Wolfred, Allison, and Masaoka, 1999).[1] Our work with nonprofits indicated that turnover in executive leadership was a significant issue, and this growing awareness prompted our research.[2]

For many respondents, being an executive director is a one-time event. Nearly two-thirds of the respondents were on their first jobs as executive directors. Of these, only 20 percent indicated they wanted their next job to be as an executive director. Tellingly, only 14 percent of their predecessors left to take another nonprofit CEO position. We found these results to be disturbing: if this is a job that most people do only once, then the possibility of hiring experienced people is greatly limited, and it raises a question about whether something is wrong with the way nonprofits typically construct the job.

The management literature was largely devoid of work in this area. "The complex process of entering and exiting a position of organizational leadership has received little attention in the management literature," wrote Michael Austin and Thomas Gilmore (1993). (Gilmore wrote an excellent book on the topic, *Making a Leadership Change* [1989], that is now out of print!) When looking for resources in 1997, we could find many articles about executive leadership in the private sector, but we could find little that gave any guidance relevant to nonprofit organizations managing the process of executive transition.

We did find help from others who were actively assisting nonprofits with this issue. The experiences of the Neighborhood Reinvestment Corporation (NRC) and the Presbyterian Church were particularly helpful. NRC is an association of two hundred housing and community development organizations across the United States. As part of an initiative funded by the Kellogg Foundation from 1990 to 1995, NRC found that it was able to increase retention and effectiveness of leadership by combining three strategies. By raising salaries an average of $10,000 per year, the group expanded and improved the pool of candidates that NRC affiliates could attract. Two additional strategies were consulting to boards in the hiring process and providing training to new executive directors once they were hired. Combining these three strategies, NRC found a significant measure of success. In 1999 Tom Adams, the lead consultant on this initiative, authored a very helpful manual informed by this experience. The lessons we drew from NRC's experience helped us to understand the discrete steps in the transition process and to develop distinct strategies for each step.

Leaders at the Presbyterian Church in Northern California shared valuable experience and knowledge with us about their formal pastor transition program. The church treats leadership transition as a naturally occurring event in the life of a congregation (rather than an unanticipated crisis to be avoided) and has developed a national program to support congregations in this transition. A central feature is the requirement that a congregation take a full year for reflection and renewal between pastors. During this process the congregation reflects on its goals and on the nature of the leadership that its members want their next pastor to provide. In order to manage during this transitional year, the church has trained a cadre of interim pastors ready to step in and provide temporary leadership—as well as guidance in hiring—to these congregations. We learned two key lessons from this model: (1) to look on the transition as an opportunity for renewal and (2) to support that transition with skilled interim leadership.

Finally, although we did not find much in the way of published research and writings about this process, William Bridges' work (1991) on the overall process of transitions proved helpful in developing our conceptual framework. Bridges makes a fundamental distinction between change, which occurs externally, and transition, the emotional process people go through as a result of a change.

A change, such as moving across the country, takes perhaps a week or two, whereas the transition, the personal adjustments needed for the individual to finally feel at home in a new city, may take a couple of years. We might say that transformation (such as the finished pottery emerging from a kiln) has been accomplished once the transition is complete.

Bridges provides a three-stage model to describe the emotional process of transitions: ending, neutral zone, and new beginnings. "All changes begin with an ending," he writes (1991, p. 19), and goes on to discuss the importance of acknowledging the inevitable loss associated with any change. The neutral zone that follows the ending describes the emotional turbulence people experience between the familiar state of the old and the reality of the new. This unsettled, in-between time is also characterized by creativity and fluidity necessary for meaningful change to take place. Finally, the new beginnings truly occur when people have let go of the past, moved through the discomfort and uncertainty of the neutral zone, and begun to accept the changes and focus on the future.

Our consulting and management experience has borne out this model: we have seen many instances in which an organization has quickly replaced a departing executive director, only to have the new executive leave within a year. (Gilmore and Ronchi, 1995, also describe this phenomenon.) Bridges' three-step description of the emotional transition that individuals and organizations confront in a major change helped us in two ways. First, it provided a practical conceptual framework for structuring our services. But far more importantly, we found that this straightforward approach resonated easily and deeply with our clients—it helped us build a shared understanding with clients about how we would approach managing this process with them.

CONSULTING MODEL

We developed the Executive Transitions Services program to reflect and build on these influences. Built on the recognition that this transition is an important opportunity for reflection, change, and agency growth, the program acknowledges that this transition is critical and that the costs of mistakes in the transition are disproportionately high. And we emphasize that the change of occupant in the office of executive director can be successful only if the organization pays attention to the transition from one leader to another. CompassPoint's Executive Transitions program provides a menu of services categorized into two types: organization development consulting and interim support services.

Organization development consulting includes one or more of the following components:

- Organization assessment
- Board assessment and development
- Transition coaching to the board and support to the process
- Executive search
- Coaching to the new executive director

Interim support services include

- Assistance in hiring an interim executive director by providing screened referrals and guidance in contracting (typically for three to six months) and
- Coaching and resource support to the interim executive director.

All clients receive an introduction to our approach and services. Our emphasis on attending to the transition means that we will assist clients with the executive search while also working with them on other dimensions of the transition. We have often seen nonprofits that had directly searched for and hired an executive and subsequently run into serious trouble—in part based on the group's failure to acknowledge the endings, make use of a neutral zone, and work to create an environment in which the new executive would succeed. We offer organization development services alone and interim support services alone, along with the combination of both. For example, if another resource for providing interim management is available (such as an internal manager), we can successfully work with the agency by providing organization development services. Similarly, we provide only interim support services when we feel that the organization, with the assistance of an interim executive director, can appropriately manage the transition work on its own. Our experience, supported by the results of the first two years, is that providing both types of services in combination leads to better outcomes.

RESULTS

In the first two years of this program (1998–1999), we worked with twenty-eight organizations. The reported results are documented in two program evaluation reports (Frank, 2000, 2001). The organizations' budgets ranged from $100,000 to $5 million, with a mean of $1.14 million. The age of the organizations ranged from one year to over thirty years, with the mean and median both over twenty years. Although most older organizations had larger budgets, two of the clients had incorporated more than twenty years before we began working with them, had smaller budgets, and were hiring their first executive directors. The 5 percent mean for consulting time was sixty-eight hours per engagement. Of the twenty-eight organizations, ten (36 percent) used both organization development and interim support services. Another ten (36 percent) used organization development services only. The final eight (29 percent) used interim support services only. Larger agencies tended to use more services.

Services Used	Median Budget
Both organization development and interim support services ($N = 10$)	$950,000
Organization development services only ($N = 10$)	$750,000
Interim support services only ($N = 8$)	$375,000

As expected, this pattern of using consulting appears to be a function of the cost of consulting. The larger agencies were more likely to have resources available from their general funds. They were also more likely to have successfully obtained a special grant for at least some part of the transition cost.

An independent evaluator gathered information about the results of the transition processes from surveys with a sample of nine of the organizations approximately one year after we finished working with them. Although evaluating the process one year in may prove too early to assess fully the outcomes of the transitions, indications are that most organizations have managed the transitions well and indeed made use of the transition to renew the organization.

For example, eight of the nine organizations reported that they are either healthier or much healthier since hiring the new executive director. (Indicators for health included financial growth, strength of board and staff, and levels of satisfaction reported by new executive directors and board members). Additionally, since they hired the new executive directors, all but one of the organizations increased their budgets; one-third of the organizations are serving new populations, with 44 percent offering new programs and 33 percent serving higher numbers of clients; and two-thirds of executive directors and board members report the board of directors is stronger than prior to the transition. Finally, two-thirds of new executive directors reported being satisfied or very satisfied with their jobs; only one reported being dissatisfied.

Our internal records and follow-up with the full population of clients appears to indicate that an organization's success is related to the comprehensiveness of services it used. Of the eight organizations that used interim services only, four are struggling or have already lost their new directors. On the other hand, of the twenty organizations that used organization development services—with or without interim services—only three are struggling or have replaced their new directors within a year. We will continue to track the development of this group to see the degree to which these early results are borne out over time.

THREATS TO SUCCESSFUL TRANSITIONS

Clients' experiences during the first two years of this program have thrown into relief several problems of governance that threaten successful transitions. Our experience working with clients on these characteristic threats gives us confidence that we can increase the organization's chances for success through structured support.

Threat 1: Boards Underestimate the Risks and Costs of Bad Hires

Selecting an executive director is arguably the most important act a nonprofit board performs. The literature on business management is crowded with books and articles about the importance and exercise of leadership.[3] Private-sector companies often pay CEOs more than one hundred times the amount they pay to the lowest-level staff. Although the hero status and myths associated with leadership in U.S. culture probably over-emphasize the value of the individual leader, many agree that the individual CEO can make or break an organization. In an article about the relationship between CEO transition and the failure of rural community hospitals, Alexander and Lee (1996) present a well-researched and compelling case that this is particularly true for small nonprofits.

However, the nonprofit sector has tended to downplay the importance of the executive director and the CEO. Perhaps because of nonprofit organizations' generally higher commitment to issues of equality and participatory democracy, much of the nonprofit management literature focuses on what organizations do or should do rather than on the role of the individual in the most influential leadership role. For example, the literature contains many more books about board roles and responsibilities or about management functions (such as financial management, program evaluation, strategic planning, and so on) than about executive leadership.[4]

Executives as well as board members seem reluctant to acknowledge the importance of the role. Without exception, at each of the initial meetings we held with prospective clients, board members would express the desire to spend as little money as possible and to replace the director as quickly as possible. Rather than seeing this executive search as the defining moment of their board terms, their opportunity and responsibility to shape the future of the organization, they often saw the task as an unwelcome and troubling burden. Surprisingly, this reaction predominated whether the outgoing director was leaving on good or bad terms.

Failure to place proper importance on this process is a major threat to the organization. The decision to hire a new executive director raises important questions about the organization's future, and about the nature of the leadership it requires to achieve success. Will the organization continue its current programs or pursue new directions? Will the organization's operational infrastructure support its programs, or does it need to grow or change in some important way? Are relationships with key constituencies healthy, or is rebuilding required with certain stakeholders? And what are the strengths and weaknesses of the current board, staff, and volunteers? Clearly, the nonprofit's response to each of these questions affects the nature of the individual and the nature of leadership in general that an organization requires at the point of hiring a new executive director.

Why, in addition to resisting any new burden, do boards underestimate the risks and costs of poorly managed transitions? In contrast, when organizations lose a major funder or experience a public relations disaster, board members are typically more attentive and willing to engage with the work of responding appropriately. Further, even when a board has made a poor choice and is facing another transition within a short period of time, board members have tended to see the situation as an unfortunate fluke rather than a failure of their approach. Finally, the cost of a poor choice is often in the form of opportunity costs, work that did not get done or growth that did not take place. The loss may be just as significant, but board members, for some of the reasons we will cite, are not typically skilled as a group at estimating lost potential.

Threat 2: Boards Are Typically Unprepared for the Task

Unfortunately, even when a nonprofit board appreciates the importance of the transition and the hire of a new executive director, boards are typically not well suited to this task. This is not due simply to ignorance; in fact, many characteristics of nonprofit boards make the process and the management of the change particularly problematic.

Many authors (Chait, Holland, and Taylor, 1996; Demb and Neubauer, 1992; Masaoka and Allison, 1995) have discussed an inherent paradox in the relationship between boards and executives. When acting as governors (hiring an executive director, setting long-term goals, and acting as ambassadors on behalf of the organization), the board is the "boss" providing leadership to the staff. However, when supporting the organization (assisting with fundraising, lending personal expertise to the development of management policies, or volunteering to support program activities), the board is in the position of accepting leadership from the staff.

Paradox, a situation with two mutually exclusive aspects, both of which are true, presents difficulties for all groups (Smith and Berg, 1985). Groups tend to choose one or the other dimension to hold as their truth, in effect denying the validity of the other aspect. Along these lines, members of the board of directors at a nonprofit often act as if the executive director is the boss, even while espousing and acknowledging their responsibilities for governing the organization.

Moreover, boards generally have too little time, too little experience with nonprofit management principles, too little expertise in the business of the organization (field of service), and too little skill at governing as a group to be able to handle the governing role well (Masaoka and Allison, 1995).

Sometimes board members assume that if they have colleagues whose professional experience lies in the private sector, the board has somehow "covered" the process of selecting a new executive. However, the work of governing a nonprofit board is different from work in the private sector (McFarlan, 1999). And researchers found that board members reported in a number of focus groups that they did not expect to play a governing role when recruited. Most board members saw their job as helping the organization rather than leading it (Wirthlin Worldwide and Alice Allen Communications, 1999).

Nonetheless, when an executive director leaves, the board has no option other than to play its governing role. As a result, the tasks of organization assessment, executive search, and transition management impose burdens that the typical board may not be prepared to shoulder. (This threat is reflected in the higher failure rate of clients who consulted us only for search or interim services rather than for organization development support.)

Threat 3: Boards Fail to Make Full Use of the Opportunity in Transitions

One of the most important lessons we learned from the Presbyterian Church program was the extent of the opportunity that a change in leadership presents. A nonprofit's executive transition process presents not only dangers but also valuable opportunities for growth and renewal.

Unfortunately, nonprofit organizations are often operating with little in the way of cushions such as financial reserves or predictable cash flows, and a disruption can tip the balance between "making it" and "falling apart."

But far from seeing the opportunity for reflection and renewal, many boards of directors are anxious to get through the disruption, get back to normal, and replace the CEO as quickly as possible. This impulse to flee from the pressure that the situation imposes sometimes manifests in board members simply disappearing and leaving the task to a few hardy souls. On the other hand, we have also seen board members who have the impulse to fight. In a number of cases, we have seen boards that are not ready for the transition devolve into heated conflict and become paralyzed with power struggles and personality conflicts. In at least two situations, the process could move forward only once one or more board members left the board.

The good news is that many board members stay around and rise to the occasion. Once they accept the importance of the job and see the opportunities in this challenge, board members are often eager to invest fully in a meaningful transition process. Finding a way to buy time for this work is essential to the success of this approach. This is why the presence of interim directors is so critical. The board cannot do the work of letting go while the departing executive is still present. And unless the incoming executive director is skilled at managing this transition, the individual is likely to fail to help an organization that has not yet let go of the past to move toward the future.

The organization must give itself the freedom to create a true neutral zone; this is one reason we counsel against having a candidate for the permanent job assume the interim role. We have found that the transition process works better for everyone if the prospective candidate makes a choice either to serve as interim director until the board hires a new director or to put a hat in the ring as a candidate for the permanent job.

Our Executive Transitions program responds to these three threats directly. To acknowledge the tendency of boards to underestimate the cost of a bad hire, we insist on a brief education process in discussions with any prospective client. This is also the reason we insist on combining consulting with the executive search. By providing board development support and doing some of the work of the executive search, our consultants help compensate for the typical board's lack of preparedness. And providing interim services along with educating boards of directors helps board members to see the opportunity that the transition presents.

CONCLUDING THOUGHTS

Even without structured assistance, the lessons for board members are clear. Leadership transition is a fact of organizational life, and one that the board of directors should accept as a normal development: one that they can prepare for, one for which resources are available, and one that should not be hurried. An important lesson for executive directors is to support independence and strength (as opposed to dependency and compliance) in their board leadership. In addition, executive directors can encourage the recruitment of board members who will be good transition leaders rather than only those who can be effective partners with the current staff. No matter how hard an executive director tries, one individual cannot ensure a safe future for the organization he or she has worked so hard to lead and build. For funders, a grant to support a thoughtful and careful process is likely to be a strong investment in grantee organizations that they want to see continue to thrive. For practitioners and researchers, an appropriate focus is to develop a deeper understanding of leadership turnover, the ways we can support effective leadership, and the unique and powerful role for boards in leading for change.

Notes

1. CompassPoint Nonprofit Services conducts more than three hundred consulting engagements with nonprofit organizations each year and has been in operation since 1976. In addition, Tim Wolfred, director of the program, served as an interim executive director with sixteen organizations prior to joining the CompassPoint consulting staff.
2. The *Chronicle of Philanthropy* reported on June 3, 1999, that the David & Lucile Packard Foundation found executive turnover among 45 percent of its grantees from 1994 to 1997 (Marchetti, 1999). See Sean Bailey's interview (1997) with Jan Masaoka on this topic. Apparently, the nonprofit sector is not alone. The study, conducted by the Center for Executive Options, a division of Drake Beam Morin, revealed that nearly 20 percent of the top U.S. corporations hired new CEOs in 1997 ("Executive Briefing," 1998). The study also found that roughly 31 percent of Fortune 100 companies had turnover in the CEO position between the fourth quarter of 1995 and 1998.
3. *The Leadership Challenge,* by Kouzes and Posner (1995), cites fifty-six references on theory and evidence for their model alone!
4. In September 2001 Amazon.com listed 709 books on nonprofit management and seventy-four on nonprofit leadership—of which only eighteen had to do with executive leadership.

References

Adams, Tom. *Executive Leadership Transitions.* Washington, DC: National Center for Nonprofit Boards, 1999.

Alexander, J., and Lee, S. "The Effects of CEO Succession and Tenure on Failure of Rural Community Hospitals." *Journal of Applied Behavioral Science,* 1996, *32*(1), 70–88.

Austin, M., and Gilmore, T. "Executive Exit: Multiple Perspectives on Managing the Leadership Transition." *Administration in Social Work*, 1993, *17*(1), 47–60.

Bailey, S. "Executive Transition: A Powerful Opportunity for Change." *Nonprofit Genie* [http://www.genie.org/op_opinion_001.htm], 1997.

Bridges, W. *Managing Transitions: Making the Most of Change*. Reading, MA: Perseus Books, 1991.

Chait, R. P., Holland, T. P., and Taylor, B. E. *Improving the Performance of Governing Boards*. Phoenix, AZ: Oryx Press, 1996.

Demb, A., and Neubauer, F. *The Corporate Board: Confronting the Paradoxes*. New York: Oxford University Press, 1992.

"Executive Briefing." *HR Magazine*, 1998, *43*(7), 10.

Frank, N. *Evaluation of the Executive Transitions Program at CompassPoint Nonprofit Services*. Oakland, CA: Nancy Frank & Associates, 2000.

Frank, N. *CompassPoint Executive Transitions Program: Client Longitudinal Survey*. Oakland, CA: Nancy Frank & Associates, 2001.

Gilmore, T. *Making a Leadership Change: How Organizations and Leaders Can Handle Leadership Transitions Successfully*. San Francisco: Jossey-Bass, 1989.

Gilmore, T., and Ronchi, D. "Managing Predecessors' Shadows in Executive Transitions." *Human Resource Management*, 1995, *34*(1).

Kouzes, J. M., and Posner, B. Z. *The Leadership Challenge*. San Francisco: Jossey-Bass, 1995.

Marchetti, D. "Managing Turnover at the Top: Charities Seek to Transform the Loss of a Leader into an Opportunity." *Chronicle of Philanthropy*, 1999, *11*(16), 1 [http://philanthropy.com/free/articles/v11/i16/16000101.htm].

Masaoka, J., and Allison, M. "Why Board's Don't Govern." In R. Turner (Ed.), *Taking Trusteeship Seriously*. Indianapolis: Indiana University Center on Philanthropy, 1995.

McFarlan, W. "Don't Assume the Shoe Fits." *Harvard Business Review*, 1999, *77*(6), 65–80.

Smith, K., and Berg, D. *The Paradoxes of Group Life*. San Francisco: Jossey-Bass, 1985.

Wirthlin Worldwide, Alice Allen Communications. *Nonprofit Board Member Self-Education Focus Group Report*. New York: Volunteer Consulting Group, National Center for Nonprofit Boards, 1999.

Wolfred, T., Allison, M., and Masaoka, J. *Leadership Lost: A Study on Executive Director Tenure and Experience*. San Francisco: CompassPoint Nonprofit Services, 1999.

—◦◦◦—

Michael Allison is director of the Consulting and Research Group at CompassPoint Nonprofit Services in San Francisco and the Silicon Valley.

CHAPTER TWENTY-NINE

Leadership and Leading
Leadership Challenges

Marcia Marsh

The number one challenge for public, not-for-profit, and for-profit organizations is leading beyond boundaries. I cannot think of a single organization I have touched in the past two decades that owns even a majority of the assets—capital, intellectual, or human—that it must lead in order to be successful. We are totally reliant on the cooperation and collaboration of partners, suppliers, contractors, governments, nongovernmental organizations (NGOs), and communities in meeting our goals. Truly excellent organizations and leaders excel in engaging all the resources required for success, but these organizations are few and far between.

I can think of no public-sector organization that can go it alone or simply collaborate within government. At the Department of Defense (DOD), the number of partners involved in the conflicts in Afghanistan and Iraq extends well beyond other governments to contractors, other agencies, NGOs, local communities, and more. At other agencies, Hurricane Katrina provided a most visceral example

---

Originally published as "Leadership and Leading: Leadership Challenges," *American Review of Public Administration, 36.* (April 2006).

of this challenge of leading across boundaries, but examples exist every day in cleaning up Manhattan project sites, creating effective land-use partnerships, delivering the new Medicare drug prescription benefits, improving our schools, and so on. We need to broadly understand partnerships and adapt our leadership to constantly build and reinforce coalitions if we are to be successful leaders.

During my time at the Partnership for Public Service, I participated in a number of studies and panels focusing on leadership of the "blended workforce." The conversation almost always devolved into a discussion of how evil contracting out is versus how we leverage all the assets federal leaders touch. At forums about partnerships and collaboration, I heard a great deal of cynicism about working with the private sector or entrusting real responsibility to state and local entities. We must develop leaders throughout these organizations who create solutions across sectors and leverage our precious dollars and resources effectively in solving highly complex problems.

Nowhere is this challenge more evident than in not-for-profit organizations. The biggest rap against not-for-profit management is the lack of accountability for real and sustainable results. The refrain you will hear in trying to set goals in this sector is "We don't have control over . . . " or "We can only do so much." I heard this from dozens of otherwise talented leaders, and my response was always, "Then why exist?" Funders and donors are extremely conscious of this leadership and accountability gap. Money is shifting to those leaders who demonstrate competency in producing results through highly innovative and effective collaborations or new ventures.

I am fortunate to work for a not-for-profit where leaders believe that they can and should be accountable for significant results outside their direct control and where they have the competencies to build and manage coalitions. I moved to the World Wildlife Fund for two reasons—mission and global business and political savvy. Through highly innovative projects and leadership, we are achieving results that not only save habitats and communities but change global markets and policies to support, expand, and sustain those results.

WHAT TALENTS AND COMPETENCIES ARE REQUIRED TO MEET THIS CHALLENGE?

It's back to the future in this case. We need to produce generations of explorers and renaissance leaders—people who can dream big dreams and produce them. This time our explorers need not only a broad education and worldview but hands-on knowledge of global technologies and communications tools.

If I were hiring leaders for critical public-sector challenges, I would look for competencies above and beyond the Executive Core Competencies for the Senior Executive Service. I would want people with a track record of:

- *Consistently creating wins across communities*—Leaders who have the ability to put themselves in others' shoes and find ways to produce solutions that create mutual success. People who have either been employed or have effectively worked across countries, sectors, and organizations. Diplomats, negotiators, deal makers. In the Strength Finders parlance—people who "woo." This is not to suggest anything other than strong leaders who demand excellence, but it does suggest leaders who create excellence through shared accountability and recognition or reward. My first stop for such experience would be the diplomats and negotiators in uniform in Iraq who, despite horrific conditions and challenges, are managing their own wins in communities there. Whatever your view of the war, the extraordinary expertise that many of our junior military officers and enlisted personnel have gained there should be shared across government and other sectors.

- *Extreme resourcefulness*—Leaders who are creative day in and day out in leveraging resources, looking for opportunities to multiply their impact through the efforts of others and unusual partnerships or solutions. The Department of Interior has exceptional examples of such leaders—most are long-time career civil servants who have leveraged their assets to create incredible results. The Department of Interior has used partnerships with volunteers, foundations, corporations, and communities to extend the reach of a shrinking employee base. They have a Partnership and Collaboration Team that is spreading that expertise across the country and creating "bureaucracy busting" tool kits that enable new leaders inside and outside government.

- *Campaign-style communications savvy*—Leaders who understand and have used multiple methods and channels to successfully pull information in and push it out. I would look for how leaders adapted their behavior, message, and perhaps strategies on the basis of those efforts, how they disseminated information, found ways to listen across the organization, and adapted both strategy and messages accordingly. Communications is key to leading across a distributed workforce and stakeholder community.

- *Self-awareness and humility*—In an environment in which you are leading resources well beyond your reach, you simply cannot know it all. Leaders who embrace this and are comfortable with their own limitations ask the right questions, involve the right people, and establish the right atmosphere for success.

- *Adaptability*—Understanding that leaders cannot know it all, the best of the best can admit they have issues or problems and address them quickly and decisively. I want people who have taken risks, stumbled, and found ways to make the best of those learnings—either with a more creative solution to that problem or a life lesson that has influenced their leadership going forward.

- *A voracious appetite for continued learning and adventure*—The greatest leaders who I have encountered are constantly looking for new trends, markets, ideas, and solutions. They are seeking new tools and techniques they can leverage in their difficult worlds. They have multiple passions that extend beyond and yet complement their professional lives: Lovers of Shakespeare, history, writing, adventure traveling, language, culture, technology, science, and so on. Advocates for many causes outside their professional lives. They feed their passions and use that information to stretch their thinking. They instill that same continued intellectual curiosity and commitment in others and inspire people to continue to grow.

HOW CAN WE DEVELOP LEADERS WITH THESE ATTRIBUTES?

For federal agencies, the answer has to come through education and disproportionate doses of rotations and assignments. The Corporate Leadership Council recently completed a study of thousands of leaders across sectors. When asked about the experiences that contributed most to leadership development, the greatest value was placed on stretch assignments, personal development plans, and mentoring.

When I think about my own development, the greatest growth spurts occurred when I was personally responsible for a major endeavor and fully accountable for results that seemed outside my reach. I learned more on late nights working with teams on seemingly insurmountable problems (simultaneously worrying about the imminent demise of my career) than I did from any other training opportunity.

The military successfully combines education with assignments and application, but how can we create the same combination of development activities outside the military ranks? We have to incorporate the right blend of just-in-time learning with immediate application. That requires a robust and accessible curriculum with succession and assignment planning. This combination is nonexistent in most federal agencies.

Beyond succession planning, the curriculum we offer must also expand. How do we expose people throughout their careers to learning about cultures, market forces, technology and innovation, global politics, trends, and so on? DOD is tackling this issue head on. Are other federal agencies? What are the continuing education requirements for our managers and leaders?

Early training and exposure to some of the soft-skill competencies I mentioned above are also important. Are we training our aspiring public-sector leaders in how to manage world-class communication campaigns? Are they learning about engaging and managing broad stakeholder communities? Do their courses include practical experience in setting and measuring mutual goals or managing performance-based ventures? These are some of the questions we must answer to create leaders capable of leading beyond boundaries.

—∿∿—

At time of original printing Marcia Marsh was senior vice president of operations for the World Wildlife Fund and had an extensive career that has included leadership and consultancy across public and private sectors with such organizations as the Partnership for Public Service and Watson Wyatt Worldwide.

CHAPTER THIRTY

Understanding the Nonprofit Sector's Leadership Deficit

Thomas J. Tierney

———

America's nonprofit sector, already expansive, is expanding. Most of us both contribute to the sector and benefit from it: we strengthen our communities when we give time and money to nonprofit organizations. Yet few of us are aware that those organizations face an insidious crisis that could undermine all their good works—a shortage of nonprofit leaders. Our collective response to the accelerating leadership deficit will have an impact on society for decades to come.

Nonprofits face unyielding pressure to make every dollar go a long way. But money is not the only resource in short supply. Many nonprofits are struggling to attract and retain the talented senior executives they need to continue converting society's dollars into social impact. This leadership challenge will only become more acute in the coming years.

Originally published as "Understanding the Nonprofit Sector's Leadership Deficit." In Frances Hesselbein and Marshall Goldsmith (Eds.), *The Leader of the Future 2.* (San Francisco: Jossey-Bass, 2006).

Bridgespan recently carried out an extensive study of the leadership requirements of U.S. nonprofits with revenues greater than $250,000.[1] The study found that in 2006, those organizations need to add more than 56,000 new senior managers to their existing ranks. Cumulatively, over the decade from 2007 to 2016, they will need to attract and develop some 640,000 new senior leaders—or the equivalent of 2.4 times the number currently employed. To put this challenge in context, filling the gap would require recruiting more than 50 percent of every M.B.A. graduating class, at every university across the country, every year for the next decade.[2]

Whether—and how well—these leadership needs are met will have an enormous impact on individual nonprofits. But that's only one aspect of the challenge. Over the next decades, charitable bequests conservatively estimated at $6 trillion will flow to the nonprofit sector, as wealth is transferred from the baby-boom generation to its heirs (Schervish and Havens, 2003). If the nonprofit sector does not address its looming leadership deficit, many of those well-intentioned charitable dollars will be wasted, to the detriment of society as a whole.

CONSTRAINED SUPPLY, BOOMING DEMAND

A growing body of research and experience defines the challenges that nonprofits face to fill leadership positions.[3] To understand the problem, and why it will intensify in coming years, we must examine the structural dynamics shaping the market for nonprofit leaders.

The supply side of the story revolves around the aging baby-boom generation. As the first wave of this cohort, nearly eighty million strong, exits the workforce or shifts to part-time employment, the reverberations will be felt throughout the economy. Their departure will create a vacuum: from 2000 to 2020, the number of men and women ages thirty-four to fifty-four will grow by only three million (Committee for Economic Development, 2005).

Nonprofits confront a corresponding demographic reality—the sector's annual executive retirement rate could climb by 15 percent or more before the end of the decade (Hinden and Teegarden, 2002). The supply of potential leaders will shrink even further as some senior managers burn out and others seek more attractive opportunities. Writing in *The Nonprofit Quarterly* in 2002, two seasoned executives estimated that at any given time, 10 to 12 percent of the country's nonprofit organizations undergo leadership transitions. The authors cited surveys indicating that 15 to 35 percent of nonprofit executives plan to leave their current positions within two years and 61 to 78 percent plan to leave within five years (Hinden and Teegarden, 2002). Whatever the precise timing of those transitions, there is little question that there will be significant sector leadership turnover in the next decade.

The demand-side dynamics are also in flux. The total number of nonprofit organizations has tripled in twenty years. The number of organizations with revenues exceeding $250,000 has increased from 62,800 to 104,700 in the nine years from 1995 to 2004—an annual growth rate of almost 6 percent.

Numerous trends contributed to this expansion. Charitable giving equaled or exceeded the organizational growth rate during most of that nine-year period. The roster of philanthropic foundations swelled by an average of 2,900 new entrants annually in the decade ending in 2002 (Foundation Center, 2004). Young people have taken a growing interest in social entrepreneurship. Many corporations have made social responsibility a greater priority. And government has turned steadily to nonprofits to deliver public services.

Some observers label the growth "proliferation" and suggest that sector consolidation is in order. Others applaud the growth as evidence of our civil society in action. By any measure, though, the nonprofit space is steadily enlarging in both the economy and our communities.

As nonprofits pay more attention to strengthening their capabilities and performance, they will both ask more of their senior management teams and require additional, specialized functional skills. Influential board members may insist that a nonprofit be run "more like a business" and urge the hiring of a chief operating officer. Stepped-up reporting standards create an urgent need for skilled finance and accounting professionals. Experienced communications and development executives are in demand as nonprofits reach out more aggressively to potential funding sources. Efforts to recruit and retain front-line staff and screen volunteers require professional expertise.

UNDERSTANDING THE NUMBERS

Bridgespan has incorporated the trends just described into an analysis of the number of new senior managers nonprofits would need through 2016. We assumed that the growth in the number of nonprofits in each revenue category would continue at historic 1995 to 2004 rates. We also assumed that retirement rates would remain constant throughout the 1996 to 2016 time period, save for an incremental six-percentage-point demographic boost from 2004 through 2009, attributable to a spike in baby-boomer retirements, and that rates of other forms of transition would be stable.

Using these assumptions, we projected that nonprofits will require 78,000 new senior managers in 2016, up from 56,000 in 2006 and more than a fourfold increase since 1996. The projected increase is attributable to growth in the number of nonprofits (42 percent); leadership transitions, retirement, or other departures (55 percent); and the trend to larger organizations (3 percent). The combined effect of these dynamics is reflected in a base-case estimate that 640,000 new senior managers will be needed over the coming decade.

Now suppose that the growth rate in the number of nonprofit organizations declines dramatically, perhaps because of changes in the flows or magnitude of charitable funding or because of widespread failures of established nonprofits. Future turnover rates might fall below recent projections. *Even with such conservative assumptions, however, the sector will still need some 330,000 new senior executives over the next decade.*

But growth will more likely accelerate, driven by the confluence of the coming wealth transfer and increased societal reliance on nonprofits. Executive burnout and the war for talent might further accelerate turnover. *If those more aggressive assumptions prove correct, the total need for new managers would increase from the base case of 640,000 to 1,250,000.*

Even in the most optimistic scenario, the need for new nonprofit leaders will be acute in the decade ahead. Nonprofit organizations will need an exceptional number of new leaders each and every year. Current practices cannot adequately address this unprecedented deficit.

UNDERSTANDING THE LANDSCAPE

The sector's challenge is complicated by the nature of nonprofits. Most nonprofits are too small to provide meaningful career development for next-generation leaders, and few can afford to invest substantially in recruiting and human resources—especially in an environment that tends to view such expenditures as wasteful overhead. Consequently, many nonprofits search outside their own organizations (but within their own networks, as we shall see) for new senior managers. The best available data indicate that non-profits fill 30 to 40 percent of senior management positions with internal candidates (in contrast, businesses fill 60 to 65 percent of their senior positions from within) (Charan, 2005; Russell Reynolds Associates, 2005; CompassPoint, 2001). The risks notwithstanding, external recruiting is more expensive and time-consuming than internal sourcing. Thus, as the war for talent intensifies, the cost of addressing the sector's leadership deficit will likely escalate.

Nonprofits also face a training and recruiting deficit. Nonprofit management programs are growing, but they are modest compared with traditional business education programs. Nor do nonprofits have a search infrastructure to rival the business world's, in which the executive search industry, job-posting platforms such as Monster.com, and outsourcing service providers such as Hewitt Associates and Convergys are all eager to help. The infrastructure exists because the rewards for serving the business sector are ample.

The nonprofit sector offers no such profit pool, so there is no comparable infrastructure to deliver a robust supply of leadership talent (Gadiesh and Gilbert, 1998). With notable exceptions, few nonprofits recruit effectively from colleges or graduate schools. The largest search firms devote only a fraction of their resources to the nonprofit sector, and they typically focus on higher-profile, higher-paying positions—an entirely rational approach given their financial incentives. A handful of medium-sized search firms, such as Isaacson Miller, concentrate on nonprofits, yet their business is skewed toward larger institutions. Thousands of outstanding independent recruiters work in the nonprofit sector but are constrained by limited capacity or access to talent. Organizations such as Action Without Borders (Idealist) are emerging to help nonprofits find talent, but their scale is dwarfed by the magnitude of the problem.

FINDING THE LEADERS WE NEED

The underlying trends of the leadership deficit are beyond anyone's control, but we can control how we react to them. It's not enough to acknowledge and understand the sheer size of the problem; we must make this challenge a top priority in nonprofit governance, planning, and day-to-day decision making. Closing the gap will require action, innovation, experimentation, and leaps of faith at both an organizational and a systemic level.

Within each organization, board members, senior managers, and major donors must commit to building strong and enduring leadership teams. Across the whole sector, foundations, intermediaries, and associations must collaborate to nurture the flow and development of management talent. In short, we must invest in leadership capacity, refine management rewards to retain and attract top talent, and expand recruiting horizons while fostering individual career mobility.

Invest in Leadership Capacity

There's a widespread belief among donors, the media, and even many of the organizations that evaluate and rate nonprofits that overhead is always bad and less overhead is always better (Lowell, Trelstad, and Meehan, 2005). Ergo, recruiting expenses, training costs, compensation, and senior-level positions themselves should be held to a bare minimum. Herein lies one of the major obstacles to remedying the leadership deficit. Donors, board members, and executive directors need to embrace the importance of investing in leadership capacity, despite prevailing pressures to the contrary.

Investment includes both money and time. Many successful business CEOs spend well over half their time on people-related issues, while the executive directors of nonprofits devote the bulk of their time to fundraising (Bossidy, 2001; CompassPoint, 2003; Whelan, 2003). Although entirely rational, this prioritization forces nonprofits to give short shrift to mentoring, training, succession planning, recruiting, and other organization-specific functions. The opportunity costs are substantial.

Refine Management Rewards to Retain and Attract Top Talent

The greatest rewards of nonprofit careers will always be intangible, but that doesn't mean that compensation doesn't matter. Indeed, as nonprofit managers face increasingly complex challenges and are judged by much more rigorous performance standards, their tougher, riskier jobs will require commensurate rewards. More competitive compensation packages would speed the sector's migration toward more professional management and help nonprofits attract, recruit, and retain talented leaders. By facing the complex realities of executive compensation, nonprofits can better equip themselves to address performance shortfalls, executive burnout, and the need for more sophisticated financial reporting. Of course, they will need the support of funders and donors to do so.

Expand Recruiting Horizons and Foster Individual Career Mobility

Nonprofits typically draw key managers from within their personal and professional networks. This isn't surprising, given the vital importance of fit and a proven affinity for an organization's mission. Candidates not only must possess technical expertise but also must be demonstrably coachable, flexible, and entrepreneurial. Factor in the sector's fragmentation and the strong local roots of most nonprofits, and it is clear why organizations prefer to hire friends or friends of friends.

But networking alone cannot ensure that we will place the right leaders in the right jobs during the next decade. Nonprofits must expand their search to several significant pools of new leadership talent.

- *The baby-boom generation.* A recent study by the MetLife Foundation and Civic Ventures (2005) indicated that many fifty- to seventy-year-olds want to work during their later years: two-thirds of those surveyed intend to continue working, and fully half hope to work in organizations with social missions.[3]

- *"Repotters."* In addition, more people at the midpoint of their professional lives are thinking about "repotting" themselves. John Gardner (1995) wrote eloquently about the value of such career shifts more than forty years ago, as have the late Peter Drucker (2005) and, more recently, Bob Buford (1994). The sector would both gain new sources of leadership and provide collegial resources for existing leaders by reaching out to these two pools of talent alone.

- *Young managers in training.* In 1990 there were seventeen graduate programs in nonprofit management in the United States. Today there are well over ninety, and more than 240 university programs offer nonprofit courses (Joslyn, 2004). Those figures alone suggest the depth of those students' commitment to service.

- *Other pools.* Strong and diverse candidates may also be found among civil servants, officers making the transition from military service to civilian life, and women reentering the workforce after working at home to raise families. Today, many such qualified people are excluded from the recruiting process simply because they lack the right personal contacts.

The nonprofit sector also needs an infrastructure designed to ensure that its talent is visible and mobile. Again, promising examples already exist. Community foundations in cities such as Chicago, San Diego, and New York are expanding programs to build local leadership capacity. The Annie E. Casey Foundation and others are tracking and attacking issues such as executive director succession. Net Impact is building a global network of MBAs, graduate students, and young professionals with a mission to grow and strengthen leaders using the power of business to make a positive net social, environmental, and economic impact. Idealist, a project of Action Without Borders, offers nonprofits and individuals opportunities to connect via job openings, volunteer opportunities, internships, events, and resources posted by organizations all over the world. CompassPoint has recently started a division to help nonprofits prepare for executive transitions, recruit strong pools of candidates, and support and train executive directors. Bridgestar, an initiative of the Bridgespan Group, collaborates with universities and many forms of professional networks to develop pools of management talent, and provides content and recruiting services, including an online job board, to help match individuals with nonprofits' needs.

IT'S UP TO US

America relies upon vibrant nonprofit organizations to create substantial social impact. The imperatives surrounding the leadership deficit must be addressed by nonprofit management teams, boards of directors, donors, and volunteers. We cannot wait: nonprofit leaders are retiring, organizations are growing, and society's demands are escalating. Without aggressive support and disciplined investment, our efforts may amount to too little, too late. Nonprofits need the best of tomorrow's leaders—today.

Notes

1. We excluded hospitals and institutions of higher learning from our sample, because of their distinctive funding mechanisms, specialized pools of talent, and well-developed infrastructure for developing talent.
2. The National Center for Education Statistics reports that 120,785 MBA degrees were conferred in the 2001–2002 school year.
3. Including the following: CompassPoint, *Help Wanted: Turnover and Vacancy in Nonprofits* (San Francisco: CompassPoint Nonprofit Services, January 2002); TransitionGuides and Management Performance Concepts, *Community Foundation CEO Survey: Transitions and Career Paths* (Silver Spring, MD: TransitionGuides, October 2003); New England Executive Transitions Partnership, *Executive Director Tenure and Transition in Southern New England* (Boston: New England Executive Transitions Partnership, January 2004); Paige Hull Teegarden, Management Performance Concepts, and TransitionGuides, *Nonprofit Executive Leadership and Transitions Survey 2004: Greater NYC* (Silver Spring, MD: TransitionGuides, November 2004).

References

Bossidy, Lawrence A. "The Job No CEO Should Delegate." *Harvard Business Review*, March 2001.

Buford, Bob. *Halftime*. Grand Rapids, MI: Zondervan, 1994.

Charan, Ram. "Ending the CEO Succession Crisis." *Harvard Business Review*, February 2005.

Committee for Economic Development. *Cracks in the Education Pipeline: A Business Leader's Guide to Higher Education Reform*. Washington, DC: Committee for Economic Development, 2005.

CompassPoint. "Daring to Lead: Nonprofit Executive Directors and Their Work Experience," 2001. San Francisco, Author. http://www.compasspoint.org/assets/5_daring.pdf (accessed July 2, 2009)

Drucker, Peter. "Managing Oneself." *Harvard Business Review*, January 2005.

Foundation Center. *Foundation Yearbook: Facts and Figures on Private and Community Foundations*. New York: Foundation Center, 2004.

Gadiesh, Orit, and Gilbert, James L. "Profit Pools: A Fresh Look at Strategy." *Harvard Business Review*, May/June 1998.

Gardner, John W. *Self-Renewal: The Individual and the Innovative Society*. New York: W.W. Norton, 1995.

Hinden, Denice Rothman, and Teegarden, Paige Hull, "Executive Leadership Transition: What We Know." *The Nonprofit Quarterly*, Winter 2002.

Joslyn, Heather. "Gaining Success by Degrees" and "Young People Fuel Demand for Nonprofit Study." *Chronicle of Philanthropy*, January 8, 2004.

Lowell, Stephanie, Trelstad, Brian, and Meehan, Bill. "The Ratings Game." *Stanford Social Innovation Review*, Summer 2005.

MetLife Foundation and Civic Ventures. *New Face of Work Survey*. San Francisco: Civic Ventures, 2005.

Russell Reynolds Associates. "The CFO Turnover Study," May 2005. http://www.russellreynolds.com/pdf/thought/CFOTurnoverSurvey .pdf (accessed July 2, 2009)

Schervish, Paul G., and Havens, John J. "New Findings on the Patterns of Wealth and Philanthropy." Boston: Social Welfare Research Institute, Boston College, 2003.

Whelan, David. "Exploring a New World." *Chronicle of Philanthropy*, January 23, 2003.

―⁕―

At time of original printing Thomas J. Tierney was the chairman and cofounder of The Bridgespan Group, a nonprofit organization established in 1999 to provide management consulting services to the nonprofit sector. Most recently, he led the development of Bridgestar, a Bridgespan initiative dedicated to talent-matching for the sector. Tierney was the chief executive of Bain & Company from 1992 to 2000. He contributed to many publications, including the Harvard Business Review, *and is the co-author of* Aligning the Stars *(Harvard Business School Press, 2002). Tierney was a director of eBay, Incorporated, and was serving on numerous nonprofit boards and advisory groups.*

The Nexus Effect
When Leaders Span Group Boundaries

Jeffrey Yip
Serena Wong
Christopher Ernst

I n this age of global interconnection, leaders need to go beyond their traditional focus on managing and protecting group boundaries and work toward boundary-spanning leadership—bridging intergroup boundaries in order to achieve a shared vision or goal. The experiences of leaders in three different sectors shed some preliminary light on the collective solutions that can be achieved when leaders facilitate collaborative practices *across* diverse and even divided groups.

nex · us

1. *CONNECTION, LINK; also: a causal link*

2. *a connected group or series*

3. *CENTER, FOCUS*

—*Merriam-Webster's Collegiate Dictionary,* Eleventh Edition.

Originally published as "The Nexus Effect: When Leaders Span Group Boundaries," *Leadership in Action,* 28 (September/October 2008).

The practice of leadership traditionally has focused on the role of leaders in managing and protecting group boundaries. Leaders often operate within their box on the organizational chart, within the interests of their unit or team, and within the mind-sets of the demographic or cultural groups to which they belong. However, in this age of global inter-connection, the opposite response is often required—the ability to bridge intergroup boundaries toward a shared vision or goal.

What can be achieved through boundary-spanning leadership? Specifically, we use the term the *nexus effect* to describe the higher, collective outcomes that can be achieved when leaders span boundaries that are above and beyond what each group could achieve on its own. In this article we explore the nexus effect through the experiences of leaders in three different sectors: Ingrid Srinath, former CEO of Child Rights and You (CRY), the leading nongovernmental organization in India dedicated to children's rights; William J. Amelio, president and CEO of Lenovo, the world's fourth-largest manufacturer of personal computers; and Mechai Viravaidya, a social entrepreneur and former politician in Thailand who is currently chairman of that nation's Population and Community Development Association, which he founded in 1974.

REFRAMING DIFFERENCES

In 2004, Ingrid Srinath was appointed CEO of CRY, then known as Child Relief and You. In this role she was given a clear but daunting task—to lead a sweeping reorganization that would transform CRY from a child relief agency to a child rights agency.

At the onset Srinath was keenly aware that this undertaking would require her to adopt a new and different model of leadership. Srinath came to CRY after eleven years of leadership in the hard-charging world of corporate advertising. When asked to describe her leadership style, she summed it up in two words: *impatient* and *unreasonable*. CRY, however, is a grassroots organization based on the principles of democracy and collective action. The groups that make up CRY span seventeen of the twenty-eight Indian states and are a microcosm of the tremendous diversity of the vast nation, differing in matters of gender, religion, region, language, ethnicity, and caste.

William Amelio, brought in to lead Lenovo after its acquisition of IBM's global personal computer operation in 2005, faced the complex challenge of leading at the crossroads of two distinct organizational cultures and also two national cultures.

Srinath and her management committee recognized that the organizational transformation would take root only if all the groups of the organization reframed their differences and identified with the new strategic direction. As Srinath explained it, "We can't create a movement [for child's rights] with over a billion people in India until we first create that movement and that understanding within our own diversity."

Guided by the principle that all groups within CRY had to be brought along on the transformational journey, Srinath and her team instituted a number of boundary-spanning practices over the next two years. One of these practices involved bringing representatives from the organization's entire system together for dialogue, planning, and implementing key change initiatives. Another practice incorporated an innovative planning process in which the CRY people in each Indian region worked collectively to create an overarching strategy. The final plan is what emerged after the regional groups cooperated to reconcile regional variations in support of an integrated strategy. A third practice leveraged the CRY's intranet to create a consensus decision-making platform through which groups could participate in decisions related to implementing the transformation.

Practices such as these, although complex and time-consuming to implement, helped Srinath to bridge groups in service of the larger transformational goal. "Investing the time up-front pays off because there is a genuine acceptance of the need for change," explains Srinath. "The sustainability will be so much greater because it becomes fully internalized."

In April 2006, CRY celebrated the transformation process with an event involving all 191 employees. On that day, CRY's name changed from Child Relief and You to Child Rights and You. True to Srinath's guiding principle, everyone in the organization was brought along on the journey. One employee poignantly described the event: "It was a day in which everyone experienced a collective vision. It was no longer different groups with different agendas but rather a powerful, integrating vision."

That same year CRY went on to affect the lives of nearly five hundred thousand children through advocacy and initiatives in more than five thousand villages throughout India.

GOING GLOBAL

William Amelio was brought in to lead Lenovo after its high-profile acquisition of IBM's global personal computer operation in 2005. Beyond the merging and streamlining of Lenovo's and IBM's systems and procedures, Amelio, an American with several years' experience heading up Dell's Asia-Pacific business from Singapore, had the complex challenge of leading at the crossroads of two distinct organizational cultures and also two national cultures. "It's hard enough just putting two companies together," Amelio told *U.S. News & World Report* in 2007. "Imagine doing that with different ideologies, backgrounds, and histories."

After the merger, Amelio and his team moved quickly to implement Lenovo-only branding of the company's products, and the company celebrated the change at a party where employees ripped IBM logo stickers off computers in unison. Employees were also encouraged not to hang onto old legacies; a "trash bin project" gave former IBM staff members the opportunity to submit examples of things they did while with IBM but did not want to continue doing.

More than just products and processes were unified under a single brand. Ken DiPietro, head of human resources at Lenovo, told *U.S News:* "We were labeling people as legacy IBM, legacy Lenovo, or new hires. At one point, [Amelio] and I got really frustrated with everybody talking about three streams. We said we need to stop doing that."

From that point on, Lenovo was positioned as a global company rather than a Chinese or a U.S. or a Sino-American company. One move was to internationalize the management team. Nowadays even the management meetings have taken on a global character. Amelio works out of Singapore; Lenovo chairman Yang Yuanqing lives in Raleigh, North Carolina; and meetings among top executives are held in different locations each month.

The Lenovo management team worked to reduce potential East-West cultural tensions among employees. A "cultural audit" of Lenovo employees was conducted. Chinese employees were encouraged to speak out more, and Western employees were taught to be less confrontational and to speak more slowly and listen more. The company also worked with its Chinese employees on improving their English skills to facilitate communication. Informal company table tennis sessions helped employees bond over common interests.

Although it is still early in the merger to make a full assessment, healthy numbers posted for the most recent fiscal year—for instance, a 17 percent increase in sales over the previous year—are encouraging. Lenovo also retained almost all of the former IBM staff, which again suggests Lenovo's success in spanning two distinct organizational and societal cultures.

WORKING TOGETHER

In the late 1980s, Mechai Viravaidya, a long-time activist for population control and family planning, anticipated that AIDS would become a crisis in Thailand but was aware that broaching the subject was not going to be easy. Yet amid the sensitivities of a conservative society and resistance from some business and government groups, Viravaidya managed to bring his fellow Thais on board to fight the spread of AIDS. The Viravaidya-led AIDS awareness and prevention campaign in the 1990s has been deemed one of the world's most successful.

Viravaidya realized early on that effectively curbing the spread of AIDS in Thailand would require many different groups with diverse interests working together. It looked like an uphill battle. Former Thai prime minister Anand Panyarachun recalled in 2004 that the tourism industry was concerned that visitors would be scared off by this highly publicized education campaign on AIDS.

> Amid the sensitivities of a conservative society and resistance from some business and government groups, Mechai Viravaidya managed to bring his fellow Thais on board to fight the spread of AIDS.

Viravaidya reached out to groups outside the government, especially those with wide influence in Thai society. As he had learned from his days as a family-planning activist, it was important to get religion on his side and win over conservatives. He gained the support of Buddhist monks, an important moral authority in predominantly Buddhist Thailand. Some religious associations trained monks and nuns to work in AIDS prevention and treatment. In 1989, Viravaidya persuaded General Chavalit Yongchaiyudh, Thai Army chief and acting supreme commander, to agree to make 126 military-run radio stations and two television networks available for the AIDS prevention campaign. The general also presided over the testing for

AIDS of all the military's personnel, including its temporary civilian staff.

When Panyarachun appointed Viravaidya as Thailand's AIDS czar in 1991, Viravaidya positioned AIDS as a societal and national challenge rather than as an issue to be handled by the health ministry and confined to a small group of Thais. He persuaded the prime minister to helm the national AIDS committee. This was an important symbolic move that also afforded Viravaidya, by extension, the power of the prime minister's pulpit with the government ministries. He used the office to engage and direct a variety of groups—including government departments, schools, television and radio stations, nongovernmental organizations, and the business community—to support the AIDS education campaign. As Viravaidya told Agence France-Presse in 2007, "Everyone was involved, every ministry—education was involved, business was involved, religion was involved, everyone."

> Organizations often fail to create an inclusive vision when the dynamics of *us* and *them* cannot be transformed into a collective *we*.

Viravaidya also found a powerful image that even if criticized by some as gimmicky was an effective tool for changing mind-sets and breaking down barriers. Back in his family-planning days, he had persuaded Buddhist monks to bless batches of condoms before they were sent out for distribution. When it came time to show people that AIDS could not be passed by casual contact, Viravaidya during a news conference drank from a cup that had been used by an AIDS sufferer.

In 2006, a World Bank report estimated that if Thailand had not pursued such an effective campaign, a further 7.7 million people would have been infected with AIDS.

FOUR PRINCIPLES

The word *nexus* comes from the Latin word *nectere*, which means "to bind." A nexus is a form of connection, a link, or a tie. In mathematical terms, Alfred North Whitehead, the late-nineteenth and early-twentieth-century English mathematician and philosopher, described a nexus as a system of relationships in which the whole is greater than its parts. In philosophical terms, Aristotle recognized that, although there will inevitably be differences of opinion about what is the common good, it is the responsibility of a leader to identify the highest possible common good for all. In organizational terms, from the examples of Ingrid Srinath, William Amelio, and Mechai Viravaidya, the Center for Creative Leadership's early research suggests four principles for the nexus effect.

The nexus effect occurs when there is a strong bridge between us and them. In CRY the nexus effect was created when a powerful, collective vision was created that could not have been achieved by any one group in the organization acting alone. For this vision to take root, Srinath and leaders throughout the organization had to bridge groups from different parts of India, representing different beliefs and cultures, to work together effectively. This required leaders to not only understand the interests, needs, and values of different groups but also to actively facilitate dialogue among those groups. Organizations often fail to create an inclusive vision when the dynamics of *us* and *them* cannot be transformed into a collective *we*. In the case of CRY, boundary-spanning practices created an effective bridge, one that allowed a collective future strategy to emerge.

The nexus effect is as much about changed mind-sets as it is about action. As seen in the example of Amelio and Lenovo, the nexus effect is manifest not only in the increased productivity of a merged company but also in the shared mind-sets of employees from different cultures. Amelio advanced a multi-group vision that produced a greater good for everyone. This is an example of how leaders can span boundaries to enhance relationships and sensitize different groups to shared concerns. An aspect of the nexus effect is that people start to think across boundaries and shift their beliefs from in-group attitudes toward a vision shared by all groups.

The nexus effect unleashes resources beyond an individual or organization. In the case of Viravaidya's campaign, the nexus effect was realized through the outcomes of AIDS prevention and the coordinated response at every level and sector of society. The nexus effect occurs when leaders such as Viravaidya tap into a diversity of knowledge and capabilities represented by different sectors of society. The energies of diverse groups are harnessed to address persistent and often previously intractable problems.

The nexus effect can create a mutually reinforcing cycle. This occurs when success in one group strengthens the other groups and creates a positive feedback loop. The effect is significant, especially when it comes to finding solutions to difficult yet important developmental problems and fostering sustainable change. In CRY, for instance, by spanning the boundaries within the organization, Srinath and her team were able to create the change they wanted to see in the groups they worked with. They were able to create a reinforcing cycle of diverse people working toward common objectives and the realization of a shared vision for social change.

CHANGING DYNAMIC

As the examples in this article suggest, groups of people who historically had remained apart now find themselves increasingly working together. Organizations today are junctions and nodes through which people, resources, and information interact and flow. Despite this reality, current leadership research and practice continue to focus on leadership *within* a defined group, assuming a traditional dynamic in which leaders and followers share a common culture and set of values.

> The nexus effect occurs when leaders tap into a diversity of knowledge and capabilities represented by different sectors of society. The energies of diverse groups are harnessed to address persistent and often previously intractable problems.

Through its research, CCL is just beginning to understand the nexus effect and the collective solutions that can be achieved when leaders facilitate collaborative practices *across* diverse and even divided groups. CCL hopes to identify methods for developing effective leadership across groups and to create frameworks for understanding boundary-spanning practices and mind-sets in varying contexts.

CCL believes that boundary-spanning leadership is particularly vital as business, government, civil society, and local communities partner to try to solve the world's most pressing societal challenges. As philosopher Martha C. Nussbaum writes in her book *Cultivating Humanity: A Classical Defense of Reform in Liberal Education* (Harvard University Press, 1997): "Citizens who cultivate their humanity need an ability to see themselves not simply as citizens of some local region or group but also, and above all, as human beings bound to all other human beings by ties of recognition and concern.... Issues from business to agriculture, from human rights to the relief of famine, call our imaginations to venture beyond narrow group loyalties and consider the reality of distant lives."

Therein lies both the challenge and the opportunity of the nexus effect when leaders span group boundaries.

—⁓—

At the time of original printing Jeffrey Yip was a research associate at CCL's Singapore campus. He holds an M.Ed. degree from Harvard University and a master of social science degree from the National University of Singapore.

At the time of original printing Serena Wong was an adjunct researcher with CCL-Asia. She holds an M.B.A. degree from INSEAD.

At the time of original printing Christopher Ernst was research director of global leadership at CCL's Singapore campus. He holds a Ph.D. degree from North Carolina State University.

CHAPTER THIRTY TWO

The Politics of Doing Good

Philanthropic Leadership for the Twenty-First Century

Leslie Lenkowsky

In his Discourses on the work of Livy, Niccolo Machiavelli recounted an episode from the history of Rome. It concerns a famine that had struck the city and the donation by a citizen named Spurius Melius of a "private stock of grain and feed" to the hungry. In return, "fearing the evil consequences that might arise" from this act of generosity, Machiavelli wrote, the Roman Senate created "a Dictator" who put this early philanthropist to death. Notwithstanding the old saying that no good deed goes unpunished, that would seem to be a bit excessive.

However, in his commentary, Machiavelli leaves no doubt that he believes the Senate was right. A republic that has "no distinguished citizens," he wrote, cannot be well governed, but at the same time, the

---

Originally published as "The Politics of Doing Good: Philanthropic Leadership for the Twenty-First Century." In William Damon and Susan Verducci (Eds.), *Taking Philanthropy Seriously: Beyond Noble Intentions to Responsible Giving.* (Bloomington, IN: Indiana University Press, 2006).

influence of such citizens often causes the public to surrender their freedoms to those who promise them great rewards. To avoid that fate, Machiavelli advised, a "well-regulated" government should offer many opportunities for such citizens to serve the public through the state. But if it allows its distinguished citizens to obtain "reputation and influence" through private means, it is asking for trouble. Indeed, warned Machiavelli, "if one such transgression were allowed to go unpunished, it might lead to the ruin of the republic, for it would then be difficult to force back the ambitious to the true path of duty" (Machiavelli, 1950, 490–493).

The lesson of this story might be, to paraphrase William Shakespeare, "First, kill all the philanthropists." And if we have not yet heard a state attorney general go quite that far, we have seen no less than the former head of the Council on Foundations, the premier association of the nation's grant-making bodies, quoted as saying that, sooner or later, she expected to see one of her members paraded before television cameras in a "perp walk." Moreover, many legal experts, such as well-known television commentator Jonathan Turley, a professor at the George Washington University law school, have argued that the time has come to extend the corporate-governance laws prompted by the scandals at Enron, Tyco, and other companies—and presumably, the penalties for breaking them as well—to large not-for-profit corporations (Turley, 2004).

In a country long accustomed to holding philanthropy and charities in regard, such proposals—and Professor Turley is by no means alone in making them—strike a discordant note. Between 1995 and 2002, a period in which the size of the nonprofit sector expanded greatly, a survey of newspaper reports by Marion Fremont-Smith and Andras Kosaras found 152 reports of criminal and civil wrongdoing (Fremont-Smith and Kosaras, 2003). In the years that followed, spurred particularly by reporters for *The New York Times*, *The Boston Globe*, and *The Washington Post*, the "bad news" continued and perhaps even increased as Congress held several widely publicized hearings to examine abuses by tax-exempt organizations and their supporters. What has happened? And what will happen? Obviously, some questionable practices have now come to light which, if not always strictly illegal, are less tolerable than they were before the corporate scandals.

But where there is smoke, there is not necessarily fire. The scandals that have recently engulfed the philanthropic world are not a sign that legal and ethical transgressions are rampant in philanthropy. But they do reveal the growing importance of philanthropy in American life—and the resulting political questions about doing good through private means.

Indeed, in light of the magnitude of the alleged transgressions (of the more than $350 billion the Internal Revenue Service [IRS] estimates is lost to the U.S. Treasury because of illegal tax avoidance, only about $6 billion might be realized by curbing the misuse of charitable organizations), the amount of attention the non-profit world has been receiving from government has been striking (Everson, 2005; Joint Committee on Taxation, 2005). In the name of increasing foundation payouts, Congress considered—and will undoubtedly do so again—a bill that would disallow certain administrative expenses—especially high salaries and excessive travel expenses—from the required spending amount (which is currently 5 percent of asset values, averaged over several preceding years). Sponsored by an unusual coalition of liberals and conservatives, the proposals resulted in the kind of lobbying effort by the philanthropic world that is generally associated with advocates for tariffs and highways, a campaign which itself became something of an embarrassment, though for now, at any rate, it has been successful.

The 2002 Bipartisan Campaign Finance Reform Act opened the door to regulating political advertising near federal elections by ostensibly nonpartisan nonprofit groups that are supported by donations. During the 2004 campaign, the Federal Election Commission considered actions to regulate contributions to issue-oriented nonprofit organizations established under Section 527 of the tax code, and rules for 501(c)(3) and 501(c)(4) groups—public charities and social welfare organizations—may come next. The PATRIOT Act, passed in the wake of the 9/11 terrorist attacks, gave broad new powers to the Departments of Justice and Treasury to monitor the flow of money to organizations suspected of supporting terrorism, including supposedly charitable ones. Several foundations and the Combined Federal Campaign (the "United Way" for federal employees) adopted rules aimed at preventing such gifts, leading to protests from groups such as the American Civil Liberties Union and higher-education institutions, which regarded them as too intrusive and burdensome.

Following the United States Supreme Court's decision in the case of Ryan v. Telemarketing Associates, the Federal Trade Commission and over three dozen state attorneys general have become more aggressive in pursuing cases of alleged fund-raising fraud. California, Minnesota, New York, Indiana, and other states have enacted new laws that give officials expanded powers to regulate charities, including, if necessary, replacing their boards of trustees if they have misused or improperly solicited gifts. Still under consideration are proposals to extend the so-called Sarbanes-Oxley rules on corporate governance to nonprofits, including by making financial records more transparent to stakeholders, curtailing conflicts of interest, and imposing greater penalties for misdeeds.[1] Legal advisors and groups such as Independent Sector are urging charities to get ready for the changes likely in store and to preempt new mandates through greater self-regulation.

High-profile lawsuits, such as one accusing Princeton's Woodrow Wilson School of Public and International Affairs of ignoring the intent of a major donor, are becoming more common, as are challenges to trustee decisions by public officials, including governors. Following court injunctions requested by the Pennsylvania attorney general, the trustees of the Milton Hershey Trust cancelled a planned sale of the stock it owned in the Hershey Foods Corporation, which comprised the bulk of its assets and 77 percent of the shares with voting rights, lest the company's operations be moved out of the state. And under pressure from state and local officials, as well as other philanthropists, the trustees of Philadelphia's Barnes Foundation successfully petitioned a court to relocate its multibillion-dollar art collection to a new locale, despite concerns that the move might be at odds with the donor's intent.

Following a widely publicized series of articles in *The Washington Post*, the IRS launched an audit of The Nature Conservancy, the largest environmental organization in the world, which led to major changes in its governance and procedures to prevent accusations of favoritism toward board members and large donors in sales of property under the organization's control. After a report by the General Accounting Office and a legislative hearing, President George W. Bush proposed and Congress enacted new rules for calculating the amount of the charitable deduction for gifts of used cars to keep donors from overvaluing them. Similar changes for other contributions of property are also under consideration.

As *The Washington Post*'s exposé of The Nature Conservancy demonstrated, far from still being a spin-off of reporting in society pages on fund-raising galas, "needy cases," and heart-warming philanthropic projects, covering charities has become a focus for investigative reporters, especially at major national and regional dailies, such as *The Boston Globe,* the *San Jose Mercury News,* and *The New York Times.* Specialized publications, such as *The Chronicle of Philanthropy,* have been doing more in-depth reports too, such as examining loans and other forms of compensation to key executives of charities.

To be sure, the developments of the past two years—and others could be listed—are not unprecedented. The 1980s and 1990s also saw a number of high-profile episodes of misbehavior in the nonprofit world: among others, the fraudulent investment practices of the Foundation for New Era Philanthropy; excessive expenditures by executives of the Freedom Forum Foundation; improprieties by the trustees of Hawaii's largest philanthropy, the Bishop Estate; and misuse of funds by the head of the United Way of America, the umbrella organization for over 1,000 employee-giving campaigns in the United States. At a 1998 American Assembly gathering on "Philanthropy in a Changing America," Duke University's Joel L. Fleishman, a veteran participant in and observer of the nonprofit world, used instances such as these to argue for the creation of a new government regulatory body to oversee charities. "The truth is," he wrote, "that there is no entity at present ... which has the authority to establish and police standards of compliance on a national scale, yet the existence of such standards and both actual and perceived compliance with them are essential if the public is to continue to feel justifiably comfortable in trusting not-for-profit organizations." While meant as a "strategy of last resort," the new agency would be designed not to replace the efforts of the IRS or state attorneys general but to add to them (Fleishman, 1999, p. 186).

Though it attracted considerable attention, Fleishman's proposal garnered very little support. (The American Assembly's final report called merely for strengthening the existing oversight agencies.) This may have been partly because the scandals were largely perceived as isolated incidents that did not reflect any deep-seated problem with philanthropy in general. They could cause—and may indeed have caused—damage to the organizations involved. They may also have produced greater public skepticism about nonprofit organizations in general. But even so, a 1994 Independent Sector poll found that more than one-third of the American public still had "a great deal" or "quite a lot" of confidence in nonprofits (even if religious groups are not counted), nearly double the level expressing such views about federal and state government (Independent Sector, 1995).

The most urgent challenges facing the philanthropic world appeared to be external more than internal. Cutbacks or policy changes in government funding in "areas of concern to nonprofits" (to use Lester M. Salamon's phrase) were putting increasing pressure on donors to "pick up the slack" (as President Ronald Reagan's advisor, Michael K. Deaver, reportedly said). At the same time, reductions in tax rates seemed likely to reduce some of the economic advantages of charitable giving. For-profit companies, such as Fidelity Investments, were establishing tax-exempt "donor-advised" funds that threatened to draw money away from more traditional forms of philanthropy, such as foundations and local branches of the United Way. And as the Baby Boom generation achieved greater financial success, its apparent preference for "bowling alone" (in political scientist Robert D. Putnam's words) and disinclination to support charities as their parents had boded ill for the likelihood they would be generous with their new wealth. Nonetheless, when, on occasion, questions were raised about the health of philanthropy (for example, the issues the Bradley Foundation's National Commission on Philanthropy and Civic Renewal raised in 1997), they were largely ignored.

And why not? Despite the scandals and challenges that beset it, the 1990s were a pretty good decade for the nonprofit world. Charitable giving kept pace with a rapidly growing economy and at times exceeded it. The number of nonprofit organizations grew, as did the number of and assets held by foundations. (By the end of the decade, holdings of $1 billion were barely sufficient to place an organization among the top fifty grant-makers in the United States.) Because of growing student interest, programs to prepare them for careers in the nonprofit sector were started or expanded. The Clinton administration sponsored what was billed as the first White House Conference on Philanthropy, and in the 2000 campaign, both Vice President Gore and Governor George W. Bush promised, if elected, to rely more on what the latter called "the armies of compassion."

Writing early in the new millennium, Salamon (2002) called "nonprofit America" the "resilient sector." In the face of challenges and opportunities in the 1980s and 1990s, it had responded, he wrote, by "strengthening its fiscal base, upgrading its operations, enlisting new partners and new resources in its activities, and generally improving its reputation for effectiveness" (p. 45). It still faced "risks," including the "potential loss of public trust," Salamon said (p. 48; emphasis added). But while he called for some changes in public policy, mostly aimed at distinguishing the charitable from the commercial activities of nonprofits, there was little suggestion of the intense public scrutiny about to come.

How much difference a short amount of time can make is apparent in a report from The Brookings Institution entitled "To Give or Not to Give: The Crisis of Confidence in Charities." In it, Paul Light notes that public opinion of the job nonprofits were doing sank in 2001 and has not recovered much since. Especially striking, he adds, is that confidence in other civic institutions went up during this period (although it has since gone down again). "Whether correctly or incorrectly," Light concludes, "the public has come to believe that substantial numbers of charitable organizations are not doing well enough or not doing enough good" (Light, 2003, p. 8).

Light attributes this largely to the aftermath of the 9/11 terrorist attacks and the criticisms leveled against the American Red Cross and other nonprofit groups for mishandling relief contributions. Undoubtedly, reports that the large sums of money Americans donated were slow in getting to the victims of the attacks (or were slated to be used for other purposes altogether) were an embarrassment for the nonprofit world. But how valid the criticisms were and what effect they really had is open to doubt. A careful review for The Century Foundation by Paula DiPerna concluded that much of the press coverage was inaccurate or incomplete and that the successful efforts of charities to respond innovatively in the face of an unprecedented disaster went virtually unnoticed (DiPerna, 2003). In any case, Light notes that public confidence in the Red Cross rebounded and surpassed that for charitable organizations in general (before a new round of criticisms were directed at its performance after Hurricane Katrina). If the negative publicity really did have a harmful effect, the fact that the respect of the Red Cross did not have more of a positive impact on the rest of the nonprofit world is puzzling.

By the same token, despite all the charges that have been leveled in the past two years, the extent of misbehavior in the philanthropic world still appears to be small. For example, of the 152 instances of wrongdoing Fremont-Smith and Kosaras found in their survey of newspapers, less than one-fifth involved foundations or giving federations such as the United Way. Donations of property—whose overvaluation, according to the Congressional Joint Committee on Taxation, costs the U.S. Treasury about $2 billion annually (Joint Committee on Taxation, 2005)—comprised less than a quarter of the contributions taxpayers who itemized their deductions reported in 2002; most of what Americans—especially non-itemizers—give is in cash, the value of which is indisputable (Parisi and Hollenbeck, 2004). Even the much-criticized used-car donations involved just 4,300 of the 160,000 charities with revenues over $100,000 and less than 1 percent of taxpayers (General Accounting Office, 2003).

Excessive foundation staffing and administrative expenses, the target of the threatened congressional action, are mostly an issue for larger grant-makers. Smaller ones, which make up the bulk of the foundation world (but account for only a small share of its spending), are apt to be leaner, though not meaner. According to a survey of its 2,900 members by the Association of Small Foundations, the median administrative expense for those with paid staff was three-quarters of a percent of their assets; for those without staff, the figure was just one-quarter of a percent. By contrast, the median grant payout came to 5 percent of their holdings, and judging from the average of 8.5 percent, many give more, which is exactly what Congress intended when it established a rate in the 1969 tax act (Association of Small Foundations, 2002).

These figures agree with those compiled by the IRS. The smaller the foundation, the more generous it is likely to be. But even the largest ones consistently give a substantial amount to charities. Between 1985 and 1997, a panel study conducted by the IRS determined the one hundred wealthiest "non-operating" (that is, mostly grant-making) foundations "consistently" allocated about 90 percent of their expenditures to grants and other kinds of gifts. They spent just 5 percent on salaries, benefits, and other forms of compensation for their officers, directors, and staffs (Whitten, 2001).

Few accusations are more likely to prompt outrage (and attract the attention of enforcement officials) than claims of excessively generous compensation payments and excessively stingy grant payments. Yet apart from egregious (and often-cited) examples, such as the foundation that gave more to its directors and staff than to its grantees or the fund that did nothing with its assets except give its donor a large charitable tax deduction, the evidence that such practices are the norm—or are even growing—in the philanthropic world is nonexistent. Such misbehavior deserves to be punished when it occurs (and the IRS catches it), and new laws should be enacted if the current ones are insufficient to deal with new problems. But the necessity for taking such steps should not lead to the conclusion that, instead of trying to do good, the philanthropic world is bent on doing bad unless it is subjected to more stringent oversight and control.

In any case, some of the practices that are now being criticized were not long ago being praised (or at least encouraged) as ways of improving the effectiveness of the nation's charities. As Peter Frumkin has pointed out, in response to the message of the 1969 tax act that they needed to become more serious about grant-making, foundations increased the size and professionalism of their staffs, thus opening themselves to attacks today for devoting too much of their budgets to personnel (Frumkin, 1999). To prevent good intentions from being mistaken for good results, grant-makers have been urged to devote more attention to evaluation, which inevitably adds to their administrative costs. In order to expand the diversity of their grantees, funders have been asked to invest more of their resources in outreach and in providing assistance to new applicants; neither is inexpensive. And in the name of fostering "high-performance grant-making," venture philanthropy gurus advised donors to become closely involved with their grantees rather than maintain an arm's-length relationship, which is likely to invite criticism in the post-Sarbanes-Oxley world of heightened sensitivity to potential conflicts of interest in corporate activity.

Good practices can, of course, be carried to such excess that they become abuses. (Whatever they might do to improve donor accountability, the demands for greater "transparency" in grant-making that are part of the current reform proposals are all but certain to increase the amount funders will have to spend on lawyers and accountants.) On the public stage, a juicy anecdote will trump a dry statistical report every time, especially for officials who pride themselves on being guardians of the public treasury. Nor have foundations (or, for that matter, government) provided the kind of support for data-gathering and research that could shed more light on the kinds of charges leveled against philanthropy. (Ironically, just as the nonprofit world was becoming the object of policymaker attention, several underwriters of research on the sector announced plans to focus their grants elsewhere.) But while philanthropy should not be immune from criticism or, when necessary, stricter rules and tougher penalties for acting improperly, the costs of such actions also need to be kept in mind.

No one in the United States Senate (or elsewhere in Washington or in state capitals) is seriously entertaining the idea of killing philanthropists nowadays. To the contrary, all who propose new laws or call for tightening the enforcement of existing ones invariably preface their remarks by claiming that their intent is to ensure that Americans will continue to trust—and thus give generously to—charities. However, if they will not kill them, new laws and regulations have the potential to curtail the independence of philanthropists. That could be nearly as deadly.

Is it entirely coincidental that this latest round of criticism—which includes the first major congressional investigations since the 1960s—comes at the end of a decade of extraordinary growth for philanthropy and just before an impending intergenerational transfer of wealth is expected to send trillions of additional dollars in gifts to foundations and other nonprofit groups? And is it a coincidence that these criticisms are being made during a period in which the public philosophy of the United States—even if not always mirrored by its actions—has grown increasingly skeptical about the value of government-run programs? In other words, could it be that the scandal-mongering of the past few years has more than a little to do with the greater size and visibility of philanthropists in American society as well as expectations of them?

As a case in point, consider a controversy that recently occurred in Colorado. The Daniels Fund was created by cable television magnate Bill Daniels, and after his death in March 2000, it became the largest foundation in the Rocky Mountain region. On the recommendation of its president, former U.S. senator Hank Brown (most recently University of Colorado president), the trustees approved a plan to eliminate the fund's offices in New Mexico, Utah, and Wyoming as a way of reducing administrative costs and increasing the amount available for grants. Criticisms ensued, led by the governors of New Mexico and Wyoming and New Mexico's lieutenant governor, who was a niece of the late Mr. Daniels and a trustee of the fund, one of two board members to object to the reorganization. They claimed that closing the offices would mean fewer grants for their states, although fund officials argued that the opposite was as likely, since under the new arrangement, applicants could apply to any of the grant-maker's programs, not just those designated for grants in their states. The fund was also accused of paying Brown an excessive salary and moving into a lavish new office building in Denver, just as it was supposedly trying to economize elsewhere (Gose, 2004).

Whatever the truth of such claims (and they were disputed), the central issue was essentially one of governance. Traditionally, directors and trustees of foundations and other nonprofit groups have been empowered to make decisions about the use of charitable resources. The results have not always been to everyone's liking, but they did receive deference, unless they were patently illegal or improper. (Even then efforts at oversight tended to give a wide berth to private discretion.) The controversy that erupted over the Daniels Fund is just one sign—and there are others—that in an era of philanthropic growth, the public impact of such decisions will not go uncontested, especially if, as in this case, those responsible for making them are divided.

Moreover, this era is still in its early stages, as University of Southern California historian Kevin Starr observed in *The Los Angeles Times*. Noting that The David and Lucile Packard Foundation had recently completed a project to set aside 342,000 acres of picturesque California landscapes for conservation, an amount about the size of Sequoia National Park, Starr envisioned a future in which more foundations would take on more and more of what had been regarded as government's responsibilities. "In the years to come," he wrote, "as governmental resources remain scarce and foundation assistance grows increasingly necessary, Californians might be expected to regard foundations as established governance structures" (Starr, 2004).

Starr is only partly correct. The developments he foresees will affect not only Californians but all Americans. They will be obvious not just in the years to come—they are already obvious and they have led to a view of foundations as institutions that are open to questioning.

Starr understands that the entry of philanthropy into the public sphere on the scale he envisions is a recipe for contention. Whose interests are really being served when private donors set aside land for public use? Or sponsor a variety of educational and social services? Who does not have an opinion about how someone else's funds should have been spent in any of these or other areas? In public life, such disputes are usually resolved—even if only temporarily—through the political process. But how can they be settled when the key decision-makers are philanthropists outside of government? And since the United States is still a nation that believes that private donors and nongovernmental organizations have at least some right to use their funds as they see fit, is it surprising that concerns about what they do are often expressed in seemingly legalistic ways, such as by faulting the accountability, governance, or administrative policies of grant-making organizations rather than faulting how the money is actually spent?

That is why, at root, the scandals engulfing the philanthropic world are about the politics of doing good through private means. The kinds of reforms now being considered—improving ethical standards, restricting the ability of donors to use charities for their own benefit, adopting "best practices" in corporate governance, and reporting to the public more adequately about the work of the nonprofit sector—might be helpful, although obtaining voluntary compliance will always be a challenge. However, they are not likely to be sufficient for those whose ultimate concern is with what philanthropic groups do, not how they operate. To the extent that the challenge is a political one, the problems facing philanthropy are likely to get worse before they get better as foundations and other grant-makers continue to grow in activity and influence.

Paul Light and others believe that if charities want to deal with the accusations that have been made against them and regain public confidence, they need to show that they are "spending money wisely, helping people, and running their programs and services effectively." To do this, Light argues, both philanthropists and their grantees should invest more in what he calls "capacity building" measures, such as strategic planning, board development, and employee training (Light, 2003, pp. 5, 7). But useful as such steps might be, they might not be enough.

In addition, leaders of the nonprofit world ought to pay more attention to how their actions are perceived by the public, whether they can be justified in terms of the charitable purposes of their organizations, and, ultimately, what impact they have. One of the putative virtues of philanthropy is its potential to be independent of public opinion, to take risks that democratically accountable officials might hesitate to embark upon or ordinary citizens might regard as dubious, if not peculiar. Yet when practiced immoderately, this virtue, like any other, can become a vice. That may be particularly likely when the distance between grant-makers and the communities in which they work grows too wide.

Useful as it has been in many respects, the professionalization of the nonprofit world has probably had that effect. Projects that seem compelling to well-educated foundation officers who are seeking new solutions to urgent problems may come to look very different to those whose welfare is apt to be affected by them. Indeed, from the very beginnings of foundations in the United States, this has been a source of concern. The advent of the Rockefeller Foundation early in the twentieth century was greeted not by praise for its donor's magnanimity but with suspicion about what the oilman and his associates were really up to (Bremner, 1988, pp. 112–113). A few early successes, mostly in addressing medical and public health problems, were required to put these doubts at least partly to rest.

Today, foundations are far more numerous and wealthy than they were a century ago, and perhaps more ambitious too. The largest have developed highly trained staffs with considerable grant-making experience (and often, as well, a commitment to what are now called "progressive" principles that a substantial portion of the public may not share). They are engaged in a variety of issues, such as reforming schools or health care, which are important and inseparable from American political and ideological disputes. Not least important, they generally work closely—in "partnership"—with public officials (especially civil servants), whose own standing in the eyes of the public is much lower than it used to be.

From one vantage point, these changes might seem to be positive ones. But from another, their very growth, expertise, aspirations, and proximity to the levers of power inevitably make philanthropists forces to be reckoned with. And if that reckoning is now under way, as it appears to be, foundations need to do much more than get their legal and financial affairs in order or even become more effective grant-makers. They need to reexamine what they are trying to accomplish with their funds and what their relationship to government in the American political system ought to be.

Machiavelli's warning about the threat to republican government posed by those who aim to do good by private means was taken seriously by this nation's founders. Indeed, early in the history of the United States, Virginia, Pennsylvania, and other states tried to abolish charities or at least any special treatment of them. James Madison expressed such fears in his famous warning about the dangers of "faction" in *The Federalist Papers: No. 10*: "The friend of popular governments never finds himself so much alarmed for their character and fate," he wrote, as when he thinks about "the violence of faction." Left unchecked, such private interests can be responsible for "many of our heaviest misfortunes," Madison added, and "particularly, for that prevailing and increasing distrust of public engagements and alarm for private rights" (Hamilton, 1961, p. 130). Or, as a more contemporary observer, National Journal's Jonathan Rauch, has put it, they can cause "demosclerosis," a hardening of the arteries of democratic government (Rauch, 1999).

But Madison understood that eliminating factions was not only impossible (since they sprang from human nature) but would also require unacceptable restrictions on individual liberty. He turned to the design of government as a way of controlling their effects, a "republican remedy" of allowing factions to contest with other factions within rules established by the Constitution and the laws derived from it, a formula that has generally served us well.

Instead of killing philanthropists, the United States took the path of encouraging them, within some minimal restraints. But if the nonprofit sector is now moving into an era in which its role and influence will loom large and the reliance of the public on its actions will grow, the delicate balance struck between doing good through the state and doing good through private means will come under increasing stress. As in Madison's day, adding to the legal restrictions placed upon donors—even the relatively innocuous ones under consideration in Congress—risks being ineffective and counter-productive, insofar as the result will be less philanthropy. But how to produce a healthier outcome is a challenge facing philanthropic leaders in the twenty-first century, not only to protect themselves but, at least as important, to maintain the equilibrium of public and private organizations that is so vital to the preservation of democracy.

Note

1. The Sarbanes-Oxley rules of the Public Accounting Reform and Investor Protection Act of 2002, which was co-sponsored by Senator Paul Sarbanes (D-Maryland) and Representative Michael G. Oxley (R-Ohio), require business corporations to adopt stricter procedures for financial reporting and assure that directors provide auditors with certain information about the financial operations of the corporation.

References

Association of Small Foundations. *Foundation Operations and Management Survey*. Bethesda, MD: Association of Small Foundations, 2003.

Bremner, Robert H. *American Philanthropy* (2nd ed.). Chicago: University of Chicago Press, 1988.

DiPerna, Paula. *Media, Charity, and Philanthropy in the Aftermath of September 11, 2001*. A Century Foundation Report. New York: The Century Foundation, 2003. [http://www.tcf.org/Publications/HomelandSecurity/diperna.pdf.]

Everson, Mark. "The $350 Billion Question: How to Solve the Tax Gap." Written testimony before the Committee on Finance, U.S. Senate, April 14, 2005. [http://finance.senate.gov/hearings/statements/metest0411405.pdf.]

Fleishman, Joel L. "Public Trust in Not-for-Profit Organizations and the Need for Regulatory Reform." In Charles T. Clotfelter and Thomas Ehrlich (Eds), *Philanthropy and the Nonprofit Sector*. Bloomington: Indiana University Press, 1999.

Fremont-Smith, Marion R., and Kosaras, Andres. *Wrongdoing by Officers and Directors of Charities: A Survey of Press Reports, 1995–2002*. Working Paper No. 20, The Hauser Center for Nonprofit Organizations. Cambridge, MA: John F. Kennedy School of Government, Harvard University, 2003.

Frumkin, Peter. "Private Foundations as Public Institutions: Regulation, Professionalization, and the Redefinition of Organized Philanthropy." In Ellen Condliffe Lagermann (Ed.), *Philanthropic Foundations: New Scholarship, New Possibilities*. Bloomington: Indiana University Press, 1999.

General Accounting Office. *Vehicle Donations: Benefits to Charities and Donors, but Limited Program Oversight*. Report to the Committee on Finance, U.S. Senate. Washington, DC: U.S. General Accounting Office, 2003. [http://www.gao.gov/new.items/d0473.pdf.]

Gose, Ben. "Changes at Denver's Daniels Fund: Politics or Prudence?" *The Chronicle of Philanthropy*, 2004, 16, 16.

Hamilton, Alexander, Madison, James, and Jay, John. In Benjamin Fletcher Wright (Ed.), *The Federalist*. Cambridge, MA: Belknap Press of Harvard University Press, 1961.

Independent Sector. *Giving and Volunteering in the United States*. Washington, DC: Independent Sector, 1995.

Joint Committee on Taxation. *Options to Improve Tax Compliance and Reform Tax Expenditures*. Report JCS-2-05. Washington, DC: U.S. Congress, 2005. [http://www.house.gov/jct/s-2-05.pdf.]

Light, Paul C. "To Give or Not to Give: The Crisis of Confidence in Charities." Policy Brief #7-2003. Washington, DC: Brookings Institution, 2003.

Machiavelli, Niccolo. *The Prince and the Discourses.* (Luigi Ricci and Christian E. Detmold, trans.) New York: Random House, 1950.

Parisi, Michael, and Hollenbeck, Scott. *Individual Income Tax Returns, 2002.* Washington, DC: Internal Revenue Service, 2004. [http://www.irs .gov/pub/irs-soi/02indtr.pdf.]

Rauch, Jonathan. *Government's End: Why Washington Stopped Working.* New York: Public Affairs Press, 1999.

Salamon, Lester M. "The Resilient Sector: The State of Nonprofit America." In Lester M Salamon (Ed.), *The State of Nonprofit America.* Washington, DC: Brookings Institution, 2002.

Starr, Kevin. "Foundation of a New Kind of Governance?" *Los Angeles Times,* January 4, 2004.

Turley, Jonathan. "Non-Profits' Executives Avoid Scrutiny, Valid Reforms." *USA Today,* February 13, 2004.

Whitten, Melissa. "Large Nonoperating Private Foundations Panel Study, 1985–1997." Statistics of Income Bulletin. Washington, DC: Internal Revenue Service, U.S. Department of the Treasury, 2001. [http://www.irs.gov/pub/irs-soi/97pfpanl.pdf.]

———

In January 2004, Leslie Lenkowsky rejoined the faculty of Indiana University after stepping down as chief executive officer of the Corporation for National and Community Service. He was appointed by President George W. Bush and confirmed by the United States Senate in October 2001. The Corporation, created in 1993, engages more than a million Americans of all ages in improving local communities through three initiatives: AmeriCorps, Learn and Serve America, and the National Senior Service Corps.

CHAPTER THIRTY-THREE

New Models of Public Leadership

Joseph S. Nye, Jr.

W hat will public leadership look like in the new century, and how should we train people for it? Politicians tell us that the era of big government is over, but they say little about what will replace it. We do know that markets and nonprofit organizations now are filling functions once considered the province of government. For example, in the United States, Britain, and Australia, private security forces greatly outnumber police forces. We also see a trend toward devolution of authority for social programs from the federal to state governments, counter to the trends of most of the twentieth century.

THE EROSION OF CONFIDENCE IN GOVERNMENT

The public's confidence in government has declined over the last three decades. In 1964, three-quarters of Americans said they trusted the federal government to do the right thing. Today, only a quarter

Originally published as "New Models of Public Leadership." In Frances Hesselbein, Marshall Goldsmith, and Iain Somerville (Eds.), *Leading Beyond the Walls.* (San Francisco: Jossey-Bass, 1999).

express such trust. The figures are only slightly better for state and local governments. Government is not alone in losing public trust. From 1965 through 1995, public confidence in many major institutions dropped by half or more: from 61 percent to 30 percent for universities; 55 to 21 percent for major companies; 73 to 29 percent for the practice of medicine; and 29 to 14 percent for journalism (see J. S. Nye, P. D. Zelikow, and D. C. King (Eds.), *Why People Don't Trust Government*, 1997). And the United States is not alone in this—many other countries are experiencing a similar predicament.

These trends suggest a crisis of public confidence in institutional leadership that has significant implications for the future of U.S. public policy schools. Paul A. Volcker, the former chairman of the Federal Reserve Board, has suggested (at the Kennedy School of Government conference "Visions of Governance in the Twenty-First Century"; see also National Committee on the Public Service [the Volcker Commission], *Leadership for America*, 1989) a connection between the loss of public trust and the declining numbers of talented young people entering government service. Restoring public confidence in our institutions may require a new kind of leadership, and public policy schools have a crucial role to play both in defining the problem and in developing the skills to address it.

Leadership requires understanding how the world is changing, how the trends of globalization, marketization, and the information revolution are shaping democratic governance. In order to prepare leaders for service in the public interest, public policy schools must provide graduates with skills that will help them address the impact of these trends in diverse institutional settings. Today they are entering a job market that demands this ability. But even more, if effective leadership means persuading people to undertake adaptive changes, as Ronald Heifetz argues (in *Leadership Without Easy Answers*, 1994), the first step in leadership is reflection and analysis to identify the changes that are needed.

Students at public and international affairs schools across the country are shifting away from the public sector to the private and nonprofit sectors, although many will follow a revolving-door pattern in which they may alternate between sectors over time. For example, in 1980 three-quarters of Kennedy School graduates receiving master's degrees in public policy took government jobs. Last year less than half did. Overall only about one-third of all M.P.P. degree holders hold jobs in the government. The lure of private consulting firms that pay six-figure salaries is particularly strong. Moreover, as *U.S. News & World Report* (P. Longman, "Lure of the Private," February 19, 1998) recently noted, "Even students who are more interested in doing good than doing well are opting for jobs with private firms or nonprofit organizations that do government work under contract."

Common sense says that if fewer bright young people choose government as a career path, then government's ability to deal with complex social problems will decline. And when the image of government as inept, distant, bloated, and corrupt is reinforced by the media, by popular culture, and paradoxically, by campaigning politicians themselves, it is small wonder that fewer graduates seek public service jobs.

A certain degree of mistrust of government and of centralized power is a long and healthy American tradition, arguably stretching as far back as Anne Hutchinson's and Roger Williams's religious-cum-political challenges to the leaders of the seventeenth-century Massachusetts Bay Colony. But all of our institutions are at risk when bad government becomes a self-fulfilling prophecy and government bashing becomes the self-serving pastime of politicians and pundits.

REDIRECTING PUBLIC POLICY SCHOOL FOCUS

The phenomenal growth of nonprofits suggests how increasingly we depend on them to address problems that governments and for-profit institutions find intractable. Roughly 25 percent of Kennedy School graduates now go into management positions in nonprofit organizations, and other public policy schools report similar trends. Those responsible for training leaders for public service need to address a variety of questions: How can nonprofits best be managed? How do corporations and nonprofits effectively collaborate? What accountability is necessary in return for public support?

Training for the nonprofit sector is one area where public policy schools need to redirect their focus. The Kennedy School, for example, has started a new center for the study of nonprofit institutions. In addition, those who enter the private sector will profit from an understanding of public policy, environmental issues, the global economy, the impact of the new technologies, and the development of public-private partnerships—training leaders in these areas will require a reformulation of the skills and knowledge we have offered students in the past. As mentioned earlier, at different stages in their careers individuals may work in each of the three sectors.

The real world of public service tomorrow will be multicultural and multidisciplinary. Public policy school graduates will need to think and analyze through the lenses of many academic disciplines— areas that have been traditionally segregated from one another in these schools. Leadership and management will also require a new practicum of teamwork and negotiation skills so that individuals can adapt to the distinct institutional cultures of the three sectors as they increasingly interact with one another. In addition, as markets become more global, leadership will require deeper understanding of various indigenous cultural and social milieus.

Public policy schools need to teach the essential skills, tools, and behaviors of policy analysis, managerial action, and democratic advocacy. Interdisciplinary curricula, case method teaching, and collaborative and project based learning are all effective pedagogic means to that end. The Venn diagram in Figure 33.1 can help us conceptualize how a curriculum should combine leadership skills and roles. Successful leadership consists of the strategic exercise of three overlapping roles and actions: analysis—understanding a situation and thinking about what choices and changes will work out

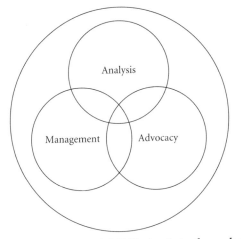

Figure 33.1.   Essential Skills Are Interdependent

best; management—mobilizing individuals, groups, organizations, and societies to work together to undertake important challenges; and advocacy—fighting for a mission that involves values, ideas, and principles and persuading others to follow. In addition, effective leadership requires the application of substantive expertise. Schools can prepare leaders by fostering basic skills and teaching about real policy issues and impacts.

In the public policy realm, we can think of the diagram's inner core in terms of roles successful leaders play: the analyst assesses policy choices using economic, statistical, institutional, political, ethical, and historical modes of analysis and thinking. The manager mobilizes his or her constituents to work together as teams by using information technology and organizational change as well as internal, financial, and human resource management. The advocate advances a mission by articulating a vision, organizing political action, participating in the electoral process, persuading, focusing media coverage, and polling. This model captures essential features of leadership that are relevant to the public, private, and nonprofit sectors beyond academia's walls.

LESSONS IN RESPONDING TO CHANGE

But above all, the quality that defines good leadership, its strategic roles and activities, is the ability to understand and respond to change. Consider the U.S. military. Despite the fact that the armed services constitute a highly centralized government bureaucracy, leaders in the military over the past two decades have vigorously adapted to change. The results have been dramatic: according to a recent Gallup poll, our armed services are among the major government institutions that still enjoy the highest confidence ratings. Despite highly visible recent controversies involving sexual harassment and adultery, a full 60 percent of those polled gave the military high confidence marks. In contrast, Congress received 29 percent and the criminal justice system just 19 percent.

The military's popularity is something of an anomaly in this era of declining public trust in government in general and in most major institutions. Why is the military different? Some say it is because the armed forces are associated with patriotism. But that was true in the 1960s and early 1970s when confidence in the military declined along with confidence in the rest of government. What is striking about the recent figures is the military's turnaround. After Vietnam the military was an institution that was drug-ridden, undisciplined, and divided by terrible racial problems. But in the mid-1970s, public confidence in it began to rise—well before its successful performance in the Persian Gulf War.

Why did the public image of the military change so dramatically? For a start, the end of the Vietnam War gave the services relief from the "baby killer" image that had resulted from the My Lai massacre, indiscriminate napalm attacks on civilian populations, and other battlefield catastrophes. But it was also incumbent on the military to take advantage of this change in circumstances. The end of the draft also provided the services with both an impetus and an opportunity to remake their public image in America. Without conscription, the military had to compete in the labor market. This required mass advertising, such as the army's highly successful "Be All That You Can Be" campaign. In an age when negative advertising in political campaigns and increasingly cynical press coverage is *demarketing* the rest of government, the military learned how to present itself in a positive light.

So, incidentally, did the U.S. Postal Service, another large bureaucracy and another example of a federal agency with high confidence ratings, one whose public image has benefited from mass marketing strategies and ad slogans like "We Deliver for You." Again, market competition helped. The Postal Service faced stiff competition from private companies like Federal Express and electronic mail systems.

But there is more to the military story than merely a tribute to the power of Madison Avenue. The military is an example of a government bureaucracy that fundamentally transformed itself. The U.S. automobile industry, another tradition-bound institution that fell on troubled times, changed in the 1980s under the impetus of intense market competition. The military, in contrast, changed because it learned from crushing defeat. After failure in Vietnam, not only did the military develop new doctrines and training that produced successful performance in war, but it also developed one of the best records of any U.S. institution on the critical social problems of race, drugs, and education.

Americans like the military because they see it as a meritocracy. Individual effort, discipline, and commitment are the clear keys to advancement and success. The public can see dramatic examples of the military's meritocratic commitment, such as General Colin Powell's rise through the Army's ranks to become chairman of the Joint Chiefs of Staff.

The military achieved racial integration not through rigid quotas but through promotion of minority candidates who met mandatory criteria. As Charles C. Moskos and John Sibley Butler have pointed out in their 1996 book *All That We Can Be: Black Leadership and Racial Integration the Army Way*, the army demands a high degree of accountability for "racial climate" from its officers. Not only is discrimination prohibited, but officers must also "resolve the perception of unfair treatment." This lesson in accountability should be portable to other institutional settings in all three sectors.

As for drugs, a zero-tolerance policy and random testing that includes everyone up through the chairman of the Joint Chiefs of Staff have produced a drug-free military. Some might object to transferring this example to other institutions or see structural problems in attempting to do so, but it is worth examining the military's experience to see what potential lessons there might be for society at large.

Another lesson from the military's success story is its commitment to its personnel to provide long-term training and education, even for those who do not intend to make the military a long-term career. Soldiers of the all-volunteer army now surpass nonveterans in education and earning power. For many of today's underprivileged youth, the armed forces have become a prime means to college education and job training—traditional high roads to increased earning power and the American dream.

Not every government agency can engage in massive advertising campaigns or demonstrate its performance in a televised war. But beyond its operational successes from Grenada to the Gulf War, the U.S. military has been able to change much of its own institutional culture. It did so by becoming labor market oriented and personnel sensitive and by stepping to the forefront of racial integration. Now it is beginning to cope effectively with problems related to gender. It is still grappling with difficulty with the issue of gay rights and participation, but even here it is arguably no worse than a reflector of the U.S. society's own deeply conflicted attitudes. The military's capacity to change is why so many people look on that institution as a success, a place where Americans can be what we all have the promise to be.

CONCLUSION

The U.S. military and the Postal Service demonstrate that even large bureaucratic organizations can evolve. Leadership can make a difference. But as the information revolution and globalization proceed, more change will be necessary for institutions. Bureaucracy itself is under challenge as the Internet and other networks increasingly facilitate unmediated communication and action. Schools of public policy must take the lead in understanding these changes and preparing people to adapt to them.

In our fractious political climate the problem of declining public confidence in our institutions has no easy fix. Therefore another contribution policy schools can make is to foster serious dialogue among academics, policymakers, and the public about what constitutes effective leadership and governance in a changing world. Such a dialogue would be a welcome departure from the rhetoric of government bashing, which in election years comes loudest from Washington, D.C., itself. And it would demonstrate the public policy schools' contribution to leadership beyond the (academic) walls.

At time of original publishing Joseph S. Nye, Jr., was dean of the Kennedy School of Government at Harvard University and the author of numerous articles and books, most recently Bound to Lead, Understanding International Conflicts, *and* Why People Don't Trust Government *(co-edited with Philip D. Zelikow and David C. King). He has appeared on programs such as* Nightline, Good Morning America, *and* The NewsHour with Jim Lehrer *and has worked in three government agencies, most recently the Defense Department, where in 1994 and 1995 he served as assistant secretary of defense for international security affairs.*

CHAPTER THIRTY-FOUR

Ties That Bind

Barbara Kellerman

I have chosen in this chapter not to focus on the constitutional and institutional contexts within which big government and big business necessarily operate. In fact, my basic argument, about the convergence between public- and private-sector leadership, might convey the impression that I consider the environments within which they are embedded of secondary importance. But let me be clear. I acknowledge the obvious: that presidents, for example, operate within the legal and political constraints of the office they hold and that chief executive officers work within a capitalist system that supports the private ownership of property for the purpose of making a profit.

I have nevertheless argued that for a variety of reasons—with the information revolution and globalization being high on the list— the theories and practices of leadership in government and business

---

Originally published as "The Ties That Bind" in Barbara Kellerman's *Reinventing Leadership*. (Albany, NY: State University of New York Press, 1999).

have converged. This book [*Reinventing Leadership*], then, makes three basic arguments: first, that individual leaders remain important; second, that political and business leadership are converging; and third, that effectively to address problems that have otherwise proved intractable, leaders in different places should join forces. This final chapter will explore the real-world implications of the ties that bind.

POLITICAL AND BUSINESS LEADERS: SIMILAR PROFILES

As we have seen, in the past, political and business leaders were distinct. They were exposed to different theories and practices. They traveled in different circles. And they claimed followers who had different expectations and demands.

As we have also seen, on the cusp of the twenty-first century the differences between political and corporate leadership have been greatly diminished. The question now is, does it matter? What impact does the closing of the gap between government and business leaders have in the real world? And what conclusions can be drawn?

Conclusion #1: Twenty-First Century Leaders Will Move from Business into Politics, and from Politics into Business, More Easily and Frequently

During the two most recent presidential campaigns, businessman-candidates were plausible players. In 1992 Ross Perot made a strong showing against Bill Clinton and George Bush (receiving a full 19 percent of the vote), and in 1996 Steve Forbes made what initially at least was a big splash in the Republican primaries. Here is why in the new millennium businessman-candidates—many of whom in fact are already in politics—are likely to have a leg up.

1. The enormous importance of money in politics, the exponential growth of corporate interest groups, and the globalization of markets have compelled business leaders to become active participants in the political process.
2. Successful executives are likely to have the financial resources necessary to run political campaigns. In the past, personal wealth and access to money more generally were considered something

of a political liability. Now they signal freedom from special interests.

3. The public sector now puts a premium on skills heretofore associated with the private sector—for example, fiscal responsibility and managerial competence.

4. The nature of foreign policy has changed. These changes, which relate primarily to globalization and privatization, equip business leaders with knowledge and experience every bit as relevant to foreign affairs as the more traditional security concerns.

5. Business leaders in their forties, fifties, and sixties are more likely than political leaders in the same age cohort to be familiar with information technology.

6. Policy areas such as welfare and education, which were viewed until recently as being entirely in the public domain, are increasingly seen as necessitating corporate involvement. Conversely, civic virtues such as equality and diversity are now shaping the ideology, if not the practice, of corporate America.

7. Because the mantras of business leadership have changed, corporate executives are now viewed as capable of a far more sophisticated approach to followers than merely command and control.

8. In comparison with political leaders, corporate leaders are credited with having an independent, can-do attitude. Unfettered by a lifetime of compromise, businessman-candidates tend to see government as a business that needs nothing so much as to be well run (Drucker, 1969).

9. The demands on business leaders now mirror the demands on political leaders. They include providing followers with meaning and purpose; standing up to public scrutiny; dealing with the media; being accountable to various and demanding constituencies; and coping with diminished authority.

Does all this mean that in the future corporate leaders will move en masse into politics, or, for that matter, that large numbers of former mayors, governors, and senators will run businesses? Am I predicting that IBM's Louis Gerstner will become president of the United States or that Texas governor George W. Bush will take over as CEO of General Electric? Of course not. But what I am saying is that in the next century a man like Gerstner could, if he chose to, make a creditable bid for elective office, even at the highest level. I am also saying that even now, public officials routinely serve on corporate boards and therefore often participate actively in running a business. (To be sure, the transition from being a political leader to being a CEO will continue to be difficult. By and large, elected officials are seen as managerial novices.)

Of course, as we have also seen, the similarities between government and business transcend those pertaining only to leadership roles. The sectors themselves now converge in two ways in particular. First, we expect government to be more efficient. This is not to say that we believe government can, or necessarily should, be a model of managerial competence. As Henry Mintzberg (1996a) put it in the *Harvard Business Review*, "I am not a mere customer of my government, thank you. I expect something more than arm's length trading and something less than the encouragement to consume."

But charges made by experts such as Paul Light (1995), who claimed that the "unwieldy, towering hierarchy" that constituted the federal government was responsible for sins ranging from inefficiency to a lack of accountability, hit hard and had an impact. (Tellingly, Light cited corporate guru Tom Peters on the evils of "bloated staffs.") And so did works like *Banishing Democracy*, in which authors David Osborne and Peter Plastrik claimed that Britain and New Zealand—not the U.S.—are the best models of government reform (Peirce, 1997).

To be sure, for all the good intentions, the task of reforming government is daunting and resistance to change remains great. While Bill Clinton and Al Gore have cut both the deficit and the bureaucracy, fiascos persist.

- "A close look at the quarter of all defense outlays that has gone into nuclear weapons suggests that a good portion was wasted," reported *The New York Times* in 1995. "Even the most useful nuclear weapons cost too much to build for the same reasons the Pentagon pays too much for toilet seats and canned ravioli" (Passell, 1995).
- "Stymied by Mismanagement," read a *Times* piece in 1996 ("Ambitious Update of American Navigation Becomes a Fiasco"), "the Federal Aviation Administration has squandered

fifteen years and at least a half billion dollars on a new air traffic control system that is still years from completion and already obsolete."

- "IRS Admits Lag in Modernization," reported the *Times* in 1997. The Internal Revenue Service conceded it had spent $4 billion developing modern computer systems that "do not work in the real world."

Just as we expect government to be more efficient, so we expect business to be more democratic. This is not to say that we now believe CEOs should poll employees before deciding how the company should be run. It is to say that virtually all large companies are now expected to mouth the new conventional wisdom: that to be virtuous is to embrace flattened hierarchies and empowered workers.

But just as public-sector organizations remain vulnerable to the charge that because of their "long-standing cultures" they "accomplish very little" (see Osborne's quote below), so private-sector organizations are still accused of failing to move far enough fast enough.

- James O'Toole (1995): "Organizations must decentralize, de-layer, and destroy bureaucracy in order to obtain the entrepreneurialism, autonomy, and innovation needed to serve customers effectively."

- Gifford Pinchot (1996): "The new organizations will be pluralistic to the core, preferring conflict between competing points of view to the illusory security of bureaucratic command and internal monopolies of function."

- Peter Senge (1996): "The basic assumption that only top management can cause significant change is deeply disempowering. Why, then, in the 'age of empowerment,' do we accept it so unquestioningly?"

Thus, while there has been over the last five decades real convergence between political leaders and their corporate counterparts, and indeed between government and business more generally, the demand for change has not let up. Government is still expected to be more efficient and business is still expected to be more democratic—which is one of the main reasons why those who cling to the idea that political and business leaders are a breed apart make a mistake.

Conclusion #2: The "Leadership Industry" Must Develop a More Integrated Approach to Leadership Education

America's anti-authority culture has always made the exercise of leadership in America difficult. Any national creed that values above all life, liberty, and the pursuit of happiness does not, by definition, worship authority. Put another way, Americans have always grappled with the tension between their wish for community and order on the one hand and their passion for individualism and independence on the other.

But since the late 1960s the exercise of political leadership in particular has become even more challenging. The assassination of John Kennedy, and campus radicals, and black power, and women's liberation, and Vietnam, and Watergate, and even change agents such as Greenpeace, caused the old order to give way. Now, sources of authority are always being challenged, and "individuals are more willing than ever to ask what justifies particular social arrangements, configurations of power, or customs" (Warren, 1996).

Arguably, this "crisis of leadership"—which, of course, affects business as well as government—should be the most fundamental concern of leadership educators. But, as we have seen, leader learning in late-twentieth-century America is not, in general, very ambitious. The flaws include:

1. The continuing segregation in the classroom between political and business (and nonprofit and military) leaders and managers—in spite of the obvious and important similarities among them (Ulmer, 1996).

2. The dearth of leadership education programs for those in the public sector.

3. The continuing distinction between content targeted at political leaders and content targeted at business leaders.

4. The failure to address honestly the perennial gap between what is being promised (for example, empowerment) and what is being delivered (for example, downsizing).

5. The reluctance to tackle precisely those social, political, and economic problems that have proved most intractable.

6. The lack of attention to collaboration. There is too little instruction on how to cross the divides of sectors, groups, interests, and nations.

7. The failed focus on character.

8. The failure satisfactorily to explore how followers can be productively engaged.

9. The feeble response to diversity in America. The divide between white men on the one hand, and women and minorities on the other, persists.

10. The failure to ask how leaders can and should be judged. What are the criteria for good leadership? And if they are not met, how should followers respond?

11. The failure to distinguish clearly between short-term tasks and long-term goals. Whereas in general followers fare better when leaders (political and corporate) adopt a long-term perspective, self-interest typically precludes their doing so.

12. The failure to distinguish between nature and nurture. The increasingly obvious importance of genetics to leadership and followership is almost entirely ignored.

13. The lack of dialogue between theoreticians and practitioners, particularly those involved in the public sector.

14. The inadequate investment in leadership education. We train men and women for many years to be doctors and lawyers. Why do we give such short shrift to educating leaders? What assumptions underlie what is, arguably at least, this neglect?

The time to overhaul leadership education in America is now. Granted, the argument for investing in leader learning is difficult to make because proving that it pays off has been notoriously difficult. Moreover, the fact that there are two different kinds of leadership education—learning about leadership (Leadership Studies) and learning how to be a good leader (Leadership Training or Development)—has tended to muddy the field. (Incidentally, in my view this distinction is generally artificial and unproductive.) But, if we are to have any kind of leader learning at all, this is as good a moment as any to create a new kind of leadership education, one that sheds many of the old assumptions and is willing simultaneously to take on the hard issues.

At a minimum, twenty-first-century leadership educators should bring leaders and managers from different places together; pay greater attention to public-sector leadership; integrate content so that all leaders can profit from all of the materials; address the divide between promise and performance; meet head-on the challenges posed by the world's most intractable problems; teach collaboration; instruct more persuasively on the importance of character; clarify the nature of follower engagement and explore how it might more effectively be realized; develop criteria for good leadership; explore the question of how to use the results of assessment; and create institutions and procedures that make it possible for the relevant players to work together. (Relevant players include leaders and managers from different places, key constituents and, arguably, leadership experts.)

Conclusion #3: The Character Issue Remains Impenetrable

Of all the problems that beset leadership in America at the end of the twentieth century, the so-called character issue is perhaps the most troubling. True, we hear more about the character flaws of political leaders than of business leaders. (The former are, of course, still much better known than the latter.) But, as the polls testify, leaders generally are considered morally deficient.

The political process clearly has been corrupted by what Gary Wills (1997) calls "the unholy trinity of polls, ads, and money." Big money is necessary to win elections, and politicians are selling themselves to the highest bidders. The distinction between the system and those who people it is critical here. Elected officials are fond of saying, in effect, "The system makes me do it." But, as Fred Wertheimer (1996) argues in an article on the 1996 presidential campaign pointedly titled "The Dirtiest Election Ever," it boils down to the men and women who themselves constitute the process. "Put simply, we've seen that the attitude of our national leaders when it comes to campaign laws is no different than that of tax evaders, deadbeat dads, and welfare cheats. The most powerful people in the country have proved in the 1996 political season that they do not believe the law applies to them. The abuses involve the Democratic president and his Republican challenger; the Democratic and Republican national party committees; Democrats and Republicans running for Congress; labor unions, corporations, wealthy individuals, and foreign-based interests. Special mention must be made of the incumbent president, who has led the way in setting the tone and unleashing an escalating money war that resembles the Cold War arms race."

Bill Clinton has played a not inconsiderable role in creating the end-of-the-century impression that politics is dirty. To be sure, as Wertheimer points out, none of the major players are pure. But for whatever constellation of reasons, the impression remains: even in the Oval Office, the man remained "slick Willie." Whether or not Bill Clinton will ever be held in any way legally responsible for Whitewater, or Travelgate, or Filegate, or sexual misconduct, or the Democratic Party's campaign fundraising practices is almost beside the point. What matters is the constant drumbeat of impropriety, and what matters even more is that the American people are now so jaded that they—we—no longer seem to care. (In 1997 polls indicated that more than 60 percent of the American people disapproved of the way presidential and congressional campaigns are financed, and more than 60 percent of the American people said they had little hope that the president or the Congress will substantively change things.)

It should be noted that business leaders are not exempt from the general sense that those in positions of authority are not to be trusted. While as individuals they are generally still able to avoid the intense day-to-day scrutiny that besets their political counterparts, as a collective their integrity has come under public attack on at least two fronts. First, they are charged with individual and corporate greed. On the one hand they are held responsible for massive layoffs, and on the other they have manifestly profited from historic rises in the prices of company stock.

To be sure, by the end of the decade there was a growing awareness that firing people while simultaneously raking in record profits was somehow unseemly. Wrote the prolific Henry Mintzberg (1996b), again in the *Harvard Business Review*, "There is nothing wonderful about firing people. True, stock market analysts seem to love companies that fire frontline workers and middle managers (while increasing the salaries of senior executives) . . . [but] lean is mean. So why do we keep treating people in these ways?" But let us not be misled. In general, business leaders will continue to do what they think they must in order to improve the bottom line. If that means letting workers go, so be it. The lesson learned is not to stop being hardnosed when necessary, but to be hardnosed in less obvious ways.

The second charge against corporate executives relates to the old saw about democracy in the workplace. Obviously, buzzwords like "empowerment" notwithstanding, notions of corporate loyalty are largely obsolete, and people are less secure in their jobs than they used to be. Too little truth and too little trust — in spite of the fact that truth and trust are considered in virtually every document on the subject the sine qua non of great corporate leadership. A "characteristic of great management," writes Thomas Teal (1996), "is integrity . . . . Integrity means being responsible, of course, but it also means communicating clearly and consistently, being an honest broker."

I said earlier that, of all the problems that plague leadership in America at the end of the twentieth century, it is the character issue that is probably the most troubling. It disturbs not only because it is so obviously corrosive, but also because what should be done about it remains entirely unclear. The apparent lack of integrity that characterizes so many of those in positions of authority is not the consequence of inattention. Forests have been felled for paper on which to write about the ethics of leadership; and there isn't a leadership education program in the country that fails to address the virtues of being virtuous. But all too often, the pious intoning falls on deaf ears. Attention should be paid.

Conclusion #4: Our Image of the Ideal Political Leader Has Converged with Our Image of the Ideal Business Leader

Popular perceptions about the differences between them notwithstanding, leaders from different sectors are, so far as our fantasies about them are concerned, virtually interchangeable. Here, then, as drawn by both the public- and private-sector literatures, is the picture-perfect leader, the Reinvented Leader for all sectors and seasons.

The Reinvented Leader

Traits/Attributes

    Considerable Experience

    Some Expertise

Good Education

Rather High Intelligence

High Level of Activity

Drive for Achievement

Rather Assertive

Independence

Extroversion

Well-Adjusted

Tolerance for Stress, Delay, Uncertainty

Willingness and Ability to Exercise Authority and Influence

Empathy and Insight

Flexibility

Creativity

Good Character

Challenges

Mastering Information

Coping with Complexity

Understanding Technology

Managing Change

Managing Conflict

Making Decisions Under Conditions of Uncertainty

Implementing

Extracting Efficiency

Developing Loyalties

Managing Crises

Creating Diversity

Creating Alliances

Addressing Resistance and Dissent

Making Time for Reflection and Analysis

Strategies

    Envisioning

    Agenda Setting

    Communicating

    Listening

    Educating

    Inspiring

    Mobilizing

    Coalition Building

    Planning

    Using Authority and Exercising Influence

    Being Ingratiating

    Adapting

    Delegating

    Collaborating

    Empowering

    Encouraging

    Enabling

    Questioning

    Evaluating

    Negotiating

    Unifying

Values

    Integrity

    Self-Knowledge

    Curiosity

    Balance and Stability

    Change (when change is in order)

    Noncoercion

Bestowing Respect

Inclusion

Mutuality of Purpose (with followers)

Now the question is whether this overlap, this composite picture of what ideal leaders look like, implies that there are no significant differences between leaders in government and business. The answer is obviously no. Clearly, men and women in politics have different interests from men and women in business. The business of politics is making public policy, and the business of business is making money. But the fact that the most obvious task of the political leader is different from that of the business leader does not, as we have by now come to see, negate or even overwhelm the commonalties.

In an interview that appeared in the *Harvard Business Review*, David Osborne acknowledged that "Yes, government is different from business. Businesses typically exist in fiercely competitive markets; most public organizations don't. Businesses have clear bottom lines; governments don't. Businesses usually know who their customers are; most public organizations don't" (Posner and Rothstein, 1994). These major distinctions did not, however, stop Osborne from teaching corporate-sector lessons to "public managers." He advised them to strengthen relationships with "customers," to create consequences (positive and negative) for how people perform, to flatten organizational hierarchies, and to work to change the public-sector culture. "In the federal bureaucracy long-standing cultures have taught people to keep their heads down, stay out of trouble," he noted. "Unfortunately, they have accomplished little."

Authors of books such as *Public Entrepreneurs* similarly exhort political leaders to act like their corporate counterparts, urging them to create change by becoming the "public-sector equivalent of private-sector entrepreneurs" (Schneider, Teske, and Mintrom, 1995). The commonalties, in short, are clear. Americans want their political and business leaders to be perfect in most of the same ways. What is not apparent in the model outlined above is that all leaders should also be ready, willing, and able to transcend their immediate concerns and domains. They should seek to make the transition from self-interest toward the public good. In fact, it is to this theme—of transcendence and integration—to which we finally turn. Put another way, the sine qua non of the Reinvented Leader is the capacity to create ties that bind between interests ordinarily considered competing. Reinvented Leaders conjure constituencies other than their own and conceive of interests other than only those preceded by the word "self."

POLITICAL LEADERS AND BUSINESS LEADERS: COMMON INTERESTS

Not long ago, Harlan Cleveland (one of the most interesting leadership scholars) bemoaned the lack of "generalist" leaders. "The problems of a nation, of a city, of a village," he wrote, "are to be seen as interconnected and therefore to be tackled simultaneously and as a complex, not separately or sequentially. The community's future comprises economic, social, cultural, and political as well as technical facets; these cannot be dealt with by the politician alone, or by the economist, the engineer, or the scientist in isolation." Cleveland (1985) went on to point out that, although real-world problems are interdisciplinary, and solutions are interdepartmental, interprofessional, interdependent, and international, our institutions—particularly our institutions of higher education— start with a heavy bias against breadth.

This section is based on Cleveland's simple assumption: that common interests demand common work. The questions are, How do these common interests manifest themselves? and How does common work get done?

Conclusion #5: Technology Has Tied Government to Business and Changed the Nature of Leadership

We know the information revolution changed the way the private sector works. And we also know that it has finally started to change the way the public sector works. Said President Clinton in his February 1997 State of the Union message, "We have only begun to spread the benefits of a technology revolution that should be the modern birthright of every citizen."

We understand less well how the information revolution is changing the relationship between the two (Yergin and Stanislau, 1998). What we can say is that, at a minimum, technology is fueling the convergence—bringing government and business closer together.

Of course, with each passing year technology matters more, if only because of the numbers. In the early 1990s, about one million people were wired. Since then, the number of Internet users worldwide has grown to an estimated fifty-seven million; by the end of the century, the number will reach 700 million. Even the telephone will still make a major difference. Early in the twenty-first century its use in previously isolated corners of the globe is expected to increase exponentially.

The sequence, then, goes something like this. Technologies change economies and economies, in turn, change politics. While in the developed world the impact of the information revolution is arguably not as dramatic as in the developing world, in fact some of the countries of Europe, and also Japan, have had problems making the economic, political, and social adjustments necessary to the nanosecond nineties. For example, in the last decade of the twentieth century, the Japanese were held back by the same patterns and practices that had only recently (in the 1970s and 1980s) built Japan Inc: groupism, conformity, and hierarchies. Indeed, the 1997 collapse of Asian financial markets testified to the domino effect. Technology made Asia's burgeoning economies possible; but when the "Asian flu" struck, national governments were forced to respond and, in one or another fashion, to change their ways.

However differently the drama is played out in different places, no leader, political or corporate, is immune to the effects of the information revolution. Above all, leaders are learning (albeit in some cases, such as China, only with great difficulty) that the attempt to control information is destined to fail. Information expands as it is used. It is easily transportable. And it leaks (Cleveland, 1997). In short, "when it comes to pure content regulation ... government authorities have lost their grip completely" (Cyberpower, 1996).

Of course, the hunger for information is driven by economic necessity. In the interest of growth, most governments—even most authoritarian ones—have shown themselves increasingly willing to assume the political risks of full disclosure.

China's recent history illustrates the dilemma. In 1978, Deng Xiaoping initiated a radical restructuring of China's economic system and a dramatic opening up to the outside world. But, as economic reforms gradually took hold, disruptive political values such as individualism, freedom of expression, and democracy made inevitable inroads into the still highly controlled society. By spring 1989, hundreds of thousands of students and other citizens were demonstrating on a regular basis in Tiananmen Square, demanding dialogue and democracy. The result was probably inevitable: On June 4 the People's Liberation Army stormed into Beijing, killing and wounding thousands of unarmed protesters.

Even now some 3,000 people languish in Chinese prisons because of their political views. But China's development in recent decades is more complex than its record on political dissidents would seem to suggest. While China is not at all free for a very small number of people, it is in nearly every way far freer than it used to be for the large majority.

This brings us to another way in which the information revolution affects those in positions of authority: controlling others is more difficult. As Cleveland (1997) pointed out in his small book *Leadership and the Information Revolution*, the people, not their "leaders," are doing the leading. The peaceful revolutions that started with the collapse of the Soviet Union were sparked not by distant visions of Utopia, "but by rapidly spreading information about neighbors who were obviously getting more goods and services, more fairness in distributing them, and firmer guarantees of human rights."

The impact of this link between technology, economics, and politics is not, of course, confined to domestic affairs. Even as political leaders nurture high-tech growth for their citizens, they face the challenge of defending national security in the age of interconnectivity. In 1997 the Pentagon's Defense Science Board urged the federal government to invest $3 billion into protection against information warfare. Why? Because the most computer-dependent nation in world, the United States, is also the most vulnerable to "cyber attack." Explains strategic analyst Ariel Sobelman, "The more dependent you are on information technology, the more you are also increasing your vulnerability not just to bombs, as in the Gulf War, but to computer viruses and worms" ("Wired World," 1997).

The information revolution has changed not only the definition of national security, but also the relevance of geography and territory in fashioning political arrangements. National leaders in particular will have to contend with the fact that the modern state is getting weaker. As Cleveland (1997) describes it, the state is "leaking power in three directions at once." It leaks from the bottom, as information and communications enable individual citizens and local authorities to take governance into their own hands. It leaks from the sides, as transnational businesses and nongovernment organizations play increasingly important roles in international affairs. And it leaks from the top, as states have to pool their sovereignty in order not to lose it altogether.

Clearly, technology has changed the way public- and private-sector leaders do their work. Increasingly, all leaders must be versed in the ways of both politics and business and, increasingly, all leaders must understand the ways in which technology complicates the task of creating change. The information revolution is one of the main reasons why the gap between the public sector and the private one has narrowed, and why leaders in different places find themselves wrestling with many of the same problems in many of the same ways.

Conclusion #6: The New Foreign Policy Demands Increased Collaboration Between Government and Business

The fact that commercial interests play a role in American foreign policy is nothing new. But, as Jeffrey Garten has pointed out in an important 1997 article that appeared in *Foreign Affairs*, during the next few decades "the interaction between them will become more intense, more important, more difficult to manage, and more complicated for the American public to understand."

Garten (1997) maintains that because government and business have been slow to respond, now there is no time to waste: they must get their "collective act" together. "Their objective should be a new partnership based on two realities of the changing global marketplace. The first is that the federal government's ability to conduct foreign policy in a world preoccupied with economic stability and progress is dwindling.... The second is that, even though business has the money, technology, and management that make today's world spin, it needs Uncle Sam's help more than ever, particularly in a world where governments are awarding big contracts abroad and companies are becoming ensnared in issues such as human rights, labor practices, environmental protection, and corruption."

Garten does not believe the interests of the country and the business community intersect at every turn. He nevertheless advocates the development of a framework that would enable the public and private sectors to "work together for their mutual benefit." Above all, the administration and the foreign policy establishment must reach consensus about the centrality of commercial interests in foreign policy.

The New Foreign Policy, one in which economic and traditional security interests coexist, is a hybrid that has by now become the norm. The evidence is everywhere.

- November 1996: At a meeting in Manila attended by President Clinton and leaders of seventeen other Pacific Rim nations, Commerce Secretary Mickey Kantor spoke of the emergence of a "Clinton Doctrine." What is the Clinton Doctrine? It is "not mutually assured destruction and a policy of containment, but mutually assured prosperity and a policy of engagement" ("In Manila, Asians Pore Over Washington's Inner Truths," 1996).

- December 1996: Thomas Friedman noted in *The New York Times* that for too long the American business community in China has behaved as if human rights and business rights were two different things. "Wrong. Human rights and business rights are just flip sides of the same coin ... and the coin is called the rule of law." As Friedman goes on to point out, we have leverage with the Chinese. "They crave Big Macs, Macintosh, Microsoft, and Mickey Mouse."

- January 1997: Jessica Mathews wrote in *The Washington Post* that, while Clinton's second-term foreign policy team faced an array of familiar challenges (NATO expansion, China, Middle East peace), new kinds of issues were also on the agenda, for example, global warming. This issue is "weighted with national and private interests, highly technical, and explosively controversial." Mathews argues that complex problems such as greenhouse warming must be considered within the purview of American foreign policy and must, therefore, be addressed with the same passion and persistence the American government used to expend on, for example, mutual deterrence.

A foreign policy shaped to a considerable degree by the imperatives of the global marketplace also has domestic implications. Donors to Clinton's 1996 campaign included the Lippo Group, based in Indonesia, and the Chaoren Pokaphand Group, based in Thailand. Both consortiums made huge investments in China, are controlled by ethnic Chinese families, and operate in countries dominated by Chinese minorities. By helping to fill Clinton's campaign coffers they sought to ensure that the United States would not constrain China's export-driven economic expansion (Lighthizer, 1997).

There is another much larger question that neither governments nor businesses have yet come to grips with: Is the uncontrolled integration of information, trade, and finance an economic threat to the have-nots in the short term and, therefore, a political threat to the haves in the longer term? Critics like Ethan Kapstein have argued that in order to protect workers from the negative consequences of globalization (for example, growing job insecurity), and to protect democracies from the unrest that such dislocations would inevitably generate, governments will be forced to provide programs such as education, training, and unemployment insurance. Kapstein (1997) puts it bluntly: "The welfare state is the cornerstone of the global economy."

What, precisely, are the implications of the New Foreign Policy for political and corporate leaders? At least three are obvious. First, the politicians and bureaucrats who constitute America's official foreign policy cadre should be as familiar with international economics as they are with international politics. Unfortunately, whatever their other merits, neither of President Clinton's two Secretaries of State, Warren Christopher and Madeleine Albright, fit the bill in this regard. Both are of a generation whose view was shaped by World War II and the Cold War that followed it. And both have been far more worried about how to expand NATO than about how to cope with global warming (clearly more of a twenty-first-century threat than Russia's now-decimated military or, for that matter, nuclear proliferation) or economic instability.

Second, U.S. foreign policy institutions and systems should be restructured to reflect the new global reality. Moreover coordination among the various economic, diplomatic, and military initiatives that now constitute American foreign policy should be accelerated and strengthened.

Finally, the business community should be brought in a more systematic way into the American foreign policy process. Inevitably, if unofficially, business leaders already have a profound impact on the conduct of foreign affairs. The question that remains is how to integrate their growing involvement into the work done by the traditional foreign policy establishment. For the time being the nation-state will survive the globalization of the economy and the information revolution that preceded it. But, as Peter Drucker (1997) has pointed out, "It will be a greatly changed nation-state, especially in domestic fiscal and monetary policies, foreign economic policies, control of international business, and, perhaps, in its conduct of war."

Conclusion #7: To Create Change Twenty-First Century Leaders Will Have to Join Forces

When Bill Clinton became president, he declared health care reform his number one priority. Moreover, 70 percent of the American people agreed with the two basic principles underlying his plan: that all American families should have health insurance and that all employers should contribute to paying for employee premiums.

What went wrong? Why was it that for all the good intentions and for all the popular support Clinton's attempt at health care reform was a political disaster? Here I will name only one of several reasons for the fiasco: the administration's failure to understand that leadership initiatives of this magnitude require extensive collaboration over an extended period of time. What we got were covert conversations and secret plans; what we got was a proposal owned by the administration and disowned by nearly everyone else. In particular, Bill and Hillary Clinton's failure to engage private-sector participation in their public-sector planning was a major mistake (Johnson and Broader, 1996).

The lesson was learned. From that point on President Clinton made it a point to involve business and industry in virtually every significant federal initiative. Listen to Clinton on the subject of welfare reform in his 1997 State of the Union speech. "Here is my plan. Provide tax credits and other incentives to businesses that hire people off welfare. . . . And I say especially to every employer in this country who has ever criticized the old welfare system: You cannot blame that old system anymore. We have torn it down. Now do your part. Give someone on welfare the chance to work. Tonight I am pleased to announce that five major corporations—Sprint, Monsanto, UPS, Burger King, and United Airlines—will be the first to join in a new national effort to marshal America's businesses, large and small, to create jobs so people on welfare can move to work."

While big government and big business have been slow to act, at the state and local levels there is a growing body of evidence in support of the proposition that joining forces—bringing the public, private, and also the nonprofit sectors together—is the most effective way to create change.

- In Connecticut, Tom Ritter, Speaker of the State House of Representatives, and Wick Sloan, a business executive, assembled a group of legislators, bankers, city and state officials, and neighborhood activists to develop legislation that would eliminate discriminatory mortgage lending practices. Their proposal was quickly passed by both houses of the state legislature (Chrislip, 1995).

- In Harlem, a confluence of city, federal, and private money rebuilt West 140th Street, by all accounts one of New York City's most ravaged blocks. The specifics of the initiative were worked out by the mayor's office. But the cornerstone of the program was a federal tax credit that entices corporations and wealthy individuals to contribute money for buildings and upkeep in poor neighborhoods ("From Harlem's Worst to City Star," 1997).

- In Colorado, the State Department of Health convened a group to develop a plan for the prevention of AIDS. Gay activists, state health officials, doctors, health care providers, educators, and representatives of conservative political and religious groups were included. Through a carefully designed collaborative process, the group was able to agree on a comprehensive plan for controlling the spread of AIDS (Chrislip, 1995).

- In Baltimore, a coalition that included community activists, business interests, school administrators, and government officials brought an integrated and ultimately successful approach to previously fragmented efforts to keep students in school (Chrislip and Larson, 1994).

- In Missoula, Montana, under the leadership of Mayor Dan Kemmis, collaborative work addressed the challenges of growth. The tensions of development were familiar: suburban sprawl and industrial development versus the desire for a more livable community, private property rights versus broader community values, and new job creation versus environmental amenities. But rather than succumbing to conflicting interests, Kemmis helped the city develop common goals and shared strategies.

Various stakeholders were involved, including leaders in government, business, nonprofit organizations, interest groups, and academia. Public forums were created to develop alternative futures, identify policy recommendations and tools, establish a credible and open process, address difficult and divisive issues, and create a broad base of support for implementation. To be sure, creating change was not easy. But over the years Missoula became a model of what a community can do to promote the public good. As Kemmis observed (and outsiders concurred), "In Missoula we went against the trend—and we have been rewarded with a tremendous strengthening in our civic culture and a heightened respect for public service" (Gerzon, 1996).

As indicated, it would be a mistake to downplay the difficulties involved in sustaining collaboration over a period of time. For example, the evidence suggests that business leaders in particular have a low level of tolerance for long and frequent meetings with community leaders (Adams, 1997). But there are ways of overcoming obstacles such as these, and there is ample evidence to suggest the hard work pays off in the end.

Indeed, this evidence is starting to accumulate. Case studies of cities and regions across the land describe "how diverse segments and sectors of the community are working together in new patterns of collaboration and partnership" (Peirce and Johnson, 1997). Consider Cleveland, one of the "Rustbelt" cities hardest hit in the 1960s and 1970s by the decline in local manufacturing. The population of the city declined precipitously, unemployment shot up, crime rates rose, poverty increased, racial tensions flared, and in 1969 the heavily polluted Cuyahoga River caught fire, fixing in the nation's mind a disastrous image of what Cleveland had become. In 1978 Cleveland hit bottom: It declared bankruptcy, thereby becoming the first American city to default on its debts since the Depression.

How to explain the urban "comeback kid"? What accounts for Cleveland's remarkable recovery in recent years—one symbolized since 1995 by the internationally famous and architecturally stunning Rock and Roll Hall of Fame? Obviously, the reasons are many and complex, but if one stands out it is the development in recent decades of scores of local organizations that initiate and then sustain multi-sector collaboration. "Cleveland has perhaps the strongest network of civic, community, religious, and nonprofit organizations anywhere in the country" (Peirce and Johnson, 1997). They include:

- Cleveland Community Foundation;
- George Gund Foundation (convenes civic players to deal with community challenges);
- Cleveland Tomorrow (a business group formed in the early 1980s that by now has expanded its reach beyond the downtown area to local neighborhoods);
- Greater Cleveland Roundtable (focuses on human relations);
- Cleveland Community Building Initiative and Neighborhood Progress, Inc. (both attack poverty in depressed neighborhoods);
- Cleveland Initiative for Education (a vehicle for coordinating business and foundation support for Cleveland's public schools).

Each of these organizations testifies to the efficacy of public/private/nonprofit partnerships. In fact, these partnerships are how the city does its work. And they have created through the years networks of individual leaders who contributed to the various institutional collaborations. During the 1980s Cleveland's leaders included Mayor George Voinovich, City Council President George Forbes, tax lawyer Carlton Schnell, business executive William Seelbach, and corporate leader George Dively (who hired McKinsey and Company to help determine how to turn Cleveland around). As the president of the Gund Foundation put it, the secrets of Cleveland's success are the people who build "constellations of trusting relationships" and "serve as the glue between the business and government communities" (Garten, 1997).

None of this is to suggest that Cleveland's work is complete. In fact, if anything at all has been learned by regional and local leaders across the country, it is that the joined efforts must be ongoing. It is, however, to say that by all accounts Cleveland's collaborations have been remarkably fruitful ones and that "a foundation for hope has been laid" (Urban Neighborhoods Task Force, 1996).

We have already seen that at the national level government and business leaders are learning only now that the common interest demands work done in common. What then can we expect at the international level? Is there any evidence that even a small number of public- and private-sector leaders understand the virtues of joining forces? Obviously it is easier to get leaders to collaborate at the state and local levels than it is at the federal one. Just as obviously, it is easier to get them to collaborate at the national level than at the international one. But, if a transnational problem—deforestation, for example, or volatile currencies—is to be effectively addressed, big government and big business must be involved both at home and abroad.

Perhaps the biggest obstacle to collaboration on this large a scale is the near-total absence of institutions designed first to generate and then to support international, cross-sectoral work. The world is full of associations of all kinds designed to address problems of all kinds. But these groups and organizations are nearly always limited in their memberships and limited therefore in what they are able to accomplish. There are public affiliations and private ones, and there are regional affiliations and global ones. But we have no instrument whose mission it is to enable political and business leaders from different places to work together in the common interest.

Arguably, there is one exception to this general rule: the World Economic Forum—known to those in the know simply as Davos. In the early 1970s, Klaus Schwab, a Swiss professor of business administration, began to gather in Davos, a world-famous ski resort, European CEOs for annual conversations about the emerging challenges of the global marketplace. A decade later these meetings had been transformed. They were now attracting political and business leaders from around the world.

By the late 1990s, the World Economic Forum was billing itself as "the foremost international membership organization integrating leaders from business, government, and academia into a partnership committed to improving the state of the world."[1] Moreover, it was able to claim several achievements of no mean consequence. They included the first joint appearance outside South Africa of F.W. de Klerk, Nelson Mandela, and Chief Buthelezi (in 1992), and the draft agreement between PLO Chairman Yasser Arafat and Prime Minister Shimon Peres on Gaza and Jericho (in 1994).

But it is the global economy that is front and center in Davos. For example, President Carlos Salinas of Mexico is said to have conceived of the North American Free Trade Agreement in Davos (1990). And, in collaboration with the Council on Foreign Relations, the World Economic Forum convened Middle East-North Africa Economic

Summits in 1994 and 1996. Moreover, at its regional summits the Forum has panels and discussions that specifically include government representatives and regulators as well as corporate executives.

Although the World Economic Forum is "committed to improving the state of the world," in fact it is, by its own proud testimony, an organization in which membership is severely restricted: "The Forum is a club, providing its members with networking opportunities at very high level throughout the world. In an informal atmosphere, Forum members meet business and government leaders to exchange first-hand information and share experiences in a given region or on a given subject. Experts from academia, the sciences and the media are integrated into these exchanges."

Who belongs? In principle, club membership is made up of the "1,000 foremost global enterprises." But the success of the Forum is explained not by its formal membership roster, but rather by the remarkable assortment of players who in fact attend the various functions. Put another way, Schwab's genius is that he transformed what was originally a regional association of business leaders into an international association of leaders from different sectors. (In 1998 the net was cast even wider. John Sweeney, president of the AFL-CIO, was in Davos—the first union official ever to come from the United States in the Forum's twenty-seven years.)

The written report on the Forum's 1996 South Africa Economic Summit observed that there is in the region a "gulf between government imperatives and those of businessmen and investors who can pick their investment targets from the entire world." The report concluded, "The challenges facing Southern Africa cannot be resolved without creating a close partnership between the public and private sectors on a regional scale." To Schwab's enduring credit, it is this logic—the logic of transectoral collaboration—that he is attempting to market worldwide.

While on paper those who gather annually at Davos are committed to "improving the state of the world," in fact, they are, of course, looking out for number one. Moreover there is a growing awareness that the globalized markets so enshrined in the Forum's world view have a downside that both political and corporate leaders have yet fully to acknowledge. Finally, there are the inevitable questions about what all the high power and hot air at Davos actually accomplish. Richard Holbrooke calls the annual meeting "the world's greatest Ponzi scheme," and Euan Baird, the head of Schlumberger Ltd., decided in 1997 not to attend, presumably on the assumption that it was not worth his time ("At Davos, Networking for the World's Most Powerful," 1997).

Still, there is about the meetings in Davos an air of excitement and energy that is singular. In 1997, Nelson Mandela, Jack Welch, Yasser Arafat, Bill Gates, Vaclav Klaus, Kofi Annan, Benjamin Netanyahu, Javier Solana Madariaga, Newt Gingrich, Andrew Grove, and Malcolm Rifkind were only a few of those who made up the heady mix. Why did they bother to go to Davos? Because it is the only place in the world that provides them with the opportunity to meet their various counterparts. Thus, while it can hardly be claimed that the World Economic Forum is perfect, it is the only institution of its kind. It is transsectoral and transnational, and it is sweeping in its ambition. As *Forbes* put it, the Forum is a business, but it is a business built on a high-minded premise: "that a continuing dialogue between businessmen and government leaders will help produce more rational decisions on both sides. At the Forum the two sides meet not as antagonists but as confrères" ("One of the Greatest Shows on Earth," 1996).

In the new millennium it will be even clearer than it is now that leaders in government and business are much more similar than they are different. There will also be a paradigm shift. Whereas in the past leaders were specialists—for example, political leaders, or business leaders, or military leaders—in the future they will be generalists. Reinvented Leaders will be leaders without borders. They will have the capacity to forge integrated strategies, make connections between individuals and institutions that have long been at odds, and conjure constituencies other than their own (Smith, 1995). If we are to avoid "applying to the present the habits of the past," there is no alternative.

Note

1. Unless otherwise noted, all the quotes in this section are from World Economic Forum documents.

References

Adams, Bruce. Unpublished memo dated February 4, 1997.

"Ambitious Update of American Navigation Becomes a Fiasco," *The New York Times*, January 29, 1996.

"At Davos, Networking for the World's Most Powerful," *International Herald Tribune*, January 30, 1997.

Chrislip, David. "Transforming Politics," unpublished paper, 1995.

Chrislip, David, and Larson, Carl. *Collaborative Leadership*. San Francisco: Jossey-Bass, 1994.

Cleveland, Harlan. *The Knowledge Executive: Leadership in an Information Society*. New York: Dutton, 1985.

Cleveland, Harlan. *Leadership and the Information Society*. Minneapolis: World Academy of Art and Science, 1997.

Clinton, Bill. State of the Union speech delivered February 4, 1997.

"Cyberpower," *Forbes*, December 2, 1996, p. 146.

Drucker, Peter. *The Age of Discontinuity: Guidelines to our Changing Society*. New York: Harper & Row, 1969.

Drucker, Peter. "The Global Economy and the Nation-State," *Foreign Affairs*, 1997, Sept/Oct.

Friedman, Thomas. "Fed Up," *The New York Times*, December 4, 1996, p. A21.

"From Harlem's Worst to City's Star," *The New York Times*, August 3, 1997, p. B29.

Garten, Jeffrey. "Business and Foreign Policy," *Foreign Affairs*, 1997, May/June, p. 67.

Gerzon, Mark. *A House Divided: Six Belief Systems Struggling for America's Soul*. New York: Putnam, 1996.

"In Manila, Asians Pore Over Washington's Inner Truths," *The New York Times*, November 24, 1996, p. A1.

"IRS Admits Lag in Modernization," *The New York Times*, January 31, 1997, p. 1.

Johnson, Hayes, and Broader, David. *The System: The American Way of Politics at the Breaking Point*. Boston: Little, Brown, 1996.

Kapstein, Ethan. "The Welfare State? An Economic Cornerstone, Not a Luxury." *International Herald Tribune*, January 30, 1997, p. 8.

Light, Paul. *Thickening Government: Federal Hierarchy and the Diffusion of Accountability*. Washington, DC: Brookings Institution: Governance Institute, 1995.

Lighthizer, Robert. "What Did Asian Donors Want?" *The New York Times*, February 25, 1997, p. A27.

Mathews, Jessica. "Tricky Talks," *The Washington Post*, January 27, 1997, p. A19.

Mintzberg, Henry. "Managing Government: Governing Management," *Harvard Business Review*, 1996a, May/June, p. 77.

Mintzberg, Henry. "Musings on Management," *Harvard Business Review*, 1996b, 74(62).

O'Toole, James. *Leading Change: Overcoming the Ideology of Comfort and the Tyranny of Custom.* San Francisco: Jossey-Bass, 1995.

"One of the Greatest Shows on Earth," *Forbes*, December 2, 1996, p. 72.

Passell, Peter. "Economic Scene," *The New York Times*, December 14, 1995, p. D2.

Peirce, Neal. "Britain and New Zealand Are Showing the Way," *International Herald Tribune*, February 19, 1997.

Peirce, Neal, and Johnson, Curtis. *Boundary Crossers: Community Leadership for a Global Age.* College Park, MD: Academy of Leadership, 1997.

Pinchot, Gifford. "Creating Organizations with Many Leaders." In Hesselbein et al. (Eds.), *The Leader of the Future*. San Francisco: Jossey-Bass, 1996.

Posner, Bruce, and Rothstein, Lawrence. "Reinvention the Business of Government: An Interview with Change Catalyst David Osborne," *Harvard Business Review*, 1994, 72, 137

Schneider, Mark, Teske, Paul, and Michael Mintrom. *Public Entrepreneurs: Agents for Change in American Government.* Princeton, NJ: Princeton University Press, 1995.

Senge, Peter. "Leading Learning Organizations: The Bold, the Powerful, and the Invisible" In Hesselbein et al. (Eds.), *The Leader of the Future*. San Francisco: Jossey-Bass, 1996.

Smith, Hedrick. *Rethinking America: A New Game Plan from the American Innovator: School, Business, People, Work.* New York: Random House, 1995.

Teal, Thomas. "The Human Side of Management," *Harvard Business Review*, 1996, 74, 37.

Ulmer, Walter Jr. "Leadership Learnings and Relearnings." Unpublished paper, Kellogg Leadership Studies Project, 1996.

Urban Neighborhoods Task Force. *Life in the City*. Washington, DC: Center for National Policy, 1996.

Warren, Mark. "Deliberative Democracy and Authority," *American Political Science Review*, 1996, 90, 58.

Wertheimer, Fred. "The Dirtiest Campaign Ever." *Washington Post National Weekly Edition*, November 11, 1996.

Wills, Gary. "The Real Scandal," *New York Review of Books*, February 20, 1997, p. 4.

"Wired World," *Time*, February 3, 1997, p. 37.

Yergin, Daniel, and Stanislau, Joseph. *The Commanding Heights: The Battle Between Government and the Marketplace That Is Remaking the Modern World*. New York: Simon and Schuster, 1998.

—∿∿—

Barbara Kellerman is the James MacGregor Burns Lecturer in Public Leadership at Harvard University's John F. Kennedy School of Government. She was the Founding Executive Director of the Kennedy School's Center for Public Leadership from 2000 to 2003; and from 2003 to 2006 she served as the Center's Research Director.

Name Index

Subject Index

Page references followed by *fig* indicate an illustrated figure; followed by *t* indicate a table; followed by *e* indicate an exhibit.